Vermont

AN EXPLORER'S GUIDE

Vermont

AN EXPLORER'S GUIDE

CHRISTINA TREE & PETER S. JENNISON

PRINCIPAL PHOTOGRAPHY BY KIM GRANT

Eighth Edition

The Countryman Press
Woodstock, Vermont

Dedications

Christopher John Davis
— C.T.

Keith Warren Jennison
—P.S.J.

Eighth Edition

ISSN 1523-9462

ISBN 0-88150-461-0 (alk. paper)

Maps by Mapping Specialists, Ltd.,
Madison, Wisconsin
Book design by Glenn Suokko
Cover photograph by Richard W. Brown
Published by The Countryman Press
PO Box 748, Woodstock, Vermont 05091
Distributed by W. W. Norton & Company, Inc.
500 Fifth Avenue, New York, New York
10110
Printed in the United States of America
10 9 8 7 6 5 4 3 2 1

Explore With Us!

We have been fine-tuning *Vermont: An Explorer's Guide* for the past 16 years, a period in which lodging, dining, and shopping opportunities have more than quadrupled in the state. As we have expanded our guide, we have also been increasingly selective, making recommendations based on years of conscientious research and personal experience. What makes us unique is that we describe the state by locally defined regions, giving you Vermont's communities, not simply its most popular destinations. With this guide you'll feel confident to venture beyond the tourist towns, along roads less traveled, to places of special hospitality and charm.

WHAT'S WHERE

In the beginning of the book you'll find an alphabetical listing of special highlights, with important information and advice on everything from antiques to weather reports.

LODGING

Prices: Please don't hold us or the respective innkeepers responsible for the rates listed as of press time in 1999. Some changes are inevitable. The 9 percent state rooms and meals tax and any built-in gratuities are included only where applicable.

Smoking: State law bars smoking in all places of public accommodation in Vermont, including restaurants, and even in bars that don't qualify as "cabarets."

RESTAURANTS

Note the distinction between *Dining Out* and *Eating Out*. In the *Dining Out* section, à la carte entrée prices are either listed or described as follows:

Moderate: $12–18 · Expensive: $18–25 · Very Expensive: over $25

By their nature, restaurants listed in the *Eating Out* group are generally inexpensive.

KEY TO SYMBOLS

The special value symbol appears next to lodging and restaurants that combine high quality and moderate prices.

The kids-alert symbol appears next to lodging, restaurants, activities, and shops of special appeal to youngsters.

The wheelchair symbol appears next to lodging, restaurants, and attractions that are partially or fully handicapped-accessible.

The dog paw symbol appears next to lodgings that accept pets (usually with a reservation and deposit) as of press time.

We would appreciate your comments and corrections about places you visit or know well in the state. Please use the card enclosed in this book, or e-mail Chris: ctree@traveltree.net.

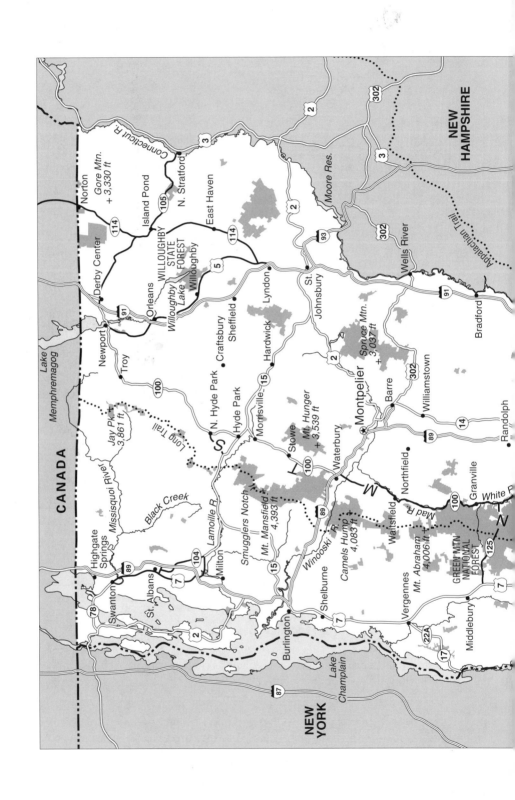

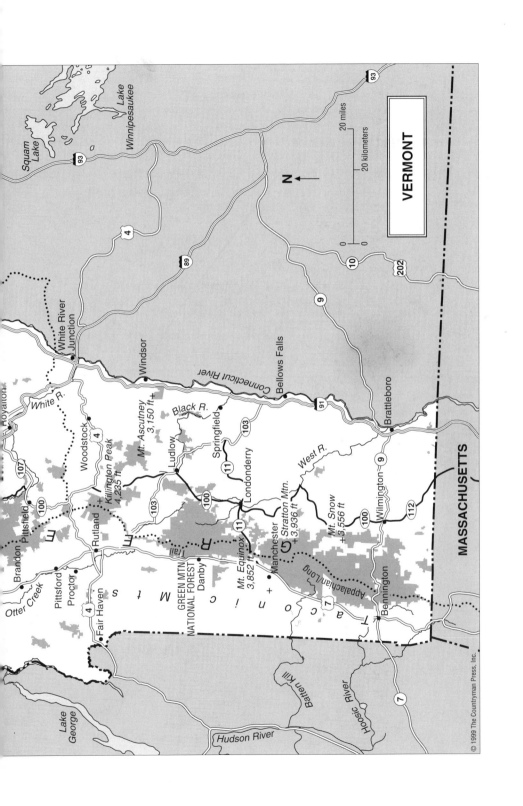

VERMONT

N ←

20 miles
20 kilometers

© 1999 The Countryman Press, Inc.

MASSACHUSETTS

Squam Lake
Lake Winnipesaukee
93
4
89
10
202
9
Lake George
Hudson River
Otter Creek
White R.
Royalton
107
Brandon
Pittsfield
100
Pittsford
Proctor
Fair Haven
4
Rutland
103
Woodstock
4
Killington Peak
4,235 ft
Mt. Ascutney
3,150 ft
Windsor
White River Junction
Black R.
Ludlow
Springfield
103
11
Londonderry
100
11
Manchester
Danby
Mt. Equinox
3,852 ft
Stratton Mtn.
3,936 ft
West R.
Mt. Snow
3,556 ft
100
Wilmington
9
112
Bennington
7
Connecticut River
Bellows Falls
91
Brattleboro
GREEN MTN NATIONAL FOREST
GREEN MTS
Taconic Mts
Appalachian/Long Trail
Battenkill
Hoosic River
7

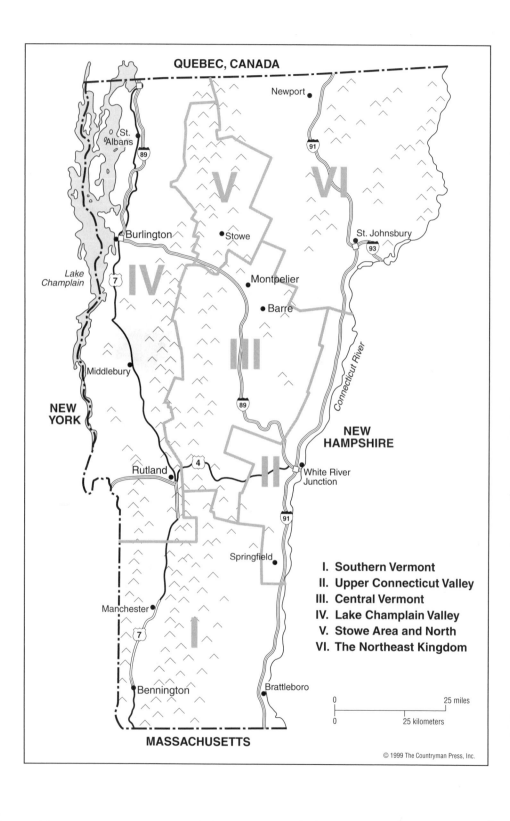

QUEBEC, CANADA

Newport

St.
Albans

89

V

VI

Burlington

Stowe

St. Johnsbury

93

Lake
Champlain

7

IV

Montpelier

Barre

NEW
YORK

III

Middlebury

89

Connecticut River

NEW
HAMPSHIRE

Rutland

4

II

White River
Junction

91

Springfield

I. Southern Vermont
II. Upper Connecticut Valley
III. Central Vermont
IV. Lake Champlain Valley
V. Stowe Area and North
VI. The Northeast Kingdom

Manchester

7

I

Bennington

Brattleboro

0   25 miles

0   25 kilometers

MASSACHUSETTS

© 1999 The Countryman Press, Inc.

Contents

Introduction

Welcome to the Green Mountain State and this eighth edition of the most comprehensive guide to its distinctive landscape, character, and places to see and stay. No other portrait of Vermont gathers so much practical information between two covers—so much, in fact, that even Vermonters find it useful.

We have divided the guide into areas whose boundaries usually coincide with those of the local chambers of commerce. Each section begins with a verbal snapshot of the area against a historical background, followed by advice on sources of information, getting around, things to see and do, and descriptions of just about every legal form of recreation, from skiing, horseback riding, sailing, hiking, swimming, canoeing, and golf to llama trekking and white-water rafting.

Then we give capsule descriptions of places to stay, representing roughly two-thirds of the resorts, inns, B&Bs, and farm stays—but omitting most motels. We try to be descriptive and reasonably candid about what we like and don't like. We visit regularly (many innkeepers tell us they see us far more frequently than they do authors of the specialized guides), and we describe many reasonably priced options, some of them real gems, that are found in no other book. We do not charge innkeepers to be included; a large percentage of lodging guides charge lodging places a "processing fee," anywhere from $250 to $2,500.

Finally, we critique upscale restaurants (*Dining Out*) and the everyday options (*Eating Out*), plus good delis, bakeries, and coffeehouses. Local entertainment, shops worth walking into, and special events round out coverage of virtually every city, town, and village.

Vermont is within a few hours' drive of 35 million people, and its popularity as a destination is growing. In summer, the whole state can be said to be a resort. In winter it offers the best skiing in the East; in fall foliage weeks, traffic congeals in places, and visitors without reservations find themselves sleeping in spare bedrooms.

Far from discouraging anyone to explore Vermont in autumn, though, we urge everyone to visit—but only with reservations and this book. Vermont, after all, invented "foliage season" and has been promoting its autumn colors as a drive-through spectacle for the past 50 years, in the process developing a better system (see *Foliage* in "What's

Where") for lodging "leaf-peepers" at peak periods than the other New England states.

Vermont harbors an inexhaustible supply of scenic routes, hundreds of miles of back roads shadowing mountain ridges and valley streams. Ironically, however, its image of ubiquitous pastoral beauty seems to discourage visitors from exploring far off the beaten path. Bostonians tend to stick to the eastern side of the Green Mountains, New Yorkers the western side, because that's where the interstates put them and they see little reason to travel far in Vermont once they get there.

Contrary to its image, Vermont's landscape varies substantially from north to south and even more from east to west. Rather than following the tried-and-true tourist routes (East/West Routes 9 and 4 and North/South Route 100), we suggest that (weather permitting) you drive the dramatic but well-surfaced "gap" roads (see *Gaps, Gulfs, and Gorges* in "What's Where") east or west across the state's relatively narrow width, bundling very different landscapes—mountain valleys and the broad sweep of farmland along Lake Champlain—into a few hours' drive.

While focusing on all the state's regions through the same lens (our format), we fervently hope that this book conveys the full spectrum of Vermont's beauty: the river roads of the Upper Valley, the high rolling farmland around Tunbridge and Chelsea, the glacially carved, haunting hills of the Northeast Kingdom, and the limestone farmsteads of Isle La Motte. Villages range from the self-consciously painted and pampering old resorts of Stowe, Woodstock, and Manchester to the equally proud but quiet villages of Craftsbury Common, Chelsea, and Newfane and the Victorian brick streetscapes of Brattleboro and Burlington.

In 1993 the National Trust for Historic Preservation named Vermont an "endangered" place, the first time an entire state has been so designated. The distinction was later rescinded, perhaps because the pace of condomania slowed considerably. Despite the inevitable inroads of today's shopping center culture, we have mostly preserved the character of the rural countryside that arouses twinges of nostalgia in many urban visitors. Currently, for every acre of open land paved for a parking lot, at least 10 acres are added to the holdings of the Vermont Land Trust and thus are shielded from development. The administrators of Act 250, the pioneering land-use program, also still exercise sensible controls over new commercial development, deflecting sporadic efforts in the legislature to dilute the act's provisions.

Vermonters, prudently, have not torn down the past. Abandoned farmhouses have been restored, and in a score of towns, adaptive preservation techniques have been thoughtfully applied to convert obsolete mills to other uses.

Vermont has never been a "rich" state. Except for machine tools, the Industrial Revolution skipped over it; as one political scientist noted, we leaped from "cow chips to microchips." Nevertheless, a few

19th-century family fortunes were made from lumber, wool, marble, and railroads. Tangible evidence of those entrepreneurs can be found in half a dozen stately homes that survive as inns, notably the Inn at Shelburne Farms, The Castle in Proctorsville, and the Hartness House in Springfield.

The 14 years of sovereignty as an independent country between 1777 and 1791 stamped Vermont with the indelible "contrary country" brand. Many examples of this spirit animated the state's subsequent history, from the years when Ethan Allen's Rabelaisian Green Mountain Boys wrested independence from the grip of Hampshiremen and 'Yorkers as well as from "The Cruel Minestereal Tools of George ye 3d," and blunted the British invasion of the Champlain Corridor. This spirit was later responsible for the abolitionist fervor that swept the state in the years before the Civil War and impelled Vermonters to flock to the colors in record numbers when President Lincoln called for troops. They voted their consciences with much the same zeal when, in both World Wars, the legislature declared war on Germany, in effect, before the United States did; and when Vermont and the United States observed their Bicentennials in 1976–77, debates about secession drew crowds to the state's town halls!

Contrary to common belief, tourism (for lack of a better word to describe the phenomenon of visitors "from away") is an integral part of Vermont's history, one that has affected its landscape—not just since the '50s but for 150 years.

Before the Civil War, southerners patronized mineral spas along the Connecticut River in Brattleboro and Newbury, and after the war Vermont's burgeoning railroads teamed up with the state's Board of Agriculture to promote farm vacations. Railroad guides also promoted Newport, with its elegant four-story Lake Memphremagog House ("one of the largest and finest hotels in New England") and Lake Willoughby ("one of the most remarkable places in the continent"). Carriage roads were built to the top of Jay Peak, Mount Mansfield, and Mount Equinox, and of course there was a summit hotel atop Mount Mansfield (highest peak in the state) as well as a large hotel beside the Green Mountain Inn in Stowe Village.

In the 1850s the Equinox House was recognized as one of New England's leading hotels. By 1862 the *Manchester Journal* could report that the previous summer, "Every house in the village was as full as a 'Third Avenue car,' almost entirely New Yorkers." Woodstock was equally well known in the right Manhattan circles by the 1890s.

All 19th- and early-20th-century visitors arrived by train (the exception being those who crossed Lake Champlain by ferry), and Vermont was slower than many other states to provide roads suitable to touring. The flood of 1927 washed out a number of major highways and bridges. In 1936 the proposal for a federally funded 260-mile Green

Mountain Parkway the length of the state—passing just below the crests of Pico, Killington, and several other peaks—was roundly defeated in a public referendum.

After World War II, however, Vermont launched what may be the world's first and most successful campaign to turn off-season into peak season.

"If you can pick and choose, there is no better time for a motor trip through Vermont than in autumn," Abner W. Coleman wrote in the first issue of *Vermont Life*, a state publication. The autumn 1946 article continued: "To the color photographer, Vermont during the autumn months offers delights indescribable. Should film become more plentiful this year, hundreds of camera enthusiasts will be roaming around these hills, knocking themselves out in a happy frenzy of artistic endeavor. For the autumn woods run the entire spectrum's course, from the blazing reds of the maple through the pale yellows of beech and birch to the violet of far-off mountain walls." The story was illustrated with the first of many vividly hued photos for which *Vermont Life* remains famous.

While Vermonters can't claim to have invented skiing, the state does boast America's oldest ski resorts. In the 1930s skiers began riding rope tows up slopes in Woodstock, at Pico, and on Mount Mansfield; after World War II Stowe became "Ski Capital of the East." Patrons at Mad River Glen built the country's first slope-side lodging, and in the early '60s nearby Sugarbush opened with the East's first bottom-of-the-lifts village. In ensuing decades more than a dozen Vermont ski areas have evolved into year-round resorts, several (Stowe, Sugarbush, and Killington) spawning full-fledged communities.

Vermont's ski communities mirror (in reverse) the story of its mill towns. Whereas mills were positioned on waterfalls—and no longer need the water to generate power—ski resorts have grown around mountains chosen for their good terrain and "dependable" snowfall. Only in recent years has it become apparent that access to enough water—to make snow—is crucial.

The question of whether skiing or any other manifestation of "tourism" (again that inadequate term) contributes to the preservation or destruction of the Vermont character and landscape can be argued interminably. But the fact is that it has been here for 150 years. Today, Vermont inns and B&Bs outnumber farms, and Vermont visitors outnumber cows. Perhaps it's time for the Departments of Agriculture and Tourism to merge once more.

Today's visitor is more likely than not to be welcomed by ex-visitors: More than 40 percent of the state's population of 570,000 came "from away," a post–World War II phenomenon that has profoundly affected the cultural and political landscapes.

Much has been made of the proverbial "Vermont mystique," that indefinable quality of life and character. It is, we are happy to report, alive and well, especially along the back roads and in villages and hamlets where "neighboring" still reigns. While the portrait of the legendary Vermont Yankee—frugal, wary, taciturn, sardonic—has faded somewhat in today's homogenized culture, independent-minded Vermonters (many of them ex-"tourists") take care of each other, tolerate eccentricities, and regard the world with a healthy skepticism.

A flatland author, born in Hawaii, raised in New York City, and living near Boston, Chris Tree claims to be a professional Vermont visitor. Her infatuation with the state began in college.

"The college was in Massachusetts, but one of my classmates was a native Vermonter whose father ran a general store and whose mother knows the name of every flower, bird, and mushroom. I jumped at her invitations to come 'home' or to 'camp' and have since spent far more time in Vermont than has my friend. As a travel writer for *The Boston Globe*, I have spent more than 30 years writing newspaper stories about Vermont towns, inns, ski areas, and people. I interviewed John Kenneth Galbraith about Newfane, Pearl Buck on Danby. I rode the Vermont Bicentennial Train, froze a toe on one of the first inn-to-inn ski treks, camped on the Long Trail and in state parks, paddled a canoe down the Connecticut, slid over Lake Champlain on an iceboat as well as paddling it in a kayak, soared over the Mad River Valley in a glider, and hovered above the Upper Valley in a hot-air balloon. I have also tramped through the woods collecting sap, ridden many miles with Vermont Transit, led a foliage tour, collided with a tractor, and have broken down in a variety of places." Chris also coauthors *Best Places to Stay in New England*.

Peter Jennison, a sixth-generation Vermonter, was born on a dairy farm in Swanton, attended one-room schoolhouses, and graduated from Middlebury College. After 25 years in the publishing business in New York City, he became a "born-again" Vermonter, returning to his native heath in 1972—"like many latter-day immigrants, tired of the City and being held hostage daily by the New Haven Railroad."

Peter and his wife, Jane, revived The Countryman Press imprint as a cottage industry in Taftsville in 1973. His other Vermont books include *The Roadside History of Vermont* and *Vermont on $500 a Day*. He also reviews inns and restaurants for *Vermont Magazine*.

"In 75 years," Peter recalls, "I have seen the state transformed from an almost wholly agrarian society to a far more sophisticated place to live—a land of infinite variety, but where people still mind their own business. We have freedom and unity, the state's motto."

Chris wishes to thank Tom Kaiden, Bobby Kyle, and Hariett Hyer for their help with Stowe, Margie Ramsdell and Darcie McCann for help with the Northeast Kingdom, also Barbara Thomke in the Lamoille Valley, Barbara Mooney in the Champlain Islands, Marree Gatani in

16

Burlington, Susan VanDeWater in Randolph, Thom and Joan Gorman and Susan Roy in the Mad River Valley, Patricia Long and William Hays in Brattleboro, and Roger Clapp for his help with Burlington and for agricultural information throughout the state. Both authors are hugely grateful to Ann Kraybill, our ever-supportive editor; to the folks at Countryman Press; and to Doris Troy, our tireless copyeditor, for piecing together this monster manuscript to make the best *Vermont: An Explorer's Guide* ever.

Christina Tree
Peter S. Jennison

What's Where in Vermont

AREA CODE

The area code for all of Vermont is **802;** we have omitted listing it at all within the text.

AGRICULTURAL FACTS AND FAIRS

Some 1,350,000 acres—of the state's total of 6 million acres—are under cultivation. The farmhouse and barn are still a symbol of Vermont and part of every Vermont visit should be a visit to a farm, whether to buy

ROBERT EDDY

syrup or cheese, wool, or wine, maybe to pick apples or berries, just to tour the dairy operation, or to stay for a night or a week. Finding farms can be an excuse to explore unexpectedly beautiful backcountry.

Of course a "farm" isn't what it used to be. Fewer than half of Vermont's 5,600 farms are now dairy, compared with 10,000 dairy farms 40 years ago. Cows are being replaced by goats and llamas, beef cattle and sheep, not to mention Christmas trees and flowers, fruit, and trout. Bear in mind that Vermont's farms were not always dairy. In the 1830s and '40s Vermont's meadowland was far more extensive, populated by millions of sheep. When the Civil War ended, so did the push for wool blankets and a significant number of sheep farms were wiped out. Luckily railroads were expanding to every corner of the state in the 1870s, and railroad companies teamed up with state agriculture departments to promote farms to "summer boarders."

Now once more farmers are looking to visitors as well as to new forms of agriculture to maintain their farms. Within "What's Where" we suggest how to find a variety of agricultural products from apples to wine. For a current packet from the Vermont Department of Agriculture, including a **"Vermont Farm Map"** covering the state, phone 828-2416 or write the department at 116 State Street, Drawer 20, Montpelier 05620-2901. The easiest web access to farms and their products is currently: www.vtcheese.com. Also inquire about regional farm maps.

Request *Vermont Agricultural Fairs and Field Days,* a pamphlet listing major agricultural events, beginning with the **Vermont Maple Festival** in St. Albans in April and filling every weekend in July, August, and September. The most famous are the **Champlain Valley Exposition,** Essex, around Labor Day; the **Orleans County Fair** in Barton (5 days) and the **Bondville Fair** (2 days), both in late August; the **Vermont State Fair** in Rutland (9 days, the biggest), early September; and the **Tunbridge World's Fair** (4 days, the most colorful of all), mid-September. See also in this chapter *Apples, Cheese, Christmas Trees, Farmers' Markets, Farm Stays, Gardens, Maple Sugaring, Pick Your Own, Sheep,* and *Wine.*

AIR SERVICE

Burlington International Airport (863-1889) currently offers most of the scheduled (largely commuter) service in Vermont. Carriers include: **Delta Express** (1-800-221-1212), **Continental Express** (1-800-525-0280), **Northwest Airlink** (1-800-225-2525), **United Airlines** (1-800-241-6522), connecting with most U.S. points via Chicago, and **USAir Express** (1-800-428-4322). **Lebanon Regional Airport,** just across the river from White River Junction, links the Upper Valley with New York and Boston; and the Albany, New York, airport, served by major carriers, is less than an hour from much of central and southern Vermont. The Rutland/Killington region is served by Continental Connection's **Colgan Air** (1-800-272-5488) from Boston and New York.

AIRPORTS

Vermont offers 16 public-use airports, 2 (above) with scheduled flights but all accessible to private and some to charter planes. Request a copy of the *Vermont Airport Directory* from the Vermont Agency of Transportation (828-5754).

AMTRAK

Amtrak service (1-800-USA-RAIL) has improved dramatically in the past couple of years. Amtrak's *Vermonter* runs from Washington to Montreal with stops (at decent hours both north- and southbound) in Brattleboro, Bellows Falls, Claremont, Windsor, White River Junction, Randolph, Montpelier, Waterbury, Burlington, and St. Albans. The *Adirondack* runs up the western shore of Lake Champlain en route from Manhattan to Montreal and stops at Port Kent, New York, across from the ferry to Burlington. The *Ethan Allen Express* connects Rutland with New York City and Albany. All Vermont trails carry bicycles in the baggage car.

ANTIQUARIAN BOOKSELLERS

The **Vermont Antiquarian Booksellers Association** (VABA) publishes a pamphlet list of its more than 50 member stores, available in those stores or (in 1998) from **Craftsbury Books,** P.O. Box 111, Craftsbury 05827; questions go to Gary Austin at **Antiquarian Books** (464-3727), Wilmington.

ANTIQUING

A pamphlet guide, *Antiquing in Vermont,* listing more than 120 members of the Vermont Antiques Dealers' Association, is available by sending a double-stamped, self-addressed, business-sized envelope to James Harley, RR 1, Box 155, Reading 05062. The association sponsors an **annual antiques**

KIM GRANT

show at Stratton Mountain base lodge early in August. Major concentrations of dealers can be found in Bennington, Burlington, Dorset, Manchester, Middlebury, Woodstock, and along Route 30 in the West River Valley. The **Weston Antiques Fair,** usually the first weekend in October, is the state's oldest and still one of its best.

APPLES

During fall harvest season, there is a demand not only for bushel baskets already filled with apples but also for an empty basket and the chance to climb a ladder and fill it with McIntosh, Red Delicious, and others among the many varieties of apples grown in Vermont—primarily in the **Champlain Islands,** in the Champlain Valley around Shoreham, and in the **Lower Connecticut River Valley** between Springfield and Putney. Listings of orchards can be found under descriptions of these areas in this book and by requesting a map/guide to farms from the **Vermont Department of Agriculture** (see Agricultural Fairs and Facts). Several apple orchards offer bed & breakfast: check out **Allenholm Farm** (312-5566) in South Hero, **Indian Trail Farm** (897-5292) in Shoreham, and **Maple Crest Farm** (492-3367) in Cuttingsville. From the earliest days of settlement through the mid-1800s more apples, it's said, were used for making hard cider and brandy than for eating and cooking. In 1810 some 125 distilleries were annually producing more than 173,000 gallons

of apple brandy. Today a half dozen wineries and cideries are once more making apple wines; we describe the most visitor-friendly of these: **Boyden Valley Winery** in Cambridge (644-8155), **Joseph Cernigila Winery** in Proctorsville (226-7575), and **North River Winery** in Jacksonville (368-7557). Contact the Vermont Department of Agriculture for the most up-to-date listing.

ART GALLERIES

Vermont's principal collections of art (painting, sculpture, and decorative arts) are found in the **Bennington Museum** (works by Grandma Moses); the **Robert Hull Fleming Museum** at the University of Vermont, Burlington; the new **Arts Center at Middlebury College;** the **Athenaeum** in St. Johnsbury; the **Shelburne Museum** in Shelburne; the **Chaffee Art Center,** Rutland; the **Southern Vermont Arts Center,** Manchester; the **Thomas Waterman Wood Art Gallery,** Montpelier; the **Helen Day Art Center** in Stowe; the **Chester Art Guild** in Chester; and the **Chandler Gallery in Randolph**. Manchester and Woodstock offer an unusual number of private galleries, and Brattleboro is another art center. Both Burlington and Brattleboro sponsor open gallery tours the first Friday of every month.

ARTS COUNCILS

Vermont's local arts councils organize films, festivals, and concerts throughout the year. Those listed here are the largest and sources of cultural happenings in their areas: **Arts Council of Windham County,** Brattleboro (257-1881); **Catamount Film and Arts Center,** St. Johnsbury (748-2600); **Crossroads Arts Council,** Rutland (775-5413); **Onion River Arts Council,** Montpelier (229-9408); **Pentangle Council on the Arts,** Woodstock (457-3981). The overall information source is the **Vermont Arts**

Council (828-3291) in Montpelier. The web site: www.state.vt.us/vermont-arts/

AUCTIONS

Most major upcoming auctions are announced in the Thursday edition of Vermont newspapers, with a listing of items that will be up for bid. Auctions may be scheduled at any time, however, during summer months, advertised primarily on local bulletin boards and in shop windows. Among well-known auctioneers and auction houses: **William Dupras** of Randolph Center; **Butch Sutherland,** Woodstock; **C. W. Gray** of East Thetford, every Monday night, year-round (livestock); **Arthur Hicks,** Hicks' Commission Sales, Morrisville.

BALLOONING

Year-round champagne flights are offered by Brian Boland at **Post Mills Airport** (333-4883). Also inquire at the **Stoweflake Resort** in Stowe (253-7355). The state's major ballooning events are the **Lake Champlain Balloon Festival,** held in early June, and the **Annual Balloon Festival** in Quechee, in late June.

BARNS

Many barns along the highways and byways have distinctive touches, such as ornate Victorian cupolas, and still more are connected to farmhouses in the "extended" architectural style that served as shelter for the farmers' trips before dawn in deep snow. Just a dozen round barns survive in Vermont, all built between 1899 and World War I. The concept of the round barn is thought to have originated with the Shakers in Hancock, Massachusetts, where the original stone barn, built in 1824, is now the centerpiece of a museum. The Vermont survivors include: the **Moore barn** in East Barnet; the **Hastings barn** in Waterford; the **Metcalf barn** (Robillard Flats) in Irasburg; the

KIM GRANT

Parker barn in Grand Isle, converted into a housing center for the elderly; two barns in Coventry; the **Powers barn** in Lowell; the **Parker barn** in North Troy; one in Enosburg Falls; and **Southwick's** in East Calais. In Waitsfield the **Joslin round barn** is now a cultural center with a swimming pool in its bowels, attached to the **Inn at Round Barn Farm;** in Strafford the **Round Barn Farm,** a 350-acre working dairy farm, takes guests. Round-barn addicts should check at local general stores for exact location and to secure permission to photograph the structures. Among other Vermont barns open to the public are the vast, five-story, 416-foot-long, Norman-style **Farm Barn** and the impressive stable and carriage house at Shelburne Farms in Shelburne. The round barn once in Passumpsic has been moved to the Shelburne Museum. Two lively, illustrated guides are *A Field Guide to New England Barns and Farm Buildings* by Thomas Visser and *Big House, Little House, Back House, Barn: The*

Connected Farm Buildings of New England by Thomas Hubka (both the University Press of New England).

BED & BREAKFASTS

The hundreds of B&Bs we have personally inspected are listed under their respective locations in this book; they range from working farms to historic mansions, from $45–270 per room.

BICYCLE TOURING

In Vermont the distance via back roads is never far from swimming hole to antiques shop to the next inn, and touring options have increased substantially since John Freidin, author of 25 *Bicycle Tours in Vermont* (Backcountry Publications), introduced the whole notion of guided bike tours for adults back in 1972. Woodstock-based **Bike Vermont** (1-800-257-2226; P.O. Box 207, Woodstock 05091) is now by far the state's largest, most respected inn-to-inn tour outfitter, offering a "sag wagon," renting 21-gear hybrid bikes, specializing in small (under 20) groups and a wide variety of

Vermont destinations. **Bicycle Holidays** (1-800-292-5388) caters to those who prefer to travel without a guide but want a route mapped, inns reserved, and luggage transferred. Guided camping tours (with a sag wagon) are offered by POMG (Peace of Mind Guaranteed) **Bike Tours of Vermont** (434-2270; 1-888-635-BIKE). **Vermont Bicycle Touring** (1-800-245-3868) offers hiking and biking tours to several destinations. **Vermont Country Inns Along the Trail** (247-3300; RR 3, Box 3115, Brandon 05733) and **Cycle-Inn-Vermont** (228-8799; Box 243, Ludlow 05149) are both composed of innkeepers whose establishments are a comfortable bike ride from each other. Participants are largely on their own, but rental equipment is available and baggage is transferred from inn to inn. Bicycle paths continue to grow and multiply in Vermont. **Stowe's "Rec" Path** and easy rentals make it an ideal place to sample the sport. The **Burlington Bike Path** follows the shore of Lake Champlain for 7 miles (rentals available); the 26-mile **Missisquoi Rail Trail** follows an old railbed from St. Albans to Richford; the **Bennington Historic Bike Route** leads bikers around local sights; and the 34-mile **D&H Recreation Trail** follows an abandoned railroad bed almost 20 miles from Castleton to West Rupert, with the remainder in New York State. Within each chapter, we have described sources for local bike rentals. Note that many inns and outfitters offer shuttle service from Amtrak stops. The Vermont Department of Travel (1-800-VERMONT) keeps a running list of bike tours and rental sources. See also *Mountain Biking.*

BIRDING

While the hermit thrush is the state bird (reclusive and not too easy to spot), Vermont offers ample opportunities for observing herons and ducks, as well as raptors like owls, hawks, falcons, osprey, even bald eagles. Outstanding birding areas include the **Missisquoi National Wildlife Refuge** (868-4781) in Swanton, the **Dead Creek Wildlife Refuge** (759-2398) in Vergennes, and the 4,970-acre **Victory Basin** east of St. Johnsbury. The 255-acre **Green Mountain Audubon Nature Center** in Huntington (434-3068) is open year-round, Tuesday through Friday 9–5 and weekends 1–4; inquire about guided walks and special programs (web site: www.thecompass.com/audubon). The **Vermont Institute of Natural Science** in Woodstock (VINS; 457-2779) open November to May except Sundays and daily the rest of the year, also has nature trails, a library, and a series of special programs (admission: $6 per adult, $3 per child 12–18, $2 5–11). The Institute's **Vermont Raptor Center** introduces visitors to the owls, hawks, and eagles of northern New England (26 species are in residence). We recommend *A Guide to Bird Finding in Vermont* by Walter G. Ellison.

BOATING

Phone 1-800-VERMONT and request a current list of boat rentals & marinas; it's updated annually and lists motor, sail, and canoe rentals. The official state map notes public boat-launch areas. A booklet, *Laws and Regulations Governing the Use and Registration of Motorboats,* is available from the Vermont Department of Public Safety, Marine Division, Montpelier 05602. (See also *Canoeing* and *White Water.*)

BOAT EXCURSIONS

If you don't own a yacht, there are still plenty of ways to get onto Vermont rivers and lakes. Possible excursions include the **Belle of Brattleboro** (254-1263), which plies the Connecticut from Brattleboro; the **Spirit of Ethan Allen II** (862-8300), an excursion vessel based in Burlington; the **M/V Caril-**

lon (897-5331), which offers narrated cruises from Larrabees Point in Shoreham up and down Lake Champlain near Fort Ticonderoga; **Newport's Princess** (334-6617), a paddlewheel riverboat offering daily cruises of Lake Memphremagog; and the **M/V Mountain Mills** (464-2975), which sails on Lake Whitingham. For details, check under respective locations in this book. See also *Ferries.*

BOOKS

For a complete bibliography, write for the *Books about Vermont* catalog from the Vermont Historical Society, 109 State Street, Montpelier 05602 (vhs@.state.vt.us). In addition to the books we mention in specific fields or on particular subjects, here are some of the most useful current titles: The *Vermont Atlas and Gazetteer* (DeLorme); *Vermont Place Names: Footprints in History,* by Esther Swift (Vermont Historical Society); and *Lake Champlain: Key to Liberty,* by Ralph Nading Hill (The Countryman Press). *The Roadside History of Vermont,* by Peter Jennison (Mountain Press, Missoula, MT), is an informal narrative of what happened where and when along main travel routes. Lovers of natural history should seek out *The Nature of Vermont* by Charles Johnson (University Press of New England). For children, *Vermont, The State with the Storybook Past,* by Cora Cheney (New England Press), is the best. A basic reference directory is *The Vermont Yearbook,* published by the National Survey, Chester. Civil War buffs will be rewarded by Howard Coffin's *Full Duty: Vermonters in the Civil War* and *Nine Months to Gettysburg: Stannard's Vermonters and the Repulse of Pickett's Charge* (both The Countryman Press). Our favorite current Vermont fiction writer is unquestionably Howard Frank Mosher of Irasburg, whose evocative novels include *Disappearances,*

Northern Borders, Where the Rivers Flow North, and *A Stranger in the Kingdom;* the last two are now also films. Joseph Citro is the author of several books about occult occurrences and ghost stories in the state; his latest is *Green Mountains, Dark Tales* (University Press of New England). The Brattleboro-based mysteries of Archer Mayor, including *Open Season,* and other titles in his Joe Gunther police-procedural series, are gaining momentum. And look for the charming little *Art of the State: Vermont* by Suzanne Mantell (Abrams).

BREWERIES

Microbreweries are multiplying. The **Catamount Brewery** in Windsor is the oldest and largest of more than a dozen and the number seems to grow weekly. Founded in 1987, Catamount (764-6700) brews a variety of porters as well as gold and amber lagers, distributes throughout the country, and offers frequent tours at its new brewery in Windsor Industrial Park, just off I-91. Other breweries that offer tours and tastings: **Black River Brewing Company** (228-3100) in Ludlow, **Golden Dome Brewing Company** (223-3290) in Montpelier, **Long Trail Brewing Company** (672-5011) on Route 4 at Bridgewater Corners, **Magic Hat Brewing Company** (658-BREW) in South Burlington (off Route 7), **Otter Creek Brewing** (1-800-473-0727) in Middlebury, and **Trout River Brewing Company** (626-3984) in East Burke. Brew pubs include the **Salt Ash Inn** in Plymouth, **Jasper Murdock's Alehouse** in Norwich, the **Shed** in Stowe, and the **Latchis** and **McNeill's**, both in Brattleboro. For the latest listing contact the Vermont Department of Agriculture, Food and Markets (828-2416).

BUS SERVICE

Vermont Transit. For a current timetable, contact Vermont Transit Co., Inc.

(864-6811; 1-800-451-3292), 106 Main Street, Burlington 05401; web site: www.vttransit.com. The major routes are (1) up the western side of the state from New York City and Albany via Bennington, Rutland, and Burlington to Montreal; (2) from Boston via White River Junction and Burlington to Montreal; you can connect to St. Johnsbury and Newport. Read the timetable carefully, and you will find that most corners of the state of Vermont—and a number elsewhere in northern New England—are served. Children under 12 years travel at half price; one child under 5 can travel free. Inquire about overnight and multiday tours to Montreal, Boston, New York, and points south. Note that the new 345 Pine Street terminal in Burlington offers ample parking but is no longer downtown.

CAMPS, FOR CHILDREN

For information about more than 50 Vermont summer camps for boys and girls contact the **Vermont Camping Association** (1-888-882-2677).

CAMPGROUNDS

A *Vermont Campground Guide* advertising some 90 private campgrounds that belong to the Vermont Campground Association is available from the Vermont Department of Tourism (1-800-VERMONT). Just one page within this publication is reserved for a graphlike presentation of the campgrounds, but full, clear, and detailed descriptions are available for each park from the Vermont State Department of Forests, Parks and Recreation (241-3655; 103 South Main Street, Waterbury 05671-0603; web site: www.vtstateparks.com); request a copy of the *Vermont State Parks Map Atlas.* Facilities include furnished cottages, unfurnished cabins, lean-tos, and tent and trailer sites. Fees vary with the class of the area. Inquire about season passes.

Anytime after January 1, a campsite can be reserved for 4 or more consecutive days until March 1, and then reservations for all parks for fewer than 4 days will be accepted. (The reservation fee is $5.) *Note:* Campsites at Branbury, Burton Island, Silver Lake, and Lake St. Catherine State Parks can be reserved for no more than 4 days at a time, regardless of the time of year. In 1999, camping fees are $11–13 per night for a tent or trailer site, and $15–17 for a lean-to. Vermont state park campsites are all screened by trees from neighboring sites and are well maintained; many parks have organized programs such as hikes, campfire sings, films, and lectures. Most parks are relatively uncrowded, especially midweek; the most popular parks are Branbury, Stillwater, Groton Forest, and Lake St. Catherine. We have provided details, including phone numbers, for each park as it appears within the text. Within the 300,000-acre **Green Mountain National Forest,** 94 fine, well-developed campsites are offered. They are available on a first-come, first-served basis for a maximum 14-day period at a modest charge, posted at the entrance to each area. Camping is also permitted, without fee or prior permission, virtually anywhere on national forest land. Before you pitch your tent, however, we recommend that you visit one of the three district ranger offices, in Manchester Center (362-2307), Middlebury (388-6688), and Rochester (767-4261), and inquire about proper places to camp. A free minimap is available from the Green Mountain National Forest (747-6700), P.O. Box 519, Rutland 05701. The **U.S. Army Corps of Engineers,** New England Division, has constructed two camping areas in Vermont. The **Winhall Brook Camping Area** at Ball Mountain Lake in Jamaica offers 108 campsites near flush toilets, showers, and swimming, free on a first-come, first-served basis; for details, contact the Basin Manager,

Upper Connecticut River Basin Office, North Springfield Lake, 98 Reservoir Road, Springfield 05156. The Corps of Engineers also built the 30-site camping area of **Quechee Gorge** near the North Hartland Dam, now maintained by the state.

CANOEING

Organized canoe trips have increased in recent years: **Battenkill Canoe** (362-2800; 1-800-421-5268; Box 65, Route 313, West Arlington 05250) offers day trips, and inn-to-inn tours throughout the state; **Paddle Vermont** (228-4957), Ludlow, tailors trips to special interests; **Clearwater Sports** (496-2708; Route 100, Waitsfield 05673) offers guided tours, instruction, and special expeditions, as does **Umiak Outdoor Outfitters** (253-2317; 849 South Main Street, Stowe). **Vermont Touring Center** (257-5008; Route 5, Brattleboro) offers canoe rentals, shuttle service, and river camping on the lower stretch of the river, just as **North Star Canoes** (603-542-5802), based in Cornish, New Hampshire, does for the scenic reach above the covered bridge, one particularly rich in camping spots (see "Upper Connecticut Valley"). The stretch of the Lamoille River around Jeffersonville is served both by **Smugglers Notch Canoe Touring,** based at the Mannsview Inn

(1-800-937-MANN), and by **Green River Canoe** (644-8336), based at Smugglers' Notch Resort. An excellent detailed guide, *Canoeing on the Connecticut River,* is available from U.S. Generating Company; phone 603-653-9200. The *Vermont Guide to Fishing* map, free from the Vermont Fish and Wildlife Department (241-3700), 103 South Main Street, Waterbury 05676, notes falls, rapids, boulder fields, dams, and other potential dangers. A *Winooski River Canoe Guide* is $3 if you pick it up; $4 by mail from the Winooski Valley Park District, Ethan Allen Homestead, Burlington 05401. Recommended books: Roioli Schweiker's third edition of *Canoe Camping Vermont and New Hampshire Rivers* (Backcountry Publications) is a handy guide, and the *AMC River Guide: Vermont/New Hampshire* (AMC Books) is good for detailed information on canoeable rivers. (See also *White Water.*)

CANOE RENTALS

Rentals are available from the canoe outfitters listed above and from the boat rental sources described in each chapter.

CHEESE

A century ago, almost every Vermont town had its cheese factory to which farmers brought their daily surplus milk. **Crowley Cheese** (259-2340; 1-800-683-2602), established in 1882 and billed as "the oldest continuously operated cheese factory in the U.S.," is the only survivor of this era, and welcomes visitors to its wooden factory just west of Ludlow on Route 103 in Healdville (open weekdays 8–4; store open daily). There only a few hundred pounds of this distinctive cheese that's creamier than cheddar is still made each day in the old traditional way. The state's most famous cheese factory is the **Cabot Creamery** (563-2231) in Cabot. This modern plant, which pro-

duces 12 million pounds of cheese a year, maintains a visitors center with a video orientation, plant tour, and gift shop, also operates an annex in Waterbury Center, south of Stowe. Far from just a familiar name brand (it's widely distributed in supermarkets), Cabot has maintained quality, winning the "Best Cheddar in the World" title in the 1998 World Championship. **Vermont Shepherd Cheese** (387-4473), a rich, tangy sheep's milk cheese from Westminster, has also won top awards and opens its "cave" to visitors from August through October, 10–2 (call for directions). The **Seward Family** produces a genuine Vermont cheddar in its East Wallingford plant; it showcases and sells it in the Seward Family Restaurant on Route 7 in Rutland. The family has been in the business since the Civil War and prides itself on a sharp cheddar, aged over 9 months. **Grafton Village Cheese Company** (1-800-472-3866) in Grafton had its beginnings around 1890 and was resurrected by the Windham Foundation in 1966; visitors view the cheesemaking from outside, through a picture window. The **Plymouth Cheese Company** (672-3650) was founded in 1890 by Colonel John Coolidge, father of President Coolidge. The factory shop is open (see "Killington/Pico Area") year-round, producing an old-fashioned Vermont granular curd cheese. At **Shelburne Farms** (985-8686; open daily, year-round), in Shelburne near Burlington, Alec Webb makes prizewinning cheddar from a single herd of Brown Swiss cows. In New Haven, **Orb Weaver Farm** (877-3755) produces a creamy, aged, Colby-type cheese made in small batches, entirely by hand (available in 2-pound wheels and 1-pound waxed wedges). The **Organic Cow** in Tunbridge produces a cheddar and a creamy Havarti made from raw milk, and **K. C. Kritters** (257-4595) in Guilford produces four varieties of goat cheese, selling it at the farm.

Sugarbush Farm (457-1757), set high on a hill in Woodstock, smokes and packages several varieties of cheddar cheese; **Vermont Butter & Cheese Company** in Websterville makes a wide variety of tantalizing goat cheeses but is not geared to visitors. **Blythedale Farm** (439-6575) in Springfield produces a fine Vermont Brie. Request a cheese brochure from the Vermont Department of Agriculture, Food and Markets (828-2416), 116 State Street, Drawer 20; Montpelier 05620-2901, or check out the Vermont Cheese Council web site: www.vtcheese.com.

CHILDREN, ESPECIALLY FOR

Alpine slides delight children of all ages at Bromley (where there is also a **DevalKart Ride**) as well as at Pico and Stowe. **Alpine lifts,** which operate in summer, are also a way of hoisting small legs and feet to the top of some of Vermont's most spectacular summits. **Mount Mansfield,** Vermont's highest peak, is accessible via the gondola. Killington Peak, second highest in the state, can be reached via gondola on weekdays; a 2.5-mile gondola ride brings you most of the way in fall. **Jay Peak,** commanding as dramatic a view as the others, is accessible on a smooth-riding tram. In southern Vermont, **Stratton's** gondola runs daily all summer and fall, and chairlifts at **Sugarbush** and **Mount Snow** run weekends in summer, daily during foliage season. **Santa's Land** in Putney is the only commercial attraction geared specifically to children. The **Shelburne Museum** has many exhibits that please youngsters, as does the **Fairbanks Museum and Planetarium,** St. Johnsbury, which is filled with stuffed animals, birds, and exhibits from near and far. The **Montshire Museum of Science** in Norwich is a real standout, with hands-on exhibits explaining many basic scientific mysteries; it's also good for waterside walks. The **Billings Farm & Museum** and **Vermont Institute of Natural Science,** both in Woodstock, are child pleasers. Over the past few years, as ski areas have come to compete for family business, most ski resorts have developed special programs for children; see the description for each ski area in the text. In summer, a growing number of ski areas—**Bolton Valley, Smugglers' Notch, Sugarbush, Stratton, Killington,** and **Mount Snow**—offer full day-camp programs for children. **The Tyler Place Family Resort** in Highgate Springs and the **Basin Harbor Club** in Vergennes are family-geared resorts with children's programs. (See also *Agricultural Fairs and Facts, Farm Stays, Boat Excursions,* and *Railroad Excursions.*)

CHRISTMAS TREES

A list of Christmas-tree growers, trees, and wreaths by mail is available from the Vermont Department of Agriculture, (see *Agricultural Facts and Fairs*) on the web site: vtcheese.com. Most farms open after Thanksgiving, inviting customers to come tag the tree they want, leaving it to cut until the last moment. Some places offer sleigh rides and one, **Wilson's Tree Farm** in Putney (387-4409), has live reindeer. The most imaginative marketer is, however, **Redrock Farm** (685-2282) in Chelsea, where you can pick out a balsam fir or white spruce (up to 6 feet) and it will be shipped to you UPS at Christmas. See "The White River Valleys" for details.

COLLEGES

For information about all the state's colleges and universities, contact the Vermont Higher Education Council (878-7466), P.O. Box 47, Essex Junction 05453-0047; vhec@aol.com; web site:www.vtcolleges.org

KIM GRANT

COVERED BRIDGES

The state's 110 surviving covered bridges are marked on the official state map, on our chapter maps, and are described in the appropriate chapters of this book under *To See*. Bridge buffs should secure a copy of *Covered Bridges of Vermont* by Ed Barna (The Countryman Press).

CRAFTS

More than 1,500 Vermonters make their living from craft work. There are also more than 100 retail craft outlets in the state, ranging from back kitchens to the four nonprofit **Vermont State Craft Centers,** principally at Frog Hollow in Middlebury, with others in Windsor, Manchester, and Burlington. Pick up a copy of the *Vermont Crafts Guide* in information centers or request it from the Vermont Crafts Council, P.O. Box 938, Montpelier 05601-0938; vt1crafts@aol.com; web site: www.vermontcrafts.com. Inquire about **Open Studio Weekends.** Within this book, we have described outstanding local crafts studios, galleries, and shops as they appear geographically. We have also included major crafts festivals. Among the best: in July, the **Woodstock Craftsmen's Fair,** the **Killington Art Show, Art on the Mountain** at Haystack Ski Area in Wilmington, and the **Southern Vermont Craft Fair** in Manchester; the **Stowe Craft Show;** in September, the **Stratton Arts Festival**

(4 weeks, until mid-October); in October, the **Apples & Crafts Show** in Woodstock, the **Mount Snow Craft Fair,** and the **Fall Festival of Vermont Crafts** in Montpelier; and in November, the **Burlington Craft Fair.**

DINERS

Vermont will not disappoint diner buffs. Hearty meals at reasonable prices can be found at the **Miss Newport** (good coffee), East Main Street, Newport; and at **Henry's Diner** (known for its Yankee pot roast, lobster roll, and generally good three squares) and the **Oasis,** both on Bank Street, Burlington. **Libby's Blue Line Diner,** Route 7 (just off I-89, exit 16), Colchester, is upscale and popular (you might dine on an eggplant burger). The **Parkway Diner** at 1696 Williston Road, South Burlington, is known for its Greek salad, lobster roll, and Parkway Special: roast beef on a pumpernickel roll. The **Miss Lyndonville Diner** on Bond Street, Lyndonville, is admired for its pies (a breakfast special) and has been augmented by the nearby **Miss Vermont** (Route 5, St. Johnsbury Center), though lines are still long on Sunday morning. **Anthony's Restaurant** in St. Johnsbury has expanded and is wheelchair-accessible but still offers great food at great prices. **Blue Benn Diner,** 102 Hunt Street in Bennington, serves imaginative vegetarian as well as standard diner fare. Add to these the **Yankee Diner** at Timber Village, Quechee; **Green Mountain Diner,** Main Street in Barre, **Cindy's Diner** in St. Albans, and **Don's Diner** in Bennington. **T. J. Buckley's** in Brattleboro may look like the battered vintage Worcester diner it is, but inside oak paneling gleams and the fare (dinner only, and only by reservation) is recognized as some of the best in the state. Brattleboro also offers **Ray's Diner,** not far off I-91, exit 1 (45 Canal Street), known for its crispy french fries; **Chelsea Royal Diner,** west on Route 9, while a bit heavy on diner decor, is still a good family bet (wheelchair-accessible). In Chester the **Country Girl Diner** has to compete with **The Other Diner** (excellent). **Miss Bellows Falls Diner** is on the National Register of Historic Places, and the **Windsor Diner** in Windsor, the **Polka Dot** in White River Junction, and the **Fairlee Diner** in Fairlee should be if they aren't; we swear by both of these last two and wouldn't think of driving by without stopping. See also *Highway Roadfood.*

EMERGENCIES
Try **911** first. This simple SOS is finally reaching most corners of Vermont. Within this book, we have furnished the number of the medical facilities serving each area in each chapter.

EVENTS
Almost every day of the year, some special event is happening somewhere in Vermont. Usually it's something relatively small and friendly like a church supper, contra dance, community theatrical production, concert, or crafts fair. We have worked up our own "Calendar of Events" but would like to mention here that detailed listings of current events are available from the Vermont Tourism Department (1-800-VERMONT), or by checking out the state's travel web site: www.travel-vermont.com. Still, many of the best events are like fireflies, surfacing only on local bulletin boards and in the Thursday editions of local papers. In Burlington check out the free and fat *Seven Days*, a funky weekly listing of local arts and entertainment, available everywhere in town.

FACTORY OUTLETS
Within the book, we have mentioned only a small fraction of the factory outlets of which

we are aware. Our bias has been to favor distinctly made-in-Vermont products. Among our favorites: **Johnson Woolen Mills** (outstanding wool clothing for all ages) in Johnson; **Bennington Potters** (dinnerware, planters, etc.) in Bennington and Burlington; **Vermont Marble** in Proctor; and **Weston Bowl Mill** in Weston. Manchester is known for its concentration of outlet stores specializing in quality clothing.

FARMER'S MARKETS
From mid-June through early October, you can count on finding fresh vegetables, fruit, honey, and much more at farm prices in commercial centers throughout the state. Check the times and places in Burlington, Enosburg, Morrisville, Newport, St. Johnsbury, Norwich, Fair Haven, Middlebury, Montpelier, Rutland, Brattleboro, Manchester, Waterbury, Windsor, and Woodstock.

FARM STAYS
Under *Agricultural Facts and Fairs* we have described Vermont's changing farm scene and the ways in which farmers are reaching out to visitors. One way that deserves special notice is the increase, once more, of farms that take in guests. A century ago, hundreds of Vermont farms took in visitors for weeks at a time. "There is no crop more profitable than the crop from the city," an 1890s Vermont Board of Agriculture pamphlet proclaimed, a publication noted by Dona Brown in *Inventing New England* (Smithsonian, 1995). Articles advised farmers how to decorate, what to serve, and generally how to please and what to expect from city guests—much as B&B literature does today. A free booklet, **Vermont Farm Vacations,** is available from the Vermont Department Agriculture (see *Agricultural Facts and Fairs*), but a half-dozen more have opened to visitors since its publication; all are listed as they appear geographically but,

KIM GRANT

probably because our own family found a farm stay so enriching, we list them all here: **Arkmont Christmas Tree Farm** (758-2300) in Bridmont, **Kimberly Farms Riding Stable** (442-4354) in Shaftsbury, **Rose Apple Acres** (525-6695) in North Troy, **Mendon Mountain Orchards** (425-2811) in Mendon, **Shadowbrook Farms** (524-7062) in Fairfield, **Maple Crest Farm** (492-3367) in Shrewsbury, **Redemption Farm** (235-2105) in Middletown Springs, **Indian Trail Farm** (247-8002) in Shoreham, **Berkson Farms** (933-2522) in Enosburg Falls, **Knoll Farm** (496-3939) in Fayston, **Liberty Hill Farm** (767-3926) and **Harvey's Mountain View** (767-4273), both in Rochester, **Allenholm Farm/Orchards B&B** (372-5566) in South Hero, **Round-Robin Farm** (763-7025) in Sharon, **Emergo Farm Bed and Breakfast** (684-2215), **Tamworth Farm** (684-3963), and **Sherryland** (684-3354), all in Danville, **Garvin Hill B&B** and **Beefalo Farm** in Greensboro, **Greenhope Horse Farm** (533-7772) in Walden, the **MacBain Homestead** in West Danville (563-2025), **Echo Ledge Farm Inn** (748-4750) in East St. Johnsbury, **Cedar Grove Farm** (592-3650) in Peacham, and the **Perry Farm** (754-2396) in Brownington. We should also mention that Shelburne Farms, the state's most elegant farm, is also the site of its most elegant inn : the **Inn at Shelburne Farms** (985-8686).

FERRIES

On Lake Champlain, a number of car-carrying ferries ply back and forth between the Vermont and New York shores, offering splendid views of both the Green Mountains and the Adirondacks. The northernmost, the **Plattsburgh Ferry,** crosses from Grand Isle, Vermont, on Route 314 (year-round; 12-minute passage). From Burlington, the **Lake Champlain Ferries** cross to Port Kent, New York (1 hour). The **Essex Ferry** crosses from Route F-5 near Charlotte, Vermont, to Essex, New York (20 minutes). Check schedules (864-9804) for hours of operation and rates. All three of these are operated by the Lake Champlain Transportation Company, descendant of the line founded in 1828 claiming to be "the oldest steamboat company on earth." Near the southern end of the lake, the **Fort Ticonderoga Ferry** (897-7999) provides a scenic shortcut between Larrabees Point, Vermont, and Ticonderoga, New York. This small, car-carrying ferry makes the 6-minute crossing continuously between 8 AM and 9 PM during the summer season and less frequently in spring and fall. Service runs from late April through the last Sunday in October. Officially, the Fort Ti Ferry has held the franchise from the New York and Vermont legislatures since 1799.

FIDDLING

Vermont is the fiddling capital of the East. Fiddlers include concert violinists, rural carpenters, farmers, and heavy-equipment operators who come from throughout the East to gather in beautiful natural settings. The **Northeast Fiddling Association** publishes newsletters that list fiddling meets around the state, the first Sunday of every month. Contact them at RR 1, Box 1, East Randolph 05401; 728-5188. Annual events include the **Crackerbarrel Fiddle Festival,** Newbury, and, in late September, the **National Championship Fiddle Contest,** Barre. Fiddle festivals tend to start around noon and end around dusk.

FILM

Two Vermont filmmakers have produced some notable low-budget films in recent years. Jay Craven's dramatizations of Howard Frank Mosher's novels—*Where the Rivers Flow North, A Stranger in the Kingdom,* and *Disappearances*—are all not only good films but evocative of life in the Northeast Kingdom not too long ago. By the same token John O'Brien's films, *Vermont is for Lovers* and *Man with a Plan,* go right to Vermont's still very real rural core. *Man with a Plan* actually launched its hero's real-life political campaign in 1998: To the amazement of the country, retired Tunbridge dairy farmer Fred Tuttle not only defeated a wealthy carpetbagger for the Republican nomination but won a respectable percentage of the vote for a U.S. senatorial seat.

FISHING

Almost every Vermont river and pond, certainly any body of water serious enough to call itself a lake, is stocked with fish. Brook trout are the most widely distributed game fish. Visitors ages 15 and over must have a 5-day, a 14-day, or a nonresident license good for a year, available at any town clerk's office, from the local fish and game warden, or from assorted commercial outlets. Because these sources may be closed or time-consuming to track down on weekends, it's wise to obtain the license in advance from the **Vermont Fish and Wildlife Department** (241-3711), Waterbury 05676; request an application form and ask for a copy of the informative *Vermont Guide to Fishing,* which details every species of fish and where to find it on a map of the state's rivers and streams, ponds, and lakes. Boat access, fish

hatcheries, and canoe routes are also noted. A list of contoured depth charts for more than 80 Vermont lakes and ponds is available from the **Vermont Department of Environmental Conservation,** Waterbury 05676; prices vary; minimum order is $1. The state's most famous trout stream is the **Battenkill River** in the southwest, focus of a fly-fishing school in Manchester Center offered by the **Orvis Company,** which has been in the business of making fishing rods and selling them to city people for more than a century (it also maintains an outstanding museum devoted to fly-fishing). Many inns, notably along Lake Champlain and in the Northeast Kingdom, offer tackle, boats, and advice on where to catch what. Landlocked salmon can be found in some northern lakes, and the Atlantic salmon has begun to return to the Connecticut and Clyde Rivers; other common species include bass, walleye, northern pike, and perch. Federal fish hatcheries can be found in **Bethel** (234-5241) and **Pittsford** (483-6618), and state hatcheries are in **West Burke** (467-3660), **Bennington** (442-4556), **Grand Isle** (372-3171), **Roxbury** (485-7568), and **Salisbury** (352-4471). Virtually every Vermont body of water has one or more fishing access areas, and they are used year-round. Ice anglers can legally take every species of fish (trout only in a limited number of designated waters) and can actually hook smelt and some varieties of whitefish that are hard to come by during warmer months; the **Great Benson Fishing Derby** held annually in mid-February on Lake Champlain draws thousands of contestants from throughout New England. The **Lake Champlain International Derby,** based in Burlington (call 862-7777 for details), is a big summer draw. Books to buy include The *Vermont Atlas and Gazetteer* (DeLorme), with details about fishing species and access; the

Atlas of Vermont Trout Ponds and *Vermont Trout Streams*, both from Northern Cartographics Inc. (Box 133, Burlington 05402); and *Fishing Vermont's Streams and Lakes* by Peter F. Cammann (Backcountry Publications).Within this book we have listed shops, outiftters, and guides as they appear within each region. *Vermont Adventure Guides* (1-800-425-8747) represents qualified guides throughout the state; web site: www.adventureguidesvt.com.

FOLIAGE

Vermont is credited with inventing foliage season, first aggressively promoted just after World War II in the initial issues of *Vermont Life.* The Department of Tourism (see *Information*) maintains a foliage "hot line" and sends out weekly bulletins on color progress, which is always earlier than assumed by those of us who live south of Montpelier. Those in the know usually head for northern Vermont in late September and the very first week in October, a period that coincides with peak color in that area as well as with the **Northeast Kingdom Fall Foliage Festival** (see "St. Johnsbury, Craftsbury, and Burke Mountain Area"). By the following weekend, central Vermont is usually ablaze, but visitors should be sure to have a bed reserved before coming, because organized bus tours converge on the state from throughout the United States, with a growing contingent each year from Canada and the rest of the world. By the Columbus Day weekend, when what seems like millions of Bostonians and New Yorkers make their annual leaf-peeping expedition, your odds of finding a bed are dim unless you take advantage of those chambers of commerce (notably Middlebury, Woodstock, Brattleboro, Manchester, and St. Johnsbury) that pride themselves on finding refuge in private homes for all comers. During peak color, we recommend that you avoid

Vermont's most heavily trafficked tourist routes, especially Route 9 between Bennington and Brattleboro; there is plenty of room on the back roads, especially those unsuited to buses. We strongly suggest exploring the high roads through Vermont's "gaps" (see *Gaps, Gulfs, and Gorges*) during this time of year.

FORESTS AND PARKS

The **Department of Forests, Parks and Recreation** (241-3665), 103 South Main Street, Waterbury 05671-0603 (web site: www.vtstateparks.com), manages more than 157,000 acres of state land, offering opportunities for hunting, fishing, cross-country skiing, mountain biking, snowmobiling, and primitive and supervised camping. The 50 exceptionally well-groomed state parks that including camping and/or day-use facilities, are described in the invaluable *Vermont State Parks Map Atlas* (revised in 1999, $5). Request individual leaflet guides to *Day Recreation Areas,* to *Vermont State Natural Areas,* and to specific hiking trails such as those in **Camel's Hump State Park,** in the **Mount Mansfield State Forest,** and in **Willoughby State Forest** (overlooking Lake Willoughby). Many of the trails detailed in current guidebooks (see *Hiking and Walking*) traverse state forests. Since its founding in 1924 the department has acquired, and continues to acquire, such a diverse assortment of properties that no one image applies. Within this book we attempt to describe each as it appears geographically. See also *Green Mountain National Forest.*

GAPS, GULFS, AND GORGES

Vermont's mountains were much higher before they were pummeled some 100,000 years ago by a mile-high sheet of ice. Glacial forces contoured the landscape we recognize today, notching the mountains with a number of handy "gaps" through which men eventually built roads to get from one side of the mountain to the other. Gaps frequently offer superb views and access to ridge trails. This is true of the **Appalachian, Lincoln, Middlebury,** and **Brandon Gaps,** all on the Long Trail and linking Route 100 with the Champlain Valley; and of the **Roxbury Gap** east of the Mad River Valley. Note, however, that the state's highest and most scenic gap of all is called a "notch" (**Smugglers Notch** between Stowe and Jeffersonville), the New Hampshire name for mountain passes. Gaps at lower elevations are "gulfs," scenic passes that make ideal picnic sites: Note **Granville Gulf** on Route 100, **Brookfield Gulf** on Route 12, and **Williamstown Gulf** on Route 14. The state's outstanding gorges include: 140-foot-deep **Quechee Gorge,** which can be viewed from Route 4 east of Woodstock; **Brockway Mills Gorge** in Rockingham (off Route 103); **Cavendish Gorge,** Springfield; **Clarendon Gorge,** Shrewsbury (traversed by the Long Trail via footbridge); **Brewster River Gorge,** south of Jeffersonville off Route 108; **Jay Branch Gorge** off Route 105; and (probably the most photographed of all) the **Brown River** churning through the gorge below the Old Red Mill in Jericho.

GARDENS

Vermont's growing season is short but all the more intense. Commercial herb and flower gardens are themselves the fastest-growing form of agriculture in the state, and many inns and B&Bs pride themselves on their gardens. Within the book we describe commercial gardens in most chapters. The Brick House (a B&B) in East Craftsbury and Sage Sheep Farm in Stowe both serve tea in their gardens; lodging places with especially noteworthy gardens include the Basin Harbor Club in Vergennes, Judith's Garden B&B

and Blueberry Hill, both in Goshen, and the Jackson House in Woodstock. Historic Hildene in Manchester also features formal gardens. Request the *Vermont Perennial & Herb Display Gardens* brochure from the Vermont Department of Agriculture (828-2416), 116 State Street, Montpelier 05620.

GENERAL STORES

Still the hub of most small Vermont communities, general stores retain some shreds of their onetime status as the source of all staples and communication with the outside world. The most famous survivor is the **Vermont Country Store** in Weston, a genuine family business that has expanded into a Vermont version of L. L. Bean. Still, its thick catalog is a source of long underwear and garter belts, Healthy Feet Cream, shoe trees, and gadgets like a kit that turns a plastic soda bottle into a bird feeder. Within each

CHRISTINA TREE

chapter, we have described some of our personal favorites. "The General Store in Vermont," an oral history by Jane Beck, is available from the Vermont Folklife Center in Middlebury. Within this book we have described our favorite generals stores as they appear geographically.

GOLF

More than 50 Vermont golf courses are open to the public and more than half of these are 18 holes, a half dozen justly famed throughout the country. A full program of lodging, meals, and lessons is available at **Mount Snow, Killington, Stratton Mountain, Sugarbush,** and **Stowe.** The **Woodstock Inn, Mountain Top Inn,** and others also offer golf packages. The Manchester area boasts the greatest concentration of courses. For a complete list of courses see Vermont's official state map, and for descriptions see the glossy *Vermont Golf Journal* (1-800-639-1941); web site: www.golf-vermont.com. *Vermont Golf Courses: A Player's Guide,* by Bob Labbance and David Cornwell (New England Press), is a useful book that describes all 50 of the courses open to the public, including detailed course maps, yardages, fees, opening/closing dates, and starting times.

GREEN MOUNTAIN NATIONAL FOREST

The **Green Mountain National Forest** encompasses more than 300,000 Vermont acres, managed by the U.S. Forest Service. They are traversed by 512 miles of trails, including the Appalachian Trail and the Long Trail, which follows the ridgeline of the main range of the Green Mountains (see *Hiking and Walking*). The forest harbors six wilderness areas. Use of off-road recreational vehicles is regulated. Information—printed as well as verbal—about hiking, camping, skiing, berry picking, and bird-watching is available from the ranger stations in Manchester Center, Middlebury, and Rochester. For details (request a free "minimap" and "Winter Recreation Map"), contact the Green Mountain National Forest (773-0300), P.O. Box 519, Rutland 05701. (See also *Campgrounds.*)

HANDICAPPED ACCESS

With this edition we have included the wheelchair symbol &. to indicate lodging and dining places that are handicapped-accessible.

HERBS

Herb farms are a growing phenomenon in rural Vermont—sources of live perennials and herbs; herbs dried into fanciful wreaths; sachets, potpourris, or seasonings distilled as scents. In our wanderings, we have happened on **Meadowsweet Herb Farm,** attached to a handsome farmhouse on a back road in Shrewsbury; **Talbot's Herb and Perennial Farm** in Hartland, east of Woodstock off Route 4; in Stowe, **Misty Meadows Herb and Perennial Farm** and **Sage Sheep Farm** both welcome visitors. A pamphlet guide, *Vermont Perennial & Herb Display Gardens,* is available from the Vermont Department of Agriculture (828-2416), 116 State Street, Montpelier 05620.

HIGH SEASON

"High season," interestingly enough, varies in Vermont. While "foliage season" represents peak price as well as color everywhere, a ski condo can easily cost four times in February what it does in July. Meanwhile, a country inn may charge half its July price in February.

HIGHWAY ROAD FOOD

As we cruise Vermont's interstate we have, over the years, developed patterns of exiting for food at places where (1) food is less than a mile from the exit, and (2) food is good, and we strongly favor diners and local eateries over fast-food chains. Recently friends have been calling, asking for advice on where to break for food. Needless to say, wherever there's food there's gas (no pun intended). All the following restaurants are described in their respective chapters.

Along **I-91,** south to north: *Exit 1* puts you on Route 5 in Brattleboro; head up to **Ray's Diner.** *Exit 2:* Route 9 is handy to downtown Brattleboro. *Exit 4:* The **Putney Inn** is good for all three meals; around the corner (right on Route 5) is **Curtis's Barbecue;** just a bit father up on your right, the **Putney Diner.** *Exit 11:* We usually pass up the chains in favor of the **Polka Dot Diner** in downtown White River Junction, or the **Four Aces Diner** just across the river in West Lebanon, New Hampshire. *Exit 13:* Turn right over the bridge into Hanover, New Hampshire, or left into Norwich to **Alice's Bakery & Cafe.** *Exit 15:* The **Fairlee Diner** is just north on Route 5. *Exit 16:* The **Bradford Village Store** is in the middle of the village (left); try for the window seat. *Exit 17:* **P&H Truck Stop** is worth a stop. *Exit 23:* Turn north onto Route 5 to find the **Miss Lyndonville Diner.** *Exit 25:* **Miss Newport Diner.** *Exit 28:* **Abbie Lane,** ½ mile west of exit 28, closed Monday.

Along I-89: *Exit 2:* **Brooksie's** is right there in the middle of Sharon. *Exit 3:* **Eaton's Sugar House** is right off the exit. *Exit 10:* Turn left, then left again, and you are in the middle of Waterbury at **Arvad's.** *Exit 13:* Burlington is just down the hill, worth a detour. *Exit 16:* **Libby's Blue Diner** is right there and great.

HIGHWAY TRAVEL

The **official state map,** updated annually (see *Maps*), comes free from local chamber of commerce information booths as well as from the state (see *Information*). **Interstate highway rest areas** with pay phones and bathroom facilities (usually open 7 AM–11 PM), indicated on the state map, are found on **I-91** at **Guilford** (a Welcome Center), northbound; at **Bradford,** north- and southbound; at **Barnet,** northbound; at **Derby,** southbound; and at **Fairfax,** southbound. On I-89 there are rest areas at **Sharon,** north- and southbound; at **Randolph,** north- and southbound; and at **Williston,** north- and southbound (these are now staffed as information centers for the Burlington area). Note the work of Vermont

sculptors commissioned for these rest areas by the Vermont Council on the Arts in cooperation with the Vermont Marble Company. In 1982, the Vermont stretch of I-89 was dedicated to honor veterans and casualties of the war in Vietnam. Picnic sites with tables and benches are scattered along most major routes throughout the state; picnic tables are clearly marked on the state map. A major welcome center is also located on I-93 in Lower Waterford. **AAA Emergency Road Service:** 1-800-222-4357. See also *Weather.*

HIKING AND WALKING

There are more than 700 miles of hiking trails in Vermont—which is 162 miles long as the crow flies but 255 miles long as the hiker trudges, following the **Long Trail** up and down the spine of the Green Mountains. But few hikers are out to set distance records on the Long Trail. The path from Massachusetts to the Canadian border, which was completed in 1931, has a way of slowing people down. It opens up eyes and lungs and drains compulsiveness. Even diehard backpackers tend to linger on rocky outcrops, looking down on farms and steeples. A total of 98 side trails (175 miles) meander off to wilderness ponds or abandoned villages; these trails are mostly maintained, along with the Long Trail, by the **Green Mountain Club** (244-7037), founded in 1910. The club also maintains 70 shelters, many of them staffed by caretakers during summer months. The club publishes the *Long Trail Guide* ($14.95), which gives details on trails and shelters throughout the system, as well as the *Day Hiker's Guide to Vermont* ($14.95; new again in 1999). These and other guides are sold in the club's **Hiker's Center,** 4711 Waterbury Road, Waterbury Center 05677 (open 9–5 daily). The **Appalachian Trail Conference** (P.O. Box 807, Harpers Ferry, WV 25425) in-

© SPORTS FILE/DENNIS CURRAN

cludes detailed descriptions of most Vermont trails in its *Appalachian Trail Guide to Vermont and New Hampshire* ($18.95), and a wide assortment of trails are nicely detailed in *50 Hikes in Vermont* (Backcountry Publications, $14.95). Backpackers who are hesitant to set out on their own can take a wide variety of guided hikes and walks. **Adventure Guides of Vermont** (1-800-425-8787) can put you in touch with guides throughout the state, and organized tours are offered by **Umiak Outdoor Outfitters** (1-800-479-3380) based in Stowe. **North Wind Inn Touring** (1-800-496-5771; web site: www.northwindtouring.com) in Waitsfield offers 3- to 7-day hiking and walking tours throughout North America as well as Vermont, as **Country Walkers** (244-1387; 1-800-464-9255), based in Waterbury, and **Vermont Hiking Holidays** (453-4816), based in Bristol, walk the world; **Four Seasons Touring** (365-7937) in Townshend and **Walking Tours of Southern Vermont** in Arlington (375-1141) are locally focused. Two groups of inns have also offered support services (route planning, baggage transfers) as well as meals and lodging: **Country Inns Along the Trail** is based at the Churchill House (247-3300; RFD 3, Brandon 05733), and **Walking Inn Vermont** involves inns between Ludlow and Chester (228-8799; P.O. Box 243, Ludlow 05149-0243). "Walking" Vermont's dirt roads and less strenuous paths has, in fact, become the "inn" thing to do in the past

couple of years. Within this book we suggest hiking trails as they appear geographically and should note the recent proliferation of trail systems. In the Northeast Kingdom check out **Kingdom Trails** in East Burke, the **Vermont Leadership Center** near Island Pond, and the **Hazens Notch Association Trails.** We should also note that both Killington and Sugarbush offer ridge hiking from the top of their lifts. (See also *Birding, Forests and Parks, Mountain Biking,* and *Nature Preserves.*)

HISTORY

Vermont's a small state, but it's had a dramatic life. In essence, the whole state is a living history museum, even though most towns were settled later in the 18th century—after the Revolution—than in other New England states. Many, often overlapping land grants issued by the royal governors of both New Hampshire and New York, were not finally sorted out until 1791, when Congress admitted Vermont as the 14th state, after 14 years as an independent republic.

Although there's an Abenaki presence in **Swanton,** little tangible evidence remains of the nomadic Native American tribes that once roamed the virgin forests. The 18th-century tavern at **Chimney Point State Historic Site,** however, has a well-mounted display that explains the territory's Native American and French colonial heritage.

Bennington, the first town to be chartered (1749) west of the Connecticut River in the New Hampshire Grants by the avaricious Gov. Benning Wentworth, became the tinderbox for settlers' resistance to New York's rival claims, confirmed by King George in 1764. The desperate grantees found a champion in the protean Ethan Allen, from Connecticut. This frontier rebel—land speculator, firebrand, and philosopher—recruited the boisterous

Green Mountain Boys militiamen, who talked rum and rebellion at the Catamount Tavern in **Old Bennington,** roared defiance of the 'Yorkers, and then fought the British. Ethan's rambunctious life is reflected in the **Ethan Allen Homestead,** the farm in Burlington where he died in 1789.

In Westminster, on the bank of the Connecticut River, the 1775 **"Massacre"** was thought, incorrectly, to have been the first armed engagement of the Revolution. But the death of William French, shot by a 'Yorker sheriff ("The Cruel Minestereal Tools of George ye 3d"), galvanized opposition to both New York and England, leading to a convention in Westminster in January 1777, where Vermonters declared their independence of everyone.

Formal independence was declared the following July, upriver in Windsor, where delegates gathered in Elijah West's tavern (now **The Old Constitution House**). They adopted a model constitution, the first to abolish slavery, before rushing off to attack the British, who had retaken Fort Ticonderoga. (While in Windsor, visit the **American Precision Museum,** a landmark reflecting early gun makers and the heyday of the machine tool industry.)

Ever since its discovery by Samuel de Champlain in 1609, Lake Champlain has been not only one of the nation's most historic waterways, but a strategic corridor in three wars. **St. Anne's Shrine** on Isle LaMotte marks the site of the first French settlement in 1666, and Champlain himself is honored here with a massive granite statue.

The lake was controlled by the French until 1759, when Lord Jeffery Amherst drove them out of Fort Carrillon (now **Ticonderoga**) and then captured Montreal. In the American Revolution, the British used the lake as an invasion route to divide the colonies, but were thwarted when Ethan Allen's Green Mountain Boys captured Fort Ticonderoga in 1775.

Facing Ticonderoga across the lake's narrowest channel, the **Mount Independence State Historic Site** near Orwell dramatizes the struggle that ended with the decisive British defeat at Saratoga in 1777. As Burgoyne's British troops marched south, the only battle of the Revolution to have been fought on Vermont soil is commemorated at the **Hubbardton Battlefield** near Castleton, where a small force of Green Mountain Boys under Col. Seth Warner stopped a far larger British contingent. The invaders were soon repulsed again in the Battle for Bennington—actually fought in New York—marked by the **Bennington Battle Monument** and by exhibits in the **Bennington Museum.**

The lake also figured in naval warfare when Benedict Arnold and a quickly assembled American flotilla engaged a heavier British squadron off Plattsburgh, New York, in the battle of Valcour Island in October 1776. One of Arnold's small gunboats, the *Philadelphia,* sunk by the British, was salvaged in 1935 and reposes in the Smithsonian. An exact replica is moored at the **Champlain Maritime Museum** at Basin Harbor near Vergennes. In 1814 the British again tried to use Lake Champlain as an invasion route. Commo. Thomas McDonough moved his headquarters from Burlington to Vergennes and a shipyard at the mouth of Otter Creek. His small fleet barely managed to defeat British ships at Plattsburgh Bay, a bloody engagement that helped end the War of 1812.

With Vermont in the vanguard of the antislavery movement of the 1840s, the Underground Railroad flourished, notably at **Rokeby,** the home of the Robinson family in Ferrisburg, now a museum. Evidences of the state's extraordinary record in the Civil War and its greater-than-average number of per-capita casualties may be seen in the memorials that dot most town and village greens. How Vermonters turned the tide of battle at Cedar Creek is portrayed in Julian Scott's huge painting that hangs in the **State House** in Montpelier. The October 1864 **St. Albans Raid,** the northernmost engagement of the Civil War, is observed annually.

There are few 18th-century structures in the state, but the settlers who poured into the state after 1791, when the population nearly tripled from 85,000 to 235,000 in 1820, built sophisticated dwellings and churches. **Dorset, Castleton, Chester** (Old Stone Village), **Middlebury, Brandon, Woodstock,** and **Norwich** are architectural showcases of Federal-style houses. Several historic, outstandingly splendid mansions built by 19th-century moguls are open to the public: the **Park-McCullough House,** North Bennington; the **Wilburton Inn** and **Hildene,** Manchester; **The Castle Inn,** Proctorsville; **Wilson Castle,** West Rutland; the **Marsh-Billings National Historical Park,** Woodstock; and **The Inn at Shelburne Farms** (built by Lila Vanderbilt Webb), Shelburne.

Vermont's Congressional delegations, especially in the 19th century, have always had more influence in Washington than the size of the state might indicate. For example, the **Justin Morrill Homestead** in Strafford, a spacious Gothic-revival stone house, reminds us of the distinguished career of the originator of the Land Grant Colleges Act, who served in Congress from 1855 to 1898.

State and local historical societies have faithfully preserved the cultural evidence. The **Vermont Historical Society Museum** in Montpelier houses permanent and thematic exhibits. Arts, crafts, architecture, and transportation are featured in the **Shelburne Museum** in Shelburne. The **Billings Farm & Museum** in Woodstock

re-creates a model stock farm and dairy in the 1890s. Outstanding collections of the ways people lived and worked can be found in town historical societies, notably the **Farrar-Mansur House** in Weston, the **Sheldon Museum** in Middlebury, and the **Dana House** in Woodstock. For a lively, popular story of the state from its origins to the present, read Peter Jennison's *Roadside History of Vermont* (Mountain Press). A pamphlet guide to Vermont historic sites is available at information centers throughout the state.

HISTORICAL SOCIETIES

Historical societies are the attics of every town and are frequently worth seeking out, but because most are staffed by volunteers they tend to be open just a few hours a week, in summer. Within each chapter we have tried to give accurate, current information, but in recent years Vermont has fallen far behind other New England states in collecting and relaying information about these village museums. Outstanding local historical societies are found in **Brattleboro, Brownington, Newfane,** and **Middlebury.**

HORSEBACK RIDING

A list of riding stables, specifying trail and sleigh rides, is included in the free booklet *Vermont Life Explorer,* available from the Vermont Department of Tourism and Marketing (see *Information*). Inn-to-inn treks are offered by **Kedron Valley Stables** in South Woodstock and the **Icelandic Horse Farm** in Waitsfield. Places that combine lodging and riding include **Greenhope Horse Farm** in Walden, **Kimberly Farms** in Shaftsbury, **Firefly Ranch** in Bristol, **Mountain Top Equestrian Center** in Chittenden, **Topnotch at Stowe Resort & Spa** and **Edson Hill Manor** in Stowe, **Stratton Mountain** and **Smugglers'**

Notch resorts, and **West River Stables** in Newfane. Better riders will also appreciate the mounts at **Rohan Farm** in East Burke. Trail rides are also offered at **Birch Meadow Rising Stables** in Brookfield, **Cedar Ridge Farm** in Barre City, **Mazza Horse Services** in Bridport, at **Flame Stables** and **Mountain View Stables** in Wilmington, **Pond Hill Ranch** in Castleton, at **Valley View Horses and Tack Shop** in Pownal, **Cavendish Trail Horse Rides** in Proctorsville, and **Winchester Stables** in Newfane. Serious equestrians interested in horse shows and horse boarding should contact the **Vermont Horse Council** (1-800-722-1419), P.O. Box 105, 400 Country Road, Montpelier 05601.

HOSTELS

The hostels in Vermont are affiliated with **Hosteling International** (formerly AYH), with New England headquarters at 1105 Commonwealth Avenue, Boston, MA 02215 (617-779-0900). Hostels are open to all travelers who are HI members (membership costs adults $25, seniors $15; children are free). Nonmembers may use hostels for an additional nominal charge per night. They supply simple lodging and cooking facilities and are geared to bicyclists and everyone on a budget. The Vermont hostels are in **Burlington** (865-3730), **St. Johnsbury** (748-1575), **East Jamaica** (874-4096), **Ludlow** (1-800-547-7454), **White River Junction** (295-3118), **Montpelier** (223-2104), **Woodford** (442-2547) and **Underhill Center** (899-1796). The HI booklet comes free with membership. Hostelers are expected to carry their own sleeping sack, to reserve bunk space ahead, and to arrive between 5 and 8 PM. Hostels customarily close between 10 AM and 5 PM; alcohol is not permitted on the premises. We should also note the **Vermont State Ski Dorm** (253-4010), built by the Civilian Conservation Corps near the top of Stowe's Mountain Road in 1933.

HUNTING

Vermont Guide to Hunting, a free pamphlet, lists and locates major wildlife management areas in the state and is available, along with a current *Digest of Fish & Wildlife Laws,* from the Vermont Fish and Wildlife Department (241-3700), 103 South Main Street, Waterbury 05671-0501. A nonresident small-game hunting license costs $35, a regular hunting license is $80, a combined hunting and fishing license is $100. A limited bow-and-arrow license is $50; a regular bow-and-arrow license is $15 on top of the regular hunting license. A nonresident trapping license is $300; an alien, nonresident trapping license is $500; both of these can be obtained only through the Fish and Wildlife Department. Of special interest may be the nonresident, 5-day small-game license for $20. A resident hunting license is $12, and trapping is $20. **Deer season** begins 12 days before Thanksgiving and lasts for 16 days. **Bow-and-arrow season** also lasts 16 days, beginning the first Saturday in October; **hare and rabbit season** extends from the last Saturday in September to the second Sunday in March; **gray squirrel season** is from the last Saturday in September to the last Thursday before regular deer season. **Partridge and grouse** may be shot between the last Saturday in September and December 31, with a limit of four daily, eight in possession. **Black bear** season is determined annually. Licenses may be secured from local town clerks or wardens or ahead of time by mail from the Fish and Wildlife Department. In order to purchase a Vermont hunting or combination license, you must show or submit either a certificate proving you have satisfactorily completed a hunter safety course or a previous hunting or combination license.

ICE CREAM

Vermont's quality milk is used to produce some outstanding ice cream as well as cheese. The big name is, of course, **Ben & Jerry's,** proud producers of what *Time* has billed "the best ice cream in the world." Their plant on Route 100 in Waterbury (featuring factory tours, free samples, real cows, and a gift shop full of reproductions in every conceivable shape) has quickly become one of the state's most popular tourist attractions. Other good Vermont ice creams include **Seward's** in Rutland, **Wilcox Brothers** in Manchester, and the **Mountain Creamery** in Woodstock.

INFORMATION

The Vermont Department of Tourism and Marketing (828-3237; 1-800-VERMONT; fax: 828-3233; e-mail: vttravel @dca.state.vt.us; web site: http://www.1-800-vermont.com), 6 Baldwin Street, 4th Floor, Drawer 33, Montpelier 05633-1301, offers excellent, free aids: (1) **Vermont's official state map** includes symbols locating covered bridges, golf courses, and picnic spots, ski areas, recreation sites, and boat-launch ramps. On the reverse side are descriptive listings of museums, galleries, and historic places, fishing and hunting rules and license fees, state and private campgrounds, state liquor stores, and hospital emergency rooms. (2) *Vermont Life Explorer,* a glossy magazine introducing the state. For information about specific parts of the state, the magazine refers visitors to 12 regional marketing associations, which we note as they apply to specific regions within each chapter of this book. On request you can also obtain the *Vermont Campground Guidebook,* and two seasonal guides to cottage rentals. The **Vermont Chamber of Commerce** (223-3443;

fax: 828-4257; e-mail: info@vtchamber.com) also publishes *Vermont Travelers Guidebook* and will send it on request, along with a *Vermont Attractions* map and pamphlet guides to shopping and country inns and B&Bs; the web site is www.vtchamber.com. **State Welcome Centers** are located at **Fair Haven** (265-4763), on Route 4A at the New York border; in **Guilford** (254-4593), on I-91 at the Massachusetts border; in **Highgate Springs** (868-3244), on I-89 at the Canadian border; in **Bradford** (222-9369), on I-91; and in **Lower Waterford** (748-3725), on I-93 on the New Hampshire line. Dial the toll-free Vermont fax line (1-800-833-9756) and you get a printout of the month's events and other current travel tips. We have noted local chambers of commerce town by town in each chapter of this book. In towns not served by a chamber, inquiries are welcomed by the town clerk. First-time visitors may be puzzled by Vermont's Travel Information System of directional signs that replace billboards (banned since 1967, another Vermont "first"). Stylized symbols for lodging, food, recreation, antiques and crafts, and other services are sited at intersections off major highways, at interstate rest areas, at incoming border Welcome Centers, and at other key points of travel interest. Travel Information Plazas should be consulted to get oriented to the system. They are indicated on the state map.

INNS

It's safe to say that we have visited more Vermont inns, more frequently, than anyone else living today. We do not charge for inclusion in this book, and we attempt to give as accurate and detailed a picture as space permits. We have described many inns in their respective towns, quoting 1999 rates. These prices are, of course, subject to change and should not be regarded as gospel. Summer rates are generally lower than winter rates (except, of course, at lake resorts); weekly or ski-week rates run 10–20 percent less than the per-diem price quoted. Many inns insist on MAP (Modified American Plan—breakfast and dinner) in winter but not in summer. Some resorts have AP (American Plan—three meals), and we have shown EP (European Plan—no meals) where applicable. We have attempted to note when 15 percent service is added, but you should always ask if it has been included in a quoted rate. Always add the 9 percent state tax on rooms and meals. It's prudent to check which, if any, credit cards are accepted. Within the text, special icons in the left-hand margin also highlight lodging places offering exceptional value 🏠, those that appeal to families ✧, those that are handicapped-accessible ♿, and those that accept pets 🐾.

KIM GRANT

LAKES

The state famed for green mountains and white villages also harbors more than 400 relatively blue lakes: big lakes like **Champlain** (150 miles long) and **Memphremagog** (boasting 88 miles of coastline but most of it in Canada), smaller lakes like **Morey, Dunmore, Willoughby, Bomoseen,** and **Seymour.** Lakes are particularly plentiful and people sparse in Vermont's Northeast Kingdom. A century ago, there were many more lakeside hotels; today just a half-dozen of these classic summer resorts survive: **Quimby Country** in Averill, **Highland Lodge** in Greensboro, the **Tyler Place** in Highgate Springs, the **Basin Harbor Club** near Vergennes, and the **Lake Morey Club** in Fairlee. There are a half-dozen smaller, informal inns on scattered lakes, but that's about it. Still, you can bed down very reasonably within sound and sight of Vermont waters either by renting a cottage (more than half of those listed

in *Four Season Vacation Rentals,* available from the Vermont Department of Tourism and Marketing, are on lakes) or by taking advantage of state park campsites on **Groton Lake, Island Pond, Maidstone Lake, Lake Bomoseen, Lake Carmi, Lake Elmore, Lake St. Catherine,** and **Silver Lake** (in Barnard). On Lake Champlain, there are a number of state campgrounds, including those on **Grand Isle** (accessible by car) and **Burton Island** (accessible by public launch from St. Albans Bay). See *Campgrounds* for details about these and the free campsites on **Ball Mountain Lake** maintained by the Army Corps of Engineers. There is public boat access to virtually every Vermont pond and lake of any size. Boat launches are listed on the state map.

LIBRARIES

The small village of Brookfield boasts the state's oldest continuously operating public library, established in 1791. Most libraries that we mention here date, however, from that late 19th-century philanthropic era when wealthy native sons were moved to donate splendidly ornate libraries to their hometowns. Notable examples are to be found in **Barre, Chester, Ludlow, Wilmington, Rutland, Newport, Woodstock, St. Johnsbury,** and **Brattleboro.** Two of our favorite libraries lie within a short drive of each other: one on the common in **Craftsbury Common,** and the second—a converted general store—in **East Crafts-**

bury, where there is a special back room for youngsters, with a Ping-Pong table amid the books. Unfortunately, visitors may not check out books unless they happen to be staying within the community that the library serves. For research, the **Vermont Historical Society Library** in Montpelier is a treasure trove of Vermontiana and genealogical resources, as is the Wilbur collection of the **Bailey-Howe Library** at the University of Vermont and the Russell Collection in Arlington. Three of the Vermont state colleges—Castleton, Johnson, and Lyndon—have collections of Vermontiana in the Vermont Rooms of their libraries.

LLAMA TREKKING
Both **Northern Vermont Llama Treks** (644-2257) in Waterville and **Cold Hollow Llamas** (644-5846), Belvidere, are described in our "North of the Notch and the Lamoille River Valley" chapter. **Heart of Vermont Llama Treks** (889-9611) are on a farm in Tunbridge in the White River Valley.

MAGAZINES
Vermont Life, the popular and colorful quarterly published by the Agency of Development and Community Affairs and edited by Tom Slayton, is an outstanding contemporary chronicle of Vermont's people and places, featuring distinguished photographers. Single issues cost $3.50; $14.95 a year; 6 Baldwin Street, Montpelier 05602. *Vermont Magazine,* the upbeat, statewide bimonthly launched in 1989, covers major issues, townscapes, new products, and personalities, and reviews inns and restaurants ($16.95 a year from Box 800, Middlebury 05753). *Vermont History,* a quarterly scholarly journal, is published for members of the Vermont Historical Society, Montpelier. *Vermont Business Magazine* (2 Church Street, Burlington 05401) is a well-written, tabloid-sized monthly that provides investigative reportage, analysis, and overviews of the state's economic doings from politically conservative and entrepreneurially aggressive points of view. *Seven Days* (864-5684), Burlington's free weekly tabloid of area arts and entertainment, is far more than a calendar of events (e-mail: sevendays@ together.net; web site: www.sevendaysvt.com.

MAPLE SUGARING
Vermont produces an average of 500,000 gallons of maple syrup each year, more than any other state. No fewer than 2,400 maple growers tap an average of 1,000 trees each. About ⅕ to ¼ gallon of syrup is made per tap; it takes 30–40 gallons of sap to make each gallon of syrup. The process of tapping trees and boiling sap is stubbornly known as "sugaring" rather than syruping, because the end product for early settlers was sugar. Syrup was first made in the early 19th century but production flagged when imported cane sugar was easy to come by. The Civil War revived the maple sugar industry: Union supporters were urged to consume sugar made by free men and to plant more and more maples. We urge visitors to buy syrup direct from the farm that has produced it any time of year (finding the farm is half the fun) but also to seriously consider making a special trip to a sugar shack during sugaring season. It's then, not autumn, that sugar maples really perform, and it's a show that can't be viewed through a windshield. Sugaring season begins quietly in February as thousands of Vermonters wade, showshoe, and snowmobile into their woods and begin "tapping," a ritual that may have changed technically as plastic tubing has replaced buckets, but the timing hasn't. Traditionally, sugaring itself begins on Town Meeting day (the first Tuesday in March). The fact is, however, that sap runs only on those days when temperatures rise to 40 and 50 degrees

KIM GRANT

during the day and drop into the 20s at night. And when the sap runs, it must be boiled down quickly. What you want to see is the boiling process: sap churning madly through the large, flat evaporating pan, darkening as you watch. You are enveloped in fragrant steam, listening to the rush of the sap, sampling the end result on snow or in tiny paper cups. Sugaring is Vermont's rite of spring. Don't miss a sugar-on-snow party: plates of snow dribbled with hot syrup, accompanied by doughnuts and dill pickles. The Vermont Department of Agriculture (828-2416) publishes the pamphlet guide *Maple Sugarhouses Open to Visitors* and also lists them by region on the web site www.vtcheese.com. Be sure to call before going to check if there is sugaring that day. The one big **Maple Festival** each spring is in St. Albans, a 3-day happening that includes tours through the local sugarbush (usually the second weekend in April; 524-5800). At **Maple Grove,** "the world's largest maple candy factory" in St. Johnsbury, factory tours are offered Monday through Friday year-round, and the **Maple Museum** and gift shop is open

May through late October. At **American Maple Products** (year-round) in Newport, you can see a movie about maple production; the story of sugaring is also dramatized in the **New England Maple Museum** in Pittsford and in the maple museum at **Sugarmill Farm** in Barton. Within this book we list maple producers in the areas in which they are most heavily concentrated.

MAPS

The **official state map** (see *Information*) is free and extremely helpful for general motoring in Vermont but will not suffice for finding your way around on the webs of dirt roads that connect some of the most beautiful corners of the state. Among our favorite areas wherein you are guaranteed to get lost using the state map: the high farming country between Albany, Craftsbury, and West Glover; similar country between Chelsea and Williamstown; south from Plainfield to Orange; and between Plymouth and Healdville. There are many more. We strongly suggest securing a copy of *The Vermont Atlas and Gazetteer* (DeLorme) if you want to do any serious back-road exploring, or *The Vermont Road Atlas and Guide* (Northern Cartographics); both are widely available at bookstores, gas stations, and general stores. The best regional maps for anyone planning to do much hiking or biking are published by **Map Adventures** (253-7489), 846 Cottage Club Road, Stowe 05672; www.mapadventures.com.

MONEY

Don't leave home without MasterCard or Visa, the two credit cards that are far more readily accepted in Vermont than American Express or personal checks. Each inn has its own policy about credit cards and checks.

MOUNTAIN BIKING

Several ski areas offer lift-assisted mountain biking: The **Mount Snow Resort Mountain Bike Center** (464-3333) was the first, offering 25 miles of trails spread over three of the ski resort's six peaks. **Stratton Mountain Resort** (297-4139), **Sugarbush Resort** (583-2381), **Killington** (422-6232), and **Jay Peak Resort** (988-2611; 1-800-451-4449) also now permit mountain biking on ski trails, accessible via lifts. In recent years, however, Vermont mountain-biking options have dramatically broadened beyond its ski mountains as the potential for its hundreds of miles of dirt and "class 4" roads as well as cross-county trail systems has been recognized. **The Craftsbury Center** (1-800-729-7751) up in the Northeast Kingdom was the first place to rent mountain bikes and offer guided tours over dirt and abandoned logging roads. A former prep school now devoted to running and rowing as well as biking in summer and cross-country skiing in winter, it's set in high, rolling farm country with mountain views. In Randolph you can arrive with your bike via Amtrak and walk up to **Bicycle Express** (728-5568), which also rents mountain bikes, offers guided tours, and sells a map to the 240 miles of trails maintained by the **White River Valley Trails Association** (728-4420). The **Three Stallion Inn** (see "The White River Valleys") in Randolph offers its own network of trails and serves as headquarters for the 3-day late-September **New England Mountain Bike Festival**. There's another magnificent trail system in the Burke Mountain area: **Kingdom Trails**. The hub of this system is **East Burke Sports** (626-3215), offering a 75-mile mix of alpine and cross-country ski trails, several loops in East Burke Village, snowmobile trails maintained by VAST, cross-country trails up on Darling Hill, and several more miles of trails specifically maintained by this nonprofit organization. For a map send $4 ($3 for the map, $1 for handling) to Kingdom Trails, P.O. Box 204, East Burke 05832. In southeastern Vermont the **West Hill Shop** (387-5718) publishes its own map to an extensive network of singletrack trails and forgotten roads. Another good bet is **Escape Routes** (746-8943), based at the Pittsfield Inn, which offers custom-designed guided and self-guided mountain biking. We describe inns and bike shops that offer bike rentals in almost every chapter, but here we should mention **Blueberry Hill Inn** (1-800-448-0707), set high in Goshen with easy access to trails in the Moosalamoo Region of the Green Mountain National Forest and to Silver Lake. In the Burlington area the **Catamount Family Center** (879-6001) and **Bolton Valley** (434-2131) both offer extensive cross-country trail networks and rentals. Nominally priced **Map Adventures Topographic Maps & Guides,** based in Stowe (253-7489), are useful map/guides outlining rides in various parts of Vermont: the Burlington and Stowe areas, the White River Valley, the Upper Valley, and southern Vermont, among others. **Adventure Guides of Vermont** (1-800-425-8747) is the way to find a guide. See also *Bicycle Touring*.

MOUNTAINTOPS

While Vermont can boast only seven peaks above 4,000 feet, there are 80 mountains that rise more than 3,000 feet and any number of spectacular views, several of them accessible in summer and foliage season to those who prefer riding to walking up mountains. **Mount Mansfield,** which at 4,343 feet is the state's highest summit, can be reached via the Toll Road and a gondola. The mid-19th-century road brings you to the small Summit Station at 4,062 feet, from which the ½-mile Tundra Trail brings you to the actual summit. The Mount Mansfield gondola, an eight-passenger, enclosed lift, hoists you from the main base area up to the Cliff House (serving light meals all day), from which a trail also heads up to the Chin. **Killington Peak,** Vermont's second highest peak at 4,241 feet, can be reached via a 1.2-mile ride on a gondola that takes you to a summit restaurant and a nature trail that even small children can negotiate. **Jay Peak,** a 3,861-foot summit towering like a lone sentinel near the Canadian border, is accessible via a 60-passenger tram (daily except Tuesday), and a "four-state view" from the top of **Stratton Mountain** is accessible via the ski resort's six-passenger gondola, "Starship XII" (daily in summer and fall). Other toll roads include the Auto Road to the 3,267-foot **Burke Mountain** in East Burke, the Toll Road to the 3,144-foot summit of **Mount Ascutney** in Ascutney State Park, and the road to the top of **Mount Equinox** in Sunderland. There are also chairlift rides to the tops of **Bromley** (you don't have to take the alpine slide down) and **Mount Snow** (weekends in summer, daily in foliage season).

MUD SEASON

The period from snowmelt (around the middle of March) through early May (it varies each year) is known throughout the state as mud season, for reasons that few visitors want to explore too deeply.

MUSEUMS

Vermont museums vary from the immense **Shelburne Museum**—with its 36 buildings, many housing priceless collections of Americana, plus assorted exhibits such as a completely restored lake steamer and lighthouse—to the **American Precision Museum** in Windsor, an 1846 brick mill that once produced rifles. They include a number of outstanding historical museums (our favorites are the **Sheldon Museum** in Middlebury, the **Old Stone House Museum** in Brownington, and the **Dana House** in Woodstock) and some collections that go beyond the purely historical: **Bennington Museum** (famed for its collection of Grandma Moses paintings as well as early American glass and relics from the Revolution) and the **Fairbanks Museum and Planetarium** in St. Johnsbury. The **Billings Farm & Museum in Woodstock** shows off its blue-ribbon dairy and has a fascinating, beautifully mounted display of 19th-century farm life and tools. A detailed, 150-page catalog, *Vermont's Museums, Galleries & Historic Buildings*, is available from the **Museum & Gallery Alliance,** c/o Shelburne Museum, Dept. VTM, Shelburne 05482 ($5.95, plus $1.50 postage and handling). Within this book, we have included all museums in their respective areas.

MUSIC

The Green Mountains are filled with the sounds of music each summer, beginning with the **Discover Jazz Festival** (863-7992), more than 100 concerts held over a week around Burlington in early June. In Putney, a late-June through July series of three evening chamber music concerts each week are presented in the **Yellow Barn** (1-800-639-3819). In July and August options include the internationally famous **Marlboro Music Festival** (254-2394), at Marlboro College, presenting chamber music on weekends, and the **Vermont Mozart Festival** (862-7352; 1-800-639-9097), a series of 20 concerts performed at a variety of sites ranging from beautiful barns at the University of Vermont and Shelburne Farms to a Lake Champlain ferry and including some striking classic and modern churches and a ski area base lodge. **The Killington Music Festival** (773-4003) is a series of Sunday concerts at Ramshead Lodge in July and August, and the **Manchester Music Festival** (362-1956) brings leading performers to various venues around Manchester. Also well worth noting: the **Central Vermont Chamber Music Festival** (728-9133) at the Chandler Music Hall in Randolph in mid-August, **Summer Music School** in Adamant (229-9297), concerts at the Town House in Hardwick by the **Craftsbury Chamber Players** (1-800-639-3443), and in Stowe, for a week in late July, at the **Performing Arts Festival** (253-7321). Other concert series are performed at the **Southern Vermont Arts Center** (Thursday and Sunday, 362-1405); at the **Fine Arts Center,** Castleton State College (468-4611, ext. 285); at the **Dibden Auditorium,** Johnson State College (635-2356); and at **Middlebury College Center for the Arts** (443-5007). The **North Country Concert Association** (43 Main Street, Derby Line) performs at sites throughout the Northeast Kingdom lake area. The **Vermont Symphony Orchestra,** oldest of the state symphonies, figures in a number of the series noted above and also performs at a variety of locations, ranging from Brattleboro's Living Memorial Park and the statehouse lawn to Wilson Castle, throughout the summer. In Weston, the **Kinhaven Music School** offers free concerts on summer weekends. The **Vermont Bach Festival** (257-4523), sponsored by the Brattleboro Music Center with performances in local churches and at Marlboro College, is a fitting climax to the season. See also *Fiddling.*

NATURE PRESERVES
In recent years the **Vermont Land Trust** and many local land trusts have acquired numerous parcels of land throughout the state. Within each chapter in this book we note these where they appear under *Green Space.* Many of the most visitor-friendly preserves are owned by **The Nature Conservancy,** a national nonprofit conservation organization that has preserved close to 7 million acres throughout the United States since its founding in 1951. A *Vermont Project Directory,* available from The Nature Conservancy (229-4425), 27 State Street, Montpelier 05602, describes more than 100 properties.

OPERA HOUSES
Northern New England opera houses are a turn-of-the-century phenomenon: theaters built as cultural centers for the surrounding area, stages on which lecturers, musicians, and vaudeville acts, as well as opera singers, performed. Many of these buildings have long since disappeared, but those that survive are worth noting. The **Hyde Park Opera House,** built in 1910, has been restored by the Lamoille County Players, who stage four annual shows—one play, two musicals, and an annual foliage-season run of *The Sound of Music.* The **Barre Opera House,** built in 1899, is an elegant, acoustically outstanding, second-floor theater, home of the Barre Players; productions are staged here year-round. In Derby Line, in the second-floor **Opera House** (a neoclassic structure that also houses the Haskell Free Library), the audience sits in Vermont watching a stage that is in Canada. The **Chandler Music Hall** in Randolph has been restored for varied uses.

PETS
This is the first edition in which we have noted lodging places that accommodate pets with a symbol ❀. We should note that while traveling with a dog or cat generally tends to rule out the possibility of staying in inns or B&Bs, some of Vermont's most elegant inns do permit them: the **Inn on the Common** in Craftsbury, **Topnotch** in Stowe, the **Basin Harbor Club** in

Vergennes, and the **Woodstock Inn and Resort** in Woodstock.

PICK YOUR OWN

A list of orchards and berry farms open to the public, as well as a *Vermont Apple* brochure detailing all major orchards, can be secured from the **Vermont Department of Agriculture** (828-2416), 116 State Street, Montpelier 05602; the information can also be accessed from the web site: www.vtcheese.com. Strawberry season is mid- to late June. Cherries, plums, raspberries, and blueberries can be picked in July and August. Apples ripen by mid-September and can be picked through foliage season.

QUILTS

A revival of interest in this craft is especially strong in Vermont, where quilting supply and made-to-order stores salt the state. For information, contact the **Green Mountain Quilters Guide,** c/o L. Leister, RD 2, Bethel 05032, which sponsors several shows a year. The **Vermont Quilt Festival** is held for **three** days in mid-July in Northfield, including exhibits of outstanding antique quilts, classes and lectures, vendors, and appraisals. **Shelburne Museum** has an outstanding quilt collection. and the **Billings Farm & Museum** holds an annual show.

RAILROAD EXCURSIONS

Vermont's rail excursions are limited, but due for expansion. The **Green Mountain Flyer** (463-3069) runs between Bellows Falls on the Connecticut River and Chester (13 miles), with special foliage runs for another 14 miles to Ludlow. Named for the fastest train on the old Rutland Railroad, the excursion is run by the employee-owned Green Mountain Railroad, which also hauls talc, lumber, and limestone slurry between Bellows Falls and Rutland (see "Grafton,

Chester, Saxtons River, and Bellows Falls" for details). The **Vermont Valley Flyer** (463-4700) runs between Manchester and Arlington in summer, and may be extended to North Bennington. The **Champlain Valley Weekender** (463-3069) operates between Middlebury and Burlington all summer; the route follows the lakes and stops in Vergennes and Shelburne.

RENTAL COTTAGES AND CONDOMINIUMS

Four Season Vacation Rentals, an annual booklet available from the Tourism and Marketing Department (828-3236; 1-800-VERMONT; Montpelier 05602), lists upward of 200 properties, most of them either lakeside cottages or condominiums near ski areas but also including a variety of other housing, ranging from wooded summer camps by streams to aristocratic brick mansions with priceless views. We have found this publication indispensable for exploring the state—as a family of five—at all seasons. Rentals average $400 per week, usually more

in winter, less in summer; incredible bargains by any standard. ***Vermont Rentals Quarterly*** (228-7158), 138 Main Street Ludlow, is also available on request.

RESTAURANTS
Culinary standards are rising every day: You can lunch simply and inexpensively nearly everywhere and dine superbly in a score of places where the quality would rate three stars in Boston or New York but is at least a third less expensive. Fixed-price menus (prix fixe) have been so noted. We were tempted to try to list our favorites here, but the roster would be too long. Restaurants that appeal to us appear in the text in their respective areas. The range and variety are truly extraordinary. Note that we divide restaurants in each chapter into *Dining Out* (serious dining experiences) and *Eating Out* (everyday places). See also *Highway Roadfood.*

ROCKHOUNDING
Rockhounding in Vermont, a good write-up of Vermont's rockhounding sites, special events, and the state's geological history, is available free from the Department of Tourism and Marketing (828-3236, Montpelier 05602). The most obvious sites are **Rock of Ages Quarry and Exhibit** in Barre and the **Vermont Marble Company Exhibit** in Proctor (a film, free samples). Major exhibits of Vermont fossils, minerals, and rocks may be viewed at **Perkins Geology Hall,** University of Vermont, Burlington; the **Fairbanks Museum** in St. Johnsbury; and the **Melendy Mineral Museum,** South Londonderry (call for an appointment). An annual **Rock Swap and Mineral Show** is held in early August, sponsored by the **Burlington Gem and Mineral Club.** Gold, incidentally, can be panned in a number of rivers, notably Broad Brook in Plymouth; the Rock River in Newfane and

Dover; the Williams River in Ludlow; the Ottauquechee River in Bridgewater; the White River in Stockbridge and Rochester; the Mad River in Warren, Waitsfield, and Moretown; the Little River in Stowe and Waterbury; and the Missisquoi in Lowell and Troy.

SHEEP AND WOOL
Sheep are multiplying quickly in Vermont and may someday again outnumber cows, as they did in the mid-19th century. Their modern appeal is primarily for their meat, but a number of farmers specialize in processing wool, among them **Mettowee Valley Farm** (325-3039) in Pawlet, **Country Casuals** (869-2360) in Cambridgeport, **Singing Spindle Spinnery** (244-8025) in South Duxbury, **Lamb and Lamb Company** in Royalton (763-2076), **Maple Ridge Sheep Farm** in Randolph (728-3081), **Spring Hill Farm** (333-9023) in Fairlee, **Magnus Wools** (592-3320) in Barnet, **Plums Knits** (334-8081) in Newport, **Diamond Ledge Handspun** (334-5115) in Newport Center, **Round Barn Merinos** (877-6544) in Ferrisburg, **Wool and Feathers** (888-7004) in Hyde Park, and **Wooly Hill Farm** (758-2284) in Bridport. Request a copy of the ***Vermont FiberWorks Directory,*** listing more than 80 producers, from the Vermont Department of Agriculture (828-2416), 116 State Street, Montpelier 05602. Inquire about the **Vermont Sheep and Wool Festival,** featuring sheep shearing, spinning, weaving, and plenty of sheep, held early October.

SHIPWRECKS
Well-preserved 19th-century shipwrecks are open to the public (licensed divers) at three Underwater Historical Preserves in Lake Champlain near Burlington. ***The Phoenix,*** the second steamboat to ply Lake Champlain, burned to the waterline in 1819. The

General Butler, an 88-foot schooner, fell victim to a winter gale in 1876. A coal barge, believed to be the **A. R. Nowes,** broke loose from a tug and sank in 1884. Contact the Division of Historic Preservation (828-3226) and the **Lake Champlain Maritime Museum** in Vergennes, which is charting underwater remains.

WOODSTOCK INN AND RESORT

SKIING, CROSS-COUNTRY

Thirty cross-country centers and tours are listed in the free *Vermont Winter Guide* published by the Vermont Chamber of Commerce (223-3443; www.vtchamber. com). At this writing the only good web site posting conditions for Vermont's cross-country centers is **Scenes of Vermont:** www.pbpub.com. Within this book we have described each commercial touring center as it appears geographically. Given the dearth of natural snow in recent years, checking current conditions is now more important than ever. Vermont's most dependable snow can be found on high-elevation trails in **Stowe**, at **Craftsbury Center** in Craftsbury Common, **Hazen's Notch** in Montgomery Center, **Bolton Valley Resort** (between Burlington and Stowe), and **Blueberry Hill** in Goshen. **Mountain Top Inn** in Chittenden (handy to Killington and Rutland) and **Grafton Ponds** in Grafton offer snowmaking on a short loop trail. All of the cross-country-ski centers mentioned above are located on the 200-mile **Catamount Trail,** a marked ski trail that runs (almost; it's now more than 90 percent complete) the length of the state. Contact the **Catamount Trail Association** (864-5794), P.O. Box 1235, Burlington 05402; web site: www.catamountrail.together.net. Members ($20 per person, $30 per family) receive a regular newsletter and discounts at participating touring centers. You might want to request area maps; *The Catamount Trail Guidebook* is $16. *Adventure Skiing,*

a map guide to cross-country trails in the Stowe/Bolton/Underhill area, is useful (253-7489). Inn-to-inn tours are possible between **Craftsbury Center Resort** and **Highland Lodge** in Greensboro; **Trapp Family Lodge** and **Edson Hill Manor** in Stowe; **Chipman House** in Ripton and **Churchill House Inn** in Brandon; and between **Village Inn** of Landgrove and **Nordic Inn** in Londonderry. **Mad River Glen** and **Bolton Valley** are two alpine resorts that specialize in telemarking. For details about marked cross-country trails in state preserves, contact the Department of Forests, Parks and Recreation (241-3655), Waterbury 05676, and for those within the Green Mountain National Forest request the **"Winter Recreation Map"** (see *Forests and Parks*).

SKIING, DOWNHILL

Since the 1930s, when America's commercial skiing began with a Model-T Ford engine pulling skiers up a hill in Woodstock, skiing has been a Vermont specialty. Fifteen ski areas are members of the Vermont Ski Areas Association and accessible with daily updated snow conditions and weather on the web site: www.skivermont.com. The Vermont Chamber of Commerce publishes a glossy *Vermont Winter Guide* (available free; see *Information*). Unfortunately, this guide includes no rates, but these are available on the above web site. In 1999, lift tickets ranged from $28 per adult at **Mad River Glen,** a famously challenging old ski area with the state's lowest percentage of snowmaking but frequently excellent conditions (especially in late winter), to $52 per adult, on holidays, at **Mount Mansfield** and **Okemo.** Daily lift tickets are, of course, not the cheapest way to ski; all resorts deeply discount multiday lifts and lodging packages. **Killington/Pico,** the largest ski resort in the East, **Mount Snow,** Vermont's second largest area, and **Sugarbush** are all owned by Les Otten's American Skiing Company; lift tickets and passes at one are honored at the others, and at ASC resorts in New Hampshire and Maine. A number of long-established Vermont ski areas have become self-contained resorts. Both **Bolton Valley** and **Smugglers' Notch** cater to families; **Okemo, Stratton,** and **Sugarbush** offer varied skiing and facilities, appealing to a full range of patrons. Though no longer Vermont's biggest, Stowe remains Ski Capital of the East when it comes to the quantity and quality of inns, restaurants, and shops. We have described each ski area as it appears geographically. A 24-hour snow condition report for the state is available by calling the Vermont Skiing Today SnowLine: 229-0531 (November through June).

SLEIGH RIDES

A list of sleigh rides is available from the Vermont Tourism Department (see *Information*). They're also contained in the *Vermont Winter Guide* (see *Skiing*) and listed in this book where they are available.

SNOWBOARDING

An international sport first popularized by Burton Snowboards (born in Manchester, long since moved to Burlington where we list details about its factory store), snowboarding lessons, rentals, and special terrain parks are offered at every major Vermont ski area except Mad River Glen (the only holdout in the East).

SNOWMOBILING

Some 2,800 miles of well-marked, groomed trails are laced together in a system maintained by the **Vermont Association of Snow Travelers (VAST).** VAST's corridor trails are up to 8 feet wide and are maintained by 200 local snowmobile clubs; for detailed maps and suggestions for routes, activities, and guided tours, contact the Vermont Association of Snow Travelers (229-0005), Box 839, Montpelier 05602; web site: www.vtvast.org. Vermont has a reciprocal registration agreement with New York, Maine, New Hampshire, and Quebec; otherwise, registration is required to take advantage of trails within the state. Snowmobile rentals and tours are listed in the *Vermont Winter Guide* (see *Information.*)

ROBERT KOZLOW

SNOWSHOEING

Snowshoeing is experiencing a rebirth in Vermont, thanks to the new lightweight equipment available from sources like Tubbs Snowshoes in Stowe. Virtually all ski-touring centers now offer snowshoe rentals, and many inns stock a few pairs for guests.

SOARING

Sugarbush Soaring (496-3730), Sugarbush Airport, Warren, is in the Mad River Valley, known as one of the prime spots in the East for riding thermal and ridge waves. The **Sugarbush Airport** is a well-established place to take glider lessons or rides or simply to watch the planes come and go. The **Fall Wave Soaring Encampment** held in early October draws glider pilots from throughout the country. Gliders and airplane rides are also available at the **Morrisville/ Stowe State Airport** (888-5150) and **Post Mills Aviation** in Post Mills (333-9254), where soaring lessons are also a specialty, along with simply seeing the Connecticut Valley from the air.

SPAS
Vermont is the setting for a select few of the country's finest spas. The oldest of these is **New Life Fitness Vacations,** directed by Jimmy LeSage at Killington. **Topnotch** and **Stoweflake** in Stowe and the **Equinox Hotel** in Manchester both offer spa programs.

SUMMER SELF-IMPROVEMENT PROGRAMS
Whether it's improving your game of tennis or golf, learning to take pictures or to weave, cook, identify mushrooms, fish, or bike, or simply to lose weight, there is a summer program for you somewhere in Vermont. See *Tennis, Golf, Canoeing,* and *Fishing* for lodging and lesson packages. Prestigious academic programs include the **Russian School** at Norwich University (Russian only is spoken in all social as well as class activities; both undergraduate and graduate courses are offered), intensive language programs at **Middlebury College,** and a writers' conference at the latter's Bread Loaf summer campus. Senior citizens can take advantage of some outstanding courses offered at bargain prices that include lodging as part of the **Elderhostel** program. For details, write to Elderhostel, 80 Boylston Street, Boston, MA 02116. The state's oldest, most respected crafts program is offered by **Fletcher Farm Craft School,** Ludlow 05149: off-loom weaving, creative needle-work, quilting, pottery, raku, and stained glass, plus meals and lodging (minimum age 18). The **Vermont Studio Center** in Johnson is relatively new but already has a national reputation. Working artists come to renew their creative wellsprings or to explore completely new directions during intensive sessions that feature guidance and criticism by some of the country's premier artists. For details, call 635-7000. **Craftsbury Center** in Craftsbury has summer programs for all ages in running and sculling, and **Lyndon State** has a running camp.

SWIMMING
On the official state map, you can pick out the 36 day-use areas that offer swimming, most with changing facilities, maintained by the Vermont State Department of Forests, Parks and Recreation (weekdays: $1.50 per person 14 years and older, $2 for Sand Bar Park; weekends and holidays: $2.50 per person, $3 for Sand Bar Park). A similar facility is provided by the Green Mountain National Forest in Peru, and the U.S. Army Corps of Engineers has tidied corners of its dam projects for public use in Townshend and North Springfield. There are also public beaches on roughly one-third of Vermont's 400 lakes and ponds (but note that swimming is prohibited at designated "Fishing Access Areas") and plenty on Lake Champlain (see Burlington, Charlotte, Colchester, Georgia, and Swanton). Add to these all the town recreation areas and myriad pools available to visitors and you still haven't gone swimming Vermont-style until you have sampled a Vermont swimming hole. These range from deep spots in the state's ubiquitous streams to 100-foot-deep quarries (**Dorset Quarry** near Manchester and **Chapman Quarry** in West Rutland are famous) and freezing pools between waterfalls (see "Sugarbush/Mad River Valley"). We have included some of our

favorite swimming holes under *Swimming* in each section but could not bring ourselves to share them all. Look for cars along the road on a hot day and ask in local general stores. You won't be disappointed.

TENNIS
Vermont claims as many tennis courts per capita as any other state in the union. These include town recreation facilities and sports centers as well as private facilities. Summer tennis programs, combining lessons, lodging, and meals, are offered at **Bolton Valley, Killington,** the **Village at Smugglers Notch, Stratton, Topnotch Resort** in Stowe, and two Sugarbush resorts (**Sugarbush Inn** and the **Bridges**). Check *Tennis* under entries for each area.

THEATER
Vermont's two long-established summer theaters are both in the Manchester area: the **Dorset Playhouse** and the **Weston Playhouse.** The **Green Mountain Guild** presents a series of summer musicals at the Killington Playhouse. Other summer theater can be found in Castleton, in Saxtons River, in Waitsfield (the **Valley Players**), in Warren **(Phantom Theater),** in Stowe (the **Stowe Playhouse** and the **Lamoille County Players** in Hyde Park), and **Northern Stage** at the Briggs Opera House in White River Junction. The **Flynn Theater** in Burlington is the scene of year-round live entertainment as well as film.

TRAINS
See *Amtrak* and *Railroad Excursions.*

VERMONT PUBLIC RADIO
Stations for those addicted to National Public Radio can be found throughout the state on the FM dial. In the Burlington area, tune into WVPS (107.9), in the White River Junction/Windsor area to WVPR (89.5), and in the Rutland area to WRVT (88.7).

WATCHABLE WILDLIFE
Throughout Vermont, nonprofits and commercial enterprises offer frequent walks, workshops, hikes, bike tours, and other ways of heightening appreciation of the birds and animals, reptiles, fish, flowers, and other natural things to be seen. Request a copy of the free *Vermont Explorer's Guide Watchable Wildlife* pamphlet listing these events, published periodically throughout the year. It's available from the Vermont Department of Fish and Wildlife (241-3295) and on the web at: www.nwf.org/northeast/index.html. See also *Birding* and *Hiking and Walking.*

WATERFALLS
Those most accessible include: the falls at **Brewster River Gorge** in Jeffersonville; in **Bristol Memorial Forest Park,** Bristol; **Buttermilk Falls** (a popular swimming hole) in Ludlow; **Carver Falls** in West Haven (126 feet high); the falls in **Clarendon Gorge; Cow Meadows Ledges** in Newbury; **Duck Brook Cascades** in Bolton; the **East Putney Falls and Pot Holes; Glen Falls** in Fairlee; **Great Falls of the Clyde River** in Charleston; **Hamilton Falls** in Jamaica; **Little Otter Creek Falls** in Ferrisburg; **Middlebury Gorge** in East Middlebury; **Moss Glen Falls** in Granville Gulf; the **seven falls on the Huntington River** in Hanksville; **Shelburne Falls** in Shelburne; **Texas Falls** in Hancock; **Cadys Falls** in Morrisville; **Bingham Falls** in Stowe; and **Northfield Falls,** Northfield. We have spent some time looking without success for **Big Falls** in Troy (we gave up after learning that a few people had died there in recent years) and could not penetrate the swampy ground around **Moss Glen Falls** in Stowe. Most of these

VDT

sites can be located on the invaluable *Vermont Atlas and Gazetteer* (DeLorme).

WEATHER REPORTS

For serious weather travel information in Vermont, check with the Vermont highway department's weather line: 828-2648. Listen to **"An Eye on the Sky"** on Vermont Public Radio. In the show, produced by the Fairbanks Museum and Planetarium, Mark Breen and Steve Maleski make their reports on life's most constant variable both entertaining and informative (see *Vermont Public Radio* for stations). The Vermont Chamber of Commerce web site (see *Information*) also carries current weather information.

WEB PAGES

We have not listed the pages of individual inns or resorts, though most of them have one, because they may change while this book is in print, but we have included those of area chambers of commerce. And here are some of the more general, state-wide web pages: **www.travel-vermont.com** is maintained by the Vermont Department of Travel and Tourism, with many informa-

tional leads and links; **www.linksvermont. com** has useful links to events, real estate, and weather; **www.vtstateparks.com** includes locator maps and special programs related to state parks; **www.scenes of vermont.com** is an independently published 'zine of general information and links; and **www.selectvt.com** is a mail-order shopping cart for many of the state's products. The Vermont Chamber of Commerce is **www.vtguides.com;** *Vermont Life* magazine is **www.vtlife.com.** The outstanding sites for southern Vermont are **www.southernvermont.com** and **www.sovermont.com.**

WEDDINGS

Destination weddings have become big business in Vermont, so big and so ubiquitous that we can no longer list individual places in this section. Within each chapter we note inns and other sites that cater to weddings. Also check the web sites and phone numbers listed under *Information.* One great wedding site that doesn't makes these listings is **Grand Isle Lake House** (865-2522) in the Champlain Islands, a turn-of-the-century summer hotel currently maintained by the Preservation Trust of Vermont.

WHITE WATER

During white-water season beginning in mid-April, experienced canoeists and kayakers take advantage of stretches on the **White,** the **Lamoille,** and the **West Rivers,** among others. **White-water rafting** is also available on the **West River** during spring dam releases.

WINE

Vermont has traditionally made apple and other fruit wines, but recently two wineries in the very northern reaches of Vermont have begun planting, harvesting, and fermenting grapes, with respectable results.

These are **Boyden Valley Winery** (644-8151)—also good for premium apple wines—in Cambridge, and **Snow Farm Vineyard and Winery** (372-9463) in South Hero. **North River Winery** (368-7557), Vermont's long-established vintner, produces fruit wine; **Joseph Cerniglia Winery** (226-7575) in Proctorsville, **Flag Hill Farm** (685-7724) in Vershire, **Grand View Winery** (456-8810) in East Calais, and **Putney Mountain Winery** (387-4610) all make cider and apple wine. **L'Abeille Honey Winery** (253-2929) in Stowe produces a honey wine.

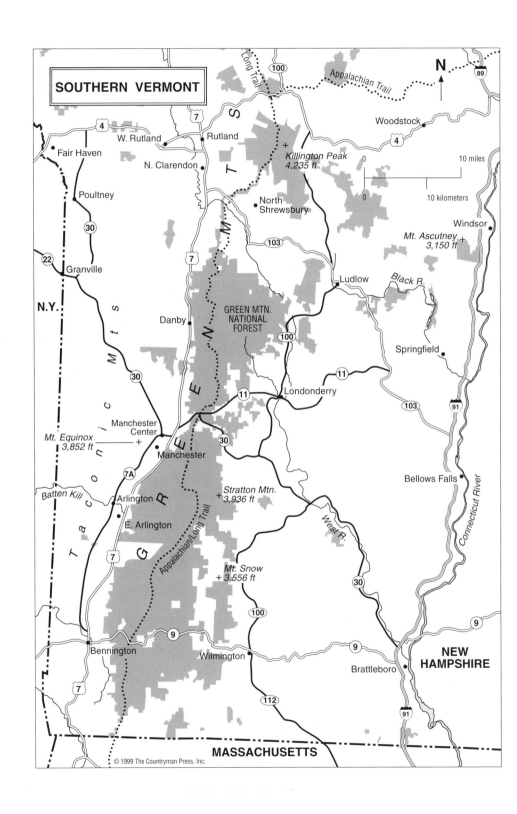

I. SOUTHERN VERMONT

The Lower Connecticut and West River Valleys
Mount Snow/Wilmington Area
Bennington/Arlington Area
Manchester and the Mountains
Grafton, Chester, Saxtons River, and Bellows Falls
Okemo Mountain/Ludlow Area

KIM GRANT

Fly-fishing on the Battenkill River

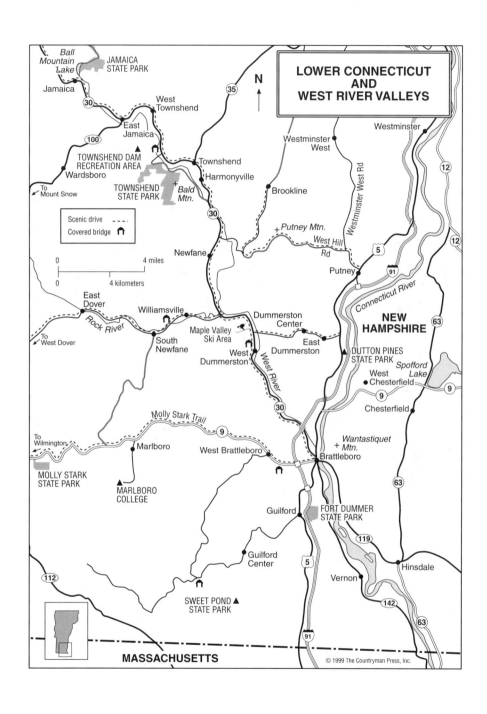

LOWER CONNECTICUT
AND
WEST RIVER VALLEYS

N

Ball
Mountain
Lake
JAMAICA
STATE PARK
Jamaica
30
West
Townshend
East
Jamaica
100
TOWNSHEND DAM
RECREATION AREA
Wardsboro
To
Mount Snow
TOWNSHEND
STATE PARK
Bald
Mtn.
Townshend
Harmonyville
Brookline
35
Westminster
West
Westminster
12

Scenic drive
Covered bridge

Putney Mtn.
West Hill
Rd
5
12

0   4 miles
0   4 kilometers
Newfane
Putney
91
Connecticut River
NEW
HAMPSHIRE
63

East
Dover
Williamsville
Rock River
To
West Dover
South
Newfane
Maple Valley
Ski Area
West
Dummerston
Dummerston
Center
East
Dummerston
West River
DUTTON PINES
STATE PARK
West
Chesterfield
Spofford
Lake
9
9
30
Chesterfield

Molly Stark Trail
To
Wilmington
Marlboro
9
West Brattleboro
Wantastiquet
Mtn.
Brattleboro
63

MOLLY STARK
STATE PARK
MARLBORO
COLLEGE

Guilford
FORT DUMMER
STATE PARK
119
Hinsdale
112
Guilford
Center
5
Vernon
142
63
SWEET POND
STATE PARK
91

MASSACHUSETTS
© 1999 The Countryman Press, Inc.

The Lower Connecticut and West River Valleys

The southeast corner of Vermont is one of the state's most interesting and varied. The classic white-clapboard, green-shuttered towns of Newfane, Townshend, and Jamaica are strung like pearls along the West River; and there are two small college towns, Marlboro on Whetstone Brook and Putney on the Connecticut. All three rivers and the roads that shadow them meet in Brattleboro, as do area residents whenever they go to a supermarket or movie.

The supermarket is actually a splendid co-op and the movie house is a lovingly restored art deco theater. While commerce continues to spread north along Putney Road (Route 5), downtown Brattleboro's brick blocks become ever more densely filled with counterculture shops, bookstores and art galleries, restaurants and coffeehouses. Everything is for local, not tourist, consumption.

"'Bratt' is a college town without a college," we were once told by a fellow customer at the Common Ground, a collective-run restaurant founded in 1971. Many of the town's movers and shakers are former members of the numerous communes that once flourished in the surrounding hills, and idealistic young people continue to arrive, drawn by the area's private educational institutions—especially World Learning—and by nonprofits. Artists and musicians add significantly to this synergy (it's said that you can't throw a stone on Main Street without hitting a poet, musician, or artist). The result is an earnest, yeasty community in which the spirit of the '60s continues to build.

Minutes from Brattleboro, in any direction, you are in the hills. Be sure to explore the heavily wooded country among the three river valleys, the hamlets, and farms.

GUIDANCE

Brattleboro Area Chamber of Commerce (254-4565; web site: www.bratcham.com; e-mail: bratchmber@sover.net), 180 Main Street, Brattleboro 05301. Open year-round, Monday through Friday 8–5. Besides the Main Street office, there are two seasonal information booths run by knowledgeable senior citizens in warm-weather months—on Route 9 in West Brattleboro and on Route 5 at the common, just north of the junction with Route 30.

Putney has its own first-rate web site: www.putney.net, featuring its many artists and artisans, as well as lodging and dining, and linking to Brattleboro cultural information. The **West River Valley towns** along Route 30 maintain: www. westrivervalley.com. Other helpful websites for attractions in southern Vermont are www.southern vermont.com and www.sovermont.com.

Newspaper: *The Brattleboro Reformer* (254-2311) publishes a special Thursday calendar that's the best source of current arts and entertainment. Pick up a copy of the free brochure *Arts in the Season,* published by the Arts Council of Windham County.

GETTING THERE

By bus: **Greyhound/Vermont Transit** offers service from New York and Connecticut. **Peter Pan Bus Company** serves Boston via Springfield. The bus stop is on Route 5 at its junction with Route 9 west.

By train: **Amtrak** (1-800-USA-RAIL) trains from Washington, D.C. and New York City stop at the old downtown railroad station, now a museum.

Note: A transportation center on Elliot Street in Brattleboro (still in the planning stages) will eventually combine taxi, bus, and Amtrak services.

GETTING AROUND

Brattleboro Taxi (254-1717) will meet trains and buses. **Thomas Transportation** (1-800-526-8143) offers shuttle service to Boston's Logan Airport, Hartford's Bradley Airport, and Manchester Airport.

Parking: Main Street has metered parking, side streets are possible, and a large parking area **(Harmony Place)** in the rear of the Brooks House accesses shops on High, Elliot, and Main Streets; access is from High Street (Route 9). Another large lot runs between High and Grove Streets.

MEDICAL EMERGENCY

911 now serves this entire area. The medical facilities are at **Brattleboro Memorial Hospital** (257-0341), 9 Belmont Avenue, Brattleboro, and **Grace Cottage Hospital** (365-7357), Townshend. Rescue: 254-1010.

TOWN AND VILLAGES

Brattleboro. Vermont's largest town, "Bratt" is a largely 1870s brick and wrought-iron commercial hub for rural corners of three states. (Population swells from 12,000 at night to 30,000 by day.)

Known as a hippie haven in the '70s, Brattleboro remains hip, a very real mix of native Vermonters, former commune members, and young people who have arrived more recently as students at one of several nearby educational institutions, including the burgeoning Brattleboro Music Center. Some 200 students enroll each year in gradu-

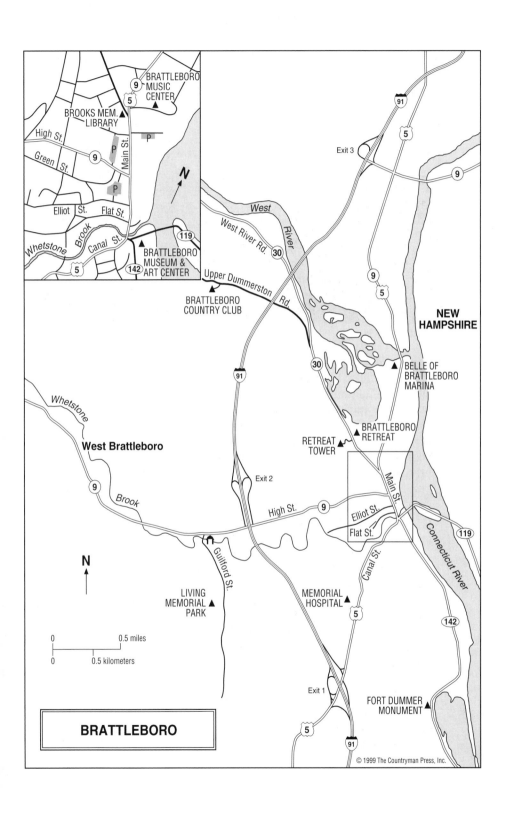

BRATTLEBORO MUSIC CENTER

BROOKS MEM. LIBRARY

High St.

Green St.

Elliot St.   Flat St.

Whetstone   Brook   Canal St.

BRATTLEBORO MUSEUM & ART CENTER

Upper Dummerston Rd.

BRATTLEBORO COUNTRY CLUB

West   West River Rd.   River

Exit 3

NEW HAMPSHIRE

BELLE OF BRATTLEBORO MARINA

Whetstone

West Brattleboro

RETREAT TOWER

BRATTLEBORO RETREAT

Brook

Exit 2

High St.

Elliot St.

Flat St.

Main St.

Canal St.

Connecticut River

N

LIVING MEMORIAL PARK

Guilford St.

MEMORIAL HOSPITAL

0   0.5 miles

0   0.5 kilometers

Exit 1

FORT DUMMER MONUMENT

BRATTLEBORO

© 1999 The Countryman Press, Inc.

KIM GRANT

Brick mill buildings as seen from the Connecticut River in Brattleboro

ate programs at World Learning, begun in 1932 and best known for its Experiment in International Living program (now the School for International Training). Alternative shops and restaurants that first softened the brick edges of this old river town are now expanding along Main and Elliot Streets to outnumber the old clothing and hardware stores. Sam's Army and Navy, Brown & Roberts Hardware, and Miller Bros-Newton, a classic men's store with awnings and a river view, are still thriving, but Twice Upon a Time and Vermont Artisan Designs have replaced more traditional downtown anchors. The first Friday of every month is now marked by open houses at a dozen galleries and studios.

This is not the first time that Brattleboro has taken on a different personality. During its long history, the town has shed many skins. The very site of Fort Dummer, built in 1724 just south of town, has been obliterated by the Vernon Dam. Gone, too, is the early-19th-century trading and resort town; no trace remains of the handsome, Federal-style commercial buildings or the two elaborate hotels that attracted trainloads of customers who came to take their water cures. The gingerbread wooden casino in Island Park and the fine brick town hall, with its gilded opera house, are also gone. And the great slate-sided sheds up on Birge Street are the sole evidence that hundreds of thousands of Estey organs were once made here.

Still, a motorist bogged down in the eternal Main Street bottleneck notices Brooks House, built splendidly in 1869 as an 80-room hotel, once frequented by Rudyard Kipling, now converted to housing, offices, and shops. If you park, you will find that Elliot Street is studded with specialty shops and good restaurants and that the Latchis Hotel, a couple of blocks down, has been restored to its 1930s high art deco glory (inside as well as out).

Brattleboro is full of pleasant surprises. Down near the national offices of the Holstein Foundation, the former railroad station is now the Brattleboro Museum and Art Center. The Connecticut River is accessible by both excursion boat and rental canoe and can be viewed from a hidden downtown park, a great picnic spot, especially when the twice-weekly farmer's market fills an adjacent space. Living Memorial Park offers extensive sports facilities. Live theater, music, and dance are presented without hoopla. The fanfare seems to be reserved for the annual winter carnival, begun aeons ago by Fred Harris, who is also famed for founding the Dartmouth Winter Carnival and the U.S. Eastern Amateur Ski Association. Brooks Memorial Library (254-5290), 224 Main Street (open daily except Sunday), mounts changing exhibits of regional art and has a fine collection of 19th-century paintings and sculpture, including works by Larkin G. Mead, the Brattleboro boy who first achieved national renown by sculpting an 8-foot-high angel from snow one night and placing it at the junction of Routes 30 and 5. **The Brattleboro Historical Society** (258-4957) maintains a "history room" (a restored 1800s classroom), a collection of Estey organs, and a collection of more than 7,000 photographs dating from the mid-1800s. It's on the third floor of the Municipal Building (230 Main Street; open Thursday 1–8 and Saturday 9–noon). Pick up the leaflet architectural walking tour of Main Street. Suggested reading: *Rudyard Kipling in Vermont*, by Stuart Murray (Images from the Past), evokes a sense not only of Kipling but also of time (1892–1896) and place during the years the author lived just north of town.

Note: The International Center on the 200-acre campus of World Learning (275-7751) is on Kipling Road (off Route 5 just north of town), offering a sense of the view across the valley to Mount Monadnock that Kipling enjoyed from Naulakha (see *Lodging*).

Newfane. A columned courthouse, matching Congregational church, and town hall—all grouped on a handsome green—are framed by dignified white-clapboard houses, including two of Vermont's most elegant inns.

When Windham County's court sessions began meeting in Newfane in 1787, the village was about the same size it is now: 20 houses and two hotels. But in 1787, the village was 2 miles up on Newfane Hill. Beams were unpegged and homes moved to the more protected valley by ox-drawn sleighs in the winter of 1824.

Newfane inns have been famous for more than a century, at first because the whitewashed jail accommodated 25 paying guests, feeding them (as an 1848 poem says) "good pies and oyster soup" in the same rooms with inmates. By the time this facility closed (in the 1950s), the Old Newfane Inn—which incorporates much of its original hilltop structure—was beginning to acquire a reputation for gourmet fare.

Economist John Kenneth Galbraith, a summer resident in the area since 1947, helped publicize the charms of both the village and the inn—whose onetime chef eventually opened the Four Columns Inn at the rear of the green.

Newfane Village is more than just an excellent place to dine, sleep, and stroll. It is the site of one of the state's oldest and biggest Sunday flea markets, and the immediate area offers an unusual number of antiques shops. Beyond the stores and the remnants of the railway station (which served the narrow-gauge Brattleboro–Londonderry line from 1880 to 1936) is a fine old cemetery.

Newfane has bred as well as fed famous people. You'll learn about some of them in the exceptional **Historical Society of Windham County** (365-4148), Route 30, south of the common. It looks like a brick post office (open Memorial Day through October, Wednesday, Sunday, and holidays noon–5, and for special events). Displays change but might highlight Eugene Field, of nursery rhyme fame ("Wynken, Blynken, and Nod," for example); a portrait of his father, Roswell, who defended Dred Scott in his famed Supreme Court case, hangs in the courtroom. However, unquestionably the most interesting tale that's frequently told in the Historical Society displays is the story of John Wilson (see Brookline, below).

Brookline. Half as wide as it is long, Brookline is sequestered in a narrow valley bounded by steep hills and the West River. (Turn off Route 30 at the Newfane Flea Market.) Its population of 410 is four times what it was 50 years ago but a small fraction of what it was in the 1820s and '30s, when it supported three stores, three schools, two hotels, and a doctor. Those were the decades in which its two landmark brick buildings were constructed. One is a church, but the more famous is a round schoolhouse, said to be the only one in the country—and also probably the only school designed by a crook.

John Wilson never seems to have mentioned his past career as Thunderbolt, an infamous Scottish highwayman. In 1820, the obviously well-educated newcomer designed the circular schoolhouse. He gave it six large windows, the better (it was later noted) to allow him to see whoever approached from any side. Wilson taught only a term before moving to the neighboring (and more remote) town of Dummerston, just about the time that an Irish felon, "Lightfoot" Martin, was hanged in Cambridge, Massachusetts. In his confession (reprints are sold at the Historical Society of Windham County; 365-4148), Martin fingered Wilson as his old accomplice, but with no obvious effect. Not long thereafter, Wilson added "Dr." to his name and practiced medicine in Newfane, then in Brattleboro, where he married, fathering a son before his wife divorced him "because of certain facts she learned." When he died in 1847, scars on Wilson's ankles and neck suggested chains and a rope. Today, several of Thunderbolt's pistols are preserved by the Historical Society and in Brattleboro's Brooks Library.

Unfortunately, the round schoolhouse is now virtually never open. In 1928, the town's first eight grades moved down the road to the current wooden schoolhouse. Then for a decade or two it served as Town Hall, until those offices were moved across the road. As the population dwindled through the '30s, '40s, and '50s, the building was used for town meeting, but that assemblage is now held in the vestry of the Baptist church, Brookline's second landmark. Built in 1836, the church has been beautifully restored, thanks to fund-raising efforts like the annual Musicale Sunday usually held late in July, sponsored by the Ladies Benevolent Society.

Townshend. The next village green on Route 30 is a full 2 acres, complete with Victorian-style gazebo. It's bordered on one side by a classic, white, 1790 Congregational church flanked by lovely clapboard houses, on others by a columned and tower-topped stucco town hall and the fine buildings of the new Leland and Gray Union High School (founded as a Baptist seminary in 1834), and by a clapboard commercial block containing a corner store (with a soda fountain) and a fish and game outfitter. The big annual event is Hospital Fair Day, when the common is filled with booths and games, all to benefit Grace Cottage Hospital, which has grown, unbelievably, out of the back side of a rambling old village home. (Known for the quality of its service, this is Vermont's first hospital to have installed a birthing bed.) West Townshend, farther along Route 30, is a three-corners with a photogenic church and general store.

The town also harbors stuffed-toy and furniture factories, a state park, a public swimming area, Vermont's largest single-span covered bridge, 15 cemeteries, and several good places to stay and to eat.

Jamaica. A small village clustered around its white Congregational church (1808) on Route 30, Jamaica is the kind of place you can drive through in 2 minutes, or easily stay a week (see the Three Mountain Inn under *Lodging*). The village buildings are few but proud, and there is swimming and plenty of hiking as well as camping in Jamaica State Park. The village, which lies within the bailiwick of Stratton Mountain's resort community, also offers some surprisingly good shopping.

Marlboro. Turn off busy Route 9 and enter another, more tranquil world. In summer, flowers brim from window boxes, and the air is filled with the sounds of the Marlboro Music Festival. In other seasons, students stride purposefully from building to building on the small, attractive Marlboro College campus, which, incidentally, maintains a fine network of cross-country-ski trails. Check *Selective Shopping—Crafts Shops* for crafts studios here. The Marlboro Historical Society (254-9152), with its collection of pictures, old farm tools, and antique furniture, is housed in the Newton House and the 1813 one-room schoolhouse on Main Street. It's open Saturday 2–5, July through Labor Day.

Putney. This village's riverside fields have been heavily farmed since the mid-18th century, and its hillsides produce more than one tenth of all the state's apples. Putney is an unusually fertile place for progressive thinking, too. Back in the 1840s, it spawned a group who practiced Bible Communism, the sharing of all property, work, and wives. John Humphrey Noyes, the group's leader, was charged with adultery in 1847 and fled with his flock to Oneida, New York, where they founded the famous silverplate company. Known today for experimental education rather than religion, Putney is the home of the Putney School, a very unusual coed, college preparatory school founded in 1935. It stresses the individual aptitudes of its students and has a regimen that entails helping with chores, which include raising animals on the school farm. Landmark College, the country's first college specifically for dyslexic students, occupies the former multimillion-dollar Windham College campus designed by Edward Durrell Stone. The Greenwood School, a prep school for dyslexic boys, and the Oak Meadow School, a pioneering support service for homeschooling, are also in town. Many young people who come to Putney for schooling never move away. The changing population is evidenced by the range of gourmet items available in the Putney Food Co-op (at the eastern edge of the village) and in the fact that dozens of established craftspeople now live in town. Putney's native sons are no slouches, either. They include the late George Aiken, who served as governor before going on to Washington as a senator in 1941, a post he held until his retirement in 1975. He was also the author of the classic *Pioneering with Wildflowers*. Frank Wilson, a genuine

Dummerston Covered Bridge

CHRISTINA TREE

Yankee trader who was one of the first merchants to enter Red China, built the first of his six Basketvilles, "The World's Largest Basket Stores," in the village. **The Putney Historical Museum** (387-5862), housed in Town Hall, is open weekdays 9–5; the curator comes in Wednesday 2–4 and by appointment.

Guilford. Backroaded by I-91 (where there is no exit between Brattleboro and Massachusetts), this old agricultural town rewards with quiet rural scenery anyone who drives or pedals its roads. Check out Sweet Pond State Park (257-7406), a former 125-acre estate with a large pond good for swimming and boating. It's circled by a nature path that leads to a 5-acre perennial display garden at Floral Gates Nursery (call for hours: 257-7406), featuring 400 varieties of flowering perennials and shrubs. The Labor Day weekend is big in Guilford, when it's the setting for the old-fashioned Guilford Fair and for the annual 2-day, free music in Guilford's Organ Barn (257-1961). A quilt show at the Guilford Center Meeting House is sponsored by the Guilford Historical Society (call Wilma Higgins at 254-9557), which also maintains exhibits in the 1822 town hall, in the 1837 meetinghouse, and in the 1797 one-room brick schoolhouse, open Sunday afternoons in July and August and by appointment.

TO SEE

MUSEUM
 ♿ **Brattleboro Museum and Art Center** (257-0124; web site: www. Brattleboromuseum.org, 10 Vermont Street (off Canal and Bridge Streets), Brattleboro. Open mid-May through early November, Tuesday through Sunday noon–6; $3 per adult, $2 for seniors and students, free under 18. The town's 1915 rail station makes a handsome home for changing exhibits that have varied wildly in recent years, from quilts to architecture to contemporary art. A historical room tells the story of Brattleboro's famed Estey Organ Co., which produced thousands of organs each year between the 1850s and the company's demise in 1961. Inquire about frequent concerts, "twilight" guided walks, and other live presentations.

See also Historical Society of Windham County in Newfane under *Villages*.

COVERED BRIDGES
In Brattleboro, the reconstructed **Creamery Bridge** forms the entrance to Living Memorial Park on Route 9. North on Route 30 in West Dummerston, a Town lattice bridge across the West River is the longest still-used covered bridge in the state (for the best view, jump into the cool waters on either side; this is a popular swimming hole on a hot summer day). The **Scott Bridge,** Vermont's longest single-span bridge, stands by Route 30 in West Townshend just below the Townshend Dam, but it is closed to traffic. There is also a covered bridge across the Green

River in Guilford and another on the South Newfane Road in Williamsville.

FOR FAMILIES

✍ **Santa's Land** (387-5550; 1-800-726-8299), Route 5, Putney. Open daily Memorial Day to Christmas 10–5. Igloo Pancake House, Christmas shops, Santa's home, reindeer, kiddie rides. A Christmas theme park with barnyard and unusual animals. $8 for adults, $6 children 3–12.

✍ **Brattleboro Retreat Petting Farm** (258-3714), 350 Linden Street, Route 30 just north of Brattleboro. Open early June through August, Wednesday through Saturday 10–4, also weekends in spring and fall. Admission: $4.50 for 12 and over, $2.50 under 12. Part of the Retreat's dairy farm (visitors are invited to milk cows); animals include llamas, pot-bellied pigs, emus, lambs, sheep, goats, oxen, donkeys, and a miniature horse. A gift shop features Vermont products.

✍ **Connecticut River Fish Ladder,** Vernon. The New England Power Company's 984-foot fish ladder helps American shad and salmon return to their spawning grounds; 51 pools in a 35-foot vertical rise. Best viewing is from late May through mid-July, 8–5 daily.

SCENIC DRIVES

The hilly, heavily wooded country between the West and Connecticut River Valleys is webbed with roads, most of them dirt. Our favorites include:

Putney Mountain Road to Brookline. At the Putney General Store on Route 5, turn left onto Westminster West Road and left again about a mile up the hill onto West Hill Road. Not far above the Putney School, look for a dirt road on your right. It forks immediately; bear right to Putney Mountain. Trees thicken and sunlight dapples through in a way that it never seems to do on paved roads. Chipmunks scurry ahead on the hard-packed dirt. The few drivers you pass will wave. The road curves up and up—and up—cresting after 2.1 miles. Note the unmarked parking area on your right (see Putney Mountain under *To Do—Hiking*). Then the road snakes down the other side into Brookline (see *Villages*).

Molly Stark Trail, Route 9 between Brattleboro and Bennington, is dedicated to the wife of Gen. John Stark, hero of the Battle of Bennington. It is a winding, heavily trafficked route, lined for much of the way with tourist-oriented shops and restaurants. We advise avoiding it in foliage season.

West Dummerston to West Dover. Beautiful in a car or on a bike, the 13 miles between Route 30 and Route 100 actually form a shortcut from Brattleboro to Mount Snow. Turn west off Route 30, 2 miles north of the covered bridge. Follow the Rock River (in summer, clumps of cars suggest swimming holes) west from West Dummerston and Williamsville, on through the picturesque village of South Newfane (the general store is a source of picnic fare); detour ½ mile into the old hill village of Dover, very different from West Dover down on busy Route 100.

Route 30 from Brattleboro to Jamaica (you can loop back on Route 100 and either of the two routes sketched above) shadows the West River, passing two covered bridges and going through exceptionally pictur- esque villages like Newfane and Townshend, as well as by the Townshend Dam (good for swimming).

East Dummerston to West Dummerston. A handy shortcut from Route 5 to Route 30 (or vice versa), just 2 miles up one side of a hill to pictur- esque Dummerston Center and 2 miles down the other. This was long known in our family as the Gnome Road because of the way it winds through the woods to Vermont's longest (recently refitted) traffic-bearing covered bridge (see *To See*). It's generally known as the East/West Road.

TO DO

BICYCLING

The combination of rail service (Brattleboro is an Amtrak stop) and some 200 miles of dirt roads and abandoned roads, also off-road trails, adds up to a well-established mecca for bicyclists. The **Putney Bicycle Club,** the oldest in Vermont, organizes weekly (hard-core) mountain- bike tours. Check with the **West Hill Shop** (387-5718), open daily, I-91 exit 4, across from the Putney Inn. Since 1971 the hub of biking information throughout this area, the shop has published its own map, detailing four tours as well as Class 4 roads and off-road routes. It also provides mountain-bike rentals.

Brattleboro Bicycle Shop (254-8644; 1-800-BRATBIKE), 178 Main Street, offers day rentals (hybrids) and plenty of advice about where to use them.

Bike Vermont (1-800-453-4811) offers weekend and longer guided inn- to-inn tours through the area.

BOATING

Vermont Canoe Touring Center (257-5008), Brattleboro. Located at the cove at Veterans Memorial Bridge, Route 5, just north of the junction with Route 30. Open Memorial Day weekend through Labor Day week- end, daily 9–7, weekends in spring and fall. John Knickerbocker rents canoes and kayaks, and offers shuttle service, guided trips, and wilder- ness camping on the river. The 32 miles from Bellows Falls to the Vernon Dam is slow-moving water, as is the 6-mile stretch from below the dam to the Massachusetts border.

Connecticut River Tours (254-1263), Putney Road, Brattleboro. The 49- passenger, mahogany-trimmed *Belle of Brattleboro* offers several kinds of cruises Tuesday through Sunday and holidays, Memorial Day through Columbus Day.

White water on the West River. Twice a year, once in spring and again in September, the Army Corps of Engineers releases water from the Ball Mountain Dam in Jamaica, creating white water fit for national kayak championships. The races are no longer run here, but commercial white-water rafters as well as white-water kayakers and canoeists take advantage of the flow, especially in fall, when many of the region's other white-water courses are dry. As many as 2,500 kayakers converge on Jamaica State Park (see *Green Space*) for the event in late September or early October; call the Springfield office of the Vermont Department of Forests and Parks (885-8855) for the precise date.

Townshend Outdoors (365-7308), Route 30 south of Townshend village. Ann Griswold's consignment shop for sports equipment has canoes and kayaks, which can also be rented for use at the nearby Townshend Recreation Area (the dam) and other nearby lakes. You can rent tubes for use in the river, too. (The shop also sells skis and snowshoes.)

FISHING

In the **Connecticut River,** you can catch bass, trout, pike, pickerel, and yellow perch. There is an access on Old Ferry Road, 2 miles north of Brattleboro on Route 5; another is from River Road on the New Hampshire shore in Westmoreland (Route 9 east, then north on Route 63).

The **West River** is a source of trout and smallmouth bass; access is from any number of places along Route 30. For a fishing license, tackle, and tips, stop by **Feather, Fin & Game Sporting Goods** (365-4306) in Townshend, on the common.

In Vernon, there is a boat access on **Lily Pond;** in Guilford, on **Weatherhead Hollow Pond** (see the DeLorme *Vermont Atlas and Gazetteer*).

GOLF

Brattleboro Country Club (257-7380), Upper Dummerston Road, has nine holes.

HIKING

In Brattleboro, a pleasant path up to the Retreat Tower, a 19th-century overlook, begins beside Linden Lodge on Route 30. Another trail follows the West River along the abandoned **West River railroad bed.** Access is off Route 5 north of town; take the second left turn after crossing the bridge (by the Maple Farms milk plant). **Wantastiquet Mountain,** overlooking Brattleboro from across the Connecticut River in New Hampshire, is a good 1½-hour hike from downtown, great for picnics and views of southeast Vermont. See also Fort Dummer State Park under *Green Space* for a wooded trail south of town overlooking the Connecticut, and Townshend State Forest for a steep trek up **Bald Mountain.**

Putney Mountain between Putney and Brookline, off Putney Mountain Road (see *Scenic Drives*), is one of the most rewarding 1-mile round-trip hikes anywhere. A sign nailed to a tree in the unmarked parking area assures you that this is indeed Putney Mountain. Follow the trail that heads gently uphill through birches and maples, then continues through firs and vegetation that changes remarkably quickly to the stunted growth usually found only at higher elevations. Suddenly you emerge on the mountain's broad crown, circled by one of the most deep-down satisfying panoramas in all of New England. The view to the east is of Mount Monadnock, rising in lonely magnificence above the roll of southern New Hampshire, but more spectacular is the spread of Green Mountain peaks to the west. In summer, you can still pick out the ski trails on Haystack, Mount Snow, and Stratton, but these are just a few among the seemingly dozens of green peaks that crowd around.

Jamaica State Park offers a choice of three interesting trails. The most intriguing and theoretically the shortest is to Hamilton Falls, a 125-foot cascade through a series of wondrous potholes. It's an obvious mile (30-minute) hike up, but the return can be confusing. Beware straying onto Turkey Mountain Road.

Black Mountain Natural Area, maintained by The Nature Conservancy of Vermont (229-4425). Cross the covered bridge on Route 30 in West Dummerston and turn south on Quarry Road for 1.4 miles. The road changes to Rice Farm Road; go another 0.5 mile to a pull-off on the right. The marked trail begins across the road and rises abruptly to 1,280 feet to a ridge, traversing it before dropping back down, passing a beaver dam on the way back to the river; best done clockwise. Beautiful in laurel season.

HORSEBACK RIDING

West River Lodge and Stable (365-7668), Hill Road, Brookline. Roger Poitras has built a barn and ring across the way from the inn (see *Lodging—Bed & Breakfasts*) and offers English riding featuring "centered riding" (using the Alexander technique), dressage, and jumping. All-day trail rides in spring and fall are a tradition, and trail rides geared to better equestrians are offered. Just 2 miles from Newfane, a short way off Route 30, this is a frequently bypassed place, a real find for anyone who loves horses. Some of the finest back-road bridle paths are right out the door.

Winchester Stables (365-9434), River Road, Newfane. Lessons and trail rides offered.

RAILROAD EXCURSION

The Green Mountain Flyer (463-3069), based just north of this area in Bellows Falls, offers a 26-mile run in-season. See also "Grafton, Chester, Saxtons River, and Bellows Falls."

SWIMMING

In Brattleboro, **Living Memorial Park,** west of downtown on Route 9, offers a public pool (mid-June through Labor Day). The nearest beach for this area is Wares Grove in Chesterfield, New Hampshire (9 miles east on Route 9, the next left after the junction with Route 63). This pleasant beach on **Spofford Lake** is good for children; there is a snack bar and makeshift changing facilities. In Guilford, there is swimming at **Weatherhead Hollow Pond.** The biggest swimming hole by far is at the **Townshend Lake Recreation Area** (874-4881) off Route 30 in

West Townshend. You drive across the top of this massive structure, completed in 1961 as a major flood-prevention measure for the southern Connecticut River Valley. Swimming is in the reservoir behind the dam, ideal for children. Changing facilities provided; small fee.

Sweet Pond State Park (257-7406), Guilford. This former 125-acre estate with a large pond is good for swimming and boating. It's circled by a nature path that leads to a 5-acre perennial garden.

The **West River** offers a few swimming holes, notably under the covered bridge on Route 30 in West Dummerston. Just off Route 30, a mile or so up (on South Newfane Road), the **Rock River** swirls through a series of swimming holes, some favored by skinny-dippers. There's parking and a small beach at the covered bridge, and cars line the road above the Rock River (there's a steep path down).

WINTER SPORTS

CROSS-COUNTRY SKIING

Brattleboro Outing Club Ski Hut (254-4081), Upper Dummerston Road, Brattleboro. Trails through woods and a golf course, 15 km machine tracked, rentals, instruction.

In **Living Memorial Park** (254-4081), Brattleboro, a 6 km trail through the woods is not only set but also lighted for night skiing.

West Hill Shop (387-5718), I-91, exit 4 (across from the Putney Inn) is the source of cross-country information for the Putney area.

Townshend Outdoors (365-7309), Route 30 south of Townshend Village, rents cross-country skis and snowshoes.

See also Grafton Ponds in "Grafton, Chester, Saxtons River, and Bellows Falls."

DOWNHILL SKIING

The big ski areas are a short drive west into the Green Mountains, either to **Mount Snow** (Route 9 from Brattleboro and then up Route 100 to West Dover—see "Mount Snow/Wilmington Area") or up Route 30 to **Stratton** or **Bromley** (see "Manchester and the Mountains").

Maple Valley (254-6083), Route 30, West Dummerston, is one those rare surviving small ski areas that are hanging in there: It offers two double chairlifts, one T-bar, 14 trails, a 1,000-foot vertical drop, and facilities that include a cafeteria, ski shop, and lounge. There are rentals, repairs, and snowmaking. It's open weekends for day and night skiing, midweek conditions permitting. In '99, lift tickets are $28 adult, $20 junior.

In Brattleboro itself, a T-bar serves the ski hill in **Living Memorial Park** (see *Green Space*), and there is a ski jump on **Harris Hill** near the Brattleboro Retreat on Route 30.

SKATING

Living Memorial Park, Route 9, Brattleboro. Rink is open daily until 9 PM.

SLEIGH RIDES

Fair Winds Farm (254-9067), Upper Dummerston Road, and the **Robb Family Farm** (254-7664; 1-888-318-9087), 827 Ames Hill Road, both offer sleigh rides within minutes of downtown Brattleboro. See also *Farms to Visit*.

SNOWMOBILES

River Bend Lodge (365-7952), Route 30, Newfane, and **Stanley Bill Sales** in Townshend (365-7375) rent machines. Guided tours are offered by **High Country Snowmobile Tours** (464-2108; 1-800-627-SLED) in Wilmington.

GREEN SPACE

Fort Dummer State Park (254-2610), RFD 3, Brattleboro. Located 2 miles south of Brattleboro on South Main Street. There are 61 campsites, including nine lean-tos, a dump station, a playfield, and a hiking trail through hardwoods with views of the river valley.

Jamaica State Park (874-4600), Jamaica. This 758-acre wooded area offers riverside camping, swimming in a great swimming hole, a picnic area, and an organized program of guided hikes. An old railroad bed along the river serves as a 3-mile trail to the Ball Mountain Dam, and an offshoot mile-long trail leads to Hamilton Falls. A weekend in spring and again in fall is set aside for white-water canoe races. There are 61 tent/trailer sites and 18 lean-tos. A large picnic shelter is handy to the swimming hole and a playground includes swings, a teeter-totter, and slides.

Ball Mountain Lake (886-8111), Jamaica. This 85-acre lake, created and maintained by the U.S. Army Corps of Engineers, is a dramatic sight among the wooded, steep mountains, conveniently viewed from the access road off Route 30. One hundred seven campsites are available on Winhall Brook at the other end of the reservoir, open mid-May through mid-September; accessible off Route 100 in South Londonderry. Free. A controlled release from this flood dam provides outstanding canoeing on the West River below Jamaica each spring and fall (see *To Do—Boating*).

Dutton Pines State Park (254-2277), Brattleboro. On Route 5, 5 miles north of town, this is a picnic area with a shelter.

Townshend State Park (365-7500), Townshend, marked from Route 30 south of town. Open early May through Columbus Day. Up a back road, an attractive, classic '30s Civilian Conservation Corps (CCC) stone and wood complex with a picnic pavilion. This is really an 826-acre state forest with 41 acres reserved for the park. The camping area (30 campsites, four lean-tos) is near the start of the 2.7-mile (steep) climb to the summit of Bald Mountain; trail maps are available at the park office.

✐ **Living Memorial Park,** just west of Brattleboro on Route 9. This is an unusual facility for any community. It includes a swimming pool (mid-June

through Labor Day), ice-skating rink (early December through mid-March), tennis courts, and playground, camping sites, lawn games, a nine-hole golf course, and a ski hill serviced by a T-bar.

See also Sweet Pond State Park under *To Do—Swimming.*

FARMS TO VISIT

One of the state's concentrations of farms and orchards is here in the lower Connecticut River Valley, some offering "pick your own," others welcoming visitors to their farm stands, sugaring houses, or barns. Call before coming.

Note: **Brattleboro Farmer's Market** is held May through late October, Wednesday 10–2 at Merchants Bank Square across from the post office, and Saturday 9–2, Route 9 in West Brattleboro. A lively community coming-together showcasing crafts and produce. Food vendors and, frequently, music and flowers are part of the scene.

Southern Vermont Working Farms, a map guide available from the Windham County Natural Resources Conservation District (254-5323), locates more than a dozen farms in this area.

APPLES AND MORE

Dwight Miller & Son (254-9158), 581 Miller Road, East Dummerston. Open daily year-round. Syrup and seasonal pick-your-own apples, strawberries, and peaches, blueberries and raspberries, also selling pears, plums, and organic produce.

Green Mountain Orchards (387-5851), West Hill Road, Putney. Open daily in-season. Pick-your-own apples and blueberries; cider available in-season. Open in winter, selling apples.

CHEESE

Major Farm (387-4473), Patch Road, Westminster West.

Vermont Shepherd Cheese holds one the country's top awards for its hand-pressed distinctive, sweet, creamy-textured sheep's milk cheese. It is made April through October, then aged 4 to 8 months and available mid-August until the year's supply runs out in spring. The Cave is open to visitors for tours and cheese tastings August through October, Thursday and Saturday 10–noon. Call for directions.

MAPLE SUGAR AND MORE

The Robb Family Farm (254-7664; 1-888-318-9087), 827 Ames Hill Road, Brattleboro. This 420-acre dairy farm has been in the same family since 1907, and visitors are welcome here in a number of ways and in all seasons. In spring the sugarhouse is a fragrant, steamy place; year-round it's also the Country Shop (open Monday through Saturday 10–5, Sunday 1–5, closed Wednesday), stocked with maple products, baked goods, and crated and floral items. Visitors are also welcome in the barn, moved here from Halifax in 1912 (50 of the 100-head herd are presently milked). Inquire about a Day on the Farm, beginning with breakfast, also about hayrides, sleigh rides, hiking, and the Apple Fritter Fest in October.

Lilac Ridge Farm (254-8113), Ames Hill Road, Brattleboro, is just before the Robb Family Farm (see above). Stuart and Beverly Thurber also milk 50 cows and produce maple syrup, and they grow Christmas trees. They invite visitors to come and walk around.

Franklin Farm (254-2228), Weatherhead Hollow Road, Guilford. A diversified family farm: dairy, maple sugaring, baked goods, fresh eggs, compost, and poultry.

Miller Farm (254-2657), Route 142, Vernon. One of Vermont's first registered Holstein farms (1887), in the Miller family since 1916. Farm tours offered.

Harlow's Sugar House (387-5852), Route 5 in Putney, is one of the most visitor-oriented operations, permitting you to pick your own apples, blueberries, and strawberries and offering sleigh rides during sugaring season.

H & M Orchard (254-2711), Dummerston Center. One of the most accessible sugar shacks to observe "boiling" during sugaring season.

Sweet Tree Farm (254-4508), Route 5, Dummerston. The sugarhouse opens in March and continues through the summer months.

OTHER

Overlook Farm (365-4088), River Road, Newfane. This sheep farm has been in agricultural production since 1776. Lamb is raised, and wool products, including natural wool-filled comforters, are sold.

Hickins Mountain Mowings (254-2146), Black Mountain Road, Dummerston. Located off the high, wooded East/West Road (see *To See—Scenic Drives*), this is an outstanding family farm, noted for the quality and variety of its vegetables, flowers, maple syrup, pickles, jams, jellies, and fruitcakes. Open year-round, except Tuesday, until sunset.

Green Mountain Llamas (365-7581), Route 35, Townshend. Jane and Conrad Grillo and their sons have 40 llamas. Jane uses the fiber to make unusual hand-felted hats. They also make and sell llama pack frames and baskets.

Walker Farm (254-2051), Route 5, Dummerston. A 200-year-old farm and garden center (open April 15 through fall), specializing in hard-to-find annuals and perennials. A full line of produce June through Thanksgiving, featuring their own organic vegetables and local fruit. Display gardens, and calves for petting.

Dutton Berry Farm and Stand (365-4168), farm stand on Route 30, Newfane. This is a large, varied stand featuring produce from the family's Dummerston farm.

Fair Winds Farm (254-9067), Upper Dummerston Road. This small, diversified family farm offers horse-drawn sleigh and hayrides through the woods. Organic produce and fresh eggs are sold at their roadside stand on weekdays.

Elysian Hills (257-0233), Tucker Reed Road, Brattleboro. Bill and Mary Lou Schmidt maintain this tree farm (available for tagging in October) and also grow rhubarb for rhubarb wine, along with Gilfeather turnip seed. Visitors welcome to walk the woodland trails.

LODGING

INNS

Three Mountain Inn (874-4140), Route 30, Jamaica 05343. Ten minutes from the Stratton access road, this 1790s inn sits in the middle of a classic Vermont village, with deep gardens behind. You enter from the rear, through a cozy pub and a living room with its original wide-plank floor and large hearth. There are 10 rooms in the main house and 6 in neighboring Robinson House, all carefully decorated. Two have working fireplaces, and the suite has a wood-burning fireplace and a garden view; the honeymoon cottage near the pool has a fireplace and Jacuzzi. Innkeeper Elaine Murray is also the chef (see *Dining Out*), and both Elaine and her husband Charles are delighted and able to advise visitors about local hikes, antiquing, and shopping. Jamaica State Park and its trails are within walking distance (see *Green Space*). The neighboring Congregational church combined with the inn's reception space make this a good spot for weddings. $180–240 per couple MAP, $125–165 B&B. Stratton is just up the road (see *To Do—Downhill Skiing* in "Manchester and the Mountains"); inquire about ski packages.

   ♿ **Four Columns Inn** (365-7713; 1-800-787-6633), Newfane 05345. Built in 1830 by Gen. Pardon Kimball to remind his southern wife of her girlhood home, this classic Greek Revival mansion fronts on Newfane's classic green. There are 15 guest rooms with private bath and antique beds, and four fireplace suites with Jacuzzi. Innkeepers Pam and Gorty Baldwin have redone the common space, adding comfortable chairs, French doors, softening the former formal feel of the place, enhancing the tavern and dining room. Guest rooms vary from crisp doubles under the eaves to a palatial suite. While it's set in a splendid village (see Newfane under *Villages*), the inn backs onto 150 steep and wooded acres, good for walking or snowshoeing. Dining is a big attraction (see *Dining Out*), and facilities include a swimming pool. $110–240 double occupancy, B&B; roll-away $25. More in foliage season.

   ♿ **Windham Hill Inn** (874-4080; 1-800-944-4080), West Townshend 05359. High above the West River Valley, this 1825 brick farmhouse offers an unusual retreat. Some of the 21 guest rooms have soaking tub, Jacuzzi, fireplace, or gas stove, and all have private bath and phone. All are carefully furnished with antiques and interesting art. Eight are in the White Barn Annex, some with a large deck looking down the valley. Common space in the inn itself include a music room with grand piano and an airy sunporch with wicker. Two sitting rooms are country elegant with wood-burning fireplaces, Oriental carpets, and wing chairs, and the dining room also has a fireplace, a formal dining table, and tables for two (see *Dining Out*). Innkeepers Grigs and Pat Markham have added a pool and tennis court. The 160-acre property also includes an extensive network of hiking paths to a waterfall and pools, groomed as cross-country trails in winter (when the frog pond freezes for skating). Inquire about weddings, both inside (there's a small conference center in the barn) and outside (for up to 150 guests). $245–370 per couple MAP, $155–280 B&B; $70 per extra person. Inquire about discounted packages.

Old Newfane Inn (365-4427; 1-800-764-4427), Newfane 05345. Closed in November and April. Two-night deposit required to confirm reservation on big weekends. The long, low-beamed dining room was a part of the original inn built up on Newfane Hill (see *Villages*), and there is a seemly sense of age to this landmark, with its formal atmosphere. The eight guest rooms and two suites, eight with private bath, are furnished with antiques and are spotless, as are the public rooms. Famous for outstanding French-Swiss cuisine (see *Dining Out*). $125–155 double with bath; the high end is for a suite (living room, bath, and bedroom). No credit cards.

The Inn at South Newfane (348-7191; e-mail: innatsouthnewfane@ sover.net), South Newfane 05351. This elegant inn is sited just off the beaten track in a picture-perfect village, complete with covered bridge. There are six large guest rooms, all with high ceilings and private bath. The rooms are nicely appointed and the porch overlooks a sweeping lawn shaded by weeping willows. Innkeeper Neville Cullen serves breakfast and dinner, also lunch in summer. The swim pond is backed by 100 acres with trails for walking and skiing. $95–125 B&B; add $25 per person for dinner. Many weekends are booked for weddings (there's a country chapel just down the road and receptions can accommodate 60 inside, 300 out).

🏮⛄**Latchis Hotel** (254-6300; fax: 254-6304), 50 Main Street, Brattleboro 05301. A downtown art deco–style hotel first opened in 1939 and resurrected after thorough restoration. It has remained in the Latchis family throughout. Push open the door into the small but spiffy lobby, with its highly polished terrazzo marble floors. Surprises in the rooms include restored 1930s furniture, air-conditioning, and soundproof windows (a real blessing). Rooms are cheerful, brightly decorated, all with private bath, phone, fridge, and coffeemaker. The 27 rooms and three 2-room suites are accessible by elevator. The rooms to request are on the second and third floors, with views down Main Street and across to Wantastiquet Mountain. The hotel is so solidly built that you don't hear the traffic below. Some smoking rooms. The hotel's Windham Brewery and Latchis Grille are described under *Eating Out*. Rates: $62–95 for double rooms, $120–150 for suites, includes continental breakfast.

🏮🐾⛄**The Putney Inn** (387-5517; 1-800-653-5517), Putney 05346. One of the

The Latchis Hotel, an art deco landmark

KIM GRANT

oldest farmhouses in the area, this red-clapboard landmark was built by the first settlers. In the early 1960s, when the land was divided for construction of I-91, it was sold to local residents, who renovated the farmhouse without disturbing the posts and beams or the central open hearth. Plants and antiques add to the pleasant setting of the entry and large dining rooms. Twenty-five guest rooms occupy a motel-like wing, each with Queen Anne reproductions, bath, color TV, and phone. Pets are permitted but "must be smaller than a cow and not left alone in the rooms." The complex is set in 13 acres, with views of the river valley and mountains. Staff are helpful and friendly, and chef Ann Cooper has won many awards for her distinctly New England fare featuring local products (see *Dining Out*). At $78–148 per couple with a full breakfast, this is one of the better deals around.

☙ **Chesterfield Inn** (603-256-3211; 1-800-365-5515), P.O. Box 155, Chesterfield, NH 03443. On Route 9, 2 miles east of Brattleboro. The original house served as a tavern from 1798 to 1811 but the present facility is contemporary, with a large attractive dining room, spacious parlor, and 15 guest rooms scattered between the main house and the Guest House. All rooms have sitting area, phone, controlled heat and air-conditioning, optional TV and wet bar, and some have a working fireplace or Jacuzzi. Innkeepers Phil and Judy Hueber have created a popular dining room (see *Dining Out*) and a comfortable, romantic getaway spot that's well positioned for exploring southern Vermont, as well as New Hampshire's Monadnock Region. $125–225 includes a full breakfast.

BED & BREAKFASTS

40 Putney Road (254-6268; 1-800-941-2413; fax: 258-2673), at that address, Brattleboro 05301. Just north of the town's common and within walking distance of downtown shops and restaurants, this house with steeply pitched, gabled roof was built in 1930 for the director of the neighboring Brattleboro Retreat. It's said to be patterned on a French château. Dan and Gwen Pasco offer three guest rooms and one suite nicely furnished with family antiques; two have fireplace, all have private bath and phone. We would request one of the two rooms overlooking the gardens, away from Route 5 (Putney Road) traffic, but front rooms are air-conditioned so noise is muted. Common space is plentiful and attractive, and landscaped grounds with working fountains border the West River. The $110–170 double rates include a full breakfast served, weather permitting, on the garden patio.

Crosby House (257-4914; 1-800-528-4914), 45 Western Avenue, Brattleboro 05301. A mansion built in 1868 and loving restored, this is a special place with marble fireplace and baby grand piano in the parlor and superb detailing, augmented by cabinets and other examples of highly skilled woodworking by Lynn Kuralt's late husband, Tom. Each of the three guest rooms is well thought out and has a magnificent bed and bath; Winifred's Summer Retreat has both a paneled fireplace and a double whirlpool with separate shower. $95–125 includes a full, heart-healthy breakfast served in the oak-paneled dining room or continental, served in your room.

The Artist's Loft B&B and Gallery (phone/fax: 257-5181; e-mail: artguys@the artistsloft.com), 103 Main Street, Brattleboro 05301. Artist William Hays and wife Patricia Long offer a middle-of-town suite with a private entrance, queen-sized bed, and river view (private bath). This is a great spot if you want to plug into all that Brattleboro offers in the way of art, music, dining, and shopping: Pat and William are tuned into everything and delight in sharing their enthusiasm for their adopted town. $88–98 includes continental breakfast.

    Hickory Ridge House (387-5709; 1-800-380-9218; e-mail: mail@ hickoryridgehouse.com), RFD 3, Box 1410, Putney 05346. An 1808 brick mansion, complete with Palladian window, set on 12 acres on a country road near the Connecticut River. There are six airy guest rooms in the inn and a two-bedroom cottage (two baths and full kitchen facilities, a wood-burning fireplace in the sitting room), painted in soft, authentic colors. They come with and without fireplace but all have private bath, phone, and (hidden) TV. The original Federal-era bedrooms are large, with Rumford fireplaces, and there's an upstairs sitting room. A first-floor room is handicapped-accessible. Hosts Linda and Jack Bisbee ran another local B&B before acquiring and refurbishing this one in 1998. In summer, a swimming hole lies within walking distance, and groomed cross-country-touring trails are out the back door. $135–165 per couple; cottage is $310–350 per day. Inquire about horse-drawn carriage rides. Weddings are a specialty.

West River Lodge (365-7745), RR 1, Box 693, Newfane 05345, off Route 30, Hill Road, Brookline. This may be the only Vermont farmhouse-turned-inn that's still dwarfed by its weathered red barn, one that hasn't been turned into "carriage house suites." Instead, since the 1930s, the inn has catered to horse lovers. In 1999 the inn was sold to Ellen Capito and Jim Wightman, who are carrying on the inn's equestrian tradition (horses are boarded) but also welcome anyone who finds his or her way here, just a couple of miles but seemingly worlds away from Route 30. Instead of a pool, there is the best swimming hole (10 feet deep with a totally private beach) in the entire length of the West River. The riding remains outstanding (see *To Do—Horseback Riding*). There are eight guest rooms. $70–95 with private bath, $60–95 with shared bath.

Boardman House (365-4086), village green, Townshend 05353. An 1840s Greek Revival house tucked into a quiet (away from Route 30 traffic) corner of one of Vermont's standout commons. Sarah and Paul Messenger offer five unusually attractive guest rooms, each with private bath. There's also a two-bedroom suite, a parlor, and an airy, old-fashioned kitchen. Breakfast usually includes fresh fruit compote and oven-warm muffins with a creative main dish. $75–110 per room. Dogs accepted with prior arrangement.

Meadowlark Inn (257-4582; 1-800-616-6359; e-mail: lark@together.net), Orchard Street, P.O. Box 2048, Brattleboro 05303. The town of Brattleboro includes some surprisingly rural corners, like this maple-walled ridge road. The large farmhouse, set in lawns, has been in Lark Canedy's family since 1958, and there is a hospitable, comfortable feel to the place. Common space includes a wraparound screened porch as well as a large living room. We prefer the old-fashioned, tastefully furnished rooms in the inn—which include three crisp, bright doubles ($85) and the Pine Room with a king bed, fireplace, and TV ($115)—to the two rooms in the 1870 coach house with Jacuzzi in the same room as the beds ($115). The coach house also has two more luxurious rooms with king beds, views, and fridges. The building has its own common space with a combination goldfish-tank/coffee-table centerpiece.

Ranney Brook Farm (874-4589), Route 30, Townshend. Diana and John Wichland reopened this B&B in the fall of '98, after greatly enhancing it. Common space now includes a den with piano, a "great room" in the rear (a 1790s barn), and a dining room in which a full breakfast is served family-style. Of the four upstairs rooms, two have private bath (one is in the room). John Wichland managers Miller Brothers-Newton, a long-established clothier in Brattleboro, and the couple moved here from Keene, New Hampshire, where his brothers manage the parent store.

Ranney-Crawford House (1-800-731-5502; 802-387-4150), Westminster West Road, Putney 05346. Arnie Glim, innkeeper of this 1810 brick Federal-style house on a quiet country road surrounded by fields, is an enthusiastic bicyclist who knows all the local possiblities for both touring and mountain biking.

🐾 **Whetstone Inn** (254-2500), Marlboro 05344. Just up the road from Marlboro College, site of the internationally acclaimed summer music festival (see *Entertainment—Music*), this is a 1786 tavern, part of the cluster of white-clapboard buildings—including the church and post office—that form the village core. Innkeepers Jean and Harry Boardman have been here more than 20 years, and there's a casually comfortable feel to the old place. It has nine guest rooms, eight with private bath. $60–85. Breakfast is extra.

MOTEL

🐾 **Dalem's Chalet** (254-4323; 1-800-462-5009), 16 South Street, West Brattleboro 05301. Set back from Route 9, this chalet-style lodge is a long-established family find, offering rooms with two double beds, TV, and phone. Facilities include a small winter indoor pool and a summer outdoor pool, a game room, a pond with swans, and a restaurant serving Swiss, German, and Austrian specialties as well as American fare (see *Eating Out*). $52–86 per couple; suites with cooking facilities are $84 for two.

CAMPGROUNDS

See *Green Space* for information on camping in Fort Dummer State Park, Jamaica State Park, Ball Mountain Lake, and Townshend State Park.

OTHER LODGING

Naulakha (254-6868), c/o the Landmark Trust, 707 Kipling Road, Dummerston 05301. In 1893 Rudyard Kipling, with his American bride, completed this long, narrow-shingled mansion (supposedly built to resemble a riverboat) high on a hill, with views east across New Hampshire to Mount Monadnock. Here he finished *Captains Courageous* and *The First and Second Jungle Books,* but a court case against his brother-in-law (shattering his beloved seclusion) caused the writer to leave for England so abruptly in 1896 that the family took only books, carpets, and select pictures. Thanks to the care with which two subsequent owners preserved the property—and the outstanding care with which a British preservation group has restored it—60 percent of the present furnishings are original (including a handsome, third-floor pool table). The house stood vacant from 1942 to 1992, when the Landmark Trust acquired, gutted, rewired, and replumbed it (a new septic system was required). Though the house is not available for functions or tours, it can be rented for $1,900 per week, not much when you consider that it can accommodate several couples. A game of tennis, anyone, on the Kipling court? Or how about curling up with the *Jungle Books* on a sofa by the fire, only a few feet from where they were written?

WHERE TO EAT

DINING OUT

T. J. Buckley's (257-4922), 132 Elliot Street, Brattleboro. Open Wednesday through Sunday, 6–9. Reservations required. From the outside this small but classic red and black 1920s Worcester diner looks unpromising, even battered. Inside, fresh flowers and mismatched settings (gathered from yard sales) brighten the tables, walls are oak paneled, and chef-owner Michael Fuller prepares the night's fish, chicken, and beef (vegetarian is also possible) in the open kitchen behind the counter. Fuller buys all produce locally and what's offered depends on what's available: On a July day the menu included bluefin tuna with roasted lobster stock, carrots, celery, fresh horseradish root, served with a risotto with a ginger/pheasant stock; and a chicken breast with white truffle and goat fontina, served with flageolet beans (white) with fresh artichoke and julienned Romano beans; the $25 entree includes salad; appetizer and dessert are extra. The wine list ranges from $20 to $60. No credit cards.

Peter Haven's (257-3333), 32 Elliot Street, Brattleboro. Open from 6 PM Tuesday through Saturday. Just 10 tables in this nifty restaurant decorated with splashy artwork, and with an inspired menu to match. The evening's entrées might include pasta del mar (a nest of linguine with a creamy pesto sauce topped with shrimp, scallops, and artichoke hearts), chicken in an Oriental sauce, and roasted boneless duck breast with a black currant and port sauce. Entrées $16.50–22.

The Four Columns Inn (365-7713), Route 30, Newfane. Serving 6–9 nightly except Tuesday, and Sunday brunch 11–2; reservations suggested. Chef Greg Parks has earned top ratings for his efforts, served in a converted barn with a large brick fireplace as its centerpiece and an evolving mural of Newfane Village. The emphasis is on herbs (home-grown), stocks made from scratch, and locally raised lamb and trout (the latter from the adjacent pond). While the menu changes frequently, it might include baked fish fillet with greens, tomato, black olives, and Chinese black bean sauce with cardamom-scented sushi rice, crispy free-range baby chicken with a porcini essence sauce, and grilled black Angus with portobello mushrooms and a sweet-and-sour dipping sauce. Entrées $20–26.

Three Mountain Inn (874-4140), Route 30, Jamaica. Dinner by reservation only. While enjoying a candlelit dinner in front of the fireplaces in the two small dining rooms of this 18th-century village house, it's easy to imagine that you're in a colonial tavern. The frequently changing menus feature innkeeper Elaine Murray's soups, breads, and desserts. You might begin with spinach pie or mussel bisque and dine on a seafood crêpe, pork tenderloin, or venison. Leave room for Kahlúa mocha fudge pie or maple mousse. Entrées are $12.50–22.50 and include breads, salad, and vegetables.

The Putney Inn (387-5517; 1-800-653-5517), just off I-91, exit 4, in Putney. Open for all three meals. An 18th-century house is now a popular restaurant, and executive chef Ann Cooper has won numerous awards and national acclaim for pastries and sauces. The menu features classic New England dishes like roast breast of turkey with maple pecan stuffing, Vermont lamb with a rosemary Merlot sauce, and a native venison sampler with sweet potato pancakes and wild mushroom sauce. A "family-fare menu" includes reasonably priced options like turkey and vegetable potpie in a bread bowl and Frank's Favorite Meat Loaf with three-onion sauce. Entrées $16–19.75.

Old Newfane Inn (365-4427), Route 30, Newfane Village. Open for dinner nightly except Monday. Reservations requested. The low-beamed old dining room is country formal. Chef-owner Eric Weindl is widely known for his Swiss-accented Continental menu with entrée choices like roast duckling au Cointreau à l'orange or *poivre verte*, Hungarian veal goulash, or scallopine of veal Marsala. Entrées are $14.95–26.

Windham Hill Inn (874-4702; 1-800-944-4080), West Townshend. An unusually attractive dining room overlooking the frog pond, open to the public by reservation. The prix fixe five-course menu ($40) might feature grilled medallion of beef with Burgundy-pear sauce or Chilean sea bass with hazelnut crust and a fragrant fennel broth; wines by the glass and a reasonably priced house wine are available.

Townshend Country Inn (365-4141), Route 30, Townshend. Open daily year-round except Wednesday for dinner, also May through October for a Sunday buffet brunch. In this pleasant country restaurant (in a house that was a summer home for Grandma Moses), Joe Peters has created a mix of ambience and quality dining at prices well below the norm. The menu might include pasta primavera, roast Vermont turkey and stuffing, and baked stuffed shrimp. There are nightly specials as well. Entrées $7.95–12.95. The Sunday buffet is $9.95 per adult, $4.95 per child.

Latchis Grille and Windham Brewery (254-4747), 6 Flat Street, Brattleboro. Open for dinner nightly; also lunch on weekends. Hidden away in the depths of the Latchis Hotel, this upbeat restaurant offers a "dining out" atmosphere (scenes of old Brattleboro spread across the walls) at modest prices. Dinner entrées might include roast chicken breast stuffed with sun-dried tomatoes, leeks, and goat cheese, served with basil oil; and Atlantic salmon broiled in a soy marinade, crusted with lemongrass, black sesame, and green onions, served over Japanese noodles. A "café menu" is also available, along with beers brewed in the Windham Brewery (see *Eating Out*) on the premises. Entrées $8–19.

Chesterfield Inn (603-256-3211; 1-800-365-5515), Route 9, West Chesterfield, New Hampshire. Open nightly for dinner. Across the river, less than 15 minutes east of Brattleboro, this attractive inn is justly known for its dining room with views of the Vermont hills. Chef Carl Warner has an enviable reputation for dishes like grilled salmon with mango-mustard glaze and shrimp, mushrooms, and sugar snap peas in a wasabi butter sauce. Entrées $16–22.

See also Flowers Cafe under *Eating Out*.

EATING OUT

In Brattleboro

Common Ground (257-0855), 25 Elliot Street. Monday through Saturday for lunch (11–2) and dinner; Sunday for brunch 10:30–1:30 and dinner (5 PM till closing); closed Tuesday year-round, also Monday and Wednesday in the off-season. Founded in 1971, a collective-run throwback to the '60s: a high-ceilinged second floor of an old industrial building, with a seasonal, glass-walled solar terrace. Each month a new menu is printed showing the specialties, which run the gamut from Russian vegetable pie to lasagne and spanakopita. Beverages range from banana yogurt shakes through beer and wine. A bar/counter serves solo diners but strangers routinely sit down at the same table and converse. Live entertainment Friday and Saturday night, anything from DJs to jazz.

Ray's Diner (254-0090), a mile up Route 5 from I-91, exit 1, at 45 Canal Street. Open 6 AM–2 PM, until 8 PM Thursday through Sunday; closed Mondays. Forget the white siding and blue roof. Ray Bachinyski swears that this is the oldest, continually operating diner in Vermont, vintage 1919, Worcester. Ray will probably both make your "hub cap burger" and hand it to you. Eat at the counter, in a booth or on the small, shaded patio. The iced sun tea is real, the french fries as crisp, Thursday's specials are always Polish (try the kapusta), and fresh seafood is available on weekends.

Shin La Restaurant (257-5226), 57 Main Street (across from the Latchis Hotel), Brattleboro. Open 11–9, a small, attractive Korean restaurant known for homemade soups, dumplings, and other Korean fare. There are sushi specials on Tuesday.

3 Seasons Cafe, 139 Main Street. Open May through Halloween, weekdays 9–5, Saturday 10–5. Tucked away in a vest-pocket park overlooking the river in downtown Brattleboro: café tables, baked goods, Moroccan specialties, and cappuccino.

Walker's Restaurant (254-6046), 132 Main Street. Open for lunch and dinner until at least 10:30. Closed Sunday except during foliage and ski season. A good downtown way-stop: a spacious dining room with bare brick walls, oak tables and bar, soft lighting. For lunch a choice of burgers, soups, quiches, and sandwiches (note that only fresh potatoes, cut on the premises, are used for the french fries). The dinner menu includes steak, seafood, fish, and chicken, basics like fried clams and sirloin steak, and not-so-basics like mustard-herbed baked chicken.

Windham Brewery (254-4747), in the Latchis Hotel (see *Dining Out*). There's a pub menu to go with the ales, porters, and lagers on tap that are made on the spot.

✍ **McNeill's Brewery** (254-2553), 90 Elliot Street. Gold medal–winning brew on tap. Games, food; children welcome.

Cafe Beyond (258-4900), 29 High Street. Open for breakfast and lunch. Back of the bookstore (see *Selective Shopping—Bookstores*), a café with delightful decor, a blackboard menu featuring panini, rollups, soups, and salads. Beverages range from espresso to microbrews. Works of local artists on display.

Back Side Cafe (257-5056), Green Street Extension (accessed from the parking lot). Open weekdays for breakfast, lunch, and dinner; Sunday brunch. A comfortable café featuring soups, salads, and Mexican specialties. Liquor license.

The Marina Restaurant (257-7563), Route 5, just north of the West River bridge. Open year-round for dinner and for lunch but closed during off-season for lunch Monday and Tuesday. Seasonal outside as well as attractive inside seating, all right on the river; a favored spot for sunset marguerites. This is a real find. The reasonably priced menu includes plenty of vegetarian choices, both at lunch and dinner.

Panda North (257-4578, 257-4486), Route 5 north of Brattleboro (exit 3 off I-91), near the Quality Inn. Chinese-restaurant buffs will delight in this excellent source of Hunan and Szechwan dishes. Lunch specials include shredded pork with black beans and shrimp with garlic sauce.

Brattleboro Farmer's Market. If you happen into town around noon on a sunny Wednesday or Saturday, head for the Farmer's Market. On Wednesday it's downtown off Main Street by the Merchant's Bank Building (look for the parking lot right there) with food vendors next to a small park overlooking the river. On Saturday it's just west of town by the Creamery Bridge. A live band and crafts, as well as produce vendors, are usually on hand.

Linda's Place (254-2713), 2 Main Street. Across from the Co-op. Open for breakfast and lunch. Located in the old brick Abbott Block, a small, pleasant café with good food and a surprisingly nice view down over the iron bridge.

India Palace (254-6143), 69 Elliot Street. Open for lunch and dinner daily, even Sundays in mud season. Reliability aside, this is good Indian food, a branch of the more famous restaurant in Northampton, Massachusetts.

Sarki's Market (258-4906), 50 Elliot Street. Open for lunch and dinner. Good Lebanese. Sit-down and take-out.

Riverview Restaurant (254-9841), Bridge Street, Brattleboro. Open for all three meals. The best river view in town. Sunday brunch is your best bet.

In Putney

Curtis' Barbeque (387-5437). Summer through fall, Wednesday through Sunday 10–dusk, follow your nose to the blue school bus parked on Route 5 in Putney, just off I-91, exit 4. Curtis Tuff cooks up pork ribs and chicken, seasoned with his secret barbecue sauce, also foil-wrapped potatoes, grilled corn, and beans flavored with Vermont maple syrup. By far the best barbecue in the Northeast!

Putney Diner (387-5433), Main Street. Open 6 AM–9 PM daily. Another pleasant option in the middle of Putney Village, open for all three meals. Good for Belgian waffles, Philly cheese steak, and homemade vegetable lasagne. Pastries made daily.

Along Route 30

Rick's Tavern (365-4310), Route 30, Newfane. Open daily except Monday for lunch and dinner. An informal, pleasant roadhouse.

Flowers Cafe (365-7861), Route 3, Newfane Village. Open for lunch daily, along with breakfast weekends and dinner Monday and Friday night. The front rooms of a village house are a pleasant space. Al Kosmal's lunch menu features salads, fresh baguettes with cheese sampler and homemade soup, and quiche. Dinner is prix fixe ($20–25) with two seatings and a multicourse menu that changes weekly.

The Townshend Dam Diner (874-4107), Route 30, 2 miles north of the Townshend dam. Open from 5 AM–8 PM. Breakfast all day. Home-made French toast, home fries, muffins and biscuits, the "best dam chili," soups, and bison burgers (from the nearby East Hill Bison Farm), dinner staples like roast turkey, spaghetti, and garlic bread, daily specials.

Route 9 West

Dalem's Chalet (254-4323), West Brattleboro. A pleasant atmosphere to match the Austrian fare, a good place for Wiener schnitzel ($16.95); lighter fare also on the menu.

Zita's Putney Inn Market & Deli (257-4994), 201½ Western Avenue (Route 9), West Brattleboro. Open Monday through Saturday 7–6, Sunday 8–6.

A deli and café featuring the pastries and specialties from the Putney Inn kitchen.

 ♿ **Chelsea Royal Diner** (254-8399), Route 9, West Brattleboro. Open 6 AM–9 PM. A genuine '30s diner that's been moved a few miles west of its original site (it's a mile west of I-91, exit 2). Plenty of parking and diner decor, serving breakfast all day as part of a big menu, also plenty of daily specials.

ICE CREAM AND CAFFEINE

Page's Ice Cream, Route 9, West Brattleboro. Outstanding ice cream with frequent special flavors, made on the spot. There's a coffee shop, too, open 6 AM–8 PM.

Jamaica Coffee House (874-7085), Route 30, Jamaica Village. Open daily 8–5 for coffees, light breakfast, and lunch.

Mocha Joe's (257-7749), 82 Main Street, Brattleboro. Coffee is taken seriously here, roasted as well as brewed. Live music on weekends.

Putney Hearth Bakery (387-2708), in the Putney Tavern Building, center of the village. Open daily. Breads, pastries, and coffee. Exhibits work by local artists, occasional live music.

Coffee Country (257-0032), on the Harmony parking lot, Brattleboro. Good coffee, good food.

See also Cafe Beyond under *Eating Out.*

ENTERTAINMENT

Note: **Arts in the Seasons,** a pamphlet guide to arts and special events throughout this area, is available at the Windham Art Gallery (257-1881), 69 Main Street, Brattleboro.

ARTS CENTER

Hooker-Dunham Arts Center (254-9276), 139 Main Street, Brattleboro. Call and check out what's going on at this brand-new venue. Offerings include theater, music, film, and lectures, and there's always a gallery show.

MUSIC

Marlboro Music Festival, Persons Auditorium, Marlboro College (September through June: 215-569-4690; summer: 254-2394). Concerts, primarily chamber music, are offered on Friday, Saturday, and Sunday, early July through mid-August. This unusual "festival" is a 7-week gathering of 70 or so world-class musicians who come to work together. It is held on this rural campus because Rudolf Serkin, one of its founders, owned a nearby farm. Pablo Casals came every year from 1960 to 1973. Some concerts are sold out in advance (for advance tickets, write to Marlboro Music Festival, 135 South 18th Street, Philadelphia, PA 19103; 215-569-4690; after June 6, call the Marlboro box office), but you can frequently find good seats before the performance (chairs are metal, and regulars bring cushions). There are (almost) always bargain-priced seats in the tent just outside the auditorium's sliding glass doors.

Yellow Barn Music Festival (387-6637; 1-800-639-3819), Putney. Begun in 1969, this is a series of 25 chamber music concerts in July and August. Performances are in a 150-seat barn located behind the Public Library in Putney Village. Artists include both well-known professionals and students from leading conservatories.

Brattleboro Music Center (257-4523), 15 Walnut Street, Brattleboro. Housed in a former convent, this burgeoning music school sponsors a wide variety of local musical events and festivals, including a Spring Festival of oratorios and pageants such as a winter/spring Chamber Music Series. Periodic concerts are presented by the Windham Orchestra and by the Community Chorus in area churches, and, most notably, the New England Bach Festival. The Festival, a series of more than a dozen October concerts and lectures, has been held since 1969 in area churches and chapels, featuring choral performances conducted by the Swiss-born Blanche Moyse (founder of the Music Center in 1951). It's reviewed and celebrated as one of the Northeast's major annual events.

Friends of Music at Guilford (257-1969, 257-1028), Guilford. A series of concerts throughout the year at various locations. Note the free Labor Day weekend concerts under *Special Events.*

Vermont Jazz Center (254-9088) 72 Cotton Mill Hill, Studio 222, South Main Street, stages frequent musical, vocal, and jazz happenings.

THEATER

Whittermore Theater at Marlboro College (257-4333) is the setting for frequent presentations.

Sandglass Theater (387-4051), Kimball Hill, Putney. October through Christmas and April/May, occasional summer performances. Housed in a historic barn in Putney Village, the resident theater company performs original work combining live theater with puppetry. Also hosts guest performers.

Wild Roots Arts Association (254-6140) stages presentations in downtown Brattleboro.

Actors Theater Playhouse (603-256-4486), corner of Brook and Main Streets, West Chesterfield (just across the river from Brattleboro), is a Vermont-based troupe staging frequent, nominally priced presentations.

MUSIC VENUES

Mole's Eye Café (257-0771), corner of Main and High Streets, Brattleboro. A live and lively music club.

Common Ground (257-0855), 25 Elliot Street. Live music Friday and Saturday night. See *Eating Out.*

Gallery Walk. The first Friday of each month features music in Brattleboro's galleries.

Note: Check the *Brattleboro Reformer*'s Thursday listings of live music and entertainment at other area restaurants and cafés.

FILM

The **Latchis Theater,** Main Street, Brattleboro, shows first-run films. For film buffs, this 900-seat movie house is itself a destination. Apollo still drives his chariot through the firmament on the ceiling; walls are graced with Doric columns, and the lobby floor bears the zodiac signs in multi-colored terrazzo.

Spinelli Cinemas (at Fairfield Plaza, Route 5 north of Brattleboro), a multiplex, also shows first-run films.

SELECTIVE SHOPPING

ANTIQUES
In Brattleboro

Twice Upon a Time (254-2261), 63 Main Street, Brattleboro. Open Monday through Saturday 10–6, Friday until 8, Sunday noon–5. "I always wanted a consignment shop that would be able to display anything that anyone wanted to give me," says Randi Crouse, proprietor of this truly amazing shop that now fills the entire three-level space created in 1906 for the E. J. Fenton Department Store. In the '50s it was chopped into smaller storefronts, but the two-story-high Corinthian columns, bubble glass, and wooden gallery are back, a setting for clothing, antique furniture, and furnishings. The markdown schedule is patterned on that of Filene's Basement. More than 100 dealers and a total of 4,000 consignors are represented. If there's something special you are looking for, chances are Crouse can find it.

La Tagge Sale (254-9224), at the Marina Restaurant, Putney Road. Open 10–6 daily. Down by the West River, a classic '50s roller-skating rink with a giant reflecting ball and music to match is filled with antiques, furniture, books, and art.

Along Route 30

More than two dozen dealers are found along this route. Pick up a copy of their pamphlet guide at the first place you stop. They include:

Black Mountain Antiques Center (254-4384), 2 miles north of Brattleboro. A mall with 70 dealers, open year-round 10–5.

Newfane Flea Market (365-4000), just north of Newfane Village, Sunday, May through October. Billed as the largest open-air market in the state; usually 100 tables with assorted junk and treasure.

West River Antiques (365-7215), Newfane. Jack Winner, a longtime local antiques dealer, specializes in equestrian art and antiques.

Nu-tique (365-7677), Newfane Village. Open May to October and by appointment. Books, including New England histories, poetry, military, children's; also old lamps, glass, sheet music, records.

Harmonyville Antiques (365-7679), south of Townshend Village. Open most days. Country furniture, china, glass.

Riverdale Antiques (365-4616), Route 30, Harmonyville (between Newfane and Townshend). Open daily year-round, 10–5. More than 60 dealers selling quality antiques and collectibles.

Townshend Auction Gallery (365-4388), Townshend, stages frequent

Window shopping on Main Street in Brattleboro

auctions. Inquire.

ART GALLERIES

Note: The first Friday of each month is Gallery Walk in Brattleboro, open house with refreshments and music at downtown businesses that hang work by local artists and at studios as well as at formal galleries, usually 5–7.

Windham Art Gallery (257-1881), 69 Main Street, Brattleboro, showcases work by 50 members of an artists cooperative. It's also the place to pick up a copy of the Arts Council of Windham County quarterly publication *Arts in the Season,* which lists current theater, poetry readings, and gallery shows throughout southeastern Vermont.

Artist's Loft Gallery (phone/fax: 257-5181), 103 Main Street, Brattleboro. Realistic landscapes of Brattleboro and Vermont are William Hays's forte.

The Art Building, 127 Main Street, Brattleboro, houses a dozen studios, open irregularly and for Gallery Walk. Visitors are welcome to stroll up any day and see whose door is open. The **River Gallery School** (257-1577) offers frequent classes and workshops here.

Tyler Gallery (257-4333), Rice Library, Marlboro College. Changing exhibits.

Elaine Beckwith Gallery (874-7234), Route 30/100, Jamaica Village. Open daily except Tuesday. Some 30 artists in a variety of styles and mediums are represented.

See also Brattleboro Museum and Art Center (under *To See*), Hooker-Dunham Arts Center (under *Entertainment*), Vermont Artisan Designs (under *Crafts Shops*), Cafe Beyond (under *Bookstores*), and Tom & Sally's Handmade Chocolates (under *Special Shops*).

BOOKSTORES

The Book Cellar (254-6026), 120 Main Street, Brattleboro. An outstanding, long-established, full-service bookstore, particularly strong on Vermont and New England titles.

Everyone's Books (254-8160), 23 Elliot Street, Brattleboro. This is an earnest and interesting alternative bookstore, specializing in women's books; also a great selection of children's and multicultural titles.

Collected Works Books & The Cafe Beyond (258-4900), 29 High Street, Brattleboro. An attractive full-service bookstore with rooms that ramble on and back into the café (see *Eating Out*). Not a bad place to spend a rainy day.

Old & New England Books (365-7074), West Street, Newfane. Open May to October. A delightful browsing place with an interesting stock of books old and new.

Mystery/Trek (254-1359), 49 Elliot Street, Brattleboro. The specialties here are science fiction and crime.

Brattleboro Books (257-0177), 34 Elliot Street, 9:30–6 daily except Sunday. An extensive selection of used and out-of-print books; has recently expanded into the adjoining storefront. Browsing encouraged.

Hearthstone Books (387-2100), at the junction of Route 5 and West Hill Road in Putney. Housed in the restored old tavern at the center of Putney Village, a full-service bookstore that invites browsing, with a frequently working hearth in the adjacent café.

CRAFTS SHOPS

Vermont Artisan Designs (257-7044), 106 Main Street, Brattleboro. Open daily. Recently expanded, southern Vermont's outstanding contemporary crafts gallery displays the work of 300 artisans. Check out the branch shop in Putney Village (below).

In Putney

Putney Clayschool (387-4395), Kimball Hill, open 10–5 daily except Thursday. A great variety of pitchers, teapots, batter bowls, and other functional stoneware and earthenware made, displayed, and sold.

Richard Bissell Fine Woodworking (387-4416), Signal Pine Road. Open Monday through Friday 8–5. Exceptional Shaker-inspired furniture, cabinetry, Windsor chairs.

Brandywine Glassworks (387-4032), Fort Hill Road. Robert Burch hand-blows glass in his studio (call to see what he's doing); seconds of distinctive paperweights and other likely gifts are sold.

Green Mountain Spinnery (387-4528), just off I-91, exit 4. Open Monday through Friday 9–5:30, Saturday 10–5:30. Labor Day through Thanksgiving, also Sunday noon–4. Founded as a cooperative more than 20 years ago, this is a real spinning mill in which undyed, unbleached wool from local flocks is sorted, scoured, picked, carded, spun, skeined, and labeled. You can buy the resulting wool in various plies—all in natural colors. Knit-kits, patterns, buttons, and blankets are also sold.

Vermont Artisan Designs (387-2883) is a branch of the Brattleboro store, open daily in the Putney Tavern Building.

Note: On the weekend after Thanksgiving, Putney's two dozen artisans open their studios to visitors. For details, call the **Putney Craft Tour** (387-4032).

Along Route 9

Turnpike Road Pottery (254-2168), Marlboro. Open Saturday 1–4. Malcolm Wright makes distinctive wood-fired pottery.

Applewoods (254-2908), Marlboro. Daily 10–6. David and Michelle Holzapfel create amazing furnishings from burls and other wood forms.

Gallery in the Woods (464-5793), Marlboro. Dante Corsano makes widely respected tables, dressers, armoires—whatever you need. The lines are simple, and the craftsmanship is so exceptional that the pieces are striking. His wife, Suzanne, crafts equally striking pottery lamps in a range of soft hues. Many other artists are also featured.

Lucy S. Gratwick Fine Handweaving (257-0181). Call for directions and hours: a colorful range of apparel and other items in cotton, silk, and wood.

Along Route 30

Botanical Castings (257-1115), West Dummerston. A variety of gifts, from sun catchers to mirrors and framed pictures, made using dried local wildflowers.

Taft Hill (865-4200), Harmonyville (Townshend). Open daily 11–5. Fine gifts and furnishings, featuring fine hand-painted glass and china created here at Crest Studio.

American Country Designs (874-4222), Jamaica Village. Open daily 9–5:30 except Tuesday. Bright, irresistible pottery is the specialty here; also personalized wedding plates and a nice selection of crafts.

FACTORY OUTLETS

The Outlet Center (254-4594), Canal Street, Brattleboro; exit 1 off I-91. Open daily 9–9. This former factory building produced handbags until a few years ago. The Factory Handbag Store still carries the brand that was made here (it's now manufactured in Massachusetts) and a variety of other bags of all sizes. Fifteen stores now fill the building; ample parking.

Townshend Furniture (365-7720). Route 30, Townshend. Open weekdays 10–4, weekends until 5. Sturdy furniture made on the premises is sold at discount.

Mary Meyer Stuffed Toys Factory Store (365-7793), Route 30, Townshend, west of the village. Open weekly in summer and fall; weekends in December. The original location of Vermont's oldest and largest stuffed-toy company; 20–70 percent off.

SPECIAL SHOPS

In Brattleboro

Sam's Army and Navy Dept. Store (254-2933), 74 Main Street, Brattleboro. Open 8–6, until 9 on Friday, closed Sunday. The business that Sam Borofsky started in 1934 now fills two floors of two buildings with a full stock of hunting, camping, and sports equipment. Prices are reasonable, but people don't shop here for bargains. The big thing is the service—skilled help in selecting the right fishing rod, tennis racket, or gun. There are also name-brand sports clothes and standard army and navy gear. On the first day of hunting season (early November), the store opens at dawn and serves a hunter's breakfast (it also sells licenses). *Tip*: There's free popcorn every day, all day.

Delectable Mountain (257-4456), 125 Main Street. Fine-fabric lovers make pilgrimages to Jan Norris's store, widely known for its selection of fine silks, all-natural imported laces, velvets, cottons, and upholstery jacquards. It's also offers a wide selection of unusual buttons.

Brattleboro Food Co-op (257-0236), 2 Main Street. Open Monday through Saturday 9–9, Sunday 9–8; deli and fresh baked products. The cheese counter could just be the best showcase for Vermont cheese in the state; cheese from around the world also knowledgeably selected and presented (note the "cheese of the week"), also local produce, grains, wines, and a café.

Tom & Sally's Handmade Chocolates (254-4200), 55 Elliot Street. Through the plate glass window at the back of this friendly chocolate factory (6 Harmony Place) you can watch chocolate being molded into "cow licks," "cow chips," and a wide of assortment of other luscious concoctions. Local artists and artisans are also displayed.

A Candle in the Night (257-0471), 181 Main Street. Donna and Larry Simons have built up a vast knowledge as well as inventory of Oriental and other handcrafted rugs over the decades.

Beadnicks (257-5114), 115 Main Street. Beads, baubles, whimsical wonders.

Adavasi Imports (258-2231), 8 Flat Street. Indian imports: jewelry, tobacco, gifts.

In Putney

Basketville (387-5509), Route 5. Open daily 8 AM–9 PM in busy seasons, 8–5 in slack seasons. Factory tours are free and available weekdays 9–2:30. The first of "The World's Largest Basket Stores" now scattered between Venice, Florida, and Milo, Maine, it is also one of the oldest crafts producers in the state. Founded by Frank Wilson, an enterprising Yankee trader in the real sense, this is a family-run business. The vast store features woodenware, wicker furniture (filling the entire upstairs), wooden toys, and exquisite artificial flowers as well as traditional baskets and myriad other things, large and small. Prices are generally 40 percent below retail. *Note*: Check out the mid-October Basketville Seconds Sale.

Silver Forest of Vermont (387-4149), in the center of the village, a clothing store worth checking out.

Offerings (387-2529), Kimball Hill. Open daily. A wide assortment of imported and jewelry, much of it reasonably priced.

Along Route 30

Newfane Country Store (365-7916), Newfane. Quilts and Vermont cheese and maple syrup, plus toys and Christmas ornaments. The quilts and other quilted things are truly outstanding.

Lawrence's Smoke House (365-7751), Newfane. Corncob-smoked hams, bacon, poultry, fish, meats, and cheese are the specialties of the house. Catalog and mail order.

Jamaica Country Store (874-9151), Jamaica Village. Just a real country store, selling cheese, syrup, and souvenirs along with everything else.

SPECIAL EVENTS

February: **Brattleboro Winter Carnival.** Many events in Living Memorial Park (see *Green Space*); a full week of celebrations, climaxed by the Washington's Birthday cross-country ski race.

Late June: **Dummerston Center Annual Strawberry Supper,** Grange Hall, Dummerston.

May through October: The **Brattleboro Area Farmer's Market,** Saturday 9–2 on Route 9 at the Creamery Covered Bridge, is a colorful happening.

July and August: **Marlboro Music Festival** in Marlboro; **Yellow Barn Music Festival** in Putney (see *Entertainment—Music* for both).

July 4: A big **parade** winds through Brattleboro at 10 AM; games, exhibits, refreshments in Living Memorial Park (see *Green Space*); fireworks at 9 PM.

Late July (last Saturday): Annual **sale and supper** sponsored by the Ladies Benevolent Society of Brookline; an old-fashioned affair with quality crafts. *Last weekend:* Events in Brattleboro both days climaxed by the **Riff Raff Regatta** Sunday, a raft competition off the Marina Restaurant at the confluence of the West and Connecticut Rivers.

Early August: **Grace Cottage Hospital Fair Day,** exhibits, booths, games, rides on the green in Townshend.

September: Guilford is the place to be on Labor Day weekend, both for the **Guilford Fair** and for the annual 2-day music festival in **Guilford's Organ Barn** (257-1961). Concerts are free. **White Water on the West River,** Jamaica State Park; see *To Do—Boating.* **Heritage Festival Benefit** in Newfane, sponsored by the Newfane Congregational Church. **Putney Artisans Festival,** Putney Town Hall. *Last weekend:* **Apple Days** in downtown Brattleboro.

October: **Newfane Heritage Fair** on Columbus Day: crafts, dancing, raffle, sponsored by the Newfane Congregational Church.

Mid-October: The **Apple Pie Festival in Dummerston** features hundreds of Dummerston's famous apple pies, also crafts, at the Dummerston Center Congregational Church and Grange. **New England Bach Festival,** a series of major concerts in area churches sponsored by the Brattleboro Music Center (257-4523; see *Entertainment—Music*). The annual **Pumpkin Festival** on Townshend common features biggest-pumpkin and best-pumpkin-pie contests, plenty of vendors, food.

Weekend after Thanksgiving: **Putney Artisans Craft Tour**—some two dozen local studios open to the public, geared to Christmas shopping.
Early December: **Christmas Bazaar** on the common, Newfane.

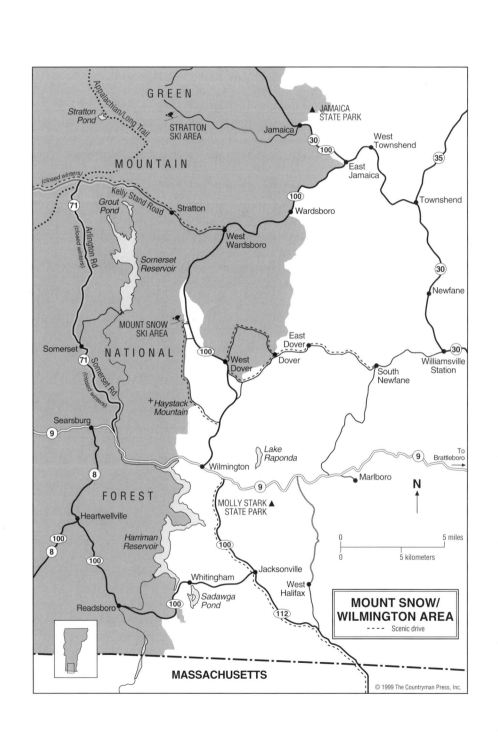

MOUNT SNOW/
WILMINGTON AREA
- - - - Scenic drive

© 1999 The Countryman Press, Inc.

Mount Snow/Wilmington Area

Mount Snow made its splashy debut as a ski destination in 1954. Reuben Snow's farm was transformed by ski lifts and trails, lodges, a skating rink, and an immense, floodlit geyser. Ski lodges mushroomed for miles around, varying in style from Tyrolean to '50s futuristic. The impact of all this hasty development on the small village of West Dover helped trigger Vermont's environmental protection law, Act 250.

By the early '70s, bust had followed boom, and the ski area was absorbed by one company after another, finally acquired in 1997 by Les Otten's American Ski Co. Mount Snow now incorporates Haystack, a few miles down the valley, and major improvements are being made, including its new Grand Summit Resort. A cross-country ski ridge trail connects the two downhill areas. There are also three commercial cross-country-ski centers maintaining an extensive system of touring trails. The town of Dover, which includes Mount Snow, now boasts hundreds of new condominium units—all neatly clustered behind screens of greenery—built in the '80s.

The village of Dover is a small knot of white-clapboard buildings on the crest of a hill. It isn't even marked from Dover Hill Road. West Dover, down on Route 100, is the actual center of town. It remains picturesque enough, a lineup of church, inn, and town offices. But much of Route 100 between Wilmington and Mount Snow is a visual history of the ups and downs of the ski industry since the late '50s.

Beyond this narrow, 9-mile-long, well-kept corridor of motels and shops, however, mountains rise steeply. On the west, the upper Deerfield Valley is edged with the backbone of the Green Mountains, and on the east, the hills rise tier upon tier. Drive north a mile beyond Mount Snow and you enter some of the least touristed countryside in Vermont. The same is true a mile south of Wilmington.

Although the surrounding hills were once lumbered extensively, they are now hauntingly empty. At one time, there were more local lumbering villages than there are ski areas today. Wilmington, the village at the junction of Routes 9 and 100, looks much the way it did when sheep were being herded down its streets.

GUIDANCE
Mount Snow Valley Chamber of Commerce (464-8092; www. visitvermont.com), P.O. Box 3, Wilmington 05363. Its recently expanded quarters on West Main Street (Route 9 west, seven doors from the junction of Routes 9 and 100) is also an official **Vermont Information Center.** Pick up the useful, comprehensive *Mount Snow Valley Visitor's Guide.* The *Deerfield Valley News,* a local weekly, is a good source for current events information.

GETTING THERE
By train or bus: You can take **Amtrak** to Brattleboro, or **Vermont Transit** to Brattleboro or Bennington, but there's no dependable way of getting from either town to Wilmington.

By car: The obvious route to Mount Snow from points south and east is I-91 to Brattleboro, then Route 9 to Wilmington. There are two scenic shortcuts that are useful to know about, especially during foliage season and winter weekends: (1) Route 30 north from Brattleboro 11.1 miles to the marked turnoff for Dover; follow the road through the covered bridge in South Newfane past Dover to West Dover; (2) turn off I-91 onto Route 2 in Greenfield, Massachusetts; follow Route 2, 3.6 miles to Colrain Road (turn at Duck Pond Tavern) and proceed 17.3 miles to Jacksonville, where you pick up Route 100 into Wilmington.

New York City to Mount Snow: **Edventures Bus Service** (464-2810; 212-921-9161).

GETTING AROUND
The Moo-ver (464-8487) is a free community bus service operated by the Deerfield Valley Transit Association (DVTA). It connects points of interest in the valley, along Route 100 from the Deerfield Valley Health Center in Wilmington, picking up passengers at DVTA stops 7 AM– 10 PM. Look for its Holstein cow logo.

MEDICAL EMERGENCY
Deerfield Valley Rescue (368-2323): includes Halifax, Jacksonville, Readsboro, Searsburg, West Dover, Whitingham, and Wilmington. East Dover (365-7676).
Deerfield Valley Health Center (464-5311).

VILLAGE

Whitingham Village. Brigham Young, the Mormon prophet who led his people into Utah and is hailed as the founder of Salt Lake City, was born on a hill farm here, the son of a poor basket maker. Two sites in town commemorate Young: One is a monument that sits high on Town Hill (the view is spectacular) near picnic benches, grills, a playground, and parking area. The second is on Stimpson Hill (turn south at Brown's General Store); on the right a few hundred yards up, there is a small marker that proclaims this to be the homestead site of Brigham Young:

BORN ON THIS SPOT 1801 . . . A MAN OF MUCH COURAGE AND SUPERB EQUIP-
MENT. Before leaving the village, note the "floating island" in the middle
of Sadawga Pond. The village was once a busy resort, thanks to a mineral spring and its accessibility via the Hoosuc Tunnel and Wilmington
Railroad. It retains an inn (see *Lodging*) and an auction barn (see *Selective Shopping*).

TO SEE

MUSEUMS

Southern Vermont Natural History Museum (464-0048), Route 9,
across from the Skyline Restaurant (see *Eating Out*), Marlboro, east of
Wilmington; part of the **Vermont Country Market** store. Open Memorial Day through October, 9–5 (winter days and hours vary). This is
a great little museum, featuring stuffed birds and animals begun as the
collection of Luman R. Nelson, a noted taxidermist. Nominal admission.

Living History Association Museum (464-5569), Route 9, Hogback
Mountain, Marlboro. Summer hours 10–5, Thursday through Sunday;
fall 10–5 daily and by appointment. Displays military memorabilia from
colonial times on, with special emphasis on World War II. Reenact-
ments and other events are scheduled.

The Crafts Inn (464-2344), West Main Street, Wilmington. An architectural landmark, this massive, wood-frame, former hotel designed by
Stanford White in the late Shingle Style so popular in Newport, Rhode
Island, was built in 1902 as Child's Tavern, catering to wealthy summer
travelers. President Taft and Admiral Dewey were among the notable
guests. It now houses time-share units.

WINERY

North River Winery (368-7557), Route 112, 6 miles south of Wilmington.
Open daily 10–5, except January through May, when hours are 11–5
Friday through Sunday. An 1850s farmhouse and barn in this small village contain an interesting, small winery dedicated to producing fruit
wines. We can speak for the full-bodied apple-blueberry, neither too
dry nor too sweet. Green Mountain apple, cranberry-apple, and a number of other blends are offered. Free samples come with the tour.

FOR FAMILIES

✒ **Adams Petting Farm** (464-3762), 15 Higley Hill Road, Route 100,
Wilmington. Open for the season July 1 daily except Tuesday; weekends
only from Labor Day to Columbus Day. The farm has around 150
animals, including Rosie, the sow, in her swimming pool; Mr. McGregor's
garden rabbits; a miniature horse; and goats, sheep, peacocks, turkeys,
and geese. Pony-, tractor-, and horse-drawn sleighs in winter. Sugarhouse
and farm store. Admission: $5 for adults; kids 2 years and under free, 3–
15 years $4.50; "Frequent Petters Cards."

✒ **Mount Snow** (464-4152) provides the themed **Mount Snow Valley Adven-**

KIM GRANT

Kelly Stand Road

ture **Programs** in summer, Monday through Friday, for the 5–12 age group, and child care for kids from 6 months to 6 years.

SCENIC DRIVES

Dover Hill Road, accessible from Route 100 via either Dorr Fitch Road in the village of West Dover or East Dover Road farther south (just below Sitzmark; see *Cross-Country Skiing* and *Golf*). The road climbs steeply past the tiny village center of Dover. Here you could detour onto gravel-surfaced Cooper Hill Road for a few miles to take in the panorama of mountains that spread away to the northwest. On an ordinary day, you can pick out Mount Monadnock in New Hampshire beyond Keene. You can either loop back down to Route 100 via Valley View Road or continue down the other side of the hill, through East Dover to the general store, covered bridge, and picturesque village center in South Newfane, returning the way you came. If you are out for a real ride, follow this road all the way to Route 30, then continue south to Brattleboro and return through Wilmington on Route 9, the Molly Stark Trail.

Handle Road runs south from Mount Snow, paralleling Route 100, turning into Cold Brook Road when it crosses the Wilmington line. The old farmhouses along this high, wooded road were bought up by city people to form a summer colony in the late 1880s. It's still a beautiful road, retaining some of the old houses and views.

Kelly Stand Road is a 20-mile road heading west from West Wardsboro through the village of Stratton (very different from the ski area by that name on the other side of the mountain), past the Daniel Webster Monument (Webster spoke here to 1,600 people at an 1840 Whig rally), through Green Mountain National Forest all the way to Arlington. The hiking trail into Stratton Pond that begins near the monument is the most heavily hiked section of the Long Trail.

TO DO

AIRPLANE RIDES
North Air (464-2196), Mount Snow Airport off Country Club Road, West Dover, offers scenic air rides.

BICYCLING
The Mountain Bike School and Touring Center at Mount Snow (1-800-245-SNOW) bills itself as "America's first and foremost mountain-bike school." Two- and 4-day sessions geared to everyone from beginners to racers are offered on local terrain ranging from back roads to ski trails.

The Cupola (464-8010), Route 100, West Dover. Open daily 8–6. Sales/rentals of Reflex mountain bikes.

BOATING
Green Mountain Flagship Co. (464-2975), Route 9 west from Wilmington. Richard Joyce offers seasonal excursions on Lake Harriman aboard the M.V. *Mt. Mills*, a twin-stacked pontoon vessel accommodating 50. Joyce caters to bus groups, but there are usually at least a half-dozen seats left over. His narration of the lumbering history of the area is often accompanied by live music. Canoes and kayaks can be rented, too.

High Country Waverunner & Boat Rentals (464-2108; 1-800-627-7533), Route 9, on Lake Harriman. Waverunner jet boats or pontoon boat, wake boards, ski tubes.

BOWLING
North Star Bowl and Mini Golf (464-5148), Route 100, Wilmington, opens daily at noon for candlepin bowling; videos and pool tables, too.

CAMPING
Green Mountain Expeditions (368-7147), Whitingham, arranges llama treks, overnight camping, inn-to-inn and picnic day trips.

CHAIRLIFT
Mount Snow (1-800-245-SNOW). The lift operates on weekends in summer and daily throughout foliage season, and the view is truly spectacular.

FISHING
Harriman Reservoir is stocked with trout, bass, perch, and salmon; a boat launch is off Fairview Avenue.

Somerset Reservoir, 5 miles west of Wilmington, then 10 miles north on the Somerset Road, offers bass, trout, and pike. There is a boat launch at the foot of the 9-mile-long lake. Smaller **Sadawga Pond** in Whitingham and **Lake Raponda** in Wilmington are also good for bass and trout; there is a boat launch on the former. Fishing licenses are available at **Bill's Bait**

Shop, Whitingham; from the Wilmington Town Clerk; and at the Orvis dealership at Taddingers, Wilmington (see *Selective Shopping—Special Shops*).

FITNESS

Sugarhouse Health and Racquet Club at Timber Creek (464-0259), off Route 100, West Dover.

GOLF

Mount Snow Country Club (1-800-240-2555). Weekend and 5-day midweek golf-school packages are offered May through October; 18-hole, Cornish-designed championship golf course also open on a daily basis.

Sitzmark Golf & Tennis Club (464-3384), Wilmington; 18 holes, club and cart rentals.

Haystack (464-8301), Mann Road, off Cold Brook Road, Wilmington; clubhouse, 18 holes designed by Desmond Muirhead, full pro shop.

Someday Golf (464-5807), Sugar Lot Road, West Dover. A distinctive, nine-hole course.

HIKING

Aside from the trails in Molly Stark State Park (see *Green Space*) and a short, self-guided trail atop Mount Snow, there are a number of overgrown roads leading to ghost towns. The **Long Trail** passes through the former logging town of Glastenbury (261 residents in 1880), and a former colonial highway in **Woodford State Park** (see *Green Space* in *Bennington/Arlington Area*) leads to a burying ground and 18th-century homesites. Somerset is another ghost town.

Forest Care Nature Walks (254-4717). Lynn Levine leads popular group and individual treks in the summer and fall, discussing the ecology and wildlife in the area. Reservations needed a week ahead.

Mount Snow Adventure Center (464-3333). Interpretive trails for day-hiking across the ridge connecting Haystack and Mount Snow.

HORSEBACK RIDING

Flame Stables (464-8329), Route 100, Wilmington. Western saddle trail rides, half-hour wagon rides.

Whitingham Horse Farm (368-2664), Route 100, Jacksonville, offers scenic trail rides, along with private and group instruction.

HUNTING

The Hermitage Sporting Clays and Hunting Preserve (464-3511), Wilmington, consists of 500 acres and provides guided shoots with dogs, or you can try your hand at a round of 100 sporting clays. It is possible to use your own dog for a shoot, but there are no kennels available for overnight lodging. Reservations required.

SWIMMING

There are two beaches on 11-mile-long Harriman Reservoir, also known as Whitingham Lake. **Mount Mills Beach** is 1 mile from Wilmington Village, posted from Castle Hill Road. **Ward's Cave Beach** is on Route 100 south from Wilmington—turn right at Flame Stables (see *Horseback Riding*) and follow signs.

Sitzmark Lodge (464-3384), north of Wilmington on Route 100, has a pool that is open to the public free of charge. Snacks and a bar are available poolside.

TENNIS

The municipal courts at **Baker Field** in Wilmington are open to the public; also eight courts at Sitzmark (see above).

WINTER SPORTS

CROSS-COUNTRY SKIING

Hermitage Ski Touring Center (464-3511), Wilmington. Outstanding 35 km, machine-tracked network (50 km total) includes a ridgetop trail with superb views, and elevations of 1,867–3,556 feet. Instruction, rental, repair, telemark guided tours (see also *Lodging—Inns* and *Dining Out*). Guided tours are offered along the ridge trail connecting Haystack and Mount Snow; inquire at the Hermitage.

Sitzmark Ski Touring & Learning Center (464-5498), Wilmington. Open fields, golf course with orchards and woodlands above, 25 km total tracked. Rentals, instruction, café, changing rooms, headlamp tours, telemark lessons, guided tours.

The White House Ski Touring Center (464-2135), Wilmington. A total of 22 groomed trails meander through the woods at elevations of 1573–2036 feet. Instruction, rentals, lodging (see *Lodging—Inns* and *Dining Out*), ski weeks.

Timber Creek Cross Country Touring Center (464-0999), West Dover. Just across Route 100 from the entrance to Mount Snow, a high-elevation, wooded system of trails that hold their snow cover; rentals, instruction available.

DOWNHILL SKIING

Mount Snow/Haystack (information: 464-3333; snow report: 464-2151; reservations, including the Country Inn-Vitation Ski & Stay Package: 1-800-245-SNOW), West Dover. Now owned by the American Skiing Company, the 767-acre area is being rapidly improved, with a new learning terrain and lifts for first-time skiers and snowboarders, an expanded Vacation Center and ski rental shop, an illuminated 400-foot halfpipe and Planet 9 center at the base of Carinthia for snowboarders, 16 new acres for classic tree skiing, a new mile-long Canyon Quad, and an enhanced Clipper Quad. The new Grand Summit Hotel and Crown Club, a big resort hotel with condos, is now open.

Lifts: 30—two quad chairs, 12 triple chairlifts, 12 double chairlifts, two T-bars, and two rope tows.

Trails: 130, including 22 "easier," 59 "more difficult," and 19 "advanced." There are five distinct areas here: the Main Mountain, the expert North Face, the Sunbrook Area, Carinthia Slopes, and Haystack.

Vertical drop: 1,700 feet.

Snowmaking: 85 percent of the mountain.

Facilities: Five base lodges, an upper lodge near the summit, a Vacation Center, the Snow Barn (nightclub with entertainment, dancing), and Planet 9 for teens; five terrain parks; The Gut (Vermont's longest lift-serviced halfpipe; Natural Life Center spa.

Ski school: 85 instructors, Perfect Turn teaching methods—two clinics.

For children: Perfect Kids—Teen Extreme (13–17); Mountain Camp (7–12); Mountain Riders (7–12); Snow Camp (4–6); Pre-Ski (3-year-olds); Child Care (6 weeks–5 years).

Rates: Adults, weekdays Mount Snow and Haystack $49, Haystack only $27; weekends, holidays $52/39; young adult, $44/19, $46/26; junior/senior, $31/33.

Special events: December 26, Jumbo Fireworks and Torchlight Extravaganza; January, Gotta Rock College Weeks, Green Mountain Snowboard Series, State Downhill Championships; February, Boarderfest; March, Northeast Snocross Championships.

OTHER WINTER RECREATION

Ice fishing is available on **Harriman** and **Somerset Reservoirs.**

Sleigh rides are offered at the **William Adams Farm** (464-3762), Wilmington, which includes a refreshment stop at a cabin in the woods; at **Flame Stables** (464-8329; see *Horseback Riding*); and at **Matterhorn Lodge** (464-8011), where dinner is also served.

High Country Snowmobile Tours (464-2108; 1-800-627-SLED), Wilmington; also **Rock Maple Snowmobile Tours** (464-3284), Route 9 east, Wilmington.

GREEN SPACE

Molly Stark State Park (464-5460), Route 9 east of Wilmington Village. A hiking trail leads through the forest of this 158-acre preserve to 2,415-foot Mount Olga, from which there is a panoramic view. See also *Lodging—Camping.*

LODGING

There are some 90 lodging facilities in the area, ranging from intimate country inns to impersonal, motel-like facilities designed to accommodate groups. The **Mount Snow Region Vacation Information Center** (1-800-451-MTSNOW, ext. 40; www.mountsnow-vt.com) operates year-round: November through March, 8–9, otherwise 8–5. The Mount Snow brochure, available by writing to the bureau (P.O. Box 757, Mount Snow 05356), includes descriptive listings of inns and lodges, plus chalet and condo rentals.

RESORT

✐ **The Grand Summit Hotel and Crown Club** (464-6600; 1-800-261-9442), Mount Snow 05356. Opened in 1998 by the American Skiing Company, this handsome—though conventional in every sense—201-room, slope-side condo, hotel, and conference center features suites with one to three bedrooms and apartments (many with kitchens) as well as the usual hotel rooms, plus a host of amenities, including outdoor pool and hot tubs, child care and arcade, and valet parking. **Harriman's Restaurant** is open for breakfast and dinner, **Harriman's Pub** has a bistro menu, and **Café 66** is handy for snacks. Rates vary seasonally as well as for midweek and weekend stays: $120–250 for a hotel room, $550–925 for the penthouse. Many packages available.

INNS

In Wilmington 05363

The White House of Wilmington (464-2135; 1-800-541-2135). Built in 1915 on a knoll off Route 9 as a summer residence for Martin Brown, founder of Brown Paper Company, this Colonial Revival mansion has a lovely setting and, with Bob Grinold as innkeeper, offers many amenities. Its public rooms are huge, airy, and light but also manage to be warm in winter—with the help of yawning hearths. It has recently been expanded, so there are a variety of accommodations: 15 luxurious rooms and one suite in the main house, all with private bath, and 7 rooms with private bath in the guesthouse. Two rooms have a balcony with fireplace, plus two-person whirlpool tub; two rooms have terrace with fireplace and whirlpool tub. There's a 60-foot outdoor pool, and an indoor pool with whirlpool and sauna. Guests gather around the sunken bar. There are 45 km of cross-country trails in winter. Full breakfast and highly rated dinner served daily (see *Dining Out*), and a buffet Sunday brunch. Skiers' lunch in winter. Cash or checks preferred for accommodations. Rates range from $59 per person, B&B, in the guesthouse, and from $74 per person double in the inn, to $89 per person in the balcony rooms, plus 10 percent gratuity. Discounts on non-holiday midweek stays in both facilities.

Misty Mountain Lodge (464-3961), Stowe Hill Road. Just 20 people can be accommodated in this informal old farmhouse set high on a hillside, surrounded by 150 acres. Its eight rooms (four with private bath, four with shared) have been recently redecorated. One has a jetted whirlpool bath, and one is handicapped approved. There is an agreeable atmosphere to the inn, which features home-cooked meals and singing around the hearth while innkeeper Buzz Cole plays the guitar after dinner; children feel welcome. This is, in fact, one of the very few inns in Vermont run by Vermonters, one of the few that look like a Vermont home. And some guests who have never stayed in a Vermont house are a bit put off at first. "A couple pulled up one night," Buzz Cole told us, "and they stayed out there in the car for the longest time, deciding whether to come in. When they did, they said they would eat somewhere else. But then they smelled the roast beef and agreed to have dinner. They got talking to other guests—lawyers, engineers, people who have been coming here for years—and they joined in the singing after dinner. The next evening they came back with champagne for everyone in the house." The farmhouse has been in the family since 1916, and Buzz and his wife, Elizabeth, have been taking in guests since 1954. $87–117 per room, double occupancy, MAP midweek, $110–150 holidays, $70–110 B&B; for a 2-day winter weekend, $170–240 double. Summer: $57–85 per room double, B&B. Dinner $20.

Nutmeg Inn (464-3351), P.O. Box 818. This delightful, 18th-century, roadside farmhouse on Route 9 west run by Dave and Pat Cerchioe is actually a B&B but feels like an inn. It's on the edge of the village and offers 10 rooms, each nicely decorated with wallpaper, quilts, and braided rugs; four spacious one- and two-bedroom suites with fireplace and color TV/VCR and two-person whirlpools. All rooms and suites have central air-conditioning. There is a cozy living room, library, and BYOB bar, plus three intimate dining rooms for full, complimentary breakfasts. Summer rates: $88–189 double; fall, $110–259; winter, $98–260. No service charge.

Trail's End, A Country Inn (464-2727; 1-800-859-2585), 5 Trail's End Lane, off East Dover Road. So fancifully designed and decorated that a gnome would feel at home. There's a wonderfully in-the-woods feel to the unusual spaces, which include a library and game room; a large living room with a two-story, fieldstone fireplace; another balcony-level sitting room; and a great dining space divided between an area with large, round, hand-carved pine tables for a number of guests to gather around and "the bar," which is lined with wooden booths. There are 13 rooms, each decorated differently, all with private bath, of which 4 have real wood-burning fireplaces; two fireplace suites have canopy beds, refrigerator, microwave, and Jacuzzi. In summer, there is a clay tennis court, a nicely landscaped heated pool, and inviting paths leading out into the gardens and up the hill to the pond. Debby and Kevin Stephens take pride in the four-course dinners served Saturday, concert night during the Marlboro Music Festival (see *Entertainment* in "The Lower Connecticut and West River Valleys"). Guests have access to their own fridge, a luxury especially in summer, when no one wants to stray too far from the pool for lunch. $125–165 daily per room with breakfast in winter, $185–195 for suites, plus 15 percent gratuity; less in summer.

The Hermitage (464-3511), Coldbrook Road. Innkeeper Jim McGovern breeds dogs and game birds and collects wines and art for this unusual and popular hostelry, which combines fine dining with cross-country skiing. There are some lovely rooms in the farmhouse annex; 14 of the 29 guest rooms are in the former Brook Bound, a mile down the road. Rates vary widely: from $60–125 double in Brook Bound, B&B, to $225–250 double, MAP, in the inn, plus 15 percent gratuity.

The Red Shutter Inn (464-3768; 1-800-845-7548), Route 9. Renée and Tad Lyon preside over this big, gracious, 1890s house on the edge of the village with six nicely furnished guest rooms, a mini-suite, and two suites with fireplace, one with a whirlpool built for two. The dining room, furnished with an assortment of old oak tables, has a good reputation and is open to the public (see *Dining Out*). From $105 double for cozy rooms in the carriage house to $145 for the spacious two-room Courtemanche Suite in the main house, B&B.

In West Dover 05356

The Inn at Sawmill Farm (464-8131), off Route 100. Closed early April to mid-May. Rod Williams is an architect, his wife, Ione, an interior decorator, and their son, Brill, an accomplished chef. Together the team has created one of Vermont's most elegant inns, a world-class hideaway in the Relais & Châteaux category, filled with antiques and splendid fabrics. The dining room is exceptional (see *Dining Out*). In summer, flowers are everywhere, inside and out; there is a swimming pool, tennis court, and two trout ponds. There are 20 beautifully appointed guest rooms, each different, 10 with working fireplace. $360–395 double occupancy, inn rooms, MAP; $420–470 double occupancy, fireplace rooms, MAP.

    Deerhill Inn (464-3100; 1-800-99-DEER9), P.O. Box 136. After a hiatus of several years, Linda and Mike Anelli, former owners of Two Tannery Road, returned to West Dover and took over Deerhill, upgrading its flexible accommodations and dining rooms (see *Dining Out*). There are 15 luxurious rooms and suites, some in the old farmhouse, others in a newer wing. From the latter—especially on the galleried second floor—you enjoy a smashing view of Haystack and Mount Snow. One comfortable sitting room adjoins the tiny bar and two spacious dining rooms, walled with the work of local artists; upstairs is another big lounge for house guests, plus a library nook. In summer, flowers abound inside and out and around the patio of the new swimming pool. The Loft Room in the main house has its own terrace and private entrance, and the Oriental Room is a stunner. A lot happens here, too, especially during the valley's pre-Christmas festivities. Midweek, daily rates in the summer are $165–275 double, MAP, $95–205 B&B; holiday periods $220–330 MAP, $150–260 B&B. A 2-day winter weekend is $150 per person B&B, $220 MAP. Ask about golf, fishing, and ski packages, and the Wine, Dine & Stay program, which includes the Doveberry Inn (see *Dining Out*).

Snow Goose (464-3984; 1-888-604-7964), P.O. Box 366, Route 100. Formerly the Shield Inn and now owned by Karen and Eric Falberg, this attractive place has 11 antiques-furnished rooms with private bath and cable TV; 6 of them have wood-burning fireplace and two-person Jacuzzi. Full country breakfasts are served. Summer rates are $110–160; fall and winter, $140–210.

    The Austin Hill Inn (464-5281; 1-800-332-RELAX), Route 100. Several of the 12 guest rooms have a balcony, and all come with private bath. There's a big common room with a fireplace, and an outdoor swimming pool. New innkeepers Debbie and John Barley serve full country breakfasts and afternoon tea. Rates vary by the season: $275–305 for 2-night fall and winter weekends for two B&B; $220–250 spring; $80–95 summer. Well-mannered children are welcome, but no pets.

Doveberry Inn (464-5652; 1-800-722-3204), Route 100. A spacious, well-built inn just a minute's drive from the Mount Snow access. There's a comfortable, large living room with fireplace and wine bar. Upstairs, each of the eight rooms is immaculate and bright, with private bath and full vanities (some of them copper), also with cable TV and video player. Request a back room overlooking the woods. Innkeepers Michael and Christine Fayette are culinary school graduates and prepare all of the Northern Italian cuisine (see *Dining Out*). $90–110 daily per room with full breakfast in fall; $110–150 in winter. $90–110 spring and $80–105 in summer. MAP is available on request.

West Dover Inn (464-5207), Route 100. Built as the village inn in 1846 and now on the National Register of Historic Places, this handsome inn has been updated by Gregory Gramas and Monique Phelan to include modern amenities and antique appointments in each of its 12 guest rooms, 4 of which are fireplace suites with whirlpool tub. All rooms have private bath and cable TV. Guests enjoy a common room, with fireplace, as well as a publike cocktail lounge and casual fine-dining restaurant, Gregory's (see *Dining Out*). Rates: $90–135 per couple in summer; $110–200 in foliage season, $90–200 in winter. All B&B. Three-night minimum required during holiday periods.

✍ **Cooper Hill Inn** (348-6333; 1-800-783-3229), Cooper Hill Road, East Dover 05341. High on a hilltop on a quiet country road with one of the most spectacular mountain panoramas in New England, Pat and Marilyn Hunt's sprawling colonial home has 10 guest rooms, all with private bath, including two-room family suites, living room, dining room, game room, and roomy covered porch. Meals served family-style; BYOB. The Hunts host "Mystery Weekends" several times a year. Rates: $36 per person (double occupancy) April through September 21, $42 in fall-foliage season; $38 winter, B&B; a 2-night winter weekend costs $105 per person with two breakfasts and a dinner; $95 in the fall, $80 in spring and summer (in spring, summer, and fall, dinner is not included); $20 per child under 12. No credit cards.

BED & BREAKFASTS

Snow Den Inn & Gallery (464-9355; 1-800-852-9240), Route 100, West Dover 05356. A small country inn—on the National Register of Historic Places—in the middle of the village, neat and cozy. Five of the eight rooms have fireplaces, and all have private bath. Works by local, national, and international artists are featured. Summer $75 per room; $100 per person for a 2-day winter weekend, breakfast included.

🏮 **Weathervane Lodge** (464-5426), Dorr Fitch Road, West Dover 05356. Well away from Route 100 with a fine view, this chalet-style lodge run by

Liz and Ernie Chabot can accommodate as many as 25 guests in nine rooms and a nice big suite. All but three rooms and the suite share baths. Two large, casual lounges with fireplaces have a rather cluttered but homey quality; the one on the lower level has a set-up BYOB bar, soda and ice machines, microwave, and a refrigerator for guests' use. Rates range from $34 per person B&B during the week to $50 per person for the suite on holidays and weekends; plus 15 percent gratuity.

Shearer Hill Farm (464-3253; 1-800-437-3104), P.O. Box 1453, Wilmington 05363, Shearer Hill Road off Route 9, 1.5 miles east of the village. Keep going on this back road, bearing left at the fork, to Bill and Patti Pusey's simple, restored 200-year-old farmhouse a stone's throw from the Massachusetts border. Popular with Marlboro Music Festival goers (see *Entertainment* in "The Lower Connecticut and West River Valleys"), it has three rooms in the main house with private baths, an annex with a ground-floor room and kitchenette, and two bedrooms and sitting room upstairs. The pleasant large living room in the farmhouse has a VCR library. $80 double, with continental breakfast buffet.

LODGES

These are distinctly different from the inns. They are larger, usually with motel-style rooms, and designed with skiers in mind—with such amenities as pools, saunas, game rooms, and lounges.

Snow Lake Lodge at Mount Snow (464-7788; 1-800-451-4211), 100 Mountain Road, Mount Snow 05356. This five-story, 92-room lodge includes 13 family suites, **Walter's Restaurant, Walt's Pub,** a game room, an outdoor pool, and tennis in summer. A 2-day winter weekend is $224 per person, lift and lodging, based on double occupancy, EP, non-holiday.

Nordic Hills Lodge (1-800-326-5130; fax: 802-464-8248), 34 Look Road, Wilmington 05363. A fairly large (27-room) lodge near Haystack with a warm, family-run feel, plenty of common space, in-room cable TV, BYOB bar, Jacuzzi, sauna, outdoor heated pool in summer. Rates: $70 double B&B May through August; bus tours only September and October; $121 per person for 2-night winter weekend, MAP.

Four Seasons Inn (464-8303; 1-800-682-2129), Route 100, West Dover 05356. Not to be confused with its deluxe namesakes in Boston and New York, but a convenient, inexpensive resting place with 24 rooms—each with private bath and cable TV—a licensed lounge and breakfast restaurant, plus outdoor heated pool. $45–55 double, summer; $75 late September through foliage season; $75 per person 2-day, non-holiday winter weekend.

The Inn at Mount Snow, a country B&B in the heart of the base lodge complex; **The Handle House,** a renovated farmhouse between Mount Snow and Haystack; **The Ironstone Lodge** and **The Matterhorn Lodge** are all under the umbrella of **The Inn at Mount Snow Properties,** Route 100, West Dover (464-3300; 1-800-577-SNOW).

MOTEL

The Vintage Motel (464-8824), Route 9, Wilmington 05363. The Vintage offers 18 pleasant rooms with bath; there's also a comfortable common room with wood-burning stove. Heated pool and some air-conditioned rooms are available. The village shops are just down the road. $49–70 per couple, B&B; higher December through April; ask about midweek and weekend specials.

CONDOMINIUMS AND TOWNHOUSES

Condominium development has been recent and intense in this area. The Mount Snow brochure describes a half-dozen major complexes. Haystack has its own mushrooming units.

Mount Snow Condominums (464-7768; 1-800-451-4211). Four villages of various units from studios to three-bedroom town houses, with pools, saunas, hot tubs, and other facilities.

Snowresort Rentals (464-2177; 1-800-451-MTSNOW [6876]), Mountain Park Plaza, West Dover, has extensive listings of vacation homes and condos, ranging from small studios to five-bedroom condos for daily, weekend, monthly, or seasonal rentals.

CAMPGROUND

Molly Stark State Park (464-5460), Route 9 east of Wilmington Village. This 158-acre preserve offers 34 campsites, including eight lean-tos. See *Campgrounds* in "What's Where" for fees, reservations, and other information.

WHERE TO EAT

DINING OUT

Inn at Sawmill Farm (464-8131), Route 100, West Dover. Open for dinner only, 6–9:30. The main dining room is the interior of a former barn, with fine chintz and old portraits. The linen-covered tables are set with sterling and garnished with fresh flowers; there is also a smaller, sun- and plant-filled dining room. The 34,000-bottle wine cellar was given the Grand Award from *Wine Spectator*. Eighteen main dishes are offered regularly; specialties include roast duck in green peppercorn sauce, rack of lamb, and soft-shell crab; generally there is also a choice of 16 appetizers and irresistible desserts. One of the best in the state. Very expensive.

Deerhill Inn (464-5474), off Route 100, West Dover. Michael Anelli presides over the kitchen of this luxurious establishment, with two attractive dining rooms lined with the work of local artists. One might begin dinner with crab-and-lobster-stuffed portobello mushrooms or steamed mussels with parsley garlic broth, and proceed to veal medallions with wild mushrooms and lemon cream sauce, or five-layer veal with roasted pepper sauce. Desserts are delectable. Expensive, and worth it.

The Hermitage (464-3511), Coldbrook Road, Wilmington. A popular, highly regarded restaurant with two dining rooms, fine art on the walls, and a mixture of arm- and wing chairs that all make for the elegance due the dishes. You might begin dinner with Norwegian smoked salmon or game bird pâté, proceed to chicken amandine, venison, or the game bird selection, with a wine chosen from among 2,000 labels. Sunday brunch. Moderate to expensive.

Le Petit Chef (464-8437), Route 100 north, Wilmington. Open daily except Tuesday, 6–9 PM. Elegant French dining in an old roadside house. This is a local favorite. Chef-owner Betty Hillman's menu might include shrimp dijonnaise (baked in mustard, garlic, and herb sauce), noisettes of venison (sautéed with shiitake mushrooms), or a fresh vegetable sauté. Moderate to expensive.

Doveberry Inn (464-5652), Route 100, West Dover. Closed Tuesday. Authentic Northern Italian cuisine. New chef-owners are making their mark on the valley. Choose from the veal chop, shrimp and scallops penne, or wild mushroom risotto. The menu is complemented by one of the largest Italian wine lists in the area. Moderate to expensive.

Gregory's (464-7264), Route 100, West Dover. In the talented hands of the new chef, the dining room at the West Dover Inn has a distinctive, and seasonally changing, menu: Start, for example, with grilled shrimp marinated in tequila and lime with tomato and avocado salsa, or mushroom caps stuffed with lobster and Boursin; follow with mesquite-grilled sirloin with fried leeks, or penne with sautéed scallops in a wild mushroom and artichoke sauce. Moderate to expensive.

Two Tannery Road (464-2707), Route 100, West Dover. Open Tuesday through Sunday. A popular and highly rated spot (once the home of Theodore Roosevelt's son) for dining on the likes of escargots l'alsacienne, smoked salmon, and angel hair frittata, followed by grilled chicken Jamaica, Bangkok shrimp, or New England veal roast. Expensive.

The Red Shutter Inn (464-3768), Route 9, Wilmington. Open Wednesday through Saturday in winter; daily except Tuesday in summer. The pleasant, oak-filled dining room provides a locally acclaimed "night-out" atmosphere, and the menu ranges from escargots with wild mushrooms to seafood, chicken, beef, duck, and veal Oscar with crabmeat and hollandaise sauce ($19.50). Moderate to expensive.

The White House of Wilmington (464-2135), Route 9 east, Wilmington. The wood-paneled dining room is warmed by a glowing hearth. The menu is ambitious, including Wiener schnitzel, veal saltimbocca, boneless duck with apple, grape, and walnut stuffing, and veal Marsala, plus 13 other entrées. Moderate.

EATING OUT

Poncho's Wreck (464-9320), South Main Street, Wilmington. Open daily for dinner; lunch Friday through Sunday. A delightful, casual atmosphere; specialties are Mexican dishes, fish, and smoked meats. Located in the village, moderately priced; tends to fill up, so it's advisable to

Wilmington

come very early or late. Live entertainment (see *Entertainment—Après-Ski*).

Dot's Restaurant (464-7284, 464-6476), Wilmington, is open 5:30 AM–3 PM; to 8 PM Friday and Saturday. This is a cheerful, pine-sided place in the middle of the village. There's a long Formica counter as well as tables, a fireplace in back, and wine by the glass. Stop by for a bowl of the hottest chili in New England. The soup and muffins are homemade, and the Reubens are first-rate. Its sibling is on Route 100 in the Dover Retail Center.

Skyline Restaurant (464-3536), Route 9, Hogback Mountain, Marlboro. For more than 40 years, Joyce and Dick Hamilton have operated this restaurant with "the 100-mile view." The knotty-pine dining room has worn, shiny tables, fresh flowers, and a traditional New England menu. In winter, there's a fire. Specialties include homemade soups; home-baked brownies, pies, and turnovers; and a Vermonter sandwich.

Truffles Restaurant (464-5141) at the Viking Motel, Route 100, Wilmington. A large, roadside dining room with a varied menu, including Wiener schnitzel and roast duckling. You can also get by for dinner with a steak sandwich or quiche and the salad bar.

Anchor (464-2112), South Main Street, Wilmington. Lunch and dinner, Sunday brunch. An informal fish place with a raw bar, fried clams, and daily specials like fried salmon slices in bacon and a sautéed mixed grill with lemon pepper sauce, plus ribs.

Fannie's Main Street Restaurant and Tavern (464-1143), West Main Street, Wilmington, has good family fare for lunch, dinner, and Sunday brunch.

Alonzo's Pasta and Grille (464-2355), at the Crafts Inn, West Main Street, Wilmington. Open daily for lunch and dinner, breakfast on weekends. "Create-your-own-grille" specials (teriyaki steak, andouille sausage, for example); homemade pastas.

Dover Forge (464-2114) at the Andirons Lodge, Route 100, West Dover, open for dinner daily except Thursday. Its seafood, chicken, and veal are especially favored by seniors.

The Silo Family Restaurant (464-2553), Route 100, West Dover, features steak, seafood, chicken, pasta, and pizzas for lunch and dinner, plus a late-night menu, satellite TV, and game room. Two dance floors, entertainment.

COFFEEHOUSES

Bean Heads (464-1208), Main and River Streets, Wilmington. Espresso, cappuccino, bagelry, soup, and sandwiches.

Freddie's (464-FOOD; 464-FLICK), Mountain Park Plaza, West Dover. Bookstores with coffee bars are familiar, but here's a video store with one, plus deli and bakery.

Julie's Cafe (464-2078), Route 100, West Dover. The former owner of the notable bakery in Wilmington serves a tasty array of coffees, desserts, soups, and salads.

ENTERTAINMENT

Memorial Hall Center for the Arts (464-8411), lodged in the McKim, Mead and White–designed theater next door to the historic Crafts Inn, Wilmington. The center sponsors a growing number of theatrical, musical, and community events. For example, in 1998: Tickle Me Tuesday, jazz and classical pianists; folk-rock and jazz concerts; and a cabaret evening. *Annie*, the musical comedy, was staged here, and the Village Light Opera Group has performed.

Mountain Park Cinema (464-6477), Route 100, West Dover, has two movie theaters for first-run films; matinees on rainy weekends.

APRÈS-SKI

During ski season, the following establishments feature live entertainment or DJs on most nights. In summer, they come to life on weekends. On Route 100, between Wilmington and Mount Snow, look for **High Tops** (464-3508), **Sitzmark Lodge** (464-3384), **Andirons** (464-2114), **Deacon's Den** (464-9361), and **Snow Barn Entertainment Center** (the old Rubin's Barn at Mount Snow). In town, check out **Poncho's Wreck** (464-9320).

SELECTIVE SHOPPING

ANTIQUES SHOPS

Left Bank Antiques (464-3224), Routes 9 and 100, Wilmington. Country furniture, old paintings, and prints.

Wilmington Antique and Flea Market (464-3345), junction of Routes 9 and 100, Wilmington. Open Saturday and Sunday, Memorial Day through Labor Day.

ARTISANS AND CRAFTS

Quaigh Design Centre (464-2780), Main Street, Wilmington. This is a long-established showcase for top Vermont crafts; imported Scottish woolens are also a specialty. Lilias MacBean Hart, the owner, has produced a Vermont tartan.

John McLeod, Ltd. (464-8175), Route 9, Wilmington. Unusual wooden shapes to decorate your home (clocks, mirrors, cutting boards) are sold in the showroom of this woodworking shop on the western verge of the village; open daily.

Anton of Vermont Quilts (896-6007), Route 100, Wardsboro. Judith Anton makes and imports quilts, wall hangings, and patchwork pillows in an old barn.

Partridge Feathers (464-3245), Tollgate Village, Route 100, West Dover, has pottery, woodenware, Simon Pearce glass, and Shaker oval boxes, among other items.

Craft Haus (464-2164), Stowe Hill Road, Wilmington. Set high on a hillside, this is a gallery in Ursula and Ed Tancrel's home. The big attractions are works by folk artist Will Moses and Ursula's cloisonné and enamel-plated jewelry, which sells for far higher prices in urban stores. Open weekends 10–5 and at other times by appointment.

BOOKSTORES

Bartleby's Books and Music (464-5425), North Main Street, Wilmington, is a cheerful shop for new books (mostly paperbacks), greeting cards, cassettes, and compact disks.

Austin's Antiquarian Books (464-3727), Route 9 west, Wilmington.

SPECIAL SHOPS

Taddingers (464-5793), Route 100, Wilmington. Seven specialty shops under one roof: antiques and fine prints, exclusive decorative accessories, Christmas Room, Nature Room, and an Orvis dealership, with gear for fly-fishing, fly-tying, and shooting, plus sponsorship of 1- and 2-day fishing schools.

Manyu's Boutique (464-8880), Main and River Streets, Wilmington, has casual, contemporary clothes and accessories for women.

Klara Simpla (464-5257), Route 9 west, Wilmington. A "holistic country store" with a following stretching the length of Route 9. Vitamins, homeopathic remedies, natural foods, a wide selection of books, and, of course, Birkenstock sandals are available. Upstairs are weekly sessions in massage therapy, yoga, chiropractic, acupuncture; also special workshops in nutrition and dowsing, for example.

Vermont Maple Farm (464-3739), West Main Street, Wilmington, has a demonstration sugarhouse; syrup and other maple goodies.

Coomb's Sugarhouse (368-2345), Jacksonville. Free tours and samples at Coomb's Candy Kitchen; pure maple syrup and candies.

1836 Country Store Village (464-5102), West Main Street, Wilmington, has an eclectic stock of decorative brasses, pierced-tin lanterns, cotton calicoes, quilting supplies, cheese, and the usual souvenirs, plus **Lyman House Restaurant,** which serves breakfast all day, and Norton House quilts.

Swe Den Nor Ltd. (464-2788), Route 100, West Dover. A long-established store with a wide selection of Scandinavian, contemporary, and country furniture; also lamps, paintings, and gifts.

SPECIAL EVENTS

Late January: **Harriman Ice Fishing Derby** on Lake Whittingham (368-2773).

April (Easter weekend): Nondenominational **sunrise service** on Mount Snow's summit with continental breakfast, eggs hidden all over the mountain, good for prizes.

July through mid-August: **Marlboro Music Festival** (254-2394; see *Entertainment* in "The Lower Connecticut and West River Valleys").

Late July through early August: **Art on the Mountain** (464-8671), Haystack. A 9-day exhibit, one of the largest and best gatherings of craftspeople and their wares, displayed in Haystack's unusual glass-and-wood base lodge, daily 10–5.

Early August: **Vermont's Green Mountain Irish Festival** (1-800-245-SNOW), Mount Snow.

Mid-August: **Deerfield Valley Farmers Day** (464-8092), Wilmington. Old-fashioned agricultural fair with midway, livestock exhibits.

November 25–December 25: **"Nights Before Christmas"** celebration— wreath sales, fashion shows, concerts, Festival of Lights, holiday tour of country inns, Living Nativity, and other events in the Mount Snow Valley.

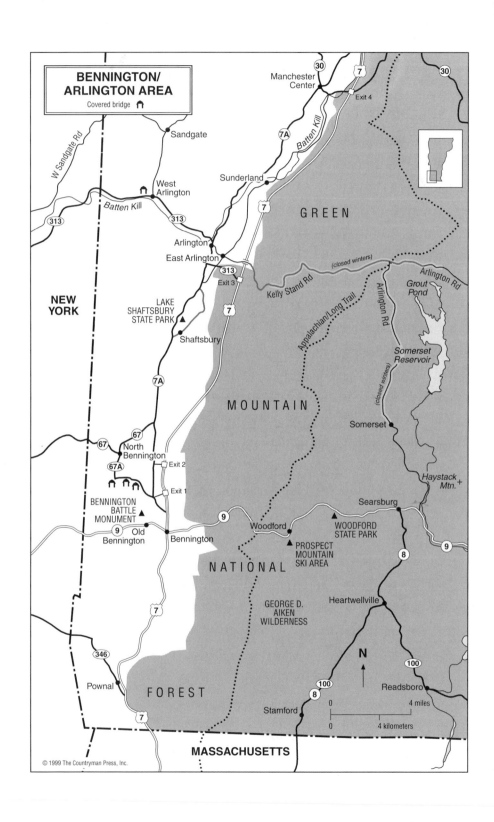

BENNINGTON/
ARLINGTON AREA
Covered bridge

Manchester Center

Exit 4

Sandgate

W Sandgate Rd

West
Arlington

Batten Kill

Sunderland

GREEN

313

Arlington
East Arlington

Batten Kill

Exit 3

LAKE
SHAFTSBURY
STATE PARK

Kelly Stand Rd

(closed winters)

Arlington Rd

Grout
Pond

NEW
YORK

Shaftsbury

Appalachian/Long Trail

Arlington Rd

Somerset
Reservoir

7A

MOUNTAIN

(closed winters)

Somerset

North
Bennington

Exit 2

Haystack
Mtn.

Exit 1

Searsburg

BENNINGTON
BATTLE
MONUMENT

WOODFORD
STATE PARK

Old
Bennington

Woodford

Bennington

PROSPECT
MOUNTAIN
SKI AREA

NATIONAL

Heartwellville

GEORGE D.
AIKEN
WILDERNESS

N

FOREST

Readsboro

Pownal

0   4 miles

Stamford

0   4 kilometers

© 1999 The Countryman Press, Inc.

MASSACHUSETTS

Bennington/Arlington Area

Vermont's southwest corner is dominated by Bennington, the state's third largest city (15,815), which is undergoing something of an industrial renaissance while retaining its historic luster. This growth has, in turn, spawned several new places to stay and eat. The first town settled west of the Connecticut River in the New Hampshire Grants in 1749 and named for avaricious Gov. Benning Wentworth, Bennington became a hotbed of sedition when the "Bennington Mob," or Green Mountain Boys, formed in 1770 at Fay's Catamount Tavern under the leadership of Seth Warner and Ethan Allen to expel both the 'Yorkers (who claimed the territory) and, later, the British.

The Battle of Bennington (more precisely, the Battle for Bennington) on August 16, 1777, deflected General Burgoyne's occupation of the colonies when New Hampshire Gen. John Stark's hastily mobilized militiamen beat the tar out of Colonel Baum's overdressed Hessians on high ground near the Walloomsac River, across the New York border.

Today, Bennington is nationally known as the home of distinguished Bennington College, established in the early 1930s. It is also remembered by collectors of Bennington pottery.

Although never formally the capital of Vermont, Arlington, on Route 7A, was the de facto seat of government during most of the Revolutionary period. Fearing British attacks in the north, Vermont's first governor, Thomas Chittenden, moved south from Williston, liberated a Tory property in Arlington (the area known as Tory Hollow), and conducted affairs of state from there.

Many older visitors to Arlington fondly remember Dorothy Canfield Fisher, the author of 50 immensely popular, warm-hearted novels and a judge of the Book-of-the-Month Club for 25 years. Five years before her death in 1958, Mrs. Fisher published *Vermont Tradition: The Biography of an Outlook on Life,* in which she captured the essence of the state's character:

> *Travel through Vermont—north, south, east, west, from Pownal to Canaan, Guilford to Highgate—nowhere will you find a township where overwhelming majority opinion does not*

support this unwritten law: that, except where the safety of others is in danger, everyone must be allowed to do, think, believe whatever seems best to him; that equality before the law is only the first step. Equality must extend to the protection of everybody's personal dignity, within the community; for the backroad farmer and his wife bringing butter and eggs to the kitchen door, no less and no more for the owner of the plywood factory.

Another famous resident was illustrator Norman Rockwell, who lived in West Arlington from 1939 to 1953. Many of his illustrations of small-town Americans were done in and around Arlington.

GUIDANCE

A good visitors guide to Bennington County is provided by the **Bennington Area Chamber of Commerce** (447-3311), www. bennington.com, Veterans Memorial Drive, Bennington 05201, which also has a well-supplied information center.

Arlington Chamber of Commerce (375-2800). An information booth on Route 7A is open May through October.

GETTING THERE

By car: Bennington lies at the convergence of Routes 7, 7A, 9, 67, and 67A. Going north can be confusing; watch the signs carefully to choose between the limited-access Route 7 to Manchester and the more interesting but slower historic Route 7A, to Shaftsbury and Arlington.

By bus: **Vermont Transit** from Albany or hubs in Connecticut and Massachusetts.

MEDICAL EMERGENCY

Bennington (911); Arlington (447-7911); **Southwestern Vermont Medical Center** (442-6361), 100 Hospital Drive, Bennington.

TO SEE

Historic Bennington Walking Tours, self-guided with a keyed map-brochure from the chamber of commerce (see *Guidance*) that describes Old Bennington, including the 306-foot, blue limestone shaft of the Bennington Battle Monument, dedicated in 1891; all the fine early houses along Monument Avenue; the Old Academy; Old First Church; the Burying Ground, where five Vermont governors and Robert Frost repose; and the venerable Walloomsac Inn, now a private home. A second walking tour of the downtown area includes the 1898 railroad depot (now a restaurant), constructed of blue marble cut to resemble granite; old mills; and Victorian homes.

Bennington Battle Monument (447-0550), Old Bennington. Open mid-April through October 31, daily 9–5, this Sandy Hill dolomite limestone shaft commemorates Gen. John Stark's defeat of General

Old First Church

Burgoyne's invading British and Hessian forces at Walloomsac Heights, 5 miles to the northwest, on August 16, 1777.

MUSEUMS

Bennington Museum (447-1571), West Main Street, Route 9, Bennington. Open daily 9–5 except holidays. This really distinguished and growing collection features memorabilia from the Battle of Bennington, especially the oldest American Revolutionary flag in existence, Early American glass, furniture, dolls and toys, historic Bennington pottery, notably an extraordinary 10-foot ceramic piece created for the 1853

Crystal Palace Exhibition, and a luxury 1925 Wasp touring car, the only surviving model of the rare automobiles made by Karl Martin in Bennington.

Particularly popular is a gallery of the largest collection of paintings by Grandma Moses (Anna Mary Robertson, 1860–1961), who lived in the vicinity. There's a gift shop and genealogical library. Admission.

The Park-McCullough House (442-5441), Route 67A in North Bennington. Open for tours late May through October and December, daily 10–3 except Tuesday and Wednesday. A splendid, 35-room Victorian mansion built in 1865 by Trenor W. Park, a forty-niner who struck it rich as a lawyer in California and later as a railroader. He built the house on part of the farm owned by his father-in-law, Hiland Hall, a representative to Congress and governor of Vermont. Park's son-in-law, John G. McCullough, became governor of Vermont in 1902 and raised his family in this capacious house. It has been open to the public since 1965 and is on the National Register of Historic Places, functioning as a community arts center. There's an appealing children's playhouse replica of the mansion and a stable full of carriages; also a gift shop, lunch counter, afternoon tea on the veranda. Admission.

Bennington Center for the Arts (442-7158), Route 9 at Gypsy Lane, houses two visual arts galleries and a theater for the Oldcastle Theatre Company, which performs April to mid-October (see *Entertainment*).

The Shaftsbury Historical Society, Route 7A, is gradually developing a cluster of five historic buildings, including two schools. Open summer weekends 2–4 and serendipitously when the curator happens to be handy.

Hemmings Motor News (442-3101), Route 9, 3 miles west of Bennington, is not really a museum, but it attracts large numbers of vintage-automobile buffs, Monday through Friday 9–5; a few of its old-timer vehicles are parked at its Sunoco station branch on West Main Street near the Bennington Museum.

Norman Rockwell Exhibition (375-6423), Route 7A, Arlington. Open daily 9–7. Housed in a Hudson River Gothic church are some 500 of the artist's *Saturday Evening Post* cover illustrations and prints. There's a 20-minute film, and a gift shop. Admission.

The Dr. George A. Russell Collection of Vermontiana, believed to be the third largest such collection, is housed in quarters behind the Martha Canfield Public Library, Arlington. Although not a museum (there are no displays), the collection is open to the public on Tuesday or by appointment with the curators, David and Mary Lou Thomas (375-6307). Dr. Russell, the country doctor immortalized in the Rockwell print that hangs in thousands of doctors' offices, collected Vermontiana for most of his long life and left his collection to the town. The collection includes Dorothy Canfield Fisher materials, a large selection of Norman Rockwell's work, many photographs from the period

1860–90, an extensive selection of town and country histories for Vermont and neighboring states, and a wealth of genealogical materials (deeds, letters, wills, account books, and diaries) for both the Arlington area and the state as a whole.

The Martha Canfield Public Library, Route 7A, Arlington (named for Dorothy Canfield Fisher's grandmother), holds a book sale under a tent on its lawn 10–5 Friday and Saturday and 1–5 Sunday from June 15 through foliage season. Books are sold at prices from 15¢ to 50¢, and records and jigsaw puzzles are also available at moderate prices. During peak holiday seasons, the sale is sometimes held weekdays as well.

WINERY

Joseph Cerniglia Winery (442-3531), Route 9 west of Bennington, open daily for tours and tastings, 10–5; gift shop.

COVERED BRIDGES

Three stand just off Route 67A in North Bennington: Silk Road, Paper Mill Village, and the Burt Henry.

TO DO

CANOEING

Battenkill Canoe Ltd. (362-2800; 1-800-421-5268), River Road, off 7A, Arlington, is the center for day trips—with van service—canoe camping, instruction, rentals, and equipment. Customized inn-to-inn tours arranged.

GOLF AND TENNIS

Mount Anthony Club (442-2617), Bank Street (just below the Battle Monument): 18-hole golf course, tennis and paddle courts, pool, lunch and dinner.

HORSEBACK RIDING

Kimberly Farms Riding Stables (442-4354), RR 1, Box 345, Shaftsbury, offers trail rides, lessons, hayrides, inn-to-inn tours.

SKIING

Prospect Mountain (442-2575, 442-5283), Route 9 east of Bennington. An intimate, friendly, family ski area, with cross-country (25 km), downhill, and telemark facilities, ski school, rentals and repairs, learn-to-ski packages, group rates, cafeteria, and bar. Moderate prices for all.

GREEN SPACE

Lake Shaftsbury State Park (375-9979), 10.5 miles north on Route 7A, has swimming, picnicking, boating, and a nature trail on 26-acre Lake Shaftsbury.

Woodford State Park (447-4169), Route 9 east of Bennington. This 400-acre area includes 104 camping sites, 16 of them with lean-tos, swimming in Adams Reservoir, a children's playground, picnic spots, canoe and rowboat rentals.

Park-McCullough House

LODGING

INNS

The Four Chimneys Inn (447-3500), 21 West Road, Route 9, Old
Bennington 05201. This stately, 1910 Colonial Revival home, once the
estate of Phillip Jennings, offers 11 luxurious rooms, all with private
bath, TV, and phone, some with fireplace and Jacuzzi. Now owned and
managed by Ron and Judy Schefkind, the Four Chimneys and its beautifully landscaped grounds is a popular wedding site. Rates $100–185
double B&B, $150–210 double MAP, depending on the season. (See
also *Dining Out*).

The Arlington Inn (375-6532; 1-800-443-9442), on Route 7A in the center of Arlington 05250, occupies the 1848 Greek Revival mansion built
by Martin Chester Deming, a Vermont railroad magnate, and has been
used as an inn off and on since 1889. Bill and Sherrie Noonan assumed
ownership in 1998. The 15 rooms and four suites in the main house and
former carriage barn are spacious and furnished with Victorian antiques, and there's a formal parlor. Sylvester's Study on the ground floor
is particularly impressive. Six new units, including two suites, have been
installed in the adjacent 1830 parsonage; they have Drexel cherry four-
posters and sleigh beds, TV, and air-conditioning. The inn is also known
as a popular spot for dinner. Rates range from $70 double occupancy to
$195, including a full breakfast. Open all year.

West Mountain Inn (375-6516), on Route 313 west of Arlington 05250.
Open year-round. A large, rambling former summer home with splen-

did views of the mountains and valley, converted and expanded into an inn. The 12 attractive rooms and six suites are named after famous people associated with Arlington, and a copy of Dorothy Canfield Fisher's *Vermont Tradition* is in every room. Breakfast and dinner are served daily; Sunday brunch on certain holidays. The inn's property includes more than 5 miles of walking and cross-country-ski trails, a bird sanctuary, seasonal gardens, and llamas in residence. A number of special events are featured, such as a St. Lucia Festival of Lights in early December, Leek and Fiddlehead days in early May, and Ethan Allen Days (Father's Day weekend). Ann and Wes Carlson give complimentary African violets to guests who promise to take care of them. $145–244 MAP. (See also *Dining Out*.) *Aunt Elsie's Room*

Hill Farm Inn (375-2269; 1-800-882-2545), RR 2, Box 2015, Arlington 05250. Located off Route 7A north of the village, this historic farmstead, owned and managed by Kathleen and Craig Yanez, is set on 50 acres of land bordering the Battenkill River. The 1830 main building, 1790 guesthouse, and four seasonal cabins hold six rooms with private bath, five rooms sharing three baths, and two suites with private bath, porch, and separate entrance. Licensed for beer and wine. Double rooms $105–176 includes full country breakfast. A four-course dinner is available for guests on Saturday evening at 6. Children welcome at special rates.

BED & BREAKFASTS

South Shire Inn (447-3839), 124 Elm Street, Bennington 05201. This turn-of-the-century Victorian mansion is a most attractive guesthouse, featuring 10-foot ceilings with plaster moldings, a library with a massive mahogany fireplace, an Italianate formal dining room, and comfortable bedrooms furnished with antiques. The five guest rooms in the main house, some with fireplace, have private bath; two can be joined as a suite. Four newer rooms, with Jacuzzi and TV, have been added in the old carriage house. $105–180 with breakfast; older children preferred.

Molly Stark Inn (442-9631; 1-800-356-3076), 1067 East Main Street, Bennington 05201. Six cozy bedrooms, all with private bath, some with Jacuzzi and/or woodstove, decorated with Americana, antiques, and quilts; wraparound porch. $70–95; $145 for the guest cottage with Jacuzzi.

Alexandra B&B (442-5619; 1-888-207-9386), Historic Route 7A at Orchard Road, Bennington. Alex Koks and Andra Erickson, former proprietors of the Four Chimneys, have redecorated this attractive 1859 farmhouse. The five guest rooms with private bath have an English country house atmosphere. As Alex Koks is a master chef, breakfasts are very special. $85–125.

The Henry House (442-7045; 1-888-442-7045), RR 1, Box 214, Murphy Road, North Bennington 05257. Don and Judy Cole have five beautiful guest rooms in this restored Historic Place, built in 1769 on 25 acres, complemented by four common rooms. Among the guest rooms, the Ballroom, with its vaulted 14-foot ceiling, four-poster canopy bed, and a sitting area with working fireplace, is the most notable ($135). The other four are also distinctive: $85–100. Pets and children under 12 are not welcome.

The Inn on Covered Bridge Green (375-9489; 1-800-726-9480; fax: 375-9046), off Route 313, West Arlington 05250. Fans of Norman Rockwell can now actually stay in his former home, a pretty white 1792 Colonial next to a red covered bridge on the village green where Ethan Allen mustered his Green Mountain Boys. Ron and Anne Weber opened the place in 1987 and offer five bedrooms and one suite, with private bath, furnished with antiques. There's a tennis court, and full country breakfasts are events, served on bone china with Waterford glass and silver. The Bicentennial and Spooners Rooms have fireplaces, and the former a whirlpool bath. Rates range from $110 to $145 (for the Norman Rockwell Suite) double.

Country Willows B&B (375-0019; 1-800-796-2585), East Arlington Road, Arlington 05250. This is a tidy, 1850s village historic landmark with four nifty guest rooms with private bath (two with claw-foot tubs), decorated in Victoriana. The West Mountain Room has a fine view, fireplace, and sitting area. Weekend rates: $75–95; $85–125 over holidays and in foliage season; midweek specials. Full country breakfasts.

Arlington Manor House (375-6784), Buck Hill Road, Arlington 05250. Kit and Al McAllister's spacious, early-1900s Dutch Colonial atop a knoll has a delightful, turn-of-the-century atmosphere, with expansive, sunny guest and living rooms. Three rooms have private bath, two have shared, two with fireplaces. There's a tennis court (with auto-server), biker's workshop, and an antiques shop (with lots of old books). $50–130 double.

The Keelan House (375-9029), 549 Route 313 west, Arlington 05250. This handsome 1825 Colonial, owned by Verrall and Don Keelan, furnished with antiques, has a third of a mile of frontage on the Battenkill River—a great spot for anglers. Five pretty rooms with private bath are $95–125, including the 9 percent tax, with full breakfast.

Ira Allen House (362-2284), Route 7A, Arlington 05250. A smartly renovated old roadside home with nine guest rooms, some set up for families. The inn's property across Route 7A fronts the Battenkill, good for trout fishing and, for the warm-blooded, a dip in a 10-foot-deep swimming hole. $65–80 per room with full breakfast.

The Willow Inn (375-9773), Route 7A, Arlington 05250, is a small, freshly decorated, "English-style" B&B with three rooms; $55 with shared bath, $65 with private.

Green River Inn (375-2272; 1-888-648-2212), 2480 Sandgate Road, Sandgate 05250 (off Route 313, 4 miles west from Route 7A, Arlington), has 14 renovated guest rooms, all with private bath, some with whirlpool and fireplace; sunroom, deck, and special children's room. Jim and Betsy Gunn have a lot of ideas about what to do outdoors on their 450 acres. $70–140 B&B, $100–210 MAP.

MOTELS

Vermonter Motor Lodge (442-2529; 1-800-382-3175), Route 9, 2 miles west of Old Bennington 05201, is an attractive mini-resort with nicely decorated rooms and cabins, cable TV, room phone, swimming, boating, bass pond, Sugar Maple Inne Restaurant; $50–75 per room.

Paradise Motor Inn (442-8351), 141 West Main Street, Bennington 05201, close to the Bennington Museum (see *To See—Museums*), has 76 rooms and a nice restaurant on the premises; $59–94.

OTHER LODGING

Greenwood Lodge (442-2547), P.O. Box 246, Bennington 05201, 8 miles east of town on Route 9. Open May 20 through October 24. This rustic lodge/hostel and its campsites occupy 120 acres in Woodford, adjacent to the Prospect Mountain ski area (see *To Do—Skiing*). There are dorms for American Youth Hostel members and private family rooms; bring your own linen or sleeping bags. Three small ponds for swimming, boating, and fishing. There are hiking trails at Prospect Mountain. Inquire about the inexpensive rates.

WHERE TO EAT

DINING OUT

The Four Chimneys Inn (447-3500), 21 West Road, Route 9, Old Bennington. Open daily for lunch and dinner in a gracious dining room and an enclosed porch. Lunch could start with a house specialty, mustard soup, and proceed with a smoked salmon croissant, chicken potpie, or omelets. Dinner (prix fixe $33.50) might include Burgundy-style snails followed by chicken breast with wild mushroom cream sauce, beef medallions and shrimp, or rack of lamb.

Bennington Station (447-1080), Depot Street, Bennington. Open for lunch and dinner daily. Train buffs love this place—a splendidly converted Romanesque railroad station built in 1897 of rough-hewn blue marble for the Bennington and Rutland Railroad. The exceptionally attractive restaurant features a collection of historic photos. For lunch, you could have Iron Horse Chili, Railroad Spikes (marinated and grilled beef strips), or a variety of salads and sandwiches. The dinner menu includes grilled duck salad, prime rib, New England chicken potpie, fish, various teriyakis, and BBQ ribs. Moderate.

Publyk House (442-8301), Route 7A north, Bennington. Dinner daily 5–9. The restaurant occupies a remodeled barn with a fine view of Mount Anthony and features western beef, seafood, and a big salad bar. Moderate.

The Arlington Inn (375-6532), Route 7A, Arlington. There's a mauve-walled formal dining room and a more casual solarium. The menu changes seasonally, but from a recent one you could select smoked seafood as an appetizer and continue to scampi with mustard sauce; salmon fillet marinated in ginger, garlic, soy, and sesame oil; and pastas.

Maryland crab cakes with tarragon and tartar sauce is among the light entrées. Moderate.

West Mountain Inn (375-6516), River Road, Arlington. Chef Larry Vellucci's dining room is open to the public by reservation 6:30–8:30 PM, Sunday through Friday, featuring a $35 prix fixe menu that might include steak *au poivre,* grilled tuna, roast quail topped with orange kiwi glaze, pasta primavera, or baked sea scallops.

East Arlington Cafe (375-6412), East Arlington. David Ingison's culinary artistry shines in this small, polished wood setting, at lunch and dinner, Wednesday through Saturday, and sometimes Sunday brunch. The focus is on seafood, with stellar crab cakes and stir-fried garlic shrimp, for example, plus pastas and vegetarian specials, ending with a Triple Chocolate Indulgence. This has become a favored spot for many local B&B guests. Inexpensive to moderate.

EATING OUT

The Brasserie (447-7922), 324 County Street, Bennington (in Potters Yard), is open daily 11:30–8, serving inexpensive, exceptional, lighter fare—imaginative combinations of hearty soups (black-eyed pea with ham hocks and vegetables), quiche, pâté, salads, and such specialties as mozzarella loaf (cheese baked through a small loaf of French bread with anchovy-herb butter) and rotelle with spinach, onions, and prosciutto in cream with Parmesan cheese.

Blue Benn Diner (442-5140), Route 7, near Deer Park, Bennington, open from 6 AM; breakfast all day, or lunch, which combines "road fare" with more esoteric items like eggs Benedict, tabbouleh, falafel, and herb teas.

Alldays & Onions (447-0043), 519 Main Street, Bennington. In this fish market and upscale deli-café, you can build your own sandwiches at lunch daily except Sunday, or splurge on rack of lamb with honey-thyme sauce for dinner (Thursday through Saturday).

ENTERTAINMENT

Oldcastle Theatre Company (447-0564), Box 1555, Bennington. This accomplished theater company offers a full summer season of plays in the Bennington Center for the Arts. April to mid-October.

SELECTIVE SHOPPING

ANTIQUES SHOPS

The Antique Center of Old Bennington (447-0039) is one of the shops in **Camelot Village,** Route 9 west, Bennington, which also houses the **Craft Center; Yesterday, Today & Tomorrow** (vintage clothing and collectibles); **Granite Lake Pottery;** and a café serving breakfast, lunch, and afternoon tea.

BOOKSTORE

Bennington Bookshop (442-5059), 467 Main Street. Vermont books, adult and children's titles, cards.

CRAFTS SHOPS

Hawkins House (442-6463), 262 North Street, Route 7, Bennington, is a crafts market complex for the work of some 400 artisans in silver and gold, unusual textiles, handblown glass, pottery, quilts, cards, books, music, prints and woodcuts, stained glass, candles, and more. Open daily except Christmas and New Year's.

Oak Bluffs Cottage Pottery (823-5161), Route 7, 8 miles south of Bennington, has a full range of stoneware, baskets, and lamps.

Mahican Moccasin Factory (823-5294), Route 7, 5 miles south of Bennington, features a variety of deerskin, elk, and cowhide footwear, made in Pownal.

Bennington Potters Yard (447-7531), downtown on County Street, Bennington, is the high-tech place to get contemporary Bennington pottery, Catamount glass, and well-designed ovenproof cookware manufactured in North Bennington, as well as to eat at the Brasserie.

GALLERIES

Images from the Past (442-3204), West Main Street, Bennington. Open daily April through December, winter weekends. Fascinating ephemera: postcards, prints, holograms, historic house boxes.

The Beside Myself Gallery, Lathrop Lane, 4 miles north of Arlington off Route 7A. Open May 15 through October 15, 2–5 daily or by appointment, this gallery displays the work of contemporary regional artists: paintings, handmade paper, sculpture, and collages.

SPECIAL SHOPS

The Chocolate Barn (375-6928), Route 7A north of Shaftsbury, is an unusual combination: two floors of antiques, 56 varieties of hand-dipped chocolates, fudge, and special orders from antique candy molds. (There's another store at Routes 30 and 100 in Jamaica.)

Candle Mill Village (375-6068) in East Arlington is a charming hamlet of specialty shops next to two waterfalls. It is located in the Candle Mill, operated locally, stocking 50,000 candles from all over the world, including one that weighs 248 pounds. There's also the **Happy Cook,** the **Rosebud Toy Company,** and the **Bearatorium.** Nearby are an **Antiques Center,** the **Village Peddler,** and the **Scandinavian Country Shop.** One of the ubiquitous Green Mountain Boys, Remember Baker—the builder and first owner of the mill—is commemorated by a monument.

The Cheese House and the Arlington Wood & Pottery Center, Route 7A, Arlington. From souvenir T-shirts to custom-stained glass and other local crafts.

Vermont Country Bird Houses (375-0226), P.O. Box 220, East Arlington

Road, East Arlington. Imaginatively hand-carved birdhouses in various architectural styles, with steeples, cupolas, bell towers, and the like, by Jim Kardas.

SPECIAL EVENTS

Late May: **Bennington Mayfest**—street festival, crafts, entertainment.
July: Annual **Bennington Museum Antique Show** (see *To See—Museums*).
August 16–18: **Bennington Battle Day Weekend.**
Mid-September: **Antique and Classic Car Show,** Willow Park, Bennington.
December 31: **First Night Bennington.** Community-wide celebrations.

Manchester and the Mountains

No Vermont community has changed more dramatically in recent years than Manchester. A summer resort since the Civil War, Manchester has also long been a place to stay while skiing at nearby Stratton and Bromley and on southern Vermont's most dependably snowy cross-country trails.

What's new is the breadth and depth of shopping in this proud old town: upward of 50 top-brand outlet stores and another 50 or so specialty stores and galleries. Manchester is also home to some of Vermont's best restaurants and places to stay, including one of its grandest resorts.

The white-columned, tower-topped, 180-room Equinox is as much a part of Manchester's 1990s appeal as it was in the 1850s, the era in which the town's status as a resort was firmly established. Mrs. Abraham Lincoln and her two sons spent the summers of 1863 and '64 at the Equinox, booked again for the summer of '65, and reserved a space for the entire family the following season. The president, unfortunately, never made it.

Other presidents—Taft, Grant, Theodore Roosevelt, and Benjamin Harrison—came to stay at the Equinox, but it was Lincoln's family who adopted the village. Robert Todd Lincoln, who served as secretary of war under President Garfield, minister to Britain under Harrison, then president of the Pullman Palace Car Company, selected Manchester Village as his summer home, building Hildene, the lavish mansion that's now such an interesting place to visit. Other opulent "summer cottages" are sequestered off River Road and nearby country lanes.

The area's summer residents continue to support several golf courses and the Southern Vermont Art Center (Vermont's oldest cultural institution), along with the Dorset Playhouse and the Weston Playhouse (the state's oldest summer theaters and still the best).

Manchester Center and Village are both down in the wide Valley of Vermont, but Mount Equinox, a stray peak from New York's Taconic range, thrusts up a full 3,800 feet from the village, rising right from the back of its namesake hotel.

Luckily the 1930s Work Projects Administration plan to carve ski

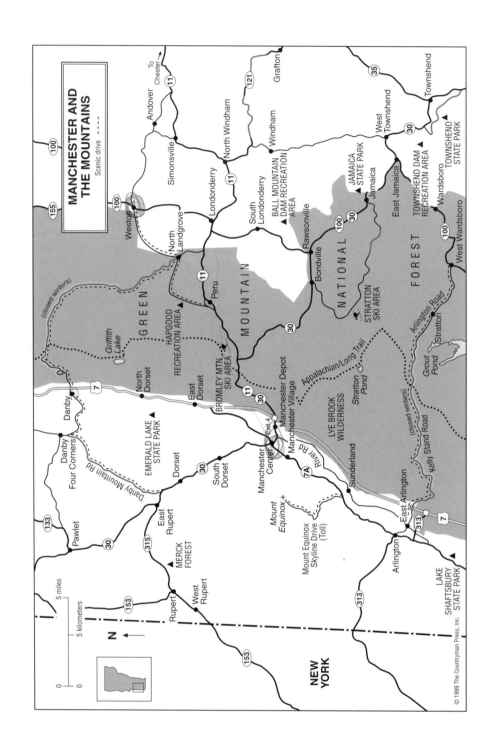

MANCHESTER AND
THE MOUNTAINS

Scenic drive - - - - -

trails on Mount Equinox never panned out, and Manchester Village retains its serene, white-clapboard good looks. The hotel faces the Congregational church and gold-domed Bennington Courthouse, and the few tasteful stores include a branch of Frog Hollow, Vermont's premier crafts shop. Public buildings trail off into a line of mansions, spaced along marble sidewalks.

Discount shopping begins a quarter mile downhill in Manchester Center, a village with a different zip code and zoning. The center was "Factory Point" in the 19th century, when sawmills, marbleworks, and a tannery were powered by the Battenkill River's flow.

Fears that the former Factory Point might become Vermont's future factory outlet capital began in the mid-1980s, with the opening of a trendy wood-and-glass shopping complex at the traffic heart of town, the junction of Routes 7A and 11/30—known locally as "Malfunction Junction."

The strip malls, however, haven't materialized. Instead, outlets along Route 7A fill old homes and house-sized compounds, blending nicely with the shopping landmarks like the Orvis Retail Store (supplying the needs of fishermen and other sportsmen since 1856).

The Green Mountains rise even within Manchester town limits to 3,100 feet on the east, then roll off into heavily forested uplands punctuated by picturesque villages like Peru, Landgrove, Weston, and Londonderry, all noteworthy for cross-country skiing and equally appealing in summer. Dorset and Danby are also well worth a visit.

GUIDANCE

Manchester and the Mountains Regional Chamber (362-2100; www.manchesterandmtns.com), at Manchester Center; this clapboard chamber of commerce information booth is walled with pamphlets, good for general walk-in information. The chamber does not make reservations but does keep a running tally on space in member lodging places and on short-term condo and cottage rentals.

Stratton Mountain maintains a reservation and information service (297-4000 in-state; 1-800-843-6867 THE-MTNS) and serves some 20 lodges, condo clusters, and inns on and around Stratton.

In winter, the **Bromley Village Lodging Service** (1-800-865-786) also makes reservations for condominiums.

Dorset Chamber of Commerce (867-2450; www.DORSETVT.com), P.O. Box 121, Dorset 05251.

Londonderry Chamber of Commerce (824-8178) maintains an information booth and office in the Mountain Marketplace (the Londonderry shopping center) at the junction of Routes 11 and 100.

GETTING THERE

By car: From Bennington, Route 7 to Manchester is a limited-access highway that's speedy but dull, except for viewing Mount Equinox. You get a more interesting taste of the area, especially around Arlington, by clinging to historic Route 7A. From the southeast, the obvious access is I-91 to Brattleboro, then Route 30 north. And from the Albany-Troy area, take NY 7 heading east into Vermont, where it becomes 9 east. In the center of Bennington, take VT 7 north to exit 4, or follow historic Route 7A.

By bus: **Vermont Transit** offers good service from New York and Montreal to Manchester; connections with Boston are via Williamstown, Massachusetts, or Rutland.

MEDICAL EMERGENCY

Manchester-Dorset Rescue Squad (911; 362-2121).

Northshire Medical Associates (362-4440), Manchester Center.

Manchester Family Medical Clinic (362-1263), Route 7A, Manchester.

Mountain Valley Medical Clinic (824-6901), Route 11, opposite the Flood Brook School, 2 miles west of Londonderry, 3 miles east of Peru.

Carlos Otis Clinic (297-2300), at Stratton Mountain.

Tri Mountain Rescue Squad (824-3166). Bondville, Landgrove, Peru, and Stratton.

VILLAGES

In addition to Manchester, the area's picturesque places include: Weston, 15 miles to the northeast; Dorset, 8 miles to the northwest; Pawlet, another 7 miles to the north on Route 30; and Danby, 8 miles north of Dorset and 10 miles east of Pawlet.

Dorset. This pristine village is visible evidence that it takes money to "prevent the future." A fashionable summer refuge for years, few signs of commerce mar its state of carefully manicured nature. Today's tranquillity, making it a haven for artists and writers as well as the affluent, contrasts sharply with the hotheaded days of its youth. In 1776, the Green Mountain Boys gathered in Cephas Kent's tavern and issued their first declaration of independence from the New Hampshire Grants, signed by Thomas Chittenden, Ira Allen, Matthew Lyon, Seth Warner, and other Founding Fathers of Vermont. Today the Dorset Inn, said to be the state's oldest continuously operating hostelry, is the village focal point, along with the Dorset Playhouse, one of New England's most venerable summer theaters. The first marble to be quarried in North America came from Dorset, and one quarry is now a popular swimming hole. There is also a nine-hole golf course, the private Dorset Field Club (billed as the state's oldest), and a fine choice of places to stay.

Pawlet. Not far north of Dorset, this hamlet on Route 30 is an unexpected delight, with a mix of architectural styles in the buildings that cling to the rather steep slopes leading up from Flower Brook, over which Johnny Mach's General Store extends. Gib Mach has harnessed the rushing brook to a turbine that generates his electricity and has built a glass-topped counter at the end of a store aisle through which you can peer down at the water, surging through the narrow gorge below. Next door, a former railroad station is now the Old Station Restaurant and Ice Cream Parlor, and a clutch of nearby shops are worth investigating.

Danby. A bypassed hamlet on Route 7 between Dorset and Wallingford, Danby is a vintage village known for fine marble quarries and as home base for Silas Griffith, an 1850s lumber baron who was Vermont's first millionaire. In the 1960s, novelist Pearl Buck bought seven buildings in the village and began to renovate them, and since her death, inns, restaurants, and some intriguing shops have opened here.

Weston. A mountain crossroads that's a logical hub for exploring all of southern Vermont, this village of just 500 souls looms large on tourist maps. It's the home of one of the country's oldest and best summer theaters and the Vermont Country Store, New England's number one nostalgia outlet. The oval common is shaded with majestic maples, and a band plays regularly in the bandstand. Free summer concerts are also presented by the Kinhaven Music School high on a back road, and visitors are also welcome at Weston Priory, a small community of Benedictine monks, nationally known for the music sung and played at Sunday liturgies. Weston was actually one of the first villages in Vermont to be consciously preserved. The theater, the unusually fine historical collection in the Farrar Mansur House, and (indirectly) the Vermont Country Store all date from the "Weston Revival" of the 1930s. Today it offers exceptional lodging and dining as well as theater and shopping.

TO SEE

MUSEUMS

♿ **Southern Vermont Arts Center** (362-1405), West Road, Manchester Center. Late May through October, daily 10–5 except Monday, and Sunday noon–5; December through mid-March, Monday through Saturday 10–5. Donation requested. This gracious old mansion, set on 375 acres of grounds, offers changing exhibits—paintings, sculpture, prints, and photography—and classes in various art forms for both adults and children, as well as a series of concerts (held in the adjacent, 430-seat Pavilion hall). Other special events throughout the year. Light lunches are served in the Artist's Palate Café (see *Eating Out*), and there are extensive trails through the woods, among them a botany trail featuring rock formations, 67 varieties of wildflowers, and birches. Limited handicapped accessibility.

The American Museum of Fly Fishing (362-3300), Seminary Avenue and Route 7A, Manchester Village. Open May through October, 10–4 daily, the museum displays the beautiful flies of Mary Orvis Marbury as well as more than 1,000 rods and reels made by famous rod builders and owned by such luminaries as Daniel Webster, Bing Crosby, Ernest

Historic Hildene, Robert Todd Lincoln's summer home

Hemingway, and presidents Hoover and Eisenhower. Don't miss it. $3 admission; students free.

HISTORIC HOMES

    Historic Hildene (362-1788), Route 7A, Manchester Village. Mid-May through October, 9:30–4; $7 adults; $3 youths 6–14. Limited handicapped accessibility. An impressive house among historic houses, this 24-room Georgian Revival manor is set on 412 acres, including formal gardens and paths that lead down into the Battenkill Valley. Bring a picnic lunch and plan to stay half the day. The tour begins with a wagon ride to the Carriage Barn, now a sophisticated visitors center with a slide show about Robert Todd Lincoln. You learn that he first came to the village as a boy with his mother for a stay at the Equinox House; his father was assassinated before the family could return, as they had intended, the following summer. It was Todd's law partner who later persuaded him to build this summer home adjacent to his own mansion. Todd died here in 1926, and members of the family lived here until 1975. Guides are familiar with at least one Lincoln and with the true character of the authentically furnished house. Tours include the restored formal gardens and a brief demonstration of the 1,000-pipe organ, which can be played both manually and with one of 240 player rolls on hand. Picnic tables outside command a view of the valley below, and there are numerous trails to stroll or—in winter, when the Carriage Barn becomes a warming hut—to explore on skis (see *Cross-Country Skiing*). In summer, Sunday-afternoon polo matches are a popular spectator sport. Inquire about organ concerts and other special events.

    Farrar Mansur House (824-4399), village green, Weston. Open weekends Memorial Day through Columbus Day; in July and August, Wednesday through Sunday 1–4. Fee. Limited handicapped accessibility. Even if you have never set foot inside a historic house, make an exception for this one, built in 1797 as a tavern with a classic old taproom and seven fireplaces. Thanks to 1930s Work Projects Administration (WPA) artists, murals of Weston in its prime—in the 1840s it was twice the size it is today—cover the living room walls, and a number of primitive portraits hang in adjoining rooms, which are filled with furniture and furnishings donated by Weston families. Upstairs in the old ballroom, a rendition of townspeople dancing—each face is painted to resemble a specific resident— conjures the spirit of a town that knew how to have fun.

Weston Mill Museum, at the junction of Routes 100 and 155, Weston. Daily Memorial Day through Columbus Day, 10–5. Donations requested. This is a working restoration of a vintage mill. Note the work of David Claggett, a skilled tinmaker who uses 18th-century methods to make exceptional chandeliers, lanterns, sconces, and folk art.

SCENIC DRIVES

Mount Equinox (362-1114). The summit of Mount Equinox is 3,825 feet high. Most of the mountain is owned by the Carthusian monks who occupy the monastery, which you can see from the top. A toll road (open May to November; $6 per car and driver; $2 per passenger) climbs more than 5 miles from Route 7 to the **Equinox Mountain Inn** (362-1113; 1-800-868-6843) on top. This can be a spectacular ride on a clear day, even more dramatic if the mountain is in the clouds and the road keeps disappearing in front of you. Be sure to drive back down in low gear and in total sobriety. There are also trails to the top.

Green Mountain National Forest Road Number 10, Danby to Landgrove. Closed in winter. The longest (14 miles) and most isolated of these byways, the road (beginning in Danby) climbs through the White Rocks Recreation Area, crossing a number of tempting hiking paths as well as the Long Trail. There are some fine views as you continue along, and you might want to picnic somewhere in the middle of the forest, as I did by a beaver pond. The road follows Tabor Brook down into Landgrove, itself a tiny, picturesque village.

Peru to Weston. From the village of Peru, an enticing, wooded road is paved as far as Hapgood Pond, then continues smoothly through Landgrove, a minuscule village with an outstanding inn (open to the public for dinner), set in rolling fields. The way to Weston is clearly marked.

East Rupert to Danby. Danby Mountain Road is the logical shortcut from Dorset to Danby, and it's quite beautiful, winding up and over a saddle between Woodlawn Mountain and Dorset Peak. Well-surfaced dirt, with long views in places. If you are coming from East Rupert, be sure to turn right at Danby Four Corners and follow Mill Brook into Danby.

TO DO

BICYCLING

In Manchester, mountain-bike, hybrid-bike, and touring-bike rentals and touring information are available from **Battenkill Sports Cycle Shop** (362-2734), open daily 9:30–5:30, in the Stone House, junction of Routes 7 and 11/30.

Stratton Sports (297-2200; 1-800-STRATTON), at Stratton Mountain, rents mountain bikes and offers terrain ranging from paved roads to cross-country-ski trails and (for expert bikers) a combination of service and ski trails down from the summit (the gondola hoists bikes as well as riders to the top); guided tours.

Viking Biking (824-3933), Little Pond Road, Londonderry, offers 16- to 18-gear rentals and self-guided bike tours along dirt roads either as day trips or with baggage transferred from inn to inn; weekends are $200 per person, lodging and meals included.

CAMPING

Green Mountain National Forest (362-2307), District Ranger Office, Manchester. A public information office serving the southern third of the 275,000-acre Green Mountain National Forest is located on Routes 30 and 11 east of Manchester; open year-round, Monday through Friday 8–4:30. Maps and details are available about where to fish, hike, cross-country ski, and camp. All national forest campsites are available on a first-come, first-served basis.

Emerald Lake State Park (362-1655), North Dorset. On Route 7, this area offers 105 campsites, including 36 lean-tos, also hiking and nature trails, among them a 3.4-mile, round-trip trek to a natural bridge.

Hapgood Pond Recreation Area, Peru. Acquired in 1931, this was the beginning of the Green Mountain National Forest. There is swimming, fishing, and limited boating on the 7-acre pond. Removed from the picnic ground and beach are 28 campsites (first-come, first-served basis). A pleasant, 8-mile forest trail threads through the woods.

Greendale Campground, 2 miles north of Weston on Route 100. There are 14 sites.

See also *Green Space* in "The Lower Connecticut and West River Valleys" for details about Jamaica State Park.

CANOEING

The **Battenkill** makes for satisfying canoeing in the spring; the Manchester-to-Arlington section is relatively flat water but it gets difficult a mile above Arlington.

BattenKill Canoe Ltd. (362-2800), Route 7A in Arlington, an outfitter offering inn-to-inn canoe trips throughout the state and as far afield as Costa Rica and England, also rents canoes and offers shuttle service on the Battenkill.

DRIVING

Land Rover University at the Equinox (362-4700), Manchester Village. No joke. An off-road instructional course and classroom area has been constructed, and expert instructors are on hand to offer tips on driving both on- and off-road.

FISHING

Fly-fishing has been serious business in the Battenkill since the mid-19th century. The Orvis Company began manufacturing bamboo rods in Manchester Village near the spot where they are still produced.

The **Battenkill** is generally recognized as Vermont's best wild trout stream; access is available at a number of places off Route 7A. Brown trout can also be found in **Gale Meadows Pond,** accessible via gravel road from Route 30 at Bondville. **Emerald Lake** in North Dorset is stocked with pike, bass, and perch; rental boats are available at the state park facility.

Orvis Fishing Schools (362-3622; 1-800-235-9763), *the* name in fly-fishing instruction as well as equipment; 3-day courses, offered twice weekly April through August.

Southern Vermont Fly Fisherman (1-800-682-0103). Chuck Kashner's guide service includes rods, reels, waders, flies, and a meal on full-day trips.

Battenkill Anglers (362-3184) is a Thomas & Thomas–sponsored fly-fishing school and outfitter.

Peter Basta (867-4103), P.O. Box 540, Dorset 05251, offers guide service and on-stream instruction.

GOLF

The 18-hole **Gleneagles Golf Course** at the Equinox Country Club (362-3223), Manchester Center, which was established in the 1920s for guests of the Equinox House, has just undergone a $3 million renovation and is open to the public. The **Dormy Grill** at the Gleneagles Clubhouse also offers pleasant noontime dining.

The Stratton Golf School (297-2200; 1-800-843-6867) offers weekend and midweek sessions, including professional instruction, use of the 27-hole course at the **Stratton Mountain Country Club,** and a special 22-acre "training site."

Tater Hill (875-2517), Popple Dungeon Road, Windham. An 18-hole course, built on the site of one of New England's largest and oldest potato farms. Facilities include a pro shop, carts, dressing rooms, and showers. The **Grille** serves a Vermont country breakfast on weekends; salads, sandwiches, and burgers at lunch; and a tavern menu from 3:30 until closing. (*Note:* There is also a swimming pool for non-golfing members of the family.)

The Practice Tee (362-3100), Route 7, Manchester Center. Open in-season, weather permitting, 9–7 weekdays, 8–7 weekends and holidays; lessons available.

HIKING

From the Green Mountain National Forest District Office, request hiking maps for **Lye Brook Wilderness,** a 14,600-acre preserve south of

Manchester with a 2.3-mile trail to the Lye Brook Waterfalls and the **Long Trail.** This Massachusetts-to-Quebec path doubles as the Appalachian Trail throughout the area; portions of the trail make good day hikes, either north over Bromley Mountain or south over Spruce Peak from Routes 11 and 30. The most heavily hiked stretch of the entire trail is the relatively level trek in from Kelly Stand Road to Stratton Pond; there are three shelters in the immediate area, and swimming is permitted. Griffith Lake, accessible from Peru and Danby, is a less crowded swimming and camping site on the trail. For details, consult the Green Mountain Club's *Long Trail Guide.*

Mount Equinox. Details about the rewarding, 6-mile Burr and Burton Trail from Manchester Village to the summit are available in *Day Hiker's Guide to Vermont* (Green Mountain Club). At 3,825 feet, this is the highest mountain in the state that is not traversed by the Long Trail. See also Equinox Preservation Trust under *Green Space.*

Walking Tours of Southern Vermont (375-1141), Route 2, Box 622, Arlington. Guided tours throughout this area are offered with lodging at local inns. Trail rides with llamas, too.

HORSEBACK RIDING

Horses for Hire (824-3750), South Road, Peru. Trail rides, sleigh rides, riding lessons, even in winter, weather permitting; $25 per person for 1½ hours, $100 per half day. English riding.

Sun Bowl Ranch (297-2200), at Stratton Mountain Resort, offers trail rides, donkey rides, lessons, and wagon rides.

Chipman Stables (293-5242), Danby Four Corners. Trail rides and lessons, both Western-style. Trail rides $12, lessons $10 per hour.

Eastbrook Farm (375-9957), Manchester. A stable specializing in English riding, dressage; lessons by appointment.

HUNTING

Orvis Company (362-3622; 1-800-548-9548) of Manchester (see *Fishing*) offers 2-day shooting courses ($775) in July and August; 3-day programs ($950) September through mid-October. Hunters move in groups of five through 10 stations in a simulated hunting course. Tuition includes guns and ammo, but not lodging.

The British School of Falconry (362-4780) at the Equinox Hotel, Manchester Village, offers introductory lessons, hawk walks, and pheasant hunting with hawks and falcons at the Tinmouth Hunting Preserve in Wallingford.

MOUNTAIN RIDES

Bromley Mountain (824-5522), Route 11, Peru (6 miles east of Manchester). This 3,284-foot-high mountain offers excellent views of Stratton and Equinox Mountains. It is traversed by the Long Trail (see *Hiking*) and is also accessible by hiking the ski trails from the midpoint exit on the chairlift. This lift, serving the alpine slide, is open Memorial Day through mid-October, weather permitting, on weekends 10–5 and daily July

Norcross West marble quarry

through Labor Day 9:30–6 (fee). The **Bromley Alpine Slide,** the first in this country, is a great ride with fabulous views whatever your age. We have yet to try the **DevalKart Ride** and the **Bromley Thrill Sleds** (similar to a winter luge), also making their American premiere at Bromley. Lunch, snacks, and drinks available at the base lodge.

Stratton Mountain (297-2200; 1-800-STRATTON) offers a four-state view from its summit, accessible by Starship XII gondolas from the ski resort (Route 30, Bondville). The gondolas run daily in summer and fall, 9:30–4:15. And there's lots of summer action in its **Adventure Zone**—skate park, climbing wall, boulders, and a cave.

NATURE WALKS AND WORKSHOPS

Vermont Institute of Natural Science (VINS), in partnership with the Equinox Preservation Trust (362-4374; see *Green Space*), offers natural-history walks and programs for adults, families, and children. The programs run year-round, geared to the season. $4–5 per adult, $1–2 for children.

SWIMMING

Dana L. Thompson Recreation Area (362-1439), Route 30 north, Manchester, is open daily in summer, but hours for general swimming are limited; nominal fee.

Dorset Quarry, off Route 30 on Kelly Road between Manchester and Dorset (turn across from Mountain Weavers), is a deep, satisfying pool but not recommended for children. The upper quarry is the local skinny-dipping spot.

Hapgood Pond in Peru, with its sand and calm, shallow drop-off, is favored by families with young children.

Emerald Lake State Park (362-1655), Route 7, North Dorset, offers clear lake swimming.

See also *Green Space*.

TENNIS

Stratton Mountain (297-2200) offers weekend and midweek clinics. There are 15 outdoor and 4 indoor courts. *Note:* Stratton Mountain offers full day care and day camp in summer for children (6 weeks to 10 years old) of parents enrolled in the golf and tennis programs. A Junior Tennis Day Camp is also offered weekdays for children ages 7–15.

Dana L. Thompson Recreation Area, Manchester. Public courts are available with weekly memberships or on a per-hour basis.

Equinox Hotel Tennis (362-4700), Route 7A, Manchester Village. Three Har-Tru courts are open to the public for an hourly fee.

Dorset Tennis Club (362-2236), Route 7A, 4 miles north of Manchester. Indoor court; lessons.

TRAIN RIDES

The *Vermont Valley Flyer* (463-3069; 1-800-707-3530), operated by the Green Mountain Railroad Corp., makes three round-trips a day between Manchester and Arlington from the first of July to mid-October. $10 for adults, $6 children 3–12.

WINTER SPORTS

CROSS-COUNTRY SKIING

Viking Ski Touring Centre (824-3933), Little Pond Road, Londonderry. The Viking trail system now includes 40 km of trails, 30 km groomed, 3 km lighted. There is a rental and retail shop and a café serving drinks, light breakfasts, and lunches. There are lessons, lunch tours to Weston, and bed & breakfast and inn-to-inn tours using a total of four local hostelries. Owner Irving Gross also offers four bedrooms at the center, $55–60 per person, including breakfast, snacks, and trail pass. Trail fee: $11.

Wild Wings Ski Touring Center (824-6793), Peru. Tracy and Chuck Black run a family-oriented touring center located within the boundaries of the Green Mountain National Forest, 2.5 miles north of Peru. Trails are narrow, geared to the intermediate skier, and adjoin an extensive public system that connects the center with Landgrove. This area tends to get a heavier snowfall than other local touring centers; the 20 km of trails are at elevations between 1,650 and 2,040 feet. Instruction, rentals, and free hot bouillon can be found in the warming hut. $9 trail fee.

Stratton Ski Touring Center (297-2200), Stratton Mountain. Based at the Sun Bowl (see *Horseback Riding*), a 20 km series of groomed loops plus adjoining backcountry trails. Guided backcountry tours as well as a variety of other tours are offered. $10 trail fee.

Hildene Ski Touring Center (362-1788), Manchester. The Lincoln Carriage Barn serves as a warming hut for this system of 12 km of groomed and mapped trails on the estate built by Robert Todd Lincoln (see Hildene under *To See*). Trails meander through woods and fields on a promontory overlooking the Battenkill Valley between Mount Equinox and Lye Brook Wilderness. Lessons and equipment are available.

Equinox Ski Touring Center (362-3223) has 35 km of groomed trails and tracked terrain, snowshoeing, instruction, and rentals. This network includes trails on the golf course, up through the forests of the Equinox Preservation Trust (see *Green Space*), and around Equinox Pond.

DOWNHILL SKIING

Bromley (824-5522). Located on Route 11 in Peru, 8 miles east of Manchester. Founded in 1937 by Fred Pabst, of the Milwaukee brewing family, this is among the oldest ski areas in the country. It was also one of the first to have snowmaking, snow farming, a slope-side nursery, and condominiums. It retains its own following of those who like its friendly atmosphere and sunny trails. A renovated and expanded base lodge is part of Bromley's current capital improvement program, which included a snowboard park and halfpipe.

Lifts: One quad and five double chairlifts, three surface lifts.

Trails: 39 trails—35 percent intermediate, 34 percent beginner, 31 percent expert.

Vertical drop: 1,334 feet.

Snowmaking: 84 percent of terrain from base to summit.

Facilities: The base lodge offers two cafeterias and two more-formal areas. Skiers unload right at the base lodge; the driver then parks in an area across Route 11 and rides back on a shuttle bus.

Ski school: ATM method.

For children: Nursery for ages 6 weeks to 6 years. Mighty Moose for ages 3–5, Mountain Club 6- to 12-year-olds; Beginners Circle for 15 and older.

Rates: $46 adults, $39 teens, $30 juniors, weekends; midweek, $35 adults, $30 teens, $25 juniors. Snowboard park $15.

Stratton (1-800-STRATTON; ski report: 297-4211; boarder line: 297-4545). Located atop a 5-mile access road from Route 30 in Bondville, Stratton is an unusually well-groomed mountain. This goes for its trails, facilities, lodges, and clientele. It ranks high among Vermont's major ski resorts, a big mountain with two separate areas: the original North Face and the distinctly sunnier Sun Bowl, focus of a current expansion program including a new base lodge, new quad chair, improved trail system, and snowmaking. There's a 3,000-foot snowboard park with two halfpipes and a retro diner. Thanks to the quantity of lifts, skiers are generally dispersed over the trail network. Stratton Village, a complex that includes 25 shops, three restaurants, a 91-room condo-hotel, a 750-car garage, and 170 condominiums, dwarfs the base facility. A sports center includes a 25-yard-long pool, whirlpool, indoor tennis courts, racquetball courts, exercise equipment, and a lounge. (See also *Lodging*.)

Stratton Mountain

SPORTS FILE

A lot happens here in summer, too: There's a 70-foot climbing wall; a skate park with jumps, ramps, and rails; and an indoor family FunZone.

Lifts: 12—a 12-passenger gondola, a 6-passenger high-speed detachable, four quads, one triple, three double chairs, and two surface lifts.
Trails and slopes: 90.

Vertical drop: 2,003 feet.

Snowmaking: 80 percent.

Facilities: A recently expanded restaurant and cafeteria in the base lodge, also cafeterias midmountain and in the Sun Bowl lodges. Chapel of the Snows at the parking lot, a little Bavarian-style church, has frequent nondenominational and Roman Catholic services. A shuttle bus brings skiers from inns on the mountain to the base lodge. Also a clinic, sports center, and shops and restaurants in the base area Village Square.

Ski school: ATM and GLM methods.

For children: Childcare Center for ages 6 weeks to 3 years. A separate base lodge for KidsKamp; combined ski and play programs are offered—Little Cubs (ages 4–6) and Big Cubs (7–12).

Rates: $48 per adult midweek, $52 weekends and holidays; $42–46 young adults and seniors; $35–37 juniors and super seniors. Many special packages.

Magic Mountain Ski Area, Londonderry, was scheduled to reopen for the 1999 season, but details were unavailable at press time.

ICE SKATING

The **Equinox Ski Touring Center** rents ice skates for use on its rink.

SLEIGH RIDES

Pfisters (824-6320) in Landgrove offers the most remote, romantic sleigh ride around.

The **Equinox Hotel** and the stables listed under *Horseback Riding* also offer sleigh rides, as does **Merck Forest and Farmland Center** (see *Green Space*).

SNOWMOBILING

A *Winter Recreation Map,* available free from the Green Mountain National Forest District Ranger Office (362-2307), Manchester, shows trails presently maintained in this area by the Vermont Association of Snow Travelers. **Classic Snow Tours** (824-6628), based at the Pinnacle Sun & Ski Lodge, junction of Routes 11 and 30, Manchester, offers tours and rentals.

GREEN SPACE

Equinox Preservation Trust (362-4700), Manchester Village. A not-for-profit organization created in 1993 by Equinox Resort Associates and administered through the Vermont Land Trust and The Nature Conservancy. Some 850 acres on Mount Equinox are now a user-friendly preserve. Secure a map/guide to the trail system (a portion is open to cross-country skiers) and inquire about the nature walks and seminars offered year-round, some geared to children, in conjunction with VINS (see *To Do—Nature Walks*). Horseback riding and mountain biking are also permitted on the ski trails in summer and fall. Be sure at least to walk the 1.2-mile loop through the hardwoods around Equinox Pond. *Note:* All parking for access to the trust property is at the parking lot of the Equinox Hotel (see *Lodging*).

✍ **Merck Forest and Farmland Center** (394-7836), Route 315, Rupert. Some 2,800 acres of near wilderness, including Mount Antone, were set aside in the 1950s as a foundation by George Merck, of the Merck Drug Company. The area is now maintained through donations, and the forest offers year-round walks, talks, and facilities: foot and horse trails, picnic areas, a spring-fed swimming pond, 12 shelters, a farm museum, and a sugarhouse that produces 400 gallons of syrup. The Merck Forest Summer Camp has six 1-week sessions for children. Reservations are required for overnight use of the shelters. An extensive network of trails is marked for cross-country skiing.

Grout Pond, west of the village of Stratton, marked from Kelley Stand Road. Deep in the Green Mountain National Forest, this is a great spot for a picnic, complete with grills and a small beach.

Ball Mountain Lake (886-8111), Jamaica. This 85-acre lake, a dramatic sight among the wooded, steep mountains, can be viewed from the access road off Route 30. One hundred seven campsites are available on Winhall Brook at the other end of the reservoir, open mid-May through mid-September; accessible from Route 100 in South Londonderry; free. It is controlled release from this flood dam that provides the outstanding canoeing available on the West River below Jamaica each spring. This area is maintained by the U.S. Army Corps of Engineers. See also *To Do—Camping*.

LODGING

RESORT

The Equinox (362-4700, 362-1595; 1-800-362-4747), Route 7A, Manchester Village 05254. The white-columned inn is composed of 17 distinct parts that have evolved over the past 229 years. It's still evolving. In the mid-1980s, it was revamped from its foundations up, an unavoidable process that left it sound but, many said, soulless. Thanks to a 1990s infusion of funds, the 136 rooms and 47 suites, most of them spacious and furnished in pine reproductions, have acquired modern plumbing and a brighter, more country inn feel. The **Charles Orvis Inn** next door (opened in 1995) is composed of suites, each with a cherry-paneled kitchen, oak floors, gas fireplace, and separate living room and bedroom. Common rooms include a paneled bar, billiards room, and meeting space. The inn's public spaces are extensive and quite magnificent, the grandest in Vermont. Meals are memorable (see *Dining Out*). Facilities for which guests pay extra include the newly revamped, 18-hole golf course, a fitness center with outdoor and indoor pool, touring bikes, a 14-acre stocked trout pond, tennis courts, a cross-country-ski network, snowmobiling, hunting with falcons, and learning to drive

The Equinox

Land Rovers ecologically off-road. You might want to make sure before booking that your stay does not coincide with one of the business groups that can preempt the public spaces. Rates: $179–319 double; suites $489–899; town houses $379–679 per night for up to six people. Weekend packages, children free; MAP available at $60 per day per person. Inquire about midweek packages that bring these prices way down.

INNS AND BED & BREAKFASTS

In Manchester

⟨ **The Inn at Ormsby Hill** (362-1163; 1-800-670-2841), 1842 Main Street, Manchester Center 05255. The inn is 2 miles southwest of Manchester Village on Route 7A, set in 2.5 acres of rolling lawns. The best views are from the back of the house. This gracious, elegant manor was the home of Edward Isham—Robert Todd Lincoln's law partner—and his family's home for 100 years. Its connection to Hildene (see *Historic Homes*) is strong, spiritually and aesthetically. Innkeepers Chris and Ted Sprague have doubled the number of guest rooms and obviously enjoyed distinctively decorating each in Waverly prints and exceptional antiques, all with fireplace and two-person Jacuzzi. The spacious Taft room, with its wood-burning fireplace and huge four-poster, is the unofficial honeymoon suite, but every one of the rooms is romantic enough to qualify. The downstairs Library suite is handicapped-accessible. Common space includes a formal parlor and an inviting library lined with bookshelves that hold many of Isham's personal volumes. The huge, many-windowed dining room with ornately carved hearth is the scene of bountiful breakfasts featuring, perhaps, strawberries with crème fraîche and wild mushroom risotto with sliced ham, capped with desserts like rhubarb crumble with vanilla ice cream. Chris Sprague is a chef of some renown, and dinner is also served to guests on Friday evenings. $115–290.

The Inn at Manchester (362-1793; 1-800-273-1793), Route 7A, Box 41, Manchester 05254. A gracious old home, set back from Main Street, with an expansive front porch, big windows, gables, and a restored, vintage-1867 carriage house in back. The 18 rooms, all with private bath and air-conditioning, are named for flowers and herbs. There are also four suites, three with working fireplace. The dining room and parlors are imaginatively and comfortably furnished, and there is a TV and game room, warmed by an antique woodstove. Summer brings use of the pool in the back meadow and plenty of wicker on the flowery porch. Breakfast is served with flair by Harriet and Stan Rosenberg, celebrating their 20th year as Manchester innkeepers. $125–155 per room, regular season; $149–209 during foliage season, including breakfast and afternoon tea, tax, and gratuity. Ask about midweek rates.

✍ **Manchester Highlands Inn** (362-4565; 1-800-743-4565), P.O. Box 1754, Highland Avenue, Manchester Center 05255. Patricia and Robert Eichorn call their spacious Victorian inn "Manchester's best-kept secret." Recently repainted Victorian gray with rose and plum accents, it's on a quiet side street, a short walk from all the shops and restaurants but with an away-from-it-all feel, especially on the back porch and lawn (with its pool), both of which command an expansive view of Mount Equinox. The 15 guest rooms, all with private bath, are nicely decorated with family antiques and personal touches, many with canopy beds. Common space includes a comfortable living room, a wicker-filled sunroom, and a TV room (with a library of movies to feed the VCR). In winter, the loss of the pool and porch is assuaged by the basement Remedy Room, with its bar and games—connected by "the tunnel" (decorated with guest graffiti) to the rooms in the carriage house, which, incidentally, are usually reserved for families. A very full breakfast featuring morning-glory muffins, maybe lemon soufflé pancakes and cheddar soufflés, is served, plus home-baked afternoon snacks and tea. $105–145 double; midweek and off-season specials. Children under 6 free; add $10 for 6- to 12-year-olds.

1811 House (362-1811; 1-800-432-1811), Route 7A, Manchester 05254. "A place to feel pampered" is the way the owners of this magnificent building describe what they offer. Parts of this mansion date back to the 1770s. It has been an inn since 1811, except for a few years during which it was owned by President Lincoln's granddaughter Mary Lincoln Isham. Public rooms are as elegant as any others to be found in New England, and the 14 guest rooms are in keeping, each with private bath, many with hearths. Innkeepers Bruce and Marnie Duff dispel any stuffiness in this rarified world. The cozy pub, replete with dartboards and a wide selection of single-malt Scotches, is open to the public from 5:30 to 8. An expansive lawn and newly redesigned English-style gardens overlook the Gleneagles Golf Course (see *To Do*—

Golf). A wonderful full breakfast is included in the room rate, from $120 for a cozy double to $230 for a suite with a king four-poster canopy bed, fireplace, and sitting room. Rates include gratuity. Children over 16 are welcome. Off-season rates available.

Reluctant Panther Inn & Restaurant (362-2568; 1-800-822-2331; fax: 802-362-2586), Box 673, Manchester 05254. Renowned for its gourmet fare (see *Dining Out*), this mauve, yellow-shuttered village home also has 13 rooms, with five suites in the adjacent Porter House, each decorated with bright wallpaper and antiques. Seven rooms and all the suites have fireplaces. Many suites feature two wood-burning fireplaces—one in front of the two-person whirlpool bath and a second in the bedroom. All have private bath, room phone, and cable TV. Breakfast is served to guests only, and, with the exception of dining hours, the living room and unique pubs make a peaceful and pleasant retreat. Innkeepers are Maye and Robert Bachofen. The inn is open year-round; the restaurant is open weekends only from November through April and closed Tuesday and Wednesday from May through October. $158–288 per couple in rooms, $245–450 in suites, includes breakfast and dinner. No children under age 14.

The Village Country Inn (362-1792; 1-800-370-0300; fax: 802-362-7238), Box 408, Route 7A, Manchester 05254. This century-old, three-story Main Street inn has a long piazza lined with wicker and rockers. There are 33 rooms (18 suites and luxury rooms), 1 with Jacuzzi, some with gas fireplace, all with private bath, and many recently refurbished in lace, antiques, and chintz. Outside is a formal garden and gazebo, swimming pool, and patio; inside, an informal tavern and formal dining room. Rates, including breakfast and a four-course dinner, are $150–350 MAP; add 15 percent service.

Wilburton Inn (362-2500; 1-800-648-4944), River Road, Manchester 05254. This is a brick, baronial, turn-of-the-century mansion set on expansive grounds with long views of the Battenkill Valley. Common rooms are richly paneled and the living room is immense, complete with piano, comfortable window seats and couches, Oriental rugs, and an enormous hearth. An unusual quantity of original art is scattered throughout. The house itself offers four suites and five bedrooms, and there are 25 rooms in outlying cottages, better suited to families as they offer more privacy and direct access to the seemingly limitless lawn—which harbors a pool and tennis courts. Breakfast is served at wrought-iron, glass-topped tables in the Terrace Room, and dinner, in the Billiard Room, is reminiscent of an exclusive men's club. Open year-round, $110–250 per couple including a full breakfast and afternoon tea. Weddings are a specialty here.

The Inn at Willow Pond (362-4733; 1-800-533-3533 outside Vermont), Box 1429, Manchester Center 05255. Located 2.3 miles north on Route 7A, this inn offers 40 spacious guest rooms and suites in three separate, contemporary, Colonial-style buildings on a hillside overlooking the Manchester Country Club's golf course. The 18th-century Meeting House reception building contains the lofty main lounge, conference facilities, and a fitness center with exercise equipment, two saunas, and a library. There's also an outdoor lap pool and a restaurant in a renovated 1780 house (see *Dining Out*). The larger guest rooms feature fireplaces and sitting areas. Winter rates are $128 (for a small suite) to $158 for multiroom suites with fireplace and full living room; off-season rates begin at $81 per room, and all include continental breakfast. Full breakfast is served in the restaurant on weekends and holidays. Midweek and special off-season weekend rates available.

River Meadow Farm (362-1602), P.O. Box 822, Manchester Center 05255. Off by itself down near the Battenkill south of Manchester Village, this is a beautiful old farmhouse with barns, built around 1797 and purchased in the 1820s by Manchester for use as a "poor farm." There are five bedrooms sharing two and a half baths, and guests have the run of the downstairs with its welcoming kitchen, pleasant living room, and dining room. Outside there is ample space to hike and cross-country ski—with a splendid view of Mount Equinox. Pat Dupree is a longtime Manchester resident who enjoys orienting her guests. Rates are $30 per person, full breakfast included.

Seth Warner Inn (362-3830), Manchester Center 05255. This imposing vintage 1800 house is set back from Route 7A, southwest of Manchester Village, and it's a beauty—carefully restored by Stasia and Lee Tetreault. Rooms with open beams and stenciling are furnished in antiques and curtained in lace. Five bright guest rooms have country quilts and private baths. Common space includes a gracious living room, a hall library, and the dining room, in which guests gather for a full breakfast. $90–100 (fall) per room including breakfast.

The Battenkill Inn (362-4213; 1-800-441-1628), Route 7A, Manchester 05254. This 1840 Victorian farmhouse sits at the foot of the Mount Equinox Skyline Drive and backs onto meadows that stretch down to the Battenkill. The 11 guest rooms all have private bath and are furnished with antiques, and the common rooms include two sitting rooms and two small dining rooms—plenty of space to relax in. One room with a double bed and fireplace is fully handicapped-accessible. Your hosts are Yoshi and Laine Akiyama. $95–165 per couple includes a full breakfast and complimentary hors d'oeuvres. Springtime midweek specials.

In Danby 05739

Silas Griffith Inn (293-5567; 1-800-545-1509), Main Street, is the renovated 1891 mansion that once housed Vermont's first millionaire. Lois and Paul Dansereau have restored the hardwood floors and the carved bird's-eye, curly maple, and cherry woodwork; scrubbed the leaded windows; painted the tin ceiling in the dining room; and created an unusually comfortable, welcoming inn. The 17 guest rooms, 14 with private bath,

The Dorset Inn

are divided between the main house and the converted carriage house, all furnished with antiques. You might want to request room 14, with its round porch (but no closet), or room 16—with a huge bed made for the room—one of several rooms that can be combined into a family suite sharing one bath. Common rooms include a large living room, well stocked with books, and a front parlor with TV, accessed by a wonderful "moon gate" door. Lois is an acclaimed chef, and the restaurant (in the carriage house) is locally popular (see *Dining Out*). Danby's intriguing shops are just down the street, there are some outstanding hiking trails just a few minutes' drive into the Green Mountain National Forest, and Emerald Lake State Park is just 3 miles down Route 7. The inn's own 11 hilltop acres include a pool. Rates are $94 for a room with private bath, $74 shared, including full breakfast ($109 and $89 in high seasons); discounts for weekdays and for a stay of several days.

The Quail's Nest (293-5099), Box 221, Main Street, is a homey, pleasant B&B in an 1835 house. Greg and Nancy Diaz offer six guest rooms (four with private bath) furnished with antiques and handmade country quilts. There's a comfy living room and an interesting gift store out back. Rates: $50–95. Nancy makes great maple-oat scones, part of a full breakfast.

In Dorset 05251

The Dorset Inn (867-5500), Church Street. A National Historic Site and the state's most venerable hostelry (in continuous operation since 1796) faces Dorset's historic green. It has been stylishly renovated by its owners, Sissy Hicks, former chef at the Barrows House and Gretchen Schmidt. Known for its excellent cuisine (see *Dining Out*) and relaxing atmosphere, the inn has 31 guest rooms. It's within walking distance of antiques shops and the theater and offers a lineup of front-porch rockers from which you might not want to stir. Rates: $180–230 double, including dinner and a full breakfast.

☀︎❦**The Barrows House** (867-4455; 1-800-639-1620), Route 30. This exceptional mini-resort, now owned by Philadelphians Linda and Jim McGinnis, features attractive, flexibly arranged accommodations (18 rooms, 10 suites) in the main house and 7 rooms in adjacent buildings. The early-19th-century house is a short walk from the center of this historic village, but there is an out-in-the-country feel to the 12-acre grounds, which include a gazebo, heated outdoor swimming pool, sauna, and two tennis courts. In summer, bikes are available; golf and hiking are nearby. In winter, cross-country-ski equipment is available. There are comfortable sitting rooms in the main house and the bigger cottages, where large families or several friendly couples can be lodged. A convivial bar is wallpapered to resemble a private library. Dogs are welcome in three separate accommodations. The dining room and a guest room in one of the outer buildings are wheelchair-accessible. The dining room is outstanding (see *Dining Out*). $175–240 per couple including breakfast and dinner, plus 15 percent service charge; less in the off-season.

❦❦ **Inn at West View Farm** (867-5715; 1-800-769-4903), Route 30, just south of Dorset, is a small, well-groomed lodge with an appealing personality, once the focus of a 200-acre farm, now known especially for its exceptional cuisine. (The dining room—see *Dining Out*—remains the focal point of the inn. Clancy's Tavern offers lighter fare.) Helmut and Dorothy Stein have added a very pleasant living room with a fireplace to the smaller, old front parlor; common space also includes an inviting, wicker-filled sunporch. One downstairs room has been fitted for handicapped access, and the nine upstairs rooms are all furnished comfortably with cheerful paper and bright, crisp fabrics; all rooms are air-conditioned. Rates: $85–140 B&B or $155–205 MAP, per couple, plus 15 percent service charge. Ask about long weekend and theater packages.

Marble West Inn (867-4155; 1-800-453-7629), West Road. This Greek Revival house has seven marble columns on its marble front porches, and there are marble walkways and three marble fireplaces. Now it offers eight well-decorated guest rooms (one a two-room suite with fireplace), an inviting living room, and a piano room that is the scene of impromptu concerts. The stencil work in the entrance hallway and on stairway walls is exceptional, and the high ceilings and bull's-eye moldings are pleasant reminders of an earlier era, as is the gracious hospitality of owners June and Wayne Erla. Guests mingle in the library for drinks (BYOB) and conversation. Dinners may be arranged but for no fewer than six people. Rates are $90–145 per couple, including a full breakfast and afternoon tea. A 15 percent service charge is added. Please, no pets or children under 12.

Cornucopia of Dorset (867-5751; 1-800-566-5751), Route 30, P.O. Box 307. This turn-of-the-century home is one of Vermont's more elegant B&Bs. Bill and Linda Ley offer four meticulously decorated, air-conditioned bedrooms in the main house, each with canopy or four-poster bed, phone, and private bath; three with fireplace. The solarium, walled in glass, overlooks gardens and a manicured back lawn. Guests can also relax in the library or small living room, both with a fireplace, and on a back terrace under an awning. The cottage suite in the rear is a beauty, with a loft bedroom (with skylights), living room with fireplace, kitchen, and sundeck. The multicourse breakfast may feature puff pancakes, gingerbread waffles, or quiche Lorraine. A welcoming flute of champagne and a morning tray of coffee or tea are among the many amenities. Rooms are $125–165 double; the cottage is $210–245.

Dovetail Inn (867-5747; 1-800-4-DOVETAIL), Route 30. An 1800s inn on the Dorset green with 11 bedrooms (all with private bath). Breakfast is served in the Keeping Room or in guest rooms. $65 for the smallest double room in low season; $195 for a two-room suite with a fireplace and TV, sleeping up to four. Ask about midweek rates.

In Weston 05161

Wilder Homestead Inn (824-8172), 25 Lawrence Hill Road. A classic, Federal-style brick house, beautifully transformed for B&B guests by warm hosts Peggy and Roy Varner. There are seven guest rooms, most with private bath, several with early-19th-century stenciling, each with a different decor. Guests gather for a full breakfast around the long table in front of a huge hearth in the dining room; there's also an attractive library and living room, along with a piano room; also a BYOB bar. Roy is a talented craftsman (check out his Vermont flamingos and window sticks in the inn's 1827 **Craft Shoppe**). All the sights of Weston are within an easy walk, and there's a waterfall across the street. $65–135 per couple B&B. No children under age 6. No smoking.

Colonial House Inn & Motel (824-6286; 1-800-639-5033), Box 138, Route 100. A rare and delightful combination of nine motel units and six traditional inn rooms (shared baths), connected by a very pleasant dining room, a comfortable, sunken sitting room with dried flowers hanging from the rafters, and a solarium overlooking the lawn; there's also a fully equipped game room. Innkeepers John and Betty Nunnikhoven make all ages feel welcome, and most guests are repeats. Rates include memorable, multicourse breakfasts. Dinners are served family-style ($19.95). The inn is 2 miles south of the village, with lawn chairs facing a classic farmscape across the road; most guest rooms overlook a meadow. Rooms are $60–90 fall and winter, $50–80 spring and summer, B&B, $8 per child 4–12 years; $35–60 single. Ramp available for wheelchairs. Golf and theater packages. Pets are accepted in the motel units.

The Darling Family Inn (824-3223), Route 100. An 1830s house, exquisitely furnished with family antiques by Joan and Chapin Darling. The five guest rooms have private baths, canopied beds, fine quilts, and artistic touches. There are wide-plank floors throughout, and Joan has expertly painted the walls. Full country breakfasts, by candlelight, are included in the rates. In summer, the pool adds a nice touch. $80–125 per couple, including breakfast, except for guests in the two attractive cottages up on the hill (where pets are welcome).

In Peru 05152

🐾 **Johnny Seesaw's** (824-5533; 1-800-424-CSAW). Built as a dance hall in 1920 and converted into one of Vermont's first ski lodges, this is a wonderfully weathered, comfortable place. Within walking distance of the slopes in winter, it offers tennis and a pool in summer. There are 28 rooms—doubles, master bedrooms with fireplace in the main house, and family suites—also four cottages with fireplaces, good for large families and small groups. There is a licensed pub (see *Dining Out*); "Yankee cuisine" dinners are à la carte and have a French accent. The living room boasts Vermont's first circular fireplace. $50–85 per adult B&B in winter, $38 per adult B&B in summer; add 15 percent service. Pets are okay.

✧ **The Wiley Inn** (824-6600; 1-888-843-6600), Route 11, just 1 mile from Bromley. Its core is an 1835 house containing a delightful living room with fireplace, library, and dining room. A motel-like wing, now refurbished, includes two rooms with fireplaces within view of the whirlpool tubs in the bathrooms. Jerry and Judy Goldman extend a special welcome to families with the configuration of a number of rooms, as well as a game room with an on-line computer, TV, piano, and toys. Couples, on the other hand, may prefer the suitably quiet and romantic rooms in the original part of this rambling inn, with its total of eight rooms and four two-bedroom suites, all with private bath. Summer facilities include a backyard heated pool and play area; there's also a year-round outside hot tub. The inn's relatively small and attractive dining room is currently the Ginger Tree (open to the public Wednesday through Sunday), an extremely popular Chinese restaurant (see *Dining Out*). Rooms, including a buffet breakfast, are $85–105 in summer and fall; suites, $145–185 for four people; in winter $95–125 for rooms, $180–200 for four people; the first child 12 or under is free in parent's room.

In Landgrove 05148

🐾✧ **The Landgrove Inn** (824-6673; 1-800-669-8466), RD Box 215, Landgrove–Weston Road. This red-clapboard building rambles back and around, beginning with the 1820 house, ending an acre or two away. The "Vermont continuous architecture" draws guests through a handsome lobby, past 18 crisp, bright rooms (16 with private bath) that meander off in all directions, through the inviting Rafter Room Lounge (huge, filled with games and books), to the attractive dining room in the original house. Our favorite rooms are tucked up under the eaves in the oldest part of the inn, papered in floral prints and furnished with carefully chosen antiques but with new baths. Many rooms are well suited to families, who also will appreciate the heated pool, tennis, a trout pond, lawn games, and paddle tennis. In winter, you can take a sleigh ride or step out onto the 15-mile cross-country trail system that leads through the picturesque village of Landgrove (just a church, former school, and salting of homes cupped in a hollow), on into surrounding national forest. Bromley Ski Area is just 6 miles away and Stratton is a 20-minute drive. Breakfast is an event here, served in the wood-beamed dining room with a many-windowed wall overlooking the garden. Dining Thursday through Sunday is by candle-light, with a choice of four entrées prepared by a well-respected local chef (see *Dining Out*). Jay and Kathy Snyder run this very special place. $85–130 per couple B&B, $5–25 per child in the same room with parent; add 10 percent for service.

White Sky Guest Farm (824-6100), RR 1, Box 212. An attractive rehabbed old farmhouse set in 55 acres of farmland, tastefully furnished with some unusual original artwork. Matt and Anna Marie Stori offer five rooms—cozy doubles and a two-bedroom suite with living room and fireplace; all have private bath. $65–87.50 for rooms, $140–195 for the suite; multi-day rates.

The Meadowbrook Inn (824-6444; 1-800-498-6445), RR 1, Box 145, Route 11. Tony and Madeleine Rundella's forested retreat has eight guest rooms, all with private bath, five of them with fireplace and two-person whirlpool tub, plus comfortable lounging areas and a dining room that's open to the public for dinner Friday and Saturday and holiday Sundays at noon. Their 26-km trail system is available to guests in all seasons for hiking, biking, nature walks, and cross-country skiing (for which they provide instruction and rentals). Rates range from $85–120 for the Magnolia Room to $140–175 for the spacious Delphinium, depending on the season.

In and around Londonderry

Frog's Leap Inn (824-3019; 1-887-FROGSLEAP), Route 100, Londonderry 05148. Formerly the Highland House and one of the oldest inns in the area, this classic Colonial built in 1842 and set well back from the road above a sloping lawn was acquired by Kraig and Dorenna Hart in 1998. The estatelike place has 32 acres of pasture and forests with 1½ miles of hiking and cross-country trails, an outdoor heated swimming pool, and a tennis court. There are eight rooms with private bath in the main house, and another eight (four of which are suites) with private bath in the annex, plus the Tad Pool House, which has a large two-bedroom suite with a kitchen and a deck overlooking the pool. B&B rates ($110–185 per room) include a continental breakfast delivered to your room as well as a full breakfast and afternoon tea; add $30 per person for MAP and a fine four-course dinner.

The Londonderry Inn (824-5226), Route 100, South Londonderry 05155. Built in 1826 as the Melendy Dairy Farm but an inn since the 1940s, about as rambling as an inn can be, with 25 guest rooms of varied sizes and shapes and 20 baths (some rooms share a bath); good for families. Public rooms are large, bright, and warm. Jim and Jean Cavanagh delight in helping plan guests' daily itineraries. Children are welcome. There is an attractive dining room; dinner on Friday, Saturday, and holidays (except in spring); a tavern, a game room with table tennis and billiards, and a swimming pool. $39–105 per couple, depending on the season, including buffet breakfast; $12–25 per extra person in a family room. Three downstairs rooms are handicapped-accessible. Cash or check; no plastic.

The Three Clock Inn (824-6327), Middletown Road, South Londonderry 05155. This gourmet getaway is tucked up on a hilly village back street. Better known as a restaurant (see *Dining Out*), it also offers four rooms, one with a fireplace ($105–129), a two-bedroom suite ($95–105 for two, $160–165 for four), and two rooms with shared bath ($75–85). In summer, the garden is a profusion of flowers, and in winter, Bromley is just a few minutes' drive. Rates include a full breakfast.

MOTELS

Palmer House Resort (362-3600; 1-800-917-6245), P.O. Box 657, Manchester Center 05255. A luxury motel with 40 rooms with color TV, free coffee, a pool, whirlpool, and sauna; plus fishing in a private, stocked trout pond, tennis, and a nine-hole golf course; there's an adjacent restaurant. Continental breakfast is included in room rates of $65–150, $150–300 for suites, depending on the season.

&. **The Manchester View** (362-2739; 1-800-548-4141), Manchester Center 05255. On Route 7A north of town with marvelous views. Thirty-five rooms with fridge, three 2-bedroom suites, and seven 1-bedroom suites (most with fireplace, living room, and two-person Jacuzzi); also handicapped-accessible units. A former barn now holds a breakfast room. Facilities include a heated outdoor pool in summer. Golf and tennis available at nearby Manchester Country Club. Rates are $80–200 based on double occupancy.

Swiss Inn (824-3442; 1-800-847-9477), Route 11, Londonderry 05148. From its exterior, this looks like a standard motel, but once inside, the differences are appealing. Joe and Pat Donahue feature Swiss dishes in their dining room (see *Dining Out*). Rooms are large enough to accommodate families, and public space includes a library as well as a sitting room and bar. There's also an outdoor pool. $50–99 includes a full breakfast.

The Barnstead Innstead (362-1619; 1-800-331-1619), Box 998, Manchester Center 05255. Just up Bonnet Street (Route 30), two blocks from the amenities of town, this is a genuine former hay barn converted into 14 motel units. It's all been done with consummate grace and charm, with many small touches like braided rugs and exposed old beams (but no room phones). There is also an outdoor pool. $55–120.

The Weathervane (362-2444; 1-800-262-1317), Route 7, Manchester 05254. Set back from the road with two picture windows in each of its

22 large units, each room has TV, free coffee, and hot chocolate. There is a "courtesy room" with books, games, and magazines; also a pool. $79–125 per couple.

CONDOMINIUMS AND SKI LODGES

Stratton Mountain Inn (1-800-STRATTON), at Stratton Mountain, Peru 05152, with 125 rooms, is the largest lodging facility on the mountain. Rooms have private bath, phone, and TV, and facilities include a large dining room, saunas, and whirlpools. On winter weekends $89–119 per room; $59 per person per day with lift ticket. Less during the week and in summer.

Stratton Village Lodge (1-800-STRATTON), adjacent to the Stratton base lodge, at Stratton Mountain, Peru 05152, has 91 studio-style units with kitchenette from $69 per person per day with lift ticket in winter. All resort guests have access to the sports center, with its indoor pool, exercise machines, and racquetball and tennis courts.

Birkenhaus (297-2000), at Stratton Mountain, Peru 05152. A modern but intimate lodge owned by Ina and Jan Dlouhy; the smallest and coziest of the lodging options on Stratton Mountain. The 18 rooms are simply, comfortably decorated, and a sitting room with fireplace overlooks the ski slopes. An appealing bar and outstanding dining room are also part of this picture. $59–159 per person MAP; add 10 percent service.

Bromley Village (824-5458; 1-800-865-4786), P.O. Box 1130, Manchester Center 05255, is a complex of attractive one- and two-bedroom units adjacent to the ski area. Summer facilities include a pool and tennis courts. In winter, you can walk to the lifts; there is also a shuttle bus. Call for rates.

Stratton Condominiums Villas (1-800-STRATTON), Stratton Mountain 05155. Roughly 100 of the resort's condominium units are in the rental pool at any given time, in a range of sizes and shapes; they run $69–99 per person per day with lift ticket. All resort guests have access to the sports center and its indoor pool, exercise machines, and racquetball and tennis courts (a fee is charged).

CAMPGROUNDS

See *To Do—Camping* for a list of campgrounds in various state forests and parks.

WHERE TO EAT

DINING OUT

Chantecleer (362-1616), Route 7A, East Dorset. Open 6–9:30, closed Tuesday. Long respected as one of Vermont's outstanding restaurants, Swiss chef Michael Baumann's establishment is known for such specialties as veal sweetbreads (prepared with sautéed shrimp and a fresh basil-tomato sauce with spaetzle; $23) and whole Dover sole ($26). Leave room for profiterole de maison or coupe Matterhorn. The setting is an elegantly remodeled old dairy barn with a massive fieldstone fireplace. There is an extensive wine list. Reservations essential. Expensive.

The Wilburton Inn (362-2500), River Road, Manchester Village. Dinner in the mansion's baronial billiard room is an event. One might start with lobster ravioli and proceed to cornmeal-encrusted trout with brown hazelnut butter sauce, poached salmon glazed with raspberry champagne, or roasted noisette of mountain lamb with garlic and rosemary. Moderate to expensive.

The Three Clock Inn (824-6327), Middletown Road, South Londonderry. Dinner daily except Monday; Sunday brunch from 11. Reserve and request directions. After a couple of up-and-down years, this dining landmark is back on dependable ground with new owners Marcie and Serge Roche, former head chef for the New York–based Restaurant Associates. The dining space has been expanded, and while the atmosphere is still rustic (low beams, glowing hearths), the decor is simpler (vanilla walls, white tablecloths). The à la carte menu changes frequently but might include sea bass in a potato and zucchini crust ($18), fettuccine with wild mushrooms ($14), or braised rabbit ($15). Desserts might include crème caramel à l'orange ($5). A wine cellar has been added.

Mistral's at Toll Gate (362-1779), off Routes 11/30 east of Manchester. Open for dinner daily except Wednesday. Reservations recommended. Chef Dana Markay and his wife, Cheryl, run this longtime dining landmark located in the old tollhouse once serving the Boston-to-Saratoga road. During warm-weather months a brook rushes along just under the windows. The menu might include roast duckling with strawberry sauce; salmon stuffed with lobster and vegetables; and sautéed veal pesto with fusilli. All are accompanied by a very long wine list. Entrées $18–24.

The Barrows House (867-4455), Route 30, Dorset. Open for dinner nightly, but weekends only in November. In a spacious, rather formal country dining room and its attached conservatory, both conscientiously appointed, diners can select from an à la carte menu that changes seasonally; nightly specials are also offered. Maine crab cakes or garlic-herb salmon roulade might be followed by pan-roasted veal tenderloin with pancetta, tomatoes, and shiitake mushrooms or grilled Vermont trout with cantaloupe-lime salsa. Entrées are $14.95–23.95; "lighter-side entrées"—maybe sautéed chicken breast with ham, mushrooms, and cheddar ($10.95), or ricotta, roasted pepper, and pesto–stuffed eggplant ($9.50)—are also available.

Inn at West View Farm (867-5715), Route 30, Dorset. Open for dinner daily except Sunday and Monday. Check ahead for winter-day closings. The Auberge Room is exceptionally attractive, and the food is dependably good. Entrées might include pan-roasted breast of duck with rhubarb, ginger, and risotto cake ($17.25); seared veal sweetbreads with pink peppercorns ($21); or smoked salmon ravioli in scallion and dill pasta with spiced tomato and fresh Romano ($17.95). In **Clancy's Tavern,** also part of the inn, you might dine on grilled bratwurst ($10.95) or crab cakes ($12.95).

The Black Swan (362-3807), Route 7A, Manchester Village (next to the Jelly Mill; see *Selective Shopping—Special Shops*). Open for dinner daily except Wednesday. The food in this crisply decorated and managed old brick Colonial house is a treat for the senses. A representative dinner might begin with chilled strawberry soup or mussels steamed in white wine, garlic, and cream sauce, and proceed to cashew chicken over white rice ($14.75) or sweetbreads of veal with ham and artichokes in a Madeira sauce ($18.50). Lighter fare is served in the **Mucky Duck Bistro.**

Silas Griffith Inn (293-5567), Main Street, Danby. This attractive, informal dining room, with a hearth and walls decorated with antique kitchen gadgets, is in the converted carriage house. Dinner, served at 7 PM by reservation, might begin with Brie baked with apple chutney or sausage-stuffed mushrooms, and the entrée (there's a sensible choice of four) might be lamb chops with rosemary and ginger, chicken breast with spicy peanut sauce, boned trout with bananas and almonds, or pork tenderloin with apples and sausage. The menu changes daily; $24 prix fixe.

Reluctant Panther (362-2568), Route 7A, Manchester Village. Open for dinner nightly except Tuesday and Wednesday. The greenhouse dining room is particularly pleasant and can be the setting for a memorable evening, beginning with hors d'oeuvres in the sitting room. The menu changes daily but the appetizers might include a trio of smoked shrimp, peppered mackerel, and mussels; the entrées, grilled tuna steak with cilantro-macadamia salsa; osso bucco with creamy garlic-Parmesan polenta; or herbed pork tenderloin with rum-soaked fruit compote. The wine list is extensive. Expensive.

The Dorset Inn (867-5500), Church Street, Dorset. Open daily for breakfast, lunch, and dinner. Chef Sissy Hicks can be relied on for outstanding New England fare. Begin dinner with steamed mussels, then follow it with a small Caesar salad and then crispy duck confit served with braised cabbage, wild rice, and plum chutney. Entrées $8–20.

Ginger Tree Restaurant at the Wiley Inn (824-5500), Route 11 between Manchester and Londonderry (1 mile east of Bromley). Open Wednesday through Sunday 6–10. The setting is a country inn dining room seating just 30, and the menu is classic Chinese. Elliott Nachwalter and Warren Hennikoff pride themselves on using only the freshest meats, poultry, and vegetables, and on preparing every dish to order. The menu changes nightly but a sample five-course meal ($17.50) might include hot and sour soup, a handmade all-vegetable egg roll, noodles in Peking sauce, Hunan spicy shrimp, and wok-stirred broccoli and straw mushrooms. Specific items are also available à la carte, as are cocktails and reasonably priced wines. The Wednesday all-you-can-eat buffet is $16.95. Reservations suggested.

The Equinox (362-4700), Manchester. Dinner is served Tuesday through Saturday in the formal, vaulted **Colonnade** dining room; Sunday brunch ($19 prix fixe) is a tradition for residents and visitors. You might dine on roast loin of lamb with parsnips and pears ($25); grilled yellow-fin tuna ($24); or grilled veal chop with corn, red pepper, and French bean ragout ($26). The attractive **Marsh Tavern** is open for lunch and dinner daily, serving hearty soups, salads, pastas, and such specials as Devonshire shepherd's pie, lobster ravioli, Yankee pot roast, and various seafood selections at moderate prices.

Bistro Henry (362-4982) at the Chalet Motel, Routes 11/30, Manchester. Open for dinner daily except Monday. Dina and Henry Bronson, who established a dynamite reputation during their stint at Willow Pond (see below), now have their own Mediterranean-style dining room with a casual atmosphere, a full bar, and a *Wine Spectator* award for excellence. You might begin with a vegetable and Vermont goat cheese strudel ($6.50) and dine on the pasta of the day or Merlot-braised lamb shank. Entrées are $13.50–21.

The Restaurant at Willow Pond (362-4733), Route 7 north of Manchester Center, has a recently revamped restaurant in a restored 1770s farmhouse. Dinner every night (but check in the off-seasons). The menu is "authentic" Northern Italian. You might begin with a spinach salad, or grilled eggplant with a three-cheese-and-spinach stuffing and a fresh diced tomato and porcini mushroom sauce. Entrées include linguine alla pesto ($12.95) and veal piccata ($19.95).

Swiss Inn (824-3442), Route 11, Londonderry. Open to the public for dinner daily except Wednesday, the Swiss Inn has a strong local following. While ownership is no longer Swiss, the current owner-chef seems to have the right touch with such dishes as Geschnetzeltes (veal à la Swiss), beef fondue, and chicken Lugano (chicken breast dipped in a Gruyère cheese batter); also Continental dishes like shrimp à la Marseilles and veal Marsala. Fondues are a specialty. Entrées run $11.99–19.99.

𝒮 **Johnny Seesaw's** (824-5533), Route 11, Peru. A Prohibition-era dance hall, then one of New England's first ski lodges, this atmospheric inn is well worth a dinnertime visit even if you don't happen to be staying there. The extensive menu usually includes a choice of veal and seafood dishes and pork chops Vermont-style, but huge prime rib of beef is the house special (children can always get hamburgers or pasta as well as half-sized portions). Adult entrées: $12.95–19.95. Soft music played live on weekends.

𝒮 **The Landgrove Inn** (824-6673), Landgrove–Weston Road, Landgrove. Dinner by reservation Thursday through Sunday. This fine old inn is off by itself up dirt roads at the edge of a tiny village. Meals are by candlelight in a delightful old dining room with windows overlooking the garden. We began with a delectable butternut squash, apple, and onion soup; dined on a moist almond-crusted salmon with Thai red curry sauce ($18.25); and sampled the vegetable strudel with saffron tomato sauce ($12.75). Children's portions and delicious desserts.

Ye Olde Tavern (362-0611), Route 7A north, Manchester Center. Open daily from 11:30 AM for lunch and dinner. A 1790 tavern theoretically specializing in "authentic American" dinner dishes like roast tom turkey and pot roast (both $12.95), but seafood fettuccine ($16.95) is also on the menu, and the Tavern Seafood Stew is laced with vermouth, tomato, and fennel ($16.95). At lunch, try the Quacker (grilled duck with sliced apple, cucumber, bacon, and mayonnaise on whole wheat toast; $6.95). One of the better values in town.

Downstairs at the Playhouse (824-5288), Weston Playhouse, on the green in Weston. Open for dinner on theater nights beginning at 5:30; 5 on Sunday. A pleasant dining room by the falls, good, moderately priced dinners, and then you're there. Reserve. (See also *Entertainment—Theater.*)

See also the "The Lower Connecticut and West River Valleys" for Three Mountain Inn in Jamaica.

EATING OUT

In and around Manchester

The Artist's Palate Café at the Southern Vermont Arts Center (362-4220), West Road, Manchester Village. Open for lunch, June through mid-October, Tuesday through Saturday 11:30–3, Sunday noon–3. The food is fine and the setting is superb: a pleasant indoor room or the outside terrace, both with views over the sculpture garden and down the mountain to Manchester Village.

Little Rooster Cafe (362-3496), Route 7A South, Manchester Center. Breakfast and lunch from 7 AM; closed Wednesday. An offshoot of Chantecleer (see *Dining Out*), an "eclectic European café" serving exquisite waffles and omelets, café au lait and cappuccino, baguette sandwiches. Expensive by breakfast and lunch standards, but special.

❧ **Laney's Restaurant** (362-4456), Routes 11/30, Manchester Center. Open from 5 PM, this is a festive, kid-friendly spot, specializing in exotic pizza from a wood-fired brick oven, hickory-smoked ribs, grilled steaks, and salads; draft beer in frosted mugs.

❧ **Savino's** (362-4389), Routes 11/30, Manchester Center. A locally popular "ristorante Italiano" with a wide range of antipasti and pasta, veal dishes, and steak from a charcoal grill; children's menu.

❧ **Sirloin Saloon** (362-2600), Routes 11/30, Manchester Center. This is a large, many-cornered, Tiffany lamp–lit, polished-brass place that's always packed; there's a huge salad bar and a children's menu.

The Perfect Wife (362-2817), Routes 11/30, one mile east of the Route 7 overpass. Open Tuesday through Sunday 5–10 for dinner. Amy Walter features crab cakes, curry-crusted calamari, grilled shrimp and scallops, and even Szechwan dim sum. There's live music in the tavern every weekend.

✒ **Quality Restaurant** (362-9839), Main Street, Manchester Center. Still the place for local gossip; also for breakfast, lunch, and dinner. Photos depict a less self-conscious Main Street, but a print of Norman Rockwell's *War News* behind the counter alerts you to the fact that in the '40s, this was no ordinary eatery. The print features Clarence Comar, former owner of the Quality, at a time when Rockwell and Lowell Thomas frequented the place. This is still a good bet for lunch and dinner. Sandwiches are served 11 AM to closing, along with blackboard dinner specials, wine, beer, and "kidsuppers." Blackboard specials: $6–12.

Candeleros (362-0836), Main Street, Manchester Center, is a Mexican cantina open daily for lunch and dinner; there's a pleasant outdoor patio in summer.

The Buttery (362-3544), second floor at the Jelly Mill (see *Selective Shopping—Special Shops*), Route 7A, Manchester Center. An attractive, welcoming spot for lunch or brunch daily, starting at 10 AM: eggs Benedict or Blackstone, chicken salad with currants, soups, and sinful desserts.

Up for Breakfast and Dinner Too (362-4204), 710 Main Street, Manchester. Breakfast Monday through Friday 6 AM–noon, weekends 7–1, dinner nightly 5:30–9. Bright, art-decked space with tables and a counter, an open kitchen, and blackboard menu specials—maybe a sausage, apple, and cheddar omelet, trout with eggs and hash browns, or wild turkey hash—and innovative specials later in the day as well. Worth climbing the stairs.

Mika's (362-8100), Avalanche Motor Lodge, Routes 11/30, Manchester. Open daily for lunch and dinner for fans of Chinese and Japanese cooking; sushi bar.

Zoey's Deli & Bakery (362-0005), Routes 11/30, Manchester, serves breakfast and lunch daily 7–4. Nearly 20 varieties of specialty breads draw faithful customers.

For pizzas: **Christo's** (362-2408) on Main Street; **Marilyn Bruno's** (362-4469) on Center Hill; and **Manchester Pizza House** (362-3338) in the Manchester Shopping Center all offer high-quality pizza as well as salads, subs, grinders, and Italian lunches and dinners. All are in Manchester; all serve beer and wine and will deliver locally.

Elsewhere

White Dog Tavern (293-5477), Route 7 north of Danby. Open for dinner Tuesday through Sunday. This is an 1812 farmhouse with a central chimney and four fireplaces, each serving as the focal point of a dining room. There's a cheery bar, and an outdoor deck in summer. The blackboard menu includes clams, shrimp, sandwiches, and the house special—chicken breasts à la Tom, served up with herbs, garlic, and melted cheese over spaghetti. Options might include blackened catfish and clams zuppa. Inexpensive to moderate.

Danby Village Restaurant (293-6003), Main Street, Danby. Open for lunch, dinner, and Sunday brunch. Closed Wednesday. We hear good things about the Greek fare and vegetarian creations. Dinner entrées include moussaka ($13.95) and lamb shanks braised in red wine, garlic, and tomatoes ($15.95). The prime-rib special Thursdays is $12.95. At lunch, try the spanakopita (spinach pie).

The Barn Restaurant and Tavern (325-3088), Route 30, Pawlet. Open year-round for dinner. This is a genuine old barn with a huge fireplace and a view of the Mettawee River. The large menu offers something for everybody—homemade ravioli, chicken Pawlet (marinated in buttermilk, breaded, and baked with lemon shallot butter), or a 20-ounce charbroiled steak. There's also a salad bar and children's menu. Moderate.

Stoddard's Market (824-5060), Main Street, Londonderry. Open 5:30 AM–10 PM; 6 AM–9 PM Sunday. An old reliable and local hangout: counter and booths, soup of the day in a real bowl (not Styrofoam), and a great turkey sandwich for $2.50.

Jake's Marketplace Café (824-6614), Mountain Marketplace at the junction of Routes 100 and 11, Londonderry. A local institution with a lively sports lounge, a lunch counter, and a pleasant pink dining room. Overstuffed sandwiches, salads, homemade soups, burgers, and New York sirloin are the order of most days, along with pizzas, hoagies, and calzones.

Gran'ma Frisby's (824-5931), Route 11 east of Londonderry. Open for lunch and dinner. When Magic Ski Area is open, you're lucky to get in the door of this wonderfully pubby place. Known for its fries and fresh-dough pizza, this is a friendly, reasonably priced find any time of year.

The Station Restaurant and Ice Cream Parlor (325-3041), School Street, Pawlet. Open 6 AM until 3 in winter, later in summer. If you think about it, railroad depots make perfect diners—with the counter and a row of stools down the length of the building and tables along the sides. This classic 1905 depot was moved here from another town and positioned above a babbling brook. It's a particularly pleasant place. Coffee cups bearing regulars' names hang by the door.

Mulligans (297-9293) at Stratton Mountain also has a Manchester Village locale (362-3663). This spacious, pleasant, family-priced restaurant is open for lunch and dinner; good for burgers, sandwiches, salads, and dinner options like Thai basil chicken and lobster and seafood manicotti. Children's specials include a Ninja Turtle Burger and Gorilla Cheese.

Outback Food & Spirits (297-FOOD), Route 30, Bondville, serves dinner daily from 7 PM, lunch on weekends, with live music on Saturday.

The Bryant House (824-6287), Route 100, Weston. Now owned by the neighboring Vermont Country Store (see *Selective Shopping—General Stores*), this fine old house belonged to one family—the Bryants—from

Weston Playhouse

the time it was built in 1827 until the family line petered out. Upstairs, a special room is set aside to look as it did in the 1890s. There are plenty of salads, sandwiches, and Vermont-style chicken pie. Lunch served 11:30–3.

ICE CREAM AND SNACKS

Wilcox Brothers Dairy (362-1223), Route 7A south, Manchester. Some of the creamiest, most delectable flavors in Vermont are made in this family-owned and -run dairy, available at the grocery store and in a variety of local restaurants.

Mother Myrick's Ice Cream Parlor & Fudge Factory (362-1560), Route 7A, Manchester Center. Open daily 11 AM–midnight in summer; fountain treats, cappuccino, sumptuous baked goods, and handmade chocolates and fudge concocted daily.

ENTERTAINMENT

MUSIC

Vermont Symphony Orchestra (1-800-VSO-9293). The new Riley Rink at Hunter Park, on Route 7A, Manchester Center, serves as the distinguished orchestra's permanent summer home. When it's not on tour, especially around the Fourth of July weekend, the symphony's concerts in the arena are major events. The acoustics are fine, and one side of the arena swings up and open to permit part of the audience to picnic on a grassy bank.

Kinhaven Music School (824-3365), Lawrence Hill Road, Weston, a nationally recognized summer camp for young musicians, presents free concerts by students July through mid-August, Friday at 4 and Sunday at 2:30. Faculty perform Saturday at 8 PM. Performances are in the Concert Hall, high in the meadow of the school's 31-acre campus. It still looks more like a farm than a school. Picnics are encouraged.

Strattonfest (297-0100), Stratton Mountain, July and August. This series usually includes folk, jazz, classical, and country-western music on successive weeks.

Manchester Music Festival (362-1956; 1-800-639-5868), West Road, Manchester Center. A seven-week series of Thursday-evening chamber music concerts in July and August, with performances at the Southern Vermont Art Center's Arkell Pavilion, Burr and Burton's Smith Center for the Arts, and the First Congregational Church in Manchester; also fall and winter performances in Manchester and Dorset.

THEATER

Dorset Playhouse (867-5777). The Dorset Players, a community theater group formed in 1927, actually owns the beautiful playhouse in the center of Dorset and produces winter performances there. In summer, the Dorset Theatre Festival stages new plays as well as classics, performed by a resident professional group. Mid-June through October, 8:30 nightly; 5 and 9 PM Saturday.

Weston Playhouse (824-5288). Not long after the Civil War, townspeople built a second floor in their oldest church on the green and turned the lower level into a theater, producing ambitious plays such as Richard Sheridan's *The Rivals*. Theatrics remained a part of community life, and in the 1930s, a summer resident financed the remodeling of the defunct church into a real theater. Now billed as "the oldest professional theater in Vermont," the Weston Playhouse has had its ups and downs over the last half century or so, withstanding fire (in 1962 it burned to the ground) and two floods. Now nonprofit, with a company composed largely of professional Equity actors, it routinely draws rave reviews. Quality aside, Weston couldn't be more off-Broadway. The pillared theater (the facade is that of the old church) fronts on a classic village common and backs on the West River, complete with a waterfall and Holsteins grazing in the meadow beyond. Many patrons come early to dine "Downstairs at the Playhouse" and linger after the show to join cast members at the Cabaret (reservations for the Cabaret are frequently necessary). Performances are every night except Monday (plus Wednesday and Sunday matinees), late June through Labor Day weekend. Tickets run $19–24.

FILM

Derry Twin Cinema (824-3331), Routes 11 and 100, includes a bar and tables in rear rows; shows two first-run movies nightly.

Manchester Cinema (362-1229), Manchester Center.

SELECTIVE SHOPPING

ANTIQUES SHOPS

See *Special Events* for the Weston Antiques Show and Stratton Antiques Festival.

The Carriage Trade Antiques Center (362-1125), Route 7, north of Manchester Center. Open daily, displaying quality antiques representing more than 50 dealers.

Weston Antiques Barn (824-4097), open daily except Wednesday. One mile north of the village. A multiple-dealer shop.

Carlson's Antiques (867-4510), on the Dorset green. This two-story shop offers Early American and Victorian furniture, paintings, glass, and china, plus textiles such as antique needlepoint pillows, hooked rugs, and fine linens. Open daily.

East-West Antiques (325-3466), Route 30, Pawlet, offers antiques and artifacts from Indonesia and Ireland; also fabrics and women's clothing.

The Danby Antiques Center (293-9984), Main Street, Danby. Open 10–5 daily April through December; Thursday through Monday from January through March. Displays American country and formal furniture and accessories from 24 dealers in 11 rooms and the barn.

Danby North Antiques (293-5864), Route 7A, Danby. The remarkable 1870s Phillips mansion, a gingerbread landmark locally known as the Haunted House, now contains Sandra LeCompte's stock of Victoriana, plus consignments from other dealers.

ART GALLERIES

The Southern Vermont Arts Center (see *Museums*). In addition to its solo shows held throughout the year, the SVA hosts a Members' Show in early summer and a National Fall Exhibition. There are also outdoor sculpture shows, May through October, and other special exhibits in winter.

The Gallery on the Green (362-2097), across from the Equinox hotel, Manchester, is a branch of the Woodstock gallery run by Janice and Jim Allmon, featuring New England artists.

Gallery North Star (362-4541), Route 7A, Manchester Village. Open daily 10–5. An offshoot of the Grafton gallery, showcasing Vermont-based artists.

The Peel Gallery (293-5230), Route 7, 2 miles north of Danby Village. Represents 50 American artists whose works are dramatically displayed in a restored 18th-century barn. Margaret and Harris Peel launched this showcase 19 years ago. Shows and receptions are scheduled between Memorial Day and Columbus Day. Among those represented are Patrick Farrow, Sidney and Barbara Willis, and Larry Webster, along with several other nationally known artists. The gallery is open daily (except Tuesday) 10–5 year-round; open daily in July and August.

Tilting at Windmills Gallery (362-3022), Routes 11/30, Manchester Center. Open daily. An unusually large gallery with a wide selection of market-geared art.

Todd Gallery (864-5606), south edge of the village of Weston. Housed in an 1840s carriage barn, this attractive gallery displays owner Robert Todd's watercolors of Vermont and Ireland. Also whimsical photography and original sculpture, and unusual pieces crafted by Vermont artists.

BOOKSTORES

The Northshire Bookstore (362-2200), Main Street, Manchester Center, is highly regarded as one of the most complete in New England. The Morrows have filled the venerable Colburn House with a wide range of unusually well-displayed volumes, and in summer books overflow onto the porch. An amazingly wide range of adult titles, children's books, and records are featured, along with an extraordinarily comprehensive stock of current and classic paperbacks. The store and the Manchester Historical Society cosponsor frequent author lectures and book signings. The Morrows also run the **Next Chapter** (362-1006), a trove of used and antiquarian books, next door to the main store.

CRAFTS SHOPS

The American Collector (362-1002), opposite the Equinox hotel in Manchester Village, carries high-quality creations of contemporary craftspeople from around the country, including redware, furniture, clothing, and paintings by local artists.

Frog Hollow at the Equinox (362-3321), a few doors north in the same complex, is the third Vermont State Crafts Center, showcasing the work of state artisans, painters, sculptors, furniture makers, and jewelers.

The Porter House of Fine Crafts (362-4789), Green Mountain Village Shops, Manchester Center. Open daily 10–6. Unusual jewelry and handcrafts, clothing, toys, fabric art, kitchenware, alternative music.

Dorset Craft Center (362-8123), Route 30, Dorset. An old farmhouse has been converted into a studio showroom for baskets, pottery, candles, woodenware, stained glass, and quilts.

D. Lasser Ceramics (824-6183), Route 100, Londonderry. Open daily 9–6. A studio showroom with potters doing their thing, and shelves—inside and out—filled with bright pitchers and platters, bowls and vases, mugs and plates, all highly original and affordable. We're delighted with the multicolored "stix" we bought that hold either candles or flowers.

Vitriesse Glass Gallery (824-6634), Route 100, Weston Village. Open daily except Tuesday. Lucy Bergamini's intricate glass-bead jewelry is very special. The gallery also carries richly colored blown-glass vessels, goblets, and perfume bottles.

The Pawlet Potter (325-3100), School Street, Pawlet. Marion Waldo McChesney works in her studio on the ground level of her restored, brick landmark house, where customers can watch her turn out one-of-a-kind pieces: vases, platters, and "seastones"—amazing floating ceramic disks. Ceramic jewelry and a variety of unusual designs make this small studio—with a rocker in which you may want just to immerse yourself in the creative atmosphere—well worth a visit.

Danby Marble Company (293-5425), Route 7 north of Danby Village, open daily May through October and from November 20 through December 30. At first glance, this is just another array of marble bookends, lamps, chessboards, candleholders, trivets, and vases. Look more closely, though, and you'll find that this is a showcase for marble from throughout the East. (Danby itself is the site of what's billed as "the largest underground marble quarry in the world.") Tom Martin, owner of this store, cuts marble to whatever sizes and shapes you may desire.

Weston House Quilt Collection (824-3636), Route 100, Weston Village. Joanne and Richard Eggert have assembled one of the state's standout selections of both hand- and machine-made quilts and quilting fabrics, books, and notions.

Susan Sargent Designs (824-3184), Route 100, Weston Village. Open daily. The store features Sargent's striking designs woven into rugs, pillows, and throws. Other rugs, spreads, and curtains are also carried.

FACTORY OUTLETS

Manchester merchants refuse to call these stores "outlets." Prices are slightly higher than at factory stores, but they're lower than retail. The list is lengthening quickly.

Manchester Commons and **Manchester Square,** the glass-and-wood anchor complex at and near the junction of Route 7A and Routes 11/30 in Manchester Center, presently house: Giorgio Armani, Emporio Armani, Baccarat, Boston Traders, Brooks Brothers, Coach, Cole Haan, Crabtree & Evelyn, Garnet Hill, Dansk, Joan & David, Calvin Klein, Levi's, Maidenform, Movado, Polo/Ralph Lauren, Seiko, and Timberland, among others.

Equinox Square, a smaller complex tucked behind Friendly's, houses Burberry's and Christian Dior, among others.

Manchester Marketplace Outlet Shops (next to Dexter Shoe) harbors London Fog, among others.

Battenkill Plaza Outlet Center (also on Route 7A south near its junction with Routes 11/30) houses six more shops, including Anne Klein and Van Heusen.

J. K. Adams Co., Factory and Factory Store, Route 30, has a complete line of its fine wood products: sugar maple butcher blocks, knife racks, spice racks, cheese and carving boards, with complementary accessories. Discounted "seconds" on the second floor.

Weston Bowl Mill (824-6219), Route 100, Weston. Open year-round, 8–6 in summer; 9–5 in winter; 10–5 on Sunday. This classic old wood mill has long produced quality woodenware, available throughout the state and here at factory prices. There is an amazing variety of boxes, furnishings, toys, and furniture, as well as bowls; request a catalog.

CHRISTINA TREE

Everyone shops at Machs' in Pawlet

GENERAL STORES

The Vermont Country Store (824-3184), Route 100, Weston Village. Open year-round, Monday through Saturday 9–5. Established by Vrest Orton in 1946 and billed as America's first restored country store, this pioneer nostalgia venture also includes one of the country's first mail-order catalogs. The original store (actually an old Masons Hall) has since quintupled in size and spilled into four adjacent buildings. The specialty of both the catalog (which accounts for 75 percent of the company's business) and the store is the functional item that makes life easy, especially anything that's difficult to find nowadays—jumbo metal hairpins, hardwood coat hangers, slippery-elm throat lozenges, garter belts. Lyman, the present Orton-in-charge, has a penchant for newfangled gadgets, such as a plastic frame to hold baseball caps in dishwashers. He's a zealot when it comes to basics that seem to have disappeared, and he frequently finds someone to replicate them, as in the case of the perfect potato masher. The store's own line of edibles features the Vermont Common Cracker, unchanged since 1812, still stamped out in a patented 19th-century machine.

J. J. Hapgood Store (824-5911), off Route 11, Peru. Daily 8:30–6. Nancy and Frank Kirkpatrick's genuine general store has a potbellied stove, old-fashioned counters filled with food, and some clothing staples; geared to locals as well as tourists.

Peltier's General Merchandise (867-4400), Route 30, Dorset Village. A village landmark since 1816: staples and then some, including almost any kind of fish on request, baking to order, Vermont products, wines, and gourmet items like hearts of palm and Tiptree jams. Because there are no lunch or snack shops in Dorset, this also serves the purpose; good for picnic fare.

Machs' General Store (325-3405), Route 30, Pawlet Village. The focal point of this genuine old emporium is described under Pawlet (see *Villages*), but the charm of this family-run place goes beyond its water view. Built as a hotel, it's filled with a wide variety of locally useful merchandise.

The Weston Village Store (824-5477), Route 100, Weston. Open daily. A standard country emporium catering to visitors.

SPECIAL SHOPS

Orvis Retail Store (362-3750), Route 7A, Manchester Center, supplying the needs of anglers and other sportsmen since 1856. Known widely for its mail-order catalog, the second oldest in the country, Orvis specializes in the fishing rods made in the factory out back; also other fishing tackle and gear, country clothes, and other small luxury items—from silk underwear to welcome mats—that make the difference in country, or would-be country, living. Don't miss the "bargain basement."

Herdsmen Leathers, Manchester Center. Open daily, year-round, calling itself "New England's finest leather shop": coats, boots, shoes, and accessories; watch for sales.

The Enchanted Doll House, Route 7, north of Manchester Center. Open daily 9–5, Sunday 10–5. Twelve rooms full of dolls, dollhouses, toys, miniatures, games, and books, for children as well as collectors.

The Jelly Mill, Route 7A, Manchester Center. Open daily 10–6. A three-story barn filled with folk art, crystal, cards, crafts, toys, and other assorted gifts.

Equinox Village Shops. This cluster of historic buildings across from the Equinox hotel in Manchester Village includes **Irish Too,** the **Claire Murray Shop,** and **Ex Libris,** an unusual collection of books, stationery, desk accessories, new and collector's writing instruments.

Equinox Valley Nursery, Route 7A, south of Manchester. An outstanding farm stand and nursery managed by three generations of the Preuss family; good for picking vegetables, berries in-season. Especially famous in the fall for the 100,000 pounds of pumpkins it produces, also for its display of scarecrows and pumpkin faces. Sells pumpkin bread, pie, ice cream, and marmalade, along with other farm-stand staples, annuals, perennials, and shrubs. During January and February, the family usually makes 1,000 jars of jams and jellies.

SPECIAL EVENTS

March: Spring skiing, sugaring.
April: **Trout season** opens; **Easter parades and egg hunts** at ski areas. **White-water canoeing** on the West River.

May: **Vermont Symphony Orchestra** performs at Hunter Park; **Hildene** opens (see *Historic Homes*).

June: **Strawberry festivals** in Dorset; the annual **Antique and Classic Car Show** at Hildene (see *Historic Homes*) and **vintage car climb** to Equinox Summit; **Southern Vermont Art** series opens (see *Art Galleries*).

July: Manchester Center's **old-fashioned Fourth** is a daylong celebration that culminates in fireworks. Hildene Meadowlands hosts the **Vermont Symphony Orchestra** at a tailgate picnic and concert on July 2 or 3.

July through mid-August: **Kinhaven Music School** concert series (see *Entertainment—Music*); **Dorset Playhouse** and **Weston Playhouse** open (see *Entertainment—Theater*); a major **antiques show** held at Hildene Meadows in even years, at Dorset in odd ones. **Manchester Music Festival** (see *Entertainment*). **Strattonfest** at Stratton Mountain (see *Entertainment*).

August: **Southern Vermont Crafts Fair**—juried exhibitors, entertainment, food, and music; **Manchester Dance** (mid-August); **Manchester Horse Show** (late August); **polo matches** and an **antiques show** at Stratton Mountain (first week). **Stratton Antiques Festival**—every August, usually the first or second weekend, the base lodge hosts a multi-exhibitor, high-quality show under the auspices of the Vermont Antiques Dealers' Association. Fine New England furniture, paintings, and decorative objects are particularly noteworthy.

September: **Annual Maple Leaf Half-Marathon, Stratton Wurstfest** on Labor Day weekend. **Stratton Arts Festival** (297-3265), beginning second weekend and running through mid-October, inaugurated in 1963, is a major display of Vermont crafts and art, along with a performing arts series, in the base lodge at Stratton Mountain. The **Manchester Autumnfest** is a concurrent presentation of dance, theater, and music. **Peru Fair:** Just 1 day (the fourth Saturday), considered one of Vermont's most colorful (and crowded), it includes a pig roast, crafts, food, and entertainment.

October: **Weston Antiques Show,** first weekend, one of the state's oldest and most respected, staged in the Weston Playhouse (see *Entertainment—Theater*).

November: **Harvest dinners** and **wild-game suppers** abound; check local papers and bulletin boards.

December: **Christmas Prelude** (weekend events in Manchester including Vermont's largest potluck dinner, first three weekends) and **Candlelight Tours of Hildene** (between Christmas and New Year's; see *Historic Homes*), including sleigh rides, refreshments in the barn, music on the organ.

Grafton, Chester, Saxtons River, and Bellows Falls

Some of Vermont's smallest villages loom large on the state's tourist map. Such is the case with Grafton, a back-road community of 600 that a nonprofit foundation has "restored"—from its centerpiece inn to its cheese factory.

To a less dramatic degree, neighboring towns have also replaced old industries with businesses catering to visitors. Chester offers more than a dozen places to stay, a half-dozen galleries, and surprisingly varied shopping and dining. Saxtons River is known for summer theater and crafts. Bellows Falls, an old railroading village in the town of Rockingham, remains an Amtrak stop; train buffs can actually switch here to the *Green Mountain Flyer* excursion train that runs up along the Connecticut and then the Williams River to Chester. But without a car, or at least two wheels, you will miss the Old Rockingham Meeting House and the delightfully unrestored villages of Windham and Athens.

GUIDANCE

Grafton Information Center (843-2255), Route 35 just south of the village center. Open May through October, 10–6. Funded by the Windham Foundation, this is southern Vermont's most inviting and complete information center (it doubles as a community center in the off-season). You can see a short video on Grafton and pick up information on just about anything of interest in the area.

Great Falls Region Chamber of Commerce (463-4280), Windham Hotel lobby, P.O. Box 554, Bellows Falls 05101. The downtown, year-round office is open weekdays 10–3, dispensing information about the town of Rockingham—which includes Bellows Falls, Rockingham Village, and Saxtons River. Request the *Guided Walking Tour* brochure to the town's historic district, and its *Building on the Past* pamphlet about the town's past.

The **Chester Chamber of Commerce** (875-2939), P.O. Box 623, Chester 05143, maintains a seasonal information booth on the green. Pick up its walking-tour guide to 14 buildings on the National Register of Historic Places.

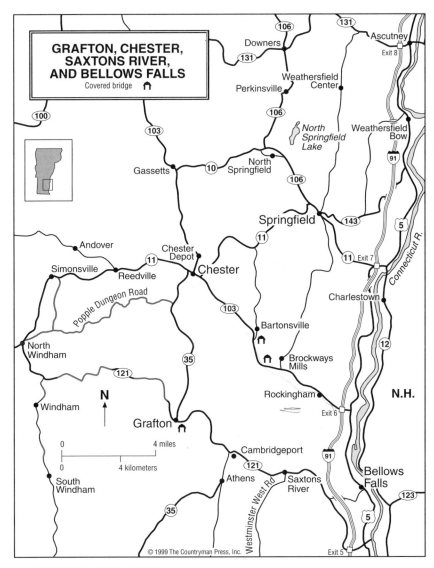

GETTING THERE

By bus: **Vermont Transit** from points in Connecticut and Massachusetts stops at Bellows Falls (at Fletcher's drugstore in the square) and in Chester (at the Rexall next to the Fullerton Inn).

By train: **Amtrak** trains stop at Bellows Falls en route to New York City and Washington. Call 1-800-USA-RAIL.

MEDICAL EMERGENCY

Chester and Gassetts (875-3200); Bellows Falls, Grafton, Rockingham (463-4223).

Health Center at Bellows Falls (463-3903), Bellows Falls.

Springfield Hospital (885-2151), 25 Ridgewood Road, Springfield.

VILLAGES

Grafton. Prior to the Civil War, Grafton boasted more than 1,480 souls and 10,000 sheep. Wool was turned into 75,000 yards of Grafton cloth annually; soapstone from 13 local quarries left town in the shape of sinks, stoves, inkwells, and foot warmers.

But then one in three of Grafton's men marched off to the Civil War, and few returned. Sheep farming, too, "went west." An 1869 flood destroyed the town's six dams and its road. The new highway bypassed Grafton. The town's tavern, however, built in 1801, entered a golden era. Innkeeper Marlan Phelps invested his entire California Gold Rush fortune in adding a third floor and double porches, and his brother Francis organized a still-extant cornet band. Guests included Emerson, Thoreau, and Kipling; later both Woodrow Wilson and Teddy Roosevelt visited.

By 1940, however, the Tavern was sagging, and nearly all the 80-some houses in town were selling—with plenty of acreage—for just $3,000–5,000.

Enter Matthew Hall, a New York financier and descendant of the town's first pastor, who had been summering here since 1936. Hall's "Aunt Pauline" Fiske, who often joined him for the summer, had financed the restoration of some fine, three-dimensional murals in the Congregational church. On her death, Miss Fiske left a fortune in trust to her two nephews, Hall and Dean Mathey, of Princeton, New Jersey. A note requested that its use be for an unusual worthy cause, something she would have liked. For five years, the men couldn't hit on a suitable scheme. Then one Vermont morning, Mathey woke Hall with the news that he had "found the answer to Aunt Pauline's money . . . Grafton."

Incorporated in 1963 under the name Windham, the foundation immediately focused on the town's rotting core. A restored version of the last store was opened, complete with lunch counter. After roofing a blacksmith shop, the foundation went on to tackle the unwinterized Old Tavern. The architects of Old Deerfield in Massachusetts left the rocking chairs on the Old Tavern's front porch and its handsome face unchanged. New heating, wiring, an elevator, 20 guest rooms, and 14 private baths were added.

The Windham Foundation has expanded the inn by adding rooms in restored homes across the way, also incorporating four complete houses and a luxurious stable for guests who want to bring a horse. It owns 50 buildings and 2,000 acres in town and, among other things, has buried the village's electric, phone, and cable TV wires. There are three museums, demonstration flocks of sheep (there's a viewing area in the new sheep barn), and marked footpaths on which visitors can wander

Grafton Town Hall

down past the sheep and pond, into the woods, and home again. Some fine B&Bs have opened around town—along with art galleries and assorted shops. Grafton has become a magnet for tourists, especially during the Columbus Day foliage weekend, so to enjoy its ambience, try to visit in the quieter weeks.

Chester (population: 2,800) encompasses three distinct villages within a few miles, each of them worth noting. The old core is centered by the historic, double-porched Fullerton Inn, which is flanked by an attractive lineup of shops and restaurants and set back from the old highway (Route 11) by a stringbean green. Across the road stands a fine old brick schoolhouse, now the Historical Society and Art Guild, in which you can see changing art exhibits and learn about the town's colorful history, including the story of Clarence Adams, a prominent citizen who broke into more than 50 businesses and homes between 1886 and 1902 before being apprehended.

Don't miss Chester's Stone Village up on North Street (Route 103): a double line of 30 buildings faced in gneiss, a rough-hewn, gleaming mica schist quarried from nearby Flamstead Mountain. Cool in summer, warm in winter, stone houses are a rarity in New England. All of these are said to have been built by two brothers in the pre–Civil War decade, with hiding spaces enough to make them a significant stop on the Underground Railroad.

Midway between Main and North Streets is Chester Depot, a pleasant old traffic center that resembles neither of these places. The well-kept Victorian depot serves as the northern terminus for the *Green Mountain Flyer* (see *To Do*), spilling more than 100 passengers at a time into the village center to browse in Cummings Hardware and Jameson's Food Market and to stroll by the steepled town hall. It's an appropriate terminus for a country railroad.

Bellows Falls, sited by one of the biggest natural falls in the entire course of the Connecticut River, itself cascades down a hill so steep that a stairway connects the commercial Westminster Street with the residential neighborhood above. Old paper mills and railroad-era buildings are crowded on yet another level down by the river—where you can still see carvings made centuries ago by members of the Pennacook tribe, who gathered by the falls to fish. You can also see the remains of one of America's first canals, built in 1802 to ease river traffic around the great falls. Most shops and businesses are contained in 19th-century brick buildings lining the widened stretch of Westminster Street (Route 5) known as the Village Square. A Florentine tower tops the town hall, which also houses the Falls Cinema and Fletcher's Drug, the bus stop. Bellows Falls was the home of Hetty Green (1835–1916), who parlayed a substantial inheritance into a $100 million fortune; she was called the Witch of Wall Street, to which she traveled by day coach, looking like a bag lady in threadbare bombazine.

Saxtons River is, like Bellows Falls, a village in the town of Rockingham. Said to be named for a surveyor who fell into the river and drowned, it's best known as the home of the Vermont Academy (founded in 1876, a private prep school since 1932). This unpretentious village of 541 souls is also not a bad place to stay, eat, and shop.

TO SEE

MUSEUMS

✒ **Grafton museums,** all within walking distance of the Grafton Information Center (see Guidance): **The Windham Foundation Barn** (open daily), in the village on Townshend Road, exhibits old carriages, tools, and artifacts; also displays on sheep farming. The **Grafton Historical Society Museum** (843-2564; across from the Village Store on Main Street; Memorial Day through Columbus Day weekends and holidays 1:30–4, and daily during foliage season) displays local memorabilia. The **Grafton Museum of Natural History** (843-2111; same periods as historical society; it's across from the Old Tavern, above the town hall/post office) focuses on local flora and fauna, with hands-on exhibits for children. The **Blacksmith Shop** (next to the Grafton School; open Thursday through Monday summer through fall) is a working smithy.

Adams Old Stone Gristmill Museum (463-3706), Mill Street, Bellows Falls. Usually open Saturday and Sunday 1–4 in July and August, and by appointment. The mill ground grain from 1831 until 1961; the old machinery is all in place, and the adjacent museum exhibits relics of the town's long and varied industrial history.

There are more relics of local history to be found in the **Rockingham Free Library and Museum** (463-4270), Westminster Street, Bellows Falls. Open year-round, Monday through Friday 2–4.

The **Saxtons River Historical Museum** (869-2657, 869-2329). A 19th-century parlor and kitchen as well as local memorabilia housed in a former Congregational church built in 1836 at the western end of the village. Open June, July, and August, as well as in foliage season, Saturday and Sunday 2–4:30.

HISTORIC SITES

Rockingham is a peaceful village just off Route 103 between Chester and Bellows Falls, worth a stop to visit the **Old Rockingham Meeting House** on Route 103 (open in summer, 10–5), Vermont's oldest unchanged public building. Built in 1787, this Federal-style structure contains "pigpen"-style pews, each accommodating 10 to 15 people, some with their backs to the minister. The old burying ground is filled with thin old markers bearing readable epitaphs.

COVERED BRIDGES

There are four covered bridges in the area: two in Bartonsville (1.5 miles north of Route 103 and the other east off Route 103); one in Grafton; and one in Saxtons River off Route 121, noteworthy for its "flying buttresses" (replaced in 1982).

FOR FAMILIES

The Fish Ladder and Visitors Center (463-3226) of the New England Power Company on Bridge Street in Bellows Falls is one of a series of ladders constructed on the Connecticut River to return Atlantic salmon and American shad to their native spawning grounds.

In Grafton: Children under 12 are invited to fish in the trout pond behind the information center (source of tackle). Youngsters are invited to pet the sheep behind the information center (see Guidance) and the cows next to the Grafton Village Cheese Co. (see Special Shops) Covered Bridge. They may also use the elaborate playground behind the Grafton School.

Rockingham Meeting House

See also the Grafton Museum of Natural History and the Blacksmith Shop under *Museums*.

TO DO

BICYCLING
Touring and mountain bikes are available May to October from the **Old Tavern** (843-2231; see *Lodging*) in Grafton. Roads radiating from the village invite biking, and the Grafton Ponds cross-country trails (see *Cross-Country Skiing*) are good for mountain biking.

GOLF
Tater Hill Club (875-2517), Popple Dungeon Road, Windham (off Route 11, 2 miles south from the junction of Windham Road and Route 121), offers 18 holes, a pro shop, instruction, and a restaurant.

Bellows Falls Country Club (463-9809), Route 103, Rockingham. Scenic nine-hole course; clubhouse with bar and lunchroom.

HIKING AND WALKING
Grafton Village is so small and compact that it's easy to tour on foot, and the Windham Foundation has outlined nine walks down dirt roads to cemeteries and cellar holes. In addition to the well-marked paths through the woods and fields, there are cross-country-ski trails that can be hiked via **Grafton Ponds** (see below).

HORSE-DRAWN RIDES
Wilbur's Horse-Drawn Rides (875-3643) in Grafton offers hay-, surrey-, and sleigh rides.

RAILROAD EXCURSION
Green Mountain Flyer (463-3069; 1-800-707-3530), 54 Depot Street, Bellows Falls. From late June through Labor Day and then in foliage

season, twice-daily rides are offered; there's a weekend schedule before and after that. Special rides all the way to Ludlow during foliage season. The regular, 13-mile (one-way) ride to the Chester Depot is exceptionally beautiful. Rolling stock includes some turn-of-the-century cars, and the route is along the Connecticut River, past covered bridges, then up the Williams River and through wooded rock cuts, which include the spectacular Brockway Mills gorge. $11 round-trip for adults, $7 per child 3–12.

[handwritten: (FRI) 11 A.m 2 hr round 9:10 2. A.m trip]

CROSS-COUNTRY SKIING

Grafton Ponds (843-2400), Townshend Road, Grafton. The program is based at the Old Tavern and the trails are just down the road: 30 km groomed trails meandering off from a log cabin warming hut, over meadows, and into the woods on Bear Hill. Night skiing, snowmaking, rentals, and instruction, plus ice skating, sleigh rides, and snowshoeing. In other seasons, it's a mountain-bike center as well.

Tater Hill Cross-Country Ski Center (875-2517), Popple Dungeon Road, Windham. A total of 40 km of trails, 20 km tracked: a mix of meadows and forests at elevations of 1,786–2,000 feet. Instruction, rentals, showers, changing rooms, and restaurant; guided and headlamp tours.

LODGING

INNS AND BED & BREAKFASTS

In Grafton 05146

The Old Tavern (843-2231; 1-800-843-1801), Main Street, where Routes 35 and 121 intersect. The brick core of this splendid building dates back to 1788, but the double-porched facade is mid–19th century. The stylish interior (vintage 1965) tastefully re-creates a formal Early American setting. The 66 rooms are divided among the inn and 11 houses, 7 of which (each with four to seven guest rooms) can be rented in their entirety. Most are in the village, but some are tucked away in the surrounding woods, offering both privacy and views. Hillside Cottage, with just a living room and bedroom and a fine view, is an ideal honeymoon haven. Guest rooms all have private bath, but no TV or phone. Common rooms are formal and elegant. The Phelps Barn has a fireplaced lounge, and a game building has pool and table tennis. In summer there are nearby tennis courts and a sand-bottomed swimming pond; in winter, cross-country skiing. Youngsters are welcome in some cottages. Pets are not permitted, but you can bring your horse (there's a stable). $145–185 per couple B&B; $580–790 for a house sleeping eight or nine people; 10 percent senior discount. Weddings are a specialty.

The Inn at Woodchuck Farm (843-2398), Middletown Road. Open year-round. This 1780s farmhouse sits high on a hill, on a back road above Grafton. The porch, well stocked with comfortable wicker, has a peaceful, top-of-the-world feel, and there are views from the elegant living room and dining room, too. Created by Ann and Frank Gabriel, the inn is now run by their son Mark and his wife, Marilyn, both psychologists in Grafton. There are six rooms, four of them corner rooms with private baths (one with a fireplace) in the main house. There is an adjoining west wing with an upstairs studio that has its own kitchen and glass doors that open onto a private deck with views of the woods. Downstairs is a spacious suite with a king-size canopy bed. Hidden away in a hand-carved armoire are the refrigerator, microwave, and coffeemaker. Just down the hill but above the pond, the old barn now offers some great spaces. You can have either a double room with fireplace, two rooms with fireplace, or the whole Barn Residence with a two-story living room, woodstove, kitchen, and view of the pond. Spruce Cottage, located on the inn property, offers privacy and seclusion. Furnished in antiques, it is fully equipped and sleeps up to seven people ($275 per day). There's a sauna in the woods next to the pond, which is good for swimming, fishing, and canoeing, and the 200 rolling acres are laced with walking trails. No smoking. $89–220 B&B.

The Wayfarer at Grafton (843-2363), Main Street. Open May through October. This 1834 brick house is up the street from the Old Tavern and has four guest rooms, three with a fireplace, all with private bath and furnished with country furniture and antiques. Dennis Scharback and Arthur Park enjoy tuning guests in to the best places to dine, shop, and explore. Open most of the year. By reservation only. $85 includes continental breakfast.

Also in Grafton: **Brandywine B&B and Antiques** (843-2250), a stately town house across from the inn, with two floors of antiques in the barn.

In Chester 05143

The Fullerton Inn (875-2444), 40 the Common, P.O. Box 188, formerly the Inn at Long Last, has Jerry and Robin Szawerda as new owners. This is a big, old-fashioned hotel, but its library/pub, the TV room, the immense old lobby, the big dining room (see *Dining Out*), and the sunny breakfast room are all lively and comfortable. Facilities include a tennis court. Each of the 21 guest rooms and two suites was recently redecorated. $89–149 double. Wedding receptions and business meetings are welcomed.

🏵 **The Chester House** (875-2205; 1-888-875-2205), 266 Main Street on the green, across from the Fullerton. This is a find. Now run by Paul Anderson and Randy Guy, its common space includes a handsome downstairs parlor with fireplace, a keeping room, and dining room decorated in Early American style. Amenities abound: For example, room 1 has a queen bed and a whirlpool bath; room 2, queen bed plus steam bath and sitting area; room 4, queen bed, sitting area, and whirlpool. They all have telephone and air-conditioning. The place is definitely gay-friendly, but not exclusively. $89–149 B&B, with various recreational packages.

Stone Hearth Inn (875-2525), Route 11 west. Janet and Don Stromeyer offer 10 comfy guest rooms, all with private bath, in this rambling 1810 farmhouse, which features an English-style pub and the Nutcracker Suite gift shop as well as a dining room for guests. $60–100 double, B&B; $20 more per person MAP.

🖉 **Henry Farm Inn** (875-2674), Green Mountain Turnpike. There's a nice out-in-the-country feel to this old place, set in 50 rolling acres with a pond. Larger than other farmhouses of the period, it was built in 1760 as a stagecoach stop and retains its pine floors, beehive oven, and sense of pleasant, uncluttered simplicity. You notice the quilts and the views. Lee and Stuart Gaw are the new owners. Children welcome. $65–85 includes a country breakfast.

🏵 **Glen Finert Farm** (875-2160; call 6–8 AM), Flamstead Road. This was the first B&B in the area, and it's still one of the most relaxing. Ruth Harvie's farm sits high on a hill with long views and a pond. There's a woodstove in the homey kitchen, a great book-lined study with fireplace, a formal dining room, and a friendly parlor with a woodstove and baby grand (Ruth plays the trumpet in the Grafton Cornet Band). The three guest rooms share a bath, but the homemade quilts and antique beds compensate. Breakfast features the farm's own eggs and home-baked breads, and after ice skating on the pond (Ruth has plenty of skates) or cross-country skiing on the property (Ruth is a PSIA-certified instructor), homemade soup is usually available. All this for $55 per couple ($50 for 2 nights or more).

♿ **The Madrigal Inn and Fine Arts Center** (463-1339; 1-800-854-2208), 61 Williams River Road. This is the 22nd home for Ray and Nancy Dressler, and they have built it from scratch, designing it as an inn and conference center. Ray is a former Navy chaplain with well-honed skills in organizing group gatherings ranging from wedding receptions to seminars in life management. The open-beamed, two-story living room and library are obviously designed for numbers, but couples are very welcome. The 11 guest rooms, all with private bath, some handicapped-accessible, have been furnished with king- and queen-sized beds and taste. $90–110 per couple includes a full country breakfast; dinner is available by reservation. The property includes a pond and 5 km of cross-country-ski trails.

♿ **Inn Victoria** (875-4288; 1-800-732-4288), on the green, Chester. Less frilly and more comfortable than under previous management, this antiques-furnished inn offers seven guest rooms and a suite sleeping six to eight. All rooms have queen-sized beds, three have Jacuzzis, and the first-floor garden room is handicapped-accessible. Norbert and Cathy Hasbrouck have added an outdoor hot tub and a deck. They serve vegetarian dinners by reservation. Rates, including breakfast and tea, are $75–95 for rooms; the suite, with kitchen, fireplaced living room, two bedrooms, and whirlpool bath, runs $150–295.

🖉 **Hugging Bear Inn & Shoppe** (875-2412; 1-800-325-0519), 244 Main Street. Though the giant teddy bear that once graced the front porch got restless and took a hike, teddy bears remain on the beds of six guest rooms (private baths). The place teems with them: teddy bear wallpaper, teddy bear sheets and shower curtains, and more than 6,000 stuffed bears in the shop behind the kitchen. Georgette Thomas believes that people don't hug enough. Everyone is invited to hug any bear in the house, and the atmosphere here is contagiously friendly. Rates are $60–75 single, $85–115 double. For extra people: $10 for children under age 15, $25 adult. Full breakfast is included.

Stone Cottage Collectables (875-6211), 196 North Street. Chris and Ann Curran are your hosts at this 1840 stone house in Chester's "Stone Village" historic district. This charming B&B is filled with antiques and collectibles and provides three sitting rooms plus patio, deck, and garden areas for relaxation. The two guest rooms each have private bath. The glorious queen-bed room, with fireplace, was created by the former owner, best-selling author Olivia Goldsmith (*The First Wives Club*), for herself. Room rates, including full breakfast, are $80 for the queen-bed room and $65 for the full-bed room. The Currans operate their antiques and collectibles shop on the premises. Radios and tubes, cameras, and stamps for collectors are among the featured items.

Night with a Native Bed & Breakfast (875-2616), P.O. Box 327 (Route 103), in the village. Doris Hastings is a sixth-generation Vermonter who obviously enjoys accommodating guests in a house that conveys a lively interest in many things. The two small, antiques-decorated bedrooms share a bath. Breakfast is included in $55–85 per couple.

Old Town Farm Inn (875-2346; 1-888-232-1089), 665 Vermont Route 10. This former "Town Farm" is in Gassetts, a village midway between Chester and Ludlow. The handsome old building with wide-board floors has 11 comfortable guest rooms (5 with private bath) furnished with quilts and antiques. It's set in 11 acres with a pond. $60–80 in summer, $75–95 in fall and winter, breakfast included; inquire about 3- and 5-day rates.

Kimberly's Cherub (875-3773), Route 103, two rooms, one with cable TV and a fireplace; **Second Wind** (875-3438), Grafton Street, two cozy suites with private baths; **Quail Hollow** (875-2467), RFD 2, Box 187, eight guest rooms with private bath and a "Great Room" for group or large-family use; **Greenleaf Inn** (875-3171), P.O. Box 188, five guest rooms with private baths.

In Andover 05143

Rowell's Inn (875-3658), Route 11, Simonsville. Open year-round except April and early November. This distinctive, double-porched, brick stage stop has been serving the public off and on since 1820. After decades of neglect it was restored by Lee and Beth Davis, who preserved its Victorian tin ceilings as well as earlier detailing and added their own Americana: a vintage soda fountain and Coke machine, for instance. There are six comfortable guest rooms with private bath, one with a working fireplace. Two spacious spaces on the third floor have been carved from the old ballroom, furnished grandly with antiques and Oriental rugs.

Located midway between Londonderry, Weston, and Chester, the inn is off by itself with some fine walks and cross-country skiing out the back door. $160–175 MAP includes a five-course dinner and afternoon tea, as well as breakfast. Add 15 percent gratuity.

❄ **The Inn at High View** (875-2724), RR 1, 753 East Hill Road. An attractive inn off by itself on East Hill with some of the best views of any inn in Vermont. Common space includes nicely paneled living and dining rooms; the 72 acres stretch away invitingly outside, beyond the rock-garden pool. In winter the big attraction is the cross-country trails, which connect with a 15-km network. There are six rooms and two suites (two rooms), all very attractively furnished. Hosts Greg Bohan and Sal Massaro serve elegant Italian fare on Saturday night ($30; BYOB). $90–135 for rooms, $135–155 for suites, includes breakfast. Pets possible.

In Saxtons River 05154

Inn at Saxtons River (869-2110), Main Street. This vintage-1903 inn with a distinctive square, five-story tower has an attractive streetside pub and a large, popular dining room (see *Dining Out*). The 16 rooms (all with private bath) are $98–108, including breakfast.

Moore's Inn (869-2020), 57 Main Street (Route 121). David Moore is a sixth-generation Vermonter who grew up in this Victorian house with fine woodwork and a spacious veranda. David and Carol offer six guest rooms, all with TV, phone, fridge, coffeemaker, and private bath, two with Jacuzzi. A three-bedroom, fully furnished family apartment with kitchen and living room is also available for short-term stays. Up to 10 people can be accommodated. Families and bicyclists (request the 25 rides Moore has mapped) will feel particularly welcome. Facilities include a 75-foot pool (protected and heated to 80 degrees March to December 1, open daily 6 AM–8:30 PM).Guest rooms are $70–90. Apartment rates vary.

In Bellows Falls 05101

Horsefeathers (463-9776), 16 Webb Terrace (Route 5 north of town). An 1890s house with garden acreage and river views. Guests can claim two sunny rooms with a library; also a tempting porch rocker. The six guest rooms, most with private bath, are $65–95, including breakfast.

🐾 **River Mist B&B** (463-9023), 7 Burt Street. This Queen Anne Victorian town house with wraparound porches reflects the way the town's onetime mill owners lived. John and Linda Maresca offer period guest rooms with private or shared baths at $32.50–55 per person, and supervised indoor and outdoor play areas for children.

🏅 **Blue Haven Christian Bed & Breakfast** (463-9008; 1-800-228-9008), Route 5, 6963 Westminster Road, south of Bellows Falls, has a distinctly French atmosphere. Helene Champagne speaks it, and the big country kitchen where guests have breakfast has the touch of a contemporary auberge. There are five comfortable rooms in this vintage-1830 schoolhouse, some with canopied beds, and four baths. The crude stone fireplace in the common room has stones from every state. $110 per couple, $45–70 single includes breakfast. AARP discount. Smoke-free. New for 1999: full-kitchen suite available (1-week minimum).

WHERE TO EAT

DINING OUT

Averill's Restaurant & Bob's Tavern (369-2327), Route 121, Saxtons River. Open Monday through Saturday 5:30–10 for dinner; 4–closing in the tavern. By far the most popular dining place in this corner of Vermont, attractive and owner-operated with a menu that might include West African peanut soup ($3.50 a bowl) and smoked trout with horseradish sauce ($5) for starters. There is a long list of entrées, maybe including spanakopita (spinach and feta cheese in phyllo pastry, $10), roast duck with apricot sauce ($15), and steak *au poivre* ($17). The tavern menu can range from a hamburger and fries ($5) or a chicken burrito ($5.50) to rigatoni or linguine with shrimp ($10). Nightly specials.

The Old Tavern (843-2231), Grafton, serves lunch, dinner, and Sunday brunch in the formal dining rooms or in the more casual sunroom. In keeping with the old New England ambience of the formal dining room, with its fine portraits and Chippendale chairs, the menu features Grafton cheddar and ale soup and Newfane trout. But the entrée choices may also include baked salmon *en croûte* ($19) and fettucine prepared with olive oil, plum tomatoes, olives, pignoli nuts, fresh basil, and aged Asiago ($14).

Bradford Tavern (875-6094), in the Fullerton Inn on the green, Chester. Open for dinner nightly except Wednesday. This pleasant place gets rave reviews from regulars. The large menu may range from baked scrod ($11.95), to barbecued baby back ribs ($11.95), to chicken Marsala ($10.95). All dinners include potato or rice pilaf and salad; children's portions available, early-bird specials until 6.

Leslie's (463-4929), Rockingham. Conveniently situated on Route 5 south of I-91, this onetime tavern with seven fireplaces and a Dutch oven serves lunch and dinner daily. There's a selection of beef entrées, including Leslie's Combo (sautéed shrimp and a 7-ounce sirloin), plus seafood (Cajun seafood, stuffed shrimp), and such specialties as veal Marsala and Leslie's specialty: strips of chicken breast sautéed with garlic, tomatoes, mushrooms, Parmesan, and cream served over fettuccine. Moderate.

Inn at Saxtons River (869-2110), Main Street, Saxtons River. Open for lunch and dinner daily; Sunday brunch. This attractive inn's dining room gets mixed reviews. Some patrons rave about it and come back again and again, and others say they have been disappointed. The à la carte menu is unusually large. You might begin with a country pâté and dine on roast Vermont turkey ($15.95) or baked stuffed shrimp ($16.95);

there's always a vegetarian dinner of the day. Salad is extra. Sunday brunch is $9.95. This is the obvious spot to dine before productions at the Saxtons River Playhouse (see *Entertainment*) around the corner.

EATING OUT

Lunch at the Old Tavern (843-2231), Grafton. The Old Tavern's glass-walled and flowery greenhouse room is the right setting for lunch creations like grilled rosemary-garlic chicken and shrimp and avocado salad.

Raspberries and Tyme (875-4486), on the green, Chester. Open daily, serving delectable breakfasts 8–11; lunches 11 AM to closing; dinner 5–9 Wednesday through Monday. In the middle of town, a delightful café with simmering soups, a wide choice of salads and sandwiches named for a variety of village establishments. The Misty Valley Books veggie bagel (spinach, tomato, grated carrots, broccoli, and sprouts with hummus on their own garlic-herb spread under melted Vermont cheddar) is a best-seller.

Common Ground Cafe (463-3150), 17 Rockingham Street, Bellows Falls. Open 10–10 Monday through Thursday, 10–3 Friday (but not to be confused with its namesake in Brattleboro), this benign place is operated by The Community, a spiritual cult. It features "south-of-the-border" dishes, creative sandwiches, and especially toothsome desserts and bakery items.

Pizza Paul and Mary (869-2222), Main Street, Saxtons River. Open daily 11–9 except Monday. Besides a catchy name, this village eatery offers unusual pizza toppings—like pesto, artichoke, and avocado—also burgers, subs, and antipasti.

Joy Wah (463-9761), Rockingham Road (Route 5), Bellows Falls. Full-service Chinese fare in a Victorian farmhouse perched on a knoll overlooking the Connecticut River; includes all the familiar dishes on its lengthy menu. Open daily for lunch and dinner.

Rose Arbour Tea Room (875-4767), just off the green, Chester. Tea served daily 10–5 except Monday. A combination gift store and tearoom in a gracious old house. Coffee and lemonade are also served to accompany the chicken salad with fruit garnish and diablo chocolate cake.

DINERS

The Other Diner (875-6006), Route 103, Chester. Open daily 5 AM–8 PM, until 9 PM Friday. At this writing, the Trombley family's cheerful, spanking-clean eatery is riding high in local opinions, and their pie won first prize at the Springfield Apple Festival. Our vegetable soup was outstanding, as was the turkey salad sandwich; dinner entrées include roast Vermont turkey ($6.50) and a 100 percent certified Angus roast beef dinner, available Sunday only, $7.25.

Country Girl Diner, junction of Routes 11 and 103, Chester, is a homey, popular spot open Monday through Saturday 5:30 AM–8 PM, Sunday 7 AM–8 PM. Classic diner and diner fare.

Father's, Route 5, just south of Bellows Falls. Open Tuesday through Saturday 5:30 AM–9 PM, Sunday 7 AM–5:30. A recently expanded diner that's favored by locals, maybe because all the bread (including sandwich bread) and pies are baked here fresh. There's a good salad bar, also. Two specials per day, both for lunch and dinner.

ENTERTAINMENT

MAIN STREET ARTS

Main Street Arts (869-2960), Main Street, Saxtons River. This 10-year-old local arts council sponsors dance and musical performances, parades, cabarets, recitals, and its own Power Singers as well as art classes and a crafts shop in its center.

MUSIC

The Grafton Cornet Band performs in either Grafton or Chester (sometimes in Townshend) on summer weekends.

THEATER

Saxtons River Playhouse (869-2030), Westminster West Road, Saxtons River. Late June through August, musicals and popular plays, Monday through Saturday at 8 PM; Sunday at 7. Also some matinees and children's theater, Friday at 2 ($3), as well as after-show cabarets.

FILMS

New Falls Cinema (463-4766), on the Square in Bellows Falls, offers first-run flicks. So does **Ellis Theatre** (885-2929), on the Square, Springfield.

SELECTIVE SHOPPING

ANTIQUES SHOPS

Antiques stores are particularly thick in this area. Among the many worth checking are:

In Grafton: **Gabriel's Barn Antiques at Woodchuck Hill Farm** (843-2509), specializing in country furniture, stoneware crocks, and primitives. **Grafton Gathering Places Antiques** (875-2309), 748 Eastman Road, open daily year-round except Tuesday. A two-story country barn filled with early country and period furniture and accessories.

In Chester: **Stone House Village Antiques Center** (875-4477), Route 103 south, is an antiques mall with 125 dealers and a touristy collection of country crafts. See also Stone Cottage Collectables under *Lodging—Inns and Bed & Breakfasts.*

In Saxtons River: **Sign of the Raven** (869-2500), Route 121 east. Open 10–5 (by chance or appointment—call ahead). Antiques and fine American paintings.

BOOKSTORES

Misty Valley Books (875-3400), on the green, Chester, open daily except Monday. Michael Kohlmann and Dwight Currie run an unusually

A sign at the Grafton Village Cheese Company

friendly, well-stocked bookshop; browsing is encouraged and book and author readings are frequent, making it a lively cultural center.

Hopewell's of Chester, on the green, open weekends. An interesting selection of used and nearly new books.

Village Square Booksellers (463-9404), 28 The Square, Bellows Falls. Open Monday through Saturday 9–6, Friday until 7, and Sunday noon–4. A new independent, full-service bookstore.

CRAFTS SHOPS

Jelly Bean Tree (869-2326), Main Street, Saxtons River. Open daily April through December, noon–5. A craft cooperative run by several local artisans and carrying the work of many more on consignment: pottery, macramé, leather, weaving, batik, and hand-sewn, -knit, and -crocheted items.

Bonnie's Bundles (875-2114), Stone Village, Route 103, Chester. Open Memorial Day through October 15; otherwise by appointment. Housed in an 1814 stone house, a doll-lover's find. Bonnie Waters handcrafts wonderfully original dolls.

GALLERIES

Gallery North Star (843-2465), Main Street, Grafton Village. One of Vermont's oldest and best galleries: Six rooms in this Grafton Village house are hung with landscapes and graphic prints, oils, watercolors, and sculpture.

Jud Hartmann Gallery (359-2544), Main Street, Grafton Village. Open daily mid-September through October. We first met Hartmann manning the cross-country-ski center in Grafton and selling his distinctive, limited-edition bronze sculptures from his house. He now maintains a gallery in Blue Hill, Maine, all summer and opens his Grafton Gallery (next to the Old Tavern) only during foliage season.

Chester Art Guild (875-3767), on the green, Chester, is open mid-June through mid-October daily except Monday, 2–5. An authentic old brick schoolhouse is the setting for exhibits by 60 member artists; opening reception the first Saturday of every month.

Crow Hill Gallery (875-3763), Flamstead Road, Chester, shows the work of Jeanne Carbonetti and other local artists. Open Wednesday through Sunday, 10–5.

Grist Mill Gallery of Fine Art (875-3415), just off Route 103, Chester Depot. This distinctive, old red gristmill lends itself nicely to exhibit space for Allison Kibbe's original landscapes.

FARMS TO VISIT

Hidden Orchard Farms (843-2499), Grafton. Pick-your-own apples, blueberries, and raspberries. Apple cider and pumpkins. Maple syrup and natural fruit and berry preserves, fruit butters. The store is in the old fire station in Grafton Village.

Allen Brothers Farms & Orchards (722-3395), Route 5, 2 miles south of Bellows Falls. Open year-round, daily. Offers pick-your-own apples and potatoes, also sells vegetables, plants and seeds, honey, syrup, and Vermont gifts.

SPECIAL SHOPS

Grafton Village Cheese Co. (843-2221), Grafton Village. The shop is open Monday through Friday 8:30–4:30; Saturday and Sunday 10–4; winter hours vary. The store sells its Covered Bridge Cheddar (the covered bridge has been positioned out back), including a classic reserve extra sharp that received the Outstanding Cheese 1993 award at an international competition. Founded in 1890 as the Grafton Cooperative Cheese Company, the factory has been revived by the Windham Foundation and produces cheddar by the traditional process: Vats of fresh milk are heated and the curd is cut by hand, tested, drained, milled, salted, molded, and pressed before aging. The six cheeses are sharp (aged one year); classic reserve (two years); smoked; dill; sage; and garlic. Tours are available by request.

The National Survey (875-2121), Chester Village, off the green. Open Monday through Friday 9–5, Saturday 10–4. Founded in 1912 by two sons of Chester's Baptist minister, the National Survey publishes maps for many states, foreign governments, industries, and other groups throughout the world. In its **Charthouse** store around the corner from the common, you can find maps, books, and old brochures.

Carpenter's Emporium (875-3267), on the green in Chester. This 1870s store carries a line of the Flamstead silk-screened skirts and dresses that were once made and sold here; the large store is filled with a variety of basic clothing, also notions, games, a room full of puzzles, toys, and souvenirs.

Forlie-Ballou (875-2090), Main Street, Chester Village. Upscale women's clothes, accessories, and gifts.

Baba-A-Louis Bakery (875-4666), Route 11 west, Chester. Closed April and November, as well as Sunday and Monday, but otherwise open 7 AM–6 PM. Stop for coffee, sticky buns, or cinnamon twists, and take home loaves of this top-drawer bakery's specialty breads.

Vermont Country Store, Rockingham Village, off Route 103. An offshoot of the famous Vermont Country Store in Weston, this is also owned by Lyman Orton and actually houses his Common Cracker machine, which visitors can watch as it stamps out the hard round biscuits. The store also sells whole-grain breads and cookies baked here, along with a line of calico material, soapstone griddles, woodenware gadgets, natural-fiber clothing, and much more. There is also an upstairs bargain room.

Caboose Corner (463-4575), 676 Missing Link Road, Route 5, Bellows Falls. Model trains and accessories in an old Rutland Railroad caboose.

SPECIAL EVENTS

July 4 weekend: A big parade in Chester is timed so as not to coincide with that in Saxtons River; usually a performance of the **Vermont Symphony Orchestra** at Grafton Ponds.

July: In Chester, **St. Joseph's Carnival; Horse Show and Community Picnic; Congregational Country Fair.** In Bellows Falls, **The Vermont State Certified Championship Old Time Fiddlers Contest.**

August: In Chester, **Outdoor Art Show.** In Rockingham (first weekend in August), **Old Rockingham Days,** a full weekend of events—dancing, live entertainment, sidewalk dining, contests, fireworks.

December: **Overture to Christmas,** Chester, usually the second Saturday. Tree-lighting and candlelight caroling procession from church to church.

Okemo Mountain/ Ludlow Area

In contrast to all other Vermont ski towns, Ludlow is neither a tiny picturesque village nor a long-established resort. It boomed with the production of "shoddy" (fabric made from reworked wool) after the Civil War, a period frozen in the red brick of its commercial block, Victorian mansions, magnificent library, and academy (now the Black River Museum). In the wake of the wool boom, the General Electric Company moved into the steepled mill at the heart of town and kept people employed making small-aircraft engine parts until 1977. Cashmere is still produced in the town's old Jewel Brook Mill, and an assortment of small industries have opened in the new Dean Brown Industrial Park. Ludlow is, furthermore, a crossroads market town, with its stores supplying most of the needs of the small surrounding towns.

The town of Ludlow has 3,300-foot-high Okemo Mountain rising from its core. The ski area here dates from 1956, but for years it was a sleeper—a big mountain with antiquated lifts on the edge of a former mill town. Ski clubs nested in the Victorian homes, and just a few inns catered to serious skiers.

Since 1982, however, when Tim and Diane Mueller bought Okemo, the old Poma lifts have all been replaced with fast-moving, high-capacity chairlifts. Snowmaking equipment and more than two dozen trails have been added, along with hundreds of condominiums. A total of 2,400 people can presently bed down on the mountain—which has doubled its number of patrons in just a couple of years. More improvements are in the works, including a passenger rail link to Rutland and Amtrak's *Ethan Allen Express* from New York City.

The effect on Ludlow has been dramatic. The old General Electric plant has been turned into condominiums, inns have multiplied, and the fire chief has tacked a tidy motel onto the back of his house. Local dining options now include six-course gourmet meals, the well-sauced dishes and stained-glass atmosphere at Nikki's, and regal surroundings at the Castle.

Summer visitors tend to own or rent cottages on Lake Pauline, Reservoir Pond, or Lake Rescue. Lake Ninevah and Echo and Amherst Lakes are just north of the town line. There are also those who come for

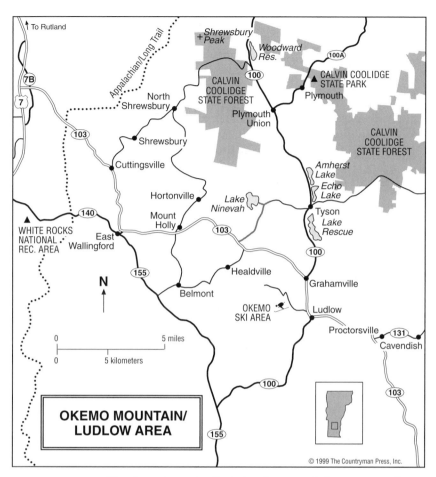

programs at Fletcher Farm Crafts School or simply because Ludlow's location makes an ideal base from which to explore much of southern and central Vermont.

"The resort business is the number one employer now," observes Bob Gilmore, owner of Nikki's. "But this is still a real town."

West from Ludlow, Route 103 climbs steeply in beautiful hill country, through Mount Holly to Belmont or Hortonville and Shrewsbury. A turnoff through Mount Holly and Hortonville will be rewarded with spectacular views of the surrounding hills.

North from Ludlow, Route 100 links the chain of lakes. South from town, it climbs Terrible Mountain for 9 full miles before its descent into Weston. To the east, Route 131 follows the Black River through the picturesque mill villages of Proctorsville and Cavendish. Route 103 follows the Williams River to Chester. Handy to Weston, Grafton, Killington, and numerous activities, Ludlow is just far enough from everywhere to retain its own unmistakable identity.

GUIDANCE

Ludlow Area Chamber of Commerce (228-5830), P.O. Box 333, Ludlow 05149. A walk-in information office in the Marketplace, Okemo, on Route 103 across from the Okemo Mountain access road (look for the clock tower) is filled with menus, events listings, and lodging brochures. During foliage and winter seasons, however, the job of finding accommodations for visitors shifts to the **Okemo Mountain Lodging Service** (1-800-78-OKEMO) at Okemo Mountain. Ask for a copy of *Off the Beaten Path*, an informative brochure listing attractions and events in southern Windsor County.

GETTING THERE

By bus: **Vermont Transit** offers direct service from Boston via Bellows Falls; for New York and Connecticut, leave from Rutland.

By train: Okemo Mountain Ski Area and the Green Mountain Railway Corp. plan special excursions and regular service to and from Rutland, connecting with **Amtrak's** *Ethan Allen Express*, but this service is still in the planning stage.

GETTING AROUND

George's Shuttle Service (1-800-208-3933) provides "seamless" transportation from the railroad stations in Bellows Falls and Rutland to Ludlow.

"The Moose Caboose" (228-4957), a local van service for shopping or shuttle service to the ski slopes from area lodging, operated by Northern Excursions.

MEDICAL EMERGENCY

Ludlow (911); Cavendish (226-7283); Mount Holly (259-2060). Proctorsville (226-7283); **Urgent Care Center** (228-5131).

TO SEE

Fletcher Library (228-8921), Main Street, Ludlow. Open Monday through Friday 10–5:30; Saturday 10–1 and 6:30–8:30. One of Vermont's most beautiful town libraries: Reading rooms contain marble inlays; fireplaces; old-style, green-shaded lights; and century-old paintings of local landscapes.

MUSEUMS

Black River Academy Historical Museum (228-5050), corner of Smith and High Streets, Ludlow. Open Memorial Day through Columbus Day, Wednesday through Sunday noon–4. A steepled, brick school building, built in 1889. The academy's reputation drew students from throughout New England. One large room is dedicated to President Calvin Coolidge, class of 1890. Other rooms in the four-story building are filled with exhibits about mining, lumbering, railroading, farming, and other segments in the history of the Black River Valley. Children and donations are welcome.

Cavendish Historical Society Museum, Cavendish. Open June through October, Sunday 2–5, housed in the former Baptist church; includes a collection of weaving implements, old photographs, farm tools, articles used or made in Cavendish, changing exhibits, and a lecture program.

Mount Holly Community Historical Museum, Belmont, open in July and August, Sunday 2–4. Even if it isn't open, the exercise of finding this appealing little museum is worthwhile. It sits just downhill from the center of the village of Belmont, as picturesque a village as any to be found in Vermont. The general store is a classic, and **Star Lake** is a great place for a swim.

WINERY

Joseph Cerniglia Winery, Inc. (226-7575; 1-800-654-6382), Winery Road, Proctorsville. The winery is open daily 10–5 year-round; there's also a gift shop. There are tours every 15 minutes and wine tastings constantly. The wines are premium apple varietal and have won prizes at both the Indiana State Fair and the International Eastern Wine Competition. A low-alcohol Woodchuck Draft Cider was introduced a few years ago.

TO DO

FOR CHILDREN

Okemo Mountain Summer Day Camp (228-4041), open mid-June through August, Monday through Friday; arts and crafts, fishing, field trips, nature walks, soccer, and softball.

BICYCLING AND WALKING

Vermont Cycle Adventures (228-5174). David Tyson, the "race across America" long-distance cyclist, arranges tours for couples or larger groups, for a day, weekend, or 5 days (including lodging), from $30 to $60 per day per person, depending on the number.

BOATING

Paddle Vermont (228-4957), P.O. Box 149, Ludlow, offers canoes, kayaks, and tubes for fishing, wildlife viewing, photography, and camping.

Echo Lake Inn (228-8602), Route 100, Tyson, rents canoes and other boats. (See *Lodging.*) Rentals are also available at Camp Plymouth State Park (see *Swimming*).

FISHING

Public access has been provided to **Lake Rescue, Echo Lake, Lake Ninevah, Woodward Reservoir,** and **Amherst Lake.** Fishing licenses are required (even for canoeing on these lakes), and this is strictly enforced. The catch includes rainbow trout, bass, and pickerel. There is also fly-fishing in the **Black River.**

GOLF

The Okemo Valley Golf Club (228-8871), Fox Lane, Ludlow. Okemo Mountain has acquired the former nine-hole Fox Run course and is expanding it. Eighteen new holes are scheduled to open in 1999. The clubhouse serves lunch.

HORSEBACK RIDING AND HORSE-DRAWN RIDES

Trail rides are offered at Hawk Inn and Mountain Resort (see *Lodging— Resorts* in "Killington/Pico Area").

Cavendish Trail Horse Rides (226-7821), Twenty Mile Stream Road, Proctorsville. Guided tours and pony rides (at the Bates Mansion at Brook Farm; see *Lodging—Special Occasions*). Reservations preferred but walk-ins allowed.

SELF-IMPROVEMENT VACATIONS

Fletcher Farm Craft School (228-8770), Route 103 east, Ludlow. Operated since 1948 by the Society of Vermont Craftsmen, this old farmstead on the eastern edge of town offers dorm-style lodging and pleasant studio space for the 86 classes held during July and August. Classes include Early American decoration, stained glass, basketry, weaving, woodcarving, quilting, oil and watercolor painting, spinning, and rug hooking and braiding. Meals are family-style. Catalogs are $2.

Green Mountain at Fox Run (228-8885; 1-800-448-8106), Box 164, Fox Lane, Ludlow. A former resort and, for the past 19 years, "an educational community for weight and health management," this was one of the first anti-diet programs in the country and continues to attract clients from 50 states and many foreign countries. With the exception of January and February, Fox Run has 1- to 4-week programs that offer a daily regimen of exercise and lectures with a remarkably high success rate. $1,150–1,800 for 1 week.

SWIMMING

✐ **West Hill Recreation Area** (228-2849), West Hill off Route 103 in Ludlow, includes a beach (with lifeguard) on a small, spring-fed reservoir; also a snack bar and playground/picnic area.

Buttermilk Falls, near the junction of Routes 100 and 103. There is a swimming hole off Route 103. Turn at the VFW post just west of the intersection.

Camp Plymouth State Park, off Route 100 at Tyson. Beach on Echo Lake, picnic area, food concession.

TENNIS

Town Recreation Park on West Hill in Ludlow (end of Pond Street). Two courts available to the public.

WINTER SPORTS

SNOWMOBILE RIDES

✐ **C&B Guided Rides** (259-2666) caters especially to families with children and groups, night and day.

CROSS-COUNTRY SKIING

Fox Run Ski Touring Center (228-8871), junction of Routes 100 and

A view of Okemo Mountain and its trails

103, Ludlow. A café and a rental shop are surrounded by the open roll of the golf course; there are also wooded and mountain trails adding up to 20 km, most of it tracked; guided tours. Trail fee $8.

DOWNHILL SKIING

Okemo (information: 228-4041, 1-800-228-4041; snow reports: 228-5222; reservations: 1-800-78-OKEMO), Ludlow. A big mountain (boasting Vermont's fourth highest vertical drop), Okemo is a destination ski area with a small-resort feel. The trails are easily accessible. Just beyond the middle of town, you turn up a short access road to a relatively little parking lot. (Additional parking lots and a shuttle service from them are also available.) You walk through a growing hotel complex, find a smallish base lodge, and are off on fast-moving chairlifts (no wait). Surprises begin at the top of these lifts, where you meet a wall of three-story condominiums and find your way down to the spacious Sugar House base lodge—from which the true size of the mountain becomes apparent. This is a mountain of many parts. Beginners and lower-intermediate skiers can enjoy both the lower southwest and upper northeast sides of the mountain—entirely different places in view and feel. From the summit, beginners can actually run a full 4.5 miles to the base. Expert skiers, on the other hand, have the entire northwestern face of the mountain, served by its own chair. There are also a number of wide, central fall line runs down the face of Okemo. Basically, however, this is upper-intermediate heaven, with dozens of trails with varying terrain. Try Upper and Lower World Cup, a long and steep but forgiving run with sweeping views across the Black River Valley to the Connecticut River. Solitude Peak, with eight totally man-made snow-covered trails served by a quad chair, is another haven. The most recent enhancements include a new 380-foot-plus halfpipe creating twin pipes, two new skier and snowboarder terrain parks, expansion of the SKIwee Snow Stars teaching terrain, and renovations to the base and summit lodges. Site work has begun at Jackson Gore, a 546-acre expansion area with its own access off Route 103.

The new Solitude Village complex has its own chairlift and trails. The Salomon Gravity Garage encourages new gear from Axendo skis to SnowBlades; demos available.

Lifts: 13—seven quad, including three high-speed, chairs, two triple chairs, and two surface lifts.

Trails and slopes: 88 trails and glades—24 percent novice, 53 percent intermediate, 20 percent adanced expert.

Vertical drop: 2,150 feet.

Snowmaking: Covers 95 percent of trails, some with top-to-bottom snow.

Facilities: Base lodge with cafeteria; midmountain Sugar House base lodge with cafeteria; summit lodge and cafeteria; hotel with restaurant, nursery, condo lodging.

Ski school: 150 instructors, Cutting Edge Learning Center for all ages. Wild Duck Snowboard Test Center.

Rates: $92–99 per adult for 2 days, $81–84 (ages 13–18), $61–65 junior. Check out pre-Christmas, Winter Carnival, and Family Value packages.

LODGING

Okemo Mountain Lodging Service (228-5571; 1-800-78-OKEMO) refers less than half of its inquiries to slope-side condominiums. A wide variety of inns can be found within a 10-mile radius. (*Note:* This seems to be the one resort area in New England in which most lodging places add a 15 percent service charge to rates. See also *Guidance.*)

INNS

In Ludlow 05149

The Okemo Inn (228-8834; out-of-state: 1-800-328-8834), junction of Routes 100 north and 103. Open year-round except for two weeks in April and November. Ron Parry has been here longer than any other local innkeeper, and this 1810 home is well kept and effortlessly welcoming. There are 11 nicely furnished guest rooms, most with two double beds, all with private bath. There is a living room with a table made from old bellows in front of the hearth and a dining room with low, notched beams; also a TV room with cable. Travel- or ski-weary muscles can be soothed in the sauna or summertime pool; 10-speed bike rentals and guide maps available. $85–95 per person MAP in winter; $75–145 per day B&B for two people. Add 10 percent for service; 5-day, SKI and STAY packages (midweek, non-holiday).

The Andrie Rose Inn (228-4846; out-of-state: 1-800-223-4846), 13 Pleasant Street, is on a quiet back street with surprisingly good views of

Okemo. This is a turn-of-the-century house in which the old detailing has been carefully preserved, but the feel—thanks to bold flowery prints, pastel colors, and skylights—is light-filled and cheerful. The 10 guest rooms have private bath and antique iron or wood beds. Four suites have marble fireplace, whirlpool tub, steam shower for two, cable TV with VCR, stereo, and phone. Two 2-bedroom suites in the guesthouse behind the main house also have full kitchen facilities. Details like a basket of "things you may need," fresh flowers, and bathroom amenities all add to the sense of someplace special. Five-course dinners ($50) are available on Saturday nights. In summer, from $70 for an inn room to $200 for a family suite; in winter, from $110 for an inn room to $500 for a family suite. Less for longer stays. Add 15 percent gratuity.

The Governor's Inn (228-8830; 1-800-GOVERNOR), 86 Main Street, open year-round. William Wallace Stickney, governor of Vermont 1900–1902, built this fine Victorian house with its ornate slate, hand-painted fireplaces. The eight guest rooms, all with private bath, are antiques-filled and coated with flowery paper, with windows fitted with European lace panels. There's a new suite with whirlpool bath, living room, and TV. Guests find cordials and other nice touches next to their down coverlets. There is a small pub and game room as well as the elegant living room and dining room, open to the public, featuring a table d'hôte menu of six courses (see *Dining Out*); five-course breakfasts and tea are served in a cheery back room, "warmed by the sun and a woodstove." $185–200 ($200–300 for the suite) double occupancy B&B; add $70 per couple MAP; add 15 percent for service. Ask about Culinary Magic Cooking Seminars on summer and fall weekends.

Black River Inn (228-5585), 100 Main Street. A fine, 1835 Federal-style home with hand-carved oak staircases and marble fireplaces is now a very gracious inn owned by Darwin and Nancy Thomas. Boasting Ludlow's first indoor tub and a 1794 carved bed in which Lincoln slept, it offers 10 antiques-furnished guest chambers, 8 with private bath. Amenities include a hot tub. Winter rates are $85–130 per couple B&B; a two-bedroom suite with two baths and a sitting room is $240. A home-style dinner is included on weekends.

✍ **Echo Lake Inn** (228-8602; 1-800-356-6844), Route 100 in Tyson, but the mailing address is P.O. Box 154, Ludlow 05149. One of the few survivors of the many Victorian-style summer hotels (although parts of the building predate the Victorian era) that once graced Vermont lakes, the inn is four stories tall with a long white porch, lined in summer with pink geraniums and red rockers. Now winterized, it offers 25 rooms, 12 with bath. There are seven condo units in the adjacent building. The least-expensive rooms are under the eaves on the fourth floor, a find for families. The top price is for spacious suites with antiques. The living room is homey and informal, with hooked rugs and wooden chairs grouped around the fireplace and TV. There's also the inviting Stone Tavern and a low-

Echo Lake

beamed dining room (see Dining Out), both open to the public. Summer facilities include tennis and swimming in the pool or at a private beach on Echo Lake across the road, where complimentary boats and canoes are available to guests. No smoking in guest rooms. Winter rates: $129–259 per room MAP; $79–209 B&B. Ask about weekend and 3-night specials. Add 15 percent for service.

🐾❧ **The Coombes Family Inn** (228-8799), East Lake Road, Ludlow. Ruth and Bill Coombes have recently celebrated their 20th anniversary as innkeepers, welcoming families to their peaceful 1891 former dairy farm home. There are 11 guest rooms, all with private bath—6 in the farmhouse and 5 in an attached unit (where pets are allowed). Guests can smoke in the privacy of their own rooms, but not in the public areas. B&B double rates: $55 spring, $82 summer, $124 winter. Ruth's hearty Vermont-style dinners are available nightly by reservation at $15 per adult and $8 for kids.

In Proctorsville 05153

The Castle (226-7222; 1-800-697-7222), P.O. Box 207, Routes 131 and 103. Quarry and timber baron Allen Fetcher, elected governor of Vermont in 1913, built this imposing neo-Jacobean stone manor on a knoll, importing European artisans in 1901 for the oak and mahogany woodwork and detailed cast-plaster ceilings. With Erica and Richard Hart as innkeepers, the Castle has 10 luxurious guest rooms, 6 with working fireplace and 2 with whirlpool bath. Even the four rooms on the third floor seem spacious. Afternoon tea and cocktails are served in the paneled library in front of a massive fireplace. Dinner is an event (see *Dining Out*). Winter rates: $130–225 per room B&B; $195–290 MAP; somewhat lower in summer.

The Golden Stage Inn (226-7744; 1-800-253-8226), 1 Depot Street, P.O. Box 218. Now with Micki Smith-Darnauer and Paul Darnauer at the helm, this handsome, historic house was an inn in the 18th century, and later the Skinner family home for 100 years after 1830. One of the eight bedrooms (also one suite) is named for the writer and performer Cornelia Otis Skinner. There are two guest rooms on the ground floor; two more and the suite are in a recent addition. The solarium, one of three intimate dining rooms, was once the inn's greenhouse. Lush summer gardens and orchards surround a full-sized swimming pool. Winter rates $95–265 B&B, $170–300 MAP; less in summer (five-course dinner served to guests).

$\mathcal{S}$ **Okemo Lantern Lodge** (226-7770; 1-800-732-7077), P.O. Box 247, 329 Main Street, Proctorsville, a former mill owner's mansion, is rich in ornately carved butternut and stained glass. The dining room takes center stage downstairs, and it's usually filled with aromas from the adjacent kitchen. Dody Button is the owner-chef, fixing generous breakfasts and multicourse dinners for guests by reservation. The 10 guest rooms range from small to large enough for a king-sized bed; all have private bath. Our favorites are on the third floor. In warm-weather months the inn is popular with bicyclists and families; it's a casual, comfortable inn with an attractive swimming pool out back. $65–80 per person MAP in winter, $40–55 B&B; less in summer. Add 10 percent service charge on MAP rate.

BED & BREAKFASTS

Fletcher Manor (228-3548), One Elm Street, Ludlow 05149. Jill and Bob Tofferi recently opened this stylish 1837 town house to guests. The music room boasts a baby grand piano, and there's a fireplace in the parlor. Continental breakfasts are served in the Victorian dining room. Four guest rooms. $65 double midweek, $95 winter weekends.

Whitney Brook (226-7460, 226-2423), Twenty Mile Stream Road, Proctorsville 05153. Jim and Ellen Parrish welcome guests to their pretty 1870 farmhouse on a quiet road. There are four guest rooms, three with queen beds and one with a double and a single. Two rooms have private bath, two have semiprivate. Guests enjoy a private living room downstairs and a sitting room upstairs. $55–95, depending on the season.

Maple Crest Farm (492-3367), RR Box 120, Cuttingsville 05738. This handsome, white-brick farmhouse sits high on a ridge in the old hilltop center of Shrewsbury. It was built in 1808 as Gleason's Tavern and is still in the same family. In the 1860s, they began taking in guests and have done so off and on ever since. The Smiths offer four antiques-filled rooms at $55 per couple ($30 single) and two charming apartments ($75), that can accommodate small families. Breakfasts may be purchased separately; no credit cards. "Every piece of furniture has a story," says Donna Smith—and she knows each one. Ask about a rocking chair or spool bed, and you'll begin to sense who has lived in this unusual house down through the years. Books and magazines are everywhere, and if you look closely, you'll see that they're carefully selected, focusing on local and Vermont tales and history. The Smiths are noted for the quality of their maple syrup, produced in the sugarhouse at the peak of the hill; the same sweeping view can be enjoyed in winter on cross-country skis. You can walk off in any number of directions.

The Buckmaster Inn (492-3485), Lincoln Hill Road, Shrewsbury 05738, was built as the Buckmaster Tavern on a hilltop in 1801. This gracious house as recently acquired by Richard and Elizabeth Davis, who have thoroughly renovated it. Eight to 10 guests can be accommodated; two bedrooms share a bath, as do the other two; all four have been freshly decorated. There is a spacious living room, a library with fireplace and TV, and a long, screened-in porch that's especially inviting in the summer and fall. The Davises are enthusiastic hosts who can tell you what to see and do. Rates are $79 and $89 double, with continental-plus breakfasts featuring home-baked goodies.

Austria House (259-2441), Bowlsville Road, Mount Holly 05758. This nicely remodeled 1812 farmhouse on a hill has four rooms; full breakfasts include "blueberry pancakes the Austrian way." $40–60 double.

Crisanver House (492-3589; 1-800-492-8089), P.O. Box 157, Wiley Hill Road, Shrewsbury 05738. Panoramic views mark this contemporary, Colonial-style post-and-beam house on 120 acres. Eight rooms with private baths; there's a porch, library, tennis, and a heated pool. $85–135 per room with private bath, $80–120 with shared, including afternoon tea, full breakfast.

High Pastures (773-2087; 1-800-584-4738), Cold River Road, Shrewsbury 05738. A 200-year-old restored farmhouse with a few antiques-furnished rooms, chickens, turkeys, game birds, and sheep in the front yard. $60–85 double.

Hortonville Inn (259-2587; 1-800-497-4091), off Route 103 in Hortonville, RFD 1, Mount Holly 05758. Ray and Mary Maglione's large white house sits high on a hill and, along with the classic church across the road, forms the center (in fact, about all there is) of Hortonville. Two rooms have private baths; the other three share another. Each room has a VCR; 250 tapes on hand. You can rent bikes. The views are magnificent, and there are 13 acres out back with trails cut for hiking and cross-country skiing. The summer rates of $50–60 per couple (foliage season and winter, $65–75) include a four-course breakfast, nightly wine and hors d'oeuvres, herbal teas, and coffee with cookies on tap all day.

The Leslie Place (259-2903), Box 62, Belmont 05730. Mary Gorman's nicely restored farmhouse on Healdville Road off Route 103 has three rooms (one on the first floor) with private bath and a small kitchenette that everyone uses. Mary gives advice on where to walk on the 100 rolling acres and beyond. You can walk to the Catamount Cross Country Ski Trail, for instance. $60–90 double B&B, depending on the season. No credit cards.

MOTELS

All Seasons Inn Motel (228-8100; 1-888-228-8100), 112 Main Street, Ludlow 05149. All 17 recently renovated units have cable TV, phone with voice mail, and refrigerator, and some have a kitchenette. Free shuttle-bus service. Winter rates: $69–119 midweek, $99–199 weekends.

Best Western Ludlow Colonial Motel (228-8188), 93 Main Street, Ludlow 05149. Originated years ago when Fire Chief Rick Harrison built a 14-unit motel onto the back of his 1825 home, this is now a 39-unit motel decorated with antiques. All units have phone, cable TV, full bath, and in-room coffee. Winter rates: $59–116 midweek, $89–194 weekends.

Cavendish Pointe Hotel (226-7688; 1-800-438-7908), Route 103, Cavendish 05142. A relatively new motor inn with 72 rooms in the $59–109 range (winter). Rooms are standard motel-style, fairly large, and there's an indoor pool, hot tub/spa room, game room; also a restaurant-bar that opens only during ski season.

CONDOMINIUMS

Okemo Mountain Lodge (228-2079; 1-800-78-OKEMO), RFD 1, Ludlow 05149. This three-story hotel at the entrance to the area is really a cluster of 55 one-bedroom condos, each with a sleeping couch in the living room. There's a compact kitchen with eating counter and a fireplace; enough space for a couple and two children. $100–295 per night per couple in winter, many packages; less in summer.

Kettle Brook Condominiums at Okemo, same phone and address as the Okemo Mountain Lodge. Salted along trails, condos range from efficiencies to three-bedroom units, nicely built. $90–520 in winter, many packages; less in summer.

Winterplace, Okemo, same phone and address as the Okemo Mountain Lodge. These are Okemo's luxury condominiums, set high on a mountain shelf with access to an indoor pool and, in summer, tennis courts. $160–590 in winter, less in summer.

Solitude Village, same phone as above, a ski-in/ski-out complex of condos and town houses plus a lodge with indoor/outdoor heated pool. Winter rates $165–995.

The Mill (228-5566; 1-800-335-MILL), 145 Main Street, Ludlow 05149. The town's centerpiece mill (see the introduction to this chapter) has been converted into one- to three-room condo units. These are attractive but rather dark rooms, although each has a fireplace; back balconies overlook the Black River. The front desk is helpful. The Mill is a half mile from Okemo Mountain and a short walk from town shops and restaurants, with shuttle-bus service to the mountain in winter. (*Note:* Vermont Transit drops you almost at the door; see *Getting There.*) From $59 per unit in summer; from $79 in winter.

CONDO RENTAL SERVICES

Rental services in the area include: **Strictly Rentals** (228-3000), 1000 South Street, Ludlow, representing 40 seasonal and 150 short-term rentals ranging from lakeside summer cottages to winter condominiums, including **Schiermeyer's Lodge**, a privately owned contemporary mansion in Shrewsbury with accommodations for as many as 30 people.

SPECIAL OCCASIONS

The Bates Mansion at Brook Farm (226-7863), Twenty Mile Stream Road, Cavendish 05142. This stately summer mansion is a great setting for weddings, family reunions, and conferences. It also has an antiques and collectibles sales barn, and offers trail rides.

WHERE TO EAT

DINING OUT

Nikki's (228-7797), Sunshine Market Place, Ludlow. Open for dinner nightly during ski season. Positioned at the foot of Okemo's access road, this is one of Vermont's most pleasant restaurants. Bob Gilmore has been in business for more than 20 years, and the dining area and menu continue to evolve. The exposed wood and brick walls are garnished with stained and beveled glass, and there are booths, an inviting bar area, and gleaming coffee machines. One table is downstairs in the wine cellar. Entrées might include fresh ribbons of garlic and black pepper pasta served with a spicy puree of red bell peppers and fresh basil, or steak *au poivre*. New England bouillabaisse (fresh salmon, littleneck clams, and scallops in a simmering tomato seafood broth) is a specialty, and there's usually stone-baked pizza. The wine selection is exceptional. Moderate.

The Governor's Inn (228-8830), 86 Main Street, Ludlow. Now owned by Jim and Kathy Kubec, this remains Ludlow's most famous restaurant. Dinner, by reservation only, is served every day except Monday and Tuesday and begins at 7 PM with hors d'oeuvres and cocktails served in the parlor. Guests then move on to the Victorian dining rooms, where they are served by waitresses in period dress. Each evening's menu is fixed. You might begin with sherried apricot soup and feast on the Governor's braised quail. Prix fixe $45.

Echo Lake Inn (228-8602), Route 100 north in Tyson. Open to the public for breakfast, lunch, and dinner. The dining room, with print wallpaper and shades of mauve, is attractive. Dining options might include hand-pounded, milk-fed veal sautéed with wild Vermont mushrooms and julienne prosciutto, and eggplant crêpes. Moderate.

Harry's Cafe (259-2996), Route 103, Mount Holly, open 5–10, Tuesday through Sunday. One of the hottest spots between Weston and Killington. Trip Pierce took the funky old Backside Restaurant and turned it into a light, airy space with good art and a woodstove. "It's open season on whatever you want to eat" is the way Pierce describes the wildly eclectic menu: Thai-style teriyaki and red curry, shrimp and tortellini, fish-and-chips, and New York sirloin. Specialties include flauta: grilled steak or chicken sliced thin, wrapped with lots of jack cheese and onion in a flour tortilla, topped with more cheese, baked until golden, and served with salsa and sour cream. Another favorite is fritto misto: a platter of deep-fried shrimp, scallops, and fish in a crispy batter served with fresh angel hair pasta with basil marinara. You can also dine on tapas like chicken and ginger wontons or Thai clear noodle salad. Cheeseburgers, pizza, and big burritos are also available all day. Inexpensive to moderate.

Priority's (228-2800), Okemo Mountain Resort. Housed right under the clock tower at the entrance to Okemo, a bright, spacious area with delightfully deep booths for lunch and a variety of spaces for dinner; also a sports bar and live music and dancing (no cover) on weekends. House specialties include chicken and steak teriyaki and seafood fettuccine Alfredo. It's a large menu ranging from fish-and-chips to prime rib. Great burgers, burritos, and pizza at lunch. Inexpensive to moderate.

The Castle (226-7222), intersection of Routes 131 and 103, Proctorsville. The interior of this stone mansion is a rich blend of American oak, Mexican mahogany, and French marble. Before dinner, guests are invited to meet in the library for cocktails, then move to the paneled dining room for a five-course meal that can commence with baked Roquefort and pear tart, pâté, or escargots, and may include rack of lamb, medallions of venison, roast duckling, or veal scaloppine. Moderate to expensive.

EATING OUT

Michael's Seafood and Steak House (228-5622), Main Street, Ludlow. A large old dining landmark with a big, upscale pub. Open for dinner nightly with midweek specials and a Sunday buffet lunch. Groups are welcome here. You might order pasta and sausage, stuffed flounder, coq au vin, or seafood Newburg for six. Moderate.

DJ's Restaurant (228-5374), 146 Main Street, Ludlow. Open from 4:30 for dinner. A former downtown eatery that's been upscaled, this place is best known for its broiled scallops and shrimp, extensive salad bar, and nightly specials. Moderate.

Cappuccino's Cafe (228-7566), 41 Depot Street, Ludlow, serves dinner Wednesday through Sunday; reservations suggested.

Pot Belly Pub (228-8989), 130 Main Street, Ludlow. Open for dinner nightly and lunch most days. First opened in a storefront in 1974, this zany place has expanded into a great space; good for live entertainment (swing and blues bands, jug band music, and rock 'n' roll on weekends), and victuals ranging from popcorn shrimp, Pot Belly chicken, or ribs to chocolate peanut butter pie. A belly burger or the Cajun chicken sandwich is a good bet at lunch, and you can always get a Belly burger at dinner, too, or go for the Pot Belly ribs or Mexican chicken.

Valente's Italian Restaurant (228-2671), Main Street, Ludlow. An old-fashioned, downtown restaurant, this is locally respected Italian food the way Mama makes it.

Archie's Steak House (228-3003), the Marketplace, Okemo, open from 4:30 daily, noon on Sunday, for prime beef, seafood, big salad bar, a cigar-friendly sports bar, and entertainment on weekends.

MICROBREWERY

Black River Brewing Company (228-3100), 207 Main Street, Ludlow, makes several ales, porters, and stouts (among them Big Buck, Fish Tale, Long Term Disability, Stump Jumper), which can be sampled and downed in its Brew House pub-restaurant. Wings and sweet potato chip nachos are among the specialties.

SELECTIVE SHOPPING

CRAFTS SHOPS

Vermont Industries Factory Store (492-3451; 1-800-826-4766), Route 103, Box 301, Cuttingsville 05738, occupies a big barn full of hand-forged, wrought-iron products—freestanding sundials, sconces, candleholders, corn driers, hanging planters, chandeliers, and a wide range of fireplace accessories. We could kick ourselves for not buying one of the distinctive floor or wall lamps that we have since seen selling for substantially more in other stores.

SPECIAL SHOPS

Singleton's Store (226-7666), downtown Proctorsville. A long-established family business in the middle (it's not hard to find) of Proctorsville has kept abreast of the demands of the area's condo owners while continuing to cover the basics. Fishing and hunting licenses, rods and reels, guns and ammo, sporting goods, outdoor wear, plus fine wines, choice meats, a standout deli, and a gun shop are all part of the scene; the specialty of the house is smoked meat (an average of 350 pounds of meat sold per day).

Green Mountain Sugar House (228-7151), Route 100, 4 miles north of Ludlow. You can watch syrup being produced in March and April; maple candy is made throughout the year on a weekly basis. This is also a place to find freshly pressed cider in September. The gift and produce shop is open daily 9–6 "most of the time."

Clear Lake Furniture (228-8395), Route 100 north, Ludlow. The workshop and showroom for custom-made pieces in cherry, curly maple, oak, and walnut by Brent Karner and Frank Procopio. Open Monday through Saturday 9–6, Sunday noon–5.

Black River Produce (226-7480), Route 103 in Proctorsville. An exceptional source of fruit, vegetables, fresh breads, cheese, seafood, and flowers.

Crowley Cheese Factory and Shop (factory: 259-2340; shop: 259-2210),

Route 103, 5 miles north of Ludlow. This highly regarded cheese is being made again; the factory is open 8–4, Monday through Friday (arrive before 2 PM), and the shop, which carries other Vermont products as well, is open daily.

Meadowsweet Herb Farm (492-3565), North Shrewsbury. The herb shed attached to Polly Hayne's handsome old farmhouse on a back road (follow the signs) is a studio and retail shop in which herb wreaths, potpourri, and culinary blends are made from more than 200 varieties of herbs. A number of perennial herbs and geraniums are grown year-round in the solar greenhouse and sold as seedlings; seeds are available too. A picnic bench overlooks the gardens, and a shop sells snacks. The farm and gardens are open daily May through October; Monday through Saturday during November and December.

Also note that the Vermont Industries Factory Store (see *Craft Shops*) is on the way to Shrewsbury.

SPECIAL EVENTS

February–March: **Okemo WinterFest** includes "the Ludlow Olympics," tobogganing, snow sculpture contest, fireworks, ski races, and torchlight parade. Call 228-4041 or 228-6110 for details.

July 1: **Fletcher Farm Arts and Crafts Fair,** Route 103, Ludlow.

August: **Vermont State Zucchini Festival,** Ludlow. Four days of "zucchini madness," such as "Give a Zucchini to a Friend or Enemy Day" (August 20, 1998); costume parade ("Snow White and the Seven Zucchini"), Z-buck auction, and other events.

Early December: **Victorian Christmas Walk and Parade,** Ludlow.

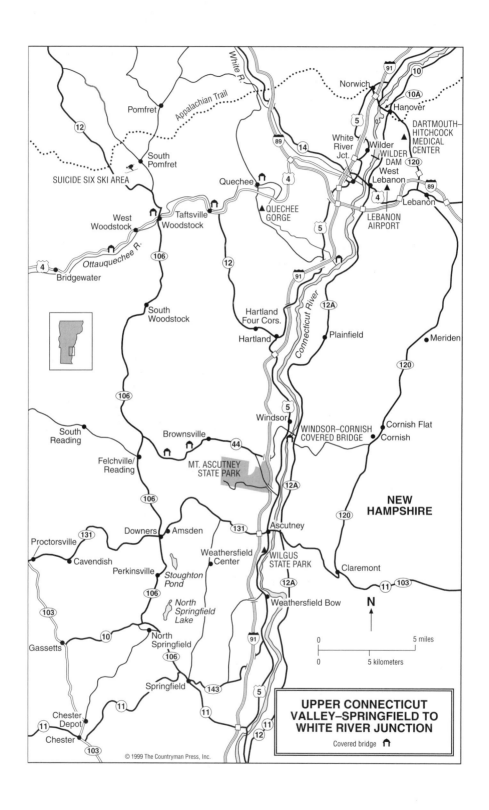

UPPER CONNECTICUT
VALLEY–SPRINGFIELD TO
WHITE RIVER JUNCTION

Covered bridge

© 1999 The Countryman Press, Inc.

II. UPPER CONNECTICUT VALLEY

Upper Valley River Towns
Woodstock

Cross-country skiers at the Woodstock Ski Touring Center

Upper Valley River Towns

The Upper Valley ignores state lines to form one of New England's most beautiful and distinctive regions. Its two dozen towns are scattered along the Vermont and New Hampshire banks of the Connecticut River for some 20 miles north and south of Dartmouth College.

"Upper Valley" is a name coined in the 1950s by a local daily, *The Valley News,* to define its two-state circulation area. The label has stuck, interestingly, to the same group of towns that, back in the 1770s, tried to form the state of New Connecticut. But the Dartmouth-based, pro–New Connecticut party was thwarted by larger powers, namely New York and New Hampshire, along with the strident Vermont independence faction, the Green Mountain Boys. On July 2, 1777, delegates met at Elijah West's tavern in Windsor to declare Vermont a "free and independent state," bounded on the east by the Connecticut River.

The Upper Valley itself prospered, a fact that's obvious from the exquisite Federal-era meetinghouses and mansions still salted through this area. And while it has had its ups and downs, it is growing now far more quickly than either Vermont as a whole or New Hampshire.

King George III's decree that the river belongs to New Hampshire still holds, which means that that state is responsible for maintaining the bridges. Of the dozens of bridges that once connected the two states, only 10 survive, but they include the longest covered bridge in the United States (connecting Windsor with Cornish), and the Upper Valley is still an undeniable entity. The Upper Valley area phone book includes towns on both sides of the river (it's a local call back and forth, although the area code is now needed), and Norwich and Hanover's Dresden School District reaches well into Vermont. Several Independence Day parades start in one state and finish across the bridge in the other. And the Montshire Museum, founded on the New Hampshire side of the river and now splendidly rooted on the Vermont bank, combines both states in its name.

The cultural center of the Upper Valley remains the Dartmouth green (now graced with a major theater and museum) in Hanover. With the nearby medical complex and the West Lebanon shopping center strip (a popular escape route from Vermont sales tax), it forms a genuine hub, handy to the highways radiating, the way rail lines once did, from White River Junction.

Since the 1820s, the Upper Valley's industrial center has been in Springfield and Windsor, both of which have produced far more than their share of inventors. And, for a century, summer inns and camps have lined the shores of Lakes Morey and Fairlee.

Beyond these redbrick towns and old resort enclaves, farms still spread comfortably along the river, all the way from Weathersfield Bow to Newbury. They are backed by steep hills, one of them (Mount Ascutney) skiable. The stretch of both road (Route 5) and river north from Wilder Dam to the oxbow in Newbury offers unexpected vistas of the Presidentials in New Hampshire (New England's highest mountains). Inns cater to bicyclists and canoeists.

Thanks to the 1970s Clean Water Act and acquisitions, greenups, and cleanups by numerous conservation groups, the Connecticut River itself is enjoying a genuine renewal, with campsites and inns spaced along the shore; visitors and residents alike are discovering its beauty.

GUIDANCE

Note: Listings are from south to north.

In Springfield, the **Chamber of Commerce** (885-2779), 14 Clinton Street (at the lights on Route 11), is open year-round Monday through Friday 8–5. The **Eureka Schoolhouse,** Route 11, near I-91, open 9–4, mid-May through mid-October, a genuine 18th-century schoolhouse, serves as an area information center. E-mail: spfldcoc@vermontel.com; the regional web site: vacationinvermont.com (877-668-1852).

The Windsor–Mt. Ascutney Area Chamber of Commerce (674-5910) answers phone queries.

The Quechee Chamber of Commerce (295-7900; 1-800-295-5451; web site: www.quechee.com). We include Quechee listings in the Woodstock chapter but the town straddles both areas and the chamber currently serves as the primary tourism information source for this part of the Upper Valley. The office is open year-round and the information booth at Quechee Gorge on Route 4 is open mid-May through mid-October.

GETTING THERE

By car: Interstates 91 and 89 converge in the White River Junction–Lebanon area, where they also meet Route 5 north and south on the Vermont side; Route 4, the main east–west highway through central Vermont; and Route 10, the river road on the New Hampshire side.

By bus: White River Junction is a hub for **Greyhound–Vermont Transit** (295-3011) with express service to Boston; the terminal itself is one of New England's few pleasant bus stations, with clean, friendly dining and snack rooms.

By air: The Lebanon (N.H.) Regional Airport has service to and from Philadelphia, Boston, and New York via **Business Express (Delta)** (1-800-345-3400) and **USAir Express** (1-800-428-4322).

By train: **Amtrak** (295-7160; 1-800-875-7245) stops in White River Junction and Windsor en route to and from New York's Penn Station and Washington, D.C. Baggage cars carry bikes. At this writing, there is one daily train southbound (10:20 AM) and one northbound (6:20 PM). Inquire about connections between St. Albans and Montreal.

GETTING AROUND

New Face Taxi (295-1500), of White River Junction, will fetch you to and from the bus, train, and plane.

MEDICAL EMERGENCY

Try **911** first in an emergency; increasingly, it's serving the entire area, but for Thetford/Fairlee/Bradford/Orford, it's still 603-333-4347.

Dartmouth-Hitchcock Medical Center (603-650-5000), One Medical Center Drive, off Route 120, between Hanover and Lebanon, is recognized as one of the best teaching hospitals in New England.

Local medical facilities include **Springfield Hospital** (885-2151), 25 Ridgewood Road, Springfield, and **Mount Ascutney Hospital** (674-6711), County Road, Windsor.

VILLAGES

Springfield. Sited at the confluence of the Connecticut and Black Rivers, Springfield boomed with Vermont's tool industry in the 19th and first half of the 20th century and suffered as that industry atrophied in the 1980s. Motorists headed for Chester on Route 11 should stop at the restored 1790s Eureka Schoolhouse and ask directions to the old downtown and the powerful falls. Gracious 19th-century residential neighborhoods are terraced above the old commercial center (see Hartness House under *Lodging*). Housed in a Victorian mansion (9 Elm Street) high above downtown, the Springfield Art & Historical Society (885-2415; open May through mid-October, Tuesday through Friday noon–5; Saturday 2–5) has collections of pewter, Bennington pottery, toys and dolls, primitive paintings, and costumes, and puts on periodic art shows.

Weathersfield Center. On a scenic, old north–south road between Springfield and Route 131 stands this nearly secret gem of a hamlet with its brick 1821 Meeting House and Civil War memorial, a particularly sobering reminder of how many young Vermonters served and died (12 boys from just this small village) in that war. The Weathersfield Historical Society, housed in the Reverend Dan Foster House (open late June to early October, Thursday through Monday 2–5), displays Civil War memorabilia, archival photos, an old forge, and the last wildcat killed in Weathersfield (1867). It was Weathersfield native William Jarvis who transformed the economy of Vermont—and the rest of northern New England—by smuggling 4,000 sheep out of Spain during his term as U.S. consul in Lisbon. That was in 1810. By 1840 there were upward of 2 million sheep in Vermont.

Windsor. In his *Roadside History of Vermont*, Peter notes that aside from

CHRIS MCKINLEY

Amtrak's Vermonter pulls into White River Junction

its title, Birthplace of Vermont (see Old Constitution House under *To See—Historic Sites*), Windsor can also claim to be the midwife of the state's machine tool industry. Windsor resident Lemuel Hedge devised a machine for ruling paper in 1815 and dividing scales in 1827. Asahel Hubbard produced a revolving pump in 1828, and Niconar Kendall designed an "under hammer" rifle, the first use of interchangeable parts, in the 1830s (see the American Precision Museum under *To See— Museums*). Windsor's 1840s prosperity is reflected in the handsome lines of the columned Windsor House, which was considered the best public house between Boston and Montreal in the mid-19th century. Saved from the wrecker's ball in 1972, it now houses the chamber of commerce and a Vermont Craftmen's Center, showcasing museum-quality craftsmanship. Just south of Windsor's brief brick commercial block stands the Old South Congregational Church, designed by Asher Benjamin and built in 1798; it was renovated in 1844, 1879, and again in 1922 but fortunately retains its classic beauty. Also worth noting is St. Francis of Assisi Roman Catholic Church, with its significant example of contemporary religious art—the series of the *Seven Sacraments* panels contributed by George Tooker, the noted American painter who lives in nearby Hartland. St. Paul's Episcopal Church, on the common, built in 1832, is the oldest Episcopal church in Vermont still in regular use. The Townsend Cottage, across the square, dating from 1847, is a striking example of Carpenter Gothic style. Two more major reasons to visit Windsor: a visitor-geared Simon Pearce Glass factory and showroom and the Ascutney Mountain Resort. Don't fail to cross the sole

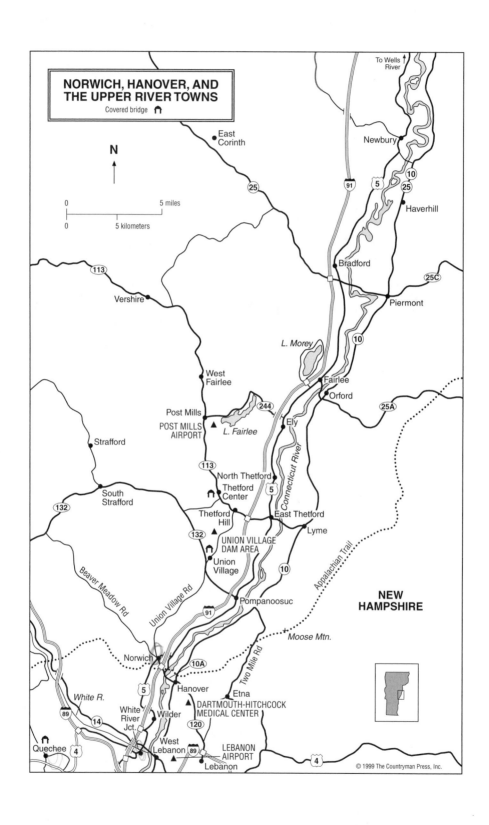

NORWICH, HANOVER, AND THE UPPER RIVER TOWNS

Covered bridge

N

0   5 miles

0   5 kilometers

To Wells River

East Corinth

Newbury

Haverhill

Bradford

Piermont

Vershire

L. Morey

West Fairlee

Fairlee

Orford

Post Mills

POST MILLS AIRPORT

L. Fairlee

Ely

Strafford

North Thetford

Thetford Center

East Thetford

Lyme

South Strafford

Thetford Hill

UNION VILLAGE DAM AREA

Union Village

Pompanoosuc

NEW HAMPSHIRE

Beaver Meadow Rd

Moose Mtn.

Norwich

Hanover

Etna

DARTMOUTH-HITCHCOCK MEDICAL CENTER

White R.

White River Jct.

Wilder

Quechee

West Lebanon

LEBANON AIRPORT

Lebanon

Connecticut River

Appalachian Trail

Union Village Rd

Two Mile Rd

© 1999 The Countryman Press, Inc.

surviving covered bridge on the Connecticut River (the longest in the United States), to Cornish, New Hampshire, where the Saint-Gaudens National Historic Site is well worth visiting.

White River Junction, located at the confluence of the Connecticut and White Rivers and the junction of Interstates 91 and 89, was once a bustling, often raucous railroad hub. While its periphery serves the interstates with brand-name motels and fast-food stops, the redbrick downtown, with its venerable Hotel Coolidge and the Polka Dot Diner, still caters to train passengers. Horace Wells of White River Junction was, incidentally, the first person to use laughing gas as an anesthetic for pulling teeth. White River Junction is actually a village in Hartford, a town that also includes Quechee, Hartford Village, Wilder, and West Hartford.

Hanover, New Hampshire—Dartmouth College. Chartered in 1769, Dartmouth is the ninth oldest and one of the most prestigious colleges in the country, and its handsome buildings frame three sides of an elm-shaded green. The fourth side is lined with visitor-friendly buildings: the large, college-owned Hanover Inn, the entertainment complex called Hopkins Center, and the Hood Museum of Art. Note the white information kiosk on the green, staffed during the summer months. Most visitors find their way into Baker Memorial Library to see the set of murals by famous Mexican painter José Clemente Orozco (which some alumni once demanded be removed or covered because of the artist's left-wing politics). When the kiosk is closed, guided tours are offered by the admission office in McNutt Hall by student members of Green Key.

Norwich, one of the prettiest towns in Vermont, was settled in 1761 by a group from Marshfield, Connecticut. It has always had close ties to Hanover (just across the bridge), with which it shares the Dresden School District. Many Dartmouth faculty members live in Norwich, which was once the home of the American Literary, Scientific, and Military Academy, founded in 1819 and named Norwich University in 1834; it moved to Northfield after the Civil War. The village is an architectural showcase for fine brick and frame Federal homes. Note the Seven Nations House across from the Norwich Inn, built as a commercial "tenement" in 1832. The big sight to see here, the Montshire Museum, is sequestered down by the river, east of I-91.

Thetford has an unusual number of post offices per capita: There are six in all. Thetford Hill, site of Thetford Academy (and the Parish Players), is one of the few almost perfect hamlets left in the state.

Fairlee Village is a plain cousin to its handsome twin—aristocratic **Orford,** New Hampshire (well known for its lineup of elegant Federal-era homes, some credited to Boston architect Charles Bulfinch), just across the river. But we like it better. Check out Chapman's, a 19th-century pharmacy that has expanded in unusual directions under more than 40 years of Chapman ownership. Summer camps and inns line nearby Lake Morey. Samuel Morey, a resident of Orford and a lumberman in Fairlee, was the inventor of the first steamboat: In 1793, 14 years before Fulton launched his *Clermont,* Morey was puffing up and down the river in a primitive craft barely big enough to hold him and his firewood. The remains of the little steamer are believed to lie at the bottom of Lake Morey, scuttled by its builder when the $100,000 in stock offered him by Robert Fulton turned out to be worthless. Morey also patented an internal combustion engine in 1825.

Bradford, where the Waits River flows into the Connecticut, is built on terraces of land above the floodplain. Buildings along the Connecticut side of its main street (Route 5) have another level below, and a golf course is sequestered down there behind the downtown. Favorite sons include James Wilson, an ingenious farmer, who made America's first geographical globes in the early 1800s, and Capt. Charles Cook, who commanded the battleship *Oregon* on its strategic 15,000-mile dash around Cape Horn from the Pacific to help defeat the Spanish at Santiago Bay in 1898. Today the town is a good way-stop for lunch and dinner, and is known for its Annual Wild Game Supper.

Newbury and **Haverhill.** The northern reaches of the Upper Valley are defined by these two unusually handsome villages. Haverhill, New Hampshire, has a covered bridge (the oldest in New England) and double commons, where all-day flea markets are held on the last Sunday of the month. Newbury, Vermont, was known in the 19th century as a mineral spa but the big old resort hotel has long since vanished. Its handsome common is the scene of the late-July Cracker Barrel Bazaar.

TO SEE

MUSEUMS

Hood Museum of Art (603-646-2808), Dartmouth green. Open Tuesday through Saturday 10–5 and Sunday noon–5; until 9 PM Wednesday. Free. An outstanding collection of art, ranging from Assyrian bas-reliefs donated by missionary graduates in the 1850s to works by Italian masters and American 18th- and 19th-century artists, is displayed in the downstairs galleries. A narrow flight of stairs rises dramatically to the high, skylit Lathrop Gallery, hung with such modern masterpieces as Picasso's *Guitar on a Table,* a gift of Nelson Rockefeller, class of 1930. Rothko, Picasso, and at least one outsized canvas by Dartmouth graduate Frank Stella are usually on display. There are frequently changing special exhibits.

Montshire Museum of Science (649-2200; web site: www.montshire.net), Montshire Road, Norwich. Open daily 10–5; admission $5.50 per adult, $4.50 per child ages 3–17. Few cities have a science museum of this quality, and the superb exhibits plus extensive trails along the Connecticut River add up to one of New England's outstanding sights. Don't be put off by the entrance fee, and stop by whether or not you have children along. Do you know which common fruits and vegetables float in water? Do you know the difference between a nebula and a nova? The museum's avowed goal is to demystify natural phenomena, and it does so in a way that's fun. Exhibits change but usually include an aquarium of northern New England fish, a display on the physics of the bubble, and another on "knot topography." All exhibits (even the boa constrictor) are "hands-on." Andy's Place, a preschool corner, includes a deep cave complete with a (stuffed) bear cub. There's also a playground and a big gift shop; inquire about workshops, guided hikes, special events, and exhibits. (See also *Green Space*.)

American Precision Museum (674-5781), South Main Street, Windsor. Open May 30 through November 1, Monday through Friday 9–5; Saturday, Sunday, and holidays 10–4; $5 per adult, $3 seniors, $2 ages 6–12. An important, expanding collection of hand and machine tools, assembled in the 1846 Robbins, Kendall & Lawrence Armory, itself a National Historic Landmark. The firm became world famous in 1851 because of its displays of "the American system" of manufacturing interchangeable parts, especially for what became the renowned Enfield rifle. Special exhibits vary from year to year.

HISTORIC SITES

Old Constitution House, North Main Street, Windsor. Theoretically open daily, late May through mid-October, but staffed by volunteers, so you can never be sure. For information call the Vermont Department of Historic Preservation at 828-3051. $2 admission. This is Elijah West's tavern (but not in its original location), where delegates gathered on July 2, 1777, to adopt Vermont's constitution. It now holds an intriguing collection of antiques, prints, documents, tools and cooking utensils, tableware, toys, and early fabrics.

The Saint-Gaudens National Historic Site (603-675-2175), Cornish, New Hampshire. Grounds open daily, dawn to dusk. Buildings open 8:30–4:30 daily late May through October. $4 adults; free under age 17. Includes the sculptor's summer home, barn-studio, sculpture court, and formal gardens, which he developed and occupied between 1885 and his death in 1907. The property was accepted by the National Park Service in 1964. Augustus Saint-Gaudens loved the Ravine Trail, a ¼-mile cart path to Blow-Me-Up Brook, now marked for visitors, and other walks laid out through the woodlands and wetlands of the Blow-Me-Down Natural Area. Saint-Gaudens was one of several artists who formed a summer colony in Cornish, a group that included poets Percy MacKaye, Witter Bynner, and William Vaughn Moody; Winston Churchill, the American novelist whose summer estate was used as the vacation White House by President Woodrow Wilson in 1914 and 1915; Ethel Barrymore, Charles Dana Gibson, Finley Peter Dunne, and Maxfield Parrish. Summer visitors can enjoy examples of the artist's work.

KIM GRANT

Windsor-Cornish Covered Bridge

Note: Bring a picnic lunch for Sunday-afternoon chamber music concerts, at 2 PM in July and August.

COVERED BRIDGES

The **Windsor-Cornish Covered Bridge** is the longest such span not only in (or partly in) Vermont but also in the United States. Constructed in 1866, it has recently been rebuilt. There are also three covered bridges across the Mill Brook (just north and south of Route 44) in Brownsville, and three in Weathersfield: The **Titcomb Bridge** is on Route 106 across from the elementary school; the **Upper Falls Bridge** is on Upper Falls Road (turn south off Route 131 about 0.3 mile west of its junction with Route 106); and the **Salmond Bridge** is on Henry Gould Road (turn north off Route 131, 2.4 miles east of its junction with Route 106). The vintage-1870 **Baltimore Covered Bridge,** originally in North Springfield, has been moved to sit beside the Eureka Schoolhouse (see *Guidance*) on Route 11 in Springfield, just off I-91.

TO DO

AIRPLANE RIDES AND BALLOONING

Post Mills Airport (333-9254), West Fairlee. Veteran balloonist Brian Boland offers early-morning and sunset rides year-round. On the summer evening we tried it, the balloon hovered above hidden pockets in the hills, and we saw a herd of what looked like brown-and-white goats that, on closer inspection, proved to be deer. After an hour or so, we settled down gently in an East Bradford farmyard and broke out the champagne. Scenic plane rides and flight instruction also offered. $200 per flight includes champagne.

BICYCLING

Route I-91 drains a large percentage of traffic from Route 5, but this old highway along the river is still fairly busy. On the New Hampshire side of the river, search out the River Road that runs 8 miles north from Route 12A just north of the Saint-Gaudens site (see *To See—Historic Sites*) on through Plainfield. Also find the River Road from Route 10 north of Hanover (just north of the Chieftain Motel) through Lyme, rejoining Route 10 in Orford. Route 10 from Orford to Haverhill is also particularly beautiful, as is Route 5 in Vermont, between Fairlee and Norwich.

For inn-to-inn guided tours in this area, contact **Bike Vermont** (802-457-3553; 1-800-257-2226), and for self-guided tours, **Bicycle Holidays** (388-2453). **Juniper Hill Inn** in Windsor and **Silver Maple Lodge** in Fairlee (see *Lodging*) cater to bicyclists, offering packages that combine biking and canoeing. **P.O.M.G.** (1-888-635-BIKE) offers vehicle-supported camping tours.

Note: **Amtrak's** *Vermonter,* serving this corridor (see *Getting There*), carries bicycles. It's possible to detrain in Bellows Falls (26 miles south of Windsor; see "Southern Vermont"), Windsor, or White River Junction and explore this area on two wheels. We suggest, however, consulting some of the above bike-geared resources before you come.

BIKE RENTALS

Ascutney Mountain Resort (484-3511) in Brownsville rents mountain bikes and offers 32 km of trails. **Wilderness Trails** (295-7620), Quechee, offers mountain-bike rentals and mapped trails.

BOATING

With its placid water and lovely scenery, the Connecticut River through much of the Upper Valley is ideal for easygoing canoeists. A flyer called *Connecticut River Primitive Campsites*, which maps 17 sites, is available from the **Upper Valley Land Trust** (603-643-6626). Canoeing the Connecticut can, admittedly, be a bit of a slog. The head wind is as infamous as the lack of current. So what? Why does canoeing have to be about going great distances? For study programs and guided educational canoe trips on the river, contact the Montshire Museum of Science (649-2200; see *To See—Museums*).

North Star Canoes (603-542-5802), Route 12A at Balloch's Crossing in Cornish, New Hampshire, just across the river from Windsor. John Hammond will shuttle patrons to put-ins either 3 or 12 miles above the Cornish-Windsor Covered Bridge so that they can paddle downstream toward the river's most famous landmark. Roughly half of North Star's patrons camp, either at **Wilgus State Park** (674-5422; see *Green Space*) or at another site in Windsor. This is probably New England's most picturesque livery: The check-in desk in the barn is redolent of bales of hay, and John Hammond may well be out front shoeing horses; the canoes are stacked behind the farmhouse.

The Ledyard Canoe Club (603-643-6709), Hanover, New Hampshire, is billed as the oldest canoe club in America. It's named for a 1773 Dartmouth dropout who felled a pine tree, hollowed it out, and took off downriver (with a book of Ovid's poems), ending up at Hartford, 100 miles and several major waterfalls downstream. Hidden beyond Dartmouth's slick new rowing center, Ledyard is a mellow, friendly, student-run place with a ratty old armchair, a phone, and a soda machine on the porch. The canoeing and kayaking center for the 40 miles above Wilder Dam, it offers kayaking clinics as well as canoe and kayak rentals. No shuttle service.

Wilderness Trails (295-7620), Quechee, offers canoe trips down the Connecticut. **Fairlee Marine** (333-9745), Fairlee, has pontoons, canoes, and rowboat rentals.

FISHING

You can eat the fish you catch in the Connecticut River—it yields brown and rainbow trout above Orford/Fairlee. There's a boat launch at Wilder Dam, another just north of Hanover, and another on the Vermont bank in North Thetford. Guides and classes in fly-tying and fly-fishing are offered by **Lyme Angler** (603-643-1263), a source of fishing gear and tips, 8 South Main Street, Hanover.

River Excitement (457-4021), P.O. Box 65, Hartland Four Corners 05049. Guided trips on the Upper Connecticut River and trout streams, good for beginners through experts. Fly-fishing to spinning, equipment, cameras and superb food provided.

GOLF

Crown Point Country Club (885-2703), Weathersfield Station Road, Springfield. 18 holes, rolling terrain. **Windsor Country Club** (674-6491); nine holes on Route 5, north of Windsor.

Hanover Country Club (603-646-2000), Rope Ferry Road, off Route 10, Hanover, New Hampshire. A classy, 18-hole course with pro shop and lounge, open May through October.

Lake Morey Inn Resort (333-4311; 1-800-423-1211) in Fairlee features an 18-hole golf course on which the Vermont Open has been played for more than 40 years.

Bradford Country Club (222-5207); nine holes down by the river.

HANG GLIDING

Mount Ascutney is one of the prime spots in the country for hang gliding. For lessons, equipment, or a shuttle or flight, check with **Morningside Flight Park** (603-542-4416) in Claremont.

HORSEBACK RIDING

See **Kedron Valley Stables** in "Woodstock and Quechee" and **Cavendish Trail** in "Okemo Mountain/Ludlow Area."

SWIMMING

Union Village Dam Area, west on Route 132 from Pompanoosuc, offers swimming, picnicking, and fishing.

✍ **Storrs Pond Recreation Area** (603-643-2134), Reservoir Road, Hanover, New Hampshire, has a pool, pond, and camping; admission.

✍ **Treasure Island** (333-9625), Thetford, on Lake Fairlee, is a pleasant public beach with lifeguards and a tennis court; admission.

The beach at **Mill Pond in Windsor** is town-owned, open to the public for a fee. **Stoughton Pond** between Downers and Amsden, south of Route 131 or north from Route 106, near Springfield Dam Lake. **North Springfield Lake** also offers picnicking and swimming.

WINTER SPORTS

CROSS-COUNTRY SKIING

Ascutney Mountain Resort (484-7711), Brownsville, maintains 30 km of cross-country trails.

Lake Morey Inn Resort (333-4800), Fairlee, maintains 12 miles of groomed trails. $8 trail fee.

See also *Cross-Country Skiing* in "Woodstock and Quechee."

DOWNHILL SKIING

✍ **Ascutney Mountain Resort** (484-7711; snow report and lodging reservations: 1-800-243-0011; web site: www.ascutney.com), Brownsville (I-91 exit 8 or 9). A family-geared ski area turned self-contained resort. Facilities include a 241-room hotel, 25 slope-side condos, a sports center—with indoor and outdoor pools and weight and racquetball rooms—a full restaurant, and a base lodge.

Lifts: Three triple, one double chairlift.

Trails: 47.

Vertical drop: 1,530 feet.

Snowmaking: 90 percent.

Nursery/childcare: 6 months to 6 years.

Rates: Adults $41, juniors $28. Multi-day and lodging packages cut the price.

See also *Downhill Skiing* in "Woodstock and Quechee."

GREEN SPACE

✍ **Wilgus State Park** (674-5422, 773-2657), 1.5 miles south of exit 8, I-91, off Route 5, Windsor. This small, quiet campground on the Connecticut River is ideal for canoeists, as many lean-tos and tent sites are on the riverbank. Car shuttle service available; playground, picnic tables, hiking trails, canoe rentals.

Springfield Nature Trail (where Weathersfield and Springfield meet). Fifty-five acres of fields and woods on the border of Springfield and Weathersfield have been developed by the Ascutney Mountain Audubon Society, an environmental group.

Ascutney State Park (674-2060). Rising out of the valley to an elevation of

3,144 feet, Mount Ascutney is set in more than 2,000 acres of woodland. The 3.8-mile paved road to the summit begins on Route 44A, off Route 5, between Ascutney and Windsor. Of the four hiking trails to the summit, we recommend the 2.9-mile ascent from Weathersfield with an 84-foot waterfall about halfway (the trailhead is on Cascade Falls Road, 3.5 miles north off Route 131). The 3.2-mile Brownsville Trail begins on Route 44 between Windsor and Brownsville; the 2.7-mile Windsor Trail starts on Route 44A in Windsor. Granite was quarried here as early as 1808, and there was a popular summit house. Tent sites, trailer sites, and lean-tos can be reserved. The ski slopes and self-contained Ascutney Mountain Resort (see *Lodging*) are accessible from Route 44 in Brownsville.

Montshire Museum of Science Trails, Norwich. The museum's 100 acres include a promontory between the Connecticut River and the marshy bay at the mouth of Bloody Brook. The ¼-mile trail leading down through tall white pines to the bay is quite magical. The 1½-mile Hazen Trail runs all the way to Wilder Village.

See also Quechee Gorge Recreation Area in "Woodstock and Quechee."

LODGING

Note: Listings are in geographical order, south to north.

RESORTS

Ascutney Mountain Resort (484-7711; 1-800-243-0011), Brownsville 05037, includes a 225-room hotel with flanking condominiums at the base of Mount Ascutney. Accommodations range from standard hotel rooms to three-bedroom suites with kitchen and fireplace and outdoor deck, furnished in reproduction antiques. Facilities include the full-service Harvest Inn Restaurant and a sports center, also indoor tennis and an outdoor pool, both cross-country and downhill trails (see *Skiing*) in winter. Summer features an activity program. Rooms: $80–110; suites: $100–260, cheaper the longer you stay.

Lake Morey Inn Resort (333-4311; 1-800-423-1211), Fairlee 05045. On the shore of Lake Morey, this sprawling, year-round landmark is geared to groups and golfers. Facilities include indoor and outdoor swimming pools, tennis courts, cross-country-ski and snowmobile trails in winter, plus a player-friendly, recently upgraded 18-hole golf course. The public rooms are informal '50s. Winter: $65 EP per room, $85–100 per person MAP; summer: $125–195 EP per room, $95–130 MAP per person, including use of sports facilities. Lakeside cottages available.

INNS

Hartness House (885-2115; 1-800-732-4789), Orchard Street (off Route 143), Springfield 05156. In 1903 James Hartness built himself a stone and shingle mansion set in 25 acres on a parklike bluff. The inventor (Hartness patented 120 machines), aviator (he held one of the first 100 pilot's licenses in the United States and built Vermont's first airport), astronomer, and governor (1920–22) installed one of the first tracking telescopes in the country at the end of a 240-foot underground corridor connected to the mansion in 1910. It's still in use (tours are daily at 6 PM), and since 1939 the mansion has been an inn with 40 individually decorated guest rooms, 10 in the main house, the remainder in a connecting annex, each with private bath, phone, and color TV. There's a formal feel to the large lobby, with its traditional check-in desk, and there is plenty of common space, including an inviting pub and dining room (see *Dining Out*). The innkeepers span two generations and six members of the Blair family. Facilities include a swimming pool and nature trails. $89–150 double. Weddings are a specialty.

The Inn at Weathersfield (263-9217; 1-800-477-4828), Route 106 (near Perkinsville), Weathersfield 05151. A columned, 204-year-old former stagecoach stop and a station on the Underground Railroad, one of Vermont's most romantic inns with a reputation for fine dining. Innkeepers Mary and Terry Carter offer 12 antiques-furnished guest rooms, all with private bath, several with working fireplace. The dining room under Chef Michael McNamara is recognized as one of Vermont's best (see *Dining Out*). Facilities include an exercise room, a game room with a tournament-size pool table and a Finnish sauna. There's also a pond and a grass tennis court. Inquire about inn-to-inn equestrian or carriage tours. $150–250 per couple, including breakfast, tea, and dinner, plus 17 percent gratuity.

Juniper Hill Inn (674-5273; 1-800-359-2541), RR 1, Box 79, Windsor 05089, off Route 5 on Juniper Hill Road. Set high on a hill above its impressive drive, with a magnificent view of Mount Ascutney and the Connecticut River Valley, this splendid 28-room mansion, built by Maxwell Evarts in 1901, combines Edwardian grandeur with the informal hospitality of innkeepers Rob and Susanne Pearl. Adult guests (and children over 12) can relax by the hearth in the huge main hall, in a second living room (with TV), or in the library, with its leather armchairs and unusual hearth. One of Vermont's most romantic getaways, the inn offers no fewer than 11 guest rooms with fireplace (all but the two on the third floor are wood-burning). All 16 guest rooms have private bath and are furnished with flair and genuinely interesting antiques. We never can decide which we like best, but #7 is a beauty, with rose floral paper, green trim, a fireplace, and a garden view. Guests gather for meals in the dining room, redecorated in deep burgundy (it works) with floor-to-ceiling fireplace. Chef Susanne offers a choice of four entrées, served by candlelight (see *Dining Out*). Inquire about the Yankee Rambler Package, using rental canoes and 18-speed mountain bicycles. On the other hand, we could easily spend a day by the pool. Rates $90–170 per room, full breakfast included; $10 less single; add $25 for additional person; MAP and 6-day midweek plans available; add 15 percent gratuity on meals and beverages.

Norwich Inn (649-1143), Box 908, 225 Main Street, Norwich 05055.

Originally built as a stage stop by Jasper Murdock in 1797, this cheerful inn now has a total of 25 rooms divided among the main building, the Vestry, and a backyard motel, all with private bath, telephone, and cable TV. Innkeeper Sally Wilson has redecorated the guest rooms, and the public rooms are attractive and welcoming. Less formal and expensive than the Hanover Inn across the river, this is very much a gathering place for Dartmouth parents, faculty, and students. A brew pub, Jasper Murdock's Alehouse, features 15 varieties of inn-made brew (see *Eating Out*). The dining rooms are open for breakfast, lunch, and dinner (see *Dining Out*). Rates run from $55 in the off-season in the motel to $129 for a two-bedroom suite in the Vestry. All three meals are served. Dogs are permitted in one twin-bedded room in the motel.

BED & BREAKFASTS

The Inn at Windsor (674-5670), 106 Main Street, Windsor 05089. Working away steadily since 1983, Larry Bowser and his wife Holly Taylor have been restoring the vintage 1790s Green Mansion, set above Main Street in downtown Windsor. Guests now enter through a landscaped garden, are asked to remove their shoes, and are then given freshly laundered slippers. The two rooms and suite are interestingly, eclectically furnished, as is the gathering space around the original kitchen hearth and a contemporary breakfast room. $105-145 includes a full breakfast.

Mill Brook Bed & Breakfast (484-7283), Box 410, Route 44, Brownsville 05037. Kay Carriere rises at dawn to create extravagant breakfasts for guests at her 1880s farmhouse near Mount Ascutney. Kay goes the extra mile to make guests comfortable in her two rooms and three suites, all with private bath and names like Columbine and Raspberry. Fresh baked goods and hot drinks are always available, and there are no fewer than four common rooms, as well as a hot tub on the back deck. Inquire about the swimming hole. Children and some pets welcome. $67–107 double.

The Pond House at Shattuck Hill Farm (484-0011; pondhouse1@aol. com), P.O. Box 234, Brownsville 05037. Vermont native David Raymond and Gretel Schuck have created a real gem of a place, an 1830s Cape by the side of a steeply rising back road, with views across fields to mountains. We love the square dining room with its pumpkin pine floors and original six-over-six windows, and we love the spare, tasteful way the three guest rooms are furnished, each with private bath. Breakfast might feature orange French toast, and the dinner menu might include tuna with artichoke hearts or wild mushroom risotto. The 10-acre grounds include a croquet court and gardens as well as the pond. Horses can be accommodated. In winter there's skating, sledding, and cross-country skiing. Dinner and full breakfast are included in $125–140 per couple.

Burton Farm Lodge (484-3300), RFD #1, Box 558, Windsor 05089-9713. An old farmstead by a large trout pond on a back road. The feel here is that of a homey farm, not your usual B&B, two rooms (shared bath). Families are welcome, and children will feel at home immediately. $60–70 includes breakfast.

See also Bailey's Mills B&B in Reading, described in "Woodstock and Quechee."

Stonecrest Farm (296-2425), 119 Christian Street, P.O. Box 504, Wilder 05088. Gail Sanderson's vintage-1810 home, 3.5 miles from Dartmouth College, offers six antiques-furnished rooms with private bath. Common space includes a large formal living room well stocked with books, along with a woodstove and French doors opening onto a stone terrace. Note the curved oak staircase. $110–120 per couple with full breakfast in high season.

Beaver Meadow (649-1053), 319 Beaver Meadow Road, Norwich. An 1850s farmhouse on a country road just a mile from the center of town (2.7 miles from Dartmouth) offers three antiques-furnished rooms; $90–100 includes breakfast.

The Stone House Inn (333-9124), North Thetford 05054, is the nearest inn in all Vermont to the Connecticut River. Art and Dianne Sharkey, both teachers, have been here since 1978, and the house, actually built in 1835 from schist quarried across the river in Lyme, has an unusually comfortable, welcoming feel. There's a piano and fireplace in the living room and rockers on the wide, screened porch. The five guest rooms share three baths; our favorite is #6, seemingly hung in the trees with its many windows facing the river. There are 12 acres in all, stretching flat and green to the water. $55 double, $32 single, breakfast included.

Silver Maple Lodge & Cottages (333-4326; 1-800-666-1946), RR 1, Box 8, Fairlee 05045. Situated just south of the village on Route 5, Silver Maple was built as a farmhouse in 1855 and has been welcoming travelers for more than 70 years. Now run by Scott and Sharon Wright, it has eight nicely appointed guest rooms in the lodge and seven separate, pine-paneled, shaded cottages. The farmhouse has cheerful sitting rooms with exposed 200-year-old hand-hewn beams in the living room and dining room, where fresh breads appear with other continental breakfast goodies. The newest cottages with kitchenette and working fireplace are real beauties. Play horseshoes, croquet, badminton, or shuffleboard on the lawn, or rent a bike or canoe. Scott will also arrange a ride in a hot-air balloon for you at neighboring Post Mills Airport. Scott grew up on a Tunbridge farm and takes pride in introducing visitors to Vermont. $54–79 per couple. Pets accepted in the cottages.

Peach Brook Inn (866-3389), Doe Hill, off Route 5, South Newbury 05051. Ray and Joyce Emery have opened their spacious 1837 home with its splendid view of the Connecticut River. What a special place! Common space includes two nicely furnished parlors with exposed beams and a fireplace, an open kitchen, and a screened porch with a view of Mount Moosilauke across the river. The house is on a country lane in the almost vanished village of South Newbury, once connected to Haverhill, New Hampshire, across the river by a long-gone covered bridge. Plenty of farm animals are within walking distance. There are three comfortable guest rooms; $50–60 with shared bath, $65–70 with private, including full breakfast. No smoking. No children under 10, please; under 18 are $10.

A Century Past Bed and Breakfast (866-3358), Route 5, Newbury 05051. Open May through November. Patricia Smith offers four rooms in her handsome, columned village house that dates in part to 1790. $65 per couple includes a breakfast of fruit and muffins.

HOTEL

The Hotel Coolidge (295-3118; 1-800-622-1124; Hotel.Coolidge@ valley.net), White River Junction 05001, deserves attention as one of the last of the old railroad hotels. Be sure to look at the splendid Peter Michael Gish murals behind the bar and in the Vermont Room, painted in 1950 in exchange for room and board while the artist was studying with Paul Sample at Dartmouth. Gish also built a great fireplace. All 53 elevator-served guest rooms have private bath, phone, and TV. Some are depressingly small, but others are quite roomy and attractive. The hotel sits across from the Amtrak station and next to the Briggs Opera House (see *Entertainment*). Local buses to Hanover and Lebanon stop at the door, and rental cars can be arranged. Owner-manager David Briggs, a seventh-generation Vermonter, takes his role as innkeeper seriously and will arrange for special needs. $59–79 per room double. Children free.

HOSTEL

The Hotel Coolidge (295-3118). In 1997 a wing of the Coolidge, described above, became a Hosteling International facility with dorm-style beds, access to a self-service kitchen, and laundry facilities. Private family rooms are also available by reservation. $18 for HI members, $21 for nonmembers; $6 for children.

LODGING WORTH CROSSING THE RIVER FOR

Moose Mountain Lodge (603-643-3529), Etna, N.H. 03750. Open June through October, December 26 through mid-March. This is the most alpine inn in all of New England, perched high on a steep hill behind Hanover, just off the Appalachian Trail with spectacular views to the west across the Green Mountains. Kay and Peter Shumway have been here since 1975 and obviously enjoy what they do, greeting guests like old friends and preparing memorable meals from the freshest ingredients. The 12 guest rooms are small but attractive, with handmade log beds and shared baths. Inside and out, the lodge has plenty of pine. It was built of stones and logs cleared from this hill. The 350 acres include a deep pond just outside the door, ample woods, and meadows with long views. $90 per person MAP in winter, $80 MAP in summer and fall; $48 for children 12 and under MAP.

Loch Lyme Lodge and Cottages (603-795-2141; 1-800-423-2141), Route 10, RFD 278, Lyme, N.H. 03768. The main lodge is open through foliage season; the cabins, Memorial Day to mid-September. There are four rooms in the inn and 26 brown-shingle cabins (12 with cooking facilities) spread along a wooded hillside overlooking a lake called Post Pond. The big attraction here is a private beach with a float and a fleet of rowboats and canoes; also a Windsurfer. Two tennis courts, a baseball field, basketball court, volleyball net, and recreation cabin are there for the using, and baby-sitting is available for parents who want time off. Lunch and dinner are served, and a take-out lunch bar is open for sandwiches and cones. Loch Lyme was founded in 1917 and has been owned and managed by Paul and Judy Barker's family since the 1940s. No credit cards. Pets permitted in cabins. From $28 per person in the off-season (which includes foliage!) to $44 per person in summer (rates include breakfast). Housekeeping cabins are $450–700 per week; cabins without kitchens are available on a B&B or MAP ($63 per adult) basis; children's rates.

Piermont Inn (603-272-4820), One Old Church Street, Piermont, N.H. 03779 (across the bridge from Bradford, Vermont). A 1790s stagecoach stop with six rooms, four in the adjacent carriage house (only the two in the inn are open year-round), all with private bath. The two in the main house are outstanding, both carved from the tavern's original ballroom, high-ceilinged and spacious, with writing desks and appropriate antiques. The carriage house rooms are simple but cheery; two are handicapped-accessible. Common space includes a living room with fireplace, TV, wing chairs, and a nifty grandfather clock. Charlie and Karen Brown are longtime Piermont residents who enjoy tuning in guests to the many ways of exploring this upper (less touristed) part of the Upper Valley, especially to canoeing the river (they offer a canoe and informal shuttle service). Breakfast is full; and dinner can be arranged. Rooms in the main house are $65–80; in the carriage house, $45–55.

The Gibson House (989-3125), RR 1, Box 193, Haverhill, N.H. 03765. Artist Keita Colton has restored one of Haverhill's classic pre–Civil War–era houses and offers five or six rooms, depending on whether someone books her own "luxury suite." The house fronts on Route 10 but back porches and terraces overlook the Connecticut River, and there are gardens. $150–250 includes breakfast.

WHERE TO EAT

DINING OUT
Note: Listings are in geographical order, south to north.

Penelope's on the Square (885-9186), Springfield. Open daily except Sunday. Polished woods, stained glass, and greenery, an attractive setting for dining from a large menu. Choices range from beef filet flambéed in brandy ($11.95) to seafood casserole ($16.95) and baked lasagne ($8.95).

Hartness House (885-2115), 30 Orchard Street, Springfield. Open for lunch and dinner weekdays, dinner only on weekends. The dining room in this venerable landmark is now in all soft, light rose hues. The chef is Michael

Hofford and the menu might include jumbo shrimp in lemon linguine, garden lasagne, and beef in vodka sauce. Entrées: $14.95–19.25.

The Inn at Weathersfield (263-9217), Route 106 (near Perkinsville), Weathersfield. A five-course, prix fixe dinner ($34.95) is served every night, with reservations recommended. This long-established dining room continues to be one of the state's most highly rated and romantic restaurants. Chef Michael McNamara is known for rack of lamb and the menu usually includes roast pork tenderloin with a maple mustard glaze as one of four to seven entrée choices. Tom McDermott plays the piano nightly.

Bennett's 1815 House (484-1815), at the junction of Routes 44 and 106, Reading. Open for dinner nightly. A handsome brick tavern actually built in 1806, serving as a public house until the 1870s and then (until the 1950s) as headquarters for Budd Hawkins' Seeds. Katherine and Peter Bennett turned it into a restaurant again. Harvard-schooled Peter specializes in his own "comfort food," dishes like Wiener schnitzel, beef stew (with red wine and garlic), and ham steak. For dessert there's crème brûlée, and chocolate mousse from a family recipe with a touch of rum. The dining room is fairly formal, and service is purposely slow. Entrées: $6–16.95. See also the Seed Cafe under *Eating Out*.

Windsor Station Restaurant (674-2052), Depot Avenue, Windsor. This was the mainline station, now decorated in natural wood plus velvet and brass. It serves reasonably priced dinner with entrées from chicken Kiev or amandine and veal Madeira to the Station Master filet mignon topped with shrimp, asparagus, and hollandaise sauce. A children's menu is available. Inexpensive to moderate.

Juniper Hill Inn (674-5273), Route 5 north of Windsor. Dinner by reservation, open for dinner nightly in-season, otherwise varying nights. Reserve. Patrons are asked to come at 6:15 for a drink before. Innkeeper Susanne Pearl is the chef, offering a four-course prix fixe menu that might include herb-crusted rack of lamb and maple-glazed salmon fillets. $32 per person. The wine list is respectable.

Skunk Hollow Tavern (436-2139), Hartland Four Corners, off Route 12 north of I-91, exit 9. Dinner Wednesday through Sunday. Reservations suggested. Carlos Ocasio's split-personality restaurant is simply one of the best places around, hidden away in a small village that's easily accessible both from the Connecticut and the Ottauquechee River Valleys. Patrons gather downstairs in the pub to play darts and backgammon and to munch on fish-and-chips, mussels, or pizza; the generally excellent, more formal dining upstairs in the inn's original parlor. The menu changes every few months but staples include roast rack of lamb, filet mignon with maple mustard cream. Variables might be red pepper shrimp with Oriental pasta or shiitake chicken; always salad of the day and homemade soups. $6.95–21. Live entertainment Wednesday and Friday night.

Karibu Tulé's A Taste of Africa (295-4243), 2 North Main Street, White River Junction. Open for dinner. "Ka-ree-bu Yu-lay" means "Welcome, let's dine" in Swahili. The menu features authentic African and world cuisine, from Moroccan couscous and Kenyan pillau (jasmine rice cooked with a blend of spices, peas and carrots) and peanut chicken stew from Mali. Chapati bread is always served and there are daily specials. This exotic restaurant is a welcome addition to Upper Valley dining. Moderate to expensive.

La Poule à Dents at Carpenter Street (649-2922), Main Street, Norwich. Open for dinner nightly from 6; reservations required. The name means "as scarce as hen's teeth," a way of noting that the best things in life are rare; this is one of the more formal, upscale places in the Upper Valley. The touch is French and the ingredients local. An à la carte menu in the beamed dining room of this 1820s house might begin with smoked breast of Peking duck with grilled red onions, followed by grilled Norwegian salmon served with hand-rolled scallion pasta and herb-infused olive oil. Expensive.

Norwich Inn (649-1143), Main Street, Norwich, popular locally for breakfast, lunch and dinner, also Sunday brunch. Although the dining rooms are traditional, they are not stuffy. The menu changes every few months but appetizers might include apple and Brie ravioli and duck confit on field greens; entrées always include a vegetarian dish like roast acorn squash and wild rice pudding and might feature fresh Maine crab cakes, sautéed veal medallions with a mustard sage crust, and green curry pork tenderloin. Entrées: $15.95–20.25.

Colatina Exit (222-9008), Main Street, Bradford. Open daily, 5-10 PM; weekends until 11. This is a real Vermont trattoria that's been here more than 26 years: candles in Chianti bottles, Italian scenes on the walls, checked (green, mind you) tablecloths, and a variety of pastas and specials like grilled shrimp primavera ($12.95) and seafood cioppino ($13.95). Note family-style specials.

Peyton Place (222-5462), Bradford. Open Wednesday through Saturday 5:30–10:30; closed Wednesday in winter. This is one place you have to know is there, back down around and under the post office. The decor is bistro and the menu surprisingly large, with blackboard specials. You might choose to begin with a fresh summer soup of peas, asparagus, wild leeks, and sorrel, followed by a breast of duck with a wild rice pancake in cherry sauce, or handmade vegetarian ravioli. Dinner for two runs $50–60. BYOB. The restaurant is named, incidentally, for owners James, Heidi, and Sophronia Peyton. Reservations recommended.

The Perfect Pear Café, (222-5912), Main Street, Bradford. A charming, chef-owned storefront bistro serving fresh, sophisticated food.

See also "Woodstock and Quechee" for the Simon Pearce Restaurant, the Parker House Inn, and the Meadows at Marshland Farm, all in Quechee.

EATING OUT

McKinley's (885-9186), on the square, Springfield. Same fern-bar atmosphere as Penelope's (see *Dining Out*) but a different menu. A good lunch stop: burgers, taco salad, sandwiches, pastas, and soups.

B. J. Bricker's (885-6050), River Street, Springfield. Open daily for breakfast, lunch, and dinner. A 14-ounce T-bone or filet mignon goes for $9.95; beer and wine; children's menu.

Country Creemee Restaurant, Downers Corner (junction of Routes 131 and 106), Amsden. Seasonal. Locals will tell you that everything tastes good here; we always get the super-long hot dog to consume at a picnic table under the trees.

Seed Cafe at Bennett's 1815 House (484-1815), junction of Routes 44 and 106, Reading. Burgers, sandwiches, salads, and ales on tap.

Windsor Pizza Chef (674-6861), 88 Main Street, Windsor. Open 11–11 most days. We've never tried the pizza but can recommend the subs and salads; we've taken them canoeing and consumed them at picnic sites (which all seem to be on the other side of the river along this particular stretch).

Windsor Diner (674-6557), Main Street, Windsor. Open from 6 AM-9 PM weekdays and Saturdays, Sunday 7 AM—4 PM. A vintage-'52 classic diner with diner food; beer served. Good chili.

Shepherd's Pie (674-9390), Route 5 north of Windsor. Open from 7 AM (Sunday from 8) for breakfast through lunch and dinner until 8 PM. Sharon Shepherd's deli and restaurant is a welcome addition, good for sandwiches, salads, and more for picnics. Outdoor seating in summer, as well as indoor seating for 25. Quiche, lasagne, and shepherd's pie are usually on the menu; wine and beer served. Children's menu.

See also Skunk Hollow Tavern under *Dining Out*.

The Polka Dot (295-9722), North Main Street, White River Junction. Open 5 AM–7 PM. A classic diner with chrome, photos of old trains, stools, and booths. Mary Shatney is known for her soups and honey-coated fried chicken, specials like tuna-noodle casserole, good pies.

River City Cafe (296-7113), 15 Main Street, White River Junction. Open weekdays 8–4, Saturday 9–3. Good for breakfast pastries, lunch soups and salads, coffee all day.

Jasper Murdock's Alehouse in the Norwich Inn (649-1143), Main Street, Norwich. Open 5:30–9. The house brew comes in 15 varieties, and we can speak for the somehat sweet, full-bodied, and slightly malty taste of Whistling Pig Red Ale. Old Slipper Pale Ale and Short 'n' Stout are particularly popular. The Alehouse is a green-walled, comfortable pub; the bill of fare changes frequently but usually includes Maine crab cakes and shepherd's pie.

Alice's Bakery and Cafe (649-2846), Main and Elm Streets, Norwich. Open Tuesday through Friday 9:30–5:30; to 3:30 Saturday. In addition to some of the Upper Valleys' best artisanal breads and pastries, you can savor cappuccino and superb sandwiches on baguettes or sourdough, pumpernickel, or raisin-pecan loaves at the limited seating inside. Or assemble a picnic from the Take-Away menu, which might include mushroom and wild rice soup, roasted vegetables and chèvre in phyllo, acorn squash stuffed with apples and brown rice, and four-bean salad.

Gilman's Fairlee Diner, (333-3569), Route 5, Fairlee. Open 5:30-2, until 7 Thursday and 8 Friday. Turn left (north) on Route 5 if you are coming off I-91. This is a classic wooden diner built in the '30s (across the road from where it stands), with wooden booths, worn-shiny wooden stool tops and good food. The mashed potato doughnuts are special and both the soup and the pie are dependably good. Daily specials.

The Potlatch Tavern (333-4629), Main Street, Fairlee. Open for lunch and dinner except Tuesday; in winter, also closed Monday. The local family restaurant with a very reasonably priced lunch menu and dinner entrées like baked Maine tuna with onions, tomatoes, and garlic and frutti di mare salad ($9.95).

The Third Rail (333-9797), Route 5, Fairlee. This popular eatery has had an on-again-off-again recent history, and it's presently open again, May through October, Tuesday through Saturday for dinner only. It's a roadside house with a friendly pub and a large menu, from seafood to steaks. A dinner of baked lasagne with homemade noodles, tossed greens, bread, and chocolate-Kahlúa mousse pie so impressed one couple that they wrote us about it. A good family restaurant.

Bradford Village Store, Main Street, Bradford. Housed in a former 19th-century hotel, this is a classic general store but with crockpots full of good soup, chili, or stew; a deli; and tables in the back—including a booth with the best river view in town.

ENTERTAINMENT

MUSIC AND THEATER

Hopkins Center for the Arts (603-646-2422), Dartmouth green, Hanover, New Hampshire. Three theaters, a recital hall, and art galleries feature year-round programs of plays, concerts, and films.

Northern Stage (291-9009), at the Briggs Opera House, White River Junction. This excellent community theater group offers semiprofessional productions year-round. Special children's theater classes and summer arts education classes.

The Parish Players (785-4344), based in the Eclipse Grange Hall on Thetford Hill, is the oldest community theater company in the Upper Valley; its repertoire includes classic pieces, original works, and summer poetry readings.

In the past few seasons, venues have burgeoned for folk, blues, and hard-to-label, idiosyncratic performers. The **Lebanon Opera House** (603-448-2498), on the green in Lebanon, New Hampshire, is one of the most active. **Opera North** (603-643-1946), headquartered in Norwich, stages semiprofessional performances of a very high standard. Opera North puts on one major opera, usually at the Lebanon Opera House, every August, and offers smaller, sometimes experimental, performances at other times of the year in various locations in the Upper Valley.

FILM
Dartmouth Film Society at the Hopkins Center (603-646-2576), Dartmouth green, Hanover, New Hampshire. Frequent showings of classic, contemporary, and experimental films in two theaters.

The Nugget (603-643-2769), South Main Street, Hanover, New Hampshire. Four first-run films nightly.

Fairlee Drive-In (333-9192), Route 5, Fairlee. Summer only; check local papers for listings.

SELECTIVE SHOPPING

ANTIQUES
Antiques Collaborative in Quechee, with 150 dealers, offers the largest selection on the Vermont side of the Valley (see "Woodstock and Quechee") and **Colonial Antique Markets** (603-298-8132) in West Lebanon, New Hampshire, is another trove representing 60 dealers (open daily 9–5 in the Colonial Plaza; flea markets year-round).

BOOKSTORES
The Norwich Bookstore (649-1114), Main Street, Norwich. This nifty, bright, very personalized shop in a classic house next to the post office has a lot going for it: knowledgeable staff, a great children's section, and frequent readings and signings by authors and illustrators.

I Wonda Book Shoppe (674-5503), Main Street, Windsor, under the Tuxbury Shops. An eclectic stock of gifts, books.

The Hundredth Monkey Bookstore (295-9397), 3 North Main Street, White River Junction. Used, antiquarian, and new books.

CRAFTS
Vermont Craft Center at Windsor House (674-6729). An attractive retail showcase-gallery for Vermont craftspeople: two floors of glass, ceramics, furniture, jewelry, prints, toys, a book corner, plus a series of instructional programs.

FACTORY TOURS AND SHOPS

Simon Pearce Glass (674-6280), Route 5, north of Windsor. Open daily 9–5. Pearce operated his own glassworks in Ireland for a decade and moved here in 1981, acquiring the venerable Downer's Mill in Quechee and harnessing the dam's hydropower for the glass furnace (see *Selective Shopping* in "Woodstock and Quechee"). In 1993 he opened a new 32,000-square-foot facility down by the river in Windsor's industrial park. Designed to resemble (theoretically, anyway) a Vermont barn and

Glass blowing at Simon Pearce in Windsor

to be visitor-friendly, it includes a catwalk viewing the gallery from above the factory floor—a fascinating place from which you can watch glass being blown and shaped. Of course, there's a big showroom-shop featuring seconds as well as first-quality glass and pottery. A riverside restaurant like the one at the Quechee facility is planned.

Catamount Brewing Company (674-6700), Windsor Industrial Park, north of town on Route 5. Open daily, year-round, 9–5; 1–5 on Sunday. Call to check the schedule of brewery tours. Catamount's new facility is next to the Simon Pearce complex. Vermont's first brewery in 100 years when it opened in 1986, Catamount is now one of 13 microbreweries in the state, but it's still the largest and its brews are the most widely distributed.

Stave Puzzles (295-5200), off Route 5, 1 mile south of Norwich and I-89 exit 13. Turn at the sign for Olcott Commerce Park, and take the drive after UPS. The handcrafted wooden jigsaw puzzles made here are the Rolls-Royces of the pastime. Some are cut and put together in multiple-choice fashion; all are mounted on mahogany. Their prices are impressive, too: A 150-piece lobster trap is $695, the 400-piece three-dimensional baseball game is $1,895. Made-to-order puzzles incorporating family photos are a specialty, but pictures of the final product never come with the puzzle pieces. Visitors are welcome to inspect display drawers filled with puzzles and to peer into the puzzle works itself.

Pompanoosuc Mills (785-4851), Route 5, East Thetford. Open daily until 6, noon–5 Sunday. Not too many years have passed since Dwight Sargeant began building furniture in his riverside house, a cottage industry that has evolved into a riverside factory employing 55, with showrooms throughout New England. Furniture is made to order, but there are seconds here.

J. J. Copeland & Sons (222-9280), Main Street, Bradford. Furniture factory outlet. Worth a detour: great clean-lined, locally made furniture at good prices.

FARMS

Cider Hill Farm (674-5293), Hunt Road, 2.5 miles west of State Street, Windsor. Growers of herbs and perennials, creators of herb wreaths, dried-flower arrangements, herbal blends, and apple cider.

Killdeer Farm (649-2852) has a farm stand on Route 5 just south of Norwich. Open every day from May through October, with a wide variety of Vermont products, baked goods, and fruit, as well as bedding plants and organic vegetables.

Norwich Farmers' Market, south of Norwich on Route 5. Open Saturday 9–1 from May through October. A real happening, this is the place to see and be seen on summer Saturdays. Local farmers bring produce, wool, baked goods, flowers, and handmade crafts; live music under the gazebo.

Cedar Circle Farm (785-4101), East Thetford. Famous for its four varieties of cantaloupes; also good for local peas and strawberries.

Crossroad Farm (333-4455), on the crossroad between Routes 113 and 244, Post Mills. Fresh local produce sold at a seasonal stand near the shores of Lake Fairlee.

4 Corners Farm (866-3342), just off Route 5, South Newbury. Bob and Kim Gray sell their own produce and flowers. An exceptionally pretty farm, just off but up above the highway.

FUNKY CLOTHING

The Upper Valley seems particularly rich in vintage-clothing stores, some of which offer more interesting and varied wares than local boutiques. **ZuZu's** (295-3557), 21 Gates Street in downtown White River Junction, open Wednesday through Saturday 11–6, is a particularly bright and interesting shop. Others include the **SEVCA Good Buy Store** (295-6373), a community thrift store at the Hartford recycling center on Route 5 south of White River Junction; **Sally's Consignments** (674-2630), 53 Main Street, Windsor; **Nouveauté** (603-448-5958), 24 Hanover Street, in Lebanon, New Hampshire; **Windfall Clothing** (353-6411) Route 10 in Orford; **Pattygram's Attic** (222-9396), Bradford; **Victorian** (989-3380) in Haverhill, New Hampshire; and our favorite, **Patricia Owens,** with a boutique on Main Street in South Strafford (765-4335) and a bargain outlet in the Colonial Plaza, West Lebanon. *Note:* Call ahead; hours tend to fluctuate.

SPECIAL SHOPS

Vermont Salvage Exchange (295-7616), Railroad Row, White River Junction, for doors, chandeliers, moldings, mantels, old bricks, and other architectural relics.

Briggs Ltd. (295-7100), 12 North Main Street, White River Junction. Hunting supplies and Orvis tackle, as well as Woolrich and Pendleton clothing for men and women.

Dan and Whit's General Store, Main Street, Norwich. Next to the Norwich Inn, a general store among general stores: great bulletin board, groceries, buttons, hardware, clothing, advice.

King Arthur Flour Baker's Store (649-3361), Route 5, Norwich. This retail outlet for the country's oldest family-owned flour company sells an array of baking equipment, cookbooks, and accessories, along with flour.

Chapman's (333-9709), Fairlee. Open daily 8–6, until 5 on Sunday. Over the years, members of the Chapman family have expanded the stock of this old pharmacy to include 10,000 hand-tied flies, wines, Mexican silver and Indonesian jewelry, used books, and an unusual selection of toys—as well as night crawlers and manila envelopes. Check out the seasonal greenhouses out back and the antiques shop in the barn.

Farm-Way, Inc. (1-800-222-9316), Route 25, Bradford. One mile west of I-91, exit 16. Open Monday through Saturday until 8 PM. A phenomenon. This family-run source of work boots and rugged clothing now includes a stock of more than 2 million products spread over 5 acres: tack, furniture, pet supplies, syrup, whatever. Shoes and boots remain a specialty, from size 4E to 16; 10,000 shoes, boots, clogs, sandals, and sneakers in stock.

SPECIAL EVENTS

January through mid-March: **Roast beef supper** at the Hartland Brick Church, Hartland Four Corners, Saturday 5–7 PM.

June through September: The ladies of Brownsville (West Windsor) have been serving up their famous **baked bean and salad suppers** since 1935, first for the benefit of the Methodist church, lately for the Grange and Historical Society. They start Saturday in late June and run through the summer. People start lining up at 4 PM for the first seating at 5.

July: **Connecticut Valley Fair,** Bradford (third weekend). **Cracker Barrel Bazaar,** Newbury (last weekend), includes plenty of fiddling, church suppers, maybe a circus. **Historic Windsor's Annual Antique Show** (usually held at Mount Ascutney). **The Big Apple Circus** comes to town for a week of performances at Fullington Farm, north of Hanover, NH on Route 10.

July 4 weekend: **Ascutney Air Carnival.** Paragliders and hang gliders congregate at Mount Ascutney.

Early August: **Lyme Summer Revels,** Lyme, New Hampshire; song and dance in a meadow.

September: Annual **Glory Days of the Railroad Festival,** downtown White River Junction.

October: The **Annual Vermont Apple Festival** (885-2779), Springfield, is held Columbus Day weekend and includes a crafts show. **Festival Windsor** is an annual autumn celebration. **Craft Festival** at Mount Ascutney.

November: **Annual Wild Game Supper** in Bradford. The town nearly doubles its population of 1,700 on the Saturday before Thanksgiving, when hungry visitors pour into the Congregational church for this feast, now in its 31st year. Some 2,800 pounds of buffalo, venison, moose, pheasant, coon, rabbit, wild boar, and bear are cooked up by parishioners as roasts, steaks, hamburgers, stews, and sausage; they are devoured along with salad, vegetables, and gingerbread with whipped cream. Tickets ($15 adults, $7 children) are limited to 1,000. Doors open at 3 PM. Reservations are accepted only on or after the "middle Monday of October," postmarked or in person. Write to: Game Supper Committee, Bradford 05033.

December: **Dickens of a Christmas** and **Christmas Revels** in Hanover, New Hampshire.

Woodstock and Quechee

A moated village cradled in hills around the Ottauquechee River 14 miles west of White River Junction on Route 4, Woodstock is one of the most cosmopolitan towns in the state and is considered, justifiably, one of the half-dozen prettiest towns in America. It has been a popular year-round resort for a century: In the 1890s, summer folk settled into the old Woodstock Inn for the season or returned for lively winter sports parties; and in the mid-1930s, it was a mecca for eastern skiers because of its rope tow—the first in America (1934).

As the Shire Town of Windsor County since the 1790s, Woodstock attracted an influential and prosperous group of professionals, who, with local merchants and bankers, built the unusual concentration of distinguished Federal houses that surround the elliptical green, forming a long-admired architectural showcase that has been meticulously preserved.

Woodstock produced more than its share of 19th-century celebrities, including Hiram Powers, the sculptor whose nude *Greek Slave* scandalized the nation in 1847, and Sen. Jacob Collamer (1791–1865), President Lincoln's confidant, who declared, "The good people of Woodstock have less incentive than others to yearn for heaven." George Perkins Marsh (1801–1882) helped found the Smithsonian; when he was serving in Congress he was the U.S. minister to Turkey and Italy, and wrote the pioneering work on environmental conservation, *Man and Nature* (1864), which has long been regarded as the ecologists' bible. John Cotton Dana was an eminent, early-20th-century librarian and museum director whose innovations made books and art more accessible to the public. The town still feels the influence of Frederick Billings (1823–1890), who became a famous San Francisco lawyer in the gold rush years and later was responsible for the completion of the Northern Pacific Railroad (Billings, Montana, was named for him in 1882). The Billings Mansion, a historic landmark and the boyhood home of George Perkins Marsh, and the prize Jersey dairy begun by Billings were owned by Billings's late granddaughter, Mary, and her husband, Laurance S. Rockefeller, who were responsible for much of Woodstock's preservation, outlying green space, and recreational assets. Most of the village itself, and the hamlet of South Woodstock, is on the National

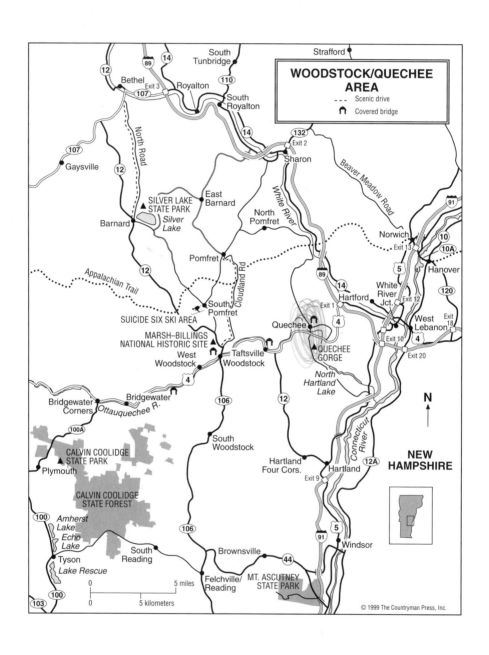

WOODSTOCK/QUECHEE AREA

- - - Scenic drive
⌂ Covered bridge

Strafford

South Tunbridge

14
89
12
Bethel Exit 3
107
Royalton
110
South Royalton

132
Exit 2
Sharon

Beaver Meadow Road

91

Gaysville
12
107

North Road

14

White River

SILVER LAKE STATE PARK
East Barnard
North Pomfret
Norwich
Exit 13
10
10A

Barnard
Silver Lake

Appalachian Trail
12
Pomfret
Cloudland Rd
89
5
Hanover

South Pomfret
14
Hartford
White River Jct.
Exit 12
120

SUICIDE SIX SKI AREA
Exit 1
West Lebanon Exit 18

MARSH–BILLINGS NATIONAL HISTORIC SITE
Quechee
4
Exit 10
4

West Woodstock
Taftsville
West Woodstock
QUECHEE GORGE
Exit 20

4

Bridgewater
Bridgewater Corners
Ottauquechee R.
106
North Hartland Lake

12

100A

CALVIN COOLIDGE STATE PARK
Plymouth

South Woodstock

N

CALVIN COOLIDGE STATE FOREST

Hartland Four Cors.
Hartland
Exit 9
12A

NEW HAMPSHIRE

100
Amherst Lake
Echo Lake

Connecticut River

Tyson
Lake Rescue
South Reading
106
Brownsville
5
91
Windsor

Felchville/ Reading
44
MT. ASCUTNEY STATE PARK

100
103

0   5 miles
0   5 kilometers

© 1999 The Countryman Press, Inc.

Register of Historic Places, and the Billings Mansion and its surrounding forest became a National Historical Park in 1998, the first in Vermont.

Quechee, on Route 4, some 4 miles east of Woodstock in the township of Hartford, was once a thriving woolen mill town, but it has been almost completely swallowed in the past 25 years by the 6,000-acre Quechee Lakes Corporation, probably the largest second-home and condominium development in the state. As such enterprises go, this one has been well planned, allowing for a maximum of green space, but hilltops crowned by town houses can't help but make rural preservationists wince. Still, it's an attractive colony of suburbanites. In the wake of this leviathan, village resources have been preserved and expanded, including a replicated covered bridge across the river near what was Downer's Mill.

GUIDANCE

The Woodstock Area Chamber of Commerce (457-3555), 18 Central Street, Woodstock 05901, keeps an information booth open on the green June through October (457-1042), which does its best to find beds in private homes for fall-foliage leaf-peepers stranded without reservations (457-2389). The chamber annually publishes a useful free brochure, *Window on Woodstock.* In summer and foliage season, **Beyond Main Street** guided walking tours of the village start from the information booth, Friday through Monday, 10 AM and 2 PM and by appointment (457-5063); $6 for adults, $3 for children.

The Woodstock Historical Society has published a walking-tour booklet, available for sale in its gift shop and in other places, and distributes another brochure called *Passport to the Past,* a guide to historic sites within a half-hour drive.

A detailed schedule of local events is posted daily on the blackboard at the corner of Elm and Central Streets by Charlotte Boggs—a custom originated by the late Frank Teagle.

For a brief history of the town, see Peter Jennison's informative booklet, *Woodstock's Heritage,* available for $4.95 from bookstores (see *Selective Shopping*) and several gift shops.

The Quechee Chamber of Commerce (295-7900) has an information booth at Quechee Gorge, open mid-May through mid-October. A useful brochure, *By the Old Mill Stream: An Architectural and Historical Walking Tour,* is available for $2.

GETTING THERE

By car: Route 4 west from I-91 and I-89.

By train: **Amtrak** to White River Junction.

By bus: **Vermont Transit** to White River Junction, with connections to and from Rutland via Woodstock; tickets at the Whipple Tree, Central Street, Woodstock (see *Selective Shopping*).

GETTING AROUND

By taxi: **Willette Cab** (295-2440).

Limousine service: **Hallmark** (295-5466).

MEDICAL EMERGENCY
Woodstock, Quechee, Hartford (911). Ottauquechee Health Center (457-3030), Woodstock.

TO SEE

NATIONAL PARK
Marsh-Billings National Historical Park (457-3368), Route 12 north of Woodstock village. Open May through mid-October. This is the first national park in the United States to focus on the twin themes of environmental conservation and the changing nature of land stewardship, linking in an extraordinary coincidence George Perkins Marsh, author of *Man and Nature,* published in 1864; Frederick Billings (1823-1890), builder of the Northern Pacific Railroad; and Laurance S. Rockefeller and his late wife, Mary, Billings's granddaughter, who donated the estate to the National Park Service. Billings, who purchased the Marsh family property in 1869 and greatly enlarged the residence, reforested the surrounding slopes of Mount Tom and built carriage roads that are open to the public along with the mansion. The Queen Anne house itself holds a notable collection of 19th-century furniture, porcelains, and American art. The guided, interpretive tour—about an hour—begins in the former carriage house, now a visitors center. Admission charge to the mansion, but not to the gardens or woodland.

MUSEUMS
Billings Farm & Museum (457-2355), River Road off Route 12 north of Woodstock, holds a beautifully mounted series of exhibits demonstrating life on Frederick Billings's model "gentleman's" farm in the 1890s: plowing, seeding, cultivating, harvesting, and storing crops; making cheese and butter; woodcutting and sugaring. The 1890 farm manager's house has been restored. Visitors can also observe what happens on a modern dairy farm based on a prize-winning Jersey herd. A 100-seat theater has been added to the visitors center, featuring *A Place in the Land,* a fine film by Academy Award–winner Charles Guggenheim. This 30-minute documentary introduces the three generations of conservation stewardship associated with the farm and the National Historical Park. Open May 1 through October 22 and for special events during the year, like apple days and wool days in fall; Thanksgiving weekend and Christmas weekend celebrations; sleigh rally in mid-February and periodic demonstrations and crafts exhibits, including quilts in mid-August. Limited capacity; admission charge.

The Dana House (the Woodstock Historical Society; 457-1822), Elm Street, Woodstock. Completed in 1807 and occupied for the next 140 years by the notable Dana family, this historic house has an interesting permanent exhibit portraying the town's economic heritage and an admirable collection of antiques, locally wrought coin silver, portraits,

The Rockefeller mansion at Marsh-Billings National Historic Park

porcelains, fabrics, costumes, and toys. The John Cotton Dana Library is a research and reference center. Open 10–5, May through October and certain winter weekends. There is a nominal admission charge.

The Norman Williams Public Library (457-2295), on the Woodstock green. A Romanesque gem, donated and endowed in 1883 by Dr. Edward H. Williams, general manager of the Pennsylvania Railroad and later head of Baldwin Locomotives. Undergoing renovations as this book went to press, the library is scheduled to reopen on Labor Day weekend, 1999. It offers children's story hours, poetry readings, and brown-bag summer concerts on the lawn. Open daily except Sunday and holidays.

The Green Mountain Perkins Academy and Institute (457-3974), Route 106 in South Woodstock, has exhibits related to its tenure as a famous school between 1848 and 1890. Open Saturday 2–4:30 in July and August and by appointment.

The Vermont Institute of Natural Science (457-2779), 1.5 miles southwest of the village of Woodstock on Church Hill Road, has a rare herbarium collection along with other exhibits of flora and fauna, the distinguished Pettingill Ornithological Library, nature trails, a bird-banding station, and a raptor center. It offers lectures and bird-fern-and-wildflower walks. Open year-round, Monday through Friday 9–4.

HISTORIC HOME

Theron Boyd Homestead, Hillside Road, off River Road, Quechee, now owned by the Vermont Division of Historic Preservation, was built in 1796 by William Burtch, a prosperous merchant specializing in the cultivation of ginseng. It remains virtually unaltered except for the addition of a two-story, brick, Federal ell with summer kitchen and carriage

KIM GRANT

The Jerseys are friendly at the Billings Farm & Museum

bays. Boyd lived there for more than 70 years without electricity or other modern conveniences, and he steadfastly refused to sell the farm to the Quechee Lakes Corporation. Open on special occasions; for tours, check with the Quechee Chamber of Commerce (see *Guidance*).

BREWERY

Long Trail Brewing Company (672-5011), Route 4 west at Bridgewater Corners, produces Long Trail Ale, Long Trail India Pale Ale, Long Trail Stout, Long Trail Lite, and Long Trail Kolsch. Tours and tasting in the pub, daily noon–5.

COVERED BRIDGES

There are three in the town of Woodstock—the **Lincoln Bridge** (1865), Route 4, West Woodstock, Vermont's only Pratt-type truss; the **Middle Bridge,** in the center of the village, built in 1969 by Milton Graton, "last of the covered-bridge builders," in the Town lattice style (partially destroyed by vandalism and rebuilt); and the notable red **Taftsville Bridge** (1836), Route 4 east, utilizing multiple king- and queenposts and an unusual mongrel truss. The Taftsville Bridge overlooks a hydro dam, still in use.

FOR FAMILIES

Quechee Gorge Village (295-1550; 1-800-438-5565), the biggest attraction at Quechee Gorge, Route 4, combines a country store, a 300-dealer antiques mall, an arts and crafts center, Basket Mart, Christmas Loft, other gift shops, an operating 1946 Worcester diner, and a carousel and miniature train ride for the kiddies.

GORGE

Quechee Gorge, Route 4, is one of Vermont's natural wonders. Its 165-foot chasm was first spanned in 1875 by a wooden bridge that carried the short-line Woodstock Railroad trains; the line shut down in 1933. The nearby **Quechee Gorge Recreation Area** (295-2990, 773-2657) has picnic grounds, tent and trailer sites, and trails leading down into the gorge, which should be approached carefully. At the north end of the gorge, under a spillway, is a fine, rockbound swimming hole, accessible by easy stages through the pine woods at the west end of the bridge.

SCENIC DRIVES

The whole area offers delightful vistas; one of the best views is from North Road, which leaves Route 12 next to Silver Lake in Barnard and leads to Bethel. Another is Cloudland Road from River Road, Woodstock, to Pomfret.

TO DO

BICYCLING

Bike Vermont (457-3553; 1-800-257-2226), Box 207, Woodstock. Weekend and 5-day midweek, inn-to-inn tours are arranged through central Vermont, including Grafton and Chester, Middletown Springs, Lake St. Catherine, Manchester, and the Connecticut River Valley. Twenty-one-speed Trek and Cannondale hybrids are available for rent.

Cyclery Plus (457-3377), Route 4 in West Woodstock, has rentals; a marked bike path leads east from the village along River Road to Taftsville and its covered bridge.

Wilderness Trails (295-7620), Clubhouse Road at the Quechee Inn. Complete outdoor equipment rental for the whole family: daily bike trips, canoeing on the Connecticut River or Dewey's Mills Waterfowl Sanctuary, and fishing on Dewey's Lake or with the Vermont Fly Fishing School (see *Fishing*).

Vermont Ski & Sports (672-3636), Bridgewater Mill Market Place, Route 4, Bridgewater, rents and sells mountain bikes.

CANOEING

See Wilderness Trails under *Bicycling* and Quechee Outdoor Adventures under *Fishing*.

FISHING

Trout on the Fly (763-7576; 1-800-441-6787), 65 Central Street, Woodstock. Brad Yoder, of Shallowford/Orvis, offers lessons and guidance.

Vermont Fly Fishing School (295-7620), centered at the Quechee Inn at Marshland Farm, provides tackle and guided trips.

Quechee Outdoor Adventures (1-800-438-5565, ext. 114), Quechee Gorge Village, offers individual and small-group canoe trips, fishing lessons, and hikes.

GOLF AND TENNIS

The 18-hole **Woodstock Country Club** (457-6674), designed by Robert Trent Jones, is part of the Woodstock Inn and Resort (see *Lodging—Resorts*). Ten tennis and two paddle courts are available.

✍ **Vail Field,** Woodstock. Two public tennis courts and a children's playground.

HEALTH SPA

Woodstock Health & Fitness Center (457-6656), part of the Woodstock Inn and Resort, Route 106, has indoor tennis and racquetball, lap pool, whirlpool, aerobic and state-of-the-art fitness equipment; flexible memberships and day-use options; pro shop.

HIKING AND WALKING

Faulkner Park, Mountain Avenue, Woodstock. Laid out by its donor, Mrs. Edward Faulkner, one of Woodstock's most thoughtful philanthropists, Faulkner Park was modeled on Baden-Baden's "cardiac" walks; marked trails lead upward around Mount Tom, where there is a fine network of walking paths.

See also Quechee Outdoor Adventures under *Fishing.*

HORSEBACK RIDING

Woodstock has been an equestrian center for generations, especially for the hardy Morgans, which are making a local comeback in South Woodstock.

Kedron Valley Stables (457-1480), Route 106, South Woodstock. Generally recognized as one of the best places to ride horseback—if you know how but don't happen to own a horse—in New England. Over the years, Paul and Barbara Kendall have pieced together a network of paths to link appealing inns. They lead riders over hiking and recreation trails, dirt roads, and meadows on 1- to 4-day tours that average 20 miles a day, 5 hours in the saddle.

The Green Mountain Horse Association (457-1509), Route 106, South Woodstock. Sponsor of the original 100-mile ride, an annual event around Labor Day that draws entrants from all over; shows, trials, and other popular events.

POLO

Quechee Polo Club. Matches most Saturday afternoons in July and August on the field near the center of the village.

SWIMMING

Silver Lake State Park (234-9451, 773-2657), 10 miles north on Route 12 in Barnard, has a nice beach, and there's another smaller one right next to the general store.

✍ **The Woodstock Recreation Center** (457-1502), 54 River Street, has two public pools, mostly for youngsters.

WINTER SPORTS

CROSS-COUNTRY SKIING

The trail system on **Mount Tom,** just outside Woodstock, ranks with some of the best groomed in New England. It's composed largely of 1880s carriage roads climbing gently from the valley floor (700 feet) to the summit (1,250 feet), skirting a small lake, and finally commanding a view of the village below and down the Ottauquechee Valley. The system offers vistas in many directions and a log cabin heated with a woodstove. Buy tickets and pick up a map at the Ski Touring Center (see below).

The Ski Touring Center (457-6674) at the Woodstock Country Club, Route 106 south of the village, part of the Woodstock Inn and Resort, has mapped, marked, and groomed 38 miles of varied trails, from gentle terrain to forest- and uplands, including Mount Tom and Mount Peg. Group and individual lessons; guided, 4-hour picnic tours; rentals; salesroom; lockers; bar-restaurant (and dogsled carts when the snow fails!).

Wilderness Trails (295-7620), Clubhouse Road at the Quechee Inn, has 8 miles of track-set trails. Most of the trails are good for "entry-level" skiers and travel through the woods and meadows around Quechee Gorge, offering fine views of its waterfalls. Complete rentals; lessons are available.

DOWNHILL SKIING

Suicide Six Downhill Ski Area (457-6661) South Pomfret, 5 miles north of Woodstock on Pomfret Road. Now nearly 60 years old, this is the heir— on the other side of the slope—to the first ski tow in the United States, which was cranked up in 1934. The face of Suicide Six, 655 vertical feet (once operated by Bunny Bertram, of the Ski Hall of Fame), is now part of the Woodstock Inn and Resort complex and has a base lodge finished with native woodwork. Its beginners area has a J-bar ($6 for all day); two double chairlifts reach 22 trails ranging from easy to The Show Off and Pomfret Plunge, plus a snowboarding halfpipe. Lessons, rentals, restaurant. Weekend/holiday lift rates are $38 for adults and $24 for seniors and children.

Quechee Lakes Ski Area (295-9356), Quechee, is open weekends and during school vacations. It "feels like a neighborhood playground devoted to introducing kids to the delights of winter," a *New York Times* writer declared. "Kids ages 4 and up can enroll in group lessons and older children roam the hill's eight trails on their own." Lift tickets: $22 for a full day, $18 for a half day; ages 6 and under, free.

ICE SKATING

Silver Lake, by the general store in Barnard.

Vail Field, Woodstock, maintained by the local hockey and skating committee. Lighted for night skating. Free.

Woodstock Sports (457-1568), 30 Central Street, Woodstock, offers skate and ski rentals.

LODGING

RESORTS

The Woodstock Inn and Resort (457-1100; 1-800-448-7900), on the green, 05091, is the lineal descendant of the 18th-century Eagle Tavern and the

WOODSTOCK INN AND RESORT

The Woodstock Inn on a winter's night

famous "old" Woodstock Inn that flourished between 1893 and 1969, putting the town on the year-round resort map. Today's grand, 146-room, air-conditioned, Colonial-style edition, owned by Laurance S. Rockefeller, reflects the owner's meticulous standards. It was extensively remodeled in 1989–91 with the addition of a townhouse wing, the luxurious **Richardson's Tavern,** and expansion of the dining and meeting rooms. The comfortably furnished main lobby is dominated by a huge stone fireplace where 5-foot birch logs blaze in winter. There's a spiffy main dining room, plus coffee shop, library, gift shop, conference facilities, putting green, and swimming pool. Guests have access to the scenic 18-hole Woodstock Country Club for golf and tennis (it's a fine cross-country-ski center in winter) and to a splendid indoor Sports Center, plus downhill skiing at the historic Suicide Six area and wagon and sleigh rides.

The creature comforts of these pearly precincts, beautifully appointed and run in most respects, make this Vermont's premier place to stay and play. Current regular-season rates rates $159–303 ($109–212 in "Value Season," such as most of March, April, and November); spacious porch and/or fireplace suites in the new Tavern Wing are $325–525; and there are special accommodations in separate cottages: the Justin Morgan House, the Timothy Knox, and Moody Heath House, which have kitchenettes. Children under 14 free when staying in the same room with an adult. MAP available at $55 per person per day.

Check out their special packages: among others, Serenity Season, Summer Sports, Wassail Weekend, and Ski Vermont Free, which includes lift tickets at Suicide Six.

Twin Farms (234-9999; 1-800-894-6327; fax: 802-234-9990), Barnard 05031. Ironically, the shades of Sinclair Lewis, whose novels satirized the materialism of American life in the '20s, and Dorothy Thompson, the acerbic foreign correspondent, hover over this 300-acre, luxurious Shangri-la that used to be their country home. Here and now, an exclusive group of corporate CEOs, heads of government, royalty, and celebrities are welcome to unwind, frolic, and be rich together in sybaritic privacy. Of the four stylish rooms in the main house, Red's is only $700 a day; Dorothy's, $850. New cottages have been added since the place opened in 1993 and range from $850 to $1,500, all including Lucullan meals at any hour, open bars, and the use of all recreational amenities, including the former Sonnenberg ski lift, a fully equipped fitness center, Japanese Furo, croquet court, pond, and mountain bikes. The common rooms and guest quarters display an extraordinary collection of modern art—by David Hockney, Frank Stella, and Roy Lichtenstein, among others. Accommodations at Twin Farms are by reservation only. There's a 2-night minimum on weekends, 3 nights over holidays, and full payment is due 30 days before arrival. The entire enclave can be yours for $13,000 a day.

INNS

The Kedron Valley Inn (457-1473; 1-800-836-1193), Route 106, South Woodstock 05071. Max and Merrily Comins have gingered up the decor, appointments, and cuisine of this venerable mini-resort without depleting its 19th-century charm. The mellow brick main house and historic tavern, plus Vermont log motel unit, are supplemented by an acre-plus swimming pond with sandy beach and the adjacent Kedron Valley Stables (see *Horseback Riding*). The 27 freshly decorated guest rooms, all with private bath, feature canopy and antique oak beds and a fireplace or Franklin stove. There are so many examples of the Cominses' collection of antique quilts on display that the dining room might have been named The Quilted Pony, reflecting both the superior quality of the food (see *Dining Out*) and the inn's popularity with the horse people drawn to South Woodstock as an equestrian center. Room rates are $120–215 double, B&B. Discounts available for May and June and midweek, off-peak periods year-round.

The Jackson House Inn (457-2065), 37 Old Route 4, West Woodstock 05091. With Juan and Gloria Florin as innkeepers, this luxuriously appointed and equipped 1890 farmhouse recently expanded to 15 exceptionally beautiful rooms and now has an outstanding restaurant as well (see *Dining Out*). Four acres of manicured grounds, gardens, and a pond add to its appeal. Rates range from $180 for the Josephine Bonaparte room on the ground floor, furnished in the French Empire style, to $290 for one of the four new mini-suites, three of which have thermal massage tubs for two. One mini-suite, the Christine Jackson on the first floor, has a Brazilian mahogany four-poster queen bed, a gas fireplace, and French doors to the brick patio and garden). Rates include a memorable breakfast and a complimentary glass of wine and hors d'oeuvres late in the day.

The Village Inn of Woodstock (457-1255; 1-800-722-4571), 41 Pleasant Street, Woodstock 05091, is an informal, purple-painted Victorian manse with fireplaces, oak wainscoting, and pressed-tin ceilings, plus bar and dining room. There are eight comfortable rooms with private baths. Daily $75–125 with full breakfast; weekend rates for two ($210–260) include 2 nights, two full breakfasts. Dine on homestyle New England fare indoors or on the veranda.

The Lincoln Inn (457-3312), Route 4, West Woodstock 05091. This 200-year-old, pleasantly renovated farmhouse on the river—next to the covered bridge—has six cheery guest rooms with bath, hand-hewn beams in the library, and a fine dining room in the hands of its Swiss chef-owner. The gazebo is popular in summer and sleigh rides in winter. Rates: $99–139 per couple B&B.

The Quechee Inn at Marshland Farm (295-3133; 1-800-235-3133), Clubhouse Road, Quechee 05059, is an extremely attractive, restored, and enlarged 18th-century farmhouse, once the home of Vermont's first lieutenant governor. It's near the Ottauquechee River just above the dramatic gorge. The sitting room and 24 guest rooms have a romantic aura, and the dining room is above average. Guests have access to the nearby Quechee Club for golf, downhill skiing, and swimming. The inn maintains its own 18 km of groomed cross-country-ski trails, bike and canoe rentals, and a fishing school (see also Wilderness Trails under *Bicycling* and *Cross-Country Skiing*). Rates range from $140 double to $260 for the Lieutenant Governor's suite, MAP.

The Sumner Mansion (436-3386; 1-888-529-8796), junction of Routes 5 and 12, Hartland 05048. Mary Louise and Ron Thorburn, who entertained so well when they owned the Inn at Weathersfield, now preside over this beautifully restored and furnished brick landmark on the National Register. Its five air-conditioned guest rooms with private baths, formal parlor, huge glass-enclosed dining room, and lofty library/music room, surrounded by extensive lawns and gardens, are often rented for weddings and other special events. $90–150.

BED & BREAKFASTS

In Woodstock Village 05091

Three Church Street (457-1925). In one of the grander Federal houses near the green, Eleanor Paine holds hospitable court, serving bountiful breakfasts (sometimes lunch in summer and fall). There are spacious sitting rooms and 11 guest rooms with private and shared baths ($75–105 B&B), plus swimming pool and tennis court. Pets welcome.

Ardmore Inn (457-3887; 1-800-497-9652), 23 Pleasant Street. A meticulously restored Victorian town house with classy Irish overtones and five spacious rooms, each with private marble bath. The Sheridan Room on the ground floor includes an extra-large bathroom with a walk-in shower and Jacuzzi. Guests use the elegant parlor, dining room, and screened veranda. Innkeeper Giorgio Ortiz serves fine breakfasts and afternoon tea. $85–150.

The Charleston House (457-3843), 21 Pleasant Street. This luxurious, recently expanded Federal brick town house is especially appealing, with period furniture in eight bedrooms, all with private bath. Rates $90–175 (the latter for two rooms with fireplace and Jacuzzi). Full breakfast in the dining room or continental breakfast bedside.

Canterbury House (457-3077; 1-800-390-3077), 43 Pleasant Street. This beautifully renovated, Victorian, antiques-furnished house has eight rooms with bath and air-conditioning. Rates from $90 up to $160 for the Monk's Tale, which has a fireplace, cable TV, and a private entrance. Chaucer's Garret is a third-floor suite with two double beds and one single ($120, plus $25 for third and fourth person). Full breakfast.

The 1830 Shire Town Inn (457-1830), 31 South Street, has three "old-worldish" rooms with private baths, wide-pine floors, hand-hewn beams, fireplace, hearty country breakfast. $75–110.

Barr House (457-3334), 55 South Street. Kay Paul, the retired Woodstock Inn bartender, and Jim, the former fire chief, offer two charming rooms with shared bath in a trim saltbox. $50 single, $60–75 double including American breakfast and afternoon tea.

The Woodstocker (457-3896; 1-800-457-3896), 61 River Street, recently redecorated, has nine rooms with private bath, plus a whirlpool; two suites with living room, kitchen, and deck; $85–155 double with big buffet breakfast.

South of the village

✎ **Woodstock House** (457-1758), Route 106, 3 miles south of Woodstock 05091. Three rooms with private bath, two shared; exposed beams, wide-board floors. Children welcome, but no pets or smoking. $70–85 with full breakfast.

🎗 **Bailey's Mills Bed & Breakfast** (484-7809; 1-800-639-3437), RR 1, Box 117, Reading 05062. As happens so often in Vermont, surprises lurk at the end of a back road, especially in the case of this venerable guesthouse, a few miles west of Route 106. With a two-story porch and fluted columns, Bailey's Mills resembles a southern antebellum mansion. The 17-room brick home includes 11 fireplaces, two beehive ovens, a dance hall, and an 1829 general store, all part of an ambitious manufacturing complex established by Levi Bailey (1766–1850) and operated by his family for a century. Today, Barbara Thaeder and Don Whitaker offer several comfortable rooms, two with working fireplaces, each with a cozy sitting area and private bath, romantically furnished with antiques. A spacious solarium makes Mom's Room an especially appealing suite. The library has an unusually interesting collection of books and is furnished, as is the dining room, with family antiques and "old stuff." $75–135, with continental breakfast; slightly higher in foliage season and over some holidays; and special rates for "Rent the Inn" extended stays and packages. (Ask about the adjacent "Spite Cemetery.")

Greystone Bed & Breakfast (484-7200), Box 85, Reading 05062, 11 miles south of Woodstock on Route 106. This restored, 1830 stone Colonial has two elegant bedrooms sharing a bath and a full-floor suite with twin beds, sitting room with queen sofa, and private bath; $85 for the bedrooms, $100 for two in the suite; lower midweek. Continental breakfast. No pets.

In the West Woodstock area

Carriage House of Woodstock (457-4322), Route 4, West Woodstock 05091. This recently refurbished Victorian farmhouse with a wrap-around porch has seven attractive guest rooms with queen beds and private baths, plus several conversation areas. Full breakfast; $95–165.

Winslow House (457-1820), Route 4, West Woodstock 05091. This restored, antiques-filled farmhouse has four spacious guest rooms, three of which are suites with sitting room, all with private bath, cable TV, air-conditioning, phone, and refrigerator. $75–115 double.

Deer Brook Inn (672-3713), Route 4, Woodstock 05091. A restored 1820 farmhouse with antique charm. Five spacious bedrooms with private bath; one is a suite. Children, but no pets. $75–125, full breakfast.

Woodbridge House (672-5070), Route 4, Bridgewater 05034, has hand stenciling in the guest rooms, original wood flooring, and country furniture. $85–110 double with breakfast. No credit cards.

North of the village

Maple Leaf Inn (234-5342), P.O. Box 273, Route 12, Barnard 05031. Gary and Janet Robison opened up this sparkling new place in a faithfully reproduced turn-of-the-century Victorian farmhouse, designed specifically as a B&B. Stenciling, stitchery, and handmade quilts decorate the five guest rooms, each with a capacious private bath, king-sized bed, sitting area, wood-burning fireplace, telephone, and TV/VCR. The parlor, library, and dining room are bright and inviting. Rates $110–175 with full breakfast. The Country Garden Room on the main floor has easy access for anyone who needs special assistance, and a whirlpool bath.

Heartacres Farm (457-2627), Old Barnard Road, North Pomfret 05053, is a Colonial-style farmhouse with two guest rooms and shared bath upstairs, at $70, and a ground-floor room with private bath for $80.

In Taftsville 05073

Applebutter Inn (457-4158), Happy Valley Road. An authentically restored and attractively decorated Federal house with five downy bedrooms, private baths, two living rooms with fireplace; $35–65 per person, with one of Bev Cook's inimitable, natural-foods breakfasts (just about the best muffins in the area).

Four Pillars (457-2797; 1-800-957-2797), Happy Valley Road. This impressive 1836 Taft family house, recently opened, has brightly decorated rooms at $75–130, depending on the season.

Eben House (457-3769), Happy Valley Road. Bob and Betsy McKaig's hearty hospitality animates this comfortable 1845 brick cottage with two guest rooms and baths; $95–135 with full breakfast; no children, pets, or credit cards, however.

In Quechee 05059

The Pippin Inn (296-3646; 1-800-9-PIPPIN), 188 Dewey's Mills Road. Mark and Patricia Pippin have renovated the mid-1800s Dewey family mansion as "an executive hideaway," preserving its fine woodwork. They have installed three two-room suites, an exercise room, lounge, and billiard parlor. $150, $200, or $300 per suite, depending on location.

Sugar Pine Farm (295-1266; 1-800-626-1266), Route 4. A reproduction 1740 house furnished with country antiques, adjacent to a gift shop; $70 and $75 shared bath, $85 private, with full breakfast.

Quechee Bed & Breakfast (295-1776), Route 4. This 1795 Colonial has eight comfortable guest rooms with private bath and a fine view over the river; rates include full breakfast and start at $94, going up to $139 for Sarah's Room, which has a king-sized four-poster, wide-pine floors, and a refrigerator.

Parker House Inn (295-6077), Main Street. An antiques-filled, restored Victorian mansion dating from 1857. Seven guest rooms, all with private bath; $105–145 double includes full country breakfast. (See also *Dining Out*.)

The Country Garden Inn (295-3121; 1-800-859-4191), 37 Main Street, has five pretty bedrooms with private baths (one with a private entrance) under its mansard roof, plus a breakfast solarium with wicker furniture. $110–200.

MOTELS

Woodstock has its share of motel units. **Braeside** (457-1366), Route 4 east 05091; 12 deluxe units, small heated pool. **Shire Motel** (457-2211), 46 Pleasant Street 05091; 33 units on two innlike floors. **Woodstock Motel** (457-2500), Route 4 east 05091; 15 units. **Pond Ridge** (457-1667), Route 4, West Woodstock 05091; 12 units plus apartments. **Ottauquechee Motor Lodge** (672-3404), Route 4, West Woodstock 05091; capacity 38.

Quality Inn at Quechee Gorge (295-7600; 1-800-732-4376), Route 4, Quechee 05059, has an attractive, campuslike setting.

OTHER LODGING

Kendall Homestead (457-2734), Route 106, South Woodstock 05071. This fine old family house on a knoll close to the Kedron Valley Stables (see *Horseback Riding*) has three bedrooms and baths, plus sitting rooms and kitchen and laundry facilities. Good spot for families or groups of horse riders; available by the day, weekend, week, or month; inquire for flexible rates.

Quechee Vacation Rentals (295-3186; 1-800-262-3186), 26 Main Street, P.O. Box 432, Quechee 05059, offers a variety of one- to six-bedroom accommodations.

Quechee Lakes Rentals (295-1970; 1-800-745-0042), Route 4, Quechee 05059, has vacation condos and homes for rent.

Quechee Gorge Recreation Area (295-2990, 773-2657) has tent and trailer sites. (See also *To See—Gorge.*)

WHERE TO EAT

DINING OUT

The Prince and the Pauper (457-1818), 24 Elm Street, Woodstock. Open daily except for late-fall and early-spring vacations. Provides nouvelle and Continental cuisine in a candlelit, elegantly rustic setting. Owner-chef Chris Balcer has, over the years, created and upheld consistently superior standards, now with daily menu changes. A recent sampling of the $35 prix fixe dinner included, for starters, smoked Ducktrap salmon garnished with Raifort sauce and capers, Vietnamese spring rolls, followed by Carré d'Agneau Royale (a "signature" rack of lamb in puff pastry), or medallions of Provini veal with Marsala. Patrons tend to linger in the premium wine bar, where you can also dine on the bistro menu (grilled Black Angus strip steak with garlic herb butter, $16.50) or on exotic pizzas ($10.50). One of the state's best; "worth every calorie and dollar," we said in the first edition of this book, and we have no reason to change our minds.

The Jackson House Restaurant (457-2065), Route 4 west, Woodstock. Open Thursday through Monday. This latest entrant in the area's world of fine dining offers sophisticated, top-drawer cuisine in surroundings of understated (but sometimes noisy) simplicity. Chef Brendan Nolan, formerly with the Four Seasons in Boston, offers a $42 prix fixe menu that could begin with ravioli or sweetbreads with leek puree, free-range chicken with truffle essence, followed by sesame-crusted monkfish and lobster with lemongrass soy broth, or grilled venison medallions with chestnut spaetzle and red cabbage, topped off by a chocolate velvet mousse torte with raspberry ice cream.

The Barnard Inn (234-9961), 10 miles north of Woodstock on Route 12, Barnard. Dinner is served in an impressive 1796 brick house in three beautifully appointed formal rooms. New owners Philip and Marie-France Filipovic took over from Sepp Schenker in 1994 and have added their French-Canadian panache to the classic Continental menu and atmosphere. Starters could include a scallop casserole and lightly smoked seafood sausages, followed by beef tenderloin with caramelized shallots, hearty veal loin chop, or an old favorite, the semi-boneless duck with various sauces. Desserts are crafted with chocoholics in mind. Closed Monday, and it's wise to call ahead anyway to check whether it's open. Very expensive; five-course tasting menu, $33.

The Woodstock Inn and Resort (457-1100), on the green, Woodstock. The cheerfully contemporary main dining room, with its alcoves and semicircular bay, is an especially attractive setting for the sumptuous Sunday brunch buffet ($23.35) and executive chef Tom Guay's really superior dinners. One might start with crabmeat cake with leeks, whole-grain mustard and tomato confit, or a "Symphony of Dining Room Appetizers" ($17.50), and continue with Dover sole napped with Grand Marnier brown butter (seldom found hereabouts), roast pork tenderloin with spinach, white bean and prosciutto ragout, plus other entrées in the $20–28 category. Pastries and other desserts, subtle or lavish, are notable. During foliage season, a buffet lunch is served in the main dining room. Lighter fare is served at breakfast, lunch, and dinner in the less expensive **Eagle Café.**

The Kedron Valley Inn (457-1473), Route 106, 5 miles south of Woodstock, has won applause for its stylish "nouvelle Vermont" cuisine. Appetizers include soups; pasta with basil pesto; oysters; and escargots in puff pastry with fennel butter. Entrées range from chicken breast with honey, peaches, white wine, and scallions to the delectable house specialty, fillet of Norwegian salmon stuffed with an herb seafood mousse and wrapped in puff pastry. Fresh vegetables are especially well prepared and subtly seasoned. Expensive.

The Lincoln Inn (457-3312), Route 4, West Woodstock. Open Tuesday through Sunday, plus Sunday brunch from 11. Fireside Continental dining on such popular selections as shrimp amoureuse, with a Pernod-scented dill sauce served in a heart-shaped pastry shell; pan-seared red snapper; and sautéed veal medallions with melted Brie. Moderate.

Wild Grass Eating Establishment (457-1917), Gallery Place, Route 4, Woodstock. Open daily for dinner, featuring an "intercontinental" menu that includes crispy sage leaves and beef carpaccio as appetizers, followed by grilled adobo-rubbed lamb, Jamaican jerk chicken, "West Meets East" cioppino of shellfish, ahi tuna, and other creative, distinctive entrées, all served in a bright, brisk, no-nonsense setting. Moderate.

The Corners Inn (672-9968), Routes 4 and 100A, Bridgewater Corners. Open Wednesday through Sunday, 5:30–9:30. A casual, highly regarded place, featuring such goodies as seafood cakes with mango chutney, lobster ravioli, veal with porcini and shiitake mushrooms, and, of course, steak. The chef gladly makes half portions on request, a neat feature. Summer dining on the deck is especially pleasant. Moderate.

The Village Inn of Woodstock (457-1255), 41 Pleasant Street, Woodstock. This Victorian guesthouse serves dinner nightly, featuring roast Vermont turkey, roast duck, prime rib, and rack of lamb. Look for seasonal early-bird specials and "Italian Nights." Moderate.

Bentley's Restaurant (457-3232), Elm Street, Woodstock, an oasis of Victoriana and plants, is open daily for lunch and dinner, featuring everything from brawny hamburgers and croissant sandwiches to veal Marsala and Jack Daniels steak. Frequent live entertainment, disco dancing weekends. Inexpensive to moderate.

KIM GRANT

The dining room at Simon Pearce overlooks the Ottauquechee River

The Meadows at Marshland Farm (295-3133), Clubhouse Road, Quechee. Open nightly, this romantically rustic dining room features, for example, cassoulet, hazelnut-crusted chicken, and sole fillets with a spinach and crabmeat timbale. Moderate.

Simon Pearce Restaurant (295-1470), The Mill, Quechee. Open daily. This is a cheerful, upbeat, contemporary place for consistently superior lunch and dinner, served with its own pottery and glass, overlooking the waterfall. The patio is open in summer, and its Irish soda bread and Ballymaloe brown bread alone are worth a visit. Lunch entrées could be spinach and cheddar cheese in puff pastry or beef and Guinness stew; at dinner, main courses might be duck with mango chutney sauce, veal with two-mustard sauce, or beef tenderloin pressed in cracked pepper and sautéed with brandy and mustard. Moderate to expensive.

Parker House Inn (295-6077), Quechee. Barbara and Walt Forrester and their boys invite you to enjoy the elegance of their main dining room or outdoor dining on the terrace overlooking the Ottauquechee River. The menu offers such signature dishes as the grilled portobello mushroom appetizer, rack of lamb, and fresh Vermont rabbit. Moderate to expensive.

See also Skunk Hollow Tavern under *Dining Out* in "Upper Valley River Towns."

EATING OUT

Spooner's (457-4022), Route 4 east (in the Sunset Farm Barn), Woodstock. Open daily for dinner; sometimes for lunch in summer. A natty, informal, relatively inexpensive family restaurant specializing in beef, seafood, and a salad bar.

Sevi's House of Seafood (295-9351), Route 4, Quechee. Closed Monday. In pleasant nautical surroundings, Mike and Sevi Guryel offer hearty, consistently well-prepared dinners, featuring lobster, broiled scrod, baked stuffed shrimp, a broiled shore dinner, steak, and tender prime ribs, plus Italian dishes, all accompanied by Greek salad. Their homemade New England clam chowder is rich, and daily specials are good values. From 4 to midnight it's pizza time, in the lounge or takeout. Moderate.

Woodstock Country Club (457-2112), Route 106 south, Woodstock. Light lunch during golf and cross-country seasons (see *To Do—Golf and Tennis*).

Mountain Creamery (457-1715), Central Street, Woodstock, serves breakfast daily 7–11:30, plus sandwiches and luncheon specials and homemade ice cream. Pies and cakes from its bakery are for sale.

The Wasp Diner, Pleasant Street, Woodstock. Join Woodstock's hardworking fraternity for breakfast or lunch at the counter.

Pizza Chef (457-1444), Route 4 east, Woodstock, has hot and cold subs, salads, and lasagna as well as pizzas.

FireStones (295-1600), Route 4, Waterman Place, Quechee. Open daily for lunch and dinner and Sunday brunch. Bill Decklebaum and David Creech, proprietors of Bentley's (see *Dining Out*), also operate this rustic, lodgelike restaurant, with a big wood-fired oven as centerpiece, featuring made-to-order flat breads, fire-roasted shrimp marinated in Long Trail Ale, fire-roasted chicken, and steaks. Children's menu; outdoor deck.

Wildflowers Restaurant (295-7051), Route 4, Quechee (near the gorge). An above-average road place for breakfast, lunch, and dinner, often crowded with bus tours during summer and early fall.

SNACKS

Pane e Salute (457-4882), 61 Central Street, Woodstock, is a traditional Italian bakery and café featuring pastries, breads, coffee, and light lunches.

Bentley's Florist Café (457-3400), 7 Elm Street, Woodstock, offers sandwiches, ice cream, cappuccino, and flowers.

The Village Butcher (457-2756), 18 Elm Street, Woodstock, provides tasty deli specials to go, along with its top-flight meats, wines, and baked goods, plus homemade fudge.

Woodstock Farmers' Market (457-3658) has a thoughtful deli case, plus soups and sandwiches, fresh fish, free-range chicken, meals to go, Baba à Louis bread, cookies.

ENTERTAINMENT

Pentangle Council on the Arts (457-3981), 1 High Street, Woodstock, sponsors plays, films, concerts, ballet performances, and other touring shows at the restored **Town Hall Theater** in Woodstock.

SELECTIVE SHOPPING

ANTIQUES SHOPS

Wigren & Barlow (457-2453), 29 Pleasant Street, Woodstock, has a large selection of fine country and formal furniture, decorative accessories, and garden appointments. Open daily April through November; by chance in winter.

Church Street Antiques (457-2628), west of the green in Woodstock, is open daily and stocks furniture, mirrors, Quimper, and porcelains.

American Classics (457-4337), 71 Central Street, Woodstock. Carefully selected, upscale folk art and antiques fill several second-floor rooms.

Pleasant Street Books, Cards, Ephemera (457-4050), 48 Pleasant Street, Woodstock, specializes in baseball cards.

Fraser's (457-3437), Happy Valley Road, Taftsville, has a good stock of Early American furniture and accessories.

Windsor Galleries & Lamp Shop (457-1797), 1211 Pomfret Road (at Route 12 north), Woodstock. Open 10–4 Monday through Saturday. Well stocked with antique furniture, porcelain, and silver, this is the place to go for lampshades and repairs as well as interior design services.

Old Dog Antiques (457-9800), 1211 Pomfret Road (at Route 12 north), Woodstock. Open Monday 10:30–2:30; Tuesday, Thursday, Friday, and Saturday 10:30–4. Here's an impressive collection of country antiques and some really outstanding examples of early folk art.

Polo Antiques (457-5837), 47 Central Street, Woodstock. Closed Tuesday and Wednesday.

The Different Drummer (234-9403), Route 12, north of Silver Lake, Barnard, features antique and reproduction dolls and doll repairs.

Antiques Collaborative (296-5858), Route 4 at the blinking light in Quechee, shows representative stock from some 80 dealers.

Quechee Gorge Village Antique Mall (295-1550), Route 4 east of

Quechee Gorge, displays antiques and collectibles from more than 300 dealers.

Bridgewater Mill Antique Center (672-3049), Route 4, Bridgewater. Many dealers, plus artisans.

ART GALLERIES

Grayson Gallery (457-1171), Central Street, Woodstock. This showcase has replaced the well-known Gallery 2, but continues to focus on the work of Vermont painters, sculptors, and glassmakers while adding regional and international dimensions.

Woodstock Folk Art (457-2012), 8 Elm Street, Woodstock, specializes in contemporary carvings, prints, and antiquities.

Stephen Huneck Studio (457-3206), 49 Central Street, Woodstock. The celebrated St. Johnsbury woodcarver's fanciful animals of all kinds adorn furniture, wall reliefs, jewelry, and other witty, uncommon pieces.

Gallery on the Green (457-4956), corner of Elm Street, Woodstock, features original art, limited-edition prints, photography, and occasionally sculpture, from New England artists.

Fox Gallery (457-3944), 5 The Green, Woodstock, is primarily a showcase for Neil Drevitson's paintings.

Open Gallery (457-1178), 8 Elm Street, Woodstock. Charlet Davenport shows her own work and that of several other local artists. Call ahead for hours.

Polonaise Art Gallery (457-5180), 71 Central Street, Woodstock, features contemporary and traditional styles in paintings and sculpture.

Robert O. Caulfield Art Gallery (457-1472), 42 Central Street, Woodstock, is the artist's studio; realistic oil and watercolor landscapes and street scenes.

Gallery at Quechee (295-3744), by the waterfall. Artist-owners Marilyn Milham and Owen McDowell show their own and others' contemporary art, including handmade papers.

ARTISANS

Peter Bramhall (672-5141), Bridgewater. The studio of this unique glass-blower may be visited by appointment.

Mark Engler Glassblowing Studio (672-3155), Woodstock. Engler's studio, near the Bridgewater Mill, is open daily; crystal Christmas ornaments a specialty, plus commissioned glass sculptures.

Woodstock Potters (457-1298), Mechanic Street, Woodstock, has a studio-workshop for stoneware and hand-painted porcelains, plus gold and silver jewelry.

Morgan Collection (457-9411), 65 Central Street, Woodstock. Here's an eclectic stock of artisans' work in glass, wood, and ceramics.

The Workshop Store (672-5175), The Mill, Route 4, Bridgewater, is the showcase for Charles Shackleton's fine furniture and accessories, and for Miranda Thomas's special pottery.

Sandra Pearl Pomeroy Cabinet Maker (296-7973), Quechee. Call for directions to her home studio/workshop for fine reproduction furniture.

BOOKSTORES

The Yankee Bookshop (457-2411), Central Street, Woodstock, carries an unusually large stock of hardbound and paperback books for adults and children, plus cards; features the work of local authors and publishers.

Shiretown Books (457-2996), 9 Central Street, Woodstock, is an intimate, very personalized shop that has a carefully selected stock of books for adults and children.

The Sun of the Heart Bookstore (672-5151), the Old Mill Marketplace, Route 4 west, Bridgewater, has an eclectic collection of new books for adults and children, with an emphasis on New Age materials. Also cards, photographs, prints.

SPECIAL SHOPS

F. H. Gillingham & Sons (457-2100; 1-800-344-6668), Elm Street, Woodstock, owned and run by the same family since 1886, is something of an institution, retaining a lot of its old-fashioned general-store flavor. You'll find plain and fancy groceries, wine, housewares, and hardware for home, garden, and farm. Mail-order catalog.

Chocolate Cow (457-9151), Elm Street, Woodstock. World-class chocolate creations: 20 flavors of truffles, gourmet fudge, and other goodies.

Shallowford & Company (457-4340), 65 Central Street, Woodstock, is chartered to sell Orvis fishing tackle and Orvis clothes for men and women, plus British sportswear.

Unicorn (457-2480), 15 Central Street, Woodstock, is a treasure trove of unusual gifts, cards, games, toys, and unclassifiable finds.

Who Is Sylvia? (457-1110), 26 Central Street, Woodstock, features vintage clothing and accessories.

The Vermont Workshop (457-1400), 73 Central Street, Woodstock, features a wide selection of gifts and crafts, furniture, rugs, and lamps.

Arjuna (457-3350), 20 Central Street, Woodstock, is a small cornucopia of unusual collectibles and items from around the world, plus funky women's clothing and jewelry.

The Whipple Tree (457-1325), 7 Central Street, has yarns, knitting, sewing, and art supplies (and Vermont Transit bus tickets).

Chapter XIV (228-4438), 47 Central Street, Woodstock, has an eclectic stock of clothing and accessories for women, plus books for children and others. There are other Chapters in Ludlow and Stratton.

Noteworthy (457-1944), 71 Central Street, Woodstock, has "themed" music and gifts: CDs, tapes, and related items, such as miniature instruments as jewelry.

Red Cupboard Gift Shop (457-3722), Route 4, West Woodstock, has a broad selection of Vermont-made gifts, jams, jellies, and a variety of maple products.

High Brook Horse and Harness (457-4677), Route 106, South

Woodstock, is a "country store" for horses and horse people—saddlery, harnesses, equestrian clothes, supplies, and gifts.

The Old Mill Marketplace (672-3332), Route 4, Bridgewater. When an 1825 woolen mill on the Ottauquechee finally gave up the ghost in the early 1970s, a local bootstrap effort was mounted to convert it into an indoor shopping center featuring a bookstore, many producers of Vermont-made articles, plus a ski and sports outlet.

Taftsville Country Store (457-1135), Route 4 east, Taftsville. Refurbished and restocked, this 1840 landmark carries carefully chosen Vermont gifts as well as a good selection of cheeses, maple products, jams, jellies, smoked ham, and bacon, plus staples, wine, and books.

Sugarbush Farm (457-1757; 1-800-281-1757), RR 1, Box 568, Woodstock (but located in Pomfret: Take Route 4 to Taftsville, cross the covered bridge, go up the hill, turn left onto Hillside Road, then follow signs. Sample seven Vermont cheeses, all packaged here. In-season, you can watch maple sugaring, walk the maple and nature trail, meditate in the Luce family's small woodland chapel, or visit with their farm animals.

Simon Pearce Glass (295-2711), The Mill, Main Street, Quechee. Pearce, who operated his own glassworks in Ireland for a decade, moved here in 1981, acquired the Downer's Mill, and is now harnessing the dam's hydropower for the glass furnace. Visitors can watch glass being blown and can shop for individual pieces from the retail shop, where seconds with imperceptible flaws are also stocked along with hand-knit sweaters, quilts, and distinctive pottery. The shop is open 10–5 daily; glassblowing and pottery throwing can be viewed weekdays 9–4:30 and on summer weekends. (See also Simon Pearce Glass under *Selective Shopping* in "Upper Valley River Towns.")

Fat Hat Factory (296-6646), at the corner of Route 4 and Clubhouse Road, Quechee, offers "spirited hats and carefree clothing."

Scotland by the Yard (295-5351), Route 4, 3 miles east of Woodstock, imports tartans and tweeds, kilts, capes, coats, sweaters, skirts, canes, books, records, oatcakes, and shortbreads.

Talbot's Herb & Perennial Farm (436-2085), Hartland-Quechee Road, 3 miles south of the blinker off Route 4. Field-grown herbs, dried flowers and wreaths, greenhouse. Open daily 9–5, from early April through October.

New England Specialties Shoppe (295-6163), Route 4, Quechee. The Laros' gorge-side store has an especially large and carefully selected stock of Vermont products, from cheese, syrup, and preserves to sweatshirts and toys.

SPECIAL EVENTS

February (Washington's Birthday): A week of **Winter Carnival** events sponsored by the Woodstock Recreation Center (457-1502)—concerts,

Fisk Trophy Race, sleigh rides, square dance, torchlight ski parade.

Late June: **Quechee Hot Air Balloon Festival** (295-7900)—ascensions, flights, races, crafts show, entertainment.

July 4: **Crafts Fair,** Woodstock—music and fireworks display in the evening at the high school. **Woodstock Road Race,** 7.4 miles (457-1502).

Mid-August: **Sidewalk sale,** Woodstock; **Quechee Scottish Festival.**

Mid-October: **Apple & Crafts Fair,** Woodstock.

Early December: **Christmas Wassail Weekend,** which includes a grand parade of carriages around the Woodstock green, yule log lighting, concerts.

III. CENTRAL VERMONT

The White River Valleys
Killington/Pico Area
Sugarbush/Mad River Valley
Barre/Montpelier Area

A farm near Chelsea

KIM GRANT

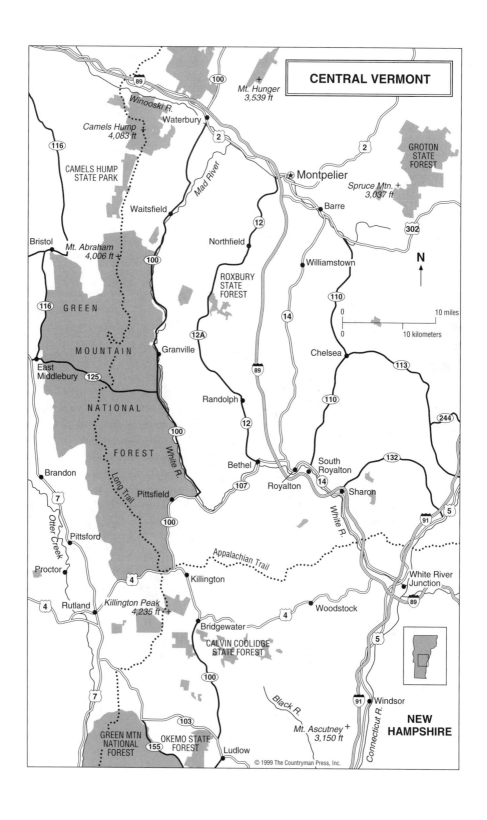

CENTRAL VERMONT

The White River Valleys

"Vanishing Vermont" could be the subtitle for this chapter. As I-89 sweeps up through central Vermont in a grand 52-mile curve (from White River Junction to Montpelier), it yields a series of panoramas. Motorists see the high wall of the Green Mountains beyond the Braintree Range on the west and catch glimpses of an occasional valley village.

What they don't see is one of Vermont's best-kept secrets: the classic old villages, abrupt valleys, and hill farms along the three northern branches of the White River. Nowhere near any ski or resort area, the farmscape around Tunbridge, Chelsea, and Brookfield still possesses a refreshingly unselfconscious beauty. The lush farmland to be seen from Route 100 as it shadows the White River through Stockbridge and Rochester suggests this still farm-based country to the east.

Route 110 follows the First Branch of the White River through the classic farming towns of Chelsea and Tunbridge, flanked by high, open country and webbed with back roads where the sky seems very near. To the east, roads slope gently off this high plateau through Vershire and Strafford. To the west, Routes 14 and 12 traverse lonely valleys that deepen in spots into gulfs and are linked by a particularly rewarding road through the photogenic village of Brookfield. Farther to the west, Route 12A follows the Third Branch of the White River along the base of the majestic Roxbury and Randolph Ranges. Three streams and their three accompanying roads (Routes 12A, 12, and 66) meet like threads in a string purse in the town of Randolph—a combination of hill farms, a gracious old village in Randolph Center, and Randolph Village itself, the area's commercial center.

In recent years Randolph has become known as the mountain-biking capital of the East. The White River Trails Association maintains trails—a vast network of Class 4 roads and grass and dirt trails, as well as country roads radiating from an Amtrak station (served by bike-carrying trains)—a bike shop that offers rentals, and an inn that maintains its own trails and serves as the setting for the annual noncompetitive New England Mountain Bike Festival, which seems to get bigger each year.

The White River proper rises high in the Green Mountains and rushes down through the villages of Granville, Hancock, and Rochester, keeping company with Route 100 until Stockbridge, where its course dictates a dogleg in the highway. Turning sharply northeast and carving a narrow valley for Route 107 (the Gaysville reach is an especially challenging one for kayakers during spring freshets), the river comes to Bethel, where it begins to parallel Route 14 and I-89. Vestiges of an old railroad connecting Rochester to Bethel can occasionally be seen from Routes 100 and 107.

As the White River courses through the Royaltons and Sharon on its way to the Connecticut River, swimming and fishing possibilities are heightened by the input of its three northern branches.

To begin exploring this region, you might exit I-89 in Sharon and climb through the Straffords to Tunbridge, north to Chelsea and west to Brookfield, then south to Randolph and on down Route 12 to Camp Brook Road (Rochester–Bethel Mountain Road), a memorable up, then down ride into Rochester. A glance through this chapter should reveal ways in which this circuit can pleasantly fill many days.

GUIDANCE

Randolph Area Chamber of Commerce (728-9027; fax: 728-4705; e-mail: mail@randolph-chamber.com; web site: www.randolph-chamber.com), 66 Central Street, Box 9, Randolph 05060. Phone answered year-round, information center maintained June through September at State Plaza just off I-89, exit 4 (next to the Mobil station); the chamber offices are just west on Route 66 across from the Montague Golf Club (see *To Do—Golf*). Request a map brochure and business directory for the area. During foliage season, the chamber refers visitors to private homes after commercial lodging is filled.

The Herald of Randolph (728-3232), Box 309, Randolph, carries local news and events for most of Orange County.

GETTING THERE

By bus: **Vermont Transit** buses stop just off I-89 at White River Junction and Randolph.

GETTING AROUND

Taxi: **JT's Taxi & Courier** (291-1754; pager: 741-5309) is based in Randolph.

Car rental: **Especially Imports** (728-4455), Route 66, Randolph, can arrange to meet you at the train.

By train: **Amtrak's** *Vermonter* (1-800-USA-RAIL). Randolph is a stop for trains from Washington, D.C., New York City, and Springfield and Amherst (Massachusetts) with connecting bus service to Montreal; the baggage car has bike racks.

MEDICAL EMERGENCY

Randolph, Bethel, and Stockbridge (728-9600); Chelsea and Tunbridge (685-4545); Rochester (767-4211).

Chelsea Family Health Center (685-4400), Main Street, Chelsea.
Gifford Medical Center (728-4441), 44 South Main Street, Randolph.

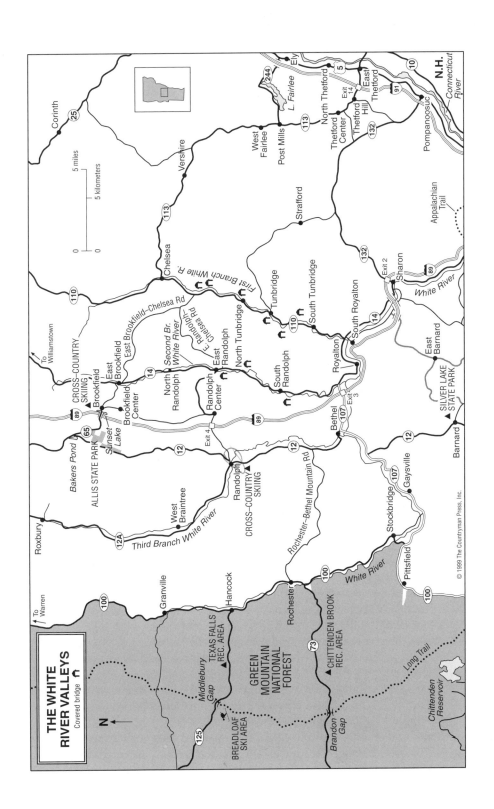

THE WHITE
RIVER VALLEYS

⌂ Covered bridge

N

© 1999 The Countryman Press, Inc.

VILLAGES

Sharon Village. An old commercial center at the junction of the river road (Route 14) and the high road (to Strafford), this remains a welcoming cluster of services, just off I-89. Brooksie's offers roadfood, the columned Sharon Trading Post is a classic general store with a serious meat department, also selling local maple products, and the Columns Motor Lodge across the street is a good way-stop with a first-rate antiques shop a few doors down. If you are lucky enough to be here on a summer Sunday, don't fail to check out the Sharon Historical Society (open July 4 through August, Sunday 1–3); its collection of vintage photos and memorabilia is particularly rich. The museum is also open on Old Home Day in early August (Sharon claims the oldest and one of the liveliest versions of this event in the country; for guests over 70, the chicken pie supper is always free). The historical society also publishes a lively newletter; for details about joining, write HCR 65, Box 102, Sharon 05065.

South Royalton Village. Cupped between a bend in the river and the straight line of Route 14, this small but unusually attractive village is gathered around an outsized green with an elevated bandstand in the middle. A granite arch at one end of the park recalls the 1780 raid on nearby Royalton by more than 300 Native Americans commanded by an English lieutenant. A stagecoach inn at one end of the green and a train depot at another recall later eras in village history. Many of the clapboard buildings within eyeshot, including the old inn, have received a new lease on life as part of Vermont's first and only law school, headquartered in a tower-topped old school building. Founded in 1972, Vermont Law School now draws students from around the country.

Tunbridge. Some 20,000 people jam into this village of 400 souls for four days each September. They come for the World's Fair, said to have originated in 1761 when the town received its charter from George III to hold two fairs each year. In fact, the fair dates back to 1867, when it was first sponsored by the Union Agricultural Society. Sited in a grassy, natural bowl by a bend in the river, the event still has everything an agricultural fair should have: a midway, livestock displays and contests, a Floral Hall, collections of old-time relics, dancing, sulky racing, a fiddlers contest, horse pulls, a grandstand, and more. Known as the Drunkards Reunion during a prolonged era when it is claimed that anyone found sober after 3 PM was expelled as a nuisance, it is now billed as a family event; drinking is confined to the parking lot and beer hall. The town also boasts four covered bridges, a fishing hole, and a photogenic brick Methodist church (in South Tunbridge).

Strafford. East from Tunbridge, the road climbs steeply through woods and fields, finally cresting and beginning its downhill run through beau-

KIM GRANT

The green in South Royalton

tifully restored farms with ponds out back (pools would be too garish), stables, and other signs of wealth not evident on the other side of the mountain. You are in Strafford, a physically beautiful community that has grown greatly in recent decades because it is within an easy commute of Dartmouth College and Vermont Law School, as well as within the outstanding bistate Dresden School District. Aristocratic homes—which include the Gothic Revival Justin Morrill Homestead, built in 1848—are clustered along and below a sloping common, above which rises the exquisite white clapboard Town House, built in 1799. South Strafford is a crossroads community with a pleasant general store.

Chelsea. Chelsea has been hailed as one of the few remaining bastions of "Vermont character." It is a town with an unusual survival rate of dairy farms and maple producers. It has a classic steepled church and a courthouse, a brick library and its own bank (since 1822), an abundance of Federal-era homes, and not one but two handsome commons. An amazing number of services—post office, restaurant, barber, food stores, and fish and wildlife office—are compressed into a small space. The commercial heart of town revolves around twin 1818 brick buildings that house general stores.

Brookfield. Easily one of the most picturesque four corners in all New England, this sleepy community belies its vivid past. Among its boasts are the state's oldest continuously operating library (established in 1791) and a house in which the Prince of Wales, father of Queen Victoria, not only slept but also received a kick in the pants. Sunset Lake is traversed by a floating bridge, buoyed by 380 barrels (the lake is too deep to support a pillared span). During the summer, much of its traffic stops midway to fish, and on the last Saturday in January, it is a coveted viewing point for one of New England's last ice harvest festivals. At the center of the village is Green Trails Inn, with extensive cross-country trails. Ariel's Restaurant across the way overlooks the pond. Allis State Park, a few miles west, offers camping, picnicking, and a sweeping view. The Marvin Newton House, Ridge Road in Brookfield Center, is an eight-room home built in 1835, now housing local historical exhibits (open Sundays in July and August, 2–5; $2).

Randolph. Randolph Center is clearly the oldest of the five Randolphs, a lineup of brick and clapboard Federal-era mansions along a main street that was cut unusually wide with the idea that this might be the state capital. Instead, it is now a soul-satisfying village in which life centers on Floyd's General Store and the nearby complex of Vermont Technical College, grown from the grammar school built here in 1806. A historical marker informs us that musician and schoolmaster Justin Morgan of Randolph Center brought a young stallion from Massachusetts to his home here in 1789 (Justin Morgan the man lies buried in the nearby cemetery; the grave of Justin Morgan the horse is marked by a simple stone off Route 110 in Chelsea). Randolph remains an unusually horsey community. With the arrival of the railroad in the mid–19th century, the population shifted from the center to the valley 3 miles west, where Amtrak now stops and a brick Main Street with a lively performance center (Chandler Music Hall, vintage 1907) serves as a shopping, dining, and entertainment center for surrounding villages. With its combination of train service and 350 miles of mapped mountain-biking trails, Randolph is emerging as one of New England's premier mountain-biking centers; the Three Stallion Inn is the setting for an annual September New England Bike Festival. A Mobil station and a McDonald's are at exit 4 off I-89 (which slices across Route 66 midway between Randolph Center and the downtown). Randolph Historical Society Museum (728-5398), upstairs in the police station, exhibits memorabilia, with the emphasis on railroading; three rooms are furnished in circa-1900 style. (Open June through October, Sunday 2–4, and by appointment. $1 per adult.)

Rochester lies on Route 100 in a narrow valley between the Green Mountains and the Braintree Range, almost equidistant between—and just far enough from—Waitsfield to the north and Killington to the south. It remains a quiet place with a large village green and reclusive summer population. A drive through the Hollows, situated above the village on the flanks of the Braintree Range, provides superb views and a delightful alternation of field and forest. The largely uninhabited western portion of the town lies within the Green Mountain National Forest and is used by sportsmen, picnickers, and hikers. The Bingo area, in particular, offers swimming holes, abandoned town roads, cellar holes, and Civil War–era cemeteries.

TO SEE

Justin Morrill Homestead (828-3211), Strafford Village. Open Memorial Day through Columbus Day, Wednesday through Sunday 11–5; $2. A striking, 17-room Gothic Revival mansion built by Justin Morrill, who served as a congressman and senator in Washington from 1855 until 1898 and is best remembered for the Land Grant Colleges Act. This was Morrill's retirement home, but he never managed to spend much time here, because he kept getting reelected. It is a fascinating Victorian house, well maintained by the Vermont Division of Historic Preservation.

Floating Bridge at Sunset Lake, Brookfield Village. First built in 1820 and replaced six times since, this is the only heavily used bridge of its kind in the country. It's quite picturesque.

Joseph Smith Memorial and Birthplace, Sharon. Open year-round during daylight hours, seasonal guided tours, late May through mid-October, Wednesday through Sunday. One mile south of South Royalton, a marker on Route 14 points you up a steep 2-mile hill to a complex maintained by the Mormon Church. A memorial to the life of the founder of the Church of Jesus Christ of Latter-day Saints, a 38½-foot-high obelisk, cut from Barre granite in 1908, marks the site of the farm on which Joseph Smith was born in 1805 and lived until he was 10. Each foot on the shaft marks a year in the life of the prophet, who was murdered by a mob in Carthage, Illinois, in 1844. The 360 well-maintained acres include picnic tables and campsites.

Braintree Meeting House (728-9291), Braintree Hill Road (off Route 12A just west of downtown Randolph). A great picnic spot with an early cemetery and views to the White Mountains. The building is open by appointment and on Old Home Day (first Sunday in August).

White River National Fish Hatchery, Gaysville (Bethel), Route 12/107 west of Bethel Village, raises imprint salmon for the Connecticut River restoration program.

FARMS TO VISIT

Vermont Technical College maintains a demonstration farm in Randolph Center (728-3395). Visitors can tour the sugarhouse, apple orchard (pick your own), and dairy barn.

The Organic Cow of Vermont (685-3123), Tunbridge. Did you know that the average milking cow in this country lives just three years? Not at Organic Cow, a 400-acre farm at which Peter and Bunny Flint allow their 80 Jersey cows to forage, change pasture twice daily, and grow old (12–16), producing a rich, pure milk available from their dairy: the milk version of a microbrew. Call to inquire about farm tours. The cheese is available at **Ken's Store** in North Tunbridge.

Maple Ridge Sheep Farm (728-3081) in Braintree, said to be the oldest and largest Shetland sheep farm in the country, produces fleece, machine-washable sheepskin, yarn, knit and woven items, meat. Call first.

Redrock Farm (685-2282), 53A Strafford Turnpike, Chelsea. Drop by any day of the year and pick out a balsam fir or white spruce (up to 6 feet) and it will be shipped to you via UPS at Christmas. A full-sized tree is $30; wreaths, too. Bev and Walt Rockwood usually take coffee breaks at .10 AM and 3 PM, good times to visit. Fishermen are welcome to test their skills on the pond.

SUGARHOUSES

These maple producers sell syrup from their homes year-round and welcome visitors into their sugar shacks during March production periods.

Silloway Farms (728-5253, 728-5503), Boudro Road, Randolph Center, welcomes up to 20 visitors at a time.

Vermont Technical College Farm (728-3395, 728-3391), Randolph, Route 66 east off I-89, invites visitors to tour sugaring operations.

North Hollow Farm (767-4255), Route 100, Rochester. Maple syrup, gift baskets.

See also *Eaton's Sugar House* under *Selective Shopping*.

COVERED BRIDGES

There are four covered bridges in Tunbridge: the **Cilley Bridge,** south of the junction of Route 110 with Strafford Road and built in 1883; the **Howe Bridge** (1879), east off Route 110 in South Tunbridge; and in North Tunbridge, the 1845 **Flint Bridge** and 1902 **Larkin Bridge,** both east of Route 110. Sadly, the historic **Mill Bridge** (1883) was crushed by ice in the winter of 1999, but is currently being rebuilt.

In Randolph, two multiple kingpost bridges, both built in 1904, are just off Route 14 between East Randolph and South Randolph.

In Chelsea, there is the **Moxley** or **Guy Bridge,** an 1886 queenpost, east off Route 110.

TO DO

BICYCLING

This is some of the most rewarding biking country in Vermont; Randoph is quickly becoming "Mountain Biking Capital of the East." The Randolph-based **White River Valley Trails Association** (728-4100), P.O. Box 455, Randolph Center 05061, publishes a map detailing 240 miles of trails including dozens of miles of Class 4 roads (public but not maintained for vehicles) and singletrack grass and dirt trails. You can take AMTRAK to Randolph (baggage cars carry bikes) and walk up to **Bicycle Express** (728-5568) to get clued in on all the possibilities; the shop rents mountain bikes and offers guided tours. In addition to the Class 4 roads, the area offers many miles of hard-surfaced dirt roads through quiet villages, woods, and farm country. The Three Stallion Inn (see *Inns*) in Randolph offers its own network of trails and serves as headquarters for the three-day New England Mountain Bike Festival in late September (see *Special Events*); for a nominal fee, participants can camp, participate in bike repair workshops, games for all ages, clinics, and group rides. Children are welcome (no dogs allowed). Green Trails Inn in Brookfield (see *Lodging*) is also a frequent stop on organized bicycle tours.

BOATING

While most of the White River is navigable in high water, the 20-mile stretch from Rochester to Bethel is especially popular with canoeists, tubers, and kayakers. A good place to put in is at the cement bridge just south of Rochester. Camping is available at **Rud Memorial Park,** 7 miles from Bethel. The river has white water in spring and some steep grades.

FISHING

Trout abound at the junction of the Tweed and White Rivers, downstream from Bethel, above Randolph, and below Royalton. Fly-fishing enthusiasts find the Bethel area good for large rainbow and brown trout, while below Royalton there are bass, spring walleye, and trout.

Fishing licenses are available at **Tracy's Midway,** a convenience store and gas station on North Main Street in Sharon.

Baker's Pond on Route 12 in Brookfield has a parking area and boat launch, good for trout fishing. There is a boat access on **Rood Pond** in Williamstown and a canoe access on **Sunset Lake** in Brookfield, also stocked with trout. The floating bridge is a popular fishing spot.

GOLF

Montague Golf Club (728-3806), Randolph. One of the oldest courses in Vermont, 18 holes. The Second Branch of the White River winds through it. Light fare is served in the clubhouse; lessons offered. *Note:* A driving range maintained by the Three Stallion Inn (see *Lodging— Inns*) is just west on Route 66.

The White River Golf Club (767-GOLF, 767-4653), RD 1, Box 137 (Route 100), Rochester. Nine holes, clubhouse with a restaurant serving lunch (dinner by arrangement). Open May 1 through October 31. Next to it is a driving range (767-3211).

HIKING

Near **Granville Gulf** there are two short nature trails. At Moss Glen Falls, the ½-mile loop on the west side of the road is more rugged than the 1-mile loop on the east side.

In **Allis State Park,** Brookfield (off Route 12; see *Green Space*), a 2½-mile trail circles down through meadows and back up through woods. Access is from the fire tower beyond the picnic area; views are exceptional. The Bear Hill Nature Trail is another reason for finding this special place.

HORSEBACK RIDING

Birchmeadow (276-3405), Brookfield. May through November. Guided hour-long trail rides geared for beginners up through experts, trail through the woods and back roads. $25 per hour.

LLAMA HIKING

Heart of Vermont Llama Hikes (889-9611), Fernwood Llama Farm, Spring Road, Tunbridge. Picnic hikes, moonrise hikes, half- and full-day hikes offered through the rural countryside. Short hikes are $25 per person. Fiber and fiber products also sold.

PICNICKING

Brookfield Gulf, Route 12 west of Brookfield. Picnic facility, nature trail. See also Allis State Park under *Green Space.*

SWIMMING

Ask locally about various swimming holes in the First, Second, and Third Branches of the White River. In Randolph Center, there is a man-made beach, bathhouse, and picnic area. At Lake Champagne, there is swimming at a private campground that charges admission. There is also a swimming pool at the recreational park in Randolph.

TENNIS

Green Mountain Tennis Center, Green Mountain Stock Farm (728-5575), Randolph.

WINTER SPORTS

CROSS-COUNTRY SKIING

Green Trails Ski Touring Center (276-3412), Brookfield. Some 35 km of trails meander around frozen ponds, through woods, and over meadows at elevations of 1,132–1,572 feet. A ski shop offering rentals and instruction is open weekends, holidays.

Green Mountain Ski Touring Center (728-9122; 1-800-424-5575), Three Stallion Inn, off Route 66, Randolph. Fifty km of groomed and tracked trails weave through woods and meadows; instruction and rentals available; marked from Route 66.

GREEN SPACE

Allis State Park (276-3175), Brookfield. Open May 30 through September 15. A camping area with 22 sites, 4 with lean-tos (no hookups), each on a wooded loop road separate from the picnic area, in which you can choose from tables on a windy hilltop or under a pavilion. A hiking trail (see *Hiking*) commands a fine view of the valley northward.

Green Mountain National Forest (GMNF). Among the highlights in the Rochester district of the GMNF are the **Long Trail** and the **Texas Falls Recreation Area** (off Route 125), offering 17 picnic sites and an interesting series of cascades hollowed through bedrock. **Chittenden Brook** (off Route 73) is the developed campground near Rochester. A good short hike is from Brandon Gap north ⅔ mile to the cliffs of Mount Horrid, where there are views to the east. Because of the abundance of other things to do in this area, be sure to drop into the district ranger's office 2 miles north of Rochester green on Route 100 (767-4261) and ask about the *Recreation Opportunity Guides.*

LODGING

INNS

☙ **The Shire Inn** (685-3031; 1-800-441-6908; explore@shireinn.com), Chelsea 05038. This is precisely the kind of Vermont country inn that everyone fantasizes about: a classic 1832 Federal-era brick mansion furnished with antiques, rooms with canopy beds and working fireplaces (all private baths), set right on the green of a handsome-yet-workaday village. It's the kind of place that could easily be too stiff and self-conscious, but thanks to Jay and Karen Keller, you'll feel right at home from the moment you enter the sunny parlor, where two parakeets chirp by the elegant hearth. Be sure to arrive in good time for dinner, a five-course candlelight event that might begin with a three-layer vegetable terrine followed by a pear sorbet, then chicken Wellington or veal Sicilian or a vegetable ravioli with basil sauce, followed by a salad and irresistible dessert (wine is served). The breakfast selection might include apple pancakes, herb-cheese omelets, and spinach quiche. The Kellers are delighted to tune in guests to the possibilities of things to see and do in this non-resortified corner of central Vermont (see Chelsea under *Villages*); bicycles and cross-country skis (snowmobile trails web the area) are provided. The six rooms are $95–145 B&B, $145–205 plus 15 percent service, including dinner. No smoking. Children inappropriate except in the nearby two-bedroom cottage, in which pets are also accepted ($130 per day).

✍ **Green Trails Inn** (276-3412; 1-800-243-3412; greentrailsinn@quest-net.com), Brookfield 05036. The unusual shape of this inn is explained by its history. It began as a scattering of rooms owned by friends and relatives of Jessie Fiske, a Brookfield native who became one of the first women professors at Rutgers University, in New Jersey. The rooms were rented to her students and associates, who spent summers horseback riding and "botanizing" with Miss Fiske. The present inn consists of 11 rooms and two suites, some in a 1790s house called the Guest House (with one particularly appealing room that retains its 18th-century stenciling), more in the Inn, which offers two comfortable sitting rooms with a large hearth and a sunny dining room. Eight guest rooms have private bath. The horses are gone, but the trails are still good for walking during the seasons that they aren't good for cross-country skiing (35 km are marked and groomed). Snowshoeing on Sunset Lake and in Allis State Park (see *Green Space*) is also possible. The inn sits just across from the floating bridge and a small beach on Sunset Pond (see Brookfield under *Villages*). The pond invites canoeing and fishing and the surrounding high, dirt roads are great for biking. Sue and Mark Erwin are your friendly hosts. Mark's passion is repairing antique clocks, a number of which decorate the inn (he also maintains the Antique Clock Shoppe here). Jessie Fiske's old riding ring up on the hillside is now a frequent site for weddings. The meadow beyond the tent (for up to 250 people) is filled with wildflowers and the view is across the village and pond. Rates are $79 per couple (shared bath) to $130 (for the two-room suites, one with a fireplace, the other with early-1800s stencils and a whirlpool bath). That includes breakfast, but add tax and 15 percent gratuity; MAP available in winter. *Note*: Ariel's Restaurant (see *Dining Out*) is across the street.

Three Stallion Inn (728-5575; 1-800-424-5575), off Route 66, Randolph 05060. Geared to sports-minded guests, especially cross-country skiers and mountain bikers, in addition to fishermen and golfers. It's set on 1,300 acres of pasture and woodland, with some 33 miles of singletrack trails, part of an old estate—the Green Mountain Stock Farm. There's a lively pub and dining room (see *Dining Out*), and the sitting rooms in the old stone farmhouse can be adapted for conference use. Facilities also include a fitness room, a whirlpool and sauna, two tennis courts, and an outdoor lap pool. The adjoining Montague Golf Club is 18 holes (see *To Do—Golf*), and the inn also maintains a driving range; swimming and brown trout can be caught in the Third Branch of the White River, which runs through the property. A trout pond also invites catch and release. (See also *Biking* and *Cross-Country Skiing*.) Rates from $79 (shared bath) to $99 double for a room with private bath, $108 for a suite accommodating up to six; MAP and group packages available. Inquire about weddings and about many special packages.

Tupper Farm Lodge (767-4243), RR 1, Box 149, Rochester 05767. An 1820s farmhouse on Route 100, known for its friendly atmosphere and good cooking. Roger and Anne Verme have been welcoming guests for more than 25 years. They accommodate 30 in 10 rooms with private bath. They cater to skiers and bicyclists with bountiful breakfasts and candlelit dinners. The swimming hole is across the road in the White River. $35–50 per person MAP, double occupancy; $25–30 per person B&B rate available in summer and fall; ski week and children's rates.

The Inn at Idlewood (763-5236), Route 132, Sharon 05065. A gracious Victorian house set high on a hillside offers three guest rooms, each with a queen-sized bed and a bath with claw-foot tub or shower. Hosts Alex Bird and Marcy Marceau are accomplished, French-trained chefs, and the kitchen and dining rooms (see *Dining Out*) form the heart of this place. There's plenty of other comfortable space, however, including 75 acres. $75–115 per couple includes breakfast.

Huntington House Inn (767-4868), on the green, Rochester 05767. Anne and John Trautlein have thoroughly renovated this gracious 1806 village home and established a reputation for the best dining in the area (see *Dining Out*). The six guest rooms include two beautifully furnished suites with sitting rooms overlooking the green ($80–125) and four more attractive rooms ($60–100), all with private bath; breakfast and tea are included in the rates.

BED & BREAKFASTS

☙ **Greenhurst Inn** (234-9474; 1-800-510-2553), Bethel 05032, a Victorian mansion on the western fringe of Bethel, across Route 107 from the river. There are 13 guest rooms, 7 with private bath, the most cheerful on the third floor; these include a spacious tower room ($90) and the Victorian Suite, tucked under the eaves with a skylight. Longtime innkeepers Lyle and Claire Wolfe have a library of 4,000 books. $50–95 double per room; $100 for Victoria's Suite, with a sitting room and private bath; breakfast included. Dogs accepted.

The New Homestead (767-4751), Rochester 05767. Don't be put off by the funky exterior of this old house in the village. Inside it's clean and comfortable, with an eclectic mix of art and attractive quilts: five rooms, three with private bath, two with shared. $40 per room all year includes a sumptuous breakfast of homegrown eggs, jams, spuds, and homemade bread. Your hosts are Sandy Haas and David Marmor.

Fox Stand Inn (763-8467), Route 14, Royalton 05063. An 1818 stage stop on Route 14, first established as a restaurant (see *Dining Out*). Jean and Gary Curley also offer five second-floor rooms (share two bath); $50–75 per room B&B.

The Shady Maple (728-4755), Prospect Avenue, Randolph 05060. Dan and Kathi Riley offer three rooms, one with private bath, in their Victorian home, full breakfast ($75–105 per couple). The house is sited on a hilltop above downtown, a steep climb up if you are on foot with luggage but otherwise handy to the Amtrak station.

Emerson's Bed & Breakfast (728-4972), P.O. Box 177, 4 Emerson Terrace, Randolph 05060. Marian and Jonathan Klenk's Victorian house offers three frilly rooms; shared bath. If you are a bicyclist with luggage arriving by train, request a pickup from the station. They'll also pick you up at the airport. $55–85 includes a full breakfast.

Brookfield Guest House (276-3146), Pond Village near the floating bridge. George and Connie Karal offer a small, unpretentious B&B in the middle of this special village. $85 per couple includes a private bath and full breakfast.

FARMS

✍ **Liberty Hill Farm** (767-3926; libertyhillfarm@quest-net.com), RR 1, Box 158, Rochester 05767. This is a working, 100-head dairy farm set in a broad meadow off Route 100—a great place for families. Bob and Beth Kennett have two sons and remain family geared, with plenty of toys, some chicks, and kittens. There are seven guest rooms and four shared baths; families can spread into two rooms sharing a sitting room and bath. Meals are served family-style, and Beth makes everything from scratch. In summer you can hear the gurgle of the White River (good for trout fishing as well as its swimming hole) from the porch, and in winter you can ski off into the village across the meadows. $70 per adult, $30 per child under 12, MAP.

❦✒**Harvey's Mountain View Inn** (767-4273), Rochester 05767. Situated in the North Hollow area, this spot offers spectacular views of the Green Mountains and the Braintree Range. Don and Maggie Harvey have been specializing in farm-style family vacations since the 1960s and enjoy a strong following. They offer 10 rooms and a two-bedroom housekeeping cottage. There are family-geared activities, along with a heated pool in summer. No smoking. Pets permitted in the chalet. Resident animals at this writing include hens, goats, a pony, geese, and rabbits. Open year-round. $35–75 per person includes a hearty breakfast and dinner.

Round Barn Farm (763-7025), Fay Brook Road, Strafford 05072. This is a 350-acre working dairy farm with one of Vermont's famous 10-sided round barns (built in 1917). It's been in the family for six generations. What's offered is the big old house or rooms therein (two rooms with double bed and two with twins) and a fridge with the fixings for making your own breakfast. Cross-country ski or walk woods and meadows. No smoking and no pets, please. A double room is $45 and a single, $25. Inquire about the price for the whole house.

Placid Farm Bed & Breakfast (728-9883), Randolph. This is an apart-ment in a hand-hewn log home (deck, kitchen, bedroom, and living room) on a large farm with its own pond. A full breakfast in Viola Frost-Lateen's plant-filled sunporch is included in $90 per couple; $40 each additional person, $14 for children ages 2–10.

MOTEL

The Columns Motor Lodge (763-7040), Sharon 05065. A small, neat motor lodge attached to an old house. Located in Sharon Village, just off I-89, it has a nice gift shop and is across from both the general store and Brooksies Family Restaurant (see *Eating Out*), a good way-stop. Cal and Joanne Keyler charge $38–46 double.

CONDOMINIUMS AND COTTAGES

Hawk North, Vermont's Mountain Hideaway (746-8911; 1-800-832-8007; e-mail: vthideaway@aol.com), P.O. Box 529, Route 100, Pittsfield 05762. Hawk homes are nicely designed vacation houses, hidden away in the woods on sites scattered among Rochester, Stockbridge, and Pittsfield. No longer related to Hawk Mountain Resort, Hawk North maintains a check-in office at the junction of Routes 100 and 107. Each of the 15 homes is individually owned, and decor varies; but all offer spacious living/dining room, full kitchen, and two to four bedrooms. Some have sauna and/or hot tub. Rates fluctuate wildly with the season: $200–800 per night for two to four bedrooms.

Birch Meadow Farm (276-3156), RD 1, Box 294A, Brookfield 05036, East Street off Route 65 south. This is Mary and Matt Commerford's woodsy hideaway, with three modern log cabins equipped for housekeeping. There are TVs and woodstoves, plus a B&B suite in the main house, which sits high on a hill with splendid views. $90 per couple, $15 each additional adult.

CAMPGROUNDS

Lake Champagne Campground (728-5298), P.O. Box C, Randolph 05061. Open Memorial Day weekend through mid-October. A 150-acre property with fields, a 3-acre swim lake, hot showers, mountain views, and facilities for tents through full-sized RVs.

See also Allis State Park and Chittenden Brook campgrounds under *Green Space*.

WHERE TO EAT

DINING OUT

Ariel's Restaurant & Pond Village Pub (276-3939), Brookfield. Open Wednesday through Sunday for dinner. Overlooking Sunset Lake in the middle of this clapboard village, this restaurant has quickly established a reputation as one of the best places to eat in central Vermont. Lee and Richard are chef-owners who specialize in Mediterranean and Pacific Rim dishes, unusual combinations of ingredients and spices. The menu changes weekly. Entrées $12–24.

The Inn at Idlewood (763-5236), Route 132, Sharon. Open Thursday through Sunday by reservation year-round. Chef-owners Alex Bird and Marcy Marceau have both studied in France and are known as caterers but have established a huge reputation for their small dining rooms. The menu changes from week to week, sometimes within the week, depending on what's fresh from the suppliers and the garden. The five-course prix fixe dinner is $38.50 and there's a long wine list, a mix of Californian and French. Inquire about weddings.

Stone Soup Restaurant (765-4301), on the green, Strafford. Open for dinner Thursday through Sunday 6–9. Reservations strongly suggested. There is no sign for this elegantly rustic restaurant that has acquired a strong following over the past two decades. You step from Strafford's handsome green into a cheery tavern room with a large hearth. The candlelit, low-beamed dining rooms are beyond. On our last visit, the blackboard menu included eggplant soup, osso buco, and garlic and lime chicken. Note the attractive herb garden. Personal checks, but no credit cards. Entrées $18.95–25.95.

Huntington House Inn (767-4868), on the green, Rochester. Open Wednesday through Sunday 6–9; reservations appreciated. Paris-trained chef-owner John Trautlein makes his own pasta, pastries, and ice cream and prepares his stocks. Specialties include seafood and Vermont loin of venison. The daily-changing menu might include a wild mushroom gâteau among its half-dozen appetizers; entrées might include homemade ravioli stuffed with artichoke hearts and pine nuts ($18) and rack of lamb with a garlic-and-mint sauce ($25). The wine list is extensive, and wine by the glass is served.

Three Stallion Inn (728-5575), off Route 66, Randolph. The dining room overlooking the swimming pool is open for lunch and dinner. The dinner menu might include veal medallions sautéed with wild mushrooms in Madeira ($16.50), a vegetarian pasta ($11.95), and a salmon fillet, pan-seared with a corn bread and fresh horseradish crust, served on grilled plantain ($15.50). A soup and sandwich menu is also served in Morgan's Pub, adjacent to the formal dining room.

Fox Stand Inn (763-8437), Route 14, Royalton. Lunch and dinner, Tuesday through Saturday; Sunday noon buffet. Homegrown beef and farm produce served in a landmark 1818 stagecoach inn. Inexpensive to moderate.

EATING OUT

Roadfood, listed geographically as they come, south to north, off I-89.

I-89, exit 2

Brooksies Family Restaurant (763-8407), Sharon. A genuine family restaurant with counter service on one side and a slightly classier addition on the other. The diner opens early for breakfast and has a full lunch and dinner menu. Meals on the restaurant side can begin with baked stuffed mushroom caps and include roast duckling flambé, filet mignon, or spaghetti with meatballs. This is a traditional stop for many ski-bound families. Good pies.

I-89, exit 3

Eaton's Sugar House, Inc. (763-8809; 1-888-VT-MAPLE). Located at the junction of Routes 14 and 107 in Royalton, just off I-89. Open daily 7–7. A good old-fashioned family-owned restaurant featuring pancakes and local syrup, sandwiches, burgers, and reasonably priced daily specials. Try the turkey club made with fresh-carved turkey on homemade bread. Vermont maple syrup, cheese, and other products are also sold (see *Selective Shopping*).

In South Royalton, between exits 2 and 3

Hannah's Cafe (763-2626), on the green in South Royalton. Open 7 AM–6 PM weekdays. A student-geared coffeehouse atmosphere, mismatched chairs and tables and changing art. Egg muffins and omelets are the breakfast specialties, along with freshly baked bagels and pastries. Soup and sandwiches at lunch, daily "hot dinner" specials for $5—maybe green spinach lasagna with salad or Irish stew with "hearty" bread.

Brew Heaven Cafe (763-7700), 28 Chelsea Street, South Royalton. Open 7 AM–9 PM, until 10 Friday and Saturday. Espresso, cappuccino, teas, breakfast scones, deli sandwiches, soups and salads, exotic dishes like Thai roast pork wrap and mandarin orange wrap (in flour tortillas).

Chelsea Station (763-8685) on the green, South Royalton. Booths, a counter, breakfast from 6 AM, a friendly atmosphere, and a basic menu; dinner served Friday and Saturday with nightly specials under $10.

In Randolph (exit 4)

Lupines (728-6062), Main Street, Randolph. Open Tuesday through Saturday 11–8. This pleasant, high-ceilinged corner storefront in the middle of town is furnished with mismatched oak tables and hung with bright quilts. Scott and Amy Berkey feature homemade soups, salads, and desserts; nightly specials. Entrées include seafood, steak, and pizza. Take home a stuffed bread or quiche. $6.95–13.

Elsewhere

Dixie's II (865-3000), Chelsea. In the middle of the village, housed in a classic old brick bank building, this cheerful spot opens at 6:30 AM for breakfast; open for lunch and dinner except on Sunday and Monday, when it closes at 2 PM.

South Strafford Cafe (765-4671), Route 132, South Strafford. This seasonal community-run café serves delicious, inexpensive fare.

ENTERTAINMENT

Chandler Music Hall (728-9133), Main Street, Randolph. A fine, acoustically outstanding music hall built in 1907 and restored to mint condition. It is now open year-round for musical and theatrical performances: chamber music, blues, jazz, opera, folksingers, the Vermont symphony, and Mud Season Talent Show.

The Playhouse Movie Theatre, Main Street, Randolph, the oldest movie house in the state. Shows first-run flicks.

Randall Drive-In Movie Theatre, Route 12 in Bethel, operates in summer only.

SELECTIVE SHOPPING

Eaton's Sugar House (763-8809), junction of Routes 14 and 107, just off I-89, exit 3. An old-fashioned, family-run, maple-focused complex in which you can watch maple candies made and find a wide selection of maple products, in addition to Vermont cheese and other products. A good place to get Christmas greens. See also *Eating Out*.

Just Vermont Shop, at the junction of Routes 100 and 125, Hancock, in the old Hancock Hotel building. Books, cards, preserves, T-shirts, Christmas decorations.

Vermont Only Village Store (767-4711; outside Vermont: 1-800-828-1005), Route 100, Granville. The **Hemenway Bowl Mill** has been making wooden salad and decorative bowls since 1857, housed in an old farmhouse; good for woodenware, toys, crafts, cards, books, clothing, baskets, smoked meats, cheeses, maple products, specialty foods, antiques. The **Rice Quartertown Clapboard Mill** is part of the complex, as is the **Country Antique Store.**

Vermont Wood Specialties (767-4253), Route 100 in Granville. Open daily 9–5. A country store with eight rooms full of gifts, souvenirs, candies, toys, and pottery, as well as wooden items.

Vermont Castings (234-2300), Route 107, 2.5 miles east of Bethel. Hours

Harvesting ice at the Floating Bridge in Brookfield

and days vary with the season; call. Even if you're not interested in buying a wood- or coal-burning stove, the showrooms are worth a stop. Since its founding in the mid-1970s, the company has established a reputation for cast-iron stoves that keep a fire overnight, ornament the house, and don't take up much space. Its first model was the Defiant, followed by the smaller Vigilant and even smaller Resolute. Gas-fired stoves are a new specialty.

Cover to Cover Books (728-5509), 27 North Main Street, Randolph. A full-service store selling new and old books, also cards, gifts; inquire about poetry readings.

Creature Comforts (728-5067), 3 Salisbury Street, Randolph. An eclectic selection of new and used housewares and antiques; also upholstery fabrics.

Old Schoolhouse Books (763-2434), 106 Chelsea Street on the green, South Royalton. An interesting selection of old and new books.

Patricia Owens (765-4335) Route 132, South Strafford. This outstanding vintage clothing store is located right in the middle of the village; it's usually open and well worth a stop. It also has its own discount branch in West Lebanon, New Hampshire.

SPECIAL EVENTS

January (last Saturday): **Brookfield Ice Harvest Festival:** ice cutting, ice sculpting, hot food, sledding, skating, skiing.

February: **Strafford Winter Carnival.**

March: Open sugarhouses.

July: **July 4 parade** in Strafford, a bigger one in Randolph. **Chandler Players** perform at Chandler Music Hall, Randolph. **Chelsea Flea Market:** 150 dealers cover both greens.

July, August: **Summer music school,** workshops at the Mountain School, Vershire. **Huntington Farm Show,** Strafford. **Brookfield Blues Festival** (off Route 65 in Brookfield, August). The South Royalton Town Band, in business for more than a century, gives free concerts on the green Thursday evening. **Sharon Old Home Day** (see *Villages*).

September: **New World Festival** (Sunday before Labor Day) at the Chandler Music Hall in Randolph features Celtic music, in addition to food and crafts. **World's Fair,** Tunbridge. **New England Mountain Bike Festival** (last weekend), Green Mountain Stock Farm, Randolph: a three-day noncompetitive event with guided rides for all ability levels.

October (Columbus Day weekend): **Lord's Acre Supper,** sale and auction, Barrett Hall, Strafford.

November: **Annual Hunters' Supper,** Barrett Hall, Strafford.

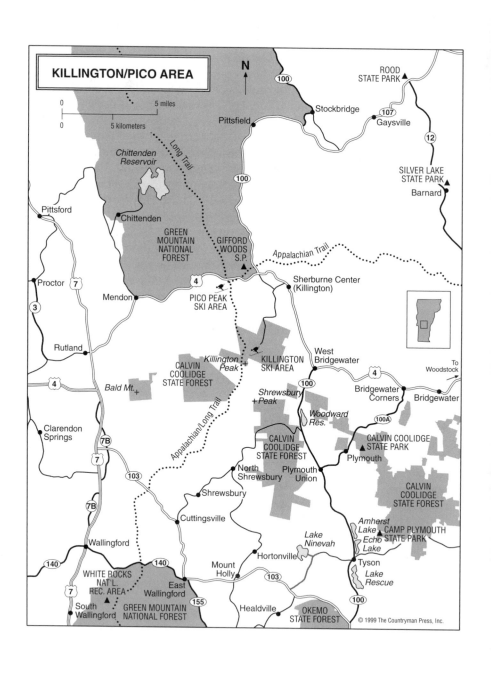

KILLINGTON/PICO AREA

N

0   5 miles
0   5 kilometers

ROOD STATE PARK

Stockbridge

100

107

Gaysville

12

Pittsfield

Chittenden Reservoir

Long Trail

100

SILVER LAKE STATE PARK

Barnard

Pittsford

Chittenden

GREEN MOUNTAIN NATIONAL FOREST

GIFFORD WOODS S.P.

Appalachian Trail

Sherburne Center (Killington)

Proctor

7

Mendon

4

PICO PEAK SKI AREA

3

Rutland

West Bridgewater

To Woodstock

CALVIN COOLIDGE STATE FOREST

Killington Peak

KILLINGTON SKI AREA

100

4

Bald Mt.

Shrewsbury Peak

Woodward Res.

Bridgewater Corners

Bridgewater

100A

Clarendon Springs

7B

7

Appalachian/Long Trail

CALVIN COOLIDGE STATE FOREST

North Shrewsbury

Plymouth Union

CALVIN COOLIDGE STATE PARK

Plymouth

CALVIN COOLIDGE STATE FOREST

103

Shrewsbury

7B

Cuttingsville

Lake Ninevah

Amherst Lake

Echo Lake

CAMP PLYMOUTH STATE PARK

Wallingford

140

140

WHITE ROCKS NAT'L. REC. AREA

East Wallingford

Mount Holly

103

Hortonville

Tyson

Lake Rescue

7

South Wallingford

GREEN MOUNTAIN NATIONAL FOREST

155

Healdville

OKEMO STATE FOREST

100

© 1999 The Countryman Press, Inc.

Killington/Pico Area

Killington is the largest ski resort in the East. It boasts six mountains, the longest ski run and season in the Northeast, and the most extensive snowmaking in the world. Just down the road is Pico, "the friendly mountain": older, smaller, family-geared. It's said that some 11,000 visitors can bed down within 20 miles of these two ski destinations, both of which were purchased in 1996 by Les Otten's American Skiing Company, which projects major new investments in their facilities, including an ambitious slope-side village.

Killington, the second highest peak in the state, is flanked by other mountains and faces another majestic range across Sherburne Pass. Although the road through this upland village has been heavily traveled since the settling of Rutland (11 miles to the west) and Woodstock (20 miles to the east), there was never much of anything here. In 1924, an elaborate, rustic-style inn was built at the junction of Route 4, the Appalachian Trail, and the new Long Trail. A winter annex across the road was added in 1938, when Pico installed one of the country's first T-bars. But the lumbering village of Sherburne Center was practically a ghost town in 1957 when Killington began.

Lodging is strung along the 4-mile length of Killington's access road and on Route 4 as it slopes ever downward through Mendon to Rutland. The hill village of Chittenden, sequestered 6 miles up a back road from Route 4, is blessed with a large reservoir and a few inns. Ski lodges are also salted along Route 100 north to the pleasant old town of Pittsfield. Killington's Skyeship gondolas from Route 100 also put the inns of Plymouth within a few miles and those of both Woodstock and Ludlow within 14 miles.

In summer, this is exceptional hiking and mountain-biking country. The view from the summit of Killington is also accessible via the K1 gondola. Other things to do include visiting the restored village of Plymouth, birthplace of Calvin Coolidge, and trying the alpine slide at Pico. Killington offers its own tennis and golf packages, and a few inns have full resort facilities; a number have tennis courts and swimming pools. There are also summer theater and ballet, a series of musical, horsey, and other events, and—because this is still primarily a winter resort area—substantial savings on summer accommodations. See "Rutland

and the Lower Champlain Valley" for more dining and lodging options.

GUIDANCE

See *Lodging* for the Killington (year-round) and Pico (ski season only) reservation services.

Killington Lodging and Travel Service (toll-free 1-877-4ktimes) serves as a central information source as well as a reservation phone line during the ski resort's unusually long season (October through May and sometimes June). Summer packages are available at 1-800-789-6676. **Wise Vacations** (1-800-642-1147), P.O. Box 231, Killington 05751. Experienced counselors arrange rentals and provide information about what to see and do.

GETTING THERE

By rail: **Amtrak,** New York City to Rutland.

By bus: **Vermont Transit** stops en route from Rutland to White River Junction at Killington Depot, Route 4 near the access road. Most inns will pick up guests, and there's a public shuttle service from Rutland's new transit center.

By plane: Airports at Rutland (**Colgan Air,** 1-800-272-5488); Burlington, and Lebanon, New Hampshire.

MEDICAL EMERGENCY

Dial **911.**

Rutland Regional Medical Center (775-7111), 160 Allen Street, Rutland.

TO SEE

Plymouth Notch Historic District (672-3650), Route 100A, Plymouth, is dedicated to Calvin Coolidge. Open Memorial Day through late October, 9:30–5; admission charged. This tiny white-clapboard hamlet is where the 30th president of the United States was born in 1872, worked on his father's farm, was awakened 52 years later at 2 AM one August morning to take the oath of office as successor to President Warren G. Harding, and was buried. A modest photo-history in the granite visitors center summarizes Coolidge's life. The old vehicles in the Wilder Barn, the plainly furnished homestead, and the re-created general store that was run by the president's father are all tangible reminders of the simplicity and frugality of the Coolidge era. The **Wilder House,** an old village home, serves soups and sandwiches in its pretty dining room, and also has counter service. Picnic tables available.

The complex includes the **Plymouth Cheese Company** (672-3650), founded by the elder Coolidge in 1890 and revived in 1960 by his grandson John Coolidge (who summers in the village). Cheese is made weekdays and sold on the premises Monday through Saturday, along with Common Crackers. They welcome visitors year-round (see *Selective Shopping*).

A stone house in the Plymouth Notch Historic District

Killington Peak. The view from the summit of the state's second highest mountain is spectacular: northwest to the Adirondacks, east to the White Mountains, and north along the spine of the Green Mountains. It's the spot on which the Reverend Samuel Peters in 1763 is said to have christened all that he could see "Verd monts." A gondola now hoists most visitors to the restaurant just below the summit, and a nature trail leads to the peak.

TO DO

OUTDOOR ADVENTURE
Escape Routes (746-8943), P.O. Box 685, Pittsfield 05762. With the Pittsfield Inn (see *Lodging—Inns*) as its home base, this center offers guided and self-guided outdoor programs and activities in every season: mountain biking May through mid-October; hiking March through December; showshoeing, backcountry skiing, and sleigh rides in winter; fly-fishing in summer; and even antiques shopping and historic tours. They range from a few hours to full-day excursions, geared to beginners as well as experts, and run $85–135 per person including lodging.

ALPINE SLIDE
Pico Alpine Slide (775-4346), Route 4, Sherburne. Memorial Day through Columbus Day. Patrons ride a triple chairlift up and then slide down a total of 3,410 feet; the slide begins near the summit with a sweeping view of the valley to the west. Lunch and snacks are served in the base lodge.

BICYCLING

Killington Mountain Bike Center (422-6232; for rental and lodging reservations: 1-800-372-2007). The Killington K1 Express Gondola operates Memorial Day through Columbus Day hoisting bicyclists and their bikes to Killington Peak, accessing 50 miles of marked trails; $8 for a trail pass, $20 for a ride on the gondola. During foliage season, the Skyeship is also available. Bike packages are offered by the Killington Resort (see *Downhill Skiing*), and touring routes of varying length and difficulty are available.

The Great Outdoors Adventure Bike Tours (1-800-345-5182), 219 Woodstock Avenue, Rutland. Two- to 5-day tours are arranged in association with the Cortina Inn (see *Lodging—Resorts*).

True Wheels (422-3234; www.truewheels.com), top of the Killington Road, Killington. Bicycle sales and service, mountain bike rentals, and guided tours.

BREWERY TOUR

Long Trail Brewing Company (672-5011), Route 4 west at Bridgewater Corners, offers tours and tastings in the pub, daily noon-5.

CANOEING

The Mustard Seed (483-6081), Dam Road, Chittenden, rents and transports canoes to the nearby reservoir.

K1 GONDOLAS AND SKYESHIP

Killington Peak. Billed as the highest point accessible by aerial lift in New England. At 4,241 feet, this is the second highest mountain in the state (see *To See*). The Killington Skyeship (422-6200), a speedy, eight-passenger system with heated cabs, operates practically nonstop during ski season; also runs daily mid-September through Columbus Day. The ride to the summit on the Killington K1 Express Gondola runs daily, Memorial Day through Columbus Day.

FISHING

Licenses are available from the Sherburne town clerk, River Road, and also from sporting goods stores and state park rangers.

Landlocked salmon and trout can be had in Chittenden Reservoir; trout are the catch in Mendon Brook. There also is fishing in Kent Pond, Colton Pond, the White River, the Tweed River, and the Ottauquechee River.

GOLF

Killington Resort (422-6700; 422-3333, ext. 586), Killington Road, Killington, has its own 18-hole, 6,300-yard, par-72 course designed by Geoffrey Cornish. Weekend clinics and golf packages. PGA professional instruction, rental clubs. **Mountain Golf School** (422-3101), at the Killington Resort, features 2-day weekend and 3-day midweek instructional programs.

Green Mountain National Golf Course (422-GOLF), Barrows-Towne Road and Route 100, Killington. This 18-hole course opened in 1996 and includes a clubhouse, three practice teeing areas, four target greens, and an 8,000-square-foot putting green.

HEALTH SPAS/FITNESS

New Life Fitness Vacations (422-4302; 1-800-228-4676), the Inn of the Six Mountains, P.O. Box 395, Killington. Early May through October: weeklong programs and "weekend samplers." Jimmy LeSage has been refining and fine-tuning his 6-day fitness program since 1978. This was one of the first such programs in the country, and it's still one of the best we know of. It combines sensible eating and exercise that can be transposed to daily living. The daily regimen begins with a prebreakfast walk and includes low-impact aerobics, body conditioning, and yoga. In the afternoon, there's usually a hike. Meals are varied, and the emphasis is on high-fiber, low-fat foods. The focus is less on losing weight than on increasing energy and stamina. $950–1,175 for 6 days double occupancy, $395 for a 3-day weekend.

Cortina Health Club (773-3333), Cortina Inn, Route 4, Killington. Heated indoor pool, whirlpool, exercise room, saunas, massage, facials, exercise classes. Open daily 6 AM–10 PM. Special short-term memberships.

Pico Health Center (733-1786), Route 4, Mendon. A 75-foot Olympic lap pool, aerobics area, fitness and cardiovascular room, Jacuzzi, saunas, tanning, massage, fitness evaluations. Monday through Friday 6 AM–9 PM, Saturday 7 AM–6 PM, Sunday 8 AM–6 PM.

Summit Lodge Racquet Club (422-3535), Killington Road. Racquetball courts, instruction, racquet rental, volleyball, whirlpool, saunas, massage, ice skating, and skate rentals.

Mountain Green Health Club (422-3000), center of Killington Village. Located in the Mountain Green complex, a club with a 54-foot indoor lap pool, Jacuzzi, aerobics classes, steam rooms, sauna, massage. Open 10–10 daily.

HIKING

Deer Leap Trail, off Route 4 behind The Inn at Long Trail (see *Lodging—Inns*), is the most popular short hike: a 2-hour round-trip trek up a winding, steep path that yields a panoramic view from the top of a 2,490-foot cliff. See *50 Hikes in Vermont* (Backcountry Publications).

For details about hiking the Appalachian and Long Trails south from Sherburne Pass (Route 4) and the Long Trail north, consult *Long Trail Guide,* published by the Green Mountain Club.

Killington's Tecnica Center (422-6232). Guided hikes twice a day (first one at 10 am): take the gondola up, hike down with a nature booklet. $15 for adults, $10 for juniors. Boots and backpacks can be rented.

Shrewsbury Peak. A rewarding, 5-hour round-trip hike begins in the abandoned Northam Picnic Area on steep, wooded North Shrewsbury Road off Route 100 south of West Bridgewater.

Bald Mountain. This 3-mile, 3-hour round-trip hike is in Aiken State Forest, off Stratton Road from Route 4 in Mendon. The blue-blazed circle trail begins opposite the entrance to **Tamarack Notch Camp.**

Two local inns, Mountain Meadows Lodge (see *Lodging—Resorts*) and Tu-

The view from Snowdon Mountain to Skye Peak at Killington

lip Tree Inn (see *Lodging—Inns*), cater to hikers on the "Hike . . . inn to inn" program; for details, write to Churchill House Inn, RD 3, Brandon 05733. The Inn at Long Trail offers hikers a special rate (see *Lodging— Inns*).

HORSEBACK RIDING

Mountain Top Stables (483-2311), Chittenden. Pony and trail rides, group and private instruction, sleigh rides.

Hawk Center (672-3811), at Salt Ash, Route 100, in Plymouth, offers lessons, trail rides, and hayrides.

TENNIS

Killington School for Tennis (1-800-417-6661), 2450 Killington Road, Killington. Weekend and 5-day, midweek packages are available Memorial Day to early September, using nine outdoor courts and the Village at Killington. It also features a Junior Tennis Academy.

Cortina Inn (773-3331), Route 4, Killington. A resort (see *Lodging— Resorts*) with eight outdoor courts, that are available to the public.

Summit Lodge (422-3535), Killington Road. Six outdoor courts are available to the public (see *Lodging—Resorts*).

Public courts are also maintained by the towns of Chittenden and Killington.

WINTER SPORTS

CROSS-COUNTRY SKIING

Mountain Meadows Ski Touring Center (775-7077; 1-800-221-0598), Thundering Brook Road off Route 4, Killington. One of Vermont's oldest and most serious touring centers, set high (1,500–1,800 feet) on the rolling acreage of the Mountain Meadows Lodge (see *Lodging—Resorts*); 60 km total, 40 km set; 1.5 miles lit; snowmaking; instruction, rentals, also telemark lessons and rentals. Tours of the backcountry available.

Mountain Top Ski Touring Center (483-6089), Chittenden. A total of 110 km of trails (70 km set) begin at Mountain Top Inn (see *Lodging—Resorts*), an ideal location at 1,495–2,165 feet, with sweeping views of Chittenden Mountain and Reservoir; rentals and lessons, limited snowmaking, and a log cabin warming hut in the woods at the intersection of trails.

Woodstock Ski Touring Center (see *To Do—Cross-Country Skiing* in "Woodstock and Quechee").

DOWNHILL SKIING

Killington Resort (switchboard: 422-3333; information: 422-6200; www.killington.com), Killington. With seven parking lots, seven base lodges, seven interconnected mountains—including Pico—and an entirely separate novice area, Killington is unquestionably big. When it was purchased by the American Skiing Company in 1996, it was dubbed the Beast of the East. Thanks to its three entry points and far-flung network of lifts and trails, the crowds are neatly dispersed throughout the area. The first of its projected new facilities is the virtually self-contained **Rams Head Family Mountain,** equipped with a family center for rentals, skier development program registration, childcare, food court emporium, and Snow Play Park. A new Needle's Eye High Speed Quad replaced the double chair, bringing Killington's quad total to 12, including 6 high-speed. A new Northbrook Quad carries skiers from the base of the Needle's Eye to the top of the Snowshed. Several crossover trails have been eliminated through the Snownet System, and the Perfect Turn Skier Development Program has been added, plus a broader range of new ski rentals.

Lifts: 35, including 12 quads plus the Skyeship and K1 gondolas, five doubles, six triples, eight surface lifts (53,288 rides per hour.)

Trails and slopes: 205.

Vertical drop: 3,150 feet.

Snowmaking: 68 miles of trails, with 1850 snowguns.

Snowboarding: Three halfpipes, 450-foot K-Pipe with 12-foot walls, lighted at night; Peace-Pie for novices; two snowboard parks, six alpine parks, one Palmer Cross park.

Facilities: Six cafeterias, five ski rental shops, one mountaintop restaurant, four lounges.

For children: Comprehensive Perfect Kids ski and snowboard coaching program based at the Family Center. Children 12 and under ski and ride free.

Special programs: School for Ski Professionals, for Snowboard Professionals, Women's Snowboard Clinics, early-December Ski Raceweek and Snowboard Freeriding and Carving Camp, Women's Ski Experience, Mogul Clinic Weekends.

Rates: One day—adult $52, young adult $47, junior $33. A Magnificent 7 Edge Card can be used at any of the American Skiing Company resorts for 7 days at $44.95 per day.

ICE SKATING

See Cortina Inn and Summit Lodge under *Lodging—Resorts.*

GREEN SPACE

Calvin Coolidge State Forest (672-3612), Plymouth. A 16,165-acre preserve that offers 60 campsites including 35 lean-tos, a dump station, picnic area and shelter, hiking, and snowmobile trails. Killington Peak is actually within this area. Primitive camping is permitted in specified parts of the forest. Facilities are handy to the Calvin Coolidge birthplace and the Shrewsbury Peak Trail.

Gifford Woods State Park (775-5354), Sherburne. One hundred fourteen acres located 0.5 mile north of Route 4 on Route 100. There are 47 campsites including 21 lean-tos, a dump station, picnic area, fishing access to Kent Pond, hiking on the Appalachian Trail (also near Deer Leap Trail; see *To Do—Hiking*).

Camp Plymouth State Park, off Route 100 at Tyson. Beach on Echo Lake, picnic area, food concession.

LODGING

Killington Lodging and Travel Service (1-800-621-MTNS), 100 Killington Road, Killington 05751, open daily 8 AM–9 PM mid-November through May, 8–5 in summer. The bureau keeps a tally of vacancies and makes reservations. A wide variety of 2- to 5-day ski packages are available.

Pico Lodging Bureau (775-1927; 1-800-225-PICO) offers a reservation service for more than 100 local lodging places during ski season.

RESORTS

The Killington Grand Resort Hotel & Conference Center (1-888-64-GRAND), 228 East Mountain Road, Killington 05751. Located at the base of the resort, this 200-room facility offers conventional hotel rooms, studios, one-, two-, and three-bedroom suites (with kitchens); outdoor heated pool, health club, on-site day care, Ovations Restaurant (see *Dining Out*), and a café. It's close not only to the base lodge, but in summer to the golf course and tennis courts as well. Summer rates range from $120 for a hotel room to $370 for the three-bedroom penthouse; in winter, from $88 per person per day, with a variety of packages.

Cortina Inn (773-3331; 1-800-451-6108), Killington 05751. This modern

luxury lodge on Route 4 is designed for the aver
to pamper themselves. Innkeepers Bob and P
prising hosts who offer a full summer progr
eight courts; a fitness center with whirlpool
and indoor pool; a game room; and special
expeditions. The grounds include an exte..
trail connecting with both the Mountain Mea..
trail networks in winter. Afternoon tea is served in the .
lobby that has a round hearth in the center and exhibit sp..
sculpture and art in the gallery. There are 97 rooms and suites, a .
of individually decorated spaces, some suites with fireplace and whirlpoo.
bath (room 215 is immense), some suites with lofts, and five rooms that
are wheelchair-accessible. Summer rates $98–159 per couple B&B (2-
day Biking Adventure from $129 per person); in winter from $257 per
couple MAP with skiing midweek; $169 midweek B&B and skiing.
Children free in the same room with parents; supervised children's
programs in summer. The Cortina dining room is Zola's Grille (see
Dining Out), open daily from 5:30; its Sunday brunch (10:45–1:30) is a
winner.

Mountain Meadows Lodge (775-1010; 1-800-370-4567), Thundering
Brook Road, Killington 05751. The main building is an 1856 barn, nicely
converted to include an informal dining room, spacious living room with
a lake view, and game room. Now run by Michele and Mark Werle and
geared to families year-round, catering to people who like the outdoors in
warm-weather months and skiers in winter, this is a hospitable, thoroughly relaxing kind of lodge. There are 18 guest rooms, many of them
great for families, all with private bath. A sauna and outdoor Jacuzzi are
among the amenities. In summer, there is a swimming pool and 100-acre
Kent Pond, which abuts the property and is good for fishing and canoeing
as well as swimming; the town tennis courts are just down the road. In
winter, this is a major ski-touring center (see *Cross-Country Skiing*). Its
Mountain Meadows Munchkins children's center is open to the public
for day care as well as to guests, and introduces kids to farm animals and
nature. Weekday rates: $71–120 per person MAP, $53–100 per person
B&B; higher on weekends, holidays, and in foliage season; singles, add
$30.

Mountain Top Inn (483-2311; 1-800-445-2100), Mountain Top Road,
Chittenden 05737. Closed April through Memorial Day and weekends
after Columbus Day until mid-December. Set on 337 rolling acres,
overlooking Chittenden Reservoir and Mountain, this is one of Vermont's
few truly self-contained resorts, recently purchased by Michael and
Margaret Gehan. There are 35 rooms, all with private bath; also 22
cottage and chalet units. Facilities include a heated pool, tennis, lawn
games, sauna, canoeing, horseback riding, chip 'n' putt golf, and, in
winter, a major cross-country skiing center and trails with limited

owmaking. $79–149 per person MAP, $49–129 per person B&B; packages and cheaper in the off-season; special rates for children.

mmit Lodge (422-3535; 1-800-635-6343), Killington Road, Killington 05751. An antique car festooned with a variety of unexpected "objects" is parked in the lobby, where one of the 45-room inn's two St. Bernards is usually majestically ensconced. Facilities include whirlpools, saunas, tennis and racquetball courts, outdoor heated swimming pool (geared for winter use, too), lawn games, and a courtesy bus to the Killington lifts. There is also a year-round dining room and rathskeller, a library, gift shop, and a game room. From $75 per person MAP; $267 per person for 2 days with skiing and breakfast; many packages.

Grey Bonnet Inn (775-2537; 1-800-342-2086), Killington 05751. Open year-round except April 15 through June 15 and October 15 through Thanksgiving. A nicely designed modern lodge set off by itself on Route 100 north, just beyond the Route 4 junction. The 41 rooms and five suites each have double, queen, or king beds and private bath, TV, phone, and flowery curtains and spreads. Bill and Barbara Flohr have created plenty of relaxing space in two comfortable, spacious living rooms. Amenities include an indoor pool, sauna, exercise room, and cross-country trails that interconnect with Mountain Meadows. In summer, there is tennis, an outside pool, and hiking trails connected with the Appalachian and Long Trails. The dining room is large and inviting, with a menu to match. In winter, $68 per person MAP midweek, $159 per person for a 2-day weekend. Add 15 percent gratuity. In summer, $49–79 per room; $89–129 per family room.

Hawk Inn and Mountain Resort (672-3811; 1-800-685-HAWK), Route 100, Plymouth 05056. Over the past four decades, hundreds of Hawk homes and condominiums have been built on four different properties throughout Vermont. The largest of these is the 1,200-acre Hawk Inn Mountain Resort complex, south of Killington's Northeast Passage entrance on Route 100. Both the freestanding homes (salted away in the woods and on hillsides with splendid views) and the condo units are architecturally striking and luxuriously furnished and equipped. The splendid, 50-room inn is the centerpiece. The resort was purchased in 1996 by Brenda and Jack Geischecker, longtime residents, who plan an ambitious series of improvements. In summer, there is tennis, horseback riding, swimming, mountain biking, fly-fishing, and canoeing, kayaking, sailing, and rowing shells on Lake Amherst. In winter, you can appreciate the new, year-round, heated outdoor pool, ice skating, cross-country skiing, and sleigh rides. Hawk prices vary widely depending on the season and special packages. In winter, rates are $239–379 per couple in the inn, $250–575 in the town houses, $290–700 in the freestanding homes; less in summer, much less in the off-season. Inn rates include breakfast in the inn. **Hawk's River Tavern** restaurant serves American cuisine and also offers a pub menu, fireside. Lunch is served poolside during the summer.

✎ **The Inn of the Six Mountains** (422-4302; 1-800-228-4676), Killington Road, Killington 05751. An ambitious, 103-room, four-story, Adirondack-style hotel with gabled ceilings, skylights, and balconies, and a two-story lobby with a fieldstone fireplace. Common spaces include a second-floor sitting room and a third-floor library. There is also a spa with lap pool, Jacuzzis, sauna and exercise room, and a dining room. The only hitch here is the building's unfortunate location, right on the access road. And when we stayed here one August, bus groups predominated. In winter, $281 per person for 2 days includes skiing, lodging, and breakfast; children free in same room with parent. In summer, $69–169 per room.

INNS

🏅✎ **The October Country Inn** (672-3412; 1-800-648-8421), junction of Routes 4 and 100A, Bridgewater Corners 05035. Handy to Killington (5 miles from the Northeast Passage lift) and Woodstock (8 miles) as well as most of the things to do and see in this chapter, yet sequestered up a back road with hiking trails that lead past the swimming pool to the top of a hill for a sweeping, peaceful view. Richard Sims and Patrick Runkel have opened up the farmhouse and created a large, comfortable living room with inviting places to sit around the hearth and at the big round table in the dining room—not to be confused with the other cheery dining room in which guests gather around long tables for Patrick's memorable meals, which can be Greek, Hungarian, Chinese, Mexican, Italian, or, occasionally, American. Candlelit dinners include homemade bread, cakes, home-grown vegetables and herbs, and wine. Breakfasts are equally ambitious, geared to fuel bikers in summer and skiers in winter. Food aside, the welcome here is unusually warm, and you find yourself quickly relaxing. The 10 guest rooms (8 with private bath) vary in size; many have queen-sized beds, and all are carefully decorated. $124–158 includes dinner and breakfast for two, $199–252 per couple per weekend. There are also single and children's rates. Inquire about summer theater packages.

The Inn at Long Trail (775-7181; 1-800-325-2540), Route 4, Killington 05751. Closed May and June and November through Thanksgiving. This is the first building in New England specifically built to serve as a ski lodge. It began in 1938 as an annex to the splendid summer inn that burned in 1968. Less elaborate than the original inn, its interior was also designed to resemble the inside of the forest as much as possible and so incorporates parts of trees and boulders. The 22-foot-long bar is made from a single log, and a protruding toe of the backyard cliff can be seen in both the pub and the dining room. (The boulders seen from the dining room are said to be the oldest rocks in Vermont.) The 14 rooms are small but cheery (2 are family suites), and there are 5 two-room suites with fireplaces. There's a hot tub and ample space for relaxing near the hearth. Dinner is served Thursday through Sunday in the candlelit dining room in fall and winter (see *Dining Out*), soup and salads in the pub during summer and fall from noon until 10 PM. There is Guinness on tap and Irish country and folk music in the pub on weekends (see *Entertainment*). Summer rates are $58–192 per room B&B; in winter, $296–384 per couple per weekend MAP; ask about ski weeks. Gratuity is 15 percent MAP.

Tulip Tree Inn (483-6213; 1-800-707-0017), Chittenden Dam Road, Chittenden 05737. This is backwoods luxury in a superb house built by the inventor William Barstow, who retired here after selling his various holdings for $40 million right before the 1929 stock market crash. Ed and Rosemary McDowell offer eight carefully furnished guest rooms, all with private bath, five with Jacuzzi. Guests gather around the big stone fireplace in the paneled den, in the comfortable living room, and at the tiny bar. Candlelight dinners are served (See *Dining Out*). There is swimming, canoeing, and fishing in the Chittenden Reservoir just down the road, and in winter you can cross-country ski in town. Rates are $170–299 MAP. Add 15 percent gratuity.

Salt Ash Inn (672-3748; 1-800-SALT-ASH), Route 100, Plymouth 05056. This is one of the few surviving small, ski-oriented inns. Built as an inn in the 1830s, it has 18 guest rooms and one suite, all with private bath. The great little union pub in the former general store retains the original grocery counter and wooden post office boxes (where Calvin Coolidge picked up his mail), and a circular hearth serves the purpose of the old potbellied stove. Facilities include a heated outdoor pool and hot tub. Glen and Ann Stanford are your friendly hosts. Daily $69–145 per room B&B; weekends $275–395 per couple, including Saturday-night dinner and two full breakfasts.

The Vermont Inn (775-0708; 1-800-541-7795), Killington 05751. Set high above Route 4 with a fine view of Killington and Pico Mountains, this is a 19th-century farmhouse with a homey feel to its public rooms—the living room with woodstove, the pub/lounge with fireplace, a game room, and an upstairs reading room, a welcome nook in the evening when the dining room is open to the public (see *Dining Out*). Summer facilities include a pool, tennis court, and lawn games. The sauna and hot tub are available year-round. Innkeepers Megan and Greg Smith offer 17 recently refurbished guest rooms, smallish but bright with brass and antique or canopy bedsteads, all with private bath. Three have a fireplace, and one is wheelchair-accessible. $110–175 per room MAP in summer, $70–135 B&B; fall, $120–225 per room MAP; winter, $120–205 MAP. Add 15 percent gratuity.

Red Clover Inn (775-2290; 1-800-752-0571), Box 7450, Woodward Road, Mendon 05701. Harris and Sue Zuckerman have renovated this handsome 1840s landmark that has 12 rooms and one suite, all with private bath, in the main house or carriage house, plus three dining rooms (see *Dining Out*) and 13 acres that include a pool and small pond. Three larger rooms have fireplaces and four-posters, two of them with whirlpools. $130–270 per couple MAP, less midweek; $55 per extra person. Pets permitted in the carriage house.

The Pittsfield Inn (746-8943), P.O. Box 685, Pittsfield 05762. Located 8 miles north of Killington in the center of the village on a handsome green, Tom Yennerell's double-porched old tavern has been a hostelry since 1835. Each of the nine rooms (all with private bath) has been individually decorated, and both breakfast and a multicourse dinner are served (see *Dining Out*). Sleigh rides and historic tours in a horse-drawn wagon are offered; Escape Routes, an outdoor adventure tour, is based here (see *To Do—Outdoor Adventure*). $70–120 per room B&B.

LODGES

Cascades Lodge (422-3731; 1-800-345-0113), RR 1, Box 2848, Killington 05751. The MacKenzie family's neat, contemporary, 47-room hostelry is practically next to the Killington base lodge. Some rooms have balconies, and there's an indoor pool, sundeck, whirlpool, sauna, lounge, and restaurant. Rates: $56–86 per room; more in winter.

Trailside Lodge (422-3532; 1-800-447-2209), Coffee House Road, Killington 05751, off Route 100. This classic Vermont farmhouse, complete with crazy window, has grown up a long way off the beaten track. A homey, old-fashioned, downhill-ski-oriented place with a loyal following. Meals and the 28 rooms are family-style, with bunk rooms (sleeping up to nine) or double beds, all with private bath. There's a hot tub and a big, comfortable living room. The place is geared to church and school groups, but families and individuals are welcome. It's a great place for a family reunion. (We suggest asking about groups that are booked for the time you plan to be there.) $45–62 per person MAP in winter, $66 double B&B in fall.

Butternut on the Mountain (422-2000; 1-800-524-7654), Box 306, Killington Road, Killington 05751. Open year-round except May and June. A family-owned motor lodge with 18 large standard rooms with color TV and phone. Facilities include an indoor heated pool, whirlpool, fireside library and lounge, game room, laundry facilities, and Mrs. Brady's restaurant (see *Eating Out*). $30–40 per person with continental breakfast; MAP and ski packages available.

BED & BREAKFAST

Fox and Pheasant Inn (422-8770), Box 305, Killington 05751. The former Sunrise Village reception center at the foot of Bear Mountain has been converted into a six-bedroom guesthouse by Charlie Brunell and Nina Tasi. Four of the oversized rooms have fireplaces; all have sitting area and private bath (one with whirlpool). Guest rooms, the fireplaced living room, TV den, and dining room are furnished with contemporary Vermont pieces. $135 double on weekends (2-night minimum), $105 Sunday through Thursday, with continental breakfast.

MOTEL

Farmbrook Motel (672-3621), Route 100A, Plymouth 05056. An unusually attractive 12-unit motel 3 miles from Coolidge's birthplace (see Plymouth Notch Historic District under *To See*); the brookside grounds have outdoor fireplaces, picnic tables. Some rooms sleep five; two kitchenettes. Rates: $45–55, $10 more during foliage season.

CONDOMINIUMS

Killington Resort Villages (1-800-621-MTNS). There are 600 condo units in a half-dozen clusters, and the complex also includes **Sunrise Mountain Village,** high on the mountain. In summer, with Snowshed Lodge offering dining and theater, this becomes a mini-resort in its own right, nicely landscaped and filled, primarily, with Florida retirees who have discovered the value of long-term rentals. Amenities include pools and whirlpools for each condo cluster. In winter you can walk to the lifts, and while the village is not "slope-side" (it's a schlep or shuttle to the base lodge), you are right at the nerve center of Killington's vast lift and trail network. Winter rates range upward from $231 per person for 2 days. In summer, Vermont Sampler Packages start at $109 per person for 2 days and 2 nights; Alpine Adventures from $125.

The Woods at Killington (422-3141; 1-800-633-0127), RR 1, Box 2210, Killington Road, Killington 05751. A complex of townhouse condominiums salted away in the woods on 100 acres around Terra Median, a combination check-in center with an unusually attractive pool (with waterfall), steam room, and sauna. The units are the ultimate in condominium-style luxury: private saunas, two-person whirlpools, sound systems, washers and dryers, the works. From $263 per person for 2 days in winter; less in summer.

Hogge Penny Best Western (773-3200), P.O. Box 914, Rutland 05701. These well-constructed, attractive units can be rented as motel rooms or as part of a one- or two-bedroom condominium suite. The buildings command a view across the Otter Valley to the Taconics and are set well back from Route 4, surrounded by grounds that include tennis courts and a pool. Each bedroom has a private bath, two double beds, and color TV, and each building includes a laundry room. The office is staffed around-the-clock. Moderate rates, year-round.

Pico Resort Hotel (775-1927; 1-800-848-7325), Route 4, Killington 05751. In recent years, 152 slope-side units have mushroomed at the base of Pico, and they are well done: one-bedroom suites in the Village Square; two-, three-, and four-bedroom units in the village, with phones and marble-faced fireplaces. The sports center offers a 75-foot indoor pool, Nautilus equipment, aerobics room, Jacuzzi, saunas, and lounge. Winter rates from $256 per person for 2 days, 2 nights.

Mountain Green Ski and Golf Resort (422-3000; 1-800-336-7754), Killington Road, has 216 condo suites, a restaurant, lounge, heated outdoor pool, health spa, and indoor lap pool; near the golf course (see *To Do—Golf*). Summer, $59–205 per unit; winter, $233 per person for 2 nights, 2 days.

Killington Accommodations Mountain Rental (773-4717; 1-800-535-8938). Deluxe to reasonably priced condos and homes, one to seven bedrooms.

CAMPGROUNDS
See *Green Space* for information on camping in Calvin Coolidge State Forest and Gifford Woods State Park.

WHERE TO EAT

DINING OUT
Hemingway's (422-3886), Route 4, Sherburne Flats, east of Killington. Closed Monday and Tuesday. Between Linda's eye for detail in the decor and service and Ted's concern for freshness, preparation, and presentation, the Fondulas have created one of the most elegant and rewarding dining experiences in Vermont, widely esteemed as perhaps the best in the state and possibly in New England. Chandeliers, fresh flowers, and floor-length table linens grace the peach-colored, vaulted main room, while a less formal atmosphere prevails in the garden room and stone-walled wine cellar. Specializes in "regional, classic cuisine" like grilled pheasant with Beaujolais wine and fillet of beef with potato galette and roasted shallots, almond-crusted swordfish, Napoleon of sea bass with tarragon pastries, and rich desserts. Four-course prix fixe menu $50; wine-tasting menu $72.

Claude's (422-4030), Glazebrook Center, Killington Road near the base lodge, Killington. Open for dinner Wednesday through Monday except in the off-season, when it's Thursday through Saturday, plus Sunday brunch. Insulated from its Choices brasserie (see *Eating Out*), Claude's is a top-drawer restaurant. Chef Claude prepares appetizers such as escargots in garlic butter and smoked salmon ravioli, and entrées of veal mignon, breast of duck cassis, and rack of lamb, with luscious Belgian chocolate mousse cake for dessert. Moderate to expensive.

The Countryman's Pleasure (773-7141), just off Route 4, opposite the Hogge Penny (see *Lodging—Condominiums*), Mendon. Open 5:30–9 daily. Known for its top-drawer Austrian/German specialties: veal schnitzel cordon bleu, sauerbraten, goulash, and so on. The attractive dining rooms occupy the first floor of a charming house. The atmosphere is cozy, informal. Moderate.

🏵⌒ **The Vermont Inn** (775-0708), Route 4, Killington. Open for dinner nightly. Chef Stephen Hatch has captured first place three times in the Killington-Champagne Dine Around Contest. It's a pleasant inn dining room with a fireplace and a varied menu that changes nightly. Entrées could include rack of lamb, Delmonico or teriyaki steak, tenderloin of pork with mushrooms, or baked Vermont veal. Children's menu available. Moderate.

Zola's Grille at the Cortina Inn (773-3333), Route 4, Killington. Open daily. Dinner in this spacious, nicely decorated dining room could start with crab cakes, goat cheese ravioli, or sliced, seared tuna, followed by grilled lamb tenderloin, apple-smoked salmon, Cajun shrimp, or steak. The Sunday buffet brunch, 10:45 AM–1:30 PM, is a winner at $13.95.

Moderate.

The Corners Inn Restaurant (672-9986), Route 4, Bridgewater Corners. Fireside dining Wednesday through Sunday 6–10; daily during holiday periods. Favored by locals, an 1890 farmhouse with a cheerful, informal atmosphere, chef owned and known for local ingredients. Specialties include chicken breast stuffed with Jarlsberg cheese; prosciutto sautéed with white wine, cream stock, mushrooms, tomatoes, and shallots; rack of lamb; and osso buco. Moderate.

Inn at Long Trail (775-7181), Route 4, Killington. Dinner served in fall and winter only, Thursday through Sunday; in summer, soups and salads all day from noon. The dining room in this unusual inn (see *Lodging—Inns*) looks out on the spotlighted face of a steep cliff. A limited choice of entrées (corned beef and cabbage, stuffed Vermont rainbow trout, Guinness stew, for example); all dinners include salad, bread, and vegetables. Inexpensive.

Red Clover Inn (775-2290), Route 4, Mendon. New chef John Wight features "healthy" American cuisine and his menu changes nightly. Entrées might include roast duckling with mango-ginger sauce, rack of lamb with balsamic porcini sauce, or pistachio-crusted salmon with a saffron orange beurre blanc, followed by a warm chocolate truffle in a phyllo crisp or the signature Red Clover Snowball (a génoise with ganache rolled in white chocolate and walnuts). Wines a specialty. Moderate.

Panache (422-8622), the Woods Resort, Killington Road, Killington, specializes in "metropolitan" cuisine, including domestic, Australian, and African wild game (tenderloin of kangaroo, seared cubes of giraffe, barbecued Texas rattlesnake); exotic seafoods (grilled New Zealand cockles); and many vegetarian selections. Moderate.

Sweet Peas (746-8943), at the Pittsfield Inn, Route 100, Pittsfield. Open Friday and Saturday for dinner. Serves wild mushroom crêpes or baked goat cheese, followed by sesame tuna, Moroccan pasta, or salmon in puff pastry. Moderate.

Ovations Restaurant (422-6111), Killington Grand Resort, is open nightly with such appetizers as roast quail on oyster mushrooms, and entrées like roast veal chop; lobster, scallops, and shrimp with angel hair pasta; and sea bass with crab and cornmeal crumbs. Moderate to expensive, with an interesting, attractively priced bistro menu as well.

Tulip Tree Inn (483-6213), Chittenden Dam Road, Chittenden. Open for dinner Tuesday through Sunday with one seating at 7 PM. The inn serves a four-course dinner ($27.50) that could start with grilled Vidalia onion and green pepper soup, followed by herb-coated fillet of beef with vodka-flambéed peppers and shallots, or chicken roulade stuffed with chèvre and herbs.

EATING OUT

Grist Mill (422-3970), at the Summit Lodge, Killington Road, Killington. Open for lunch and dinner. This is a new building, nicely designed to look like a gristmill that has always stood on Summit Pond (there's a 90-year-old waterwheel). The space within is airy and pleasing, dominated by a huge stone hearth. The menu ranges from steaks and veal dishes through grilled swordfish to vegetable stir-fry. Inexpensive to moderate.

Casey's Caboose (422-3795), Killington Road, Killington. Open daily from 3 PM. The building incorporates a circa-1900 snowplow car and a great caboose to house the coveted tables in the place, but you really can't lose: The atmosphere throughout rates high on our short list of family dining spots. Free Buffalo wings in the bar 3–6. Good for Italian and seafood dishes, as well as burgers, and the taco salad is a feast.

Choices Restaurant (422-4030), Glazebrook Center, Killington Road, Killington. Open Wednesday through Sunday for dinner; Sunday brunch 11–2. This combination bistro-brasserie-pub has a huge menu of savory appetizers, salads, soups, raw bar, sandwiches, pastas, and such entrées as Shaker-style smoked pork loin with knockwurst and Cornish Hen Calvin Coolidge.

Cascades Lodge Restaurant (422-3731), top of Killington Road at Killington Village. Open daily, featuring big breakfasts (two eggs, two pancakes, bacon, and sausage for $5.25), lunches, and dinners: scallops Cascades, followed by roast duck or Caribbean-style crab cakes, for example. Pub fare also available.

Charity's 1887 Saloon Restaurant (422-3800), Killington Road, Killington. Open daily for lunch and dinner; brunch (11:30–3) Saturday and Sunday. Decorated with hanging plants, Tiffany shades, and plenty of gleaming copper and shiny wooden booths, this place is good for a Reuben or vegetarian casserole at lunch; try steak teriyaki or just onion soup gratiné for dinner. Informal, satisfying.

Mother Shapiro's (422-9933), Killington Road, Killington. The most popular place on the mountain for breakfast (open at 7:30 AM), good for lunch and dinner, too. A pubby, friendly place with big burgers and monster deli sandwiches, homemade soups, specials.

Back Behind Saloon (422-9907), junction of Routes 4 and 100 south, West Bridgewater. Open for dinner nightly and for lunch Friday, Saturday, and Sunday. A zany atmosphere (look for the red caboose and antique Mobil gas pump), barn board, stained glass, a big hearth. Specialties like venison Jack Daniels and Texas spareribs augment basic American fare: steaks and chicken, generous portions. Entrées on the high side ($10.95–18.50).

Sugar & Spice (773-7832), Route 4, Mendon. Open 7–2 daily. A unique pancake restaurant housed in a large replica of a classic sugarhouse and surrounded by a 50-acre sugarbush. Besides dining on a variety of pancake, egg, and omelet dishes, along with soups and sandwiches, you can watch both maple candy and cheese being made several days a week. Gift shop.

Blanche & Bill's Pancake House, Route 4, just 1 mile east of the junction with Route 100 south. "Serving breakfast anytime," 7–2, but closed Monday and Tuesday. Blanche has been serving reasonably priced meals in the front rooms of her small house by the side of the road for more than a dozen years.

Marge & John's Country Breakfast, Route 4, Mendon. Closed Tuesday, otherwise open 7–3. Specializing in fresh sourdough French toast. Another roadside house with reasonable prices.

Mrs. Brady's (422-2020), Killington Road at Butternut on the Mountain. The atmosphere is casual and colorful, and the menu features a salad bar, steak, and seafood; includes a great American burger platter and gobbler (turkey on a grinder with stuffing and gravy), as well as baked stuffed lobster. There are also pasta, veal, and steak dishes; stir-fries; plus pizza and a children's menu.

Ppeppers Bar & Grill (422-3177), in the Killington Mall, is a popular spot for breakfast, lunch, dinner, and take-out food.

Chinese Gourmet & Sushi Yoshi (422-4241), Killington Road, Killington. Open daily from 11:30 AM. We thought (in the previous edition) that Japanese cuisine had finally made its way to the mountain, but it's now primarily Chinese plus sushi specials. They deliver, too.

See also "Rutland and the Lower Champlain Valley." Rutland is an exceptionally good "eating out" town.

ENTERTAINMENT

MUSIC
The Killington Music Festival (773-4003), a series of mostly chamber music concerts in Snowshed Lodge and at a scattering of other local sites; weekends in July and August.

APRÈS-SKI
The Wobbly Barn (422-3392), Killington Road, Killington. A steakhouse (dinner 5–11) with plenty of music, dancing, blues, rock 'n' roll. Ski season only.

The Nightspot (422-9885), Killington Road, Killington. Dancing nightly to a DJ. Free ski tuning and happy-hour hors d'oeuvres nightly.

McGrath's Irish Pub at the Inn at Long Trail (775-7181), Route 4, Killington. Live Irish music on weekends to go with the Gaelic atmosphere and Guinness on tap. It's a great pub with a 22-foot-long bar made from a single log and a boulder protruding from the back wall.

Pickle Barrel (422-3035), Killington Road, Killington. "Some of the finest rock 'n' roll bands in the East."

SELECTIVE SHOPPING

Bill's Country Store (773-9313), at the junction of Routes 4 and 100, Killington, stocks a broad spectrum of Vermont products, including cheese, maple goodies, deerskin gloves, and woodwork.

The Ski Shack (773-3600), Route 4 at Killington Road, Killington. Open daily 9–5:30. This place has just about everything in the way of sports clothes and equipment for adults and kids, much at discount prices.

See also the Marketplace at Bridgewater Mill in "Woodstock and Quechee."

The Plymouth Cheese Company (672-3650), Box 1, Plymouth. Open year-round but call ahead in winter. John Coolidge, son of Calvin, remains president of this business, which has been in the family since 1890. It's a true, old-fashioned Vermont granular curd cheese, available in five flavors, artfully aged, available by mail order as well as by trip to the factory store.

Long Trail Brewing Company (672-5011), Route 4 west at Bridgewater Corners, produces Long Trail Ale, as well as India Pale Ale, Stout, and Kolsch. Tours and tastings in the pub, daily noon—5.

SPECIAL EVENTS

January through March: Frequent **alpine ski races** for all ages at Killington and Pico. **Fireworks** every Thursday.

July 4: **Calvin Coolidge Birthday memorial,** Plymouth.

July 4 weekend: Vermont Symphony Orchestra **Picnic and Pops Concert** (422-6200), Killington.

July and August: **Killington Music Festival** (773-4003).

Labor Day weekend: **Killington Stage Race** (773-0755; 1-800-621-MTNS)—cyclists compete for big stakes in the 3-day event.

Sugarbush/Mad River Valley

Sugarbush is Vermont's most interesting and genuinely year-round resort community spawned solely by skiing (Stowe began as a summer resort in the 1870s).

There were farms and lumber mills in this magnificent valley before Mad River Glen began attracting skiers in 1948, but the unique look and lifestyle of this community have evolved in the past 50 years, shaped by three ski areas, just as truly as the earlier villages grew around their commons. Its present character has evolved from the '60s, when Sugarbush and then Glen Ellen (the two have since merged) triggered an influx of ski-struck urbanites who formed polo and fox hunt groups, built an arts center and airport, and opened and patronized specialty shops and fine restaurants. Young architects eager to test new theories of solar heating and cluster housing designed New England's first trailside homes, first bottom-of-the-lift village, and unconventionally shaped, hidden homes and condominiums. Most of these settling skiers have remained, their numbers now augmented by their grown children and second-home owners who have come to retire. It's an unusually ecological and community-minded group.

Only in the '90s did it become painfully clear that natural snow in northern New England is too fickle a base for the big business that skiing has become, and that to make snow you need water. The Valley's ski areas have faced up to this challenge in their own ways.

Mad River Glen has simply ignored it. But then this is the "ski it if you can" mountain that still operates the nation's oldest lift, is the country's only cooperatively owned ski area (1,700 shares are divided among 1,400 shareholders), and remains the only area in the East that bars snowboarders, featuring telemarking instead. Sugarbush, by contrast, from its 1958 opening has been one of New England's major commercial ski areas, a year-round resort that's a centerpiece for hundreds of condos and dozens of inns and B&Bs.

In 1995 the issue of drawing water from the Mad River was addressed by New England ski czar Les Otten, who bought the resort and built a 63-million-gallon snowmaking pond to store water siphoned from the Mad River during peak flows. Otten's American Ski Company also installed a dramatic 2-mile-long chairlift across the Slide Brook

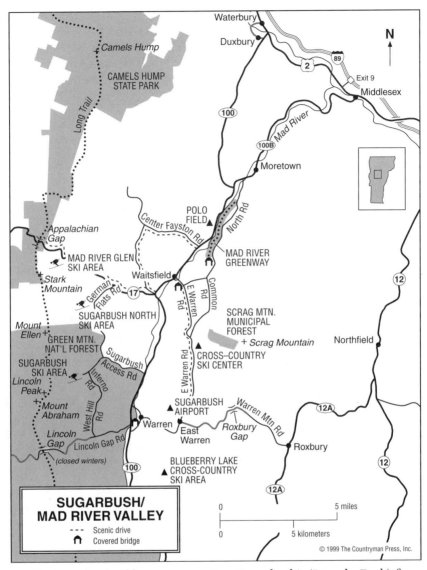

Basin, a semi-wilderness separating Sugarbush's (Lincoln Peak) from Mount Ellen.

Sugarbush skiers will tell you how fortunate their resort was to be sidelined during the era in which a large percentage of New England's best ski trails were smoothed, widened, and generally homogenized. In particular they are thankful that the Castle Rock trails, recognized throughout the country as some of the meanest, most natural, and most interesting expert terrain at any major American ski resort, survive.

Today "the Valley" (still known by two names—Sugarbush and Mad River) can accommodate more than 6,000 visitors on any given night, but it's far from obvious where. Visitors tend to drive right through on Route 100 (the Valley spine), seeing nothing more than the clump of roadside shops in Waitsfield, missing Warren Village (6 miles south) entirely.

The 7-mile-wide valley itself is a beauty: Meadows stretch away from the banks of the river, rising to the Green Mountains on the west and the Roxbury Range on the east. In summer and fall, there is hiking on the Long Trail over some of the highest peaks in the Green Mountains, soaring above the valley, mountain biking on ski trails and high woods roads, a choice of horseback-riding options, fishing and swimming in the Mad River itself, not to mention outstanding golf, tennis, polo, and cricket.

GUIDANCE

Sugarbush Chamber of Commerce (496-3409; lodging: 1-800-82-VISIT; e-mail: chamber@madriver.com; web site: www.madrivervalley.com), Box 173, Waitsfield 05673. A walk-in visitors center in the General Wait House, Route 100, Waitsfield, is open year-round 9–5 weekdays, Saturday 9–1. During crunch times, vacancies are posted after 5 PM, in the lobby, near the courtesy phone. Request the free guide.

GETTING THERE

By bus: Waterbury is the nearest **Vermont Transit** stop.

By train: The closest **AMTRAK** station is in Waterbury.

By air: Burlington Airport is 45 miles away; see *Getting There* in "Burlington Region" for carriers.

By car: Valley residents will tell you that the quickest route from points south is I-89 to Randolph and 15 miles up Route 12A to Roxbury, then 8 miles over the Roxbury Gap to Warren. This is also the most scenic way (the valley view from the top of the gap is spectacular), but be forewarned that this high road can be treacherous in winter. In snow, play it safe and take I-89 to Middlesex, exit 9, then 100B the 13 miles south to Waitsfield.

GETTING AROUND

During ski season, shuttles circle between condos at the top of the access road and restaurants and nightspots. Many inns have their own transport to the lifts.

C&L Taxi (496-4056) offers local long and distance, 24 hours.

Note: Waitsfield–Champlain Valley Telecom offers free local calls on some pay phones (but not all, so check) scattered around the Valley.

MEDICAL EMERGENCY

911 or ambulance (496-3600). **Mad River Valley Health Center** (496-3838), Route 100, Waitsfield.

VILLAGES

Note: The Mad River Valley includes **Moretown** (population: 1,507) to the north and **Fayston** (population: 1,024), an elusive town without a center that produced potatoes in the 1860s and was an important lumbering presence into the early 20th century. It's home to Mount Ellen and Mad River Glen ski areas and to inns along Route 17 and the German Flats Road.

Warren Village. The village center of the long-established farm town of Warren (population: 1,317) is a compact clapboard cluster of town hall, steepled church, and bandstand, with a double-porched general store by a waterfall across from an inn. At first glance the village doesn't look much different from how it did in the 1950s when Route 100 passed through its center, but the effect of Sugarbush, the ski resort that's way up an access road at the other end of town, has been total. The Pitcher Inn's self-consciously plain face masks an elegant restaurant and some of the most elaborate (and expensive) themed rooms in Vermont (see *Dining Out* and *Lodging*); the Warren Store (once a stagecoach inn itself) stocks a mix of gourmet food and upscale clothing and gifts (see *Selective Shopping—Special Shops*). Arts, antiques, and crafts are within an easy walk, and a covered bridge spans the Mad River. The village is the setting for one of Vermont's most colorful July 4 parades.

Waitsfield. The most populous (around 1,500) of the Valley's towns and its commercial center, home to Mad River Canoe, among several companies, and to two small, tasteful shopping malls that flank Route 100 on land that was farmed until the 1960s. The old village center is a half mile up Route 100, a gathering of 19th-century buildings, including a library and church, on and around Bridge Street (it's a covered bridge). Much larger and denser than it first looks, the village offers a sophisticated mix of boutiques and services, a movie house with a wine bar, and several first-rate restaurants. Changing historical exhibits are displayed in the **General Wait House.** Benjamin Wait, you learn, had been a member of Vermont's famed Rogers' Rangers and weathered dozens of French and Indian Wars battles, as well as serving in the Revolution before founding the town at age 53 in 1789. He later was pitted against his fellow settlers on the question of where to put the common. He wanted it just about where the commercial center is today (the original common has been left high and dry out on Joslin Hill Road). Largely denuded of its woods during its era as a lumbering and sheep-farming community, it's now mostly wooded and home to more people than ever. Pick up the leaflet *Waitsfield Village Historic District Walking Tour* at the General Wait House (see *Guidance*).

TO DO

In winter, the Valley's magnets are its alpine and cross-country ski areas, but in summer a ski lift runs weekends only and there are no slides, no factory outlets, really no focal points. Aside from two covered bridges, there are no attractions as such, just an unusual number of activities to pursue. Check the following list!

BICYCLING

The Valley's wide variety of terrain, from smooth dirt roads to technical singletrack, lends itself to mountain biking. For rentals and service, check the **Mad River Cyclery** (496-2708) and **Clearwater Sports** (496-2708) in Waitsfield. **Sugarbush Resort** (583-2381) offers lift-served mountain biking at the Lincoln Peak base area June through Columbus Day, Friday through Sunday. Rentals and tours available. **Bike Vermont** (1-800-257-2226) offers weekend tours based at the 1824 House Inn (see *Lodging—Bed & Breakfasts*).

Mad River Greenway. A 3-mile trail follows the Mad River from a parking area on Trembly Road (turn off Route 100 north of Waitsfield at the sign for the Mad River Inn).

CANOEING

Clearwater Sports (496-2708), Route 100, Waitsfield. Barry Bender offers learn-to-canoe and -kayak programs, full-moon canoe cruises on Waterbury Reservoir, camping excursions, also a children's day program (ages 9–13) and a 5-day wilderness camp program for 9- to 13-year-olds. **Vermont Pack & Paddle Outfitters** (496-9006), based in Waitsfield, offers kayaking and canoeing tours.

CHAIRLIFT

Sugarbush Resort (583-2381), Warren, operates its high-speed Super Bravo Express June through Columbus Day, Friday through Sunday.

FARMS

Guest House at Knoll Farm (496-3939), Bragg Hill Road, Waitsfield 05673. Open in summer for B&B and yoga and poetry workshops, slated to be run by the Vermont Land Trust as of 2001 as a sustainable agricultural learning center, which may still well include a B&B. Ann Day's historic (listed on the National Register of Historic Places), 150-acre working farm sits high above the valley, a half-mile off Route 17. There is a classic old barn out back, a swim pond, and nature trails through the woods and high pastures. The property includes organic gardens, pastures, and animals (Scotch Highland cattle, hens, horses, and pigs). Ann, a respected poet and photographer, began taking in guests in 1957. Inquire about rates and present status.

Rootswork (496-2474; e-mail: rootswork @madriver.com), East Warren Schoolhouse. This nonprofit organization is devoted to promoting and nurturing local agriculture. A retail store sells farmstead cheeses, vegetables, and appropriate books.

FISHING

Numerous streams offer good fly-fishing. The chamber of commerce (see *Guidance*) keeps a list of a half-dozen guide services. *Note:* A Vermont fishing license is required. See *To Do—Fishing* in "Stowe and Waterbury" for information about instructional tours and packages. Also check out Waitsfield-based **Vermont Pack & Paddle** (496-9009).

FITNESS CENTERS

Sugarbush Health & Racquet Club (583-6700), Sugarbush Village, Warren. An outstanding complex consisting of indoor and outdoor pools, indoor and outdoor Jacuzzis, whirlpool, sauna, steam room, exercise room, indoor squash, tennis and racquetball courts, massage room, aerobics studio, 11-station Nautilus, and a full range of cardiovascular equipment. The **Valley Rock Gym** (583-6754), part of this complex, features an indoor climbing wall, open 3–9 PM.

The Bridges Family Resort and Tennis Club (583-2922; 1-800-453-2922), Sugarbush Access Road, Warren. A year-round health and tennis club with indoor and outdoor tennis, heated pools, fitness center, hot tub, and sauna.

GOLF

Sugarbush Golf Course (583-6725), Warren, at the Sugarbush Inn (see *Lodging—Resorts*). An 18-hole, Robert Trent Jones Sr. course, PGA rate 42, par 72; car and club rental, lessons, practice range, café. Inquire about golf/lodging packages.

HIKING

Walks & Rambles in Vermont's Mad River Valley ($2.95), available at the chamber of commerce (see *Guidance*), unlocks the area's many superb hiking secrets.

The Long Trail runs along the ridge of the Green Mountains here and is easily accessible from three places: the two gap roads and the Sugarbush Bravo chairlift (weekends only). From the Lincoln Gap Road (4.7 miles west of Route 100) you can hike south to the Green Mountain Club's **Sunset Lodge** for a view of the Champlain Valley and Adirondacks. The more popular hike, however, is north from the gap (be advised to start early; parking is limited) to the **Battell Shelter,** on to **Mount Abraham** (5 miles round-trip), a 4,052-foot summit with spectacular views west, south as far as Killington Peak, and north as far as Belvidere Mountain. From Mount Abraham north to **Lincoln Peak** (accessible by the Sugarbush Resort chairlift) and on to **Mount Ellen** (4,135 feet) is largely above tree line; 3,600-foot **General Stark Mountain** to the north is best accessed (still a steep 2.6-mile hike) from Route 17 at the Appalachian Gap. For details about the four shelters (**Glen Ellen Lodge** and the **Theron Dean Shelter** as well as the two above), contact the Green Mountain Club (244-7037).

The Sugarbush Biking and Trekking Center (583-2385) offers guided hikes around the mountain and on the Long Trail. Hiking boot rentals available. The Super Bravo chairlift (operating Friday through Sunday) helps hikers access the Long Trail, from which they can walk the 4,000-foot-elevation ridgeline to Mount Ellen and back and descend a ski trail.

Mill Brook Path (3 miles one-way) follows the Mill Brook from German Flats Road uphill to Mad River Barn (blue blazes).

Vermont Icelandic Horse Farm in Waitsfield

HORSEBACK RIDING

Vermont Icelandic Horse Farm (496-7141), Common Road, Waitsfield. Year-round. These strong, pony-sized mounts were brought to Iceland by the Vikings, but are still relatively rare. Karen Winhod uses them for half- and full-day trail rides and (seasonal) inn-to-inn treks from her stable in Waitsfield Common. The horses have an unusually smooth gait (faster than a walk, gentler than a trot). Skijoring is offered in winter.

Navajo Farm (496-3656), Route 100, Moretown. Riding instruction and trail rides by reservation.

Dana Hill Stable (496-6251), Route 17, Fayston. Clinics, extensive coaching weeks.

MINI-GOLF

Lots-O-Balls (244-5874), Route 100, in Duxbury, between Waitsfield and Waterbury. Open in-season from 11 AM, a great 19-hole miniature golf course. $2 per adult, $1 per player age 5 and under.

POLO

Sugarbush Polo Club. The oldest and most active polo club in Vermont holds matches every Thursday, Saturday, and Sunday during summer months and USPA-sanctioned tournaments on Memorial Day, July 4, and Labor Day. Lessons available. Call the Sugarbush Chamber of Commerce (496-3409) for current dates and contacts.

SCENIC DRIVES

East Warren Road. If you miss this road, you miss the heart of the Valley. From Bridge Street in Waitsfield Village, cross the covered bridge and bear right onto East Warren Road and continue the 8.8 miles to East Warren. The views are of the Green Mountains set back across open farmland. For an overview of the Valley, take the Roxbury Gap Road up to the pullout (be careful, because there are not many places to turn around). From East Warren, loop back through Warren Village to Route 100.

Bragg Hill Road. The views from this peerless old farm road are magnificent: down across pastures and the narrow valley cut by the Mill Brook to Mount Ellen. Begin at Bragg Hill Road (off Route 100 just north of the Route 17 junction) and drive uphill, continue as it turns to dirt, and follow it around (bearing left); it turns into Number 9 Road and rejoins Route 17.

Appalachian Gap. Even if you are not continuing down the other side, be sure to drive up Route 17 past the Mad River Glen base area to its high point (there's parking at the trailhead for the Long Trail) and look down across the Champlain Valley, across the lake, to the Adirondacks in the distance. This is a great sunset ride.

SOARING

Sugarbush-Warren Airport (496-2290; 1-800-881-SOAR), Warren. Respected as one of the East's prime spots for riding thermal and ridge waves. Glider lessons, rides, food; open daily May through October. Solo and private lessons, rides, vacations available for all ages.

SUMMER DAY CAMPS

Sugarbush Resort (583-2381), the **Bridges Family Resort and Tennis Club** (583-2922; 1-800-453-2922) in Warren, **Clearwater Sports** (496-2708) in Waitsfield, and the **Sunrise Montessori School** (496-5435) in Waitsfield all offer summer day camps. For ages 13 and up there's even a weeklong Junior Soaring Camp (492-2708) at the Sugarbush Airport (see *Soaring*).

SWIMMING

South of Warren Village, the Mad River becomes a series of dramatic falls and whirlpools cascading through a gorge. The most secluded swimming hole is by the **Bobbin Mill** (the first right off Route 100 after Lincoln Gap Road, heading south); park by the gravel pit and follow the path through the pines to a series of pools, all icy cold. Ask locally about **Warren Falls** and the best spot for skinny-dipping. The **Old Lareau Farm Swimming Pond** (now a town park) in the Mad River, south of Waitsfield on Route 100, is best for kids. Also check **Blueberry Lake** (496-6687) in Warren and the **Ward Fishing Access** area on Route 100B in Moretown. **Bristol Falls** is just about 10 miles from Warren via the Lincoln Gap Road. The **Sugarbush Sports Center** (see *Fitness*) features a large, L-shaped outdoor pool with adjacent changing facilities, café, bar, and Jacuzzi; the **Bridges Family Resort and Tennis Club** (583-2922; 1-800-453-2922) offers indoor and outdoor pools and swimming lessons. Many inns also have outdoor pools. At the **Inn**

at Round Barn Farm (496-2276), East Warren Road, Waitsfield, the pool is in the barn.

TENNIS

New England Tennis Holidays (1-800-869-0949), using facilities at the Sugarbush Inn (see *Resorts*), offers clinics with 5 hours of daily instruction. Many local inns also have their own courts.

The Bridges Family Resort and Tennis Club (583-2922; 1-800-453-2922), Sugarbush Access Road, Warren, offers indoor and outdoor courts and year-round tennis clinics for both adults and juniors.

WALKING AND RUNNING

The Mad River Path Association (583-8181) maintains several ever-evolving recreation paths in the Valley, namely: the **Warren Path,** beginning near Brooks Field at Warren Elementary School (Brook Road, Warren); the **Millbrook Path** in Fayston, running along the hill through the woods (blue blazes) between Millbrook Lodge and Tucker Hill Lodge, on up across German Flats Road to the Inn at Mad River Barn; the **Mad River Greenway** (see *Bicycling*); and the **Village Path,** which begins at Fiddlers' Green and heads south to the Irasville Cemetery and beyond. See also *Hiking* and *Scenic Drives*

WINTER SPORTS

CROSS-COUNTRY SKIING

Ole's Cross-Country Center (496-3430), near the airport, Warren. Forty-five km of machine-tracked trails at elevations ranging from 1,120 to 1,640 feet.

Blueberry Lake Cross-Country Ski Center (496-6687), Plunkton Road, Warren. On the scenic, east side of the Valley, a total of 60 km of trails; also the source of information about Ole's Cross-Country Center at the airport on the East Warren plateau at altitudes of 1,200–2,450 feet (64 km). $10.

Inn at Round Barn Farm (496-2276), East Warren Road, Waitsfield. A total of 30 km of tracked, groomed trails across open meadows with mountain views, also some upland woodland. Lessons, rentals.

Local trail: **Puddledock** in Granville Gulf State Reservation on Route 100, south of Warren: 3½ miles of ungroomed trails marked with red metal triangles; map available at the registration box.

Clearwater Sports (496-2708), Route 100, Waitsfield, offers guided backcountry and telemark ski tours.

Note: Telemarking is a longtime specialty at **Mad River Glen** (496-3551). Inquire about midweek rentals, lesson and lift packages, and special events.

DOWNHILL SKIING

Sugarbush (information: 583-2381; ski report: 583-SNOW; www.sugarbush.com; lodging reservations: 1-800-53-SUGAR). Two separate trail sys-

SUGARBUSH RESORTS/DAVID BROWNELL

The slopes of Mount Ellen rise behind the Waitsfield Federated Church

tems on two major peaks—3,975-foot Lincoln Peak at Sugarbush South and 4,135-foot Mount Ellen at Sugarbush North—originally two different ski areas—were linked in 1995 by a 2-mile (9½-minute) quad chair traversing the undeveloped Slide Brook Basin which separates them. Snowmaking coverage, long adequate at Mount Ellen, was also tripled to cover substantially more terrain at Lincoln Peak.

Lifts: 18—7 quads, 3 triples, 4 doubles, and 4 surface. Lifts operate 9–4 weekdays, 8:30–4 weekends and holidays.

Trails: 112; 20-acre tree skiing; 423 skiable acres.

Vertical drop: 2,650 feet.

Snowmaking: 285.5 acres overall.

Facilities: Cafeterias, lounges, ski shops, rentals, restaurants, sports center, condominiums.

Ski and snowboarding school: Perfect Turn clinics, special teen program; women's clinics, guided backcountry skiing.

Snowboarding: Rentals, lessons, terrain parks.

For children: Nursery from infancy, special morning and afternoon programs.

Rates: In 1998–99, $49 adults; $28 juniors. *Note:* Lower rates are available with multi-day cards good for 12 months at all eight American Skiing Company resorts.

Mad River Glen (496-3551; in-state snow reports: 1-800-696-2001; outstanding web site: www.madriverglen.com). One of New England's oldest major ski areas (the first to offer slope-side lodging), in 1995 it became the first to be owned cooperatively by its skiers, retaining its enviable reputation as one of the most challenging yet friendliest places to ski. Its vertical drop puts it in the big league, but the number of lifts and trails remains consciously limited. The Sunnyside Double Chair was replaced in 1998, the first capital improvement since 1982, and access to the summit of Stark Mountain (3,836 feet) is via the vintage-1948 single chair (the only single lift left in the country). All trails funnel into the central base lodge area, the better for families—many of whom are now third-generation Mad River skiers—to meet. Many trails are off the ski map. A favored place for telemarking, it's the only place in New England in which snowboarding is outlawed. Although completely lacking in snowmaking, on a good snow day it's the region's best ski buy.

Lifts: Four chairs, including the single.

Trails and slopes: 19 expert, 10 intermediate, 14 novice, a total of 800 skiable acres.

Vertical drop: 2,000 feet.

Snowmaking: 15 percent on novice slope.

Facilities: Base lodge, cafeteria, and pub; also the Birdcage, halfway up the mountain, serving sandwiches, drinks; ski shop, rentals, ski school.

For children: Cricket Club Nursery for 3 months to toddlers, SKIwee (4–12) Junior Racing Program, and Junior Mogul Program.

Rates: $29 weekdays–36 weekends adults, $20–24 juniors (14 and under); half-day, multi-day rates.

SKIJORING

Inquire about this sport (also about winter horseback riding) at **Vermont Icelandic Horse Farm** (496-7141) in Waitsfield (see *Horseback Riding*).

SNOWSHOEING

Clearwater Sports (253-2317), Route 100, Waitsfield, offers rentals, along with custom and group tours. Check out the *Mad River Valley Snowshoe Trails* map/guide ($2.95) published by Map Adventures (253-7489) in Stowe, detailing 15 tours and identifying local animal tracks. **Crisports Service Center at Sugarbush** (583-6517) also offers snowshoe rentals and guided tours, and **Inn at Round Barn Farm** (496-2276) rents snowshoes and permits them on its property.

SNOWMOBILING

Eighty miles of local trails are maintained by the Mad River Ridge Runners; snowmobile registration can be purchased at **Kenyon's Store**, Route 11, Waitsfield. **Rentals and Guided Tours** (583-6725) at the Sugarbush Golf Course (see *To Do—Golf*), across from the Sugarbush Inn.

ICE SKATING

Sugarbush Inn (583-6100; 1-800-537-8427) in Warren offers skating on flooded tennis courts. The **Skatium** at Mad River Green Shopping Center in Waitsfield (lighted too); rentals from neighboring Inverness Ski Shop (496-3343); also free day and night skating on the groomed hockey rink at **Brooks Recreation Field** off Brook Road in Warren.

SLEIGH RIDES

The Inn at Round Barn Farm (496-2276), East Warren Road, Waitsfield, **Whispering Winds Farm** (496-2819) on South Hill Road in Moretown, and **Mountain Valley Farm** (496-9255) in Waitsfield all offer sleigh rides.

LODGING

Note: There are two major reservation services for most of the same places in the Valley. The Sugarbush-based service (1-800-53-SUGAR) represents more of the condos and offers ski, golf, and tennis packages, but the chamber of commerce (1-800-82-VISIT) also represents most inns and B&Bs, in addition to the Sugarbush Inn and many condos.

RESORTS

Sugarbush Inn (583-6100; 1-800-537-8427), Warren 05674. The centerpiece of this complex is the fairly formal, 46-room Sugarbush Inn, with a 24-hour front desk, room phones, a library and sitting room, tennis courts, and an outdoor pool. It's adjacent to an 18-hole Robert Trent Jones golf course (see *To Do—Golf*). $120 with breakfast, $90 in the off-season. See also *Condominiums*.

The Bridges Family Resort and Tennis Club (583-2922; 1-800-453-2922), Sugarbush Access Road, Warren 05674. A self-contained resort just down the access road from the Sugarbush main lifts and base lodge. Facilities include indoor tennis, squash, an indoor pool, saunas, Jacuzzi and exercise room, and 100 condo-style units ranging from one to three bedrooms, each with fireplace, sundeck, TV, and phone, some with washer and dryer. $160–180 for a one-bedroom, $165–255 for a two-bedroom, and $320–780 for a three-bedroom unit; cheaper the longer you stay; inquire about ski and tennis packages.

INNS

The inns listed below serve dinner as a matter of course; B&Bs may serve dinner on occasion.

Pitcher Inn (583-6100; 1-888-TO-PITCH; fax: 583-3209; e-mail: lodging@sugarbush.com), Warren 05674. Designed by architect David Sellers to look like it's been sitting here in the middle of Warren Village for a century, the white-clapboard inn just opened in the 1997–98 winter season, replacing a building that had burned. Inside, however, the inn offers some extraordinary spaces, notably a cozy small library with books and a hearth, far from the large, elegant dining room that's open to the public (see *Dining Out*). Each guest room was designed by a different architect to convey a different aspect of local history. The Lodge, for instance, suggests a Masonic lodge (once a major social force in the Valley), with a ceiling painted midnight blue and delicately studded with stars, and obelisk-shaped posts on the king-sized bed. From a bedside switch in the Mountain Room, you can make the sun rise and set over the mountains painted on the facing wall. Bathrooms are splendid. Two of the 11 rooms are suites. $200–350 includes breakfast in the inn, $425 in the suites.

Millbrook Inn & Restaurant (496-2405; 1-800-477-2809; fax: 496-9735; e-mail: millbrkinn@aol.com), Route 17, Waitsfield 05673. Open year-round except April, May, and late October to Thanksgiving. This 19th-century farmhouse is a gem. You enter through the warming room, actually heated by a woodstove in winter. The living rooms invite you to sit down. The heart of the ground floor, however, is the dining room, well known locally as one of the best places to dine in the Valley (see *Dining Out*). Each of the seven guest rooms is different enough to deserve its own name, but all have stenciled walls, bureaus, antique beds with firm, queen-sized mattresses, and private bath. A ski lodge since 1948, Millbrook has become a true country inn since Joan and Thom Gorman took over in 1979. They are constantly redecorating and landscaping the garden (breakfast is served on the patio, weather permitting) and in '98 they bought the small ski house on the wooded hillside across the brook. $100–190 per couple MAP in winter, $98 MAP per couple $68 B&B ($50 single) in summer. Children ages 6 and older are welcome. No smoking. Pets by prior approval.

Inn at Mad River Barn (496-3310; also in-state: 1-800-834-4666), RR 1, Box 88, Waitsfield 05673. Betsy Pratt, former owner of Mad River Glen Ski Area, preserves the special atmosphere of this classic 1940s ski lodge, with its massive stone fireplace and deep leather chairs, and a dining room filled with mismatched oak tables and original 1930s art. The food (breakfast only in summer, dinner too in winter) is fine, as are the pine-walled guest rooms, all with private bath (those in the annex come with small kitchenette). In summer, the appeal of the place is enhanced by the pool, secluded in a grove of birches, and by the deck overlooking landscaped gardens, a setting for weddings and receptions. In winter, a trail connects with Mad River Glen. In summer, rates with breakfast are $59–69 per couple; inquire about the 3-day special. In winter, $38–49 per person includes breakfast. Dinner is $15 extra; special children's rates.

Tucker Hill Lodge (phone/fax: 496-3983; 1-800-543-7841; e-mail: tuckhill@madriver.com), RFD 1, Box 147, Waitsfield 05673. A home built along traditional lines with a fieldstone hearth in the inviting living room and 22 nicely furnished rooms with handmade quilts, stenciling, and flowered wallpaper, 16 with private bath. There are two suites, one with a king-sized feather bed and a fireplace. Handy to both Waitsfield Village and Mount Ellen, it has an away-from-it-all feeling enhanced by 14 acres of wooded land. Innkeepers Giorgio (a former member of the Italian ski team) and Susan (a Canadian who met Giorgio in Italy) Noaro have revitalized this old landmark, preserving its reputation for good food (see Giorgio's Cafe under *Dining Out*). $60–115 per couple B&B; $110–190 MAP; children 10 years and younger stay free in same room with parents.

Inquire about special ski-and-stay packages. Pets possible.

BED & BREAKFASTS

The Inn at Round Barn Farm (496-2276; e-mail: roundbarn@madriver. com), East Warren Road, Waitsfield 05673. Named for its remarkable round (12-sided) barn built in 1910, now a cultural and reception center with a lap pool and greenhouse on its ground floor, this old farmhouse is one of New England's most elegant bed & breakfasts. Innkeeper Anne Marie DeFreest offers 11 antiques-furnished rooms, 6 with gas fireplace, several with steam shower and/or Jacuzzi, all overlooking the meadows and mountains. Guests who come in winter are asked to leave their shoes at the door and don slippers to protect the hardwood floors. Common space includes a sun-filled breakfast room, a stone terrace, a book-lined library, and a lower-level game room with pool table, organ, TV, VCR, and a fridge stocked with complimentary soda and juices. From $135 midweek for the Jones Room, with a double spool bed and regular shower, to $220 on weekends for the Richardson Room, with a white-marble fireplace, canopied king bed, and Jacuzzi. Prices include gourmet breakfast and afternoon edibles. No smoking. A series of workshops ranging from cooking classes to watercolor and photography are offered mid-April through mid-August. Weddings are a specialty of the barn, which also serves as a venue for summer concerts (see *Entertainment*). In winter, the inn maintains an extensive cross-country network. Children 15 and older accepted.

The Lareau Farm Country Inn (496-4949; 1-800-833-0766), Route 100, Waitsfield 05673. A 150-year-old farmhouse set in a wide meadow by Route 100 and the Mad River offers 12 guest rooms and a suite with Jacuzzi, all nicely furnished with antique beds, quilts, and rockers. Susan Easley is a warm host. Guests feel right at home, checking in via the kitchen and settling into the two sitting rooms (one with a fireplace) or onto the broad, columned back porch, which overlooks an expansive spread of lawn that stretches down to a great (10-foot-deep) swimming hole and backs into a steep wooded hill. Guests are free to walk or ski the 67 acres. $70–110 for a double room with private bath, $60–80 with shared bath, includes a full breakfast (2-night minimum on weekends). $100–135 for the suite. Children are welcome "with well-behaved parents," and families occupy rooms along an ell off the main house. Weddings are a specialty; dinner on weekends is served in the American Flatbread Kitchen (see *Eating Out*) in the adjoining barn.

West Hill House (496-7162; 1-800-898-1427; e-mail: westhill@madriver. com), West Hill Road, RR 1, Box 292, Warren 05674. A gabled farmhouse off in a far corner of the golf course but convenient both to Sugarbush lifts and to the village of Warren. Dotty Kyle and Eric Brattstrom offer seven guest rooms (private baths, most with gas fireplace) and like to gather guests around their dining room table for multicourse breakfasts (with, perhaps, a vegetable soufflé), also for candelight dinners (on request). The house offers an unusual amount of common space: a living room, library with fireplace, and sunroom with views to the mountains. Step out the front door to cross-country ski or play golf, out the back into 9 wooded acres. $90–150 year-round. Inquire about family reunions and weddings.

Mountain View Inn (496-2426), RR 1, Box 69, Waitsfield 05673. A typical Vermont house by Route 17 that can accommodate 14 in seven nicely decorated rooms. Guests gather around the wood-burning stove in the living room and at the long harvest table for breakfast. Fred and Susan Spencer are genial hosts. Handy to Mount Ellen, Mad River Glen, and the Mill Brook Path. $80–110 per couple B&B, $50–65 for singles.

1824 House Inn (496-7555; 1-800-426-9866; e-mail: 1824house@ madriver.com), 250 Main Street (Route 100), Waitsfield 05673. North of the village, the 10-gabled house is a beauty, freshly redone with an eye to room colors, Oriental rugs, and well-chosen antiques, in addition to comfort. New owners Jack Rodie and Carol Davis have both led bike tours in their varied careers and they cater to outdoor-minded guests, hikers as well as bikers, recommending routes and offering shuttle service at the end of trails. The six bedrooms vary, but all have private bath and feather beds. There are gracious drawing and dining rooms with fireplaces and an outside hot tub. The 22-acre property invites walking and cross-country skiing, and horses can be stabled in the barn. There's also a good swimming hole in the Mad River, just across the road. $85–115 in low seasons, $115–125 in high seasons includes a gourmet breakfast and evening refreshments.

The Featherbed Inn (496-7151; fax: 496-7933), Route 100, Waitsfield 05673. Clive and Tracey Coutts devoted three years to restoring this early-19th-century farmhouse before hanging out their shingle as a B&B. Back in the 1950s, it was one of the first Valley homes to take in skiers, but the Valley is different today and so are skier expectations. The two-room Beatrice Suite features a pencil-post canopy bed and wet bar; the Ilse Suite offers a cathedral ceiling and a queen-sized sleigh bed. All the rooms have feather beds, of course. There are also eight more traditional rooms. Common spaces are tasteful and inviting, from the living room with its woodstove and grand piano to the cozy den with TV. Set way back from Route 100, the house overlooks lawn and fields. Rates include a full breakfast. $75–135.

✎ **The Mad River Inn** (496-7900; 1-800-832-8278; e-mail: madriverinn@ madriver.com), P.O. Box 75, off Route 100, Waitsfield 05673. A house with turn-of-the-century detailing, like fine woodwork and large picture windows with lace etchings in the living room. The 10 guest rooms are furnished with an eye to Victorian fabric, color, and antiques. The house overlooks a gazebo, meadow, and the Mad River, and it's handy to a good swimming hole. Facilities include an outdoor Jacuzzi and a downstairs game room/BYOB bar. Rates from $69 for the smallest room with a

private but hall bath to $125 for the largest with private bath on a weekend; a three-course breakfast and afternoon tea are included. Children welcome. Weddings a specialty.

✍ **Waitsfield Inn** (496-3979; 1-800-758-3801), Waitsfield Village 05673. This Federal-era parsonage in the village is handy to shopping. It offers 14 hand-stenciled, antiques-furnished rooms, varying in size but all with private bath. Two with lofts are good for families. The common rooms are in the former 1839 barn and woodshed, now an attractive area with a huge hearth in front of which warm cider is served. From $79 per room B&B in summer, $89 in winter, $99 weekends; $15 less for singles.

Beaver Pond Farm Inn (583-2861), Warren 05674. Open summer and fall only. This Vermont farmhouse overlooks a beaver pond and the rolling expanse of a golf course. This was Bob and Betty Hansen's vacation home, and now it's a welcoming inn with five guest rooms and an emphasis on good food. $82–118 per couple includes special breakfasts. Dining by reservation ($20–25 prix fixe).

Honeysuckle Inn (496-6200; 1-800-526-2753; e-mail: merritt@madriver. com), RD 1, Box 740, Route 100, Moretown 05660. A 200-year-old Vermont house that rambles back from the road, surrounded by fields. Jerri Merritt's roots in this area are as deep as those of the maples her family taps up the road. There are five guest rooms, two downstairs sharing a bath and three up, two with private bath. $75–15 includes a three-course country breakfast and afternoon tea before the fire.

✍ **The Schultzes' Village Inn** (496-2366), Moretown 05660. On Route 100 in the middle of Moretown village (5 miles north of Waitsfield), John and Annette Schultz maintain a friendly, homey place with six guest rooms, all good for couples and then some. A spa room with whirlpool and sauna overlooks meadows. A good place for children, also for groups who want to do their own cooking. A buffet dinner is served (optional) Saturday night in winter. $25–50 per person, depending on day and season, includes a full breakfast and tax; special children's rates.

The Sugartree Inn (583-3211; 1-800-666-8907; e-mail: sugartree@ madriver.com), Sugarbush Access Road, Warren 05674. This is a modern ski lodge, but Frank and Kathy Partsch have done their utmost to create a country-inn atmosphere. The nine rooms have quilts, canopy and brass beds, and private bath; a large oak-furnished suite has a gas fireplace. Guests gather by the fireplace in the living room, and breakfast is served in the adjoining dining room. Breakfast specials include chocolate chip pancakes. $80–135 per couple B&B.

Weathertop Lodge (496-4909; 1-800-800-3625), Route 17, Box 151, Waitsfield 05673. The atmosphere is that of a ski lodge rather than a country inn, but it's appealing any time of year. The common room has a fieldstone fireplace, stereo, piano, cable TV, video games, and VCR. There's also a fitness center with an array of exercise machines and the hot tub and sauna. The nine rooms are standard—two double beds and a full bath—but Bill and Gail Mulconnery have redecorated with country inn–style fabrics and furnishings. $78–115 per room.

Note: See also Guest House at Knoll Farm under *Entertainment—Farms*.

MOTEL

Wait Farm Motor Inn (496-2033; 1-800-887-2828), Waitsfield 05673. Paul Lavoie's eight motel units, four with kitchenettes, as well as two double rooms in the main house, constitute this friendly family business. $48–68 per couple.

CONDOMINIUMS

The Valley harbors more than 400 rental condominium units, many clustered around Sugarbush (Lincoln Peak), more scattered along the access road, and some squirreled away in the woods. No one reservation service represents them all.

Sugarbush Village Condominiums (583-3333; 1-800-537-8427). The resort manages a total of 250 condominium units in the rental pool, ranging from suites to four-bedroom mountain homes. Winter rates: $300 for a slope-side two-bedroom condominium, from $200 if not slope-side; from $70 per night, $420 per week for a one-bedroom condo in summer.

Sugarbush Resort Condos (583-6100; 1-800-537-8427; fax: 583-3209). A total of 200 units, some slope-side, with health club access. $204–522 in regular season; value season: $118–230.

The Battleground (496-2288; 1-800-248-2102), Route 17, Fayston (Waitsfield) 05673. An unusually attractive cluster of 26 town houses, each designed to face the brook or a piece of greenery, backing into each other and thus preserving most of the 60 acres for walking or ski touring (the area's 60 km network of trails is accessible). In summer there is a pool, tennis, paddle tennis, and a play area for children. Mad River Glen is just up Route 17. Summer rates (2-night minimum) for two-, three-, and four-bedroom units are $135–200 per night, $700–950 per week. In winter: $235–345 per night; $1,140–1,530 per week.

Powderhound Lodge (496-5100; 1-800-548-4022; fax: 496-5163), Route 100, Warren 05674. The old roadside farmstead now serves as reception, living, and dining rooms—with a downstairs pub—for the 44 condo-style apartments clustered in back. Each of these consists of two rooms, one with two beds and another lounging/dining space with two more daybeds and a TV; token cooking facilities. There are also four motel units with phone and TV. It's all nicely designed and maintained, nothing fancy but a good deal for families and couples who like the privacy of their own space with an option to mix with fellow guests. Summer facilities include a swimming pool, a clay tennis court, and lawn games, and there's a hot tub for year-round use, plus a winter shuttle to the mountain. $60–145 in winter, with many 2- and 3-day (also midweek) ski packages; $70 in summer. Pets are $5 per night.

WHERE TO EAT

DINING OUT

Note: The Valley restaurants are unusual in both quality and longevity. Most have been around for quite some time and, like most culinary landmarks, have their good and bad days. A number of inns and B&Bs keep dining logs to which guests contribute their comments. Inquire.

Pitcher Inn (496-6350), Warren Village. Open for dinner and Sunday brunch. The elegant formal dining of this new inn features a menu to match, orchestrated by well-known Vermont chef Tom Bivins. You might begin with potato and leek chowder with smoked Vermont bacon and dine on grilled duck breast with pinot noir and wild mushroom sauce, roasted potatoes, and winter vegetables, or pan-seared medallions of venison loin with a sun-dried tomato–burnt orange brown butter, mustard spaetzle, and winter vegetables. Entrées $20–27. The choice of wines by the glass is large and the wine list itself is long and widely priced.

Chez Henri (583-2600), Sugarbush Village. Open for lunch, brunch, and dinner. (Check in the off-season.) A genuine bistro. In 1963 Henri Borel relinquished his position as food controller for Air France to open this snug, inviting café with a fireplace, marble bar (imported from a Barre soda fountain), and terrace for dining out front in summer. After dinner, the back room becomes a disco, open until 2 AM (nightly in winter, Friday through Sunday in summer). Dinner entrées usually include roast duck with a fruit and pepper sauce ($18.50) and bouillabaisse ($19.50), but most items change frequently so that longtime patrons can always find something new. Lunch on pasta provençal or French onion soup.

Millbrook Inn & Restaurant (496-2405), Route 17, Waitsfield. Open for dinner except April, May, and late October to Thanksgiving. For 20 years Thom Gorman has been the chef and Joan Gorman the pastry chef, hostess, and waitress in their attractive dining room, a double parlor with hearth and French doors opening on a garden. (The couple reenergize during the months they close by hiking, backpacking, kayaking, and camping in the world's far corners). They offer an eclectic, changing menu that might range from eggplant Parmesan to scampi and always includes a fish of the day and an "innkeeper's choice," along with a few Indian dishes, a legacy of Thom's Peace Corps days. We recommend the badami rogan josh, a wonderfully spiced (local) lamb dish. All dinners include Joan's anadama bread, as well as salad and starch—but save room for one of her freshly made pies, cakes, or ice creams. Wine and beer are served. Entrées: $9.95–16.95.

The Spotted Cow (496-5151), Bridge Street Marketplace, Waitsfield. Open for lunch and dinner daily except Monday. Reserve for dinner. This is Jay Young's latest project (Bermuda born and bred, Young owned the Sugarbush Inn for many years, in addition to Jay's in the Mad River Green; see *Eating Out*). Small and stylish, this is very much the current in spot. The Bermuda fish chowder we sampled for lunch was superb. Dinner might be grilled breast of duck with blueberries, port, and wild rice polenta, or sautéed grouper en papillote. Entrées: $15.75–19.50.

The Common Man Restaurant (583-2800), German Flats Road, Warren. Dinner only, closed Monday in the off-season. A mid-19th-century barn hung with chandeliers and warmed by an open hearth, this is another local dining landmark (Mike Ware first opened in 1972), with a respected French chef. Appetizers might include a crab and scallop mousse with a mushroom and white wine sauce and entrées range from ricotta ravioli to a ragout of Vermont venison in ale. Desserts are tempting and the wine list is extensive. Entrées $12–21.

Bass Restaurant (583-3100), Sugarbush Access Road, Warren. Open nightly for dinner. This chef-owned culinary landmark gets high marks for dependable quality. African-raised Beth Bass is in the kitchen and her Athens-born husband, Stratis, oversees the dining room, a stepped space that's pleasantly lit with a long, inviting bar and dining areas decorated with African sculpture. Patrons are presented with a tray of delectable appetizers—dainties like poached salmon quenelles, fava bean paste, and a choice of terrines. Entrées might include slow-roasted lamb shank served with bean cakes and finished with mint (delicious!) and baked eggplant and Swiss chard timbale finished with artichokes and lemon. The dessert tray is fairly irresistible. Entrées: $10.25–18.50.

Michael's Restaurant at the Powderhound (496-3832), Route 100, Warren. Open for dinner Thursday through Sunday. Michael Flanagan, one of the Valley's favorite chefs, has a loyal following, and his latest endeavor is getting rave reviews, featuring "Vermont ingredients, global flavors." It's an eclectic menu, maybe Chiang Mai chicken (free-range local chicken simmered with coconut milk, chiles, and lime juice, served on thin noodles with a variety of mix-in garnishes, $8.50) or pistachio-crusted fresh trout, sautéed with garlic-seared greens, crispy potato cake, and a roasted red pepper sauce ($12.50). The Vermont Vegetable Experience is "a serious, not-for-wimps platter featuring organic produce from our farm partners. I've been cooking for my vegetarian wife for 19 years—trust me on this one."

Giorgio's Cafe (496-3983), Tucker Hill Lodge, Waitsfield. Open for dinner and brunch year-round. Former Italian ski team member Giorgio Noaro hails from Cervinia, Italy, and the menu is rich in antipasti and pastas. The atmosphere is bright, Mediterranean, and informal, and the menu offers dishes like saltimbocca with a sweet Dubonnet demi-sauce over garlic-seared spinach and osso buco in a tomato sauce with white wine. Entrées are $14.95–17.95, but the other specialty of the house is wood-oven pizza (American Flatbread—see *Eating Out*—began here and the oven survives). Live entertainment most Friday nights. Breakfast is also served.

The Warren House Restaurant & Bar (583-2421), Sugarbush Access Road, Warren. Open for dinner daily from 5:30. Formerly Sam Rupert's, this attractive place still offers inviting, low-key bar and fine dining: entrées like Mediterranean roast chicken and smoked Cornish game hen, but you can also sup on a vegetable terrine. Entrées: $7.95–21.95.

EATING OUT

The Den (496-8880), just north of the junction of Routes 100 and 17 in Waitsfield. Open daily for lunch and dinner, sandwiches until 11. The cheerful, pubby heart of the Valley; booths, stained glass, a summer patio. The menu is large and always includes a homemade soup, a wide choice of burgers, and a salad bar; dinner entrées might include a grilled half duckling and jerk pork as well as house steak. A wide selection of beers.

American Flatbread Kitchen (496-8856), at the Lareau Farm Country Inn, Route 100, Waitsfield. Open Friday and Saturday 5:30–9:30, year-round (more or less). George Schenk's distinctive pizza is baked in a primitive, wood-fired oven heated to 800 degrees; the results are distributed to stores from Florida to Chicago. On weekends the kitchen becomes an informal dining space featuring flatbread (toppings include cheese and herb, sun-dried tomato, homemade sausage with mushroom) and exceptional salads whose dressing boasts homemade fruit vinegar. Also specials such as grilled vegetables with garlic-herb sauce, and oven-roasted chicken. Dine in or take out. Beer served. Each night Schenk writes a dedication, always food for thought.

Jay's (496-8282), Mad River Green Shopping Center, Route 100, Waitsfield. Open for breakfast, lunch, dinner, and Sunday brunch. A family restaurant with real flair. The space is bright and spacious, the menu is immense and reasonably priced. Dinner might be chicken pesto, pasta pillows filled with broccoli and Vermont cheddar in a curry cream sauce, or Jay's Giant Burger. Children's menu, pizzas; full liquor license.

Miguel's Stowe-Away (584-3858), Sugarbush Access Road, Warren. Serving meals 5:30–10. An offshoot of Stowe's successful Mexican Stowe-Away. Pollo and pescado augment a choice of fajitas, chiles, enchiladas, and burritos; also good for sopas, ensaladas, and cerveza.

Egan's Big World Pub and Grill (496-5557), Madbush Falls Motel, Route 100, Waitsfield (near the Sugarbush Access Road). Named for local extreme skier John Egan (who skis the world). The atmosphere is casual and lively—a brew pub with booths and a more formal (but not really) dining area: pastas, salads, a great marinated eggplant (served with spinach, red peppers, and Vermont goat cheese), and (winter only) a dynamite Hungarian goulash. Egan's Extreme Ale is the house brew.

Hyde Away Inn (496-2322), Route 17, Waitsfield. Pub open from 4:30, dining room 5:30–9:30. An informal, affordable restaurant with plenty of appetizers and soups, sandwiches, and burgers. The dinner menu might include crab cakes, Mexican lasagne, and broiled salmon, priced from $8.95 and served with homemade bread and salad.

Warren Store (496-3864), Warren Village. Open daily 8–7, Sunday until 6. Year-round the bakery produces French and health breads, plus croissants and great deli food and sandwiches; in summer a deck overlooks the small waterfall.

✎ **Juniper's Fare** (496-5504), Fiddler's Green, off Route 100, Waitsfield. A cheerful, reasonably priced lunch spot featuring healthy soups and sandwiches, salads, and $2.50 children's sandwiches.

Three Mountain Cafe, Mad River Green Shopping Center, Waitsfield. The café and espresso bar features croissants, pastries, and chocolate truffles to go with the coffee.

See also Michael's Restaurant at the Powderhound under *Dining Out.*

ENTERTAINMENT

Green Mountain Cultural Center (496-7722) at the Joslyn Round Barn, Waitsfield. This concert and exhibit space in a classic round barn is the setting for a series of summer concerts, along with workshops and a major foliage-season art exhibit. The **Valley Players** (583-1674), a community theater company, produces three or four plays a year in its own theater just north of Waitsfield Village, Route 100. The **Phantom Theater** (496-5997 in summer), a local group with New York City theater community members, presents original plays and improvisational performances for children and adults at Edgecomb Barn in Warren. Also note **Mad River Chorale** performances in June and December (check with the chamber of commerce: 496-7907). The **Mad River Flick** (496-4200), Route 100 north, Waitsfield: first-run films; wine, snacks served; video games.

APRÈS-SKI

The Blue Tooth (583-2656), Sugarbush Access Road, Warren. A ski season "mountain saloon"; open from 3 PM in ski season for après-ski snacks and drinks, moderately priced dinners, live entertainment, dancing. **Mad Mountain Tavern** (492-2562) and **Gallaghar's Bar & Grill** (496-8800) also offer entertainment (both are at the junction of Routes 17 and 100) and are prime boy-meets-girl scenes.

SELECTIVE SHOPPING

ANTIQUES

Warren Antiques (496-4025), Warren Village. Open daily 10–5 May through October, then by appointment. Victoriana, furniture, ephemera.

Barn-It All Antiques and Collectibles (496-7007), Warren Village. Two stories of nostalgia: furniture, glassware, pottery, and so on.

ART GALLERIES

The Millhouse-Bundy Fine Arts Center (496-5055), Bundy Road (off Route 100), Waitsfield. Open Thursday–Friday 10–4, Saturday 11–6,

Sunday 12–6. An interesting building that offers a mix of good art, in addition to a sculpture garden around and beyond a reflecting pond.

Kristal Gallery (496-6767), East Warren Road. Open year-round, daily 10:30–6. Hanni Saltzman mounts a genuinely interesting mix of oils and watercolors; in summer there's also a sculpture garden.

Parade Gallery (496-5445) in Warren Village offers an affordable selection of prints and original art.

Black Newt Ironworks Sculpture Studio (496-5843), Route 100, Waitsfield Village. A converted town barn and former blacksmith shop is studio space for John Matusz, who sculpts in steel and stone.

Bridge Street Bakery (496-0077), Bridge Street, Waitsfield. Artist owned, a café most notable for its local paintings, prints, and photography (all for sale).

Bridge Street Studio & Gallery (496-4917), Bridge Street, Waitsfield. Artist-owned gallery upstairs in an old hotel.

CRAFTS SHOPS

Tulip Tree Crafts (496-2259), Village Square, Waitsfield. Judy Dodds runs this exceptional store featuring folk art, pottery, antiques, cards, and quilts. Judy herself is a fiber artist, specializing in quilted wall hangings. Her husband silk-screens T-shirts, and the shop offers an unusual variety.

Artisans Gallery (496-6256), Route 100, Waitsfield. Open daily 10–6. A highly selective collection of furniture, baskets, canes, rugs, glass, decoys, ornaments, photography, and much more.

Cabin Fever Quilts (496-2287), the Old Church, Waitsfield. Closed Tuesday, otherwise open 10–5. Machine-sewn, hand-tied quilts come in a range of sizes and patterns, priced $175–400; also pillows, gifts, and quilt fabrics.

Waitsfield Pottery (496-7155), Route 100 across from Bridge Street. Ulrike Tesmer makes functional, hand-thrown stoneware pieces, well worth a stop.

Luminosity Stained Glass Studio (496-2231), the Old Church, Route 100, Waitsfield. This is a very special shop. Since 1975, Barry Friedman has been fashioning Tiffany lampshades and a variety of designs in leaded and stained glass; the shop also carries some interesting jewelry. Items are priced from $15 for great necklaces to $15,000 for an exquisite lamp.

Warren Village Pottery, Warren (across from the covered bridge), displays handcrafted stoneware pieces by Amalia Verrali.

Bradley House in Warren Village showcases work by an amazing variety of local craftspeople. It's a trove of hand-loomed rugs, woven baskets, quilts and pillows, wooden bowls, metalwork, furniture, fabric art, pottery, handblown glass, and more. Open daily.

Baked Beads (496-2440), Route 100 and Bridge Street, Waitsfield. A large and reasonably priced selection of earrings, necklaces, make-your-own jewelry, and funky gifts.

FARM STAND

Hartshorn's Farm Stand (496-5816) sells maple products, Christmas trees, pumpkins, and locally respected produce, and stages a Halloween haunted happening.

SPECIAL SHOPS

Warren Store and More, Warren Village. Staples, wines, and the deli and bakery are downstairs (see *Eating Out*); upstairs is one of Vermont's best-kept secrets, an eclectic selection of clothing, jewelry, and gifts from sources Carol Lippincott has been refining over the past 30 years. We treasure everything we have bought here, from earrings to a winter coat.

Alta (496-ALTA), Route 100, Waitsfield. Laurie Roth Bartlett characterizes this unusual creation as a "day spa": a source of haircuts, manicures and facials, acupuncture, and massage, along with a gift boutique featuring cosmetics, handcrafted jewelry, and fabulous floppy hats.

All Things Bright and Beautiful (496-3397), Bridge Street, Waitsfield. There are an incredible number of stuffed animals and unusual toys on two floors of this old village house.

The Store (496-4465), Route 100, Waitsfield. Since its 1965 opening, this exceptional shop has grown tenfold, now filling two floors of an 1834 meetinghouse with superb Early American, French, and English antiques, cookware, tabletop gifts, collectibles, lifestyle books, Vermont gourmet products, and children's toys and books from around the world.

Mad River Canoe, Inc. (496-3127), Mad River Green, Route 100, Waitsfield. This is the home of the internationally known line of Mad River fiberglass, Kevlar, and Royalex canoes.

Tempest Book Shop (496-2022), Village Square, Waitsfield. This family-run bookstore is a trove of titles in most categories, including children's books. We like their motto: "A house without books is like a room without windows" (Horace Mann).

SUGARHOUSES

Eastman Long & Sons (496-3448), Tucker Hill Road, Waitsfield. "Sonny" Long sets 6,000 taps high on 100 wooded acres that have been in his family for generations. He maintains that the higher the elevation, the better the syrup, and he welcomes visitors to his roadside sugarhouse (featuring a new Vermont-made, totally lead-free evaporator and two reverse osmosis machines used to reduce the sap by 70 percent) during sugaring season. "A sugarmaker has to be a plumber and electrician these days," Long jokes, relating hair-raising stories of what one small animal can to to an intricate web of tubing, at night, in the middle of a sap flow. "On summer weekends, I sit in my van and sell syrup down at the junction of Route 100 and 17 for far less than anyone can buy it at local stores," he says, "and still people tell me I'm charging too much."

Merritt Family Sugar House (496-3268; 1-800-52-MAPLE), Cox Brook Road off Route 100, Moretown. A 50-acre sugarbush; visitors welcome (please call ahead). See also Honeysuckle Inn under *Lodging—Bed & Breakfasts*.

Palmer's Maple Products (496-3675), East Warren Road, Waitsfield. Delbert and Sharlia Palmer sell syrup from their farm on this scenic road.

SPECIAL EVENTS

Note: Check with the chamber of commerce (see *Guidance*) and its web site (www.sugarbushchamber.org) for weekly listings of special events.

February: **Winter Carnival,** Sugarbush.

March: Annual **New England Telemark Festival,** Mad River Glen.

April: **Sugarbush Triathlon**—canoe, kayak, bicycle, cross-country-ski races (more than 400 competitors), Sugarbush.

July 4: Outstanding **parade,** Warren Village.

July and August: **Summer productions** by the Valley Players and by the Phantom Theater (see *Entertainment*). **Vermont Summer Horse-show** at Sugarbush and **Green Mountain Polo Tournament,** Warren.

August: **Vermont Festival of the Arts** runs 10 days throughout the Valley.

Labor Day weekend: 2-day **crafts exhibits**.

Early October: **Soaring Encampment** throughout the Valley. **Sugarbush Antique Car Show.**

December: **Christmas celebrations** throughout the Valley.

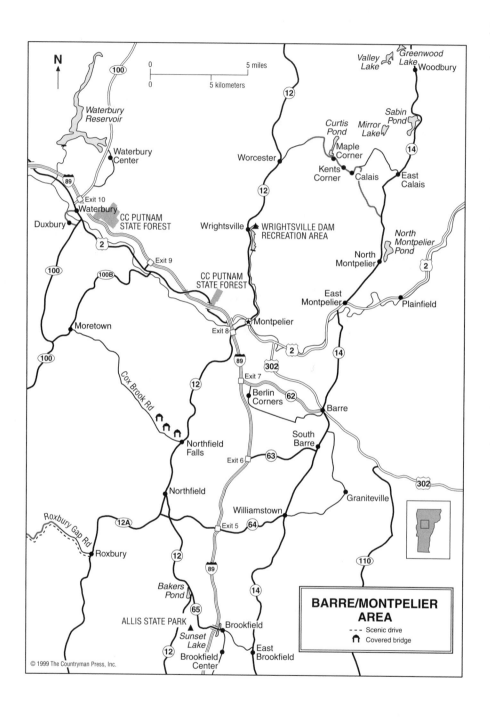

N

0 _____ 5 miles
0 _____ 5 kilometers

Waterbury Reservoir

Valley Lake   Greenwood Lake   Woodbury

100

Sabin Pond

Waterbury Center

Curtis Pond   Mirror Lake

Worcester   Maple Corner

14

89

Exit 10
Waterbury

12

Kents Corner   Calais   East Calais

Duxbury

CC PUTNAM STATE FOREST

Wrightsville   WRIGHTSVILLE DAM RECREATION AREA

North Montpelier Pond

2

Exit 9

North Montpelier

2

100   100B

CC PUTNAM STATE FOREST

East Montpelier   Plainfield

Moretown

Montpelier   14

100   Exit 8

89

2

Cox Brook Rd

12   302

Exit 7

Berlin Corners   62   Barre

Northfield Falls   South Barre

Exit 6   63

Northfield   Graniteville

302

Roxbury Gap Rd   12A   Williamstown

Exit 5   64

110

Roxbury   12

89   14

Bakers Pond   65   BARRE/MONTPELIER AREA

ALLIS STATE PARK   Brookfield

- - - Scenic drive

Sunset Lake   Covered bridge

12   Brookfield Center   East Brookfield

© 1999 The Countryman Press, Inc.

Barre/Montpelier Area

Montpelier is the smallest and possibly the most livable of the nation's state capitals. It is a town of fewer than 9,000 people, with band concerts on summer Wednesdays, high school playing fields just a few blocks from the capitol, and a bus depot so small that patrons frequently wait on the sidewalk. The gold dome of the statehouse itself is appropriately crowned by a green hill rising steeply behind it, and unless you follow the commercial strip along Route 302 to Barre, you are quickly out in the country—in the wooded Worcester Range to the north or the wilderness to the west; East Montpelier is a crossroads village.

Any attempt to understand the character of Vermont entails a visit to Montpelier: a stroll through the Vermont Museum (an extraordinary collection of things past, housed in a replica of a steamboat Gothic hotel) and into the fine statehouse built of Vermont granite and marble. The surrounding 19th-century brick business and state office buildings harbor an increasing number of good restaurants and pleasant shops.

Precisely why this narrow floodplain of the Winooski was selected as Vermont's statehouse site in 1805 is uncertain, as is why it was named for a small city in the Languedoc region of France. The fact is, however, that Vermont's first legislators picked a town noted for its unusual number of whiskey distilleries and named it for a town best known for its wine and brandy. It's also true that Montpelier is unusually accessible, by roads both old and new, from every corner of central and northern Vermont.

A city of 9,900 people, surrounded by a town of 7,000, Barre (pronounced *Barry*) is larger than Montpelier, to which it is linked via the 5-mile commercial strip of Route 302. Barre's Main Street is a perpetual bottleneck, and motorists caught in it may ponder the conspicuous absence of granite in the facades of the commercial buildings, most of which date from the 1880–1910 period when Barre became known far and wide for granite memorials. During that era, the community's population jumped tenfold, swollen by stonecutters and craftsmen from Scotland, eastern Europe, Italy, and French Canada, not to mention England, Scandinavia, Spain, Germany, and the Middle East—a volatile mix of largely underpaid workers who elected a socialist mayor and were not afraid to strike for their rights or to shelter victims of strikes elsewhere. Around the time of World War I, the famous anarchist and feminist Emma Goldman was arrested here. The quarries continue to employ some 2,000 people.

The granite quarries are southeast of town, primarily in Granite-ville, where Millstone Hill has been chipped and chiseled since 1812, when the bedrock was turned into millstones, door stoops, and posts. In the 1830s, huge slabs were hauled by oxen to build the statehouse. It was only after the Civil War that the railway and a series of inventions enabled Barre to make its mark. The memorial stone business esca-lated after 1888, when the branch railroad finally linked the quarries to finishing sheds in the valley and to outlets beyond. Today, Barre contin-ues to produce one-third of the country's memorial stones, for which its own Mount Hope Cemetery serves as a museum. All but one of the major quarries are owned by Rock of Ages, a company that has long made its operations a showcase for visitors, who can view the unforget-table, surrealistic landscape of the quarries themselves, hear the roar of the drills, and watch ant-sized men chip away at the giant pits.

GUIDANCE

Central Vermont Chamber of Commerce (229-5711), 33 Stewart Road, Berlin 05602.

Vermont Chamber of Commerce (223-3443), www.centralvt.com, Box 37, Montpelier 05601, is located off I-89, exit 7, near the junction of the access road with Airport Road in Berlin. Open 9–5 weekdays.

Vermont Department of Tourism (828-3237; 1-800-VERMONT) has its main information center at 134 State Street, Montpelier. It's open 7 AM–8 PM weekdays.

GETTING THERE

By bus: **Vermont Transit** from Boston to Montreal, connecting with New York and Connecticut service, stops in Montpelier.

By train: See **Amtrak** in "What's Where."

By air: Eastern Express to Knapp Airport in Berlin; flights from Boston.

Ground transfers: **Norm's Taxi** (223-5226); **Limousine by Jules** (476-8658, 476-6845).

MEDICAL EMERGENCY

Barre (476-6675); Montpelier (911); Northfield (485-6666). **Central Ver-mont Medical Center** (229-9121), Berlin (off Route 62; exit 7 off I-89).

VILLAGE

Northfield. This town's mid-19th-century commercial blocks suggest the prosperity that it enjoyed while native son Charles Paine served as governor. Paine actually railroaded the Vermont Central through his hometown instead of the more logical Barre. The old depot, now a bank, stands at one end of the handsome common. Today, the town's pride is Norwich University, a private, coed college of 1,000 cadets, which bills itself as "the oldest private military college in the United States." In the Norwich University Museum in White Memorial Chapel, you learn that this institution sent more than 300 officers into the Civil War. It wasn't until 1867, however, that the college moved to Northfield from its original site in Norwich. More Northfield memorabilia as well as changing exhibits can be seen in the Northfield Historical Society Museum housed in the Old Red Brick Schoolhouse, Stagecoach Road (open June through Labor Day, Sunday 2–5).

TO SEE

Vermont Statehouse (828-2228), State Street, Montpelier. Open Monday through Friday 8–4, closed holidays. Friends of the Vermont Statehouse offers tours Monday through Friday 10–3:30, Saturday 11–2:30, July through mid-October, when the gift shop is open; otherwise by appointment. In 1805, when Montpelier was chosen as the "permanent seat of the legislature for holding all their sessions," it was on the condition that the town give land for the capitol and get it built by 1808. The resulting building was nine-sided, of three stories, with a cupola, and warmed by a two-story stove. Legislators sat on plank seats at pine desks that were said to have been "whittled out of use" by the representatives' jackknives. The whole building had to be demolished in 1836 and was replaced by a granite Grecian temple designed by the Federal-era architect Ammi Young. After it was virtually destroyed by fire, it was rebuilt along the same but larger lines and completed in 1857. Visitors are welcome to watch the legislature in action, January through mid-April. Note that the 150 state representatives and senators talk with their constituents while standing in the Hall of Flags or seated on the black walnut sofas (which cost $60 apiece in 1859) at either end. Larkin Mead's statue of Ethan Allen on the steps is Danby marble, and the handsome black-and-white floor of the lobby was quarried on Isle La Motte. The lobby is lined with portraits of Vermont-born heroes including Adm. George Dewey, Adm. Charles Clark (like Dewey, a hero of the Spanish-American War), and Calvin Coolidge, 30th president of the United States. Note especially the enormous oil painting by Julien Scott, *The Battle of Cedar Creek, 1864.* The cannon on the front steps was captured from the Hessians at the Battle of Bennington in 1777. The Roman lady atop the gold-leafed dome is Ceres, goddess of agriculture, also sculpted by Larkin Mead.

The Vermont Historical Society Museum (828-2291), 109 State Street, Montpelier. Open weekdays except Monday, year-round 9–4:30; weekends also during July, August, and foliage season, 10–5. Admission is $2 adults, $1 students and seniors. This outstanding state museum is maintained by the Vermont Historical Society and housed on the ground floor of the replica of the Pavilion Hotel, which occupied this site between

The Vermont Statehouse in Montpelier

1870 and 1966. Children and adults alike can enjoy the recently redesigned displays dramatizing Vermont history, and relics ranging from the
state's first printing press to Ethan Allen's gun. There are also changing
exhibits, an impressive Victorian parlor, a small gift store, and a large,
excellent library of sourcebooks and genealogies.

T. W. Wood Art Gallery at the Vermont College Art Center (828-
8743), College Street, Montpelier, open Tuesday through Sunday noon–
4. The gallery displays Civil War–era art by local artist Thomas
Waterman Wood and has excellent shows of contemporary Vermont
artists and craftspeople. Admission $2.

Mural of Vermont Life, National Life Insurance building, Montpelier.

This huge mural fills a wall of the lobby of the home office of National Life Insurance (founded by Admiral Dewey's father) on Memorial Drive, just off I-89; open weekdays 9–4:30. It is a monumental piece, by Paul Sample, depicting the sweep of the state's present and past.

Barre Opera House (476-8188), corner of Prospect and Main Streets, Barre. Built in 1899, after fire destroyed its predecessor, this elegant, acoustically outstanding, recently restored theater occupies the second and third floors of City Hall. Performances are scheduled mid-April through mid-October.

Barre Historical Society Museum (476-7550), Aldrich Library, 6 Washington Street, Barre. An outstanding collection of 19th-century paintings, furnishings, and articles relating to Barre's stormy labor history are displayed upstairs in this unusually fine library; open by appointment. The collection, but not the archives, may be in storage in 1999 while the historical society renovates the Old Labor Hall.

Rock of Ages Quarry Complex (476-3119), 773 Main Street, Graniteville. Here, in what is probably Vermont's most dramatic attraction, you'll find the "Rock of ages, cleft for me . . ." hymn running through your head. From the observation deck of the Manufacturing Division (formerly the Craftsmen Center), you'll see stone polished and sculpted into memorials. Open year-round, Monday through Friday 8–3:30. The Visitors Reception Center, a mile up the road, is open May through October weekdays 8:30–5 and has displays explaining the geology of granite; a path leads you the short way out back to the state's oldest, 27-acre-wide quarry. Free, self-guided tours; narrated tours for a modest fee. From June through mid-October, an open-car shuttle departs every half hour, 9:30–3:30, for the working quarries farther up the hill.

In the **Mount Hope Cemetery,** Route 14 just north of Barre, the memorials that stonecutters have sculpted for themselves and their families are among the most elaborate to be found anywhere in the world.

Goddard College (454-8311), Plainfield. Founded in 1863, this is a progressive college with several buildings designed by students. Frequent live entertainment, films, concerts.

✐ **East Roxbury Fish Hatchery,** 2 miles south of Roxbury on Route 12A. This is a state hatchery in which salmon species are raised; children are allowed to feed the fish.

COVERED BRIDGES

Off Route 12 to Northfield Falls stand three covered bridges: the **Station Bridge,** spanning 100 feet, and the **Newell Bridge** are within sight of each other; farther along Cox Brook Road is the **Upper Bridge,** with a span of 42 feet.

SCENIC DRIVE

Roxbury to Warren. The road through Roxbury Gap, while not recommended in winter (when it's usually closed), is spectacular in summer and fall, commanding a breathtaking view of the Green Mountains from the crest of the Roxbury Range. Do not resist the urge to stop, get out, and enjoy this panorama. Ask locally about the hiking trail that follows the ridgeline from the road's highest point.

TO DO

BOATING AND FISHING

Wrightsville Dam, just north of Montpelier; **North Montpelier Pond,** with a fishing access off Route 14; and **Curtis Pond** and **Mirror Lake** in Calais (pronounced *Callus*). **Nelson Pond** and **Sabin Pond** in Woodbury are both accessible from Route 14, as are **Valley Lake** and **Greenwood Lake** (good for bass and pike). The **Stevens Branch** south of Barre offers brook trout.

GOLF

Montpelier Elks Country Club (223-7457), Country Club Road, Montpelier, nine holes. **Barre Country Club** (476-7658), Plainfield Road, Barre, 18 holes. **Northfield Country Club** (485-4515), Roxbury Road, Northfield, nine holes.

HIKING

Guidance: The **Green Mountain Club** (244-7037), RR 1, Box 650, Route 100, Waterbury Center 05677. Encourages general inquiries and trail description updates (see *Hiking* in "What's Where").

Spruce Mountain, Plainfield. An unusually undeveloped state holding of 500 acres, rich in bird life. The trail begins in Jones State Forest, 4.2 miles south of the village; the 3-hour hike is described in *50 Hikes in Vermont* (Backcountry) and in *Day Hiker's Guide to Vermont* (Green Mountain Club).

Worcester Range, north of Montpelier. There are several popular hikes described in the above books, notably **Elmore Mountain** in Elmore State Park (a 3-mile trek yielding a panorama of lakes, farms, and rolling hills), **Mount Worcester** (approached from the village of Worcester), and **Mount Hunger.**

Green Mountain Outdoor Adventures (229-4246), HCR 32, Box 90, Montpelier 05602, provides equipment and information on trails.

Outdoor Bound of Vermont (223-4172; 1-800-639-9208), P.O. Box 135, Calais 05648, provides equipment and arranges inn-to-inn tours.

HORSEBACK RIDING

Breckenridge Farm (476-8077), RR 1, Box 3490, Barre. **East Hill Farm** (479-0858), Plainfield, year-round lessons, no trail rides. **Whispering Winds Farm** (496-2819), South Hill, Moretown.

SWIMMING

Wrightsville Dam Recreation Area, Route 12 north; also numerous swimming holes in the Kents Corner area.

CROSS-COUNTRY SKIING

Montpelier Elks Ski Touring Center: Contact Onion River Sports, Inc.

Stone cutters' memorials at Hope Cemetery in Barre

(229-9409), 20 Langdon Street, Montpelier. This facility uses gently rolling golf course terrain and offers 10 km of set trails, instruction, rentals, food.

FITNESS
Wedgewood (223-6161), Granger Road, Berlin, has tennis, racquetball, swimming.

GREEN SPACE

Hubbard Park. More than 110 acres in the upper reaches of Montpelier; primarily leafy, windy roads, good for biking, jogging.

LODGING

INNS
Capitol Plaza (223-5252; 1-800-274-5252), 100 State Street, Montpelier 05602. The former landmark Tavern, thoroughly renovated after flood damage, is a full-service hotel with a two-tiered café and conference facilities. Its executive suite includes a large bedroom, Jacuzzi, optional living and dining room, and adjoining second bedroom. From $82 for a regular double room, to $99 for a Colonial queen, to $149 for a suite (higher in foliage season).

The Hollow Inn and Motel (479-9313; 1-800-998-9444), 278 South Main Street, Barre 05641. Jack Galloway's impressive, 41-room establishment combines the amenities of a suburban hotel with the convenience of a motel. From the south, use I-89, exit 6, to Route 14, then go 0.5 mile north; from Barre and north, it's 1 mile south of the center of the city. The outdoor heated pool and Jacuzzi are surrounded by plantings, wood fences, and a natural stone wall, and the facility boasts a summer kitchen and gas grill. The indoor Swallow Relaxation Center is equipped with whirlpool, sauna, and fitness gear. All of the rooms have VCR as well as TV, and videotapes can be rented. Fifteen rooms in the inn have microwave and refrigerator. Double room rates: $67–85 in the motel units, $75–100 (for a suite) in the inn ($5 less for single), depending on the season, including continental breakfast.

The Autumn Harvest Inn & Restaurant (433-1355), Clark Road, Williamstown 05679, Route 64 east from exit 5 off I-89. Perched on a knoll with a panoramic view across rolling pastures to distant ridges, Autumn Harvest—a 46-acre horse farm—with Carolyn White as innkeeper has 18 guest rooms that are cheerful and comparatively plain (a refreshing change from so many other inn rooms that have been overdraped with Laura Ashley and other flowery fabrics), all with private bath and TV. Willow, on the ground floor, is equipped for the handicapped. One of the two semi-suites has a fireplace; Pine is the prettier. There's a big fireplace in the spacious living room, and two dining rooms are open to the public (see *Dining Out*). Guests enjoy the swimming pond, two night-lit tennis courts, and horseback riding in summer; sleigh rides and 27 miles of cross-country-ski trails in winter. Rates: $69–139 EP.

Comfort Inn at Maplewood (229-2222; 1-800-228-5150), RR 4, Box 2110, Montpelier 05602. Take exit 7 off I-89 for 0.2 mile. This handsome and relatively new motor inn has 89 rooms, 18 two-room suites with kitchenette, and a VIP suite with kitchenette and whirlpool. Rates are $59 single, $69 double, suites $99–210 ($10 more during foliage season), with continental breakfast.

BED & BREAKFASTS

The Inn at Montpelier (223-2727), 147 Main Street, Montpelier 05602. Vermont's capital city has an exceptional, truly capital place to stay. Two stately, adjacent Federal houses have been beautifully renovated and luxuriously furnished by Maureen and Bill Russell. Amenities include central air-conditioning, downstairs guest pantries for coffee and tea at any hour, in-room cable TV, bar service, small conference facilities. A marvelous Colonial Revival veranda wraps around the brick Lamb-Langdon house for relaxing in mild weather. Of the 19 rooms, the deluxe chambers with fireplaces ($155) are just about the most handsome guest quarters in the state. The smaller king-, queen-, and twin-bedded rooms from $99 (more in foliage season) are also lovely; all with private bath and continental breakfast. Children over 10 welcome; no pets.

Cherry Tree Hill (223-0549), Cherry Tree Hill Road, East Montpelier 05651, is a restored Dutch-roofed farmhouse with views, a pool, greenhouse breakfast room, and a studio with yarns, hand-knit jackets, and refinished antiques. $60–100.

Evergreen's Chalet (223-5156), Box 41, Calais 05648, has three bedrooms and two baths, and miles of nature, cross-country, and snowmobile trails. From $35 per person.

✍ **Betsy's Bed & Breakfast** (229-0466), 74 East State Street, Montpelier 05602, is an impressive, restored Queen Anne house in the town's historic district. With added Victorian house providing 12 rooms with private baths, cable TV, and phone (with voice mail and data ports); five suites with full kitchens; exercise room; generous breakfasts. $55–85 ($10 additional during foliage season) double, with discounts for 3 nights or more. Children welcome, but no pets.

The Northfield Inn (485-8558), 27 Highland Avenue, Northfield 05663. A beautifully renovated, grand old 1902 hillside mansion, nicely landscaped with a gazebo overlooking the town and comfortable guest rooms that can be combined into family suites. Antiques, brass or carved-wood beds, European feather bedding. From $55 single to $140 for a suite, including hearty country breakfast.

WHERE TO EAT

DINING OUT

🏵 **The Chef's Table** (229-9902), 118 Main Street, Montpelier. Open for dinner 6–10, Monday through Saturday. The New England Culinary Institute shuttered its marvelous Tubbs Restaurant in 1995 and reopened this upscale, upstairs establishment over the Main Street Grill and Bar (see *Eating Out*). Student chefs and instructors ply their craft in the new location as in the old, but some of the panache is missing. The main courses may include sautéed shrimp and scallops or hickory-smoked duck under a Bourbon giblet gravy. Moderate to expensive (there's a $30 tasting menu).

A Single Pebble (476-9700), 135 Barre-Montpelier Road, northeast side near Twin City Lanes, Berlin. Closed Sunday and Monday and all of August. Classic Chinese dinners here are outstanding, probably the best in the state. The imaginative menu (mock eel made from shiitake mushrooms, for instance, and fried green beans) is designed for group enjoyment, with many dishes hot from the wok. Reservations strongly recommended. Unusually moderate prices considering the exceptional quality.

The Autumn Harvest Inn & Restaurant (433-1355), Route 64, Williamstown. The superb views from the main dining room and wraparound porch complement dinners here Tuesday through Saturday. One could begin with baked stuffed mushrooms or crab cakes with honey mustard sauce, and follow with mushrooms Alfredo over linguine, honey Dijon chicken, bay scallops, or duck with cranberry Armagnac glaze. Moderate.

EATING OUT

The Main Street Grill and Bar (223-3188), 118 Main Street, Montpelier, the New England Culinary Institute's nouveau version of the former Elm Street Cafe, is roomier—also as crowded but noisier—serving breakfast, lunch, and dinner; brunch on Sunday. The carvery is fine. Bistro menu at the downstairs bar.

Sarducci's (223-0229), 3 Main Street, Montpelier. Open Monday through Saturday 11:30 AM–midnight; Sunday 4–midnight. Above-average Italian dishes blossom in this very popular, spacious, columned, yellow-walled restaurant with an open wood-fired oven. There's an extensive menu of daily specials, antipasti, customized pizzas, salads, and 18 pasta choices, including shrimp with angel hair, tomatoes, and garlic ($6.95). At dinner, several chicken, salmon, and veal selections are added. Inexpensive to moderate.

Fiddleheads (229-2244), 54 State Street, Montpelier. Roasted vegetable crêpes, grilled coconut chicken, and other imaginative dishes distinguish this newcomer. Moderate.

Horn of the Moon Café (223-2985), 8 Langdon Street, Montpelier. Open Monday 7–3; Tuesday through Saturday 7–9; Sunday 10–2. Smoking and sugar are out; innovative, vegetarian dishes are definitely in: Herb teas, local organic products, wheat bread, pancakes, tofu, soups, and salads predominate on the inexpensive menu. Beer and wine served.

La Brioche Bakery & Cafe (229-0443), City Center, Main Street, Montpelier, is another tasty offspring of the New England Culinary Institute.

Country House Restaurant (476-4282), 276 North Main Street, Barre, serves modestly priced Italian specialties at lunch and dinner Monday through Saturday.

Green Mountain Diner (476-6292), 240 North Main, Barre. Open Monday through Friday 6 AM–9 PM; Saturday 6 AM–7 PM; Sunday 6 AM–2 PM. Friendly booths, a blackboard menu with specials like stew and Spanish pork chops; beer and wine served.

ENTERTAINMENT

The Onion River Arts Council (229-9408) arranges various kinds of performing arts events (see *Special Events*). See also the Barre Opera House under *To See.*

FILM

Savoy (229-0509), 26 Main Street, Montpelier, presents art films.

Capitol (229-0343), 93 State Street, Montpelier, is a duplex showing feature films.

Paramount (479-9621), 241 North Main Street, Barre, shows feature films.

THEATER

Barre Opera House (476-8188), corner of Prospect and Main Streets (see *To See*).

Lost Nation Theatre Company (229-0492), 128 Elm Street, Montpelier. Periodically stages plays by a professional troupe.

SELECTIVE SHOPPING

ARTISANS

Thistle Hill Pottery (223-8926), Powder Horn Glen Road, Montpelier, is Jennifer Boyd's functional cobalt stoneware studio.

Mary Azarian (464-8087) has opened the **Farmhouse Press** in Plainfield as a studio shop featuring her woodcut prints, cards, paintings, and books.

BOOKSTORES

Bear Pond Books (229-0774), 77 Main Street, Montpelier. One of the state's most inviting bookstores, heavy on literature, art, and children's books; authors' readings.

Rivendell Books (223-3928), 100 Main Street, Montpelier, features a wide stock of new books for adults and children at discount, plus selected remainders and some interesting used titles.

Capitol Stationers (223-2393), 54 Main Street, Montpelier, includes new books, with a strong Vermont and New England section.

Annie's Bookstore (442-5059), Main Street, Barre, has a personally selected stock of new books for adults and children.

Barre Books (476-3114), 158 North Main Street, Barre, has a good array of general books.

ARTS AND CRAFTS SHOPS

The Art Gallery of Barre (476-1030), 171 North Main Street, Barre, sponsored by the Paletteers, a group of central Vermont artists. Open Tuesday through Friday and Saturday morning; but call ahead in winter.

The Artisans' Hand (229-9492), City Center, 89 Main Street, Montpelier. Open Monday through Saturday 10–5. An exceptional variety of quality Vermont craftwork by a cooperative of some 125 artisans in many media.

SPECIAL SHOPS

Woodbury Mountain Toys (223-4272), 24 Main Street, Montpelier. This independent specialty toy store carries major lines and some locally made items.

Morse Farm (223-2740), County Road (the western extension of Main Street), Montpelier. Open daily, year-round except holidays. The farm itself has been in the same family for three generations. This is a place to come watch sugaring off in March; a large farm stand sells Vermont crafts and cheese as well as produce in summer and fall; Christmas greens in December. Sugar on snow.

Bragg Farm (223-5757), Route 14, East Montpelier. Open daily, March 15 through December 24, for maple products, Vermont crafts.

Danforth's Sugarhouse (229-9536), Route 2, East Montpelier. A fourth-generation sugaring operation and maple product gift shop open daily year-round.

Knight's Spider Web Farm (433-5568), off Route 14 on Cliff Place, Williamstown Village. Open daily 9–6; January through March by appointment. In-season, visitors can see spider webs being collected and mounted; gifts and pine accessories.

SPECIAL EVENTS

Early June: **Vermont Dairy Celebration,** statehouse lawn in Montpelier.

June through August: **Montpelier City Band Concerts,** statehouse lawn Wednesday at 4 PM.

July: **Midsummer Art and Music Festival,** Vermont College campus, Montpelier, sponsored by the Onion River Arts Council (229-9408).

Labor Day weekend: In Northfield, pageant, parade of floats, and Norwich cadets.

Late September: **Old Time Fiddlers' Contest,** Barre Auditorium—one of the oldest contests, attracting some of the East's best fiddlers.

Early October: **Vermont Apple Celebration,** statehouse lawn, Montpelier.

Late October: **Festival of Vermont Crafts,** Montpelier High School (call Central Vermont Chamber of Commerce, 229-5711).

December 31: **First Night** celebrations, Montpelier.

IV. LAKE CHAMPLAIN VALLEY

Rutland and the Lower Champlain Valley
Addison County and Environs
Burlington Region
The Northwest Corner

KIM GRANT

Sunset at Perkins Pier on Lake Champlain

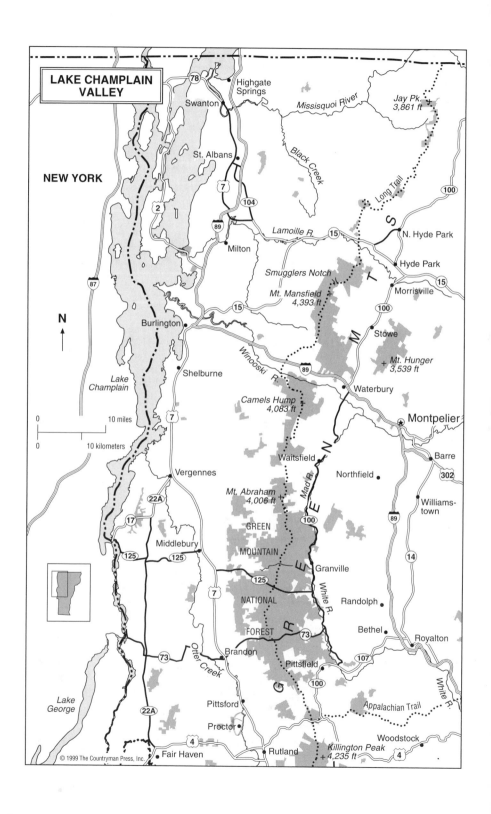

LAKE CHAMPLAIN
VALLEY

NEW YORK

Highgate
Springs

78

Swanton

Missisquoi River

Jay Pk.
3,861 ft

St. Albans

Black Creek

Long Trail

7

104

100

2

89

Lamoille R.

15

N. Hyde Park

Milton

Hyde Park

Smugglers Notch

Morrisville

15

Mt. Mansfield
4,393 ft

100

N

Burlington

Winooski R.

Stowe

Mt. Hunger
3,539 ft

89

Lake
Champlain

Shelburne

Waterbury

Camels Hump
4,083 ft

Montpelier

0   10 miles

7

Waitsfield

Barre

0   10 kilometers

Vergennes

Northfield

302

22A

Mt. Abraham
4,006 ft

Mad R.

Williams-
town

17

89

GREEN

100

14

125

Middlebury

MOUNTAIN

Granville

White R.

125

125

125

Randolph

7

NATIONAL

Bethel

Royalton

73

73

FOREST

107

Brandon

Otter Creek

Pittsfield

100

Lake
George

Pittsford

Appalachian Trail

White R.

22A

Proctor

Woodstock

4

Killington Peak
4,235 ft

4

© 1999 The Countryman Press, Inc.   Fair Haven   Rutland

Rutland and the Lower Champlain Valley

Rutland, Vermont's second largest city (Rutland County has a population of some 61,000), is more than just a convenient commercial adjunct to the Killington-Pico ski resorts. Stolid, early-Victorian mansions and streets crisscrossed with railroad tracks testify to its 19th-century prosperity—when Rutland was known as "the marble city"—and it has retained its industrial base.

Today, city fathers are trying hard to reconstitute the downtown core, buoyed by the return of railroad passenger service. The daily *Rutland Herald,* the oldest newspaper in the state, continues to win frequent journalism awards.

The long-established shops along Merchant Row and Center Street have held their own in recent years and number upward of 100 within just a few square blocks; they include some genuinely interesting newcomers. This is, moreover, a good restaurant town.

Rutland is the business and shopping center for the Lower Champlain Valley, a broad, gently rolling corridor between New York State and the Green Mountains. In contrast to the rest of the state, this valley is actually broad enough to require two major north–south routes. Route 7 is the busier highway. It hugs the Green Mountains and, with the exception of the heavily trafficked strip around Rutland, is a scenic ride. Route 30 on the west is a far quieter way through farm country and by two major lakes, Lake Bomoseen and Lake St. Catherine, both popular summer meccas.

Route 4 is the major east–west road, a four-lane highway from Fair Haven, at the New York line, to Rutland, where it angles north through the middle of town before turning east again, heading uphill to Killington. Route 140 from Wallingford to Poultney is the other old east–west road here, a quiet enough byway through Middletown Springs, where the old mineral waters form the core of a pleasant park.

GUIDANCE

The Rutland Region Chamber of Commerce (773-2747; 1-800-756-8880; www.rutlandvermont.com), 256 North Main Street, Rutland 05701; visitors center (775-0831) at the junction of Routes 7 and 4,

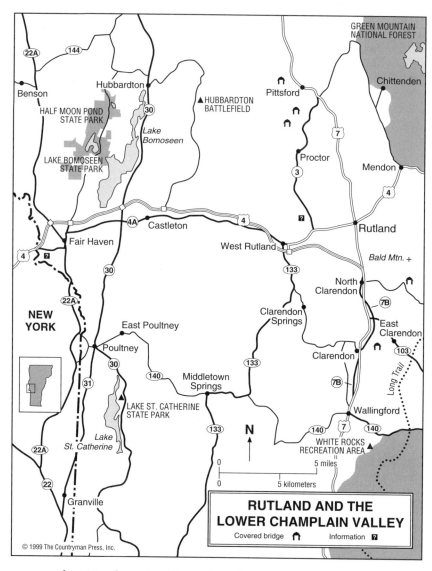

RUTLAND AND THE
LOWER CHAMPLAIN VALLEY
Covered bridge   Information

© 1999 The Countryman Press, Inc.

open late May through mid-October. The chamber supplies an illustrated *Visitor's Guide*. The self-guided *Views through Time: A Walking Tour of Historic Downtown Rutland* has been published by the Rutland Area Cultural Alliance and is available for $2 in various locations, including the Chaffee Art Center (see *Museums*) and the Book King (see *Selective Shopping—Bookstores*). There's a companion driving guide for the area, too.

The Vermont Office of Vacation Travel maintains a Welcome Center (open 8:30–5:30) on Route 4 near the New York line.

Lakes Region Marketing Corporation (1-800-655-4213; www.gwriters.com/lakes.html), P.O. Box 196, Poultney 05764.

Area Chambers of Commerce: Fair Haven (265-3855); Poultney (287-2010).

GETTING THERE

By train: **Amtrak** (1-800-USA-RAIL). Daily service to and from New York City on the *Ethan Allen Express.*

By air: **Colgan Air** (1-800-523-3273; 1-800-523-FARE), Continental Connection with daily service to Logan International Airport, Boston.

By car: Routes 7 and 4; Route 103 from Bellows Falls.

By bus: **Vermont Transit,** from Albany, Boston, and other points.

GETTING AROUND

By bus: **Marble Valley Regional Transit District** (773-3244). "The Bus" connects Killington, Castleton, the Rutland airport, and other points in the area.

MEDICAL EMERGENCY

Rutland Regional Ambulance Service (911); **Rutland Fire Department Rescue Paramedics** (911); **Rutland Regional Medical Center Fast Track Emergency Service** (747-3601), 160 Allen Street. *Rescue squads:* Fair Haven/Castleton (265-8800); Poultney (287-9510); Pittsford (773-1700); Wallingford (775-5555).

VILLAGES

Fair Haven, located where Routes 4, 4A, and 22A intersect, is at the core of Vermont's slate industry. One of its earliest developers in the 1780s was the controversial Matthew Lyon, who started an ironworks and published a newspaper called *The Scourge of Aristocracy,* in which he lambasted the Federalists. Elected to Congress in 1796, Lyon had scuffles on the floor of the House and criticized President Adams so violently that he was arrested and jailed under the Alien and Sedition Act. Lyon's case caused such a national uproar that this patently unconstitutional censorship law was soon rescinded. Lyon was reelected to Congress while still in jail and took his seat in time to cast the tie-breaking vote that made Thomas Jefferson president instead of Aaron Burr.

Around the spacious green are three Victorian mansions (two faced with marble) built by descendants of Ira Allen, founder of the University of Vermont.

Poultney, on Route 30, the home of Green Mountain College, also has significant journalistic associations: Horace Greeley, founder of the *New York Tribune,* lived at the venerable Eagle Tavern in East Poultney while he was learning the printing trade at the East Poultney *National Spectator* in the 1820s (and organizing a local temperance society). Working with him was George Jones, who helped to found the *New York Times* in 1851.

It's **East Poultney** that's the picturesque village worth detouring to see. The fine white Baptist church, built in 1805, is the centerpiece, standing on a small green surrounded by late-18th- and early-19th-century houses. The general store is also a classic and a source of good deli sandwiches. Its picnic benches are within earshot of the Poultney River, here a fast-flowing stream.

Castleton, at Routes 4A and 30, has triple historical significance: Ethan Allen and Seth Warner planned the capture of Ticonderoga here; on a nearby hill in Hubbardton, Colonel Warner's scrubby militiamen made a valiant rear-guard stand while halting the British invasion force on July 7, 1777, the only Revolutionary War battle actually fought on Vermont soil; and the town itself is a showcase of Greek Revival houses. One offshoot of the conspiratorial meeting in Remington's Tavern in 1775 was the exploit of the blacksmith Samuel Beach—Vermont's own Paul Revere—who reputedly ran some 60 miles in 24 hours to recruit more men from the countryside for the raid on Ticonderoga.

After the Revolution, Castleton grew rapidly. Thomas Royal Dake, who arrived in about 1807, left his hallmark of design and workmanship on the pillared houses that line Main Street, including the Ransom-Rehlen mansion, with its 17 Ionic columns; and Dake's masterpiece, the Congregational Meeting House, now the Federated Church, with the lovely pulpit that Dake completed with his own funds. These heirloom houses are open for tours during Castleton's Colonial Days, usually held in late July. Between 1850 and 1870, the West Castleton Railroad and Slate Company was the largest marble plant in the country. During these years, a large Welsh community grew up in the area. The town is also the site of Castleton College, part of the Vermont State College system, which has an active arts center.

Benson, west of Route 22A, 8 miles north of Fair Haven, is one of those tiny proverbial villages "that time forgot" except as a scenic photo op, but which in recent years has developed a creative personality with its artisans and special shops.

TO SEE

MUSEUMS

Chaffee Center for the Visual Arts (775-0356), 16 South Main Street, Rutland. Closed Tuesday, otherwise open 10–5, noon–4 Sunday. One of the state's outstanding art galleries, representing 250 Vermont artists, in a former private house listed on the National Register of Historic Places. It has permanent and periodic exhibits and a youth gallery for school displays. Traditional and contemporary paintings, sculpture, crafts, graphics, and photography are included. (See also *Special Events.*) Donation expected.

Vermont Marble Exhibit (459-2300; 1-800-427-1396), Route 3 from West Rutland, Proctor. Open daily 9–5:30, mid-May through mid-October. Admission charge. The first commercial marble deposit was discovered and quarried in Vermont in 1784. The Vermont Marble Company, formed in 1870 when Redfield Proctor merged several quarries, has mined one of the state's principal resources. Marble from Proctor and Danby was used for the U.S. Supreme Court building, the Lincoln Memorial, and the Beinecke Library at Yale, among many other notable edifices. Proctor himself served as governor, U.S. senator, and secretary of war. Several other members of the Proctor family and chief executives of the company also filled the governor's chair, forming a political dynasty that lasted nearly a century. The company, run by the Swiss-based Pleuss-Staufer Industries since 1976, was closed down in 1991, but nearly 100,000 people still visit the marble exhibit every year, making it one of the biggest tourist attractions in New England. Featured are a special geological display, a film dramatizing the origins and uses of marble, a gallery of bas-reliefs of American presidents, a gift shop, **Dorothea's Cafe,** replicas of the *Pietà* and the *Last Supper,* a sculptor in residence, and a factory viewing site from which to watch the various stages of transformation from rough-cut blocks to polished slabs.

The New England Maple Museum (483-9414), Route 7 north of Pittsford. Open daily 8:30–5:30 in November and December; March through May, 10–4; closed January and February. The museum has an attractive display of the history, production, and consumption of maple syrup, once called "sweet water," and its by-products. You can view the Danforth Collection of antique equipment, murals, and a 10-minute slide show, and there is a tasting area and gift shop. Mail-order service. $1.50 admission; group rates.

The International Doll and Model Railroad Museum (773-8800), Route 4 east, Mendon (above the **Sugar and Spice Pancake House**), is open July through December, 10–4, Friday through Monday. Phil and Libby Moore have installed appealing, fantasy model railroad system layouts plus an extensive, thematic doll collection. Admission charge.

Norman Rockwell Museum (773-6095), Route 4 east, Rutland. Open daily 9–6. The chronological display of all his magazine covers, many ads, posters, portraits, and other published illustrations make this an interesting documentary of changing American graphic styles. Gift shop. Admission charge.

Slate Valley Museum (518-642-1417). Just across the Vermont border on Water Street in Granville, New York, in the heart of the historic slate industry's base, on a site where immigrant quarry workers once lived in tenements, this 19th-century Dutch barn reflects the many colors and shapes of slate. It includes a quarry shanty, tools, a mural, paintings, photographs, family artifacts, and a gift shop. Call ahead for hours.

Rutland Historical Society (775-2006), 96 Center Street, Rutland. The distinctive, 1860 Nickwacett Fire Station serves as the society's home, open for public use Monday 6–9 PM, Saturday 1–4 PM, and by appointment.

HISTORIC SITES

The Hubbardton Battlefield is in East Hubbardton, 7 miles north of the posted Route 4 exit. A small, hilltop visitors center is open mid-May through mid-October, Wednesday through Sunday 9:30–5:30. Battle buffs won't want to miss the diorama and audiovisual display of this 1777 battle, detailing how a small force of Green Mountain Boys led by Col. Seth Warner, together with a Massachusetts militia and a New Hampshire regiment, managed to defeat a far larger British contingent led by General Burgoyne.

Paul P. Harris Memorial, Route 7 south of Rutland, Wallingford. Paul Harris (1868–1947), who founded Rotary International while he was working in Chicago, went to school here in the small brick building on Main Street, where the local club meets Monday at 6:30 PM.

Wilson Castle (773-3284), Route 3 from West Rutland toward Proctor. This 32-room, 19th-century stone "château" on a 115-acre estate is furnished with elaborate European and Oriental pieces, stained glass, and a variety of wood paneling. Guided tours given daily, late-May through mid-October. Admission charge.

COVERED BRIDGES

There are six in the area: the 1836 **Kingsley** or **Mill River Bridge,** East Street, off Airport Road, East Clarendon; the 1880 **Brown Bridge,** off Cold River Road, Shrewsbury; the 1840 **Depot Bridge,** off Route 7 north, Pittsford; the 1849 **Cooley Bridge,** Elm Street, Pittsford; the 1843 **Gorham** or **Goodnough Bridge,** Gorham Bridge Road, off Route 3, Pittsford; and the 1830 **Twin Bridge,** East Pittsford Road, off Route 7 north, Rutland.

FISH HATCHERY

Pittsford National Fish Hatchery (483-6618), Furnace Road, Pittsford. Open 8–4 daily. The Fish and Wildlife Service raises landlocked salmon and lake trout here.

TO DO

BOATING

Boats can be rented from the state parks on Lake Bomoseen and Lake St. Catherine (see *Green Space*).

Sailing Winds Marina (287-9411), Route 30, Lake St. Catherine, Wells. Rents boats, wet suits, and fishing supplies, and offers a speedboat tour.

FISHING

Green Mountain Fishing Guide Service (265-3721). Rod Start's customized outings, plus services through the Lake St. Catherine Inn (see *Resort*), including a special Children's Clinic in July.

GOLF

The Rutland Country Club (773-9153), a mile north of the business section on North Grove Street, Rutland. An 18-hole golf course on rolling terrain; restaurant.

Proctor Pittsford Country Club (483-9379), Corn Hill Road, Pittsford. 18 holes, lounge, and restaurant.

Lake St. Catherine Country Club (287-9341), Route 30, south of Poultney. Enlarged from 9 to 18 holes; lounge and restaurant.

The Bomoseen Country Club (468-5581) in Castleton offers nine holes.

Stonehedge Golf (773-2666), Route 103 west, North Clarendon, is a nine-hole, par-3 public course.

HIKING

White Rocks Recreation Area, Route 140 off Route 7 in Wallingford. Follow signs from the White Rocks Picnic Area. The big feature here is a 2,600-foot, conical white peak surrounded by quartzite boulders that retain ice and snow into summer. We advise picking up a hiking guidebook (see *Hiking* in "What's Where") before starting out.

HORSEBACK RIDING

Pond Hill Ranch (468-2449), Pond Hill Road, Castleton, offers trail rides and hayrides.

Mountain Top Stables (483-2311), Chittenden. Guided trail rides and pony rides; instruction. Also see Mountain Top Inn under *Lodging.*

HUNTING

Tinmouth Hunting Preserve (446-2337), East Road, Wallingford, has 800 acres of varied cover where individual and group pheasant, partridge, and quail shoots can be arranged from September through March (except on Sunday). Five sporting clay-shooting areas have been added.

SWIMMING

Elfin Lake beach, off Route 140 west, 2 miles southeast of Wallingford. (See also *Green Space.*)

SKIING

See *To Do—Skiing* in "Killington/Pico Area."

SLEIGH RIDES

Pond Hill Ranch (468-2449), Castleton. One- to 3-hour rides.

FITNESS CENTERS

The Gymnasium (773-5333), 30 Merchants Row, Rutland. A complete wellness and cardiovascular center, open Monday through Friday 6 AM–9 PM, 7–7 Saturday and Sunday.

Vermont Sport & Fitness Center (775-9916), 40 Curtis Avenue, Rutland. Outdoor pool, indoor/outdoor tennis, racquetball, cardio equipment.

GREEN SPACE

Lake Bomoseen, just north of Castleton, is a popular local summer colony. The lake gained notoriety in the 1930s because of Alexander Woollcott's summer retreat on Neshobe Island. The portly "Town Crier" entertained such cronies as Harpo Marx, who was known to repel curious interlopers by capering along the shore naked and painted blue.

Bomoseen State Park (265-4242, 483-2314), Route 4 west of Rutland, exit 3, 5 miles north on Town Road. Its 60 campsites and five lean-tos are set in a lovely wildlife refuge; beach, picnic area, nature program, trails, boat ramp, and rentals.

Half Moon Pond State Park (273-3848, 483-2314), Fair Haven, off Route 4 west of Rutland, exit 4, 7.5 miles north on Route 30, 2 miles west on Town Road, 1.5 miles south on Town Road. Wooded campsites around a secluded pond; rental canoes; hikes to **High Pond,** a remote body of water in the hills.

Lake St. Catherine State Park (287-9185, 483-2314), 9.5 miles south of Poultney on Route 30. Fifty-two campsites, sandy beaches, fishing, boat rentals, nature trails.

LODGING

RESORT

&✎ **Lake St. Catherine Inn** (287-9347; 1-800-626-LSCI), Route 30 south, Poultney 05764. Open May through October. Here's a peaceful, cheerful, lakeside family retreat that might remind oldsters of happy days at a traditional summer camp. Set in a grove on the shore of this placid little spring-fed lake, this rustic 1920 inn offers a total of 35 rooms in the main lodge and motel-like units. Guests can use paddleboats, Sunfish, and canoes without extra charge and relax on the sundeck or dock. There's a big, comfortable living room/game room and an inviting lakeside deck. Patricia and Raymond Endlich are the friendly hosts. Rates $82–97 daily, per person, double occupancy, including gratuities, full breakfast, and five-course dinner, mid-June through October; $71–91 mid-May to mid-June. Special rates for midweek, weekly, and getaway, golf, and fishing packages; a housekeeping cottage is available for $900 per week.

INN

The Victorian Inn at Wallingford (446-2099), 9 North Main Street, Route 7, Wallingford 05773. This fine, restored, historic village mansion has just four very comfortable guest rooms with private bath, and the atmosphere is family-friendly, thanks to the upbeat proprietors, Constantine and Soo Schonbackler. There's a cozy, publike bar and three dining rooms that are both formal and casual, fine settings for superior food (see *Dining Out*). Room rates $120–140 ($20 foliage supplement) with full breakfast.

BED & BREAKFASTS

The Inn at Rutland (773-0575; 1-800-808-0575), 70 North Main Street, Rutland 05071. This is a large, 1890s town house on Route 7 just north of the center of town, now owned by Bob and Tanya Liberman. All 12 distinctive guest rooms have phone, private bath, and antiques, plus color TV. The differences are in size and position. We suggest a room in the back, away from Route 7. The woodwork in the dining room is exceptional, and the fireplaced living room is attractive. $49–119 ($79–

179 September 1 through October 31 and December 16 through March 31), full breakfast included.

The Phelps House (775-4480; 1-800-775-4260), 19 North Street, Rutland 05071. Eight bedrooms, plus a private apartment that sleeps eight; playroom and tennis court. Betty Phelps's wonderfully primitive murals are worth the visit to what has been called "the first Frank Lloyd Wright house built in Vermont." $65–80.

Baker's Bed & Breakfast (775-4835), 80 Campbell Street, Rutland 05071 (off Dorr Drive, south of the business district), is a spacious 1826 redbrick house with an inviting veranda and a swimming pool. Steve and Leslie Baker offer three large bedrooms with private baths. There's a living room, library, and dining room for brunchlike breakfasts, included in the $125 rate.

I. B. Munson House (446-2860), P.O. Box 427, Route 7, Wallingford 05773, has been refurbished by owners Karen and Phil Pimental. It is now furnished with classic Victorian antiques and period decor, including claw-foot bathtubs. There are seven guest rooms and a suite, all with private bath, two with working fireplaces. Rates range from $55 single to $135 double, including full breakfast ($15 additional in foliage season and during holidays).

Maplewood Inn (265-8039; 1-800-253-7729), Route 22A south, Fair Haven 05743. Cindy and Doug Baird's historic 1843 Greek Revival farmhouse (on the National Register of Historic Places), set in fields, is decorated in period style with common rooms that ramble on and on. There is a breakfast room with hot-beverage bar, and a parlor with complimentary liqueurs. The Blue Room and the Rose Room and Hospitality "Pineapple" suites are especially attractive. The latter, with a fireplace, may be combined with the Rose Room at $199 for four people. Regular rates are $75–140, including a continental-"plus" breakfast buffet. Four rooms have fireplaces; all have private bath, cable TV, and air-conditioning.

Memory Lane (468-5394), Main Street, Castleton 05735. Antique furniture, toys, dolls, and china fill this Federal-style house, originally the home of the cofounder of the medical school at Castleton College. Now Barbara and Thomas Ettori offer three guest rooms, one with a private bath, at $55–90.

Fair Haven Inn B&B (1-800-325-7074; in Vermont, 1-800-649-1212), 18 Main Street, Fair Haven 05743. Owned by the proprietors of the popular restaurant (see *Dining Out*) but in a separate town house with a wraparound veranda, the inn has three bedrooms with private bath ($85), cable TV in the den, fax and copier service, wet bar (BYOB), and a sitting room with fireplace.

Priscilla's Victorian Inn (235-2299), 52 South Street, Middletown Springs 05757, has vintage gingerbread charm, six large Victorian rooms with private bath, a game room, and English gardens. $85 per room.

White Rocks Inn (446-2077), RR 1, Box 297, Route 7, Wallingford 05773.

June and Alfred Matthews's elegantly furnished farmhouse and its spectacular, landmark barn are on the National Register of Historic Places. The five guest rooms, each with private bath, have either king, queen, or double canopy beds (one has twin beds) and can be had for $75–100 double occupancy, including full breakfast. The Milk House Cottage (with a whirlpool bath, living room, and full kitchen) is $130 EP. Weekly rates are $5 less, slightly more in foliage and holiday seasons. Children over 8 are welcome.

See also Maple Crest Farm and Buckmaster Inn under *Bed & Breakfasts* in "Okemo Mountain/Ludlow Area."

MOTELS
In Rutland 05071

Motel at Mendon Mountain Orchards (775-5477), Route 4 east, is not really a motel but rather a series of pleasant, old-fashioned cabins, surrounded by orchards, with a pool and a shop for homemade goodies, apples in-season, cider, and flowers. $55–60 double.

Holiday Inn (775-1911; 1-800-HOLIDAY), Routes 7 and 4 south, includes **Paynter's Restaurant,** an indoor pool, **Centre Stage** lounge.

Comfort Inn at Trolley Square (775-2200), Route 7 south; **Howard Johnson's Motor Lodge** (775-4303), Route 7 south; **Days Inn** (formerly Rutland Lodge; 773-3361).

CAMPGROUNDS
See *Green Space* for information on campgrounds in Bomoseen State Park, Half Moon Pond State Park, and Lake St. Catherine State Park.

WHERE TO EAT

DINING OUT
See also "Killington/Pico Area."

Casa Bianca (773-7401), 76 Grove Street, Rutland. Open 5–10 for dinner nightly except Tuesday; Sunday brunch. Now in the hands of owners Joe and Sharon Valente after many years of Lee Bove Ryan's stewardship, Casa Bianca's reputation for fine homestyle Italian cuisine has been maintained, but in redecorated quarters. Featured are such specialties as cioppino, chicken Cara Mia, and veal Sorrentino, plus a mix-and-match Sunday "Pasta Nite" and a Tavoli munchies table in the bar. Moderate.

Bistro Café (773-2806), Three Center Street, Rutland. Open daily for lunch and dinner. This spiffy place connected to the Coffee Exchange (see *Coffeehouse/Wine Bar*) is known for its midday beef stew. At dinner, consider Caribbean roast pork, veal roulade (smoked mozzarella and roasted leeks stuffing under a herb mushroom demi-glace), or special pastas, finishing up with a sinful Grand Marnier chocolate mousse cake. Moderate.

Royal's 121 Hearthside (775-0856), 37 North Main Street (junction of

Routes 4 and 7), Rutland. Open 11–11. The legendary Ernie Royal is no longer alive, but his spirit lives on, maintained by the owner of what was 121 West. Mesquite and hearthside grill specialties: prime rib, chops, seafood, and lobsters. Moderate.

Little Harry's (775-4848), 121 West Street, Rutland. Open 5–10 Wednesday through Sunday. This offspring of the popular Harry's Cafe in Mount Holly occupies the old space of the Vacant Chair. Owner Harrison Pearce calls his venture the "general store of ethnic eating." Besides pad thai, a "signature" noodle dish, Little Harry's offers such fare as lamb chops, trout, Greek salads, and lively Spanish dishes plus burritos and steak sandwiches from what Pearce calls a "user-friendly" menu. Inexpensive to moderate.

The Victorian Inn at Wallingford (446-2099), 9 North Main Street, Route 7, Wallingford, serves dinner Tuesday through Saturday and a bountiful Sunday brunch buffet laid out in the kitchen. Closed in November until Thanksgiving. Swiss-born chef-owner Constantine Schonbachler's really exceptional Continental specialties have won a strong local following. Moderate.

The Fair Haven Inn (265-4907), 5 Adams Street, Fair Haven. In a spacious, neo-Colonial setting, the Lemnotis family serves hearty, tasty Greek and Italian dishes at lunch and dinner. Specials include spanakopita, an appetizer of pastry filled with spinach, feta cheese, and egg; moussaka; and seafood souvlakia. Inexpensive to moderate.

EATING OUT

The Palms (773-2367), 36 Strongs Avenue, Rutland. At dinner, Italian cooking by the fourth generation of the Sabataso family.

The Seward Family Restaurant (773-2738), Route 7 north, Rutland. Family-run and -geared, Seward's began as a dairy bar in 1946. Its own ice cream (34 flavors) is still the specialty of the house, along with Seward's cottage cheese, sour cream, and the cheddar cheese the family has been producing (see *Selective Shopping—Special Shops*) since the Civil War. The coffee shop has expanded into a full-scale restaurant, open for all three meals.

South Station (775-1736), at the Trolley Barn, 170 South Main Street, Rutland. Open daily for lunch and dinner, specializing in prime ribs of beef and such munchies as fried potato skins, zucchini sticks, stuffed mushrooms, chicken wings, hearty soups, salads, burgers, and teriyaki beef or chicken, all at moderate prices.

Sweet Tomatoes (747-7747), 88 Merchants Row, Rutland, has the same northern Italian flair as its siblings in Burlington and in Lebanon, New Hampshire—wood-fired pizzas and all. Open for lunch Monday through Friday from 11 AM, for dinner nightly from 5 PM. Shrimp sautéed with tomato, Greek olives, basil, garlic, crushed red chiles, and white wine, tossed with linguine, is but one sample dish.

✒ **Sawdi's Steak House** (773-8124), Route 7 north, Rutland. Open for dinner

Center Street in downtown Rutland

daily. This roadside landmark specializes in charbroiled steaks, lamb, and seafood; an extensive children's menu.

The Sirloin Saloon (773-7900), Route 7 south, Rutland. One in a Vermont mini-chain (there are three), this colorful restaurant (lots of glasswork, art, and gleaming brass) is a good bet for family dinners. The menu runs from ground sirloin to prime rib.

Panda Pavilion (775-6682, 775-6794), at the entrance to the Rutland Mall, Route 4 east. Open 11:30–11 Monday through Saturday, 1–10 Sunday. Highly praised Szechwan-Hunan-Mandarin cuisine, like Double Happiness Chicken. Take-out service.

Birdseye Diner (468-5817), Main Street, Castleton. This restored 1940s Silk City diner, open all day, is a justifiably popular spot for college students and local residents alike.

LakeShore Pub & Grill (273-3000), Route 30, on Lake Bomoseen. This locally popular place features live music on summer weekend evenings.

Wheel Inn (537-2755), Lake Street at Stage Road, Benson. Open 6 AM–9 PM, this family-friendly place has a loyal following.

COFFEEHOUSE/WINE BAR

Coffee Exchange (775-3337), 101–103 Merchants Row, Rutland. Open Monday through Thursday from 6 AM, from 8 AM Friday through Sunday. "Jazz, java, and jabber" is the theme of this upbeat coffee bar and sophisticated Wine Room orchestrated by Kevin Lefter at a key downtown intersection. Patrons sip and nosh on exotic beverages and pastries at outdoor tables in summer—perhaps macadamia cream coffee and orange-poppyseed scones. Salads, soups, and sandwiches at lunch.

ENTERTAINMENT

Crossroads Art Council (775-5413), 39 East Center Street, Rutland, sponsors a series of concerts, theater and ballet performances, and an arts education program.

See also LakeShore Pub & Grill under *Eating Out*.

Movieplex 9 (775-5500), downtown Rutland Plaza and **Westway 1-2-3-4** (438-2888), Route 4 in West Rutland show first-run flicks.

SELECTIVE SHOPPING

BOOKSTORES

Charles E. Tuttle Company (773-8930), Main Street, Rutland, facing the park, has one of the largest stocks of used and rare books in New England. Charles Tuttle began his publishing company in Tokyo right after World War II and built it into a major supplier of beautifully produced books on Oriental art and other Asian subjects.

The Book King (773-9232), Merchants Row, Rutland, is a bright, well-stocked store for new adult and children's books, paperbacks, and cards.

Annie's Book Stop (775-6993), Trolley Square, 120 South Main Street, Rutland. Annie's has a large selection of new books and preread paperbacks; specializes in children's books and storytelling cassettes, plus educational puzzles and games.

The Unnamed Bookstore and Antique Center, 110 West Street, Rutland. Clint and Lucille Fiske, former owners of the Haunted Mansion Bookstore in Cuttingsville, have moved their stock of secondhand books, antique maps, and such to downtown Rutland.

SPECIAL SHOPS

Great Outdoors Trading Company (775-6531), Woodstock Avenue, Rutland, is a vast, complete sporting goods store, with a bike shop, gun shop, archery center, and fly-rod department, among others.

The Seward Vermont Dairy Deli Shop (773-2736), 224 North Main Street (Route 7), Rutland. One corner of this vast restaurant (see *Eating Out*) showcases the cheddar cheese that has been produced by this family since the Civil War. The specialty is sharp cheddar, aged more than 9 months. Smoked cheddar and herbed cheddars are also available in wheels, blocks, and sticks and via mail order (call 259-2311 or write to Hill Country Food Products, P.O. Box 218, East Wallingford 05743). Maple syrup and creamed honey are also available. This is also the only source of old-fashioned cheese curd.

Vermont Canvas (773-7311), 179 Woodstock Avenue, Route 4 east, Rutland, makes customized luggage and handbags.

Truly Unique (773-7742), Route 4 east, Rutland, has an uncommon collection of country antiques, Vermont products, and gifts.

Rocking Horse Country Store (773-7882), Route 4 east, Rutland, combines Vermont food products (including its own homemade wine jelly), gifts, antiques, and collectibles.

Fred's Dollhouse and Miniature Center (483-6362), Route 7 north, Pittsford. Open Monday through Saturday 9:30–5, Sunday 11–5, and by appointment. This is where you can get dollhouses and miniature furnishings, accessories, scaled lumber, hardware, electrical systems, and wallpaper, plus dollhouse and furniture kits.

Farrow Gallery & Studio (468-5683), Old Yellow Church, Main Street, Castleton, shows Patrick Farrow's limited-edition, award-winning bronze sculptures, along with the work of other Vermont artists.

SPECIAL EVENTS

Late February: **Great Benson Fishing Derby,** sponsored by the Fair Haven Rotary Club—many prizes in several categories, including best ice shanty. Tickets for the Derby: P.O. Box 131, Bomoseen 05732.

Late July: **Colonial Days,** Castleton (see *Villages*).

Early August: **Art in the Park Summer Arts Festival,** sponsored by the Chaffee Center (775-0356), in Main Street Park, junction of Routes 7 and 4 east.

Labor Day weekend: **Killington Stage Race,** three events for bicycle racers.

Early September: **Vermont State Fair** (775-5200). Midway, exhibits, rodeo, races, demolition derby, and tractor pulls animate the old fairgrounds on Route 7 south, Rutland.

Mid-October: **Art in the Park Fall Foliage Festival,** sponsored by the Chaffee Center (775-0356).

December 31: **Rutland's First Night Celebration.**

Addison County and Environs

Including Middlebury, Vergennes, Brandon, and Bristol

Addison County packs as much contrasting scenery within its borders as any county in the country. On the east it includes the high wall of the Green Mountains, laced with hiking trails and pierced by four of the state's highest, most dramatic "gaps" (passes). The mountains drop abruptly through widely scattered hill towns—Lincoln, Ripton, and Goshen—into a 30-mile-wide, farm-filled valley, Vermont's largest concentration of dairy farms and orchards. Lake Champlain is far narrower here than up around Burlington, and the Adirondacks in New York seem higher and nearer, forming an improbable but spectacular backdrop to cows, water, red barns, and apple trees.

This stretch of the Champlain Valley is particularly popular with bicyclists, not only because it's the flattest piece of Vermont, but also because its quiet old farm roads wind through orchards to discoveries like the "Fort Ti Ferry" ("serving people and their vehicles since Mozart was three months old") and "the world's smallest bank" in Orwell.

Middlebury, the hub of Addison County, is among New England's most sophisticated towns, the home of one of its most prestigious private colleges and many interesting shops.

Summer visitors should take advantage of the *Sugarbush Express* train service from Middlebury up the spine of the valley, but we hope that this book will also lure them to explore the valley fringes: the Lake Champlain shoreline, notched at regular intervals with quiet and accessible bays, and the Green Mountain forest roads, with their occasional but spectacular lake and valley views.

GUIDANCE

Addison County Chamber of Commerce (388-7951; 1-800-SEE-VER-MONT; www.midvermont.com), 2 Court Street, Middlebury 05753, in the Painter House (see *Villages—Middlebury*), offers information about every corner of its domain, from Vergennes and Bristol on the north to Orwell on the south. Open Monday through Friday 9–5. This unusually large walk-in information center publishes a map/guide, stocks brochures, and refers visitors to a wide variety of lodgings, from inns and bed & breakfasts to seasonal cottages on Lake Dunmore. During foliage season, it is unusually resourceful in finding lodging for all comers.

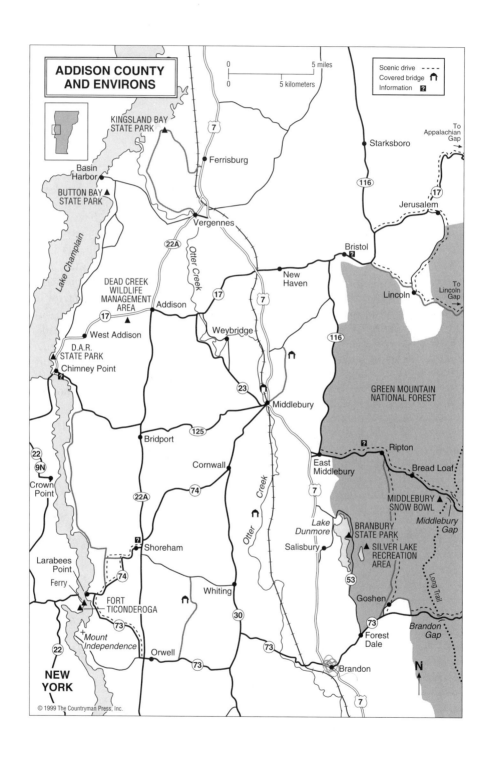

ADDISON COUNTY
AND ENVIRONS

Scenic drive - - - -
Covered bridge 🛉
Information ?

0   5 miles
0   5 kilometers

KINGSLAND BAY
STATE PARK

7

Ferrisburg

Starksboro

To
Appalachian
Gap

Basin
Harbor

116

BUTTON BAY
STATE PARK

22A

Otter Creek

Vergennes

Jerusalem

17

Bristol
?

New
Haven

To
Lincoln
Gap

Lake Champlain

DEAD CREEK
WILDLIFE
MANAGEMENT
AREA   Addison

17

17

7

Lincoln

West Addison

Weybridge

116

D.A.R.
STATE PARK

Chimney Point
?

23

GREEN MOUNTAIN
NATIONAL FOREST

Middlebury

125

Bridport

22
9N

Cornwall

Ripton
?

East
Middlebury

Bread Loaf

MIDDLEBURY
SNOW BOWL

Crown
Point

22A

74

7

Middlebury
Gap

Lake
Dunmore

BRANBURY
STATE PARK

Otter Creek

?

Shoreham

Salisbury

SILVER LAKE
RECREATION
AREA

Larabees
Point

74

Whiting

53

Long Trail

Ferry

FORT
TICONDEROGA

30

Goshen

73

Brandon
Gap

+Mount
Independence

73

73

Forest
Dale

22

Orwell

73

Brandon

N

NEW
YORK

7

© 1999 The Countryman Press, Inc.

Vergennes Chamber of Commerce (877-0080), P.O. Box 335, Vergennes 05491, has an information booth on the common.

Brandon Area Chamber of Commerce (247-6401), P.O. Box 267, Brandon 05735; visitors booth on Park Street with brochures and information in front of the library across from the Brandon Inn. There's an informative self-guided walking tour guide to the town's rich architectural heritage.

"Moosalamoo," from the Abenaki word possibly meaning "the moose departs," is a dandy map and guide, with site signage, to the trails and other natural features of some 20,000 acres of Green Mountain National Forest, published and distributed by the Moosalamoo Partnership, available at chambers of commerce, the Catamount Trail Association, other outdoor recreation organizations, and several inns. Or call 247-6735; 1-800-448-0707.

GETTING THERE

By bus: **Vermont Transit** (864-6811; 1-800-451-3292) stops in Brandon and Vergennes as well as Middlebury. This is the Burlington-to-Albany run, so New Yorkers and Bostonians must change in Rutland.

By car: The major north–south highway is Route 7, but we advise anyone from Boston to approach through the Middlebury Gap (see *Scenic Drives*). From the west you can take the toll bridge at Chimney Point year-round or the seasonal ferries described below.

By ferry: **Lake Champlain Ferry** (864-9804) from Essex, New York, to Charlotte operates spring through fall, takes 20 minutes, and puts you just above Vergennes.

Fort Ticonderoga Ferry (897-7999), Larrabees Point to Fort Ticonderoga. Memorial Day weekend through June, 8–6 daily; July through Labor Day 8 AM–9 PM, then 8–6 through the last Sunday in October. Cars $6 one-way, $10 round-trip. (See the chapter introduction.)

MEDICAL EMERGENCY

Middlebury (388-3333); Shoreham (897-7777); Bristol (453-2401); Brandon (247-6828); Vergennes (877-3191).

VILLAGES

Middlebury (population: 8,000) is the county seat and hub of Addison County. It's also the home of prestigious Middlebury College and one of Vermont's handsomest, liveliest, most welcoming communities. Inns and restaurants serve visitors as well as potential students and their parents, and in recent years it has become a great place to shop. Middlebury College (founded in 1800 and now one of the most sought-after private colleges) owes much to the energy and vision of Gamaliel Painter, a surveyor who settled here before the Revolution. Painter accompanied Ethan Allen on the Fort Ticonderoga raid and returned to Middlebury to become the town's principal landowner, sheriff, judge, and assemblyman. The fine mansion on Court Street, presently housing the visitors information center and the Vermont Folklife Center (see *To See—Museums*), belonged to Painter. Another benefactor was Joseph Battell, who owned thousands of acres of forest and mountain land that he left to the college and the state when he died in 1915. He was the proprietor of the famous old summit house, Bread Loaf Inn, now the nucleus for the summer Bread Loaf School of English and the Bread Loaf Writers Conference. Battell also owned a weekly newspaper in which he fulminated against the invasion of motor cars. Emma Hart Willard, who pioneered in the education of women, was another Middlebury luminary.

The town's proudest buildings—the courthouse, Middlebury Inn, the Battell House, and the fine Congregational church—are grouped, along with compact business blocks, around the common. It's a short walk down Main Street to the churning Otter Creek falls, a centerpiece for dozens of shops that have proliferated in the old mills and marbleworks on both banks of the river, connected by a footbridge. With the Vermont State Craft Center (see *Selective Shopping—Crafts Shops*) as its anchor store, this is now one of Vermont's most interesting places to shop.

Brandon. A peaceful town of some 4,000 inhabitants and a heretofore underrated appeal, Brandon has an unusual array of 19th-century houses in an eclectic and intriguing mix of Federal and Victorian styles. Sited between Otter Creek and the Neshobe River, it was the home of Thomas Davenport, who invented and patented an electric motor in 1838, and the birthplace of Stephen A. Douglas (1813–1861), the "Little Giant" of the famous debates with Abraham Lincoln in 1858, when Douglas was a senator from Illinois. Brandon's hospitality to travelers is growing with the addition of some interesting new places to stay.

Bristol. Billing itself as the "Gateway to the Green Mountains," Bristol is nestled at the foot of Lincoln Gap, at the junctions of north–south Route 116 (less heavily trafficked than Route 7) and east–west Route 17. Its broad Main Street is lined with a delightful mix of stores and restaurants, housed in a 19th-century building that leads to a square green, complete with fountain, park benches, and old cannon. The local site to see is the **Lord's Prayer Rock** (on the south side of Route 17 entering Bristol from the east), a flat rock inscribed with the Lord's Prayer. A physician named Joseph C. Greene commissioned the inscription in 1891, presumably because he was still thankful for having reached that point safely when, as a youth, he was hauling logs over steep roads.

Vergennes, midway between Middlebury and Burlington, is the smallest city (2,300 residents) in the United States. Although 5 miles inland, its history and its present activities are linked closely to Lake Champlain. Otter Creek winds from the "city" to the lake, and the road leads to Basin Harbor, site of the area's premier resort (see *Lodging—Resort*) and the Lake Champlain Maritime Museum (see *To See—Museums*). We recommend the lake road south from Basin Harbor, by Button Bay State Park and the D.A.R. State Park to Chimney Point. The ruins of the 18th-century fort at Crown Point in New York are just across the Lake Champlain Bridge.

Vergennes's site on an impressive falls and its handsome, early-19th-century commercial buildings suggest an unusual history. This is, in fact, one of the oldest, as well as the smallest, cities in the country. It was founded by Donald McIntosh in 1764 and later named by Ethan Allen for Charles Gravier, comte de Vergennes, the French minister of foreign affairs who was a strong supporter of the American Revolutionary cause.

In 1811–12, Thomas Macdonough used the Otter Creek Basin just below the falls to build—in record time—three ships, including the 734-ton, 26-gun *Saratoga*. He also equipped nine gunboats, using them all to defeat the British fleet in Lake Champlain off Plattsburgh in 1814.

Shoreham is known for its many orchards. Shoreham Village is a beauty, with a classic Congregational church (1846), a Masonic temple (built in 1852 as the Universalist church), and the graceful St. Genevieve Catholic Church (1873), as well as the old inn and general store (see *Lodging—Inns*). Follow Route 74 southwest from the village through the orchards; or continue straight on Witherell Road where 74 jogs south, then turn south (left) onto Smith Street along the lake. Either way, you get to Larrabees Point, the site of Teachout's Store, built in 1836 from stones taken from Fort Ticonderoga just across the lake. The excursion boat M/V *Carillon* now departs from this spot; next door, the small, car-carrying "Fort Ti" cable ferry makes the crossing to the fort itself in 6 minutes flat. It has held the franchise from the Vermont and New York legislatures since 1799, but records indicate the service was initiated by Lord Jeffery Amherst in 1757 for use by his soldiers in the campaigns against the French. Continue south on Route 73 to the turn-off for Mount Independence.

Orwell. Best known for Mount Independence (see *Historic Sites*), the small village at the center of this orchard and dairying community circles a long, sloping green with a brick Congregational church (1843) on a rise by the white-clapboard town hall (built in 1810 as the Baptist church). It all overlooks a brief line of shops with the First National Bank of Orwell, billed as "the world's smallest bank," in the middle. Chartered in 1863 (but known as the Farmers Bank for many years, before Lincoln granted it the country's 212th official charter), the bank remains a real center of town, with notices of upcoming events tacked to the authentic old teller's cages. The other village nerve center is **Buxton's Store,** the genuine article.

TO SEE

MUSEUMS

Middlebury College Center for the Arts (443-6433), Route 30, Middlebury. Open Tuesday through Friday 10–5, weekends noon–5. The college's small but distinguished permanent collection of paintings and small sculptures plus changing exhibits are displayed in galleries within the multitiered arts center, which also includes a café and several performance areas.

The Sheldon Museum (388-2117), Park Street, Middlebury. Open year-round, Monday through Friday 10–5, also Saturday late May through October. Guided and self-guided tours. This 1829 marble merchant's house has no fewer than six black marble mantels and holds an intimate collection of furnishings, tools, household articles, clothes, books, games, and other artifacts portraying Vermont folkways, displayed in period rooms. A modern research ell has been added, with a gallery for changing exhibits. There are also frequent special events. $3.50 per adult, $3 for seniors and students over 12.

The Vermont Folklife Center (388-4964), 3 Court Street, Middlebury (in Masonic Hall). This growing organization (founded in 1984) collects and presents the traditional arts and folkways of Vermont, primarily through taped interviews. It mounts changing exhibits and sells its publications.

Lake Champlain Maritime Museum (475-2022), RR 3, Box 4092, Vergennes, at the entrance to the Basin Harbor Club off Panton Road west of Vergennes. Open daily 10–5 mid-May through late October; $7 adults, $6 students, $3 ages 6 and under. This museum has been evolving steadily over the last decades. It began with the gift of a local schoolhouse constructed from native limestone in 1808, moved stone by stone (2,000 of them) and reconstructed to house exhibits. The museum's 10 buildings, spread over 3 acres, now house dozens of small craft built around the lake over a period of 150 years, and exhibits on a number of chapters in the lake's story, including the saga of the hundreds of wrecks still beneath the surface. Attempts to raise them, you learn, began in the 1930s but have been abandoned because divers and historians have accepted the obvious: Wood that's been submerged in fresh water quickly disintegrates when exposed to air. Instead, the state of Vermont has created five underwater parks; inquire about guided scuba tours, lectures, field trips, and demonstrations and courses in boatbuilding. A working replica of Benedict Arnold's 54-foot gunboat *Philadelphia*, built on the spot, is also on view. The bookstore carries a good selection of maritime-related books, prints, clothing, and gifts.

HISTORIC HOMES

Rokeby Museum (877-3406), 3 miles north of Vergennes on Route 7 in Ferrisburg. Open for guided tours at 11, 12:30, and 2, Thursday through

The gunboat replica Philadelphia under sail

KIM GRANT

UVM Morgan Horse Farm, Middlebury

Sunday, May through October, and by appointment year-round. $4 adults, $3 students and seniors. Exhibits evoke the lives of four generations of a Quaker family whose members included pioneers, farmers, and Rowland E. Robinson, the 19th-century author, illustrator, and naturalist. Rokeby was an important stop on the Underground Railway for freedom-seeking slaves before the Civil War.

The John Strong D.A.R. Mansion (759-2309), Route 17, west of 22A, West Addison, open mid-May through mid-October, Friday through Sunday 9–5. $2 per adult, $1 seniors and students. This is one of several substantial houses and buildings made of stone taken from the ruins of Fort Crown Point and skidded across Lake Champlain by oxen. General Strong, an early settler and Green Mountain Boy, built his (third) residence here in 1796, with brick from his own clay pits on the "Salt Lick" where he first hunted deer. Furnishings reflect five generations of the family.

HISTORIC SITES

Mount Independence State Historic Site (948-2000) 8 miles west of Orwell on the shore of Lake Champlain, marked from the junction of Route 73 off Route 22A. Grounds open year-round; museum open Memorial Day through Columbus Day, Wednesday through Sunday 9:30–5:30. Opened in 1996, a boat-shaped visitors center exhibits archaeological artifacts and tells the story of the thousands of men who weathered a brutal winter on this fortified peninsula in 1776–77, facing Fort Ticonderoga across a narrow strip of lake. Eventually they defeated the British at Saratoga, one of the most decisive victories of the Revolution. Four marked trails begin at the information center and wander down to the lake through 400 wooded acres.

Fort Ticonderoga (518-585-2821), Ticonderoga, New York. Open mid-May through mid-October daily. $6 per adult, $4 children ages 10–13. The 18th-century stone fort has been restored and includes a museum displaying weapons and uniforms. It was built by the French (named Fort Carillon), captured by English Gen. Jeffery Amherst, and held by the British until 1775, when Ethan Allen and his Green Mountain Boys took the fort by surprise, capturing the guns that eventually helped free Boston. The fort is easily accessible from Larrabees Point on the Vermont shore (see *Getting There* and *To Do—Boating*).

Crown Point State Historic Site (518-597-3666), Crown Point, New York. Open mid-May through October, Wednesday through Saturday 10–5, Sunday 1–5. Free. Just across the Lake Champlain Bridge from Chimney Point, West Addison, Vermont. Fifteen miles north of Fort Ticonderoga, Crown Point was once a far larger, more important fortification, and in 1775 it was the source of 29 pieces of cannon captured by the colonists and hauled off to Boston. The complex includes 18th-century ruins and a visitors center.

Chimney Point State Historic Site (759-2412), at the Vermont end of the Lake Champlain Bridge, Route 125. Open Memorial Day through Columbus Day, Wednesday through Sunday 9:30–5:30. An 18th-century tavern houses a well-mounted display on Native American and French colonial heritage.

GARDENS

Edgeview Antique Rose Garden (247-6095), 27 Marble Street, Brandon, features 200 different antique roses—for viewing, not for sale. Open Saturday through Monday and holidays, 10–4, Memorial Day through Columbus Day.

Rocky Dale Gardens (453-2782), 62 Rocky Dale Road, Bristol. Open daily 9–6 except Tuesday. Extensive displays on 3 acres with dramatic rock outcroppings, plus retail nursery.

FARMS AND ORCHARDS

The UVM Morgan Horse Farm (388-2011), open May through October, 9–4 daily. From Middlebury town square, head west on Route 125, then turn right onto Route 23 (Weybridge Street) and follow signs. Admission. The first "Morgan" was born in the late 1790s and is recognized as the sire of an entire breed of Vermont horse. Col. Joseph Battell began breeding Morgans on this farm in the 1870s and is credited with saving the breed (America's first developed breed of horse) from extinction. The farm is now a breeding and training center operated by the University of Vermont. Guided tours of the stables and paddocks are available, along with an audiovisual presentation about the Morgan horse and farm.

Yankee Kingdom Orchard (759-2387), Lake Street, West Addison. Overlooking Lake Champlain, pick-your-own apples, strawberries, and pumpkins; also a petting zoo, children's play area, wagon rides, cider pressing.

✍ **Blue Slate Farm** (758-2577), Crown Point Road, Bridport. Harold and Shirley Giard invite visitors to participate in daily activities at the 640-acre farm that has been in their family for three generations. Learn to milk cows, feed, care for (and perhaps help deliver) calves, manage young cattle, prepare land for planting, harvest crops, and repair and maintain equipment. Farm animals include miniature donkeys, horses, ducks, and pigs.

See also *To Do—Apple Picking* and Indian Trail Farm under *Lodging*.

BRIDGES OF ADDISON COUNTY

The **Pulp Mill Covered Bridge,** between Middlebury and Weybridge, spanning the Otter Creek near the Morgan Horse Farm (see *Farms and Orchards*), is the oldest in the state (1808–20) and the last two-lane span still in use.

Halpin Bridge (1824), Middlebury, 2 miles east of Route 7, off Halpin Road, is Vermont's highest bridge above the streambed.

Station Bridge, across Otter Creek in Cornwall (2 miles east of Route 30 on Swamp Road), is a 136-foot Town lattice bridge built in 1836.

Shoreham Covered Railroad Bridge, East Shoreham off the Whiting/ Shoreham road (turn south onto Shoreham Depot Road); the bridge is marked on area maps. A Howe bridge built in 1897 by the Rutland Railroad, spanning the Lemon Fair River.

SCENIC DRIVES

Middlebury Gap. This is our favorite approach to Addison County from the southeast, and this stretch of Route 125 is more dramatic driving east to west. Begin in Hancock and stop at Texas Falls. The road quickly crests at its junction with the Long Trail, near the Middlebury Snow Bowl. Then it's all downhill through the woods until the huge, wooden Bread Loaf Inn (now part of Middlebury College) improbably appears. The Robert Frost Wayside Picnic Area and the Interpretive Trail are a short way beyond. We also like to stop in the small, 19th-century cemetery a bit farther down, where a wind chime strikes softly in a row of maples. The picturesque hill town of Ripton is just below, and as the road continues to plunge into the valley, you briefly glimpse the Adirondacks in the distance.

Brandon Gap. Route 73 is a high road over Goshen Mountain and through Brandon Gap. At the height of land, several wooded hiking trails are posted, and a rest area has been sited to catch the full majesty of Mount Horrid's Great Cliff. The road then rushes downhill with Brandon Brook, joining Route 100 and the White River below Rochester.

Note: A well-surfaced woods road (Goshen Road) runs south from Ripton through the National Forest, past the turnoffs for Silver Lake (see *Green Space*) and past Blueberry Hill (see *Lodging, Bicycling,* and *Cross-Country Skiing*) to Route 73 in the Brandon Gap.

Appalachian Gap. East from Bristol, Route 17 climbs steadily for 4 miles (past the Jerusalem General Store), eases off for a couple of miles, and then zigzags steeply to crest at more than 3,000 feet, yielding some spectacular views before dropping into the Mad River Valley. It's even more spectacular heading west.

Lincoln/Appalachian Gap Loop. From Bristol, follow Routes 17/116 to the turnoff for Lincoln 2 miles east of Bristol, past Bartlett's Falls (be sure to stop) to Lincoln and out the Dowlingsville Road to Jerusalem, back down on Route 116 to Route 17.

Lincoln Gap. Follow Routes 17/116 east from Bristol, as above, but from Lincoln continue on the narrow Gap Road, unpaved in sections. Again there are beautiful views, and you are quickly down in Warren (see "Sugarbush/Mad River Valley"). *Note:* Unsuitable for trailers and RVs.

Along Lake Champlain. See *Villages* for Shoreham and Orwell.

TO DO

APPLE PICKING

September and October is apple time in Addison County, where you are welcome to pick your own (PYO). The orchards are particularly thick in and around Shoreham: **Atwood Orchards** (897-5592) on Barnum Hill, a half mile from its stand on Route 22A (3 miles south of Shoreham Village), offers PYO, also a picnic area and views of Lake Champlain. **Douglas Orchards,** 1 mile west of the village on Route 74, does the same and has a cider press; as does **RidgeView Orchards** (897-5991), another mile west on Route 74, with PYO plus honey, blueberries, and raspberries. **Larrabees Point Orchard** (897-2626), farther west on Route 74, offers PYO. See also *Farms and Orchards.*

BICYCLING

It's no coincidence that the country's first bicycle touring company was founded in this area. According to Bruce Burgess, a pioneer tour leader and current owner of Bicycle Holidays (see below), there just isn't a more rewarding place to bike anywhere than this swath of the Champlain Valley, with its relatively flat terrain and mountain views, its wealth of back roads leading through covered bridges, connecting historic sites and comfortable inns with ample swimming holes, ice cream, and antiquing stops en route. Burgess shares a word of warning: Beware deceptively quiet but narrow, truck-trafficked roads like Route 22A and Route 30.

Bicycle Holidays (388-BIKE), RD 3, Box 2394, Middlebury 05753, offers custom-designed, self-guided tours—both inn-to-inn and camping—for solos, couples, and groups. Rental equipment, airport pickup, and luggage shuttle can be arranged.

Bike Vermont (1-800-257-2226), based in Woodstock, gets good reviews for guided, small-group inn-to-inn tours in this area.

Vermont Bicycle Touring (VBT) (453-4811), Box 711, Bristol, the state's oldest bike tour company, offers guided group inn-to-inn tours.

Bike & Ski Touring Center (388-6666), 74 Main Street, Middlebury, is a source for a variety of rental bikes.

Country Inns along the Trail (247-3300), Van Cortland Road, Brandon 05733. Bike tours usually begin and end at Churchill House (see *Hiking*), which has a fleet of bikes for rent at $15 per day, including helmet. Other inns are on the itinerary. Brochure from Churchill House (see *Lodging—Inns*).

Mountain Biking at Blueberry Hill (247-6735), Goshen. An extensive network of ski trails and woods roads that are well suited to mountain biking; rentals, lessons.

BIRDING

Otter Creek (see *Boating*), near Lake Champlain in Vergennes, and the **Dead Creek Wildlife Management Area** in Addison (off Route 17) are particularly rich in bird life, especially during migration seasons. See also *Watchable Wildlife* under "What's Where."

BOATING

The M/V Carillon, a 60-foot, 49-passenger replica of a 1920s Thousand Islands luxury motor yacht, operates daily Father's Day through Labor Day. Geared to groups in spring and fall but walk-ons accepted (call ahead), from Teachout's Lakehouse Store and Wharf (897-5331) at Larrabees Point. The 1½-hour cruise goes up to Hand's Cove, then across to Fort Ticonderoga (you can debark and catch a later boat), and on to Mount Independence and Mount Defiance, while the captain tells you what was happening along the route in the 1770s. $8.50 per adult, $4.50 per child; group rates.

Boat rentals are available from **Vermont Houseboat Vacations** (948-2375), Route 73A, Orwell; **Buoy 39 Marina** (948-2411), Route 73A, Orwell; **Waterhouses** (252-4433), West Shore Road, Lake Dunmore (rents rowboats, canoes, motorboats, sailboats); **Champlain Bridge Marina** (759-2049), West Addison (boat access, pump-out station for boats less than 35 feet); **Chipman Point Marina & Campground** (948-2288), Route 73A (dockage for 60 boats, grocery store, pump-out station, game room, swimming, boat rentals); and **Lake Dunmore Kampersville** (352-4501), in Salisbury, which also rents rowboats, canoes, sailboats, and motor bugs.

FACTORY TOURS

Otter Creek Brewing (1-800-473-0727), 85 Exchange Street, Middlebury. Open daily for free guided tours. Free samples, retail sales of its Copper Ale, Stovepipe Porter, and lagers.

FITNESS CENTER

Vermont Sun (388-6888), 88 Exchange Street, Middlebury, is a spacious indoor sports and fitness center with training equipment, an Olympic-sized pool, and racquetball courts. Open daily for members; guests by the day or week.

Middlebury Fitness Center (388-3744), Wilson Road, Middlebury, features state-of-the-art equipment.

FISHING

Otter Creek is a warm-water stream good for smallmouth bass and northern pike. The cooler **Neshobe River,** especially in Forest Dale, is better for trout, and rainbows can be found in the **Middlebury River** just below Ripton. The **New Haven River** between Lincoln and Bristol and South of New Haven Mills is also good trout fishing.

GOLF

Ralph Myhre Golf Course (388-3771), Route 30 just south of the Middlebury campus, is owned and operated by the college; 18 holes.

The Basin Harbor Club (475-2311), Vergennes, 18 holes (see *Lodging—Resort*).

Neshobe Golf Club (247-3611), Town Farm Road (just off Route 73), Brandon. Open April through October. A full-service club; 18 holes.

HIKING

The Green Mountain National Forest District Office (388-4362), Route 7, Middlebury, offers a pamphlet guide to 28 day hikes.

Country Inns along the Trail. Eight other inns collaborate with Churchill House (247-3300) to provide lodging along an 80-mile stretch of the Long Trail and some of its side trails, including the section over Mount Mansfield.

Middlebury Area Land Trust (388-1007) publishes "Trails Around Middlebury," a map and guide to 14 miles of trails.

HORSEBACK RIDING

Mazza Horse Service (758-9240), Hemenway Road, Bridport. Trail-ride lessons.

Firefly Ranch (453-2223), Bristol. Open May through October for riding. Really a mini-ranch set off a back road high in the mountains, an expanded chalet with just three guest rooms (private baths), eight horses. Guests must be experienced riders (children 10 and older are accepted); guided trail rides over dirt roads and woods trails, all meals included.

Krawczyk Horse Farm (758-2655), East Street, Bridport. Trail rides, leasing, boarding, lessons, tack shop.

RAILROAD EXCURSION

Champlain Valley Weekender (463-3069; 1-800-707-3530), P.O. Box 498, Bellows Falls. Operating between Middlebury and Burlington Saturdays and Sundays only, July 4 through September 27 in 1998 (the schedule may be expanded in 1999). Two round-trips per day with stops at Vergennes (Kennedy Brothers Marketplace; a shuttle connects with town) and Shelburne (walk to the Shelburne Museum). A free trolley meets the train in Burlington, or you can transfer right to a ferry or cruise boat. $12 per adult, $8 per child round-trip. The route follows the lake and gets rave reviews from all who take it. Bicycles can be carried aboard.

SWIMMING

Middlebury Gorge, East Middlebury, off Route 125 just above the Waybury Inn (see *Lodging—Inns*), where the road suddenly steepens beyond the bridge. Paths lead down to the river.

See also Branbury, Button Bay, D.A.R., and Kingsland Bay State Parks and
Silver Lake under *Green Space.*

WINTER SPORTS

CROSS-COUNTRY SKIING

Carroll and Jane Rikert Ski Touring Center at the Bread Loaf Campus of Middlebury College (388-2759), Route 125, Ripton, 12 miles
from the main campus, is owned and operated by Middlebury College.
It has more than 42 km of groomed trails in the area of the Robert Frost
Farm and the college ski bowl. Elevations range from 975 to 1,500 feet.
Rentals, accessories, repairs.

Blueberry Hill Inn (247-6735), Goshen, has 50 km of tracked and
groomed trails plus another 20 km of outlying trails on elevations of
1,400–3,100 feet. This is a surefire cross-country mecca during even
marginal seasons. The ski center has retail and rental equipment, waxing, and repairs.

DOWNHILL SKIING

Middlebury College Snow Bowl (388-4356), 13 miles east of Middlebury
on Route 125, at Bread Loaf. A throwback to a less commercial era of
skiing: well-maintained, winding trails with a library in the base lodge!
Two double chairs, one triple, a total of 15 trails; 40 percent covered by
snowmaking. It also offers a ski school, rentals, restaurant. Closed December 25.

GREEN SPACE

Note: Public preserves are clustered on the eastern and western fringes of
the valley.

On or near Lake Champlain

Button Bay State Park (475-2377, 483-2314), on Panton Road just below
Basin Harbor. Named for the unusual, buttonlike clay bank formations,
with a splendid view across the lake to the Adirondacks; 72 campsites,
picnic areas, swimming, fishing, nature museum, and trails. Rocky Point
juts into Lake Champlain like the prow of a ship.

Kingsland Bay State Park (877-3445), Ferrisburg. Marked from Route 7.
Facilities include a picnic area on Lake Champlain, also a tennis court
and hiking trails.

Dead Creek Wildlife Management Area (759-2397), 7 miles east of the
D.A.R. State Park on Route 17, is a 2,800-acre, semi-wilderness tract.
Except for certain refuges, it is open to the public. The information
booth is not always staffed, because the supervisor is generally in the
field, but a self-guided tour folder is available.

D.A.R. State Park (759-2354, 483-2314), 8 miles west of Addison on Route
17, has a campground with 71 sites and a picnic area. Steps lead down

to a smooth shale beach for swimming.

In or near the Green Mountain National Forest

Lake Dunmore, in Salisbury between Brandon and Middlebury on Route 53 off Route 7, is a tranquil, 1,000-acre lake that has licked its once infamous mosquito problem. It is lined with summer cottages at the foot of Mount Moosalamoo and along its hiking trails. On the east shore road is **Branbury State Park** (247-5925), with a sandy beach, boating, snack bar, picnic grove, museum nature trail, and hiking to the Falls of Lana. The trail begins just south of the Branbury Park entrance, and it's just a half mile to the picnic area and falls. From Route 53, it's 1.6 miles past these falls up to **Silver Lake,** a mountain lake that was the site of religious camp meetings in the 1880s; a large hotel (actually constructed as a seminary) occupied the site of the present picnic area and stood until around 1940, when it was destroyed by fire. About 1 mile long, it is now part of the Green Mountain National Forest, accessible only by foot and mountain bike (0.6 mile via the Goshen Trail from the second parking lot on Forest Road 27, off Goshen Road). There are 31 primitive campsites and a nature trail around the lake; swimming is permitted.

"Robert Frost Country" in the Green Mountain National Forest is a title officially bestowed in 1983 on a wooded piece of the town of Ripton because it is here, in a log cabin, that the poet summered for 39 years. This section of Route 125, between the old Bread Loaf Inn (part of the Middlebury College campus) and the village, has been designated the Robert Frost Memorial Highway; there is also a Robert Frost Interpretive Trail and a Robert Frost Wayside picnic area near the road leading to the farm and cabin. The picnic area has grills and drinking water, and it's shaded by red pines that were pruned by Frost himself. Just east of the wayside, a dirt road leads to the Homer Noble Farm, which Frost bought in 1939. Park in the lot provided and walk past the farm to Frost's cabin (it's not open to the public). The Robert Frost Interpretive Trail, a bit west on the opposite side of Route 125, is an easy walk, just ¾ mile. It begins with a bridge across Beaver Pond (we actually saw a beaver here one time) and winds through woods and meadow, by seven Frost poems mounted along the way. This trail is also popular with cross-country skiers and snowshoers, and with July and August blueberry pickers.

Texas Falls, in Hancock, is easily accessible from the marked road, 3 miles east of the Middlebury Gap. It's a short drive to the parking area, and the succession of falls are just across the road, visible from a series of paths and bridges. There's also a picnic area.

LODGING

Historic Lake Champlain/Middlebury Region Lodging Association (388-0800; www.vermont-lodging.com), P.O. Box 711, Middlebury

05753, issues a descriptive brochure of places to stay in the area.

RESORT

✿♨🐾**Basin Harbor Club** (475-2311; 1-800-622-4000), Box 7, Vergennes 05491, located on Lake Champlain 5 miles west of town, off Panton Road. Open mid-May through mid-October. This is Vermont's premier family-run resort. The 700-acre retreat offers 136 rooms, most in cottages scattered along the shore. Since 1886, when they began taking in summer boarders, the Beach family have assiduously kept up with the times. Over the years, a large swimming pool, an 18-hole golf course, and even an airstrip have been added. Still, the handsome old farmhouse has been preserved. In summer, Dutchman's-pipe climbs as it always has around the porch pillars, and three grand old maples shade the lawn, which slopes to the extensive flower gardens and the round harbor beyond. There are 18 rooms in the inn, 13 more in the attractive stone Harbor Homestead. The 77 cottages, geared to families (and well-behaved pets), vary in rate depending on size and location. All have phone, fridge, and wet bar; many have fireplace. Eight cottages are handicapped-accessible, with ramps and bathrooms, as are all public areas. The lakeside units are worth the little extra, with views of the lake and the Adirondacks so extraordinary that it's difficult to tear yourself away from the window or deck, especially at sunset.

Basin Harbor manages to please both children and elderly couples. Youngsters can take advantage of the beach, elaborate playground, and lively, supervised (complimentary) children's program available 9 AM–1 PM for ages 3–15, and younger children can also dine together and play until 9 PM. For those ages 10–15, there are golf and tennis clinics, movies, mixers, and video games in the Red Mill, the resort's informal restaurant off by the airstrip. Those who like to dress for dinner have ample opportunity; at the main restaurant, men and boys over 12 must wear jackets and ties. The food is fine (see *Dining Out*). Daily rates per couple $130–250 B&B; with a full American plan, $110–198 per person; add 15 percent gratuity. Less for children. There are also golf, tennis, and fall-foliage packages; inquire about kayaking, horticultural workshops, and birding and nature treks.

INNS

  🦽 **Swift House Inn** (388-9925; fax: 802-388-9927), 25 Stewart Lane, Middlebury 05753, formerly the family estate of the legendary philanthropist Jessica Stewart Swift, who lived to be over 100. Antiques, elaborately carved marble fireplaces, formal gardens with more than 20 rosebushes, and other gracious amenities add to the charm of this 1814 mansion. Common space in the inn itself includes a cozy pub as well as two attractive living rooms. Dinner and breakfast are served in the cherry-paneled main dining room or in the library. There are 10 guest rooms in the main house, 6 in the renovated 1886 carriage house, and 5 more in the less desirable gatehouse. One room is wheelchair-accessible, as is the dining room. Dinner is served Thursday through Monday year-round (see *Dining Out*). Rates per room with continental breakfast from $90 to $185 for suites with fireplaces, sitting area, whirlpool tub, and cable TV.

Historic Brookside Farms Country Inn & Antiques (948-2727), P.O. Box 36, Route 22A, Orwell 05760. White Ionic columns distinguish the front of this stately Greek Revival mansion, enlarged in 1843 and now on the National Register of Historic Places. It's still a 300-acre working farm, owned and operated by the Joan and Murray Korda family. In the main house, guests can browse in the 10,000-volume library, relax in the TV den, and enjoy afternoon tea and a five-course dinner. Here, too, is a two-room suite with a private bath ($165). In the restored tenant farmhouse that doubles as antiques shop are four more guest rooms, two with private bath and two shared ($85–135, including breakfast). The grounds are great for nature hikes in summer and fall, cross-country skiing in winter. Cash and traveler's and personal checks accepted; no credit cards.

  ♿ **Lilac Inn** (247-5463; 1-800-221-0720), 53 Park Street, Brandon 05733. One of New England's most romantic inns, this grand old mansion has been totally restored (and then some) by Melanie and Michael Shane (he a contractor, she an interior decorator, both from California). Built with an imposing five-arched facade in 1909 by a Brandon-born financier, the mansion has some splendid common spaces (a glassed-in ballroom is the scene of chamber concerts and wedding receptions) and a wide entrance hallway with a grand staircase. There is also a formal garden with a gazebo and cobbled patio, a small living room with a fireplace and floor-to-ceiling bookcases, and a bar with comfortable seating. The nine ample guest rooms all have luxurious bathrooms with deep, claw-foot tubs; each is furnished in antiques and has a hidden TV. The bridal suite has a pewter canopy bed, whirlpool bath, fireplace, and dressing area. There is one handicapped-accessible room. Weddings are a specialty. Melanie herself makes wedding dolls (displayed throughout the house) and wedding cakes. Rates include a full breakfast, served in the oak-paneled dining room, where dinner is also served Wednesday through Saturday. Rates $185–265 in October, otherwise $120–185. Inquire about MAP, winter weekends featuring music or dramatic readings, and the cottage for four.

  ✎ **Blueberry Hill Inn** (247-6735, 247-6535; 1-800-448-0707), Goshen 05733, on Forest Road 32 in Ripton. Over the past 27 years, Tony Clark has turned this blue 1820 farmhouse on a high, remote back road into one of New England's most famous country inns. The big lures are fine food, hiking and mountain biking, and, in winter, cross-country skiing. But there is more to it: a sure touch. The rooms—some with lofts, all with full bath—have their share of antiques. The common rooms are sunny and inviting with geraniums blooming in the greenhouse off the kitchen and a stone fireplace in the dining room. Guests are encouraged to mingle, from morning coffee to evening hors d'oeuvres and dinner. This inn has

KIM GRANT

The Inn at Blueberry Hill in Goshen

long been known for its food, and current chefs more than deserve the reputation, producing elaborate, creative dinners featuring fresh, local ingredients. The cross-country-ski center, with 75 km of groomed trails, tends to be snowy, thanks to its elevation, if there is any snow in Vermont. MAP rates per person: $95–164 depending on the season, plus 15 percent gratuity; half price for children 12 and under in same room with parent. BYOB. No smoking.

The Middlebury Inn (388-4961; 1-800-842-4666), 14 Courthouse Square, Middlebury 05753, has been the town's imposing chief hostelry since 1827. The Emanuel family have now completely renovated the 75 guest and public rooms. Rooms in the main house are on two floors (there's a 1926 Otis elevator) and are furnished in reproduction antiques. They have private bath, cable TV, air-conditioner/heaters, and direct-dial phones. There are also 20 motel units with inn-style furnishings, and the adjacent Porter Mansion, full of handsome architectural details, has 10 Victorian rooms. The common rooms include a vast, comfortable lobby with a formal check-in desk and portraits of the Battell family and Robert Frost. Elegant afternoon tea and light dinners are available in the pubby Morgan Tavern; dinner and buffet breakfast are served in the pillared, Wedgwood blue, formal dining room (see *Dining Out*). Lunch is served in the Rose Room and on the front porch in summer and early fall. Thoughtful touches include readable books on shelves near guest rooms and umbrellas for guests to use next to the door. Continental breakfast is included in rates that run $86–275 double, including afternoon tea (plus $38 per person MAP). Inquire about packages. Pets are welcome in the motel units for a small daily fee, and arrangements for baby-sitting can be made.

The Shoreham Inn & Country Store (897-5081; out-of-state: 1-800-255-5081), Route 74 west, Shoreham 05770. This friendly, comfortable place is a great antidote if you've overdosed on Laura Ashley wallpaper and mints on the lacy coverlets of antique beds. Jim and Julie Ortuno offer, instead, a comfortable, country atmosphere. Rooms are whimsically decorated, some with daybeds for families, and plenty of singles for the many bicyclists and hikers who frequent the inn. There are 10 guest rooms, each with private bath. The many-windowed inn, which dates from 1790, sits in the middle of a small village, surrounded by apple country and not far from Larrabees Point, Mount Independence, and the college town of Middlebury. The common rooms are filled with pictures, plants, and, frequently, the aroma of coffee, soup, or other things cooking and baking in the kitchen. The inn's original fireplace is in the dining room, where guests gather around the long table surrounded by photos of previous visitors. This is a great place for solo travelers and people who like to read (books are everywhere), to talk (Cleo will always listen), and to eat. $65 single with full breakfast, $85–95 double. Closed November. The Country Store is next door, a source of great deli sandwiches.

The Churchill House Inn (247-3300; fax: 802-247-6851), RD 3, Brandon 05733. Located west of the Brandon Gap on Route 73, this old farmhouse has eight guest rooms furnished in 19th-century style. There are zesty dinners and breakfasts, and canoeing, hiking, bicycling, and cross-country-ski expeditions (see *To Do—Bicycling* and *Hiking*). MAP rates are $70–90 per person plus 15 percent gratuity; inquire about 3- and 5-day packages.

The Waybury Inn (388-4015; 1-800-348-1810), Route 125, East Middlebury 05740. A historic, 14-room village inn, open all year. Bob Newhart never did sleep here, though guests sometimes ask for "the Loudons" because the exterior served as the "Stratford Inn" on a veteran CBS series. There's no pool, but a swimmin' hole under the nearby bridge serves the purpose. Dinner and Sunday brunch are served year-round. The innkeepers are Marcia and Marty Schuppert, and rates are $80–115 double, including a continental breakfast. Two-night minimum stay on busy weekends and holidays.

Chipman Inn (388-2390; 1-800-890-2390), Route 125 on the way to or from Bread Loaf and the Middlebury College Snow Bowl ski area, in the center of the tiny village of Ripton 05766 (population: 400), which consists of a schoolhouse, a community meetinghouse, church, and a general store. This is an exceptionally attractive 1828 house with nine guest rooms of varying sizes (we suggest requesting one at the back of the house), all with private bath. Guests gather in the lounge/bar and around a very large old hearth or settle into the sunny sitting room near the woodstove. The dining room is lit by candles and decorated with stenciled wallpaper. Innkeepers Joyce Henderson and Bill Pierce offer a five-course dinner on request (prix fixe $25), and both dinner and breakfast guests are encouraged to sit together at long tables. There is also a table for two. Rates are $85–125 per couple ($65–80 single), with breakfast. Closed April and November.

Mary's at Baldwin Creek (453-2432), Routes 116 and 17, Bristol 05443. Open year-round. A classic Vermont farmhouse set in 15 acres including a perennial garden with paths down to Baldwin Creek. There's a large restaurant (see *Dining Out*). Five guest rooms (shared baths), $65–85 double.

🐾✒ **The Brandon Inn** (247-5766), 20 Park Street, Brandon 05733. A large brick landmark overlooking the village green. It dates from 1892 and is on the National Register of Historic Places. Innkeepers Sarah and Louis Pattis have scaled down the number of guest rooms from 46 to 37, refurbishing them nicely. Number 217, a two-room suite, is especially attractive ($155 MAP). Other MAP rates: $65–80 per person for a double; September 18 through October 18 rates are $83.75–100 per person double, MAP, and a 2-day minimum stay is required on weekends. The B&B rate is $45–77.50 per person. Children under 12 are free in their parent's room (except for meals), and are welcome. There are TV rooms upstairs as well as large living rooms downstairs, and some of the 19th-century furniture and a good deal of the atmosphere survive. The inn's 5 landscaped acres include a swimming pool (with Jacuzzi) and a stretch of the Neshobe River, good for trout fishing. An 18-hole golf course is just up the way. Buses from New York, Boston, and Montreal still stop, as stages once did, at the front door.

BED & BREAKFASTS
In and around Middlebury 05753

  ♿ **The Inn on the Green** (388-7512; 1-888-244-7512), 19 South Pleasant Street. A recent addition to the downtown hospitality scene, this very attractive 1803 Federal town house has two impressive, colorfully decorated suites in the main house, plus eight other spacious rooms, each with private bath, phone, cable TV. There's also a more contemporary carriage house, same amenities. Rates: $75–125.

Brookside Meadows (388-6429; 1-800-442-9887), RD 3, Box 2460, Middlebury. A handsome and comfortable, traditional-style house with spacious lawns and perennial gardens, set back from a quiet country road, just 3 miles from the center of town and Middlebury College. Linda and Roger Cole pride themselves on the warmth of their hospitality. They offer four bedrooms and a two-bedroom suite, all with private bath. The guests' living room, with cable TV and a glass-front woodstove, overlooks the garden and a small pond in a roll of meadow at the foot of the mountains. Rooms $85–135, suite $125–150, with full breakfast.

Linens & Lace (388-0832), 29 Seminary Street, Middlebury. This crisply decorated, yellow and white village house has five guest rooms, three with private baths; spacious sitting and dining rooms; and an inviting kitchen. Rates: $89–119.

Fairhill (388-3044), P.O. Box 2300, Middlebury, located on East Munger Street, 4 miles east of Middlebury, on 75 acres of woodland, marsh, and meadows. Russell and Fleur Laslocky's 1825 center-chimney cape has three guest rooms, one with a four-poster double and private bath. The breakfast area is in an 18th-century granary. Rates: $70–90.

In and around East Middlebury 05740

The Annex (388-3233), Route 125, East Middlebury. This 1830 Greek Revival home was originally built as an annex to the Waybury Inn (see *Inns*). It offers six rooms, four with private bath. There are two small living rooms with cable TV, and a dining room with several tables. Rooms are $50–75, $115 for the suite sleeping four, Teedee Hutchins's hearty continental breakfast included. Smoke-free; no pets; some restrictions apply for children.

Elizabeth's October Pumpkin B&B (388-9525; 1-800-237-2007), P.O. Box 226, East Middlebury. A charming 1850 Greek Revival (you can't miss the color) with stenciling; four rooms, $70–90.

By the Way B&B (388-6291), P.O. Box 264, East Middlebury. Nancy Simoes provides two spacious guest rooms with private bath, air-conditioning, $65–85; the wraparound veranda is appealing, and an in-ground swimming pool is set in the orchard.

In and around Vergennes 05491

The Strong House Inn (877-3337), Route 22A, Vergennes. This is a real beauty, built in the 1830s by Samuel Paddock Strong, a local worthy, in the graceful Federal style, with fine workmanship such as curly maple railings on the freestanding main staircase. Mary and Hugh Bargiel offer six bedrooms, all exceptional, as well as Samuel's Suite—a library with queen-sized sofa bed and fireplace and an adjoining bedroom with queen-sized poster bed, plus an enclosed sunporch with Adirondack views ($185). The Empire Room has mahogany furnishings (queen-sized bed), a working fireplace, and a private half bath ($120); and the sunny English Garden Room with its brass bed (shared bath) is a find at $75. We also wouldn't mind settling for the English Hunt Room, with its sleigh bed ($85). The Victorian Suite has a double four-poster plus a sitting room with a double tapestry sofa bed, cable TV, and air-conditioning ($125). Rates include afternoon tea and a full breakfast and increase by $15 per room in foliage season. Inquire about quilting weekends.

Emersons' Guest House (877-3293), 82 Main Street, Vergennes. Six bright and airy guest rooms in this Victorian town house are named for New England writers and poets. $55–90 with full breakfast.

&. **Whitford House** (758-2704; 1-800-746-2704), RR 1, Box 1490, Vergennes. On Grandey Road between Nortontown and Townline Roads off Route 22A (ask directions!). Sited 2 miles east of the lake in the middle of rich farmland, it's set among flower gardens on 2 acres of mowed lawns with spectacular views of the Adirondacks from an outdoor deck. Tranquillity and warm hospitality are the hallmarks of Bruce and Barbara Carson's 18th-century farmhouse, with three simple upstairs bedrooms (shared baths) and a spacious first-floor bedroom with a four-poster and private bath. The Great Room, with its fireplace made from local Panton stone, is a great place for relaxing. There is also a cottage with a large bedroom (king-sized bed), sitting room, and full bath. Rates: $70 single, $80–150 double (plus $25 in October), including afternoon tea and a full breakfast. The Carsons loan their canoe and bicycles. Breakfasts are events in themselves, and chef Karen Colvin-Rathbun's memorable dinners can be served to guests Sunday through Wednesday, and to the public Thursday through Saturday by 48-hour advance reservation. Hands-on culinary weekends with guest chefs and field trips to Vermont specialty food makers are available (at $225 per participant in 1998).

South and west of Middlebury

Indian Trail Farm (897-5292), RD 1, Box 49, Shoreham 05770. A vintage-1830 farmhouse overlooking Lake Champlain, with panoramic views also down the valley across open fields to the Green Mountains. May and Phil Small have lived here for 37 years, raising their children and maintaining their surrounding apple orchard. Guests enter through the big open kitchen/den with a woodstove, old loft in the timbers, and huge south-facing window. The living room, with its grand piano, is quite elegant, and the three upstairs rooms (one with twins or king-sized bed, one double with a window seat and lakeside view, and a third that sleeps three) are all charming. The big bath is shared. A retired schoolteacher, May also keeps busy making appealing felt hats. In winter there's cross-country skiing out the back door. Rates are $50 double, $15 extra per child in the same room, including a gourmet breakfast like cheese soufflé or sausage quiche.

Quiet Valley Bed & Breakfast (897-7887), RD 1, Box 175, Shoreham 05770. A new house built along traditional lines with wide pine floors to maximize the light and views across the Lemon Fair River to the hills. Bruce Lustgarten burns only applewood in the large, shallow, Rumford-style fireplace in the living room, and Jane enjoys preparing "healthy" breakfasts for guests, who never number more than seven. Four guest rooms, one with a wood-burning stove, two with handmade four-posters and a private bath, the other two with twin beds and shared bath. $85–105 double.

Buckswood Bed & Breakfast (948-2054), 633 Route 73E, Orwell 05760. Open year-round. Linda and Bob Martin offer two guest rooms (private baths) and ample common space in their 1814 home, set in pleasant grounds just east of the appealing village of Orwell. Dinner by reservation. Rates of $55–65 per couple include breakfast. Polite pets accepted.

Others: **The Willow & Lotus** (462-2519), 3958 Route 30, Cornwall 05753; **Carousel Farm** (623-6069), Route 30, Whiting 05778, open May 15–

October 31; **The Inn at Lovers Lane** (758-2185), Route 125, Bridport 05734; **Lemon Fair** (758-9238), Crown Point Road, Bridport 05734.

In and around Brandon 05733

The Old Mill Inn (247-8002; 1-800-599-0341), Route 73, Stone Mill Dam Road, East Brandon. Owned by Ed and Cindy Thomas, this is an attractive farmhouse set above the Neshobe River, adjoining the Neshobe Golf Club (18 holes; see *To Do—Golf*). Guests enter through a sunny breakfast room and find two large living rooms with wing chairs, a piano, TV, and Cindy's artwork. There's a sense of space here, both inside and out—a porch with wicker chairs is new. The four guest rooms have private baths, stenciling, and carefully chosen antiques. Daisy the golden retriever, two barn cats, miniature horses, chickens, and a rooster are also in residence, and guests can take advantage of the swimming hole in the neighboring rushing stream. $75–95 per couple includes a full country breakfast.

Rosebelle's Victorian Inn (247-0098), 31 Franklin Street, Route 7, Brandon. This nicely restored, mansard-roofed house has a high-ceilinged living room with fireplace and TV and a large dining room—the setting for afternoon tea and full breakfasts that feature gourmet coffees and fresh-baked breads and muffins. Guests with small musical instruments are especially welcome. Hostess Ginette Milot speaks French. All but one of the six guest rooms share baths. Rates: $75–95 double, slightly higher during foliage season.

The Gazebo (247-3235; 1-888-858-3235), 25 Grove Street (Route 7), Brandon. This is another attractive in-town, circa-1865 classic house, with a wood-burning stove in the sitting room. It's decorated with folk art and antiques and has four comfortable guest rooms, private baths. Antiques shop on premises; families welcome. Hosts Joel and Janet Mondlak include a full breakfast at $55–85 per couple; $10 less single.

🐾 **Hivue Bed & Breakfast Tree Farm** (247-3042; 1-800-880-3042), 730 High Pond Road, Brandon. A contemporary lodging that offers on-site trout fishing and walking trails in a 76-acre wildlife habitat. Picture windows in the living room and the deck overlook Pico Peak and the Killington Mountains. One of two guest quarters has a king-sized bed and sleep sofa with a Jacuzzi in the private bath; the other, a king bed and studio couch with bath. $60 per night with continental breakfast. Polite pets accepted.

Moffett House B&B (247-3843), 69 Park Street, Brandon. Full of antiques, collectibles, and 200 stuffed bears; $70–125.

Judith's Garden (247-4707), Goshen-Ripton Road, Goshen 05733. Locally noted for its lovely perennial gardens in a mountainous setting appealing to hikers, walkers, and cross-country skiers who want to take advantage of the Moosalamoo region. Proprietors Judith Irven and Dick Conrad serve smoked salmon and dill quiche among other breakfast dishes. This restored 1830s farmhouse has three attractive bedrooms with private baths; $70–90.

❋ **Salisbury Village Bed & Breakfast** (352-6006), P.O. Box 214, Salisbury 05769. Not far from Lake Dunmore, this restored farmhouse has four guest rooms with shared bath ($65–75), and welcomes polite pets at $10 per night and even provides day care for them.

In Bristol 05443

Crystal Palace Victorian B&B (453-4131), 48 North Street, Bristol. This impressive 1897 mansion with a tower provides six guest rooms, $70–95.

See also Firefly Ranch under *To Do—Horseback Riding*.

COTTAGES

Lake Dunmore. Some cottagers hope that the lake will remain off the beaten track; however, it's being "discovered." Here are some good bets:

✍ **Dunmore Acres** (247-3126; off-season: 207-499-7491), Brandon 05733, a former summer camp in a lovely setting, has nine two- and three-bedroom housekeeping cabins, a swimming pool, basketball, rec hall, boat dock with canoe and rowboat. $65 per night for a two-bedroom cabin, $70 for a three-bedroom (2-night minimum), and $425 and $450 per week, respectively.

North Cove Cottages (352-4236 summer; winter: 617-354-0124), P.O. Box 76, Salisbury 05769. Nine housekeeping cottages, sanded beach, free rowboats; $45–75 per day, $240–430 per week.

Note: The Addison County Chamber of Commerce (388-7951; see *Guidance*) has a list of rental cottages on both Lake Dunmore and Lake Champlain.

MOTEL

⑤ **The Adams Motor Inn and Restaurant** (247-6644; 1-800-759-6537), RR 1, Box 1142, Brandon 05733. Open late spring to November. Located on Route 7, 1 mile south of Brandon, this isn't really a motel but rather a shady campus of 20 cozy, one- and two-room cottages of the kind so familiar in premotel motoring days. Most of the cottages have fireplace and cable TV, and there's a stocked trout pond, swimming pool, and miniature golf across the highway. Rates for two: $55–70, without meals (extra $25 a day per person with breakfast and dinner).

FARM VACATION

Cream Hill Farm (897-2101), P.O. Box 205, Shoreham 05770. Rene and Paul Saenger welcome families to their 1,100-acre diversified farm, with beef cattle. This is very much a working farm (meaning it smells like a farm, and its owners may be preoccupied with farm chores). The 1830s renovated farmhouse has two large guest rooms, one with private bath. $40 double, $10 per additional person.

CAMPGROUNDS

See *Green Space* for information on campgrounds in Button Bay State Park, D.A.R. State Park, and Lake Dunmore.

WHERE TO EAT

DINING OUT

Swift House Inn (388-2766), 25 Stewart Lane, Middlebury. Dinner is served Thursday through Monday year-round. Dine either in the paneled main dining room or in the more intimate library on elegant fare: perhaps grilled duck sausage, savory polenta, and chutney ($6) to start, then maybe rack of lamb with roasted hazelnuts, baby red lentils, and a rosemary–port wine sauce ($22 full rack, $14.50 half). Save room for the chef's famous coffee toffee pecan torte ($4). Wine specials are available by the glass.

The Storm Café (388-1063), 3 Mill Street, Middlebury. This intimate, casual spot by the river is considered by many to serve the most imaginative food in town, if not in the state. Open for lunch Monday through Saturday, 11–3; dinner 5–9. Reservations definitely recommended. Moderate.

Fire & Ice Restaurant (388-7166; 1-800-367-7166), 26 Seymour Street, Middlebury. Open 11:30–9:30 daily except Monday. "Good Food & Legal Vice," it says of itself; excellent lunch and dinner plus Sunday brunch in an informal stained-glass and mahogany setting that has recently been enlarged. A local favorite since 1974, specializing in steaks ($14.95–20.95), prime rib ($14.95–19.95), and chicken dishes like a fresh boneless breast sautéed in a champagne and mushroom cream sauce ($14.95). The name was inspired by a Robert Frost poem.

Roland's Place (453-6309), Route 7, New Haven. A grand old tower-topped mansion, this 1796 house is the setting for dinner and Sunday brunch year-round, lunch May through October. Lunch on seafood crêpes with Newburg sauce ($7.75). Dine on a Vermont game sampler with mushroom risotto ($17.95), vegetable seacake with marinara sauce ($11.50), or one of the other moderately priced entrées. Owner-chef Roland Gaujac has a Provençal background. (Guest rooms available at $65.)

Basin Harbor Club (475-2311), Basin Harbor, off Panton Road, 5 miles west of Vergennes. If you don't stay at Basin Harbor, there's all the more reason to drive out for lunch or dinner, to see the lakeside setting and savor the atmosphere. The food is fine, too. The menu and dining room are both large. At dinner (reserve) you might begin with Green Mountain smoked trout, then enjoy seared breast of ginger-soy-marinated duck. The prix fixe is $28 plus 15 percent service charge. The wine list is extensive and excellent.

Woody's (388-4182), Five Bakery Lane, Middlebury, open daily 11:30 AM–midnight; Sunday brunch. Closed Tuesday in winter. You have the sense of being wined and dined on a small, three-decker art deco ship beached on the bank of Otter Creek. Owner-chef Woody Danforth serves up salads and quiches midday, homemade breads and desserts, and lists among dinner entrées spicy Cajun or bourbon shrimp. The menu changes nightly, and both the wine list and the selection of beers are extensive. The à la carte menu begins at $6, and inclusive dinner at $11.

Mr. Up's (388-6724), on the Bakery Lane plaza, Middlebury, open daily, lunch–midnight; Sunday brunch buffet 11–2. Dine outdoors on the riverside deck or in the brick-walled, stained-glass, oak-and-greenery setting inside. The menu is equally colorful, ranging from the Ultimate Salad Bar and Bread Board ($6.50) to prime rib ($14.75).

The Middlebury Inn (388-4961, 388-4666), 14 Courthouse Square, Middlebury, serves breakfast and dinner in the Wedgwood blue Founders Room. Lunch is served in the Rose Room and on the front porch in summer and early fall, and light dinner is served in the **Morgan Tavern**. A popular appetizer here is fried Cabot cheese (deep-fried Vermont cheddar served with apple maple sauce for dipping). The moderately priced menu includes fresh seafood, Angus steaks, and a rotating market special each evening. Dinner includes hot popovers.

Christophe's on the Green (877-3414), 5 Green Street, Vergennes. Open for dinner Tuesday through Saturday. Reservations suggested. Housed in the old hotel in the middle of town, a first-class French restaurant. You might begin with Cornish hen baked in phyllo, then dine on braised rabbit with mushrooms and tomatoes, served with a garlic flan and *pommes gauffrettes,* and finish with espresso crème caramel served with cardamom cream. All appetizers are $6, entrées $17.50, desserts $5.50. The prix fixe for three courses is $25.

Mary's at Baldwin Creek (453-2432), at the junction of Routes 116 and 17, Bristol. Open year-round except Monday for dinner, and Sunday brunch (10:30–2); lunch served in summer. Highly and widely regarded, Mary's moved a few years ago from a village storefront, expanding to fill three rooms of a classic old Vermont farmhouse on the banks of Baldwin Creek. Entrées run $10–22 and the menu changes seasonally. Local rabbit, venison, produce, and brews are featured.

The Dog Team Tavern (388-7651), a jog off Route 7, 4 miles north of Middlebury. Moderately priced, traditional New England fare (sticky buns, relish trays, et al.). Open for dinner daily except Monday; for lunch late spring through foliage season. Gift shop. Opened in the 1930s by Sir Wilfred Grenfell (1865–1940), the British medical missionary who established hospitals, orphanages, schools, and cooperative stores in Labrador and near the Arctic Circle.

The Brandon Inn (247-5766), 20 Park Street, Brandon. Open for dinner daily except Tuesday and Wednesday. Austrian-trained owner-chef Louis Pattis and David Bofhinger make moderately priced dinner in this grand old multi-pillared dining room something of an event, with appetizers like crab cakes with a mango-habanero fruit sauce and entrées like roast duck served with wild blueberry-ginger sauce.

EATING OUT

Rosie's Restaurant (388-7052), 1 mile south of Middlebury on Route 7, is open daily (6 AM–9 PM in winter, until 10 May through November) and serves a lot of good, inexpensive food. This family mecca is said to expand every eight months or so to accommodate its fans. There's a friendly counter for those in a hurry or interested in the local gossip, and three large, cheerful dining rooms . We lunched on a superb beef and barley soup and a turkey salad on wheat. Dinner choices run from fish-and-chips to Smitty's top sirloin, and there are always stir-fries.

Noonie's Deli (388-0014), 2 Maple Street (in the Marble Works), Middlebury. Open Monday through Saturday 9–9, Sunday 11–9. Good soups, the best sandwiches in Addison County (a half sandwich is plenty)—on homemade bread, you design it. Eat in or take out.

Squirrel's Nest Restaurant (453-6309), Route 116, Bristol. Open daily for breakfast, lunch, and dinner; Sunday brunch. Good family dining. Creemees and takeout year-round.

Tom's Riverside Grill (453-6633), Route 116, Bristol. Open daily for breakfast, lunch, and dinner with a pleasant decor, seats by the river. Owner-chef Tom Goulette offers dinner specials like grilled salmon ($11.50) and pesto ravioli ($8.95).

Amigo's (388-3624), on the green, Middlebury, serves Mexican specials from light snacks to full dinners, weekdays from 11:30, Sunday from 4.

Patricia's Restaurant (247-3223), Center Street, Brandon, open daily from 11 for lunch and dinner; 1–8 Sunday, when there's a senior citizen discount on complete dinners. Traditional fare like grilled pork chops, fried haddock, and Italian dishes ranging from cheese ravioli to spaghetti with hot sausage.

Bristol Bakery & Café (453-3280), 16 Main Street, Bristol. Open daily from 5 AM, except Sunday when it opens at 6. An inviting storefront filled with the aroma of coffee and breads. Stop at least for a muffin and espresso and take home a loaf of sourdough bread; there are also black-board luncheon specials.

Beth's Bakery, village green, Vergennes. A good bet for lunch, with daily specials.

Main Street Bistro (877-3288), 253 Main Street, Vergennes. Open summer and early fall Monday through Saturday, 5–9:30 PM, this intimate place has earned favorable reviews. Limited seating; no credit cards.

Cubbers (453-2400), Main St., Bristol. A local favorite for red-and-white sauce pizza. Eat in or take out.

MICROBREWERY

Otter Creek Brewing (388-0727; 1-800-473-0727), 85 Exchange Street, across the railroad tracks from the Marble Works, Middlebury. Open Monday through Saturday 10–6, Sunday 11–4. Guided tours Saturday 2–4 and Sunday at 2. Ales and other beers can be sampled in the Tasting Room.

ENTERTAINMENT

Middlebury College Center for the Arts (388-3711, ext. SHOW). The theater and concert hall in this dramatic new building on the college campus (Route 30) offer a full series of concerts, recitals, plays, dance companies, and TV and film programs.

SELECTIVE SHOPPING

ART GALLERIES

Woody Jackson's Holy Cow (388-6737) studio and workshop at 52 Seymour Street, Middlebury, is a short walk beyond the Marble Works (cross the Frog Hollow footbridge to this shopping plaza). Woody himself, a Middlebury graduate whose Holstein products have become almost more of a symbol of Vermont than the maple tree, is usually on the premises. His black-and-white Holstein cows, immortalized on Ben & Jerry's ice-cream cartons, decorate T-shirts, aprons, coffee mugs, boxer shorts, and more.

Norton's Gallery (948-2552), Route 73 in Shoreham. The small red gallery overlooking Lake Champlain houses an amazing menagerie of dogs, rabbits, birds, and fish, along with flowers and vegetables—all sculpted from wood in unexpected sizes, unquestionably works of art and a visual delight for children and adults alike.

ANTIQUES SHOP

Middlebury Antique Center (388-6229; in Vermont: 1-800-339-6229), Route 7 at the junction of Route 116 in East Middlebury. A fascinating variety of furniture and furnishings representing 50 dealers.

BOOKSTORES

Vermont Bookshop (388-2061), 38 Main Street, Middlebury, was opened in 1947 by Robert Dike Blair, who retired several years ago as one of New England's best-known booksellers and the publisher of Vermont Books, an imprint for the poems of Walter Hard. John and Laura Scott are now the proprietors. Robert Frost was a frequent customer for more than two decades, and the store now specializes in autographed Frost poetry collections as well as current and out-of-print books about Vermont.

Deerleap Books (453-4062), Main Street, Bristol. Open daily except Monday. A small, friendly, and carefully stocked bookstore that entices you to browse and to buy. Author readings are held.

Otter Creek Old and Rare Books (388-3241), Main Street, Middlebury, is a book browser's delight: 25,000 very general titles.

Monroe Street Books (388-1622), 7 Monroe Street, Middlebury. Open 10–6 Memorial Day through October, but it's a good idea to call. Dick and Flanzy Chodkowski have some 20,000 titles; specialties include children's books and cartoon, comic, and graphic art.

Frog Hollow shops in Middlebury

Bulwagga Books and Gallery (623-6800), corner of Route 30 and Shoreham Road at the Whiting post office. More than 10,000 titles plus an art gallery, handcrafted furniture, and a reading room with mountain views and coffee.

CRAFTS SHOPS

The Vermont State Craft Center at Frog Hollow (388-3177), Middlebury. Open Monday through Saturday 9:30–5, Sunday afternoon, spring through fall. This nonprofit shop combines the natural beauty of Otter Creek falls, just outside its windows, with a dazzling array of the best art and crafts work in Vermont. More than 200 Vermont artisans are represented, and you can come away with anything from a 50¢ postcard to a magnificent, handcrafted $14,000 harpsichord. A feast for the eyes, it's also a serious shopping source with an outstanding selection of pottery, woven clothing, wall hangings, jewelry, and woodwork, among other things.

Sweet Cecily (388-3353), Frog Hollow Lane, Middlebury. Nancy Dunn, former Frog Hollow gallery director, has assembled her own selection of ceramics, folk art, hooked rugs, and other items from 100 craftspeople, including Mexican and Amish artisans.

Danforth Pewterers (388-0098), 52 Seymour Street, Middlebury, is best known for its distinctive pewter buttons, found in stores throughout New England. Fred and Judi Danforth actually continue a family tradition begun by Revolutionary War hero Thomas Danforth II. They also make pewter jewelry, oil lamps, and tableware.

Robert Compton Potter (453-3778), Route 116, Bristol. Open May through October 10–6. Visitors are welcome to watch Robert Compton fashioning his stoneware pottery (plates, vases, lamps, aquasculpture) and Christine Homer at work at her loom, weaving place mats and napkins to complement her husband's dinnerware.

SPECIAL SHOPS

Wood Ware (388-6297), Route 7 south of Middlebury, is the home of solid butternut door harps and dozens of other items. Open daily, May through October, and by appointment.

Kennedy Brothers Marketplace (877-2975), Vergennes, just off Route 7, no longer produces its own oak and pine woodenware, but a Factory Marketplace serves as cooperative space for many woodworkers and craftspeople.

SPECIAL EVENTS

Early February: **The American Ski Marathon,** Goshen, a 25 or 50 km challenge that draws as many as 600 skiers.

Late February: **Middlebury College Winter Carnival** (388-4356). Ice show, concerts, snow sculpture.

Mid-March: **The Pig Race** winds up with a fine pork barbecue. Further information from Blueberry Hill, Goshen (see *Cross-Country Skiing*).

July 4: Bristol hosts one of the most colorful **Independence Day parade**s around.

Early July: A 6-day **Festival on the Green,** Middlebury, featuring individual performers and groups such as the Bread & Puppet Theater.

Early August: **Addison County Field Days** (545-2257), New Haven. Livestock and produce fair, horse show, lumberjacks, demolition derby, and other events.

Burlington Region

Superbly sited on a slope overlooking Lake Champlain and the Adirondack Mountains, Burlington is Vermont's financial, educational, medical, and cultural center. While its fringes continue to spread over recent farmland (the core population hovers around 40,000 but the metro count is now more than 140,000), its heart beats ever faster. Few American cities this size offer as lively a downtown, as many interesting shops and affordable, varied restaurants, or as easy an access to boats, bike paths, and ski trails.

"Downtown Vermont" may sound like a contradiction, but that's just what Burlington is. Vermont is known for mountains, white-steepled churches, and cows, for rural beauty and right-spirited residents. Its only real city is backed by and overlooks mountains, has more steeples than high-rises, and plenty of green space (more about the cows later). Burlington actually pushes the possibilities of the sophisticated, urban good life—the ecological, healthy, responsible good life, that is.

The community was chartered in 1763, four years after the French were evicted from the Champlain Valley. Ethan Allen, his three brothers, and a cousin were awarded large grants of choice lots along the Onion (now Winooski) River. In 1791 Ira Allen secured the legislative charter for the University of Vermont (UVM), from which the first class, of four, was graduated in 1804 (UVM now enrolls more than 9,000); it is now just the largest of the city's five colleges.

Ethan and Ira would have little trouble finding their way around the city today. Main streets run much as they did in the 1780s—from the waterfront uphill past shops to the school Ira founded and on to Winooski Falls, site of Ira's own grist- and sawmills.

Along the waterfront, Federal-style commercial buildings house shops, businesses, and restaurants. The ferry terminal and neighboring Union Station, built during the city's late-19th-century boom period as a lumbering port—when the lakeside trains connected with myriad steamers and barges—are now the summer venue for excursion trains, ferries, and cruise boats. The neo-Victorian Burlington Boathouse is everyone's window on Lake Champlain, a place to rent a row- or sailboat, simply to sit sipping a morning coffee or sunset apéritif, or to

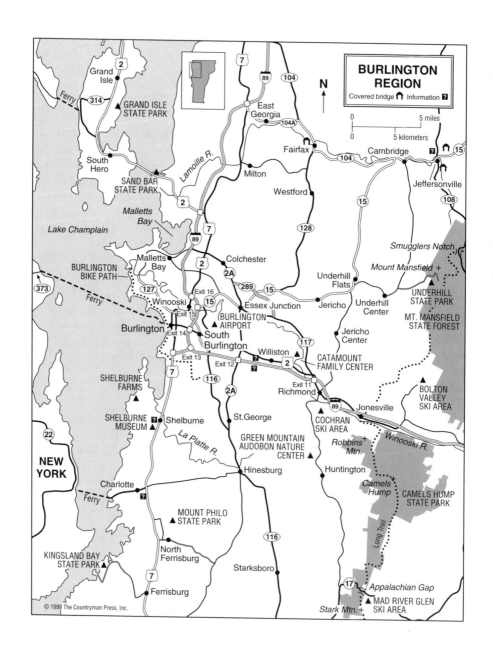

BURLINGTON REGION

Covered bridge ♁ Information ⬛

N

0   5 miles
0   5 kilometers

Grand Isle
GRAND ISLE STATE PARK
South Hero
SAND BAR STATE PARK
Malletts Bay
Lake Champlain
BURLINGTON BIKE PATH
Malletts Bay
Winooski
Burlington
South Burlington
BURLINGTON AIRPORT
SHELBURNE FARMS
SHELBURNE MUSEUM
Shelburne
NEW YORK
Charlotte
MOUNT PHILO STATE PARK
North Ferrisburg
KINGSLAND BAY STATE PARK
Ferrisburg
Ferry
Ferry

East Georgia
Fairfax
Cambridge
Jeffersonville
Milton
Westford
Colchester
Essex Junction
Jericho
Underhill Flats
Underhill Center
Mount Mansfield +
Smugglers Notch
UNDERHILL STATE PARK
MT. MANSFIELD STATE FOREST
Jericho Center
Williston
CATAMOUNT FAMILY CENTER
Richmond
St.George
GREEN MOUNTAIN AUDUBON NATURE CENTER
Hinesburg
Jonesville
COCHRAN SKI AREA
Robbins Mtn. +
Huntington
Camels Hump +
CAMELS HUMP STATE PARK
BOLTON VALLEY SKI AREA
Winooski R.
Long Trail
Starksboro
Appalachian Gap
MAD RIVER GLEN SKI AREA
Stark Mtn. +

Lamoille R.
La Platte R.

Exit 16
Exit 15
Exit 14
Exit 13
Exit 12
Exit 11

© 1999 The Countryman Press, Inc.

lunch or dine on the water. The adjacent Waterfront Park and promenade are linked by bike paths to a series of other lakeside parks (bike and in-line-skate rentals abound), which include swimmable beaches.

Halfway up the hill, the graceful Unitarian church, designed in 1815 by Peter Banner, stands at the head of Church Street—now a bricked, traffic-free marketplace for four long blocks, a promenade that's become a '90s-style common, the place everyone comes to graze.

Theater and music are constants, but Burlington is best when winter winds soften to cool breezes. The city celebrates summer with an exuberance literally trumpeted from the rooftops in its opening salvo to summer: the Discover Jazz Festival. The weeklong celebration includes some 200 performances: Stars perform at the Flynn Theater for the Performing Arts but jazz venues include buses, trolleys and ferries, street corners, parks, rooftops, and restaurants. This festival is followed by the Mozart Festival (also in varied venues) and a variety of music, both indoor and out, all summer.

Burlington in the 1950s and '60s was a different place. Docks and waterside rail yards had become privately owned wastelands, littered with rusting debris. The few public beaches were closed due to pollution, and the solution was seen as "urban renewal." In the '70s some 300 homes and 40 small businesses were demolished, and large luxury condo/retail development was planned. Then in 1981, Burlington elected as mayor Socialist Bernard Sanders, who had campaigned on the slogan, "The Waterfront Is Not for Sale."

The present waterfront includes several new parks, like Oakledge (formerly a General Electric property), just south of downtown, and Leddy Park (a former rendering plant) in the North End, and the waterside green space is linked by a 7-mile recreational path.

Downtown lodging options are mysteriously limited. Still, it is possible to walk from one high-rise hotel and several pleasant B&Bs to sights and water excursions, dining and shopping. Of course it's also appealing to bed down in the real countryside that's still within minutes of the city, so we have included B&Bs in nearby Jericho, Williston, Richmond, and Shelburne.

A couple of decades ago the Shelburne Museum, 6 miles south of the city, was the big sight-to-see in the area, although in recent years this "collection of collections" has been upstaged by Burlington itself. The museum's treasures range from a vintage Champlain Lake steamer to outstanding art and folk art, and at neighboring Shelburne Farms, New England's most fabulous estate, there are plenty of prizewinning cows (and cheese), miles of lakeside walks, and a mansion in which you should dine, sleep, or at least breakfast.

GUIDANCE

The Lake Champlain Regional Chamber of Commerce (863-3489; web site: www.vermont.org/chamber), 60 Main Street, Burlington

05401. Request brochure guides. Open Monday through Friday 8:30–5 year-round, also weekends 10–2 Memorial Day through Labor Day. Not the most obvious place for an information center (it's housed in the former motor vehicles building, halfway between Church Street and the waterfront), this one is augmented by a staffed information booth in the I-89 Williston rest area, northbound between exits 11 and 12, and at the airport. Both are staffed daily.

Newspapers: The daily **Burlington Free Press.** For current entertainment happenings, pick up **Seven Days,** a fat, free weekly published Wednesday and available in most shops and cafés.

GETTING THERE

Note: Burlington is Vermont's single most car-free destination, accessible by bus from Boston and Montreal and by train from New York City and Montreal, blessed with good local public transport and little need to use it.

By air: **Burlington International Airport** (863-2874) is just 3 miles from downtown, served by Continental Express, United Airlines, USAir, and Delta Connection. A half-dozen auto rental firms are at the airport.

By bus: **Vermont Transit Company** (1-800-451-3292 in New York and New England; within Vermont: 1-800-642-3133; from Canada: 1-800-552-8737), headquartered in Burlington, offers service to Albany, Boston, New York City, Montreal, Portland, and many points between. Buses depart from 345 Pine Street, south of the downtown area; plenty of parking.

By car: I-89, Routes 7 and 2.

By ferry: **The Lake Champlain Transportation Company** (864-9804; web site: www.ferries.com), King Street Dock, Burlington. Descended from the world's oldest steamboat company, offers three local car-ferry services. Between mid-May and mid-October, the LCTC car ferries make the 75-minute crossing between Burlington and Port Kent, New York. April through early January they also ply between Charlotte, just south of Burlington, and Essex, New York. Year-round service is offered on the 15-minute run between Grand Isle (see "The Northwest Corner") and Plattsburgh, New York.

By train: **Amtrak** (1-800-USA-RAIL; in Canada: 1-800-4-AMTRAK). The *Vermonter* (Washington to St. Albans via New York and Springfield, Massachusetts) stops at Essex Junction, 5 miles north of Burlington. (The station is served by two cab companies and by Burlington CCTA buses; see *Getting Around.*) Faster, more scenic service from New York City is available via the *Adirondack* to Port Kent, New York, connecting with the ferry to Burlington, connecting with the free trolley up Main Street. See *To Do—Rail Excursion* for details about the summer excursion train from Middlebury.

GETTING AROUND

By bus: **Chittenden County Transportation Authority** (864-0211). CCTA bus routes radiate from the corner of Cherry and Church Streets

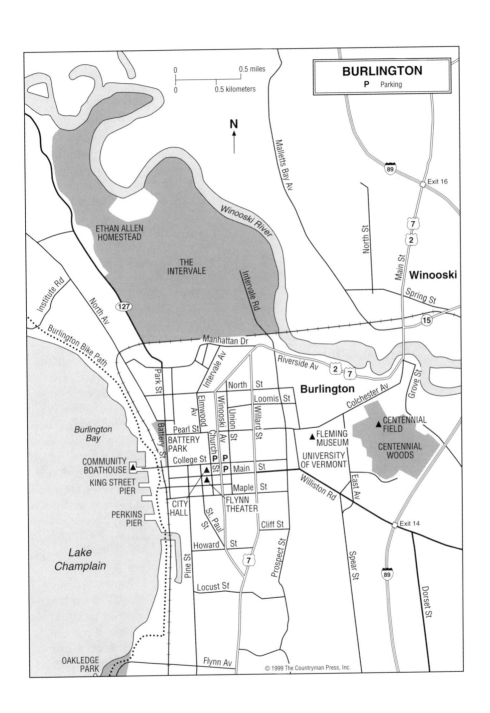

BURLINGTON

P Parking

0   0.5 miles

0   0.5 kilometers

N

Mallets Bay Av

89
Exit 16

7
2

ETHAN ALLEN
HOMESTEAD

Winooski River

THE
INTERVALE

Intervale Rd

North St

Main St

Winooski

Spring St

Institute Rd

North Av

127

Burlington Bike Path

Manhattan Dr

Riverside Av

2   7

Colchester Av

Grove St

15

Park St

Intervale Av

North   St

Loomis   St

Burlington

Elmwood Av

Winooski Av

Union St

Willard St

CENTENNIAL
FIELD

FLEMING
MUSEUM

Burlington
Bay

Pearl St

BATTERY
PARK

Church St

College St   P

P

Main   St

UNIVERSITY
OF VERMONT

CENTENNIAL
WOODS

COMMUNITY
BOATHOUSE

Battery St

Maple   St

Williston Rd

East Av

KING STREET
PIER

PERKINS
PIER

CITY
HALL

St Paul St

FLYNN
THEATER

Cliff St

Prospect St

Spear St

Exit 14

Lake
Champlain

Howard   St

7

Pine St

Locust St

89

Dorset St

OAKLEDGE
PARK

Flynn Av

© 1999 The Countryman Press, Inc.

(hub of the Church Street Marketplace), serving the Shelburne Museum, the airport, the ferry, and the Champlain Mill in Winooski as well as all the colleges and shopping areas. The fare is 75¢, and transfers are free. The CCTA also operates the **College Street Shuttle,** a free trolley on wheels circling among the waterfront, Church Street, and UVM. *By trolley:* A free, year-round trolley runs up and down the length of College Street, from the medical complex and UVM at the top of the hill to Union Station and the ferry dock on the lake. Stops are marked.

MEDICAL EMERGENCY

Burlington (911); Colchester (655-1412); Winooski/Williston (655-3212); Shelburne (911); South Burlington (656-4444); Charlotte (985-3233). In Burlington, the 24-hour emergency room is at **Fletcher Allen Health Care** (656-2450) on the UVM campus, Colchester Avenue.

NEARBY VILLAGES

Jericho. Northeast of Burlington, Jericho is best known for the **Old Red Mill** (Jericho Historical Society: 899-3225), on Route 15 at Jericho Corners (open Monday through Saturday 10–5, Sunday 1–5, except January through March when it's open only Wednesday, Saturday, and Sunday). This tower-topped, 1800s red mill set above a gorge is one of the most photographed buildings in Vermont and appropriately houses prints and mementos relating to one of the state's most famous photographers, Wilson A. "Snowflake" Bentley. A Jericho farmer who was the first person in the world to photograph individual snowflakes, Bentley collected more than 5,000 microphotos. A basement museum also tells the story of the many mills that once lined six sets of falls. Sales from the crafts store benefit the preservation of the building, which is owned by the Jericho Historical Society. A 20-acre park behind the mill, along the river, offers picnic tables and hiking trails. Ask directions to nearby Jericho Center, with its oval village common and **Desso's General Store** (899-3313), which occupies a gray, wooden building that's architecturally difficult to describe. It's just a genuine, old-fashioned general store. Lil and Gerry Desso carry the usual fresh, frozen, and canned produce, plus socks, mittens, gloves, boots, and so on. The syrup and beans (which, we can attest, bake up nicely) are local.

Richmond. East of Burlington on Route 2 (I-89, exit 11) and the Winooski River, Richmond was badly damaged in the flood of 1927 but still has a brief, architecturally interesting downtown. Turn down Bridge Street and drive by the old Blue Seal grain store (now a restaurant; see *Dining Out*) and the library (a former church) to the **Old Round Church.** This 16-sided building, one of the most unusual in the state, was constructed in 1812–13 as a community meetinghouse to serve five denominations (open daily July 4 through Labor Day 10–4, also weekends in spring and fall).

Shelburne. Beyond the commercial strip that's Shelburne Road (Route 7 south from Burlington) lie two of Vermont's greatest treasures, both the legacy of 19th-century railroad heirs William Seward and Lila Vanderbilt Webb. In the 1880s the couple hired Frederick Law Olmsted to landscape their 4,000-acre lakeside model farm and in 1946 their daughter-in-law founded a major museum of Americana. Today 1,400 acres of the estate—Shelburne Farms—survive as a combination inn and demonstration farm, complementing the exhibits in no fewer than 37 buildings in the nearby Shelburne Museum. Inevitably shops and attractions continue to multiply along Route 7; the latest, the Vermont Teddy Bear Company Factory and Museum, threatens to draw more visitors than either Shelburne Farms or the Shelburne Museum. (See *To See* for details about all three.)

Winooski. Just across 32-foot Winooski Falls from Burlington. Ira Allen was the first to harness the water that subsequently powered several mammoth, brick, 19th-century mills, attracting the workers from Ireland, Canada, and Eastern Europe who settled in the cottages that line its streets. The falls, with its art deco–style bridge, and the common, framed by the vintage-1867 Winooski Block and the handsome **Champlain Mill** (now a shopping/dining complex), still form the center of town. **St. Michael's College** (1,700 undergraduates, 750 graduate students), with its Playhouse (presenting a variety of stage performances) and an art gallery (654-2535), is just up Allen Street (Route 15).

TO SEE

MUSEUMS AND ATTRACTIONS

🖉👍 **Shelburne Museum** (985-3344; web site: www.shelburnemuseum.org), Route 7. Shelburne (6 miles south of Burlington) is open daily 10–5 late May through late October, with daily tours of selected buildings at 1 PM the rest of the year. $17.50 adults, $7 youths (6–14). Family cap: $45. Tickets are good for two consecutive days. This fascinating "collection of collections" features American folk art but also includes paintings by Rembrandt, Degas, Monet, and Manet. The 37 buildings, many of them historic transplants from around New England, each house a different collection. They are set in 45 landscaped acres that include flower and herb gardens, an apple orchard, and more than 90 varieties of lilacs (the annual Lilac Festival is usually Memorial Day Weekend; see *Special Events*).

An adequate description of the collections (more than 80,000 objects) would fill a separate chapter. Highlights include a 1915 steam locomotive and a vintage-1890 private Palace Car; the sidewheeler *Ticonderoga,* in her basin near the Colchester Reef Lighthouse; the amazing folk art in the Stagecoach Inn (weather vanes, cigar-store figures, trade signs, and figureheads); the American paintings (Fitz Hugh

The Ticonderoga is on permanent display at the Shelburne Museum

Lane, Winslow Homer, and many other lesser-known but superb 19th-century New England painters); the Webb Memorial Building, with its elegant rooms (originally in a New York penthouse) hung with Impressionist paintings (including a portrait of the museum's founder, Electra Havemeyer Webb, by Mary Cassatt); and the heirloom quilts (the collection includes some 900 American quilts). There are also the Horseshoe Barn's marvelous carriages; the Castleton Slate Jail; Shaker Shed; Dorset House and its decoys, Audubon game-bird prints, and fowling pieces; a General Store; an up-and-down Sawmill; an old-fashioned carousel, and much more. The ticket is good for two days because you may well want to allow time to absorb it all.

Acquisitions continue but this is still substantially the collection of one woman, at a time when few people were collecting Americana. Electra Havemeyer was 18 in 1910 when she bought her first cigar-store figure. Three years later she married James Watson Webb, of Shelburne (son of the wealthy couple who had built Shelburne Farms; see below). Over the next 30 years she raised five children, traveled widely, and managed homes on Long Island and in Manhattan, and a 50,000-acre "camp" in the Adirondacks, as well as the Shelburne estate. Gradually she filled all her holdings (even her indoor tennis court) with her collections, founding the museum in 1947 when her husband retired to Shelburne. The couple both died in 1960 but their vision for the museum was fulfilled by their son J. Watson Webb Jr.

The **Owl Cottage Family Activity Center** gives kids some hands-on time; a number of displays such as a model circus parade are also geared to children. There's a museum shop and cafeteria, picnic areas, and electric trams for the disabled or just footsore. The visitors center is a rare round barn. Inquire about gallery talks, classes in traditional crafts, and frequent special events.

Shelburne Farms (985-8686), marked from Route 7, Shelburne. **The Farm Store and Visitors Center** (985-8442), with an exceptional introductory film, are open daily year-round, 9–5 (10–5 in the off-season). Mid-May through mid-October, a day pass to the walking trails and children's farmyard and cheesemaking operation on the 1,400-acre lakeside property costs $5 adults, $4 seniors, $3 children 3–14; full 1½-hour wagon tours are offered five times daily mid-May through mid-October. November through April, no charge for the walking trails. Inquire about inn and garden tours, breeding-barn tours, and special events.

Much of this grand 1880s lakeside estate is now a nonprofit experimental farm and educational and cultural center. Comprising 3,800 acres at its zenith, this "duchy" was landscaped by Frederick Law Olmsted (who also designed Central Park) and pioneer forester Gifford Pinchot. It was designed for William Seward Webb and Lila Vanderbilt Webb (it was their daughter-in-law Electra Havemeyer Webb who founded Shelburne Museum). It included, and still does, a model farm with magnificent Norman-style barn buildings and a 110-room brick summer "cottage" on a bluff overlooking Lake Champlain.

The mansion is now the Inn at Shelburne Farms (open late May through mid-October; see *Lodging* and *Dining Out*). The immense, five-story, 416-foot Farm Barn (housing pigs, chickens, and other farm animals) is now a place for children to collect eggs, learn to milk a cow, or enjoy a hayride. It also houses the cheesemaking facility; the Coach Barn, once occupied by locally bred Hackneys, now houses changing art exhibits and frequent workshops. The farm's prizewinning cheddar cheese, made from its own herd of Brown Swiss cows, is sold, along with other Vermont products, in the Farm Store. A walking trail winds from the visitors center about 1 mile to the top of Lone Tree Hill for sweeping views of Lake Champlain and the Adirondacks. Inquire about naturalist-led bird walks and special events.

Tip: The Inn at Shelburne Farms is open to the public by reservation for breakfast as well as dinner. (No admission fee.) Enjoy the most elegant breakfast in the area, and then stroll the lakeside perennial, herb, and rose gardens.

Burlington waterfront: As noted in the chapter introduction, Burlington's waterfront revival is relatively recent and dramatic. The handsome (vintage-1915) **Union Station** at the base of Main Street is now public space (changing art exhibits) and the King Street Dock remains home to the Lake Champlain Transportation Company (LCTC), established in 1826 (see *Getting Around* and *Boating*). At the base of College Street at the College Street Pier, the (1991) Community Boathouse (see *Boating* and *Eating Out*) echoes the design of the Lake Champlain Yacht

Club built on its site in 1889; it's flanked by a waterfront park and by the Lake Champlain Basin Science Center (864-1848, open mid-June through Labor Day 11–5, otherwise weekends and school vacations 12:30–4:30), an "ecomuseum" devoted to the ecology, history, and culture of the Champlain Basin. The Burlington Bike Path (see *Bicycling*) links these sites with the nearby Waterfront Park to the north (it includes a promenade and picnic shelter) and with Perkins Pier (parking, boat launch, and picnic area) just to the south and to several more beaches and parks in both directions. Not surprisingly, shops and restaurants have proliferated along neighboring Battery Street; Battery Park is the setting for free summer concerts (Thursday and Sunday; see *Entertainment*) and for frequent special events.

Church Street Marketplace. The city's shopping and dining hub, the Church Street Marketplace extends four traffic-free blocks, from the graceful Unitarian church designed in 1815 by Peter Banner to City Hall at the corner of Main Street. A fanciful fountain plays at its head and the bricked promenade is spotted with benches and boulders from different parts of the state. The marketplace buildings themselves, a mix of 19th-century and art deco styles, house more than 100 shops and an ever-increasing number of restaurants. Walk through one storefront and you are in the Burlington Square Mall, a multilevel (stepped into the hillside), 60-shop complex resembling many in Montreal but few in New England. Unlike Boston's Quincy Market, Church Street is a public thoroughfare, geared as much to residents as to tourists.

Robert Hull Fleming Museum (656-0750), Colchester Avenue, on the University of Vermont campus. Open September through April, weekdays 9–4; Saturday and Sunday 1–5; closed Monday May through August and holiday weekends year-round. Limited parking. $3 per adult; over 54 and under 18, $2. Varied collections of art, natural history, archaeology, and geology. Holdings include ancient primitive art from several cultures and continents, a collection of American portraits and landscapes, from the 18th century to contemporary works, and frequent special exhibits, plus a gift shop. The building was designed by the renowned firm of McKim, Mead and White, which also designed UVM's Ira Allen Chapel (1927) and Burlington's City Hall. $2 suggested donation.

Fire House Center for the Arts (865-7165), 135 Church Street, Burlington, next to City Hall. Open Wednesday through Sunday noon–6, but noon–8 on Friday. A nonprofit community space showcasing work by top Vermont artists. Inquire about First Friday Art Trolley Tours, a free tour of local art galleries the first Friday of every month, April through November (5–7 PM).

The Ethan Allen Homestead (865-4556), off Route 127 just north of the downtown Burlington waterfront (take the North Avenue Beaches exit). Open for tours mid-May to mid-October: in spring, daily 1–5; summer,

Ethan Allen Homestead

Monday through Saturday 10–5, Sunday 1–5. Vermont's godfather is memorialized here in the timber farmhouse in which he lived out the last years of his turbulent life; he died in 1789. The visitors center offers interesting descriptive and multimedia exhibits, and the setting is a working garden and an extensive park with some 4 miles of walking trails along the Winooski River (see also *Green Space*). $3.50 per adult, $3 seniors, $2 ages 17 and under; family rate $5.

FOR FAMILIES

Vermont Teddy Bear Company Factory and Museum (985-3001; 1-800-829-BEAR), 2236 Shelburne Road (Route 7), Shelburne. Open daily 9–6, Sunday 10–5. A phenomenon in its own right, the huge, fanciful new birthplace of well over 100,000 teddy bears a year now includes a museum depicting teddy bear history; visitors are also invited to make their own teddy bear ($24.50) and to take the highly entertaining tour ($1). There is, of course, also a huge teddy bear store (see *Selective*

Shopping—More Special Stores).

⚘ **University of Vermont Dairy Farm** (862-2151), 500 Spear Street, Burlington. Open daily 9–4; milking 2:30–4. The university's working farm, with its large herd of Holsteins and Jersey cows, along with some horses, is student-run, visitor-friendly, and the site of frequent horse shows and dog shows.

⚘ **The Birds of Vermont Museum** (434-2167), adjacent to the Green Mountain Audubon Center (see Green Space) on Sherman Hollow Road, Richmond. Open May through October daily, except Tuesday, 10–4; by appointment in winter. Carvings of more than 200 species of birds by Robert Spear Jr.; also nature trails, recorded birdsongs. $3.50 adults, $1.50 children.

⚘ **Justin Morgan Memorial Museum** (985-8665), Route 7 at Bostwick Road, Shelburne. Open Monday through Friday 8–5, Saturday 10–2. A small museum depicts the Morgan horse story in illustrations and video. Token admission.

TO DO

BICYCLING

The **Burlington Bike Path** runs for almost 7 miles along the waterfront, connecting eight different parks, from Oakledge Park on the south (see *Green Space*) to the Flynn Estate at the mouth of the Winooski River. Fun side trips include Ethan Allen Park, the Ethan Allen Homestead, Intervale Community Farms, and the Salmon Hole Fishing Area off Riverside Avenue (see *Green Space*). **Rental bikes** (including tandems, trailers, and trail-a-bikes) and in-line-skate rentals are available from the **SkiRack** (658-3313), 85 Main Street. This path is used for walking, running, and in-line skating as well as biking. Note that CCTA buses and trolleys have bicycle racks. For serious bicyclists, we recommend the "Burlington Vermont Hiking and Biking Map," published by Map Adventures (253-7489) in Stowe, which details several Burlington area loops and longer tours on both sides of Lake Champlain, using ferries. Mountain bikers should check out the **Catamount Family Center** (879-6001), Governor Chittenden Road, Williston: a 40-km trail system, also rentals and food in the 1796 house built by Vermont's first governor. There is also the **Essex Transportation Trail,** a 3-mile rail trail from the Essex Police Station to Route 15 (Lang Farm); the **Shelburne Recreation Trail,** from Bay Road through Shelburne Bay Park to Harbor Road; the unpaved **Intervale Bikepath,** from Gardener's Supply on Intervale Avenue to the Ethan Allen Homestead; and **Causeway Park** in Colchester (a packed gravel trail that follows an old railroad bed out into Lake Champlain). **Bolton Valley** (see *Winter Sports*) also offers mountain biking on its cross-country and alpine trails

BOATING

Note: The regular LCTC 75-minute ferry crossing from Burlington to Port Kent, New York, is a great ride and a bargain.

Burlington Community Boathouse (865-3377), foot of College Street, Burlington. Rowboats, Rhodes and Laser sailboat rentals, captained day sails, sailing lessons, fishing charters, June through October. **Winds of Ireland** (863-5090), based here, offers day and sunset sails, bareboat charters, and instruction.

Spirit of Ethan Allen II (862-8300). Seasonal, daily scenic cruises aboard a triple-deck, 500-passenger excursion boat, departing from the Burlington Community Boathouse (see above) mid-May through mid-October. Narrated sight-seeing, plus sunset cruises, dinner, murder mystery, and variety show cruises. Sight-seeing cruise fare: $7.95 adult, $3.95 ages 3–11.

Lake Champlain Cruise & Charter (864-9804), King Street Dock, Burlington. Two regular ferries offer sunset, dinner, brunch, music, and other specialty cruises.

Northern Spy (343-3645), Perkins Pier. Whistling Man Schooner Company offers day sails.

Also note: Day sails and local marinas are listed with the Lake Champlain Chamber of Commerce (see *Guidance*).

DIVING

Lake Champlain Historic Underwater Preserves (457-2022). The Vermont Division for Historic Preservation maintains five shipwrecks, identified by Coast Guard–approved buoys, at various points on Lake Champlain, open to scuba divers. The *Horse Ferry*, the *Coal Barge*, and the *General Butler* are off Burlington. The *Phoenix* and the *Diamond Island Stone Boat* are in Colchester and Vergennes, respectively. **Waterfront Diving** (865-2771), 214 Battery Street, Burlington, provides equipment rentals, instruction in snorkeling, underwater archaeology, video, and scuba, and charters to historic preserved shipwrecks.

See also *Boating*.

FISHING

Champ Charters (864-3792), Burlington, offers charter boats. Check out **Schirmer's Fly Shop** (863-6105), 34 Mills Avenue, South Burlington, specializing in Ed Schirmer's own flies, instruction, tackle, and accessories. The **Salmon Hole fishing area** off Riverside Avenue, just beyond Tortilla Flats Mexican Restaurant, is a popular local watering hole.

GOLF

Burlington Country Club (864-9532), South Prospect Street, Burlington, 18 holes; **Marble Island Resort** (864-6800), Marble Island Road, Mallett's Bay, Colchester, 9 holes; **Rocky Ridge Golf Club** (482-2191), St. George (5 miles south on Route 2A from exit 12 off I-89), 18 holes; **Kwiniaska** (985-3672), Spear Street, Shelburne, 18 holes; **Williston Golf Course** (878-3747), Williston, 18 holes; **Essex Country Club**

Lake Champlain Boathouse

(879-3232), Old Stage Road, Essex Junction, 18 holes. **Winter Links** (864-8300), 123 Industrial Avenue, Williston (near Tafts Corner), offers instruction and high-tech simulators for playing Pebble Beach, Spyglass Hill, and Pinehurst. Pro shop and 19th Hole lounge.

HIKING
See Camel's Hump State Park under *Green Space.*

HORSEBACK RIDING
Georgia Stables (524-3395, 893-7268), Beebe Hill Roads, Georgia. Trail riding for all abilities.

KAYAKING
True North Kayak Tours (860-1910). Jane and David Yagoda are an experienced Burlington-based mother-and-son team who offer instruction and guided tours from a variety of locations on Lake Champlain. Inquire about multi-day paddles through the Champlain islands with B&B lodging.

PaddleWays (660-8606). Burlington-based Michele Rose offers 3-hour tours, instructional classes, full-day and multi-day tours on Lake Champlain.

Umiak Outfitters (253-2317), based in Stowe, also offers guided kayaking on Lake Champlain in the Burlington area.

RAIL EXCURSION
The Champlain Valley Weekender (463-3069; 1-800-707-3530) operates weekends, July through Labor Day, between Middlebury and Burlington with stops in Shelburne and Vergennes. It's run by Bellows Falls–based Green Mountain Railways.

SPECTATOR SPORTS
The Vermont Expos (655-4200), Burlington's minor league baseball team, play at Centennial Field (off Colchester Avenue) all summer. You can

park at UVM and take a shuttle bus to the game. The season is mid-June through September 1, tickets are cheap, the park is lovely, the concession food is pretty good, and there's a giant Day-Glo dancing Champ mascot for the kids. All in all a great time—and the baseball isn't bad. The Expos operate a souvenir store in the Champlain Mill (655-9477), Winooski (see *Selective Shopping—More Special Stores*).

SWIMMING

North Beach Park (862-0942), off North Avenue at Institute Road, Burlington (turn at the high school), provides tent and trailer sites plus swimming from a long, sandy beach, mid-May through October; vehicle charge. (Just before the park is the entrance to Rock Point, where the Episcopal Diocese of Vermont maintains Bishop Hopkins' Hall School, the bishop's residence, a conference center, and an outdoor chapel.)

Other beaches: **Leddy Park**, also off North Avenue; **Oakledge Park**, off Route 7 south of the city, at the end of Flynn Avenue; **Red Rocks Park**, South Burlington's public beach on Queen City Park Road.

WINTER SPORTS

CROSS-COUNTRY SKIING

"Northern Vermont Adventure Skiing," a weatherproof map ($6.95) detailing cross-country trails throughout the region, is available at local outlets and from Map Adventures (253-7489), 846 Cottage Club Road, Stowe 05672.

Bolton Valley (434-3444), Bolton. Ownership changed but this 105 km network of trails didn't. Ranging in elevation from 1,600 to 3,200 feet, this is Vermont's highest cross-country system, with snow that usually lasts well into April. A total of 45 km are machine groomed, meaning tracked for the most part, rolled elsewhere. There is a wide and gently sloping 3.6-mile Broadway and a few short trails for beginners, but most of the terrain is backwoods, much of it splendidly high wilderness country. You can take an alpine lift to the peak of Ricker Mountain and ski Old Turnpike, then keep going on cross-country trails for a total of 7 miles. There are rentals in the cross-country center, and experienced skiers are welcome to stay in the area's high huts by reservation. Telemarking is a specialty here, along with guided tours.

The legendary 12-mile **Bolton-to-Trapp trail** originates here (this is by far the preferred direction to ski it), but requires spotting a car at the other end or on Moscow Road. Inquire about the exciting new telemark/backcountry trail beginning at the top of Bolton's Wilderness Chair and meandering down into Little River State Park in Waterbury/ Stowe. Again, a car needs to be spotted at the other end.

Catamount Family Center (879-6001), 421 Governor Chittenden Road, Williston. The 40 km of trails—30 of them machine tracked, 2 km lit—

are on rolling terrain, geared to all abilities. Guided tours, rentals, instruction, warming hut. $12.

Note: See *Green Space* for more about local parks with trails that lend themselves to cross-country skiing.

DOWNHILL SKIING

Bolton Valley (434-3444), Bolton. This substantial ski mountain has the highest base elevation in the East. It changed hands in '98 again but now seems firmly financed by a consortium of local businessmen, and its base facilities have been renovated in '99. The 50 ski trails and slopes (seven lifts, including one quad and four double chairs) here are on 3,680-foot Bolton Mountain, which towers above its neighbors in a lonely stretch of country 20 miles east of Burlington, 20 miles west of Montpelier. Set atop a 4-mile access road that is, in turn, a long way up Route 2 from anything else, it offers a genuinely self-contained resort atmosphere guaranteed to make you want to stay put for a week (see *Lodging—Beyond Burlington*). Half-day and night-skiing prices also available.

Cochran Ski Area (434-2479), Cochran Road, Richmond. A small, family-owned and -oriented ski area founded by two former Olympic skiers.

Note: See also Smugglers Notch in "North of the Notch and the Lamoille River Valley," "Stowe and Waterbury," and "Sugarbush/Mad River Valley." Five major alpine areas are within easy striking distance of Burlington.

ICE SKATING

Leddy Arena (864-0123), Leddy Park, Burlington. Rentals.

Skating from **Waterfront Park** on Lake Champlain is also a special rite of winter; flags indicate ice safety.

SLEIGH RIDES

Shelburne Farms (985-8442) offers rides in 12- to 15-passenger sleighs. For a description of the setting, see *To See—Museums and Attractions*.

GREEN SPACE

Burlington Parks and Recreation (865-7247). Request a copy of the Burlington "Bike Paths & Parks" map or pick it up at the chamber of commerce (see *Guidance*). Burlington's lakeside parks are superb (see chapter introduction). **Oakledge Park** (take Flynn Avenue off Pine Street or Route 7) offers swimming and picnicking (parking fee, but you can bike or walk in). **Red Rocks Park** just south, occupying the peninsula that divides Burlington from South Burlington (take Queen City Parkway off Route 7), offers walking trails (no bikes allowed) as well as a beach. See also *Bicycling* and *Swimming*. **Ethan Allen Park** (North Avenue) is a 67-acre preserve, once part of Ethan's farm (it's near the Homestead; see *To See*) and webbed with trails that climb to the Pinnacle and to a stone tower built on Indian Rock in 1905 (open

Memorial Day to Labor Day, Wednesday through Sunday noon–8); both high points offer panoramic views of Lake Champlain.

Winooski Valley Park District (863-5744) consists of more than two dozen well-run parks, including beaches (see *Swimming*), boat launches, tennis courts, and an extensive riverside bike path (see *Bicycling*). **The Intervale** (entrance on Riverside Avenue) along the Winooski River offers walking as well as bike trails and includes Intervale Community Farms (660-3508), Gardener's Supply (retail and catalog outlet; see *Selective Shopping—More Special Stores*), and a seasonal organic farm stand. Also along the Winooski: a children's discovery garden and walking trails in the 67-acre park around the Ethan Allen Homestead (park headquarters), at **Macrea Farm Park,** and **Half Moon Cove Park. Delta Park** at the confluence of the Winooski River and Lake Champlain is a magical place with a sandy trail traversing woods to a wetland observation platform. **Centennial Woods** offers nature trails; access is from East Avenue.

Bayside Park (655-0811), Colchester. The site of a 1920s resort, the park now offers sports facilities, a beach, and walking trails. In winter this is also a popular spot for ice fishing, ice windsurfing, and skating.

For Sand Bar State Park and other green space to the north, see "The Islands" chapter.

To the East

Underhill State Park (899-3022), within the Mount Mansfield State Forest, offers camping (mid-May through mid-October), a Civilian Conservation Corps log picnic pavilion, and four trails to the summit ridge of Mount Mansfield. It's accessed from the Pleasant Valley Road west of Underhill Center.

The Green Mountain Audubon Nature Center (434-3068), Huntington. (Turn right at Round Church in Richmond; go 5 miles south to Sherman Hollow Road.) Trails wind through 230 acres of representative habitats (beaver ponds, orchards, and woodlands). Interpretive classes are given. Groups are welcome to watch (and help in) the wood-fired sugaring conducted each year. Open all year, but call ahead to confirm.

Camel's Hump State Park. Vermont's most distinctive and third highest mountain (4,083 feet) is best accessed from Huntington via East Street, then East Street to Camel's Hump Road. Request a free map and permission for primitive camping (at lower elevations) from the Vermont State Department of Forests, Parks and Recreation in Essex Junction (879-6565) or in Waterbury (241-3678). The **Green Mountain Club** (244-7037) on Route 100 in Waterbury Center also has maps and maintains shelters, lodging, and the Hump Brook Tenting Area. Camping facilities are also available in nearby Little River State Park. The name "Camel's Rump" was used on Ira Allen's map in 1798 but by 1830 it was known as "Camel's Hump." *Note:* All trails and roads within the park are closed during mud season.

To the south

LaPlatte River Marsh Natural Area, Shelburne; parking on Bay Road. Managed by The Nature Conservancy of Vermont, this 211-acre preserve at the mouth of the LaPlatte River is rich in bird life. It is traversed by an easy trail (45 minutes, round-trip).

Shelburne Bay Park, Shelburne. (Park on Bay Road, across from the entrance to the Shelburne Farms Visitors' Center; see *To See.*) The Shelburne Recreation Department maintains a blue-blazed trail along the bay through mixed woods.

Shelburne Farms. See *To See.* Five miles of easy trails on 1,400 acres landscaped by Frederick Law Olmsted.

H. Lawrence Achilles Natural Area, Shelburne, access off Pond Road. A short hiking trail leads to Shelburne Pond.

Mount Philo State Park (425-2390, 372-5060), Charlotte. A small mountaintop picnic area and campground, with spectacular views of the valley, lake, and Adirondacks. A short but steep ascent off Route 7 (not recommended for trailers or large RVs); 15 campsites; $1 per adult admission.

Kingsland Bay State Park (877-3445), Ferrisburg. West from Route 7 on Little Chicago Lane, about 1.5 miles north onto Slang Road, 3 miles to Lake Champlain. Picnic areas, tennis courts, on 130 acres.

LODGING

In Burlington 05401

HOTELS

♿ **The Radisson Hotel** (658-6500; 1-800-333-3333), 60 Battery Street. The view and location can't be beat. It's worth paying a slight premium for a room overlooking the lake and its backdrop of the Adirondacks. Families may prefer the cabana rooms, however, handy to the indoor swimming pool, Jacuzzi, and fitness room. Complimentary parking is offered in the adjacent garage, and the shops and restaurants of downtown Burlington are steps away. Request a corner room, facing south as well as west. In the hotel itself, the Oak Street Café serves three daily meals, and Seasons on the Lake, the hotel's upscale dining room, has a spectacular view. November to April $89–129; June through October $119–189; inquire about B&B packages, free shuttle service to the airport.

🐾 **The Sheraton-Burlington** (865-6600; 1-800-325-3525), 870 Williston Road. With 309 rooms, this is Vermont's largest hotel and the city's convention and trade center. It's set on campuslike grounds in South Burlington at the top of the hill behind the UVM campus and the medical center, near the I-89 (exit 14W), Route 2 interchange with easy bus access to downtown. $145–175 per room. Small pets permitted.

BED & BREAKFASTS

Willard Street Inn (651-8710), 349 South Willard Street. The classiest place to stay in Burlington, a brick mansion built grandly in the 1880s up on the Hill (adjoining the UVM and Champlain College campuses). It offers 15 guest rooms (12 with private bath, 3 that share). Guests enter a cherry-paneled foyer and are drawn to the many-windowed, flower-filled solarium with a woodstove, where guests breakfast. There is also a spacious living room with a grand piano and hearth, and a dining room. Guest rooms are decorated individually and range in size and detailing from the master bedroom to former maids' rooms but all are tastefully done and equipped with phone and TV. Top dollar is for a canopy bed, lake view, and private bath (but lake views can also be enjoyed for far less). Owner Beverly Watson also operates Isabel's on the Waterfront, a popular restaurant (see *Dining Out*). $75–150 includes a full breakfast.

288 Maple Street (863-2033). Maple Street runs uphill from the waterfront (it's the second street south of Main) and 288 is a cupola-topped town house on its upper reaches, which puts it within an easy walk of both the UVM campus and Church Street shops and restaurants. Built in 1872 with soaring ceilings and a double living room, this fine house has been restored by John and Susan O'Brien. The two guest rooms both have private bath, TV, fridge, and phone. One is downstairs and the second upstairs, sunny and spacious, with an iron bed, and rooftop and lake view. $80 year-round except foliage season ($95) includes a full breakfast.

Howard Street Guest House (864-4668), 153 Howard Street. Available by the night July through late October. A beautiful space in a detached carriage barn: a sunny, open living room, dining area/minimal kitchen with skylights, furnished with flair, a queen bed, and a pullout sofa. Andrea Gray's house is in a quiet residential area, within easy walking distance of the waterfront and Church Street Marketplace (see *To See—Museums and Attractions*). $115 includes a continental breakfast, $105 without. Good for a romantic getaway or a businessperson requiring space to spread out. 10 percent less for stays of more than 4 days.

Burlington Redstone (862-0508), 497 South Willard Street. A long but possible walk from downtown, nearer to UVM, a handsome mansion built in 1906 of local redstone. Helen Sellstedt offers two guest rooms with shared bath and one with private, along with gracious common spaces, including an invitingly landscaped garden. No children under 13, please. $75–95 includes a full breakfast.

Beyond Burlington

RESORT

Bolton Valley Resort (phone/fax: 434-3444), Bolton Valley 05477. A mountaintop cluster of condominiums, lodge, restaurants, shops, and a sports center set on 5,000 wooded acres. In winter, Bolton Valley is a ski resort (see *To Do—Downhill Skiing* and *Cross-Country Skiing*), and in summer the focus is on tennis, mountain biking, and golf, with formal programs for children. An outdoor pool, an extensive network of hiking trails, and a nearby 18-hole golf course are also part of the summer picture. Facilities include the newly renovated (in 1999) 150-room slope-side hotel (some rooms have a fireplace and kitchenette) and more than 120 one- to four-bedroom condominium units. The sports center houses an exercise room, pool, tennis courts, and game room. Rates for the hotel rooms range from $89–319; for a condominium unit, $149–649.

INNS

Inn at Shelburne Farms (985-8498), Shelburne 05482. Open mid-May through mid-October. Guests are treated to a peerless taste of Edwardian grandeur. The 45-room, Queen Anne–style mansion was built by William Seward and Lila Vanderbilt Webb on a bluff overlooking Lake Champlain. Completed in 1899, the house is the centerpiece of a 1,400-acre estate (see Shelburne Farms under *To See*).

Perhaps because its transition from mansion to inn in 1987 entailed a $1.6 million restoration but no sale (the Webb family have turned the estate into a nonprofit environmental education organization), there is a rare sense of a time as well as place here. Turn-of-the-century furnishings predominate (most are original), and you feel like an invited rather than a paying guest. You can play billiards in the richly paneled game room, leaf through one of the 6,000 leather-bound books, or play the piano in the library. Common space includes the Main Hall, a magnificent space divided into sitting areas with fireplaces and dominated by a very grand staircase. There's also an elegant tearoom (tea is served daily) and the Marble Room, a formal dining room with silk damask wall coverings, a marble floor, and long windows overlooking the formal gardens and lake. Don't miss the third-floor playroom, with its dollhouses.

Guest rooms vary in size and elegance, from the second-floor master bedroom to servants' quarters, which means room prices also vary. The Green Room, in which we slept, was painstakingly but far from fussily decorated (its wallpaper was specially made) to echo the mauve-and-green fabric in a splashy '20s screen. With its alcove desk, free-standing old mirror, fresh flowers, luxurious turn-of-the-century bath, and water view, there was a sense of comfort and space. Guests have access to tennis, boating, a swimming beach, and walking trails. Rates for the 24 luxurious, individualized bedrooms (17 with private bath): $195–350 double with private bath, $95–185 with shared bath (rates include a 15 percent service charge). Breakfast and dinner are extra, and memorable. No smoking.

   ♿ **The Inn at Essex** (878-1100; 1-800-727-4295), 70 Essex Way (Route 15 east), Essex Junction 05452. There are innlike common spaces and the 97 rooms and suites are decorated with country-chic wallpapers and fabrics; 30 have working fireplace and 2 have Jacuzzi. The large, neo-Colonial complex is set in landscaped gardens in a commercial, suburban area handy to IBM, 10 miles northeast of downtown Burlington. Facilities include a conference center and an outdoor heated swimming pool. A free shuttle to the airport is also offered. $139–199 includes continental breakfast. Inquire about special packages. Butler's, the inn's formal restaurant (see *Dining Out*), and the more casual Café are both staffed by students from the New England Culinary Institute.

BED & BREAKFASTS

Willow Pond Farm (985-8505), 20 Cheesefactory Lane, South Burlington 05403. Open early spring to late fall. If we had special sections for birders and gardeners, Sawyer and Zita Lee's elegant home would top both lists. Zita inherited the 200-acre farm and in 1990 the couple designed and built this exceptional retirement house, a blending of old lines and modern spaces. Many windows let in the view of rose and perennial gardens, with their many bird feeders, and the small pond. The property also borders Shelburne Pond, a haven for ospreys, pileated woodpeckers, mergansers, bluebirds, and wild turkeys, among others. The living room/dining room overlooks the gardens and ponds and conveys an unusual sense of light and space. A woodstove, wing chairs, and sofas invite you to sit, surrounded by books, art, and treasures well chosen by several discerning generations. A full breakfast and the Lees' special cappuccino blend are served at the formal, oval table in the dining area or out on the terrace. The upstairs master bedroom overlooks the Adirondacks and there is a sleeping loft for kids, and the two smaller rooms are also furnished in fine antiques, Oriental carpets, and handmade quilts on the king- and queen-sized beds. All have private bath. Just minutes from downtown Burlington and from Shelburne Farms (see *To See—Museums and Attractions*), with a way-out-in-the-country feel. $80–95 with breakfast for 2 nights or more, more for 1 night.

  ♧ **Heart of the Village Inn** (985-2800), 2130 Shelburne Road, P.O. Box 953, Shelburne 05482-0953. A handsome 1880s home next to the town green and library (1816) and across from Town Hall. Cohosts Bobbe Maynes and Pam Pierce, it turns out, both coveted this house for years and when it came on the market found themselves bidding against each other—then discovered they shared precisely the same vision for the place. Some $500,000 in renovations later, this is a comfortable showplace of a B&B with hosts who never seem to run out of energy, perhaps because they take turns. The two living rooms, dining room, and 5 guest rooms are all carefully, comfortably decorated. All have air-conditioning and in-room connections for phone and cable (there if desired), as well as private bath; the carriage barn houses the four most deluxe rooms, a honeymoon suite with a whirlpool bath and two rooms with wheelchair access. Breakfast and afternoon tea are included.

  ✳ **Homeplace** (899-4694), RR 2, Box 96, Old Pump Road (off Route 15), Jericho 05465. The sprawling house is set in a 100-acre wood with hiking paths. Guests can meet horses, sheep, ducks, chickens, cats, dogs, and a donkey. The guest area is separated from the family quarters and includes a large library and living room. Four rooms with two private baths and two shared (twin or double beds). Mariot Huessy asks $55 single, $65 double, $75 with private bath, full breakfast included. $10 per extra person in the room; pets possible for a small fee.

 ⛴ **Sinclair Inn Bed & Breakfast** (899-2234; 1-800-433-4658), 389 Route 15, Jericho 05465. This is a very Victorian "painted lady" with period wallpaper, chair rails, crown moldings, and a village setting. Furnishings are appropriate to the house. All six rooms have private bath and air-conditioning, but you may prefer to cool off on the ample porch or by the Japanese pond in the elaborately landscaped garden. One room is fully wheelchair-accessible. Andy and Jeannie Buchanan are your hosts. $80–115 per couple includes a full breakfast. Children over 12 welcome.

🐾 **Mansfield View B&B** (899-4793), 58 Sand Hill Road, Underhill Center 05490. A handsome, vintage-1981 garrison-style home set in 5 acres with views east to Mount Mansfield. There are two guest rooms with a shared bath, one with a double, the second with twin beds, individual heat control. The house is furnished in antiques and there's a player piano, a sunroom, and an open porch overlooking busy bird feeders as well as the mountains. Breakfast is included in $55–70 per room. Pets negotiable.

The Richmond Victorian Inn (434-4410; 1-888-242-3362), 191 East Main Street, P.O. Box 652, Richmond 05477. On Route 2 in the village of Richmond (1 mile off I-89), this exceptionally clean and classy house was formerly owned by the Harringtons of ham and other specialty food fame (the home store is still across the street). There are six comfortable guest rooms, all with private bath, all individually decorated with antiques and equipped with good reading lights. Two connecting rooms with shared bath work for families (children over 12, please). Gail Clark will pick up Long Trail hikers. Rates: $55 double with shared bath, $75–95, including full breakfast.

🐾 **Maple Grove Farm B&B** (878-4875), 741 Oak Hill Road, Williston 05495. Open year-round. Ginger and David Isham are the fourth generation of the Isham family to operate this 120-acre farm, one of the last four in this historic town just east of Burlington. While they have sold their dairy herd, the Ishams still raise cattle, and the vintage-1852 Gothic Revival farmhouse retains its surrounding fields and sugarhouse. Guests are comfortably bedded in three rooms vacated by the family's six grown children. One room has a double bed, and the other two have queen beds. Baths are shared, breakfast is full, and children are welcome. Common space includes a big living room and a den with piano. $45–60, discounts for more than 3 nights.

🐾 **Black Bear Inn** (434-2126; 1-800-395-6335), Bolton Valley 05477. Built in the '60s as a ski lodge, now very much a hilltop country inn known for its fine food. Chef-owner Ken Richardson is a Culinary Institute of America grad (see *Dining Out*). The 24 rooms all have private bath and country decor and range from standard to luxurious (hot tubs and gas fireplaces).

Richardson has weathered the changing fortunes at Bolton Valley Resort (it has changed hands three times in the past three years), with which he shares this hilltop, and continues to offer access to the resort's many facilities. This is also a favorite place for groups (one family group has been coming for 30 years), at which time the dining room is closed. From $59 per room in the off-season to $175 in-season includes full breakfast.

Elliot House (985-1412), 5779 Dorset Street, Shelburne 05482. This 1865 Greek Revival farmhouse adjoins conservation land with a view west to the Adirondacks. Susan and Nicholas Gulrajani offer an informal, three-room suite upstairs in the renovated carriage house: a bedroom with a queen-sized maple Shaker bed and a small room with twins (crib available), and a large sitting room with fridge, coffeemaker, and microwave. There is also a one-room (with bath) cottage by the swimming pool. Guests are welcome to walk the meadows; sheep, chickens, and ducks are in residence. Suite: $85 per couple, $10 per child; cottage: $65. Rates include a full breakfast; 2-night minimum.

The Millhouse Bed & Breakfast (453-2008; 1-800-859-5758), Starksboro 05487 (just off Route 116, south of Hinesburg). Open mid-May through mid-October. While it's 25 miles from Burlington, this gem of a bed & breakfast run by Pat and Ron Messer isn't really in any other region (as defined by our chapters) either. The friends who tipped us off to it found it convenient enough to use while visiting their daughter at UVM. The house retains its graceful 1831 lines and sits just above a rushing brook, near enough so that the sound of the water is constant. The sleeping arrangements include the upstairs master bedroom (shared bath) and two suites, one with three bedrooms (a large twin bedroom and two small single rooms) and another composed of two double bedrooms plus private baths. The house (on the National Register of Historic Places) is tastefully, comfortably decorated with plenty of common space, including a great back porch. The downstairs suite is handicapped-accessible. Rates, including a continental-plus breakfast, are $35–40 per person. Inquire about the studio cottage on the falls ($95 per couple).

By the Old Mill Stream (482-3613), RR 2, Box 543, Hinesburg 05461. We never connected with innkeepers Michelle and Steve Fischer and so failed to check this one out, but it sounds and looks (from its pictures) like a pleasant place: an 1860s rambling farmhouse with wide, wooden floorboards and tin ceilings. There are three upstairs guest rooms and a double living room and dining room; grounds include gardens that border a waterfall (it powered the mill for Isaiah Dow, who built the house). $70–85 includes a full breakfast.

MOTOR INNS

Hawthorn Suites (860-1212; 1-800-527-1133), 401 Dorset Street (just off Route 2), South Burlington 05403. Opened in 1998 by Chuck and Ralph DesLauriers, with an open timbered lobby, featuring suites with separate living rooms (containing foldout couches) and bedrooms: 73 one-bedroom suites and 6 two-bedroom. Facilities include an indoor pool, a spa/ Jacuzzi, and fitness machines. While it's located in the heart of South Burlington's strip malls, it's just minutes from downtown Burlington. Ralph Deslauriers developed Bolton Valley Resort and ran it for 30 years and Chuck's background is in hotel management; both men grew up in South Burlington on the family farm on which their parents ran one of the area's first motor inns. $99–179 (depending on length of stay) includes a breakfast buffet.

🐾✏️♿**The Wilson Inn** (879-1515; 1-800-521-2334), 10 Kellogg Road, Essex Junction 05452. The 32 units all include a bedroom, living room, and full kitchen. Handy to IBM rather than Burlington (10 miles away), it can work for families as well as businesspeople. Amenities include a free breakfast buffet, a grocery shopping service, and access to the neighboring fitness center. Some handicapped-accessible units available. One-bedroom units are $69–124; two-bedroom, $89–144. Inquire about winter weekend getaway packages.

🐾✏️♿**Marriott Residence Inn** (878-2001; 1-800-331-3131), Route 2A, Williston 05495. At exit 12 off I-89, this glossy, all-suite motor hotel has an indoor pool, spa, and Sport Court; free breakfast buffet. The one-bedroom-plus living room and kitchen suite is as low as $99 on weekends; the duplex, two-bedroom suite is $160 in high season. There's a pet charge.

🐾✏️ **Hampton Inn** (655-6177; 1-800-HAMPTON), 8 Mountain View Drive, Route 7 north, Colchester, exit 16 off I-89. North of Burlington, one of the chain's latest: 188 well-furnished one- and two-room suites, indoor pool, Jacuzzi, fitness facilities, free airport shuttle, and continental breakfast. From $79 for a room with a king bed.

WHERE TO EAT

DINING OUT

Inn at Shelburne Farms (985-8498), Shelburne. Open for dinner by reservation from mid-May to late-October. This turn-of-the-century manor offers imaginative cuisine in a magnificent setting: walls covered in fin de siècle silk damask from Spain, a black-and-white marble floor, and a stunning sunset view of Lake Champlain and the Adirondacks. You might begin with Shelburne Farms cheddar and ale soup and dine on roast rack of Vermont lamb served with layered asparagus, cheddar, and shiitake mushrooms ($28) or pan-roasted chicken with Yukon Gold potato, artichoke, and lemon ragout with roasted tomato relish ($20). Dessert might be a chocolate mousse torte with hazelnut ganache, cherry amaretto, white peach brandy, and raspberry sauces. Smokers can have coffee served on the terrace. Breakfast, open to the public by reservation, is also an event: five-grain pancakes, brioche French toast, or poached eggs with herbed hollandaise and red pepper homefries.

Café Shelburne (985-3939), Route 7, Shelburne. Open for dinner daily except Monday. Located across the road from the Shelburne Museum, this chef-owned and -operated authentically French bistro serves consistently fabulous fare. Sweetbreads in a port wine and mushroom sauce served in puff pastry could be a starter, followed by fricassee of rabbit in a red wine sauce with homemade fettuccine and prunes, or boneless quail stuffed with spinach in a grape sauce. It's one of the better restaurants in the state. Entrées: $17–19.50.

Pauline's Café & Restaurant (862-1081), 1834 Shelburne Road (Route 7 south). Open daily for lunch, brunch, and dinner, also Sunday brunch. It is worth braving the strip development traffic. In the elegant simplicity of the downstairs café or the more formal upstairs dining rooms, subtle cuisine featuring wild and local ingredients (mushrooms, cattail shoots, sea beans, fresh black and white truffles, for example) is artfully presented in sensible portions. Entrées might be pork loin scaloppine with apricot, sherry, and herb sauce; loin of Vermont rabbit with artichoke hearts and mushrooms; or veal tenderloin with wild mushrooms. Dinner entrées begin at $10.95 for early-bird specials (5:30–6:30); regular entrées: $14.95–22.95.

Note: Burlington offers the best choice of restaurants and cafés between Boston and Montreal, but the best are not all downtown.

Isabel's on the Waterfront (865-2522), 112 Lake Street, Burlington. Open for lunch weekdays, brunch (10:30–2) weekends, dinner nightly. Beverly Watson's attractive restaurant is housed in a 19th-century brick lumber company building across from the waterfront park, with views—especially in summer when there is dining on the terrace—of Lake Champlain and the Adirondacks. The menu changes frequently but is known for American fare like chicken Monterey (boneless, skinless chicken breast baked with artichoke hearts, roasted red peppers, fresh herbs, white wine, and butter; $13.50) and orange-sesame-glazed salmon ($17.95).

Butler's (878-1100), the Inn at Essex, Route 15, Essex Junction. Open for dinner nightly. In the deft hands of the New England Culinary Institute, the cuisine in this elegantly formal, green-walled room with high-backed, upholstered chairs is a visual as well as gustatory treat. Dinner might start with asparagus leek soup ($3.75) and Chef Jacques's rich country pâté ($5.75); proceed to grilled breast of duck with fig chutney ($16), crisp-skin salmon with fennel risotto ($17), or grilled rack of lamb with polenta and broccoli rabe ($21). Elaborate desserts might include a caramelized phyllo Napoleon with cranberry compote.

Smokejacks (658-1119), 156 Church Street, Burlington. Open daily for lunch and dinner. The decor is understated, almost stark in contrast to what even the menu describes as "bold food." Culinary Institute of America–trained Leslie Myers and Don Kelp obviously strive to be creative. Chances are we will never again have the opportunity to lunch on black bean turkey chili soup with sour cream, corn, and pumpkin seeds.

We're glad we did! Dinner entrées like balsamic-grilled Cavendish quail and "paella" (including a crispy duck leg as well as the usual seafood and sausage) are $14.95–18.95. Request a cheese plate and a glass of wine (the wine selection is long and interesting); also great martinis.

Blue Seal Restaurant (434-5949), Bridge Street, Richmond. Open Tuesday through Saturday 5:30–9:30. Reservations suggested. Housed in a vintage-1854 feed store, chef-owner Debra Weinstein's casual restaurant may not look—or charge—the part, but it's right up there with the Burlington area's finest. The menu changes frequently, but you might begin with a savory tart (sweet potatoes, apples, and grilled red onions) and dine on pan-roasted salmon with roasted garlic mashed potatoes, herb oil, and salsa, or marinated portobello mushrooms with grilled new potatoes, sautéed spinach, and goat cheese. A favorite dessert is double-layered devil's food cake with coffee swirl ice cream. Entrées: $10.50–16.

Black Bear Inn (434-2920), at the Bolton Valley Resort, off Route 2 in Bolton. Reservations requested. Chef-owner Ken Richardson is a Culinary Institute of America graduate who has turned his hilltop lodge into a dining destination for Burlington residents. The menu, which changes nightly, is limited to five entrées so you might want to call to check, and to reserve. You might begin with escargots sautéed with roasted garlic and red wine (or a cream of carrot and red pepper soup), then dine on a center-cut rib pork chop with wild rice and cranberry relish or a confit of duck with broccoli rabe, sausage, and sage. Entrées run $12.95–17.95.

Opaline (660-8875), One Lawson Lane. This new French restaurant has replaced the Iron Wolf. We have not been able to check it out ourselves but we have word of "haute cuisine" and favorable reviews.

EATING OUT

Note: Thanks to their largely student patronage, many of the following restaurants offer "dining-out" quality at "eating-out" prices. All are in Burlington.

Sweetwater's (864-9800), 120 Church Street (corner of College Street). Open Monday through Saturday 11:30 AM–1:30 AM, Sunday 10:30–1 AM. Housed in a former and splendidly restored 1920s bank building, this is a deservedly popular spot. Note the fresco depicting a number of recognizable Burlingtonians cavorting down Church Street with Bacchus. You might lunch on a burger, a salmon sandwich, or a choice of daily specials; dine on wood-grilled chicken served with sun-dried tomatoes and shiitake mushrooms. Dinner entrées run $10.95–14.95; sandwiches, flatbread pizza, and salads are always available. The square bar is one of Burlington's prime rendezvous.

Trattoria Delia (864-5253), 152 St. Paul Street. Open daily 5–10. A dimly lit, nicely decorated space with a helpful, knowledgeable waitstaff, tempting antipasti and pasta, a wide choice of entrées (ranging from chicken to wild boar), nightly specials, and regional Italian wines. Entrées $7.95–14.50; appetizers and desserts $3.50–6.95.

Daily Planet (862-9647), 15 Center Street. Open Monday through Saturday 11:30–3 for lunch, 3–5 for the bar menu, 5–10:30 for dinner; also a weekend brunch. The atmosphere is bright and casual with a solarium and airy dining room, both filled with small tables covered in bright oilcloths at lunchtime, linen for dinner. Unusual soups of the day are a specialty, along with tapas, nachos, burritos, and entrées ranging from grilled lamb loin to Vietnamese seafood and a variety of pastas. Planet burgers and fajitas are also usually on the menu. Dinner entrées from $11.95 for tempeh vegetable stir-fry to $19.95 for rack of lamb.

NECI Commons (862-6324), 25 Church Street. Open daily for light breakfast, lunch, dinner, and take-out. The former Mayfair Women's Clothing Store's three-story space is now filled with New England Culinary Institute students both learning and putting what they've learned into practice. The space includes several dining rooms, varying in tone, all hip and inviting. Generally excellent and innovative cuisine.

Sakura (863-1988), 2 Church Street. Lunch Monday through Saturday, dinner daily. Vermont's first Japanese restaurant is a resounding success. At lunch its soothing ambience is an oasis of calm (a good place for conversation), an appropriate setting for savoring sushi and sashimi dishes or simply deep-fried salmon served with a tangy sauce. Vegetarians will appreciate dishes like avocado, bean curd, boiled spinach, vegetable tempura, and hijiki (cooked seaweed). Lone diners appreciate the seats lining the long sushi bar.

Sweet Tomatoes (660-9533), 83 Church Street, in the cellar of the old Howard Opera House at the marketplace. A fine, busy place with an excellent northern Italian menu, plus top-drawer, wood-fired pizzas. You might lunch on the pasta of the day and dine on fusilli sautéed with wood-smoked chicken, sweet peas, mushrooms, plum tomatoes, black pepper, rosemary, and light cream. Outdoor tables in summer. Italian mineral water and wines featured.

Five Spice Café (864-4045), 175 Church Street. Open Monday through Saturday for lunch and dinner, Sunday 11–3 for dim sum brunch. The dishes are from a variety of Asian countries—Thailand, Vietnam, Indonesia, and India, as well as China—and the spices are as hot as you care to take them. The atmosphere is appealing. Try the ginger-tangerine cheesecake.

Parima Restaurant (864-7917), 185 Pearl Street. Open for lunch and dinner. Polished wood and brass and ornate glass lamps are the unlikely but pleasing decor for a wide selection of classic Thai dishes.

Halvorson's Upstreet Cafe (658-0278), 16 Church Street. Open for lunch, dinner, and brunch. An old landmark that's expanded its basic all-American menu has added beer and wine to meet the changing nature of the street. In summer, check out its hidden courtyard; inquire about Thursday-night jazz.

Red Square Bar and Grill (859-8909), 136 Church Street. Open after-

A sidewalk cafe on Church Street

noons for people-watching and for dinner. Jack O'Brien's attractive space features a copper bar, local art, music six nights a week, and is best known for its Sunday gospel brunch: $13.95 includes the music.

Stone Soup (862-7616), 211 College Street. Open Monday through Friday 7–7, Saturday 8–5, closed Sunday. A hugely popular storefront café specializing in vegetarian dishes, great soups, salads, and breads. Inexpensive.

Cobblestone Deli & Market (865-3354), 152 Battery Street. Open daily, 7–7 weekdays, Saturday 8–6, Sunday 8–5. No view (wrong side of Battery Street) but a pleasant café with a good deli: soups, sandwiches, coffees, wines, and microbrews. Pick up a sandwich to take on the bike path or to picnic by the lake.

Leunig's Bistro (863-3759), Church and College Streets. Open daily for breakfast, lunch, and dinner. Recently upscaled under new ownership from café to bistro. Leunig's retains its dark wood, gleaming coffee machines, streetside tables, and status as the hub of Church Street. Frequent live entertainment.

Henry's Diner (862-9010), 155 Bank Street, is a long-established, authentic diner around the corner from the Church Street Marketplace. Here you can get the meat loaf and thick gravy you've been hankering for. Closed Monday.

Nectar's (658-4771), 188 Main Street. A basic eatery for breakfast and lunch but famed for its french fries with gravy and its owner's association with the musical group Phish. Because it has a cabaret license (nightly music), it's the only restaurant in town that allows smoking.

Carbur's (862-4106), 115 St. Paul Street, has a 16-page menu, offering a hundred or so sandwich combos and many entrées. Lunch and dinner daily amid wood panels and stained-glass lamps.

Bove's Cafe (864-6651), 68 Pearl Street. Open Tuesday through Sunday for lunch and dinner. An old favorite with booths and a row of tables between; traditional Italian menu, full bar. Inexpensive.

The Vermont Pub and Brewery (865-0500), 144 College Street. Open daily 11:30 AM–1 AM. Housed in a modern building but with an old beer-hall atmosphere (tile floor, huge bar, brass), specializing in ales and lagers brewed on the premises. The menu includes Cornish pasties, cock-a-leekie pie, bratwurst, and fish-and-chips.

India House (862-7800), 207 Colchester Avenue. Lunch and dinner Tuesday through Saturday; Sunday brunch. This warm and hospitable restaurant serves traditional curries, tandoori chicken, and the like, plus puffy poori bread.

Sai-Gon Cafe (863-5637), 133–135 Bank Street. Lunch and dinner in this attractive eatery, serving authentic Thai cuisine.

Penny Cluse Cafe (651-8834), 169 Cherry Street, in the old Ben & Jerry's building. Innovative, healthy, hearty breakfasts and lunches. Famous for black beans, polenta, great biscuits.

On the waterfront
See also Isabel's on the Waterfront under *Dining Out.*

Mona's (658-6662), 3 Main Street. Open daily for lunch and dinner and Sundays for brunch. An open kitchen sets the tone in this casual place with a great view of the lake and the Adirondacks, good for southern flatbread pizza, cheddar and ale soup, or herb-roasted chicken with cornbread stuffing, sun-dried tomatoes, and artichoke hearts. Save room for the chocolate Grand Marnier mousse served in an almond cookie tulip with white chocolate and coconut macaroons.

Dockside Cafe (864-5206), 209 Battery Street. Open for lunch and dinner; Sunday brunch. Housed in the depths of one of the city's oldest waterfront buildings, with outdoor dining in good weather. A variety of tapas (appetizer-sized dishes) are featured, along with high-priced entrées.

The Ice House (864-1800), 171 Battery Street. Open for lunch and dinner daily, Sunday brunch, with seasonal open-air decks overlooking the ferry slip and marina. This was a pioneer of the city's upscale restaurant scene, a 19th-century icehouse with massive walls and timbers. American regional dishes feature seafood and Vermont lamb. We recommend the shrimp pico (shrimp and crabmeat stuffing in puff pastry with lobster-cream sauce; $18.50). You might lunch on sautéed chicken with garlic, herbs, and white wine in a tomato-cream sauce on tortellini ($6.95). Save room for hot cheesecake.

Shanty on the Shore (864-0238), 181 Battery Street. Open daily 11–11. Handy to the ferry with great inside and outside lake views; good for burgers and sandwiches as well as seafood platters, even escargots. A children's menu and choice of exotic drinks also offered.

Breakwater Cafe & Grill (864-9804), King Street Dock. Part of the LCTC ferry complex, an informal dockside space serving sandwiches, fried baskets, soups, and salads all day and evening in summer; inquire about frequent live music.

Whitecaps (862-1240), at the Boathouse. Open Memorial Day through Labor Day, 7:30 AM–sunset. This relaxing, casual spot is owned and managed by Isabel's on the Waterfront. Small menu; bar; moderate prices.

ALFRESCO

Beansie's Bus, Battery Park. Early April through autumn, this old yellow school bus parks daily by the lake and dispenses its famous french fries; the hamburgers, dogs, and grilled cheese on a bun are incidental.

The Hot Dog Lady. Lois Bodoky has her imitators, but she was the first and she's still the most reasonably priced and all around best. Look for her cart at noon every day at the Church Street Marketplace: $1 hot dog with kraut.

CAFFEINE/SNACKS

Mirabelle's (658-3074), 198 Main Street. A delightful bakery-eatery featuring special teas, espresso, pastries, sandwiches, and light fare. Look for the waterfront offshoot.

Muddy Waters (658-0466), 184 Main Street, just up from Church Street. Excellent coffee, homemade desserts, vegan specials, smoothies, beer and wine by the glass, brick walls, sofas, lots of reading material and earnest conversation.

Uncommon Grounds (865-6227), 42 Church Street. They roast their own here, and also sell tea and pastries. A good people-watching spot.

Speeder and Earl's. A small counter and café tables at 104 Church Street, a zany shop at 412 Pine Street, same complex as the Fresh Market, featuring their own blends and assorted pastries.

Ben & Jerry's (862-9620), 36 Church Street. This isn't the original location, but the world's legendary ice-cream makers did get their start in the neighborhood.

In Winooski

Papa Frank's (655-2433), 13 West Center Street. Open Monday through Friday 11–10, Saturday 4–10. A red-sauce Italian neighborhood restaurant that caters to families as well as students. Good for pizza, calzones, but also classic dishes. The vegetables are fresh, and garlic bread comes with your order. A bit tricky to find if you're driving because of one-way streets, but it's just a couple of blocks from the Champlain Mill.

Sneakers (655-9081), 36 Main Street, serves a great breakfast and lunch Monday through Friday, dinner Monday through Saturday, weekend brunch. Locals consider this the best breakfast in the area; options include eggs Benedict and freshly squeezed orange juice. The dinner special may be seafood or lamb. Inquire about live music on weekends.

Waterworks (655-2044), the Champlain Mill. Open for lunch, dinner, and Sunday brunch. Occupying the prime space in the turn-of-the-century mill, overlooking the dam spillway and rapids of the Winooski River.

You can dine outside in a greenhouse area or savor the view through the mill's long windows. The large menu ranges from sandwiches to Wiener schnitzel, steak, stir-fries, and nightly specials.

In Colchester

Colchester Reef Lighthouse (655-0200), 8 Mountain View Drive, adjacent to the Hampton Inn just off I-89, exit 16. Lunch, dinner, and Sunday brunch. Nowhere near the water, but a bustling, cheerful, steak-and-seafood place, with the biggest salad bar around; good for families (kids menu). Full bar.

Libby's Blue Line Diner (655-0343), One Roosevelt Avenue, Route 77, Colchester, with its tile floor and marble counters, attracts itinerant diner buffs and area fans for breakfast, lunch, and dinner daily. Try the banana bread French toast.

Williston Road to Richmond

Daily Bread Bakery Café (434-3148), Richmond Center. Open daily 8–4. People leave I-89 south (turn right at the Cumberland Farms and look for the aqua sign at the end of a parking lot on your left) just to drop by for breakfast, lunch, or Saturday and Sunday brunch, or even for a slice or two of maple bread.

Al's French Fries (862-9203), 1251 Williston Road, South Burlington. Open daily 10:30 AM–midnight. Burlington's own (amazingly fast) fast-food joint, spanking clean and small-town friendly with first-class fries, burgers, dogs, and shakes. Handy enough to I-89, exit 14, to work well as roadfood.

On Shelburne Road (Route 7 south)

Perry's Fish House (862-1300), 1080 Shelburne Road. Open Monday through Saturday 5–10, Sunday 4–10 A big, bustling, landlocked pier with an extensive menu of moderately priced, first-rate seafood that attracts large numbers of Burlingtonians. Specialties include batter-fried clams. Children's menu.

Harrington's (985-2000), Shelburne. Across from the Shelburne Museum, a good bet if you can snag one of the few tables and don't mind the Styrofoam at the excellent deli here. Specialties include the "World's Best Ham Sandwich" (Harrington's is known for its corn-smoked ham), also smoked turkey, quiche, homemade soups, sausage chili made with Harringon's own pork sausages ($2.50!), and chocolate mousse.

ENTERTAINMENT

Note: For current arts and entertainment in Burlington, call the **Burlington City Arts line** at 865-7166, or check *Seven Days*, a free weekly publication that's available everywhere around town.

MUSIC

Vermont Mozart Festival performances (862-7352; web site: www.vtmozart.together.com). Summer concerts in various settings—on ferries, at the Shelburne Museum and/or Shelburne Farms (see *To See—*

Museums and Attractions), at the Basin Harbor Club, in churches. Winter chamber series.

Vermont Symphony Orchestra (864-5741), 77 College Street, Burlington. One of the country's first statewide philharmonics presents a five-concert Chittenden County series at the Flynn Theater; outdoor summer pops at Shelburne Farms (see *To See—Museums and Attractions*) and elsewhere.

Saint Michael's College concerts (655-2000), in Winooski, feature jazz, pop, and classical productions.

Burlington Oratorio Society (864-0471). A volunteer, 50-voice choir presents several concerts a year.

The Discover Jazz Festival (Flynn box office: 86-FLYNN; web site: www.discoverjazz.com), Burlington, 10 days in early June, a jazz extravaganza that fills city parks, clubs, restaurants, ferries.

Battery Park Summer Concert Series, Burlington, Thursday and Sunday night.

Magic Hat Concert Series at the Old Lantern in Charlotte. Call 658-2739.

THEATER

Flynn Theater for the Performing Arts (86-FLYNN), 153 Main Street, Burlington. The city's prime stage for music and live performance is a refurbished art deco movie house, now home to plays, musical comedies, jazz concerts, and lectures, in addition to movies.

Royall Tyler Theater (656-2095), at the University of Vermont, Burlington, stages an eclectic, top-notch seasonal repertory of classic and contemporary plays.

Saint Michael's College Theater Department (654-2000), Winooski, presents two major productions, fall and spring; also an excellent summer playhouse series (654-2281).

George Bishop Lane Series (656-4455) sponsors major musical and theatrical performances around Burlington fall through spring.

DRIVE-IN

Sunset Drive-In (862-1800), Route 127 off North Avenue, Colchester. It's for real: three screens, a snack bar, and a kiddie playground.

MUSICAL VENUES

For jazz, blues, rock, and dance clubs, check out these nightspots, all in Burlington: **Nectar's** (658-4771), 188 Main Street, and above it, **Club Metronome** (865-4563). **Sh-Na-Na's** (865-2596), 101 Main Street, has dance music Friday and Saturday, live acts other nights. **135 Pearl Street** (863-2343) is the area's gay and lesbian rallying point; dance floor and cabaret theater downstairs, bar and dining room up. **Red Square Bar and Grill** (see *Eating Out*) offers frequent nightly music and a Sunday gospel brunch. **Leunig's Bistro, Halvorson's Upstreet Café,** and **Sweetwater's** on Church Street (see *Eating Out*) also frequently offer live entertainment. **Higher Ground** (654-8888), One Main Street, Winooski (next to the Champlain Spectrum Mall) offers live music.

Church Street pedestrian mall in downtown Burlington

KIM GRANT

SELECTIVE SHOPPING

In downtown Burlington

The Church Street Marketplace. Nearly a hundred stores, restaurants, and services line several blocks of Church Street, nicely paved, landscaped, closed to traffic, and enlivened by seasonal arts and crafts shows, weekend festivals, and wandering entertainers (and street people).

Pine Street area. A small yet delectable cluster of businesses on Pine Street between Marble Avenue and Howard Street, just south of the Vermont Transit terminal. Parking is never problematic. Highlights include the Fresh Market, the Burlington Futon Co., Speeder and Earl's Coffee, and Beverly's Cafe; a number of smaller craft businesses are behind Speeder and Earl's.

Burlington Square Mall. This vast indoor agora, mostly underground, has 80 stores stocking just about everything, linked to a parking garage and the Porteous Department Store. A Filene's is planned for 2000. Several food stalls for grazers.

ART GALLERIES

Fire House Art Gallery, 135 Church Street, Burlington. Pick up a copy of the *First Friday Art Trolley Tours* pamphlet guide (see *To Do—Museums and Attractions*). The trolley only runs first Fridays, but the map is a good gallery locator any day. On our own tour we were most impressed with the **Doll-Anstadt Gallery** (864-3661), 91 College Street. Ruby Anstadt offers a mix of striking paintings (changing shows) and decorative art.

Furchgott & Sourdiffe Gallery (985-3848), 86 Falls Road, Shelburne. A tasteful gallery in an old farmhouse, offering local art.

Also check out the **Exquisite Corpse Artiste,** 47 Maple Street (864-8040), just off Battery Street.

ANTIQUES SHOPS

Ethan Allen Antique Shop (863-3764), Williston Road, Route 2 east of Burlington, has a large stock of Early American and country furniture and accessories. Open daily; Sunday by appointment.

Architectural Salvage Company (658-5011), 212 Battery Street, offers artifacts from old houses and buildings.

Burlington Centre for Antiques (985-4911), 3093 Shelburne Road, south of Burlington. Open daily year-round. Two large floors offer quality antiques in every size and shape from more than 70 dealers.

Three Old Bats (860-1480), 207 Flynn Avenue, off Shelburne Road in the south end of town. Open Tuesday through Sunday. An intimate collection of elderly and antique items, reasonably priced. They also offer primitive-rug-hooking classes. Also visit their second-floor neighbor, **Upstairs Antiques,** open the same hours.

BOOKSTORES

Adventurous Traveler Bookstore (860-6776), 245 South Champlain Street (near the waterfront), is really a warehouse for its thick catalog. It's also a great place to browse, though, and conveys a sense of where Burlingtonians travel (there's far more on Nepal and Central and South America than most stores carry). The small **Everyday Book Shop** (862-5191) on College Street is the lone surviving independent downtown. **Waldenbooks'** branch is in the Burlington Square Mall, lower level. **Barnes & Noble** (864-8001), 102 Dorset Street, is a two-story book department store in South Burlington, and **Borders Books** (865-2711) is on 29 Church Street.

Antiquarian books can be found at **Bygone Books** (862-4397; 31 Main Street), Burlington's oldest and most appealing antiquarian bookstore; also at **North Country Books** and **Crow Book Shop,** both on upper Church Street. In Williston, **Beliveau Books** (482-2540), at Goose Creek Farms, specializing in Vermont, military history, and nature, is open by appointment.

CRAFTS SHOPS

Frog Hollow on the Marketplace (863-6458), 86 Church Street, is a branch of the Vermont State Craft Center of Middlebury, a showcase for fine things crafted in the state, from furniture and art glass to handwoven scarves.

Designers Circle (864-4238), 52 Church Street, features beautifully crafted jewelry. **Bennington Potters North** (863-2221), 127 College Street, sells kitchenware, home furnishings, glass, and woodenware, and Bennington pottery at "factory prices." **Church and Maple Glass Studio** (863-3880), 225 Church Street. Closed Sunday. Bud Shriner, a former emergency-room physician, bought the old Yellow Cab garage several years ago and has transformed it into a glassblowing studio with a reasonably priced array of crafted glass.

FARM

Vermont Wildflower Farm (425-3500), Route 7, Charlotte (5 miles south of the Shelburne Museum). Open May to October, 10–5 daily. A multimedia show; 6 acres of wildflowers in test fields and woodland settings; flowers and trees labeled along paths; a large gift shop; and "the largest wildflower seed center in the East." Nominal admission.

FOOD AND DRINK

Lake Champlain Chocolates (864-1807), 750 Pine Street, Burlington. Open 7 days. The home of the American Truffle and other expensive candy, discounts some of its premium chocolates. Tours possible with advance reservations.

Snowflake Chocolates, Route 15, Jericho Corners. Bob and Martha Pollak's handcrafted chocolates are so good. Try the dark, liqueur-laced truffles.

Fresh Market (863-3968; 1-800-447-1205), 400 Pine Street, Burlington. Formerly the Cheese Outlet, this market still specializes in Vermont and many other cheeses. Also most other Vermont products, and a source of sandwiches, baked goods, wines, and deli meats.

Magic Hat Brewing Company (658-BREW), 5 Bartlett Bay Road, South Burlington (turn off Route 7 at the Jiffy Lube). A microbrewery offering free tours and samples, Wednesday through Saturday; also a retail store.

Note: The Saturday Farmer's Market in City Hall Park (8:30–2:30) is good for baked goods, clothes, and art as well as fruits and veggies.

SPORTS STORES

Burton Snowboards (862-4500), 80 Industrial Parkway (near Oakledge Park), Burlington. Open Monday through Friday 8–6, Saturday noon–5. The factory's retail and factory outlet for Vermont's name-brand snow- and skateboards. Also check out the downtown Burlington store (863-0539) at 145 Cherry Streeet.

The Outdoor Gear Exchange (860-0190), 191 Bank Street, Burlington. Recently expanded and relocated, featuring used and new equipment: cross-country skiing, snowshoeing, rock-climbing, hiking, and backpacking gear. It's rock-climbing central.

The Downhill Edge Store (862-2282), 65 Main Street, Burlington, features high-performance sailboards, gives lessons, and offers rentals at Leddy Beach and the Marble Island Resort.

Skirack (658-3313), 85 Main Street, Burlington. A major source of cycling, running, in-line-skate, and cross-country-ski gear and wear, rentals.

VINTAGE CLOTHING AND FURNISHINGS

Old Gold (864-7786), 180 Main Street, is a fun and funky store. Battery Street Jeans (865-6223), 182 Battery Street, offers more grungy but cool clothing. Recycle North (appliances, furniture, books) and Garment Gallery (clothing and jewelry) are similar shops at 266 Pine Street. All are in Burlington.

MORE SPECIAL STORES

In Burlington

Peace and Justice Store (863-8326), 21 Church Street, run by the city's active Peace and Justice Coalition, a source of alternative publications and Third World–crafted items—jewelry, cards, clothing—all purchased from wholesalers committed to nonexploitation and social justice. The bulletin board is also worth checking.

Gardener's Supply (660-3505), 128 Intervale Road. One of the largest catalog seed and garden suppliers in New England, with a new store adjacent to demonstration gardens along the Winooski River.

Apple Mountain (658-0500), 30 Church Street, is a Vermont products gift and food shop; on the touristy side, but fun.

In the Charlotte-Shelburne area

The Dakin Farm (425-3971), Route 7, Ferrisburg (and the Champlain Mill, Winooski), is one of the principal purveyors of cob-smoked hams and bacon. This roadside store also stocks a variety of other Vermont food products and gifts.

Shelburne Farm Store and Visitors Center (985-8442), open daily year-round 9–5 (10–5 in the off-season; see a full description of what this place is about under *To See*). The store features the prizewinning cheddar cheeses made from the milk of the estate's own Brown Swiss herd. A variety of Vermont products are also stocked.

Harrington's, Route 7, across from the Shelburne Museum, Shelburne, has been known for years for its delectable (and expensive) corncob-smoked hams, bacon, turkey, pork chops, and other goodies. The shop also displays an array of cheese, maple products, griddlecake mixes, jams, fruit butters, relishes, baked goods, wines, and coffees. Harrington's headquarters (Route 2, Richmond) include a smaller store.

The Shelburne Country Store, Route 7, Shelburne, encloses several gift galleries under the same roof—a sweets shop, foods, lampshades.

The Vermont Teddy Bear Factory Store (985-3001; 1-800-829-BEAR), 2236 Shelburne Road (Route 7), Shelburne (see *To See*) is immense.

In Winooski

The Champlain Mill (655-9477), One Main Street, a creatively converted woolen mill, holds 30 smart shops, including the **Book Rack and Children's Pages** (655-0231), a well-stocked bookshop, plus two good restaurants, a bakery, and a deli; also several interesting clothing stores.

Blackthorne Forge (655-7676), 94 West Canal Street. Assorted traditional fixtures, plus unusual sculptured clocks.

Also in greater Burlington

University Mall (863-1066), Dorset and Williston Streets (I-89, exit 14E), South Burlington. Your basic shopping mall with 70 stores; Ames, Sears, and Penneys are the anchors. The **Essex Outlet Fair** (657-2777), Routes 15 and 289 in Essex, includes Polo Ralph Lauren, Jones New York, Levis, Jockey, and Bali.

SPECIAL EVENTS

February: **Burlington Winter Festival,** at Waterfront Park—dogsled rides, snow and ice sculptures (864-0123).

Saturday before Lent: **Magic Hat Mardi Gras**—a parade and block party at the Church Street Marketplace.

March: **Vermont Flower Show** at the Sheraton in South Burlington: 3 days of color and fragrance mark the end of winter.

May: **Lilac Sunday** at Shelburne Museum (985-3346). A festival of 19th-century food and games when the museum's many lilac bushes are in peak bloom.

Memorial Day weekend: **Lake Champlain Balloon & Craft Festival**—45 hot-air balloons hover over the Champlain Valley Fairgrounds, dawn to dusk; many special events including sky divers, crafts fair, children's rides, fireworks.

Early June: **Arts Alive,** a showcase of Vermont artists. Vintage auto rally at the Shelburne Museum (985-3346). **Discover Jazz Festival**—for 9 days, the entire city of Burlington becomes a stage for more than 200 musicians (see *Entertainment*). **Lake Champlain International Fishing Derby**—for details about registration and prizes, check with the chamber of commerce (see *Guidance*).

Late June: **Green Mountain Chew Chew,** Burlington, a 3-day food festival featuring more than 50 restaurants; continuous family entertainment. **Showcase of Agriculture** at the American Morgan Horse Association (985-4944), adjacent to the Shelburne Museum.

Early July: Gala **Independence Day celebrations** on the Burlington waterfront; fireworks over the lake with live bands in Battery Park, children's entertainment, a parade of boats, and blessing of the fleet.

Mid-July through mid-August: **Vermont Mozart Festival** performances in various locations, including Lake Champlain ferries (see *Entertainment*).

Mid-August: **The Shelburne Craft Fair** at Shelburne Farms features dozens of exhibitors.

Late August: **Champlain Valley Exposition,** Essex Junction Fairgrounds. A big, busy, traditional county fair with livestock and produce exhibits, trotting races, midway, rides, spun-sugar candy—the works.

Mid-September: **Annual Harvest Festival,** Shelburne Farms (985-8686). **Fools-A-Float**—a parade of land and sea craft, downtown Burlington. **Art Hop**—Open-studio weekend in Burlington.

Early October: **Marketfest**—celebrates Burlington's cultural diversity.

Early December: **Christmas Weekend** at the Shelburne Museum—a 19th-century festival; call 985-3344 for dates and details.

December 31: **First Night** (863-6005); the end-of-the-year gala—parades, fireworks, music, mimes, and other performances that transform downtown Burlington into a happy "happening."

The Northwest Corner

Interstate 89 is the quickest but not the most rewarding route from Burlington to the Canadian border. At the very least, motorists should detour for a meal in St. Albans and a sense of the farm country around Swanton. We strongly recommend allowing a few extra hours—or days—for the route up through the Champlain islands, Vermont's Martha's Vineyard but as yet unspoiled.

THE ISLANDS

The cows and silos, hayfields and mountain views couldn't be more Vermont. But what about those beaches and sailboats? They're part of the picture, too, in this land chain composed of the Alburg peninsula and three islands—Isle La Motte, North Hero, and South Hero.

The Champlain islands straggle 30 miles south from the Canadian border. Thin and flat, they offer some of the most spectacular views in New England: east to the highest of the Green Mountains and west to the Adirondacks. They also divide the northern reach of the largest lake in the East into two long, skinny arms, freckled with smaller outer islands. It's a waterscape well known to fishermen and sailors.

This is Grand Isle County, Vermont's smallest (with a year-round population of 4,000). It was homesteaded by Ebenezer Allen in 1783 and has been a quiet summer retreat since the 1870s.

In the 19th century, visitors arrived by lake steamer to stay at farms. Around the turn of the century, a railway spawned several hotels, and with the advent of automobiles and Prohibition, Route 2—the high road down the spine of the islands—became one of the most popular roads to Montreal, a status it maintained until I-89 opened in the 1960s.

Happily, the 1960s, as well as the '70s, '80s, and '90s, like the interstate, seem to have passed these islands by. The selection of North Hero as summer home of the Royal Lipizzan Stallions (see *Entertainment*) in the 1990s is the biggest thing that's happened here since Theodore Roosevelt's visit in 1901. (Roosevelt was vice president at the time he accepted an invitation to speak on Isle La Motte, where he received the news that President McKinley had been shot.)

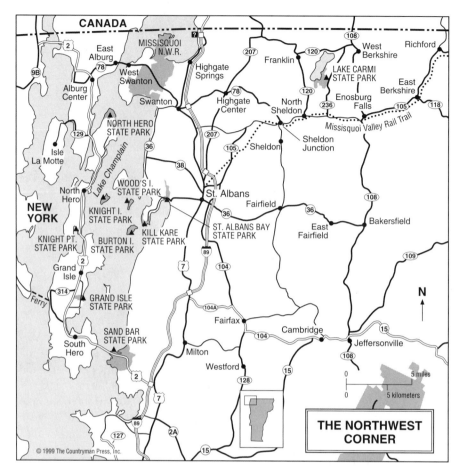

Isle La Motte is the smallest and quietest of the islands, and it's crossed and circled by narrow roads beloved by bicyclists. St. Anne's Shrine near the northern tip marks the site of a 17th-century French fort, and a rocky, tree-topped hump in the middle of a cow pasture at the southern end of the island is said to be the oldest coral reef in the world. Other evidence of the island's geological distinction can be seen in its stone houses, as well as in the marble facades of New York's Radio City Music Hall and the U.S. Capitol building. Unique, black Isle La Motte marble is once again being quarried, after years of closure.

The rural, laid-back beauty of these islands is fragile. Their waterside farms and orchards are threatened, not by tourism, but by quiet, steady suburbanization. Burlington is just south of Grand Isle, and Montreal is just 60 miles north.

Viewed primarily as a summer destination, this is a great place to visit in September and October when its many orchards are being harvested and bicycling is at its best. Roads are little trafficked, mysteriously overlooked by mainstream leaf-peepers.

GUIDANCE

Champlain Islands Chamber of Commerce (372-5683; e-mail: info@champlainislands.com; web site: www.champlainislands.com) P.O. Box 213, North Hero 05474, in the Hero's Welcome General Store (see *Selective Shopping—Special Stores*), maintains a year-round office and publishes a list of accommodations, restaurants, marinas, camp-grounds, and trailer parks.

GETTING THERE

From New York State and Montreal, Route 2 from Rouses Point, and from Vermont, Route 78 from Swanton (an exit on I-89). From Vermont on the south, I-89 exit 17 to Route 2, which runs the length of the islands.

Lake Champlain Transportation (864-9804) offers year-round, 12-minute ferry crossings between Gordon's Landing, Grand Isle, and Cumberland Head, New York.

MEDICAL EMERGENCY

North and South Hero (911). Marine emergencies (372-5590).

TO SEE

St. Anne's Shrine (928-3362), Isle La Motte, Route 129. An open-sided Victorian chapel on the shore marks the site of Vermont's first French settlement in 1666. There are daily outdoor Masses in summer and Sunday services as long as weather permits. The shrine is a pleasant and peaceful place with a public beach, a cafeteria, and a picnic area in a large pine grove, presumably descended from what Samuel de Champlain described as "the most beautiful pines as I have ever seen" near this spot. Champlain himself is honored here with a massive granite statue, which was carved in Vermont's Pavilion at Montreal's 1967 Expo. The complex is maintained by the Edmundites, the order that runs St. Michael's College in Winooski.

Hyde Log Cabin, Route 2, Grand Isle. Open July through Labor Day, 11–5 Wednesday through Sunday. Built by Jedediah Hyde in 1783, the cabin was restored by the Vermont Board of Historic Sites in 1956 and leased to the Grand Isle Historical Society, which has furnished it with appealing 18th-century artifacts—furniture, kitchenware, toys, tools, and fabrics. $1.

Isle La Motte Historical Society. Open July through August, Saturday 2–4. This old stone school building and blacksmith shop is on Route 129, 4 miles south of the bridge. Displays include a sculpture of local stone that's been partially polished, graphically illustrating that the stone used in many local buildings is marble. The nearby Chazian Reef, said to be the oldest coral reef in the world, is 450 million years old. Coral rock can harden into limestone that, over millennia, can turn to marble.

The Coral Reef at Fisk Farm. The reef noted above actually comprises 1,000 acres underlying the entire southern third of Isle La Motte. The

St. Anne's Shrine on Isle La Motte

one place that its various strata have been exposed, thanks to 19th-century and recent quarrying, is behind Fisk Farm, a bed & breakfast (see *Lodging*) with a summer-Sunday tea garden and art gallery. Currently owned by the Vermont Preservation Trust, the quarry is studded with fossils that represent some of the most primitive life on earth.

Fish Culture Station (372-3171), Bell Hill Road, Grand Isle. Just beyond the Plattsburgh, New York, ferry on Route 314, look for the large hatchery (it's precisely 2 miles up Route 314 from Route 2), open 8–4 daily. Fish are brought to the facility as freshly spawned eggs (up to 2.2 million eggs at any one time), incubated, then transferred to a series of tanks; well worth checking out.

TO DO

BICYCLING

With its flat roads (little trafficked once you are off Route 2) and splendid views, the islands are popular biking country. Isle La Motte is especially well suited to bicycling. For rental bikes check with **Hero's Welcome General Store** (372-4161; see *Selective Shopping—Special Stores*), North Hero Village, and **Bike Shed Rentals** (928-3440), Isle La Motte, West Shore Road, 1 mile south of St. Anne's Shrine. Open daily July through August, weekends in June, September, and October. Both Ruthcliffe Lodge and Terry Lodge (see *Lodging*) offer bikes to their guests.

BIRDING

Located on one of the major flyways, the islands are particularly rich in bird life: Herons, eagles, ospreys, cormorants, among others, migrate through the area. Prime birding sites include the South Hero Swamp and Mud Creek in Alburg and the Sand Bar Wildlife Refuge across from Sand Bar State Park. See also Knight's Island under *Green Space*.

BOATING

Rental boats are available in North Hero from **North Hero Marina** (372-5953), **Anchor Island Marina** (372-5131), **Charlie's Northland Lodge** (372-8822), and **Hero's Welcome** (372-4161; kayaks and canoes only). In South Hero, **Apple Tree Bay** (372-3922) offers canoes, sailboats, and pontoon boats. **Tudhope Sailing Center and Marina** (372-5320), at the bridge in Grand Isle, also offers boat slips, sailing instruction, and charters.

BOAT EXCURSIONS

Hero's Welcome General Store (372-4161), North Hero, offers several summer cruises in a 25-foot boat holding six passengers: Summer Sun, Sunset, Nature, and History Tours. Box lunches, beer, wine, and soft drinks available.

Ferry Cruise (864-9804), Route 314, Grand Isle. If you don't get out on the water any other way, be sure to take the 20-minute ferry to Plattsburgh, New York, and back.

FISHING

Lake Champlain is considered one of the finest freshwater fisheries in America. With the right bait and a little luck, you can catch trout, salmon, smelt, walleye, bass, pike, muskellunge, and perch. Don't expect area fishermen to give away their favorite spots, but you can find hints, maps, equipment, bait, and advice from local fishing pundit Charlie North at **Charlie's Northland** in North Hero (see *Boating* and *Selective Shopping—Special Stores*).

GOLF

Alburg Country Club (796-3586), Route 129, 3 miles west of South Alburg; 18 holes, gentle, shady terrain, snack bar. **Appletree Bay** (372-5398), South Hero; nine holes, rentals. **Wilcox Cove** (372-8343), Route 2, Grand Isle; nine lakeside holes, golf carts, pro shop, rentals.

Barcomb Hill Country Club at Apple Tree Bay (372-5398), Route 2, South Hero. Open May until late October. A par-3 executive golf course. Rental carts and clubs.

Wilcox Golf Course (372-8343), Grand Isle, offers nine holes.

Beaver Creek Mini Golf (372-5811), Route 2, North Hero. Open Memorial Day through Labor Day. An 18-hole miniature golf course that also features a farm-animal petting zoo. Horse-drawn hayrides by appointment.

GREEN SPACE

Alburg Dunes State Park (796-4170), Alburg. Recently opened, features a sandy beach, rare flora and fauna; limited day use only. Call for directions or ask locally.

✒ **North Hero State Park** (372-8727) has 99 wooded tent or trailer sites and 18 lean-to sites arranged in three loops, each with a rest room and hot showers (no hookups); mostly in lowland forests with access to open fields, a beach, boat launch, boat rentals, and picnic and children's play areas.

Grand Isle State Park (372-4300) has 155 campsites, including 33 lean-tos (no hookups) on 226 acres, with a beach, nature trail, and recreation building.

Knight's Island State Park (524-6353 at Burton Island State Park on the Vermont shore for information and ferry service, or Larry Tudhope, who offers a Knight Islander taxi service from North Hero: 372-6104). As Tudhope tells it, his great-uncle won mile-long Knight's Island in a crap game decades ago. He homesteaded himself on the island for nine years and built the island's only house, now home for the naturalist who oversees local tern rookeries as well as the nature trails and primitive campsites on the island. Taxi service is offered from North Hero Village.

✒ **Knight Point State Park** (372-8389), located on the southern tip of North Hero, is the best place to swim, especially if you have small children. A former farm facing The Gut, a quiet, almost landlocked bay, its grounds include a fine brick house and a nature trail that loops around the point, through maple and oak groves. From the sandy beach you can watch sailboats and yachts pass through the drawbridge between the islands.

Sand Bar State Park (372-8240) fills to capacity on sunny weekends in summer, but this oasis with its sandy beach and adjacent waterfowl area is a fine place to relax on weekdays.

See also *Green Space* in "St. Albans and Swanton" for the Missisquoi National Wildlife Refuge.

LODGING

Note: See *Green Space* for information on campgrounds in North Hero and Grand Isle State Parks. Families who don't camp tend to rent cottages for a week or more. The chamber of commerce (see *Guidance*) can furnish details about numerous old-fashioned lakeside cottage clusters.

INNS AND BED & BREAKFASTS

⚜ **Thomas Mott Homestead** (for the United States and Canada: 1-800-348-0843; otherwise, 796-3736), RFD 2, Box 149B, Alburg 05440. This 1838 white farmhouse with a splendid view of the Green Mountains is a real find. Host Patrick Schallert came from California to welcome guests to Vermont's "West Coast" in 1988 and has built up an enviable clientele.

KIM GRANT

Overlooking Lake Champlain in North Hero

Guests gather around an intriguing old Canadian tailor's table for outstanding breakfasts, maybe an omelet (15 varieties), or quiche with shrimp, or French toast with fresh raspberries. They tend to linger in the common room, with its hearth and games, or on the glassed-in side porch. The fridge is full of complimentary Ben & Jerry's ice cream. There are five bedrooms, each with private bath or shower. The Corner Suite downstairs has a cathedral ceiling, a queen bed and a twin daybed, plus full tub bath ($89). Ransom's Rest, the honeymoon suite upstairs with a balcony and fireplace, is charming ($95); Carrie's Room, a cozy little room at the top of the stairs, has a small sitting area ($75). Laura's Room has two queen beds under the eaves, catching the sunrise ($85); and the California King Hideaway, upstairs with a private entry, is designed for "very tall people" ($85). Guests are welcome to use the canoes and the swimming/fishing dock. Cross-country skiers and snowmobilers are at home here in winter (local rentals available), with 40 miles of dedicated trails adjacent. More-daring guests can try skydiving or paragliding from the Franklin County Airport in Swanton.

    ♿ **North Hero House** (372-8232; 1-888-525-3644), Route 2, North Hero 05474. Open year-round. This century-old summer hotel has a new lease on life thanks to New York investment manager Walt Blasberg, who put almost $1 million into renovations in 1997. Now it's a prim gray with black shutters and masses of red geraniums. All the rooms—the 9 upstairs and 15 more across Route 2—have been totally refurbished and many baths now have Jacuzzi. The inn offers a comfortable sitting area, also an inviting pub and small library, and a large public dining room and table-filled solarium beyond (see *Dining Out*). Facilities include a long, grassy dock at which Champlain steamers once moored; canoes, kayaks, power- and pedal boats are available. Our favorite (alas, the most expensive) rooms are in the buildings that face, even extend out over the lake, so that you fall asleep to lapping water. In summer: $79–179 per couple B&B weekdays, $110–235 weekends; $8 per child. In winter (November 20 through May 15): $79–139 weekdays, $99–159 weekends, $5 per child; just $10 extra per couple for MAP in winter.

Fisk Farm (928-3364), 44 West Shore Road, Isle La Motte 05463. Open late spring through fall. The clapboard home that once served as a store and post office is a now an attractive B&B with three guest rooms, two facing the lake. Common space includes a pleasant library, living room, and dining room. The ruins of a gray stone mansion have been pre- served in the front garden, the scene of Sunday teas, and the barn has been restored as an art gallery. It was here at Lt. Gov. Nelson Fisk's estate that Theodore Roosevelt (who was attending a Vermont Fish and Game League banquet) learned that President William McKinley (who had also been a visitor here) had been shot in Chicago. The banquet itself was in a huge tent. The mansion burned in 1924, but there is no sense of pathos about this place. Instead, thanks to Linda Fitch, who has dedicated the last few years to restoring the property, it's an excep- tionally tranquil place that offers a window into not only the history of Vermont but also the world (see Coral Reef at Fisk Farm under *To See*). In addition to the rooms in the house, there is a rustic Shore Cottage (said to have been built as a playhouse in North Hero and brought across the ice). The Ice House, built of wood and stone next to the main house, is a beauty, a place we would like to reserve for a special occasion, but only in warm weather (it has a fireplace but no other heating). Rates are $65 in the house with breakfast, $85 for the Shore Cottage, and $110 for the Ice House, both of which have their own kitchen. Guests can help themselves in the herb garden.

Ruthcliffe Lodge & Restaurant (928-3200; 1-800-769-8162), Isle La Motte 05463, open Mother's Day through Columbus Day. Way out at the end of Old Quarry Road, this lakeside compound includes a small motel and lodge with a total of nine rooms and a suite, seven of which feature lakeside panoramas and private baths. Mark and Kathy Infante are warm hosts, and the food is well known and highly rated (see *Din- ing Out*); three meals a day are served. There's a new 40-foot water's- edge patio for dining, as well as the cozy dining room in the lodge. Swimming and fishing are out the front door; rental boats and bikes are available. Rates range from $65 for a double room with a half-bath to $96.50 for a two-room adjoining unit with 1½ baths, including a full country breakfast.

The Ransom Bay Inn (1-800-729-3393), 4 Center Bay Road, Alburg 05440. A stone house built beautifully in the 1790s, originally a stage- coach stop, set back from Route 2 within walking distance of a small beach. Plenty of common space: an open-beamed living room area opening on a patio and a more formal parlor, two large airy and two smaller guest rooms, all nicely furnished and with private baths. $75 per couple, $15 per extra person, includes full breakfast. Dinner served to guests with advance notice.

Paradise Bay Bed & Breakfast (372-5393), 50 Light House Road, South Hero 05486. This is a very gracious new house in a secluded setting with plenty of deck space overlooking the lake. The two large, nicely furnished guest rooms share a bath in a separate wing. $75–100 per couple.

Farmhouse on the Lake (372-8849; 1-800-372-8849), 116 West Shore Road, Route 314, Grand Isle 05458. Built in 1801 by Capt. Daniel Wilcox, famous as the builder of many of the early packet boats on Lake Champlain, this lakeshore, brick landmark retains its original atmosphere. Teri Malkin offers six guest rooms (two shared baths), five with queen-sized beds, one with twins. Request a lake view. A broad, sunny deck faces the lake, fitted with lounge chairs, picnic tables, and a grill. The property adjoins a nine-hole golf course and a private beach. $75–85 per room.

Charlie's Northland Lodge (372-8822, 372-3829), Route 2, North Hero 05474, open all year, built by Charlie's grandparents early in the 19th century. Two guest rooms, furnished in country antiques, share a bath, a private entrance, and guest parlor. $55–65 double includes continental breakfast. It's part of a nifty little complex that includes a sporting and gift shop; boat and motor rentals, fishing licenses, bait, and tackle. Housekeeping cottages available.

Terry Lodge (928-3264), Isle La Motte 05463. Open May 15 through October 15. A friendly, family kind of place in a superb location: on a quiet road not far from St. Anne's Shrine, across a narrow road from the lake with a fine lakeside deck and swim raft. Most of the seven rooms in the lodge itself have lake views. Breakfast and dinner (family-style) are served. There's also a four-unit motel, a housekeeping cottage ($475 per week), and a housekeeping apartment ($425 per week) in the rear. Bikes and rowboats are available. Lodge rooms are $80–85 with breakfast, $100–105 per couple MAP (dinner too). Request one of the front rooms with a lake view.

The Allenholm Orchards Bed & Breakfast (372-5566), 150 South Street, South Hero 05486. Pam and Ray Allen offer a guest suite—a bedroom furnished in family antiques, including a queen-sized canopy bed, and a large living room with a TV, VCR, board games, and full-sized pool table, plus a full private bath, patio, and rose garden. A country breakfast is served upstairs in the dining room or, if preferred, on your patio. The suite is on the lower level of the Allens' modern home; it opens onto more than 100 acres of apples, billed as Vermont's oldest commercial orchard. Established in 1870s, it's now owned and operated by the sixth generation of Allens. $85 per couple for the bedroom, $125 for the entire suite.

FARM VACATION

☙✍ **Berkson Farms** (933-2522), Route 108 north, Enosburg Falls 05450. A mile north of the village, this 600-acre working dairy farm welcomes families year-round. The renovated, nicely maintained, 130-year-old farmhouse, managed by Dick and Joanne Keesler, can accommodate 8 to 10 people in four bedrooms, one of which has a private bath. There's a spacious living room and a library as well as a comfy family and game room with TV and VCR. But the main attractions, especially for kids, are the cows, ducks, sheep, and goats, along with sugaring in-season. Cross-country skiing can be enjoyed, along with hayrides and local swimming holes, and there's golf at the nearby 18-hole Enosburg Falls Country Club (see *To Do—Golf*). Rates are $55–65 per couple, including a full breakfast. Dinner is available for $15 per adult, $10 per child. A weeklong vacation including three meals a day costs $330 per adult, $180 per child (ages 2–12). Well-behaved pets accepted.

OTHER LODGING

☙✍ **Shore Acres Inn and Restaurant** (372-8722), Route 2, North Hero 05474. Motel rooms open May through early October. This pleasant motel commands one of the most spectacular views of any lodging place in Vermont. Set in sweeping, peaceful, beautifully groomed grounds, 19 comfortable rooms face the lake and the Green Mountains. There's a bar/lounge; breakfast and dinner are served (see *Dining Out*). There are also four guest rooms in the garden house, away from the lake. Susan and Mike Tranby have worked hard to make this an exceptionally friendly as well as comfortable place. Amenities include lawn chairs, two clay tennis courts, a driving range, lawn games, and a half mile of private shore for swimming. All rooms have been upgraded and have either a queen, king, two twins, or two doubles, TV, and ceiling fans or air conditioners when lake breezes fail. $89.50–124.50 June 12–July 2 and September 8–24; $94.50–129.50 between those dates and during foliage season (September 25 through October 18); less in spring and late October. Pets accepted (extra charge).

Wilcox Cove Cottages & Golf Course (372-8343 in summer; 879-7807 in winter), Route 314, mailing address: 3 Camp Court, Grand Isle 05458. Open June through mid-September. This homey, lakeside cottage colony and nine-hole public golf course, less than a mile from the ferry, is a real find (adults preferred). Each of the 11 cottages has a living room, dining area, fully equipped kitchen, one bedroom with twin beds, bathroom with shower, and one or two screened porches. They are completely furnished except for sheets, pillowcases, and bath and kitchen towels, and can be rented for about $400 a week including greens fees. Occupancy is limited to two people unless arrangements are made in advance.

WHERE TO EAT

DINING OUT

Shore Acres (372-8722), Route 2, North Hero. Reservations for dinner are a must much of the time. Also open for breakfast May through October and for lunch in July and August; dinner also served weekends until New Year's. The dining room's large windows command a sweeping view of the lake, with Mount Mansfield and its flanking peaks in the distance. It's a very attractive room with a large fieldstone hearth. You might begin with coconut-beer-battered shrimp ($5.25) or grilled homemade polenta ($3.95) and dine on apple island chicken or roast rack of lamb. Entrées ($12.95–21.95) come with home-baked bread, a salad, and seasonal vegetables. The chocolate pie is famous.

Ruthcliffe Lodge (928-3200), Old Quarry Road, Isle La Motte. Open mid-May through Columbus Day for dinner, July and August for lunch. Overnight moorings available for dinner guests. Be sure to reserve for dinner before you drive out to this rustic building, way off the main drag and overlooking the lake. Dine in the pine-paneled dining room or outside on the deck. Owner-chef Mark Infante specializes in Italian dishes like chicken Marsala and veal Sorrentina, but the menu might also include pan-fired Cajun swordfish or a full rack of lamb. Entrée prices include soup, salad, and vegetables. Entrées $16.95–25.95.

North Hero House (372-8237), Route 2, North Hero. Open mid-May through September. This historic old inn is known as a good bet for lunch as well as dinner (reserve). Although the dining room does not overlook the lake, it does feature a flower- and plant-filled greenhouse. The menu changes constantly, with entrées like salmon and steaks prepared in a variety of ways and a choice of pastas. Friday night there's always a lobster feast down on the dock. Entrées $13.95–18.95.

WEDDING RECEPTIONS

Grand Isle Lake House, East Shore Road, Grand Isle. For details and reservations, contact Bev Watson at 865-2522. Built on Robinson's Point as the Island Villa Hotel in 1903, this is a classic mansard-roofed 25-room summer hotel with a wraparound porch, set in 55 acres of lawn that sweep to the lake. From 1957 until 1993, it was a summer girls camp run by the Sisters of Mercy. Since 1997 it has been owned by the Preservation Trust of Vermont, which is currently attempting to raise funds to restore the upstairs rooms as it has the lobby, kitchen and dining rooms. It is currently available as a site for wedding receptions (80 can sit down in the dining room and another 125 guests on the porch; tents on the lawn can accommodate 250 guests).

EATING OUT

Hero's Welcome (372-4161), Route 2, North Hero Village. Open daily, year-round, an upscale general store with a good deli, a bakery, and café. Great sandwiches and freshly made soups.

Birdland, Route 2 at the Carrying Place, North Hero. Open June through August, 8 AM–9 PM, this tiny shop offers pure 1950s—or is it 1930s?—decor; great sandwiches, shakes, and legendary strawberry shortcake. You can inquire about the 12 adjoining waterside (vintage-1920s) cabins, but they tend to be booked at least a year in advance.

Margo's (372-6112), Route 2, Grand Isle. Behind this simple facade lies a cozy, popular bakery-café serving continental breakfast and light lunches indoors, outdoors, or to go, and featuring the work of local artists.

Grand Isle Ferry Dock Snack Bar, South Hero. Breakfast, 7–11 AM; open until 8 PM on Friday, otherwise until 6. Don't miss the french fries or the homemade bread that Chuck and Ruth Hager make for sandwiches. Check out the orange and peach julep. Tables inside and picnic tables outside.

Sandbar Restaurant (372-6911), Route 2, South Hero. This is a large, attractive dining room with views up the lake. Steak is a specialty of the house—T-bone, top sirloin, and filet mignon all top the menu. Chicken cordon bleu and scallops au vin are also on the menu.

Northern Café (796-3003), Route 2, Alburg. Open daily 7 AM–9 PM. Nothing special from the road, but it can hit the spot when a grilled cheese or homemade soup is what you want. Dinner specials as well as predictable fare.

Note: See also Fisk Farm under *Lodging* and inquire about Tea Garden Art Shows with music on summer Sundays, 1–5.

ENTERTAINMENT

Royal Lipizzan Stallions (372-5683), mid-July through August, performing Thursday through Saturday at the Herrmann Farm, Route 2, North Hero. Tickets through the chamber of commerce (see *Guidance*). Visitors welcome every day. These are elegant and unusually strong white horses bred in the 16th century for battle and show, known for their intricate maneuvers, many executed while in midair. Only a few hundred representatives of the breed survive. Colonel Herrmann's family have been training Lipizzans since 1618, when their ancestors received some as a gift from Hapsburg Austrian Emperor Ferdinand II. The Herrmanns winter in Florida and come to North Hero for 6 weeks each summer.

SELECTIVE SHOPPING

ANTIQUES

Pick up a current copy of the pamphlet guide *Antique the Champlain Islands* at **Hero's Welcome General Store** (see *Special Stores*). The usual count is a half-dozen shops but they are all seasonal and tend to close as one thing, open as another. Standbys include the **Alburg Coun-**

try Store, Main Street (Route 2), middle of Alburg Village, the **Back Chamber Antiques Store,** North Hero Village, and **Simply Country,** south of the village. Also check with **Alburg Auction House,** Lake Street, Alburg, open Saturday 2–6 and 7–midnight.

Richford Antique and Craft Center (848-3836), 66 Main Street, Richford. Open daily 10–5. Twenty rooms filled with antiques, crafts, and collectibles.

CRAFTS

McGuire Family Furnituremakers (928-3118), Route 129, Isle La Motte. Open year-round but call. Two generations of this talented family are involved in the day-to-day production of stunning furniture in spare, heirloom Early American designs: beds, tables, grandfather clocks, dressers—anything you want designed, and some surprisingly affordable. The showroom fills the common rooms of a classic old brick house in the village of Isle La Motte.

Country Linens (372-3306), 1 Hyde Road, corner of Route 2, Grand Isle. Patty Gentile makes the quilts displayed in this former general store and we could kick ourselves for not buying one. They really are outstanding and reasonably priced. **Black Cat Baskets & Gourds** (796-3845), showcasing Elizabeth Sloan's unusually shaped and woven baskets, shares the space.

Island Craft Shop, located next to the Hero's Welcome main store and open daily mid-May through mid-October. Works of local and area artisans.

ORCHARDS

Allenholm Farm (372-5566), 111 South Street, South Hero. Open July through December 24, 9–5. A sixth-generation, 100-acre apple orchard with a farmstead selling Vermont cheese, honey and maple syrup, jams and jellies, and papa Ray's famous homemade pies. There's also a petting paddock with rabbits, goats, horses, and donkeys. See also *Lodging* and *Special Events* (the Allens are the power behind the October Apple Fest).

Hall's Orchard (928-3418, 928-3226) , Spaulding Road, Isle la Motte. The 1820s brick house sits across from the orchard that has been in the same family since the house was built. The apples we bought here on a crisp October morning are the best we can remember finding anywhere.

Hackett's Orchard (372-4848), 86 South Street, South Hero. Perennials, syrup and pies in spring; small fruits and fresh-picked vegetables in summer, apples, cider, and pumpkins in fall. The farmstand has a family picnic and play area. Fresh cider doughnuts are a specialty.

SPECIAL STORES

Hero's Welcome General Store (1-800-372-HERO; fax: 802-372-3205), P.O. Box 202, Route 2, North Hero. Former Pier 1 CEO Bob Camp and his wife, Bev, have transformed this 19th-century landmark into a bright, smart, multilevel emporium: café and bakery, gift shop, art gallery, grocery, Vermont gourmet food products, sports clothes, wine shop, and bookstore, retaining its flavor as a community gathering spot.

They offer canoe and bike rentals as well as lake cruises (see *Boating*), and have plans for other magnetic features and services.

Charlie's Northland Sporting and Gift Shop. A serious fishing-gear source, but also assorted sportswear and gifts.

WINERY

Snow Farm Vineyard (372-9463), 190 West Shore Road (follow signs from Route 2 or Route 314), South Hero. Open Memorial Day through October 31, 10–4:30. Vineyard tours are offered daily at 11 and 2. This pioneering Lake Champlain vineyard is the fruition of several years' hard work by lawyers Molly and Harrison Lebowitz. Visitors enter a barnlike building that is the winery/showroom with a tasting counter. There they learn that this is still a relatively new operation (opened in 1997). Initially it is processing and bottling wine from grapes grown in New York's Finger Lakes, gradually mixing these with the harvest from vines on Snow Farm's 10 acres. The farm's blanc de noirs was awarded a bronze medal at the 1998 Eastern International Wine Competition. At this writing, five grape wines and an apple dessert wine are offered.

SPECIAL EVENTS

Note: Check with the chamber of commerce (see *Guidance*) about weekly events. See **Fisk Farm** under *Lodging;* inquire about Tea Garden art shows with music, summer Sundays.

July 4: **Parades** and **barbecues** in South Hero and Alburg.

July through August: **Lipizzan Stallions** (see *Entertainment*).

August: **Grand Isle County Art Show & Sale,** first weekend. **Northumbrian Pipers Convention Community Dance and Concert,** North Hero Town Hall; last weekend.

October: **Apple Fest,** the first weekend—crafts fair, a "press off," plenty of food and fun.

ST. ALBANS AND SWANTON

Once an important railroad center and still the Franklin County seat, St. Albans (population: 8,082), on Route 7, is showing signs of revitalization. Its firm place in the history books was assured on October 19, 1864, when 22 armed Confederate soldiers, who had infiltrated the town in mufti, held up the three banks, stole horses, and escaped back to Canada with $201,000, making this the northernmost engagement of the Civil War. One of the raiders was wounded and eventually died, as did Elinus J. Morrison, a visiting builder who was shot by the bandits. The surviving Confederates were arrested in Montreal, tried, but never extradited; their leader, Lt. Bennett H. Young, rose to the rank of general. When he visited Montreal again in 1911, a group of St. Albans dignitaries paid him a courtesy call at the Ritz-Carlton!

Swanton was settled by the French about 1700 and later named for a British captain in the French and Indian Wars. Swanton (population: 4,622) is growing again after a long period of relative stagnation. During World War I, the long-abandoned Robin Hood–Remington Arms plant produced millions of rounds of ammunition for the Allied armies. At one end of the village green dwell a pair of royal swans. This park is the focus for the Swanton Summer Festival (see *Special Events*). The tribal headquarters of the Abenaki are in the old railway depot.

GUIDANCE

The St. Albans Area Chamber of Commerce (524-2444; www.stalbanschamber.com), 2 North Main Street, St. Albans 05478, provides brochures and general information.

The Swanton Chamber of Commerce (868-7200), Swanton 05488, has an information booth at the north end of the village green.

MEDICAL EMERGENCY

Northwestern Medical Center (524-5911; 1-800-696-0321), St. Albans.

TO SEE AND DO

Franklin County Historical Society (527-7933), facing Taylor Park, open June through September, Tuesday through Saturday 1–4. This museum was established by the St. Albans Historical Society in 1971 in a three-story brick schoolhouse erected in 1861. The Beaumont Room has been fitted up as a fascinating, old-time country doctor's office. Another room has period costumes, a third houses Central Vermont Railroad memorabilia. Upstairs are farm tools, a maple sugaring exhibit, and other artifacts of the region. Admission is free; contributions appreciated.

Chester A. Arthur Birthplace, North Fairfield. A replica of the little house where the 21st (and usually underrated) president was born can be found 10 miles east on Route 36 to Fairfield (open June through mid-October, Wednesday through Sunday and holidays, 9:30–5:30). In the visitors center, exhibits examine the controversy over the actual site of Arthur's birth, which had an impact on the question of his eligibility to serve as president. Arthur's conduct as president in light of his reputation as a leading New York State political boss is also examined.

Marble Mill Park, Swanton (868-2559). Open year-round 8–4. The headquarters of the Abenaki Trial Council are on the banks of the Missiquoi River; the site of an ancient Abenaki camp. In the 19th century marble and limestone industries flourished and trains transported the finished product over a 386-foot covered bridge that's still partially visible. Swanton remains the hub of current tribal activities, centered in the former Central Vermont Railroad Station across the bridge from the park.

GOLF

Champlain Country Club (524-9895), Route 7, 3 miles north of St. Albans. Nine holes, some terraced. Snack bar.

Enosburg Falls Country Club (933-2296), Routes 105 and 108, Enosburg Falls, 18 holes.

Richford Country Club (848-3527), 84 Intervale Avenue, Richford, 9 holes, established 1930.**Enosburg Falls Country Club** (933-2296), Routes 105 and 108, Enosburg Falls, 18 holes.

Richford Country Club (848-3527), 84 Intervale Avenue, Richford; 9 holes, established 1930.

GREEN SPACE

Missisquoi Valley Rail Trail (524-5958), 140 South Main Street, St. Albans. The Northwest Regional Planning Commission supervises this 26.5-mile-long trail converted from the abandoned Central Vermont Railroad bed into a path for cross-country skiing, bike riding, hiking, snowmobiling, dogsledding, snowshoeing, and just plain strolling, but not for ATVs or dirt bikes. It leads from St. Albans to Sheldon Junction, from there to Enosburg Falls, and winds up in Richford. A free map-guide shows trailside facilities.

St. Albans Bay State Park, 4 miles west on Route 36, is a good place for picnics, but the water is too shallow and weedy for decent swimming.

Kamp Kill Kare State Park (524-6021), once a fashionable summer hotel site and then, for years, a famous boys summer camp; on Point Road off Route 36, St. Albans Bay. It can be crowded on weekends, but it's usually blissfully quiet other days; swim beach, playgrounds, boat rentals, access to Burton Island.

Burton Island State Park (524-6353), a lovely, 350-acre island reached from Kill Kare by park boat or by your own. Facilities include 42 campsites, including 22 lean-tos, and a 100-slip marina with electrical hookups and 20 moorings. Campers' gear is transported to campsites by park vehicle. Fishing off this beautiful haven is usually excellent. Also accessible for day use; swim beach, food concession, hiking trails, boat rentals.

Lake Carmi State Park (933-8383), exit 19 off I-89, 2 miles on Route 104; 1.5 miles north on Route 105; 3 miles north of Route 108, in Enosburg Falls. Set in rolling farmlands, the 482-acre park has 178 wooded campsites, including 35 lean-tos and some on the beach of this sizable lake; nature trails; boat ramp and rentals.

Wood's Island State Park (879-6565), 2 miles north of Burton Island. Primitive camping on an island of 125 acres. Five widely spaced campsites with no facilities; fires are not allowed. The island is unstaffed, although there are daily ranger patrols; reservations for campsites must be made through Burton Island State Park (see above). There is no public transportation to the island; the best boat access is from Kill Kare.

Gathering sap in Fairfield

The Missisquoi National Wildlife Refuge (868-4781), on the river's delta, lies 2 miles west of Swanton on Route 78 to East Alburg and the islands. Habitats are about equally divided among brushland, timberland, and marsh, through which wind Black Creek and Maquam Creek Trails, adding up to about 1½ miles or a 2-hour ramble; both are appropriately marked for the flora and fauna represented. It's open most of the time, but call ahead to confirm.

LODGING

RESORT
The Tyler Place Family Resort (868-4000), Route 7, Highgate Springs 05460. Open late May through mid-September. One of the country's oldest and most popular family resorts continues to thrive on 165 acres of woods, meadows, and a mile of undeveloped lakeshore. At the height of the season, it is rather like a jolly, crowded cruise ship with a lively crew; its faithful partisans have been returning year after year for three generations of the Tyler family's management. (Mrs. T, the grande dame, passed away in 1996—over 90—but the tradition continues.) They provide just about every conceivable form of recreation for adults and children 2–17 years of age, with separate programs and dining for each group (special arrangements for infants). The children's recreation centers are exceptional.

There are heated indoor and outdoor swimming and wading pools, six tennis courts, and equipment for kayaking, fishing, and windsurfing. Accommodations vary: the contemporary inn, plus 27 fireplaced cottages, a farm, and a guesthouse, a total of 58 cottages and family suites. Each unit has two or more bedrooms, air-conditioning, and a pantry or kitchen unit. The inn has a spacious dining room with good food, and a big lounge with bar. Call or write for rates, which range upward from $123 per adult per day from late June to early September; special rates for children; lower prices during the spring, early summer, and fall, plus learning retreats for the whole family.

BED & BREAKFASTS

High Winds (868-2521), Hog Island, Campbell Bay Road, off Route 78, West Swanton 05488. The Fournier family's working dairy farm welcomes guests in the pleasant 19th-century farmhouse, well off the main road but near the wildlife refuge. There's a comfortable double bedroom with private bath, flexible enough for a child or two. The Loft, with a double bed and whirlpool bath, has a private entrance; $65, including Susan Fournier's farm-fresh breakfast.

Country Essence B&B (868-4247), RD 2, Box 95, Swanton 05488, 1.5 miles north of the village on Route 7. Armand and Cheryl Messier provide two pretty rooms with private bath, reached by a private staircase entrance in their 1850s homestead on 12 groomed acres. There's an in-ground swimming pool. $60 double occupancy with country breakfast.

Reminisce B&B (524-3907), RD 3, Box 183, Lake Road, St. Albans 05478. Mary and Michele Boissoneault's lovely 1830s farmhouse located on a 550-acre working dairy farm was once a stagecoach stop and now features a three-room suite, individual rooms with shared bath, and a swimming pool. The suite is $70, rooms $45; weekly rates available.

Bay View B&B (524-5609), RD 3, P.O. Box 245, St. Albans 05478. Located on Hathaway's Point amid the colony of bayside cottages, this simple remodeled farmhouse with a nice screened-in porch has a few rooms at $50–60.

Wagner Road B&B (849-6030; 1-800-842-6030), 92 Fairfield Street, St. Albans 05478 (on Wagner Road, off Route 104, near Silver Lake). Gail and Ned Shulman's 1806 Cape Cod has a suite at $75–85 and a double at $60–70 with full breakfast; swimming pool in summer, cross-country trails in winter.

The Old Mill River Place (524-7211), Georgia Shore Road, St. Albans 05478, is a classic five-bay brick Federal built in 1799 as a wedding present for Sarah Allen Evarts, Ethan Allen's niece, occupied by the Neville and Bright families since 1926. There are three antiques-furnished rooms with private baths: Evarts has a lake view; Wheeler has twin cannonball low-post beds; Percival features a queen-sized four-poster and fireplace. $55–65 per double, including afternoon tea and generous country breakfast.

The Inn at Buck Hollow Farm (849-2400), RR 1, Box 680, Fairfax 05454, on Buck Hollow Road off Route 104, occupies a renovated 1790s carriage house on 400 spectacular acres. Each of the four rooms (with two shared baths) is decorated with antiques, queen-sized four-poster, and TV. Guests are encouraged to use the two-person Jacuzzi, and children have a fenced-in play area and can ride the pony. $58 per room, or $78 per night for one to three people in the suite, $88 for four, including full country breakfast.

The Hillside View Farm (827-4480), Box 2860, South Road, Fairfield 05455. Albert and Jacqueline Tetrault open up their farmhouse, especially welcoming French-speaking guests. There are cross-country-ski trails on their 236 acres. $45–55 double.

OTHER LODGING

Comfort Inn & Suites (524-3300; 1-800-228-5150), 167 Fairfax Road, Route 104, at exit 19 off I-89, St. Albans 05478. This new branch of the well-known chain has 63 guest rooms and suites, complimentary continental breakfast, indoor pool, and fitness room, at $59.95–114.95 with special rates for families, seniors, and business groups.

The Cadillac Motel (524-2191), 213 South Main Street, St. Albans 05478, is a pleasant cluster of 54 units surrounding a swimming pool, with minigolf, badminton, and a coffee shop in summer. $49–79 double.

CAMPGROUNDS

See Burton Island State Park, Lake Carmi State Park, and Wood's Island State Park under *Green Space*.

WHERE TO EAT

Jeff's Maine Seafood Market (524-6135), 56 North Main Street, St. Albans, obviously began as a fish shop and deli and has expanded into an attractive restaurant with specialties like grilled salmon with pesto butter ($9.95) and a blackened mahimahi burrito with sour cream ($5.95). Open for lunch and dinner Monday through Saturday. (This is one of the top chowder houses in the state.)

The Old Foundry Restaurant (524-9665), 3 Federal Street, St. Albans. Housed in one of the city's few 1840s buildings to have escaped the town's big 1895 fire, this is a great setting for traditional fare, like charbroiled rib steak and filet mignon (both $13.25), fried seafood, and charbroiled salmon steak ($12.95).

Chow!Bella (524-1405), 28 North Main Street, St. Albans. An intimate wine-bar with an eclectic menu, especially vegetarian dishes and fish. Open for lunch and dinner daily except Sunday.

Simple Pleasures Cafe (527-0669), 84 North Main Street, St. Albans. Cappuccino, sandwiches, baked goods.

Uncle Sam's Restaurant (527-7340), 51 South Main Street, St. Albans. A bright, casual place serving breakfast all day, plus lunch and dinner.

My-T-Fine Creamery Restaurant (868-4616), 73 First Street, Swanton. Open daily for homestyle breakfast, lunch, and dinner.

The Pines Restaurant (868-4819), Route 7, Swanton.

SELECTIVE SHOPPING

Better Planet (524-6835), 44 North Main Street, St. Albans, is a bright place for books, toys, games, puzzles, hobby kits, and art supplies.

SPECIAL EVENTS

Early through mid-April: **Maple Sugar Festival,** St. Albans. For 3 days the town turns into a nearly nonstop "sugarin' off" party, courtesy of the local maple producers, augmented by arts and crafts and antiques shows and other events.

Last week of July: **Swanton Summer Festival**—parades, band concerts, square dancing, arts and crafts shows.

Mid-September: **Civil War Days** (524-2444), St. Albans. A lively weekend of encampments at Taylor Park, a tour of an Underground Railroad home, echoes of the 1864 Confederate Raid, parade, barbecue, music, and a crafts show.

V. STOWE AREA AND NORTH OF THE NOTCH

Stowe and Waterbury
North of the Notch and the Lamoille Valley

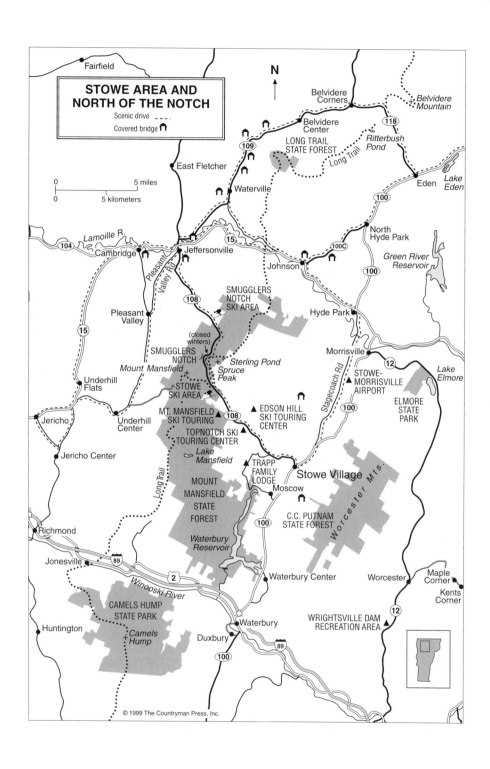

STOWE AREA AND
NORTH OF THE NOTCH

Scenic drive ----
Covered bridge

© 1999 The Countryman Press, Inc.

Stowe and Waterbury

Known as the "ski capital of the East," Stowe is the state's premier summer resort as well. A 200-year-old village that looks like a classic Vermont village should look, it's set against the massive backdrop of Mount Mansfield, which looks just like Vermont's highest mountain should look.

By the mid-19th century, men were already taxing their imaginations and funds to entice visitors up onto the heights of Mount Mansfield—which bears an uncanny resemblance to the upturned profile of a rather jowly man. In 1858 an inn was built under the Nose, a project that entailed constructing a 100-yard log trestle above a chasm and several miles of corduroy road made from hemlock. In Stowe Village at that time, a hotel, the Mansfield House, accommodated 600 guests.

Swedish families moved into Stowe in 1912 and began using their skis to get around. Then, in 1914, the Dartmouth College librarian skied down the Toll Road. Serious skiing, however, didn't begin until 1933, when the Civilian Conservation Corps cut a 4-mile-plus trail for just that purpose. The following year the town formed its own Mount Mansfield Ski Club, setting up basic lodging near the bottom of the ski trail in a former logging camp. By 1937, a rope tow had been rigged from the camp to the top of the trail, powered by a Cadillac engine. It cost 50¢ per day, $5 per season.

While its name keeps changing, the Mount Mansfield Company (also known as Stowe Resort Co.) is still the same outfit formed in 1951 from the various small concerns that had evolved in the 1930s and 1940s to serve skiers, and it's still owned by the same insurance company. The good news is continuity and an immense sense of pride and history. The bad news is a sometimes slow response to the demands of this quickly changing industry.

What the "Mountain Company" does, it always does first-class. Just as it was a Cadillac engine (not the Ford used elsewhere) that first hauled Stowe skiers, the eight-passenger gondola, installed in 1991, is one of the world's fastest, and the Cliff House in the summit Octagon offers a prix fixe, five-course menu. On the other hand, a small '50s base lodge still serves the mountain's primary trail network and, lacking snowmaking as it does, the area's best intermediate terrain (accessed by a long, slow ride on a vintage-'54 chairlift) may not be open.

The Mountain Company is finally focusing on its most basic need: water. In the '90s it became painfully clear that natural snow in northern New England is too fickle a base for the huge business that skiing has become. Ski operators and skiers alike are not about to invest big bucks unless they can depend on snow, and to make snow you need water.

Stowe has submitted a proposal for environmental review for a $9 million, 7-mile pipeline to the Waterbury Reservoir, to secure four times the water the resort now draws from the Little River. It also proposes a "hamlet" at Spruce Peak, replacing the present base lodge there with a four-story, wood-and-stone version; a 100-room lodge, shops and golf course, a sports center, and more than 500 lodging units are also planned.

In the meantime, the quality of alpine skiing and snowboarding at Stowe remains high. The more than 150 km cross-country-ski network is outstanding not only in its extent but also in its quality, thanks in good part to its elevation: Many trails meander off the high walls of the cul-de-sac in which the resort nestles, and you can usually count on snow on many miles of trail through April.

Stowe actually now attracts more visitors in summer and fall than it does in winter. From June through mid-October, it offers a superb golf course, tennis, theater, an alpine slide, and gondola rides to the top of the mountain, as well as hiking, biking, fishing, and special events every week of the summer and fall. Year-round it boasts more than 2,200 rooms, accommodating a total of 7,500 visitors on any given night. There are also more than 50 restaurants and 100 or so shops.

What's most amazing about Stowe is the way it has managed to keep its commercial side low-key and tasteful, a sideshow to the natural beauty of the place. Even in non-skiing months, most visitors are lured from their cars and onto their feet and bicycles, thanks to the 5.3-mile Stowe Recreation Path, which parallels "the Mountain Road" from the village (albeit at a more forgiving grade) to Mount Mansfield, through cornfields, wildflowers, and raspberry patches.

In warm-weather months, Stowe is also an excellent pivot from which to explore northern Vermont: 30 miles from Burlington, just over the Notch from the little-touristed Lamoille Valley, and a short drive from both Montpelier/Barre on the one hand and the Northeast Kingdom on the other. Lodging options range from funky to fabulous, including a number of self-contained resorts as well as inns, lodges, motels, and condominiums. The Stowe Area Association has been in business since 1936, matching visitors with lodgings they can afford and enjoy.

Most Stowe-bound visitors know Waterbury, 10 miles down Route 100, simply as an I-89 exit; they know the strip just to the north as the home of Ben & Jerry's ice-cream factory, one of the state's most popular

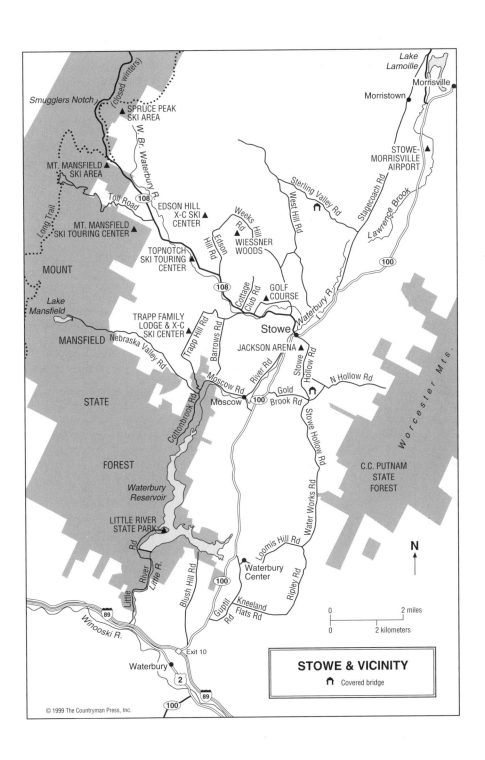

Lake
Lamoille

Smugglers Notch

(closed winters)

▲ SPRUCE PEAK
SKI AREA

Morrisville

Morristown

STOWE-
MORRISVILLE
AIRPORT ▲

MT. MANSFIELD ▲
SKI AREA

W. Br. Waterbury R.

Sterling Valley Rd

Stagecoach Rd

Lawrence Brook

Toll Road

108

Long Trail

MT. MANSFIELD
SKI TOURING CENTER ▲

EDSON HILL
X-C SKI ▲
CENTER

Weeks
Hill
Rd

West Hill Rd

100

TOPNOTCH
SKI TOURING
CENTER ▲

Edson Hill Rd

▲
WIESSNER
WOODS

MOUNT

Lake
Mansfield

108

Cottage Club Rd

Waterbury R.

GOLF
COURSE ▲

TRAPP FAMILY
LODGE & X-C ▲
SKI CENTER

Stowe

MANSFIELD

Nebraska Valley Rd

Trapp Hill Rd

Barrows Rd

JACKSON ARENA ▲

River Rd

Stowe Hollow Rd

N Hollow Rd

W o r c e s t e r   M t s .

STATE

Cottonbrook Rd

Moscow Rd

Moscow

100

Gold
Brook Rd

Stowe Hollow Rd

C.C. PUTNAM
STATE
FOREST

FOREST

Waterbury
Reservoir

Water Works Rd

LITTLE RIVER
STATE PARK ▲

River
Rd

Little R.

Loomis Hill Rd

Ripley Rd

Blush Hill Rd

100

Waterbury
Center

N

Little River

Guptil Rd

Kneeland
Flats Rd

0   2 miles

89

Winooski R.

0   2 kilometers

Exit 10

Waterbury

2

89

100

© 1999 The Countryman Press, Inc.

STOWE & VICINITY

⌂ Covered bridge

attractions. The old town itself lies along a southward bend in the Winooski River, and several interesting shops and restaurants are housed in the brief downtown between the traffic light and the railroad station. Waterbury Reservoir, accessible from Waterbury Center, is the obvious place in this area to swim and paddle a canoe or kayak.

GUIDANCE

The Stowe Area Association (253-7321; for toll-free reservations: 1-800-247-8693; web site: www.stoweinfo.com/saa), Box 1320, Stowe 05672. Open daily November through March, 9–8; the rest of the year 9–5. This service, housed in its own building in the middle of Stowe Village, provides information on more than 60 local lodging places and will make reservations; it also publishes seasonal guides listing most things in the area and is a walk-in source of advice about what's going on.

GETTING THERE

By bus: **Vermont Transit/Greyhound** stops in Waterbury with connections from Boston, New York, and points south.

By train: **Amtrak** from Washington, D.C., New York City, and Springfield, Massachusetts, stops in Waterbury.

By plane: The Stowe-Morrisville Airport, 7 miles north, provides private plane services and charters. Burlington Airport, 34 miles away, is served by major carriers (see *Getting There* in "Burlington Region").

Taxi: **Peg's Pickup/Stowe Taxi** (1-800-370-9490), also **Countryside Transportation:** 888-5405.

By car: From most points, I-89 exit 10, and 15 minutes north on Route 100.

GETTING AROUND

During winter season, the Town Trolley circles the 7 miles between the village and the mountain every 20 minutes, 8–10 AM and 2–5 PM; hourly between 11 and 2 and between 5 and 11. Pick up a schedule. Trolley tokens are $1 and 1-week passes cost $10. Tuesday and Thursday shopping runs to Morrisville are also offered; in summer inquire about trolley tours.

MEDICAL EMERGENCY

Stowe Rescue Squad, police (911); Waterbury (244-5511); **Copley Hospital** (888-4231), Morrisville.

TO SEE

Mount Mansfield, the highest point in Vermont—4,395 feet (it gained 2 feet when it was remeasured in 1998) at the Chin—yields a truly spectacular view, accessible primarily in summer, unless you can clamber up to the summit from the Cliff House restaurant at the top of the gondola over ice and snow. In summer there are two easy ways up: the Toll Road and an eight-passenger gondola.

The Toll Road (253-3000) begins 7 miles up Route 108 from the village of Stowe; look for the sign on the left just before the Inn at the Mountain (see *Lodging*). Open late May through mid-October, weather permitting, 10–5. $12 per car and $7 per motorcycle; bikes and foot traffic free. First laid in the mid-19th century, this steep, winding road led to a hotel that served the public until 1957. (It was demolished in the mid-1960s.) This also serves as a ski trail in winter. The road terminates at the Mount Mansfield Summit Station just below the Nose (4,062 feet). A half-mile Tundra Trail follows the Long Trail (red-and-white blazes on the rocks) north to Drift Rock (the trek should take 20 minutes); another mile along the trail brings you to the summit of Mount Mansfield (round-trip: 2 hours).

The Gondola (253-7311) at Stowe operates mid-June through mid-October, weather permitting, 9–5; $10 per adult, $6 per child ($25 for a family of five) round-trip. The eight-passenger gondola runs from Midway Lodge to the Cliff House (see *Dining Out*); a half-hour's trek brings you up to the Chin. However you get there, the view from the summit (the Chin) is spectacular on a clear day: west across 20 miles of farmland to Lake Champlain; east to the Worcester Range across the Stowe Valley; north to Jay Peak (35 miles distant) across the Lamoille Valley; and south, back along the Green Mountains, to Camel's Hump. Mount Washington is visible to the east, Whiteface to the west.

Stowe Village. A classic, early-19th-century Vermont village with a spired white meetinghouse at one end of Main Street and a brick stagecoach inn at the other, a satisfying variety of stores and restaurants all within an easy stroll. The former wooden high school (one block up School Street from Main) is now the Helen Day Art Center (253-8358), open in summer daily noon–5 except Monday, closed Sunday too in winter. The changing art exhibits are frequently well worth checking out ($2 per adult, $1 seniors, and $.50 students). The mid-19th-century Bloody Brook Schoolhouse next door is open on request in summer months.

Smugglers Notch is the high (elevation: 2,162 feet), extremely winding and narrow stretch of Route 108 just north of Mount Mansfield, with 1,000-foot cliffs towering on either side. The first carriage road through this pass wasn't opened until 1894, but the name dates its heavy use as a route to smuggle cattle down from Canada during the War of 1812. One of two formally designated State Scenic Roads in Vermont, Smugglers Notch is known for rock formations like Smugglers Head, Elephant Head, the Hunter and His Dog, the Big Spring, Smugglers Cave, and the Natural Refrigerator. The Notch is closed in winter, inviting cross-country skiing and snowshoeing. See also *To See* in the "North of the Notch" chapter.

Ben & Jerry's Ice Cream Factory Tours (244-8687), Route 100, Waterbury. No American ice cream has a story, let alone a taste, to match that of the totally Vermont-made sweet and creamy stuff concocted by high school buddies Ben Cohen and Jerry Greenfield. More than a decade ago, they began churning out Dastardly Mash and Heath Bar Crunch

At the Ben & Jerry's ice cream factory in Waterbury

in a Burlington garage; they have now outgrown this seemingly mammoth plant, which threatens to outstrip the Shelburne Museum (see *Museums* in "Burlington Region") as Vermont's number one attraction. A half-hour tour of the plant is offered all year, Monday through Saturday 9–4. The big store, selling an amazing number of things relating to cows and Vermont, is open 9–5, and the Scoop Shop is open 9–9 in summer, 9–5 in winter. The tour includes a multimedia show, a look (from an observation platform) at the production room, and a free sample of one of the 34 "euphoric flavors." The grounds include picnic facilities and some sample black-and-white cows. Nominal fee, children free.

COVERED BRIDGES

The **Gold Brook Bridge** in Stowe Hollow, also known as Emily's Bridge because Emily is said to have taken her life from it (in different ways and for different reasons in the different stories) and reportedly returns to haunt it on occasion. There is another picturesque bridge across the Sterling Brook, off the Stagecoach Road, north of the village.

SCENIC DRIVES

Not only is Stowe pleasantly sited for touring in all directions, but it is also organized to offer visitors well-researched printed tours. Pick up a copy of *Roads and Tours* from the Stowe Area Association (see *Guidance*). Don't fail to drive Smugglers Notch (see *To See*).

TO DO

AIR RIDES

For **hot-air ballooning,** inquire at Stoweflake Mountain Resort and Spa (253-7355; see *Lodging—Resorts*). Whitcomb Aviation, based at the

Stowe-Morrisville State Airport (888-7845), offers **glider rides,** instruction, and rentals (see *Getting There*).

Alpine slide (253-7300), Spruce Peak Base Lodge, Mountain Road, Stowe. Open late June to early September, 9:30–5. $7.50 per adult, $6 per child; $25 and $20 for five rides.

BIKING

The equipage here is a mountain bike, and the rental sources are the **Mountain Bike Shop** (253-7919), **AJ's Mountain Bikes** (253-4593), **Stowe Action Outfitters** (253-7975), and **Topnotch Resort** (253-8585), all on the Mountain Road (Route 108) in Stowe. **Stowe Hardware Inc. (253-7205),** offers rentals, and **Stowe Mountain Resort** (253-3000) offers rentals and lessons for its lift-assisted trail system. Neophytes usually head for the **Stowe Recreation Path** (see *Hiking and Walking*); next there's a 9-mile loop through part of the Mount Mansfield State Forest (see *Green Space*) and into the Cottonbrook Basin. The **Mountain Biking Center** (253-300), **Mountain Bike Shop,** and the **Inn at Turner Mill** (225-2062), all along the Mountain Road, offer mountain-biking tours. Pick up a copy of the *Mt. Mansfield/Stowe Area Biking Map/Guide* published by Map Adventures in Stowe (253-7489); it maps and describes 32 local mountain-bike trail and road rides.

BOATING

Canoes can be rented from **Stowe Action Outfitters** (253-7975) and from **Umiak Outfitters** (253-2317), Stowe, which offers rentals at Waterbury Reservoir; Umiak also offers kayak rentals, lessons, and guided trips on the Winooksi and Lamoille Rivers, on Lake Champlain, and throughout the state.

CAMPING

Little River Camping Areas (244-7103), RFD 1, Waterbury 05676. Six miles north of Waterbury on the Waterbury Reservoir: 64 campsites, including six lean-tos, swimming, hiking, rental boats, snowmobile trails in Little River State Park.

See also *Green Space* for information on camping in Smugglers Notch and Elmore State Park.

CARRIAGE RIDES

Edson Hill Manor, Golden Eagle Resort, and **Stowehof Inn** in Stowe (see *Lodging*) all offer carriage rides. **Charlie Horse** in Stowe offers carriage and wagon rides.

FISHING

The Little River in Stowe is a favorite for brook trout, along with Sterling Pond on top of Spruce Peak and Sterling Brook. Contact **Reel Vermont** (223-1869), geared to guiding everyone (families included) from neophytes to pros.

GOLF

Stowe Country Club (253-4893), an 18-hole course with a 40-acre driving range, putting green, restaurant, bar, pro shop, lessons; inquire about the Stowe Golf School. **Stoweflake Mountain Resort and Spa** (253-

7355), adjacent to the Stowe Country Club, also offers instruction. The **Farm Resort** (888-3525), Route 100, 6 miles north of Stowe in Morrisville, offers nine holes and a driving range.

Blush Hill Country Club (244-8974), a nine-hole course in Waterbury, has marvelous views.

Country Club of Vermont (244-1800), Waterbury. Just opened in 1998, this 18-hole course gets rave reviews.

HEALTH SPAS

The Stowe Athletic Club (253-2541) at the Green Mountain Inn, the **Spa at Topnotch** (253-8585), **Golden Eagle Resort Motor Inn** (253-4811), and **Stoweflake Spa & Sports Club** (253-7321) all offer spa facilities.

HIKING AND WALKING

Green Mountain Club (GMC) headquarters (244-7037), a few miles south of Stowe Village on Route 100, maintains a Hiker's Center stocked with hiking maps, guides, and gear. Inquire about workshops and special events.

Stowe Recreation Path is a 5.3-mile paved path that begins in Stowe Village behind the Community Church, winds up through cornfields, wildflowers, and raspberry patches, and parallels Mountain Road (but at a more forgiving pitch). It's open to walkers, joggers, bicyclists, etc. Note the **Quiet Path** along the Mayo River, a mile loop off the main path (it begins across from the Golden Eagle; see *Lodging—Resorts*) reserved for walkers (no mountain bikers or in-line skaters).

Mount Mansfield. See the introduction to this section and *To See* for a general description of Vermont's highest mountain. For walkers (as opposed to hikers), it's best to take the Toll Road or gondola up and follow the Tundra Trail (see *To See*). Serious hikers should at least purchase the weatherproof map of the Mount Mansfield region and can profit from the *Long Trail Guide,* both published by the Green Mountain Club. A naturalist is on hand May through November along the heavily traveled, 2½-mile section of the Long Trail between the Forehead and the Chin; the Green Mountain Club maintains Butler Lodge, a half mile south of the Forehead, and Taft Lodge, below the Chin, as shelters for hikers.

Smugglers Notch. The Long Trail North, clearly marked, provides an easy, mile-plus hike to Sterling Pond, a beautiful spot at 3,000 feet, and fish-stocked, too. The Elephant's Head can be reached from the state picnic area on Route 108; a 2-mile trail leads to this landmark—from which you can also continue on to Sterling Pond and thence out to Route 108 only a couple of miles above the picnic area. No one should drive through Smugglers Notch without stopping to see the **Smugglers Cave** and to clamber around on the rocks.

Other local hikes are detailed in *Day Hikers Guide to Vermont,* which is published by the Green Mountain Club and available from the Stowe Area Association (see *Guidance*): **Belvidere Mountain** in Eden,

Cyclists on the Stowe Recreation Path

a 3½-hour trek yielding good views in all directions; **Ritterbush Pond** and **Devil's Gulch,** also in Eden, about 2½ hours round-trip (see *Hiking* in "North of the Notch"); and **Elmore Mountain** in Elmore State Park (see *Green Space*), a 2- to 3-hour hike with spectacular views.

Camel's Hump, from Waterbury. See "Burlington Region" for details. This trail is also detailed in *50 Hikes in Vermont* (Backcountry Publications). One trail starts from Crouching Lion Farm in Duxbury; it's a 6½-hour round-trip hike to the unspoiled summit of Vermont's third highest mountain. Pick up a map at the GMC Hiker's Center (see above).

Little River Trail System, Mount Mansfield State Forest, Waterbury. There are seven beautiful trails through the Ricker Basin and Cotton Brook area, once a settlement for 50 families who left behind cellar holes, stone fences, cemeteries, lilacs, and apple trees. Accessible from both Stowe and Waterbury. Pick up the self-guiding booklet from the Vermont State Department of Forests, Parks and Recreation in Waterbury (241-3678).

See also the "Barre/Montpelier Area" chapter for hiking in the Worcester Range.

Note: The *Northern Vermont Hiking Trails Map/Guide* published by Map Adventures (253-7489) in Stowe is worth picking up.

HORSEBACK RIDING

Topnotch Stables (253-8585), Mountain Road, Stowe, offers trail rides and carriage lessons. **Edson Hill Manor** (253-8954), Stowe (see *Lodging—Resorts*), gives private lessons, trail rides. Also **Stowehof Inn** (253-9722; see *Lodging—Resorts*), and the **Mt. View Equestrian Center** (253-9901), both in Stowe.

IN-LINE SKATING

Stowe-in-Line Skate Park (253-3000) at the base of Spruce Peak features a speed oval, a halfpipe, freestyle ramps, and a timed downhill slalom course; $7 half day, $10 full day. Rentals available.

POLO

Mid-May through Columbus Day weekend, Sunday-afternoon polo matches begin at 1 PM at various locations around town; check the weekly calendar in the front foyer of Mr. Pickwick's Pub Restaurant (see *Eating Out*) on the Mountain Road in Stowe.

ROCK CLIMBING

Check with **Umiak Outfitters** (253-2317) in Stowe for instruction and ropes course.

SWIMMING

Waterbury Reservoir is the obvious local beach (see Little River State Park in *Green Space*). **Forest Pool** on Notchbrook Road, **Sterling Falls,** and the swimming holes in **Ranch Valley** are all worth checking; ask locally for directions. Many lodging places also have their own pools that nonguests may use for a fee.

TENNIS

The Racquet Club at Topnotch (253-9308), Stowe. Four indoor and 11 outdoor courts, pro shop, instruction, videotape, 8 AM–11 PM.

Stowe Mountain Resort Tennis Courts (253-7311), six well-maintained clay courts adjacent to the Inn at the Mountain (see *Lodging—Resorts*), 8–6, available by the hour (dress: whites required).

Free public courts can be found at the town recreation area off School Street. A number of inns have courts available to the public; inquire at the Stowe Area Association (253-7321; see *Guidance*).

WINTER SPORTS

CROSS-COUNTRY SKIING

A 150 km network of trails that connect ski centers in this area adds up to some of the best ski touring in New England. Given the high elevation of much of this terrain, the trails tend to have snow when few other areas do, and on windy, icy days, cross-country can be better in Stowe than downhill. All four touring centers (in Stowe) honor the others' trail tickets (if you ski, not drive, from one to the next). In February 1997, the interchangeable trail fee was $8 for guests of Stowe-area lodging.

Trapp Family Lodge Cross-Country Ski Center (253-8511). Located on the Trapp Hill Road, off by itself in the upper reaches of the valley, this is one of the oldest and most beautiful commercial trail systems— 40 km of set trails and a total of 85 km of trails at elevations of 1,100–3,000 feet. The basic route here is up and up to a cabin in the woods, a source of homemade soups and chili. Start early enough in the day and you can continue along ridge trails or connect with the Mount Mansfield

Cross-country skiers at the Trapp Family Lodge

system. Lessons, equipment rental and sales, and outstanding pastries are all available, as well as guided tours.

Stowe Mountain Resort Touring Center (253-7311), Mountain Road. Located near the Inn at the Mountain (see *Lodging—Resorts*), this center offers 40 km of set trails, plus 45 km of backcountry trails, at elevations of 1,200–2,800 feet. It's possible to take the Toll House lift partway up the Toll Road and ski down (a good place to practice telemarking). You can also take the quad close enough to the summit to enable you to climb to the very top (via the Toll Road) for a spectacular view out across Lake Champlain; the descent via the Toll Road is relatively easy. Another beautiful trail circles Sterling Pond high in the saddle between Spruce and Madonna Mountains (accessible via chairlift). Connecting trails link this system with the Trapp Family Lodge trails (see above) along some of Stowe's oldest ski trails, such as Ranch Camp and Steeple, dating to the 1920s, now backcountry trails winding along the curved inner face of the mountain.

Edson Hill Ski Touring Center (253-8954), Edson Hill Road. Relatively uncrowded on the uplands north of the Mountain Road, the area offers 30 miles of set trails, 25 more on outlying trails at elevations between 1,200 and 2,150 feet; instruction, rental, sales, full lunches, and guided tours available.

Topnotch Touring Center (253-8585), Mountain Road, Stowe. Novice to expert trails, a total of 25 km; instruction, rental, café, and restaurant available, also changing rooms.

Spruce Peak Alpine/Nordic Area (253-7311), Mountain Road, Stowe. Cross-country is available on downhill trails with the purchase of a regular lift ticket.

Backcountry tours are offered by the Stowe Mountain Touring Center (253-7311) and Trapp Family Lodge (253-8511).

"Northern Vermont Adventure Skiing," a weatherproof map ($6.95) detailing cross-country trails throughout the region, is available at local outlets and from Map Adventures (253-7489), 846 Cottage Club Road, Stowe.

DOWNHILL SKIING

Stowe Mountain Resort (253-3000; 24-hour snow report: 253-3600), Stowe. See the chapter introduction for the history and proposed future of the ski resort. At present the amazingly small, 1950s-era base lodge continues to serve the mountain's primary trail network: the legendary expert Front Four trails that plunge down the mountain's face, and a half-dozen intermediate trails that snake down its more forgiving slopes. A quad (wear a neck warmer and/or face mask) goes up to the '40s Octagon. With the exception of Starr and Goat, which are too steep to cover or groom, most trails here are coated with man-made as well as natural snow, and conditions are usually fine. It's an easy traverse from this side of the mountain to the trails served by the gondola up to the Cliff House, from which long, ego-building runs like Perry Merrill sweep to the valley floor. Stowe regulars ski Mount Mansfield in the morning, switching after lunch to south-facing Spruce Peak across Route 108. The Spruce Lodge (connected by shuttles) serves as home to the ski school and children's programs, and several lifts access extensive novice trails.

Lifts: Eight-passenger gondola, quad chairlift, triple chairlift, six double chairlifts, one surface.

Trails: 47, also glade skiing; 16 percent expert, 59 percent intermediate, 25 percent novice.

Vertical drop: 2,360 feet on Mount Mansfield, 1,550 feet on Spruce Peak.

Snowmaking: Covers 73 percent of the terrain trails served by 9 of the 10 lifts.

Facilities: Eight restaurants including those in the Inn at the Mountain (see *Lodging*), three base lodges, plus the Octagon Web Cafe (you can send free e-mail postcards), the Cliff House at the top of the busiest lifts; cafeterias, rentals, ski shops, shuttle bus.

Ski school: 200 instructors; a lift especially designed for beginners at Spruce Peak, where novices learn to make the transition from easy to intermediate trails.

Night skiing: More than 20 acres on Mount Mansfield are lighted Thursday through Saturday nights 5–9.

For children: Daycare from 6 weeks in Cubs Infant Daycare. The Children's Learning Center offers daycare or a combo of care and lessons at Spruce Peak.

Rates: $52 per adult midweek and weekend; $30 per child under 13; 5 and under free.

(*Note:* For downhill skiing at **Smugglers' Notch,** see "North of the Notch"; it is possible to ski back and forth between the two areas when the Spruce Chair is working.)

ICE CLIMBING

See Expedition Stowe under *Special Events.* Smugglers Notch itself is favored by ice climbers. Check with the Inn at Turner Mill (1-800-992-0016; see *Lodging—Inns and Bed & Breakfasts*).

ICE SKATING

Ice skating is available at the **Jackson Arena** (253-4402) in the village and on the pond at Commodores Inn (253-7131; see *Lodging—Motels*). Skates can be rented from Shaw's General Store (253-4040; see *Selective Shopping*). All are in Stowe.

SLEIGH RIDES

In Stowe, sleigh rides are found at **Stowehof Inn, Edson Hill Manor**, and the **Trapp Family Lodge** (see *Lodging—Resorts*); **Pristine Meadows** (253-9901); and **Charlie Horse Sleigh Rides** (253-2215).

SNOWMOBILING

Stowe Snowmobile Tours (253-6221) offers rentals and tours, and is also a source of information about local trails. **Smugglers Notch Snowmobile Tours** (1-800-347-8266), based at Sterling Ridge Inn on the other side of the Notch in Jeffersonville (see "North of the Notch and the Lamoille River Valley"), also offers guided trips from the Stowe side, conditions permitting.

SNOWSHOEING

Tubbs, New England's leading snowshoe manufacturer, is located in Stowe but at this writing it offers no retail store or visitor outreach program. On the other hand, **Trapp Family Lodge Cross-Country Ski Center** (see *Cross-Country Skiing*) has designated more than 15 km of its trails as snowshoe-only. The **Stowe Mountain Resort Touring Cen-**

ter (see *Cross-Country Skiing*) has cut 10 km of dedicated trails and permits snowshoers on all 80 km of its cross-country trails. **Topnotch at Stowe Resort** has also designated 10 km of snowshoe-recommended routes, and permits snowshoes on all 20 km of its trails. The obvious place to go is, of course, up the unplowed stretch of Route 108 into Smugglers Notch (see *To See*), and the more adventurous can also access more than 40 miles of hiking terrain on and around Mount Mansfield, but it's best to check with the Green Mountain Club (see *Hiking*), which also sponsors a mid-February Snowshoe Festival (see *Special Events*). **Umiak Outfitters** (253-2317) in Stowe offers guided tours. Local rental sources are so plentiful that they beg naming. Pick up a copy of **"Northern Vermont Adventure Skiing,"** a weather-proof map/guide detailing trails throughout the region. It's available at local stores and from Map Adventures (253-7489) in Stowe.

GREEN SPACE

For fees and reservation rules, see *Campgrounds* in "What's Where."

Mount Mansfield State Forest. The largest state forest in Vermont—27,436 acres—much of which lies on the other (western) flank of the mountain.

Smugglers Notch State Park (253-4014), RFD, Stowe 05472; 10 miles up Mountain Road (Route 108) from Stowe Village, open mid-May through mid-October. Thirty-eight campsites including 14 lean-tos. A few miles beyond the camping area, just beyond the highest point on this high, winding road—open only late May through November, weather permitting—is a turnoff with parking, toilet, and an information center. For details on the trails from this area, see *Hiking and Walking;* for background, see "North of the Notch."

Elmore State Park (888-2982), Lake Elmore 05657. Open mid-May through mid-October, 14 miles north of Stowe on Route 100, then east to Morrisville, south 5 miles on Route 12; 709 acres with a beach, bath-house, rental boats, 64 sites for tents and trailers including five lean-tos, picnicking, hiking trail up Elmore Mountain.

Wiessner Woods. An 80-acre preserve with nature trails maintained by the Stowe Land Trust. The entrance is on Edson Hill Road, the next right after the entrance to Stowehof Inn (see *Lodging—Resorts*).

LODGING

Most accommodations are found either in Stowe Village or along—or just off—the 7.2-mile Mountain Road (Route 108), which connects the village with the ski slopes. Unless otherwise noted, all are in Stowe 05672.

RESORTS

The Trapp Family Lodge (253-8511; 1-800-826-7000), Trapp Hill Road, is an alpine-modern version of the fabled Austrian schloss built by the baroness of *Sound of Music* fame. Johannes Von Trapp lives nearby and remains involved in the property's day-to-day operations. The 73-room lodge (a 17-room luxury wing is planned for completion by the year 2000) offers ample common space: a charming greenhouse sitting room, three common rooms with fireplaces, and a library, cocktail lounge, large dining room, and conference facilities. Twenty more rooms are in the motel-style Lower Lodge, and 100 guesthouse time-share units (inquire about vacancies) are ranged in tiers on the slope below, commanding sweeping views of the Worcester Range. The inn's 2,700 acres are webbed with cross-country-ski trails, also good for splendid walks. There are tennis courts and a spring-fed pool as well as an indoor pool, sauna, and workout room in the Sports Center. Come in late March (when the sugarhouse is operating and the sun is warm but there is still snow on the high and wooded trails) or in early December (when there is usually snow), and you can pay $98 for the same room that costs $180 (per couple) during foliage season. A 3-day minimum is mandatory in peak periods like foliage and Christmas. Inquire about family packages (children 16 and under stay free), and about nature walks, snowshoeing, sleigh rides, and children's, exercise, and cross-country-ski programs. $98–225 EP; the one-bedroom suites, two connected family rooms, and Maria's own former quarters go for $265–525 (no meals).

Edson Hill Manor (253-7371; 1-800-621-0284), 1500 Edson Hill Road. Set in 225 cultivated acres on a high slope, the manor was built in the 1940s with brick from the old Sherwood Hotel of Burlington. Most of the living room beams were hewn for Ira and Ethan Allen's barn, which stood in North Burlington for more than a century. In the inn itself, the nine guest rooms are each very individual, most with fireplace and with hand-painted mural in the bath. The honeymoon suite with a view over the gardens is room 3, and room 5 has gables, a canopy bed, and the same view. Four carriage houses, each with three or four units, are ranged in tiers behind the main house; these have knotty-pine walls, wing chairs and reproduction antiques, fireplaces, sitting areas, books, and a comfortable, spacious, in-the-woods feel. Under the ownership of Jane and Eric Lande, the small dining room has acquired an enviable reputation (see *Dining Out*). Living rooms are furnished in genuine antiques, hung with exceptional art. Facilities include a stable and trails for horseback riding, outdoor pool, stocked trout pond, and 40 km of cross-country trails. Rates are $110–210 per couple B&B; MAP and multi-day packages available, more expensive during foliage season; add 15 percent for service.

Green Mountain Inn (253-7301; 1-800-253-7302), Main Street. The brick-and-clapboard face of this landmark dates back to the 1830s, when it was built as a private home. In the 1850s it became a hotel, and it last changed ownership in 1982, when it was acquired by a Canadian, Marvin Gameroff, who has since tastefully renovated the rooms in the inn itself, outfitting them with country furniture especially made for the inn, adding niceties like salt-glaze stoneware lamps and appealing art. Public spaces have also been tastefully redecorated, settings for the collection of striking watercolors of local scenes by Walton Blodgett. The Clubhouse rooms, each with queen-sized four-poster, fireplace, VCR, and Jacuzzi, have been added in landscaped grounds beyond the swimming pool, a couple also with fully equipped kitchens. The 15-room Annex Building has been renovated, too. The dining options: a formal Main St. Dining Room, and the downstairs Whip Bar & Grill, which offers a poolside patio in summer and a fire in colder months (see *Eating Out*). Afternoon tea and cookies are served in the living room. $115–259 per room in winter and summer (2-night minimum stay on weekends), less in the off-season. Guests enjoy complimentary use of Athletic Club facilities, located just the other side of the pool.

Inn at the Mountain and Condominiums (253-7311; 1-800-253-4754), Mountain Road. The Mount Mansfield Company's luxurious 32-room lodge, also a number of town houses, and truly luxurious one-, two-, and three-bedroom Mountain Club condominiums are currently the closest lodging to the lifts. Facilities include H.H. Bingham's restaurant, clay tennis courts, swimming pools, and the Toll House Health Spa. From $145 EP per room in the inn to $385 for a three-bedroom three-bath condo sleeping up to eight people comfortably (children under 12 stay free). More in holiday periods, less in the off-season and through numerous packages.

Stowehof Inn (253-9722; 1-800-932-7136), 2 miles off Route 108. A fantasy world from the moment you step through its sod-roofed porte cochère, supported by two maple trees. No two of the 45 guest rooms are alike (some suites, a few fireplaced demi-suites with optional kitchenette). The public rooms are quixotically furnished with mementos like the divining rod that located the water source for the building. Windows everywhere let in the view. Facilities include a taproom, a dining room known for nouvelle French dishes, tennis courts, a putting range, a pool with a view, a sauna, and cross-country-ski trails connecting with the larger network. On the adjacent working farm, guests can see cattle and ride horses. Rates are $90–220 per couple B&B, from $70 in the off-season and from $150 during holidays and foliage.

Topnotch at Stowe Resort (253-8585; 1-800-451-8686), P.O. Box 1458, Mountain Road. Uncommonly comfortable rooms, luxurious areas for lounging, the Bistro for lunch and light suppers, the convivial Buttertub Bar, and the stately, glass-sided, highly rated main dining room (see *Dining Out*). The health-and-fitness spa (see *To Do—Health Spas*) offers a program as well as superb facilities, including an indoor pool with a waterfall. Contemporary sculpture surrounds the outdoor swimming pool. A red barn down across the Mountain Road serves as a cross-country- ski center in winter (50 km of groomed trails and connecting with three other trails in Stowe); riding stable, indoor and outdoor tennis courts, and a handy skating rink.

Rates begin at $150 for a double room, run $276–576 for a suite, and town houses are $275–555 per unit. Rates include use of the pool and Jacuzzi; the exercise program is $15 extra. A $52 MAP plan is offered; inquire about spa packages. Pets welcome.

Golden Eagle Resort Motor Inn (253-4811; 1-800-626-1010), 511 Mountain Road. The 12-unit motel that Herb and Ann Hillman bought in 1963 has evolved through two generations into an amazing 60-acre complex with 71 rooms, 11 efficiencies, five condominiums, and two houses. Family geared as well as owned, it offers a lot for children. In summer, there's a formal hiking and crafts program on selected days for 3- to 12-year-olds, and on certain nights, year-round, there are movies with popcorn. Amenities include a playground as well as an attractive health spa with indoor pool, large whirlpool, sauna, Universal exercise equipment, massage service, and exercise classes (see *To Do—Health Spas*). There are also outdoor heated pools (swimming lessons are offered); a clay tennis court; fish-stocked ponds; shuffleboard, badminton, lawn games, and game rooms; and a coffee shop and restaurants. Throughout, you have the sense of a well-run resort. A 50-acre wildlife area with walking trails adjoins the property. Breakfast is included in $70–179 per room in low season, $84–199 in high; fully handicapped-accessible rooms; also shuttle service to Amtrak station.

Stoweflake Mountain Resort & Spa (253-7355; 1-800-253-2232), Mountain Road. The small ski lodge that the Baraw family opened more than 30 years ago has mushroomed into a full-facility, 95-room resort (including 40 new luxury suites) and 25 townhouses. There are bright, comfortable, inn-style rooms in the original lodge and many nicely furnished motel rooms (besides its own motel wing, the resort includes the former Nordic Motor Inn). All rooms have cable TV, phone, and private bath, and common space includes a library and lobby with fireplaces and sitting area, along with a large living room with a sunken fireplace. The Spa & Sports Club includes a Cybex Circuit, racquetball/squash court, indoor pool, Jacuzzi, sauna, and steam and massage rooms. There are also tennis courts, badminton, volleyball, croquet, horseshoes, and a professional putting green and driving ranges. The links at the Stowe Country Club adjoin the property (see *To Do—Golf*). Dining options include formal Winfields and the pubby Charlie B's. $106–275 per room or suite; $140–575 for townhouse units; MAP rates and many packages.

INNS AND BED & BREAKFASTS

The Gables Inn (253-7730; 1-800-422-5371), Mountain Road. Sol and Lynn Baumrind are warm, personable hosts who have created one of Stowe's most relaxing and welcoming inns. Common rooms include a comfortable living room with fireplace, a plant-filled solarium, and a downstairs

Thatcher Brook Inn

KIM GRANT

game room/lounge (BYOB). There's a swimming pool in the landscaped grounds, which angle off from Mountain Road, across from an open stretch of the Stowe Recreation Path (see *To Do—Hiking and Walking*). The hot tub is right outside the door, the better to hop into in winter. Each of the 13 rooms (all with private bath) in the main house is different. Four in the carriage house (handicapped-accessible) feature whirlpool and fireplace; the two Riverside suites in the neighboring house across the brook have a fridge, microwave, and coffeemaker, as well as a fireplace and double Jacuzzi. After skiing, there is always a pot of soup in the den; dinner at 6:30 (by reservation) is candlelit. The famously good breakfasts are also open to the public and generally considered the best in town (see *Eating Out*). Rates are $95–200 B&B in winter, $65–145 in summer; dinner is optional.

🖉 **Fiddler's Green** (253-8124; 1-800-882-5346), Mountain Road. Less than a mile from the lifts, this pleasant, yellow, 1820s farmhouse can sleep no more than 18 guests (making it great for small groups) in seven comfortable guest rooms tucked under the eaves. Guests gather around the fieldstone hearth in the living room and at the long table off the sunny kitchen. BYOB. Hammocking and hiking or skiing, depending on the season, are close by. In summer and winter longtime owners Bud and Carol McKeon cater to bicyclists and cross-country skiers, $110–70 per room. In winter, B&B $40–90; $40–70 off-season B&B; dinner possible on request. Families welcome.

🏵✍ **The Inn at Turner Mill** (253-2062; 1-800-992-0016), 56 Turner Mill Lane. Sequestered in the pines by Notch Brook, off Mountain Road just a mile from the lifts, this complex was splendidly built in the 1930s by a woman doctor. Its 10 wooded acres include a mountain stream and "refreshing" swimming hole; there's also an outdoor pool. The family-geared efficiencies and apartments are nicely decorated, with cable TV, some with hearth, access to sauna, Jacuzzi, and cross-country trails. Greg and Mitzi Speer are friendly hosts who can find a baby-sitter and help with transfers from Burlington or Waterbury. Greg's passions are hiking and biking, cross-country skiing, snowshoeing, and ice climbing and he offers guided tours. (He also frequently just accompanies guests.) Snowhoe rentals are available and guests get a half day free. When it was built, this was as high as a car could drive up the Mountain Road, and the Civilian Conservation Corps ski trails (now cross-country-ski trails) are within easy striking distance. Rates: $35–45 per couple in low, $48–80 in regular, and $70–105 in high season.

🏵✍ **Ski Inn** (253-4050), Route 108. Harriette Heyer has been welcoming guests to Stowe's oldest ski lodge—one of the handiest places to the lifts—since Pearl Harbor Day. Designed as a ski lodge, the inn is set back from the Mountain Road amid hemlocks and evergreens. The 10 guest rooms are bright and meticulously clean, each with both a double and a single bed; shared and private baths. There is a pine-paneled BYOB bar and attractive sitting and dining rooms. Stowe's cross-country network can be accessed from the back door. $55–65 per person MAP in winter; $40–60 per person for a room in summer.

Brass Lantern Inn (253-2229; 1-800-729-2980), 717 Maple Street (Route 100), is a welcoming B&B at the northern edge of the village. Your host is Andy Aldrich, a Vermonter raised on a Richmond dairy farm, a builder of prizewinning homes. His work is evident in this nicely renovated

1800s building, with its planked floors and comfortable common rooms. The nine stenciled or papered guest rooms are furnished with antiques and hand-stitched quilts; all have private bath, some have whirlpool tub, some a wood-burning fireplace. Guests enjoy gym privileges at the Stowe Athletic Club (see *To Do—Health Spas*). Breakfast is a serious affair, maybe sourdough French toast, apple crêpes, or broccoli and mushroom quiche. $80–135 in low season, $90–160 in regular, and $100–210 per couple in high season. Weddings a specialty.

☙ **Walkabout Creek Lodge** (253-7354; 1-800-426-6697), Edson Hill Road off Route 108. "Walkabout," according to innkeeper Joni Gaines, is an Australian Aboriginal invitation to relaxation and good times. This distinctive log-and-fieldstone lodge, dating from 1941, is set on 5 wooded acres and rooms are within earshot of the mountain creek flowing through the backyard. In summer there's a pool and flower beds; in winter, cross-country trails are out the back door. The lodge accommodates up to 60 guests in varying ways, from regular rooms through family suites to a three-bedroom town house. A full breakfast is served year-round and the Billabong Pub is fully licensed. $70–150 per couple B&B. Pets accepted.

❧ **Bittersweet Inn** (253-7787; 1-800-387-8789), 692 South Main Street. This 18th-century brick farmhouse and converted carriage house is a find. Barbara and Paul Hansel offer eight rooms, including one suite, six with private bath. The house is right on Route 100, but there is a view and a sense of space in the back. Amenities include a comfortable living room, a game room with BYOB bar, a good-sized swimming pool, a large lawn, and a hot tub. Rates include a substantial continental breakfast with homemade pastries. $56–86 per couple.

♿ **Ten Acres Lodge** (253-7638; 1-800-327-7357), Luce Hill Road. Under the same ownership as Edson Hill Manor, this 1840s red-clapboard inn has a luxurious feel and a reputation for fine dining. We recommend the suites with fireplace, sitting area, and deck in Hill House, a newish complex up behind the old inn. The two cottages, one with two and the other with three bedrooms, and with kitchen and fireplace, are also exceptional. The grounds include a pool, tennis court, and hot tub. Doubles are $75–220; MAP and multi-day rates available. Add 10 percent service charge.

Olde England Inn (253-7558; 1-800-477-3771), 433 Mountain Road. Anglophiles can revel in the English accent, decor, and menu. The rooms are unabashedly luxurious, from the 17 Laura Ashley–style rooms in the inn to the two 2-bedroom English "cottages" beside the swimming pool (each with fireplace, Jacuzzi, and kitchen). There are 10 suites on a rise behind the inn, each with a four-poster, Jacuzzi, deck, and lounge with a fireplace, wet bar, fridge, and microwave. A full English breakfast and tea are included in $98–295, $178–455 during peak periods. Mr. Pickwick's Pub & Restaurant (a source of mulligatawny stew, Cornish pasties, and fish-and-chips; see *Eating Out*) and Copperfields (beef

Wellington and broiled pheasant) are also in the inn.

Foxfire Inn (253-4887), Route 100 north of Stowe Village. This early-19th-century farmhouse is set on 70 wooded hillside acres. The five guest rooms have wide-board floors (several have exposed beams) and are furnished with antiques, each with private bath. Downstairs there is plenty of space for guests away from the large, public dining room, well respected for its Italian fare (see *Dining Out*). $75–90 per double room includes a full breakfast.

In Waterbury 05676

The Inn at Blush Hill (244-7529; 1-800-736-7522), Blush Hill Road, off Route 100, hidden away on 5 hilltop acres with spectacular views across the valley and reservoir (good for boating and swimming). All five rooms have private bath, one has a fireplace, another has a 15-foot-wide view of the mountains, and a third, a Jacuzzi bath. The handsome wine red, gabled cape dates to 1790 and the living room has that nice snug feel (there's a vintage-1840 hearth and an oak armoire that opens into an entertainment center). Country breakfasts are served on an old farmhand's table in the sunny, many-windowed kitchen. Your hosts are Pam and Gary Gosslin. $59–130 per couple includes a full breakfast and evening refreshments; less in the off-season.

✿✍ The Old Stagecoach Inn (244-5056; 1-800-262-2206), 18 North Main Street. A classic stagecoach inn built in 1826 with a triple-tiered porch but substantially altered in the 1880s, when a millionaire from Ohio added oak woodwork, ornate fireplaces, and stained glass. Renovated since 1993 by the Barwick family, there are now eight guest rooms and three efficiency suites, all tastefully furnished but varying widely—from a room with a sitting area, daybed, fireplace, and private bath, to small rooms with a shared bath. One efficiency suite is a studio; the other has two bedrooms. All are large, family-geared, with connecting rooms. Coco, the African gray parrot, sits by the fireplace in the living room adjoining the library, with its fully licensed bar. Summer rates are $45–90 per couple; foliage season and winter holidays $55–130. A full breakfast, including a selection of hot dishes, is included and dinner is served to the public as well as guests. Pets possible.

Grünberg Haus (244-7726; 1-800-800-7760), Route 100 south of Waterbury. This secluded, Tyrolean-style chalet has 11 truly cozy, beamed guest rooms, all opening onto an exterior balcony. Downstairs, innkeeper Chris Sellers may be at the grand piano (guests are welcome to play), if he isn't serving a hearty breakfast, maybe ricotta-stuffed French toast or pumpkin–apple streusel muffins and maple-poached pears. The dark wood–beamed common rooms include a massive fieldstone fireplace, a large window overlooking the mountains, and a book-lined BYOB bar with stenciled booths. Two nicely designed, self-contained cabins are along the wooded path above the inn, part of a 20 km cross-country trail system. Facilities include a tennis court, warm-weather

Jacuzzi, and cold-weather sauna. In winter the inn offers discounted tickets to Stowe, Sugarbush, and Mad River Glen (all within easy striking distance) and keeps four sets of snowshoes. Rates are $59–89 in low season, $79–145 in high. $20 less single. Chickens and ducks as well as cats are in residence.

In Waterbury Center 05677

       The Black Locust Inn (244-7490; 1-800-366-5592), 5088 Waterbury/Stowe Road (Route 100). This is an 1832 three-gabled home with six rooms that have private bath, polished wood floors, stained-glass transoms. One twin-bedded room is handicapped-accessible. Len, Nancy, and Valerie Vignole (assisted by golden retriever Lady) get great reviews for hospitality. $95–135 includes three-course breakfasts.

MOTELS

In Stowe 05672

Commodores Inn (253-7131; 1-800-44-STOWE), Route 100 south. Longtime Stowe residents Bruce and Wendy Nourjian are usually around to greet guests. The 72 rooms are large (request one in the back, overlooking the lake), and there's a living room with a fireplace; also two Jacuzzis and saunas and an outdoor pool. The Stowe Yacht Club Steakhouse and Sport Lounge (a popular watering hole and spot for an evening burger) overlooks a 3-acre lake on which model sailboat races are regularly held. $88–128 per person in winter; less in summer and multi-days year-round.

Buccaneer Country Lodge (253-4772; 1-800-543-1293), Mountain Road. This is the former home of Olympian Billy Kidd. Karen and Rod Zbikowski offer 12 rooms, all with private bath, recently renovated and furnished in antiques, equipped with TV and a small fridge. Four rooms have fully equipped kitchens; three have a fireplace. Common space includes a game room, pool table, and outdoor pool. Amenities include fieldstone fireplaces and a hot tub. $45–125 per couple in summer, $69–225 in winter.

      Alpenrose (253-7277; 1-800-962-7002), Mountain Road. A pleasant, small motel with just two rooms, three efficiencies; direct access to cross-country network. $54–60 per room in winter.

In Waterbury 05676

    Holiday Inn (244-7822; 1-800-HOLIDAY), exit 10 north, I-89. There are 79 rooms, three suites, and a restaurant serving three meals. Amenities include an indoor pool, tennis court, and sauna. Positioned just off the interstate, this is a popular way-stop with family-geared rates and access to Sugarbush as well as Stowe. $79–129 per couple; many family-sized rooms; rates include continental breakfast. There's also tennis, and pets are accepted.

CONDOMINIUMS

Stowe Country Rentals (253-8132; 1-800-639-1990) handles condos and houses. **Country Village Rentals** (253-8777; 1-800-870-8771) specializes in upscale homes, both old and new. **All Seasons Rentals** (253-7353; 1-800-54-STOWE) and **Rentals at Stowe** (253-9786; 1-800-848-9120, ext. 624) also rent homes and condos.

The Village Green at Stowe (253-9705; 1-800-451-3297). 1003 Cape Cod Road, Stowe, 05672. Seven nicely designed buildings set on 40 acres (surrounded by the Stowe Country Club links; see *To Do—Golf*) contain 73 two- and three-bedroom town houses, all brightly furnished. A recreation building has a heated indoor pool, Jacuzzi, sauna, game and changing rooms; also an outdoor pool and two tennis courts. Winter rates begin at $260 per night for a two-bedroom unit with a minimum of 2 nights; less for additional nights. From $215 per night in summer, more for three-bedroom units; weekly rates.

❀ **Notch Brook Resort** (253-4882; 1-800-253-4882), 1229 Notch Brook Road, Stowe 05672. In the shadow of Spruce Peak with a spectacular view of Mount Mansfield, an unusually well-built (though no one seems to know why Vermont architect Robert Burley designed them with flat roofs) complex of 36 rooms and 35 condominiums ranging from doubles through three-bedroom town houses. Most rooms are available by the day and week. Amenities include saunas, tennis, an outdoor pool that's heated for winter use, and complimentary continental breakfast. $62–299 per unit in winter, $59–175 in summer; more in peak holiday periods.

1836 Cabins (244-8533), Box 128, Waterbury Center 05677, are tucked into a pine forest whose logging roads become cross-country-ski trails in winter. Completely furnished one- and two-bedroom units with kitchen, TV; telephones on request. Rates $79 for two, standard; $99, deluxe (gas fireplaces); more over holidays, less in the off-season.

HOSTEL

🐾 **State Ski Dorm and Hostel** (253-4010) on Mountain Road, Stowe 05672. Open to the public (all ages) September to April. Owned by the state's Department of Forests and Parks, this is the nearest lodging to the slopes, well built by the Civilian Conservation Corps in the 1930s with a big fireplace and a warm, woody look. Accommodations are in two dorm rooms (male/female) sleeping roughly 22 each. $20–25 per person (bring your sleeping bag or rent sheets); $12–15 per person in the off-season. Meals are hearty and from scratch: $7 for dinner, $5 for breakfast. Obviously this is a great place for groups, but individuals are welcome (the only hitch is that they can reserve no earlier than a week ahead of time).

CAMPGROUNDS

See *Green Space* for information on campgrounds in Smugglers Notch.

WHERE TO EAT

DINING OUT

Blue Moon Cafe (253-7006), 35 School Street, Stowe. Open for dinner daily. A very small candlelit bistro with a huge reputation. Former Ten

Acres Lodge chef Jack Pickett prepares "contemporary American" dishes. The menu changes weekly but you might begin with Maine crab cakes with roasted fennel and sauce verde or French lentil soup and Vermont feta cheese, then dine on braised Craftsbury rabbit with foraged mushrooms and wild leeks or polenta-leek pie with a sauté of summer vegetables. Dinner for two with wine is about $80.

Villa Tragara (244-5288), 6 miles south of Stowe on Route 100. Open for dinner Tuesday through Sunday. Ask any Stowe residents what their favorite restaurant is and they will note the place or two that happen to be "best" this season—but inevitably they will also mention this 1820 farmhouse. Capri-born chef Antonino Di Ruocco gives new meaning to fine Italian cuisine, creating pastas (like squash ravioli) and combining vegetables, fish, and meat in ways that simply have to be sampled. His Italian tapas are plenty for one person, and three can be split among four. We can recommend the scaloppine di Cero alla Vermontese (a tender, thin slice of venison sauteed with grilled apples, maple syrup, mustard seeds, and wine) and the roast quail on a bed of risotto in wine sauce (both $12.50). Inquire about Friday dinner theater (see *Entertainment*) in the attached barn (now also an attractive dining room) and periodic live music.

Cliff House (253-3000, ext. 2317), in the Octagon at Mount Mansfield's summit. If dinner is being served (theoretically it's year-round but varying days, 5:30–9), it's impossible to beat the view, and the gondola ride up is included in the $42 per person prix fixe. You might begin with a pan-fried crab cake or escargots sautéed with mushrooms, served with Pernod cream sauce, and dine on half a roasted duck or marinated Vermont venison. Lunch is also served Monday through Sunday in-season.

Edson Hill Manor (253-7371), 1500 Edson Hill Road, Stowe. Open for dinner nightly in-season; reservations required. Under Eric and Jane Lande, the small, gracious dining room at this low-key resort has soared to the top of local restaurant ratings. The menu might feature seared salmon with rock shrimp risotto and grilled duck breast with dried fig port glaze. Entrées from $15.50 for Mediterranean spinach pie to $24 for roast rack of New Zealand lamb.

Isle de France (253-7751), 1899 Mountain Road, Stowe. Open for dinner nightly except Monday. A classic French restaurant in the grand manner, with a formal dining room worthy of a Ritz. You might begin with escargots ($7.50) and dine on entrecôte béarnaise ($22.50). Claudine's Bistro offers less formal and expensive options, with entrées from $12.75.

Foxfire Inn and Italian Restaurant (253-4887), Route 100, north of Stowe Village. Dinner nightly. Favored by local residents for a predictably good night out. The setting is a 1850s country farmhouse and the menu is large. You might begin with rolled eggplant (baked with ricotta and prosciutto, mozzarella and Romano cheese and dine on saltimbocca

($18.95) or chicken stuffed with Gorgonzola cheese, pancetta, and figs sautéed in a creamy Marsala wine sauce ($15.95).

Seasons at Stowehof Inn (253-9722). American nouvelle cuisine in a dramatic dining room. In winter you might dine on a cassoulet of confit of duck leg, andouille, shrimp, ancho chiles, black and white beans, and a cilantro crème fraîche ($19.95). Inquire about sleigh-ride and dinner packages in winter. The Tap Room offers less formal fare.

Trapp Family Dining Room (253-8511) Trapp Hill Road, Stowe. The lodge offers noteworthy formal dining with a five-course prix fixe menu ($36); always includes Austrian specialties like Wiener schnitzel with spaetzle but also varied fare like fresh sea scallops sautéed in a Riesling cream sauce and roasted stuffed quails with pear schnapps served with braised red cabbage. Lighter meals are served in the lounge.

Mist Grill (244-2233), 95 Stowe Street, Waterbury. A vintage-1807 gristmill houses this "New England bistro," good for breakfast and lunch (see *Eating Out*), also for Sunday-night dinners (entrées under $11) and for $35 prix fixe five-course "Distinctive Dinners," $15 more for paired wines. The restaurant was newly opened in 1999 and we have not yet had a chance to check it out, but the reviews are rave.

EATING OUT

In Stowe

Gracie's Restaurant (253-8741), Main Street, Stowe Village. Open from 11:30 to "closing," this richly paneled pub with booths, a hearth, and heavily dog-themed decor, is squirreled into the depths of a commercial building in the middle of the village. We have enjoyed dining alone on one of Gracie's outstanding burgers at the bar, and on the nightly special (shrimp jambalaya) with friends. At lunch we recommend the chicken-apple sausage on a garlic bun with maple mustard. Gracie, who by the way was owners Paul and Sue Archdeacon's dog (his picture hangs at the bottom the stairs), a fixture at the Shed all those years Paul worked there as bartender.

✍ **McCarthy's Restaurant** (253-8626), Mountain Road. Open 6:30–3 daily. The local gathering place: quick, cheerful service, an open black-and-white-checked tile kitchen, oilcloths on the tables, wood skis on the walls, and deep wooden booths. Daily specials for both breakfast and lunch plus a big breakfast menu and a wide selection of soups and sandwiches on homemade breads. Kids' menu, boxed lunches to go. Great all around.

✍ **Restaurant Swisspot** (253-4622), Stowe Village. An old reliable, open nightly for dinner, lunch weekends and holidays. Soups, quiche, and fondue are lovingly prepared. For lunch, there are tempting burgers with Swiss cheeses, and a wide variety of sandwiches. Swiss cheese fondue and beef fondue bourguignon for two are moderately priced; other options range from Wiener schnitzel to pesto shrimp. Children's menu. Try the Matterhorn sundae with hot Tobler sauce.

Trapp Family Austrian Tea Room (253-8511), Trapp Hill Road, 10:30–

5:30 daily, is fully licensed and specializes in hot *glühwein* and café Viennese, soups, Austrian wursts, sandwiches, and Bavarian desserts, served up by dirndl-clad fräuleins. This attractive building is a part of the Trapp family complex. The view is spectacular, especially in summer from the terrace.

The Gables Inn (253-7730), 1457 Mountain Road. Breakfast served 8–noon daily, Sunday brunch, July and August barbecue until 2, BYOB dinners by reservation. Breakfast is an event, served under yellow umbrellas on the inn's front lawn in summer as well as on the front porch and in the cheerful country-inn dining room. The daily blackboard breakfast specials might include French toast stuffed with cream cheese, walnuts, and molasses; a Vermont cheddar cheese omelet with mushrooms, peppers, onions, and garden herbs; or chipped beef and spinach on toast. Summer lunches might range from "best wurst" (with sauerkraut) through a choice of salads. At night the atmosphere changes and the dining room becomes the **Gables Tables,** with longtime Stowe chef Bumpy Grennan manning the kitchen, producing dependable staples like sautéed breast of chicken with apple and shallots in a cider sauce and fresh salmon poached in a court bouillon, topped with roasted red pepper and hollandaise. Special children's menus (12 and under).

The Shed (253-4364), Mountain Road, open daily for lunch and dinner, also Sunday buffet brunch and a late-night menu (10–midnight). Ken Strong's old landmark pub has expanded over the years into a complex that includes a microbrewery as well as a large, greenhouse-style dining room. The varied menu includes salads, tacos, baked onion soup, zucchini boats, barbecued ribs, seafood strudel, and, of course, Shedburgers. Children's menu.

Whip Bar & Grill (253-7301), Main Street. Open daily 11:30–9:30; Sunday brunch is a specialty. For charm and good food at palatable prices, the Whip is difficult to beat. The antique buggy whips, brass dumbwaiter, and vintage photos recall the tavern's status. It boasts Stowe's first liquor license, from 1833. In summer there's patio dining and a view of lawns and the pool, and in winter the focus is on a roaring hearth. There is a blackboard menu, always a choice of grilled meats or fish, a raw bar, and specials ranging from pan-blackened fish to Montreal smoked meat with hot mustard. Dinner specials include marinated Oriental black-tip shark and fresh Vermont veal with fines herbes and cream.

Miguel's Stowe-Away Lodge and Restaurant (253-7574), 3148 Mountain Road. This snug old farmhouse, the original Miguel's, is a reliably good bet featuring innovative Mexican fare like pescado mango poblano (fresh salmon fillet grilled with a sweet and tangy mango poblano salsa, served with rice and back beans) as well as the usual Tex-Mex "especiales" and a gringo and full children's menu.

Mr. Pickwick's Pub & Restaurant at Ye Olde England Inn (253-7558), 433 Mountain Road. Open for breakfast, lunch, dinner, and Sunday brunch. "A Dickens of a place" offers Vermont bangers and mash, Cornish pasties, and steak-and-kidney pie. Also Belgian waffles for breakfast, pesto pasta for lunch, and a large dinner menu, including such game dishes as kangaroo, boar ribs, and buffalo rib-eye steak. Dinner entrées range from $7.95 for Cajun alligator medallions to $26.95 for the buffalo rib-eye.

Trattoria La Festa (253-8480), 4080 Mountain Road. Dinner served daily except Sunday (open on long weekends). On the upper reaches of Mountain Road with terrace dining in summer, a pleasant dining room that's owned by three experienced chefs, two of them brothers born and raised in Apulia, a small coastal town not far from Rome. True to the nature of an Italian trattoria, the food is varied. Reliably delicious antipastis like carpaccio di carne (thin slices of filet mignon with onions, capers, extra-virgin olive oil); specialty pastas like penne Michelangelo (penne sautéed with fresh vegetables and grilled shrimp in a garlic wine sauce); and four-course, family-style dinners can be preordered.

Sage Sheep Farm (253-2955), 2346 West Hill Road, Stowe. Open May 30 through October 8, Tuesday through Saturday, 12:30–4:30. Homemade pastries and savories are served with herbal and regular teas on the veranda and in the combination tearoom/gift shop with dried herbs and flowers hanging from the rafters. Elizabeth Squier sells fresh lamb and sausages, also yarns made from the wool shorn from her sheep and llamas, as well as finished sweaters, herbs, and cut flowers.

Dutch Pancake Cafe (253-8921), 900 Mountain Road at the Grey Fox Inn. Open daily 8 AM–10:30 AM, for Sunday brunch (in-season), and for dinner 5:30–8:30. Dutch émigré Michael Diender and his Tennessee-born wife, Debi, have married the traditional Dutch *pannekoeken* with southern breakfast specials like sausage and gravy. The results are more than 75 huge and decadent pancakes including Italian sausage, tomato, and cheese.

Depot Street Malt Shop (253-4269), Depot Street, Stowe Village. A consciously '50s decor with a reasonably priced menu to match, a great lunch stop with old-style fountain treats like malted frappes, egg creams, and banana splits.

The Mountain Roadhouse R&B Grill *(253-2800), Mountain Road, Stowe. The former Green Doors has been reborn as a dating bar/cheap eats and good music place. Burgers, ribs, and "tavern pizza" are the best food bets, specials are reasonably priced, and the average age necessitates almost universal carding. Rhythm and blues live on weekends, no cover.*

In Waterbury

Arvad's (244-8973), 3 South Main Street. Open daily 11:30–11:30. A great way-stop (just off I-89, exit 10), an attractive brick-walls-and-hanging-plants decor, varied lunch and dinner menus, a full bar. Dine on pasta primavera ($8.50) or chicken stir-fry ($9.50). Nightly specials; try the Cabot fries (made with the local cheddar).

Mist Grill (244-2233), 95 Stowe Street. Open daily. Baked goods and coffee from 6:30 AM to 4 PM; breakfast 7–10:30; lunch 11–2:30; Sunday dinner 5–8. Housed in a vintage-1807 mill, this new restaurant offers good atmosphere and food. Lunch features soups, salads, grilled panini, sandwiches, burgers, and cold cuts. Reasonably priced Sunday-night suppers are family-style, a choice of four entrees—maybe roast chicken, beef Burgundy, polenta lasagne, and seafood risotto. See also *Dining Out.*

ENTERTAINMENT

Stowe Cinema (253-4678), at the Stowe Center, Route 108. Standard seats and bar viewing area for first-run films.

The Lamoille County Players (888-4507) stage plays at the Hyde Park Opera House, Hyde Park.

Stowe Theater Guild (253-3961), staged upstairs at the Akeley Memorial Building in Stowe Village, offers a series of summer musicals and Broadway favorites.

Stowe Performing Arts (253-7792) presents a series of three summer Sunday-evening concerts followed by three **Vermont Mozart Festival** concerts held in the natural amphitheater of the Trapp Family Meadow. Patrons are invited to bring a preconcert picnic. The setting is spectacular, with the sun sinking over Nebraska Notch.

The Villa Tragara Ristorante (244-5288), Route 100, Waterbury Center, stages music and theater, usually Friday nights in-season.

APRÈS-SKI

There are reputedly 50 bars in Stowe. Along the Mountain Road, look for après-ski action at the **Matterhorn** (253-2800) with live music every weekend during ski season, at the **Mountain RoadHouse** (253-2800), featuring rhythm and blues without a cover on weekends. **Charlie B's,** at Stoweflake, is also usually lively, as is **Mr. Pickwick's Pub,** source of one of Vermont's largest selections of beers (the better to wash down its steak-and-kidney pie).

SELECTIVE SHOPPING

ARTISANS

Stowe Crafts Gallery, Mountain Road, Stowe, near the covered bridge. Outstanding crafts from throughout the country, winnowed from Jean Paul Patnode's many years of experience here. Jean Paul, who also operates the adjacent game shop, once explained to us how he happened to settle in Stowe: "I turned the corner at the light here one day in 1967 and felt like I was stepping into a tub of hot water. You know the nice comfortable feeling you get sometimes?"

Little River Hotglass Studio (253-0889), 593 Moscow Road, Moscow. We are kicking ourselves for not stocking up on the lovely, reasonably priced glass Christmas balls that Michael Trimpol creates in this small and very attractive studio just off Route 100. The specialty is exquisite colored glass creations: weights, bowls, balls, and perfume bottles.

Shimmering Glass Studio (244-8134), Route 100 north, Waterbury, also in the Cabot Creamery complex (see *Food and Drink*), shows a glittering collection of custom-made, stained-glass lampshades, doors, fused-glass boxes, vases, bowls, stained-glass panels, and jewelry by Susan Bayer-Fishman and other artists.

Ziemke Glass Blowing Studio (244-6126), Route 100, Waterbury Center. Showroom open daily 10–6. Glass is usually blown Thursday through Sunday.

Stowe Gems (253-7000), in the village near the Helen Day Art Center. Barry Tricker polishes and sets exquisite stones, many from New England.

Samara (253-8318), Red Barn Shops, Route 108, Stowe. An exceptional selection of work by Vermont artisans: quilts, soft sculpture, jewelry, wooden toys, batik, stained glass, and more.

Vermont Clay Studio (244-1126), Route 100, Waterbury, open daily 10–6. Pottery sold, made, and taught.

Vermont Rug Makers (253-6208), Stowe Village. A branch of the Johnson store: distinctive, locally handwoven rugs and hangings, also a stock of imported Turkish and Oriental rugs.

Moriarty's Hats & Sweaters (253-4052), Route 100, Stowe. Many long years ago, Mrs. Moriarty began knitting caps for Stowe skiers, and her distinctive style caught on. It is now widely imitated, but the originals remain a Stowe tradition.

FOOD AND DRINK

Cabot Creamery Annex Store (1-800-881-6334), Route 100, Waterbury, 1.4 miles north of Ben & Jerry's, same complex as the two following stores. Open daily, year-round. While the prizewinning cheese isn't made here, this is its major showcase, displaying a full line of dairy products (plenty of samples), along with other Vermont specialty foods and crafts.

Green Mountain Chocolate Company (244-8356), Route 100, Waterbury, under the same roof as Cabot (see above), is where former White House pastry chef Albert Kumin and his family create delectable truffles, fudge, cakes, and cookies. Closed Tuesday.

Green Mountain Coffee Roasters (244-5621), 33 Coffee Lane, Waterbury. Sample these famous blends at the factory outlet.

Cold Hollow Cider Mill (244-8771; 1-800-3-APPLES), Route 100, Waterbury, is one of New England's largest producers of fresh apple cider; visitors can watch it being pressed and sample the varieties. The retail stores in this big red barn complex stock every conceivable kind of apple jelly, butters, sauces, natural fruit preserves, honey, pancake mixes, pickles, and mustards, plus Vermont books and other gifts. Open daily 8–6, year-round.

L'Abeille Honey Winery (253-2929), 638 South Main Street, Stowe. Open daily 11–5 except Tuesday and Wednesday. The mead may be sampled; other honey products are sold, from honey candy to beeswax candles.

OTHER

Bear Pond Books (253-8236), Depot Building, Stowe Village. Open daily. An excellent full-service bookstore; calendars, cassettes, and cards, too.

Shaw's General Store (253-4040), 54 Main Street, Stowe Village. Established in 1895 and still a family business, a source of shoelaces and cheap socks as well as expensive ski togs and Vermont souvenirs.

Lackey's Variety Store (253-7624), Main Street, Stowe Village, open 8:30–8:30 daily. An 1840s building that has housed many enterprises and is now "just a variety store," according to Frank Lackey, its owner of more than 48 years. An anomaly in this resort village, it still stocks nail clippers, India ink, shoe polish, scissors, not to mention patent medicine and magazines. The walls are hung with posters for '30s ocean liners and long-vanished local movie houses and lined with antique bottles, boxes, and other fascinating ephemera.

Stafford's Country Store and Pharmacy (253-7361), Main Street, Stowe Village. The village's full-service pharmacy (parking in the rear), also a selection of European music boxes, toys, books, and Vermont products.

Stowe Street Emporium (244-5321), 23 Stowe Street, Waterbury. A large, eclectic selection of clothing and gifts.

The Fly Rod Shop (253-7346), Route 100, 2 miles south of Stowe, carries such name brands as Hardy, Marryat, and Cortland, as well as its own Diamondback rods, which may be tried out at its casting pool. Rentals and fishing-spot brochure.

Evergreen Gardens of Vermont (244-8523), Route 100, Waterbury Center, open March 1 through December 24, displays a large collection of hardy perennials, annuals, herbs, shrubs, and trees around a pond and picnic area. Greenhouse and gifts.

Misty Meadows Herb and Perennial Farm (253-8247), 785 Stagecoach Road, Stowe. Open mid-May through fall, 9–5 daily. Display gardens feature herbs and perennials in a farm setting; also potpourri, everlasting wreaths, seasonings, and herbs.

Nebraska Knoll Sugar Farm (253-4655), 256 Falls Brook Lane. The sugarhouse is open in-season and syrup and maple cream are available year-round. We advise calling before, especially in winter when the steep back road (especially if you come via Trapp's) is advisable to four-wheel-drive only (we chickened out three-fourths of the way there).

See also the **Johnson Woolen Mill** in "North of the Notch"; the short and scenic drive there is certainly worth the effort.

SPECIAL EVENTS

Mid-January: **Winter Carnival** is one of the oldest and most gala village winter carnivals in the country: a week of snow sculptures, sled-dog races, ski races, public feeds.

February: **Expedition Stowe,** "A Mountain Adventure Festival": Three weekends celebrating the less organized, more adventurous winter sports available in Stowe: a **Snowshoe Weekend**, then an **Ice Climbing Weekend**, and (last weekend of the month) the long established cross-country weekend climaxing with the **Stowe Derby**, the country's oldest downhill/cross-country race: a 10-mile race from the summit of Mount Mansfield to Stowe Village, which usually attracts about 300 entrants.

Easter festivities: an **Easter parade** at Spruce Peak; **Easter egg hunt.**

May: Lamoille County Players present **musicals** at the Hyde Park Opera House.

Late June: **Stowe Flower Festival.**

July 4: **Parades, fireworks, Stowe Marathon,** the world's shortest marathon; separate festivities in the village of Moscow, too small for its own band, so they parade to the music of radios.

Mid-July: **Stoweflake Hot-Air Balloon Festival,** Stowe Country Club. **International Food and Wine Festival,** Stoweflake Resort Field.

Late July: **Stowe Performing Arts Summer Festival,** a week of concerts ranging from chamber to symphony music, including bands and choral groups, presented in a number of places. **Lamoille County Field Days,** a weekend agricultural fair in Morrisville—tractor pulling, crafts, children's rides. **Annual Stowe Craft Show,** 3 days.

Early August: **Annual antique and classic car rally,** 3 days.

Late August: Lamoille County Players stage a **musical** in the Hyde Park Opera House.

September (last weekend): **Stowe Foliage Craft Fair,** Topnotch Field.

October (Columbus Day weekend): **Stowe Foliage Antique Show and Fair.**

North of the Notch and the Lamoille Valley

Vermont's most dramatic road winds up and up from Stowe through narrow 2,162-foot-high Smugglers Notch, then down and around cliffs and boulders. Just as it straightens and drops through woodland, motorists are startled by the apparition of a condominium town rising out of nowhere (Smugglers' Notch Resort, a self-contained, family-geared village that accommodates some 2,000 people). However, as Route 108 continues to descend and finally levels into Jeffersonville on the valley floor, it's clear that this is a totally different place from the tourist-trod turf south of the Notch. This is the Lamoille Valley.

Smugglers Notch, as well as the village of Jeffersonville, is in Cambridge, one of several towns worth exploring along the Lamoille River. Jeffersonville has been a gathering place for artists since the 1930s, and Johnson, 9 miles west along Route 15, is also now an arts center. It's easy to see why artists like this luminous landscape: open, gently rolling farm country. The Lamoille River itself is beloved by fishermen and canoeists, and bicyclists enthuse about the little-trafficked roads.

While Smugglers Notch is the more dramatic approach, the prime access to the Lamoille Valley region is Route 100, the main road north from Stowe, which joins Route 15 (the major east–west road) at Morrisville, the commercial center for north-central Vermont. Just west on Route 15 is Hyde Park, the picturesque county seat, famed for its year-round theater.

North of the Lamoille Valley is the even less trafficked Missisquoi River Valley, and between the two lies some beautiful, very Vermont country.

GUIDANCE

Smugglers Notch Area Chamber of Commerce (644-2239; e-mail: info@smugnotch.com), Jeffersonville 05464, publishes an area directory and distributes information by mail and phone. The excellent web site is: www.smugnotch.com.

Stowe–Smugglers Notch Regional Marketing Organization (1-877-247-8693; www.stowesmugglers.com), Morrisville. A source of information for the entire region.

Lamoille Valley Chamber of Commerce (888-7607), P.O. Box 45, Morrisville 05661. A summer information booth is at the junction of Routes 15 and 100 at the Morrisville Mobil station. Open May through October.

GETTING THERE

By air: See "Burlington Region." Given 48 hours' notice, Smugglers' Notch Resort (see *Lodging—Resort*) arranges transfers for guests.

By train: **Amtrak** stops at Essex Junction (1-800-872-7245).

By car: When the Notch is closed in winter, the route from Stowe via Morrisville is 26 miles, but in summer via Route 108 it is 18 miles from Stowe.

MEDICAL EMERGENCY

Jeffersonville, Johnson (635-7511).

Cambridge Regional Health Center (644-5114).

Cambridge Rescue: Dial **911.**

TO SEE

Smugglers Notch. During the War of 1812, Vermonters hid cattle and other supplies in the Notch prior to smuggling them into Canada to feed the British army—who were fighting the U.S. Army at the time. A path through the high pass has existed since Native American days, but it wasn't until 1910 that the present road was built, which, with its 18 percent grade, is as steep as many ski trails and more winding than most. Realizing that drivers are too engrossed with the challenge of the road to admire the wild and wonderful scenery, the state's Forests and Parks Department has thoughtfully provided a turnoff just beyond the height of land. An information booth here is staffed in warm-weather months; this is a restful spot by a mountain brook where you can picnic, even grill hot dogs. The Big Spring is here, and you can ask about hiking distances to the other local landmarks: the Elephant Head, King Rock, the Hunter and His Dog (an outstanding rock formation), Singing Bird, the Smugglers Cave, Smugglers Face, and the natural reservoir. See *To Do—Hiking and Walking* in the "Stowe and Waterbury" chapter for details about the easy trail to Sterling Pond and about the trail to the Elephant Head.

COVERED BRIDGES

In and around Jeffersonville. Look for the **Scott Bridge** on Canyon Road across the Brewster River near the old mill that's now Kelly's Restaurant; the 84½-foot-long bridge is 0.1 mile down the road. To find the **Poland Bridge** (1887) from the junction of Routes 108 and 15, drive north and turn onto Route 109, angling off on the road along the river; the bridge is in 0.2 mile. Heading west on Route 15 toward Cambridge Village, look for Lower Valley Road; the **Gates Farm Bridge** (1897) is a few hundred feet from where the present road crosses the river.

KIM GRANT

A landscape painter in Johnson

In Waterville and Belvidere. Back on Route 109, continue north to Waterville and at Waterville Town Hall (on your right), turn left; the **Church Street Bridge** (1877) is in 0.1 mile. Back on Route 109, continue north; the **Montgomery Bridge** (1887) is east of the highway, 1.2 miles north of Town Hall. Go another 0.5 mile north on Route 109 and turn right; the **Kissin' Bridge** (1877) is in 0.1 mile. Continue north on Route 109, and 1.5 miles from the Waterville Elementary School (just after the bridge over the North Branch), turn left and go 0.5 mile to the **Mill Bridge** (1895). Back on Route 109, continue north 0.9 mile and turn left to find the **Morgan Bridge** (1887). See the "Jay Peak Area" chapter for a description of six more covered bridges another dozen miles north in Montgomery. *Note:* For detailed descriptions of all these sites, see *Covered Bridges of Vermont,* by Ed Barna (The Countryman Press).

In Johnson. Take Route 100C north from its junction with Route 15 for 0.4 mile; the **Power House Bridge** (1872) is visible to your left. Continue another 1.1 miles and turn right; the **Scribner Bridge** (around 1919) is 0.3 mile on your right.

GALLERIES

Mary Bryan Memorial Art Gallery (644-5100), Main Street, Jeffersonville. Open early June to late October, daily 11–5. Built by Alden Bryan in memory of his wife and fellow artist, Mary Bryan, this mini-museum has changing exhibits featuring artists who have worked in Jeffersonville.

Vermont Studio Center (635-2727), Johnson. Over the past 16 years, this nonprofit center has absorbed 20 buildings in the village of Johnson. The lecture hall is a former meetinghouse, and the gallery, exhibiting the work of artists in residence, is in a former grain mill one street back from Main, down by the river. Some 50 professional artists and writers from throughout the country are usually here at any given time. They come to take advantage of the studio space and the chance to learn from each other through lectures and critiques. Inquire about gallery openings and evening slide shows and lectures.

Dibden Gallery (635-2356), Johnson State College, Johnson. Open during the academic year, Tuesday through Saturday 10–3. Changing solo and group shows.

SCENIC DRIVES

Four loop routes are especially appealing from Jeffersonville:

Stowe/Hyde Park (44-mile loop). Take Route 108 through Smugglers Notch to Stowe Village, drive up the old Stagecoach Road to Hyde Park (be sure to see the old Opera House), and head back through Johnson.

Belvidere/Eden (40-mile loop). From Jeffersonville, Route 109 follows the North Branch of the Lamoille River north (see *Covered Bridges*) to Belvidere Corners; here take Route 118, which soon crosses the Long Trail (see *To Do—Hiking*) and continues to the village of Eden. Lake Eden, 1 mile north on Route 100, is good for swimming and boating; return on Routes 100, 100C, and 15 via Johnson.

Jericho/Cambridge (38-mile loop). From Jeffersonville, drive southwest on Pleasant Valley Road, a magnificent drive with the Green Mountains rising abruptly on your left. Go through Underhill Center to the junction with Route 15 but continue south on Jericho Center Road; return via Jericho (see the "Burlington Region" chapter for a description of Jericho and Jericho Center) and Route 15 to Cambridge Village, then drive back along Route 15 (see *Covered Bridges*) to Jeffersonville.

Jeffersonville/Johnson (18-mile loop). From the junction of Routes 15 and 108, head north on Route 108, but turn onto Route 109 (note the Poland Covered Bridge on your right). Take your first right, Hogback Road, which shadows the north bank of the Lamoille River most of the way into Johnson. Return via Route 15.

HISTORIC HOUSE

The Noyes House Museum (888-7617), Route 100, Morrisville. Open mid-June until September, 1–5 or by appointment. Suggested donation: $3 adult, $1 student. The 18 rooms of this brick, Federal-style house are furnished and filled with varied memorabilia, including an 1,800-piece pitcher and Toby jug collection.

TO DO

BICYCLING

Rentals: Mountain-bike rentals are available in Jeffersonville at **Foot of the Notch Bicycles** (644-8182) and in Morrisville at **PowerPlay Sports** (333-6557), Route 100.

Bicycle touring: **Smugglers Notch Inn** (644-2412; see *Lodging—Inns and Bed & Breakfasts*) owners Cynthia Barber and John Day met as bike tour leaders and are delighted to share their knowledge of local bike routes. **Mannsview Inn** (644-8321; see *Lodging—Inns and Bed & Breakfasts*) offers canoeing/cycling packages.

The **Cambridge Greenway** recreation path runs 1.3 miles along the Lamoille River from Jeffersonville east.

Missisquoi Valley Rail Trail, a 26.5-mile-long rec path, traverses the northern tier of this region, following the Missisquoi River from Enosburg Falls to Richford. For a map, call the **Northwest Regional Planning Commission** (524-5989).

CANOEING AND KAYAKING

The **Lamoille River** from Jeffersonville to Cambridge is considered good for novices in spring and early summer; two small sets of rapids.

Smugglers Notch Canoe Touring (1-800-937-6266), based at the Mannsview Inn, Jeffersonville, rents canoes and kayaks and offers shuttle service. Paddles are 6–11 miles, all flat and Class 1 water.

Green River Canoe (644-8336), based at Smugglers' Notch Resort (see *Lodging—Resorts*). Peter Salinger and Sal Zabriskie offer guided canoe and kayaking trips, also instruction and rentals.

See also Sterling Ridge Inn under *Lodging—Inns and Bed & Breakfasts.*

FISHING

The stretch of the Lamoille River between Cambridge and Johnson is reputedly great fly- and spin-fishing for brown trout.

Smugglers' Notch Resort (644-8851) offers twice-weekly fly-casting clinics in-season.

The Fishing Hole (888-6210), Bridge Street, Morrisville offers year-round fishing supplies, and guide service May through September. For fly-fishing, see also the Golden Maple on the Lamoille in Wolcott (see *To Do—Fishing* under "St. Johnsbury, Craftsbury, and Burke Mountain Area").

HIKING

Prospect Rock, Johnson. An easy hike yields an exceptional view of the Lamoille River Valley and the high mountains to the south. Look for a steel bridge to the Ithiel Falls Camp Meeting Ground. Hike north on the white-blazed Long Trail 0.7 mile to the summit.

Belvidere Mountain–Ritterbush Pond and Devil's Gulch. These are basically two stretches of the Long Trail; one heads north (3½ hours round-trip) to the summit of Belvidere Mountain, the other heads south (2¾ hours round-trip) to a gulch filled with rocks and ferns. Both are described in the Green Mountain Club's *Long Trail Guide.*

HORSEBACK RIDING

Vermont Horse Park (644-5347), 4306 Route 108, Smugglers Notch, Jeffersonville. the privately owned Smugglers Notch Stables, offers guided trail rides, pony rides for kids, hay- and sleigh rides, year-round.

KIM GRANT

Smugglers Notch

LLAMA TREKS
Northern Vermont Llama Treks (644-2257), Waterville. Treks depart
   from the Smugglers' Notch Resort (see *Lodging—Resort*) and head into
   the Mount Mansfield State Forest (see *Green Space* in "Stowe and
   Waterbury"). Day treks are $60 per person (picnic and snack included)
   and half-day treks are $30 per person (including snacks). Family rates
   available.
& **Cold Hollow Llamas** (644-5846), Belvidere. Early May through October.

Laurie and Bill Samal have nine llamas at their farm and offer treks that feature gourmet picnics; a half day for one or two is $90 (geared to ages 3–83) and a full day is $160.

Applecheek Farm (888-4482), 367 McFarlane Road, Hyde Park. Trek on "wilderness trails," with or without a picnic.

PICNICKING

There are several outstanding roadside picnic areas: On Route 108, 0.2 mile north of the junction with Route 15 at Jeffersonville, picnic benches on the bank of the Lamoille; on Route 108 south of Jeffersonville Village on the east side of the highway; on Route 108 in Smugglers Notch itself (see the Notch description under *To See*); on Route 15, just 1.5 miles east of the Cambridge/Johnson line.

SWIMMING

Brewster River Gorge, accessible from Route 108 south of Jeffersonville (turn off at the covered bridge).

Smugglers' Notch Resort (644-8851; 1-800-451-8752; see *Lodging*) features an elaborate summer waterpark as well as a winter pool.

TENNIS

Courts at Smugglers' Notch Resort (see *Lodging*), and a summer program of clinics for adults and children and daily instruction.

WALKING

See the Cambridge Greenway recreation path under *Bicycling*.

Lamoille County Nature Center (888-4965), Cole Hill Road, Morrisville. Two nature trails offer easy walking and the chance to see deer, bear, and a variety of birds, also lady's slippers in early summer. Inquire about programs offered in the outdoor amphitheater.

WINTER SPORTS

CROSS-COUNTRY SKIING

Sugarhouse Nordic Center (644-8851), Smugglers' Notch Resort (see *Lodging*). Narrow trails wind up and down through the trees, then climb meadows away from the resort complex, a total of 14 miles of set trails; rentals; also telemark, skate skiing, and snowshoe rentals; lessons and tours; repairs in the warming hut, where there is cocoa on the woodstove.

Smugglers Notch. The stretch of Route 108 that is closed to traffic for snow season is open to cross-country skiers. Guided tours are offered by the Sugarhouse Nordic Center (see above).

DOWNHILL SKIING

Smugglers' Notch Resort (644-8851; U.S.: 1-800-451-8752; Canada: 1-800-356-8679), Jeffersonville. In 1956 a group of local residents organized Smugglers' Notch Ski Ways on Sterling Mountain, a western shoulder of 3,640-foot-high Madonna. In 1963 a high-powered group headed by IBM board chairman Tom Watson gained a controlling interest and began developing the area as Madonna Mountain, a self-contained, Aspen-style resort. Only two owners later, with 463 condominiums, Smugglers' is a major ski resort sporting a natural snow bowl with a satisfying variety of terrain: beginners trails on Morse Mountain (2,250 feet), some world-class trails and glade skiing on Madonna itself, along with intermediate runs that predominate on Sterling Mountain.

The only way to the summit of Madonna, which commands one of the most spectacular views in New England—from Mount Washington to Mount Mansfield—is a 17-minute ride on the longest (and coldest) chairlift in the East, and the way down can be via some of the region's steepest or longest runs. The ideal time to ski this mountain is early March, when it's relatively warm, and midweek, when it's empty. Obviously, this is a place you come, anytime during ski season, for a 5-day ski week—which automatically includes lessons for all family members.

Lifts: Five double chairlifts, four surface.

Trails: 60, including two 3.5-mile trails; 27 percent expert, 40 percent intermediate, 21 percent beginner.

Vertical drop: 2,610 feet.

Snowmaking: 60 percent.

Facilities: Mountain Lodge, base lodge with ski shop, rentals, cafeteria, pub. The reception center/ski shop at Morse Mountain has a Village Center, source of rentals and tickets; the complex also includes a ski shop and deli. Top of the Notch warming hut is at the Sterling chair terminal. Snowboarding. A new double chair and beginner area is planned for 1999/2000.

Ski school: Group and private lessons at Morse and Madonna, beginners at Morse; Star Test to rate your own level of ability. Children's ski and snowboarding camp.

For children: Day care for infants. Discovery Ski Camp for 3- to 5-year-olds—all day with hot lunch and two lessons, mountain games, and races. Adventure Ski Camp for 6- to 12-year-olds: all day with hot lunch and two lessons; games and races. Explorer Ski Program for 13- to 17-year-olds begins at 1:15; lesson and evening activities; teen center.

Rates: $42 per weekday for adults; $46 weekends; youths 7–17, $30 weekdays, $32 weekend. Kids 6 and under ski free. *Note:* Lodging packages greatly reduce ski-week rates.

ICE SKATING
Smugglers' Notch Resort rink (flooded tennis courts) is lighted at night.

SLEIGH RIDES
Applecheek Farm (888-4482), 367 McFarlane Road, Hyde Park. Sparky and Sam, gentle Belgians, take you through the woods by day or night. $4 adults, $3 children and seniors.

Vermont Horse Park (644-5347), Route 108 across from Smugglers' Notch Resort. Sleigh rides offered all winter. See also *Horseback Riding.*

SNOWMOBILING

Sterling Ridge Inn (644-8265; 800-347-8266), Junction Hill Road, Jefferson. Guided tours are offered, both on the property and from Smugglers' Notch Resort.

LODGING

RESORT

Smugglers' Notch Resort (644-8851; 1-800-451-8752; UK: 0800-89-7159), 4323 Vermont Route 108 South, Smugglers' Notch 05464. More than 460 condominium units in a variety of shapes accommodate a total of 2,000 people. Geared to families and groups (facilities include a conference center), the resort offers a year-round combination of good things: skiing, swimming (the pool is protected by a heated bubble in winter), tennis, and a varied program of summer activities, including a supervised children's schedule of fishing, horseback rides, movies, hikes, and games. Summer tennis and other packages are offered. The resort excels at catering to children, with a variety of very distinct facilities and programs geared to different ages. Alice's Wonderland, the nursery for newborns and tots, is particularly impressive, as is the program for teens. In winter, a Club Smugglers' 5-day ski week includes lodging, skiing, snowboarding, lessons, use of tennis courts, pool, sauna, a dinner out, and other extras from $89 per adult per day, from $75 per youth (7–17), kids 6 and under stay free. In summer, a comparable program, including Familyfest Camp Programs for youngsters, begins at $979 per week for a two-child family. Add 12 percent for combined state tax and service charge. *Note:* Condominium units are all individually owned and vary from fairly basic (just what you want with kids) to luxury units with TV as well as Jacuzzi in the bath. Units also vary widely in location, from roadside to slope-side to up in the woods.

INNS AND BED & BREAKFASTS

Smugglers Notch Inn (644-2412; 1-800-845-3101), Church Street, P.O. Box 286, Jeffersonville 05464. Dating in part from the 18th century, this is a comfortable village inn that's been gentrified without losing its old-fashioned appeal. The living room retains its decorative tin ceiling as well as its brick fireplace, and remains a casual, inviting space with plenty of books and games. A fully licensed, half-circular bar with a copper footrail fills a corner on the way to the columned dining room (see *Dining Out*), which is hung with paintings by artists who have stayed here over the years, a good place for weddings and reunions. The 11 guest rooms all have private bath and country quilts; the room we slept comfortably in was warmed by a gas fireplace. Facilities include an outdoor hot tub and swimming pool. Innkeepers Cynthia Barber and John Day, avid hikers and bicyclists, are delighted to orient guests to 20 different cycling routes from the door. $60–125 per room includes a full breakfast.

✐ **Sterling Ridge Inn** (644-8265; 1-800-347-8266), Junction Hill Road, RR 2, Box 5780, Jeffersonville 05464. Built in 1988 expressly as a small inn, with a wall of windows in the spacious living room/dining room commanding a magnificent mountain view. There are four cheerful bedrooms with private bath and four that share two baths, making it ideal for families or weekend house parties. Back beyond the pond, Scott and Susan Peterson have built 8 one- and two-bedroom log cabins, each nicely designed with a fireplace, cathedral ceiling, fully equipped kitchen, and outdoor grill. The inn's 80 acres are webbed with 20 km of trails; facilities include a hot tub and outdoor pool. Mountain bikes and a canoe (with shuttle service) are also available. Full breakfast; $50–89 double in the inn; $65–150 per cabin for two, 2-night minimum rental; weekly $400–595 in the off-season; $575–875 in-season.

Mannsview Inn (644-8321; 1-888-937-6266), Mountain Road, Jeffersonville 05464. The most popular spot in the house is the solarium, a greens-filled dining area off the open kitchen with a view of the mountains. There's also a library and a billiard room. Kelley and Bette Mann offer canoe trips on the Lamoille River (see *Canoeing*). Four of the six guest rooms share two baths ($75 B&B); two others have gas fireplace and private bath (one has a Jacuzzi; $110–125).

Jefferson House (644-2030; 1-800-253-9630), Main Street, Jeffersonville 05464. Three bedrooms in a Victorian village house with original woodwork throughout the home, also a wraparound porch with swings and an upstairs deck. $60–65 double with complete breakfast.

Windridge Inn (644-5556), Main Street, Jeffersonville 05464. Open year-round except November and April. Lori Dunn now operates this pleasant old inn that's primarily a restaurant (see *Dining Out*), but with four exceptionally attractive upstairs guest rooms. $85 includes a full breakfast next door at the Windridge Bakery & Cafe (see *Eating Out*).

Fitch Hill Inn (888-3834; 1-800-639-2903), 258 Fitch Hill Road, Hyde Park 05655. Handy to many parts of the North Country, this hilltop house is elegantly maintained. The four double guest rooms, each named for a state (our favorite is Vermont), are all nicely furnished and equipped with ceiling fans; a studio apartment and a suite can be combined to sleep up to six. There is ample common room, an outdoor hot tub, and a library of 300 videos for the VCR. $75–179, depending on season, includes a breakfast that might be a spinach–goat cheese frittata. Four-course candlelight dinners by reservation are $60 for two.

Also see **Berkson Farms** under *Lodging—Farm Vacation* in "The Northwest Corner."

CAMPGROUND

Brewster River Campground (644-2126), 110 Campground Drive, off Route 108, Jeffersonville. Just 20 "low-tech" tent sites and several lean-tos on 20 secluded acres with a firepit and picnic tables, a modern bathhouse (hot showers); no pets (but there's a local kennel).

WHERE TO EAT

DINING OUT

Windridge Inn (644-5556), Main Street, Jeffersonville. Open for dinner daily. The former Cheval d'Or, long respected as the best restaurant this side of the Notch, is now retaining its reputation for fine dining, albeit at more reasonable prices. In the low-beamed old dining room you might begin with a mushroom-leek soup ($4.25) and dine on duck roasted crisp and finished with a Dijon mustard sauce ($19.95) or on turkey potpie ($10.95).

Tomatillos Mexican Cafe (888-6991), Fairground Plaza (next to Grand Union), Morrisville, Route 100 north of the village. Open for dinner Tuesday through Sunday. Mexican food aficionados rave about this restaurant. The owners spent nine years in Mexico and combine staple entrées like mole poblano (chicken in chocolate sauce, $10.95) with more obscure but authentic dishes. Children can feast on pizza Mexicana ($4.95). Wine and beer are served.

Hearth & Candle (644-2900), Smugglers' Notch Resort, Jeffersonville. Housed in a New England–style house, one of the first structures built in the condo village, this is the most formal place to eat in town. The atmosphere is upscale English pub. Moderate.

Hungry Lion (644-5848), Route 108 between Jeffersonville and Smugglers. Open daily 4–9. This restaurant keeps changing names and owners but continues to be a good bet for moderately priced dinners (roast turkey is $10.95). Fully licensed.

Smugglers Notch Inn (644-2412), Church Street, Jeffersonville. Dinner nightly. This large, old-fashioned, and appealing dining room (see *Lodging—Inns and Bed & Breakfasts*) may or may not be open when you visit. At this writing it's open weekends for dinner and the food is great, but chefs come and go. Inquire about music.

See also Persico's Plum & Main, below.

EATING OUT

Persico's Plum & Main (635-7596), Main Street, Johnson. Open 6 AM–8 PM weekdays, until 9 Friday and Saturday, 8–1 Sunday. Culinary Institute of America–graduate Pat Persico could be writing his own ticket in Stowe, but this Johnson native would rather serve local folks along with the stray skier and leaf-peeper. The breakfast specials might include apple cinnamon griddle cakes with homefries and syrup, or a bacon, cheddar, and onion omelet. The lunch menu covers the basics, but the ingredients are fresh and locally grown and the soup homemade. The dinner menu changes nightly but could include baked fresh haddock with a spinach seafood stuffing ($10.95) or prime rib of beef ($9.75–12.95, depending on the cut). BYOB. Inquire about specialty nights (Mexican or Italian, for example).

Windridge Bakery & Café (644-8207), Main Street, Jeffersonville. Open 8–4. This was a dry-goods store until it became one of New England's outstanding bakeries and coffee shops. Great breakfasts; homemade soups and sandwiches for lunch. Breads are still a specialty, along with breakfast omelets.

   ♿ **Hillary's** (888-5352), Route 100, Northgate Plaza, Morrisville. Breakfast, lunch, dinner, and Sunday brunch are all served in this pleasant place that's good for everything from sandwiches to seafood, from vegetarian dishes to steak. Fully licensed.

   ✍ **Café Banditos** (644-8884), Route 108, Jeffersonville, across from the Village at Smugglers Notch. A spacious old house offers yet another family- and skier-geared dining option: Ver-Mex. Burgers, ribs, and homemade soups augment tacos, fajitas, and enchiladas, plus Chinese dishes. Children's menu. Live music most Fridays.

   ✍ **Three Mountain Lodge** (644-5736), Route 108, Jeffersonville. Open year-round, daily from 4 PM. The dining room of this log lodge is exceptionally attractive, with a large hearth and quilted tablecloths. Fish specials like grilled tuna with salad greens, light fare, children's menu, music on weekends. Inexpensive to moderate.

   ✍ **Jana's** (644-5454) at the junction of Routes 15 and 108, Jeffersonville. Open 5 AM–9 PM weekdays, from 6 AM weekends. A family restaurant that's nicely decorated, Jana's has a coloring menu for children and a collection of antique sleds. Try a pita rabbit for lunch and Vermont chicken cordon bleu ($9.95) for dinner. Fried baskets, pizzas, and most staples are served.

The Cupboard (644-2069), junction of Routes 15 and 108, Jeffersonville. Open from 5 AM weekdays, 6 AM–11 PM Saturday, until 10 Sunday. Good for a wide variety of hot and cold subs, deli chili, French bread pizzas, maple baked beans, and other goodies, especially its maple-frosted cinnamon-raisin bread.

French Press Café (635-2638), Johnson. Open 8 AM–9 PM. A middle-of-the-village place to linger at the counter or around tables over coffees, teas, and pastries. Poetry readings, live music on occasion.

ENTERTAINMENT

Lamoille County Players (888-4507); call for summer schedule of productions.

The Cambridge Arts Council stages theater, concerts, and coffeehouses in Jeffersonville. Check local bulletin boards.

Vermont Studio Center Lecture and Reading Series. For a schedule of the frequent presentations by artists and writers, call the center (635-2727).

SELECTIVE SHOPPING

ANTIQUES

1829 House Antiques (644-2912), Route 15, Jeffersonville (2.5 miles east of the village). Open year-round daily except Sunday. Carolyn and Richard Hover's great old barn is filled on two floors with a wide assortment of country furniture and furnishings representing 35 dealers.

The Buggyman Antiques Shops (635-2110, 635-7664), Route 15, Johnson. Open daily 10–5. A big old barn and 18th-century farmhouse filled with antiques, including wagons, buggies, and sleighs.

Victorian House Antiques (635-9549), Johnson. A multi-dealer and consignment shop.

By Vermont Hands (635-7664), Route 15, Johnson (1 mile west of the village) carries fine antiques and some locally made furniture.

ART GALLERIES AND CRAFTSMEN

Quilts by Elaine (644-3438), Main Street, Jeffersonville. Open 9–5 daily except Wednesday. Elaine Van Dusen makes great quilts.

Wool and Feathers (888-7004), One Main Street, Hyde Park. Open Wednesday through Saturday; ring the doorbell on off days. Gisela Gminder is well known for her fleece, raw wool, yarn, and knitted items.

Vermont Rug Makers (635-2434), Route 100C, Johnson. Open Monday through Saturday 10–5. Judy Paulette creates handwoven rugs in original designs and vibrant colors in her small house (just beyond the Power House Covered Bridge; see *To See—Covered Bridges*). No two rugs are alike; all are machine washable and reportedly durable. Stock also includes a variety of imported decorative carpets.

Silver Wing Art Gallery and **Milk Room Framery,** Main Street, Jeffersonville. Two different concerns in the same place: quality art and crafts, and custom framing and monogramming.

Boyden Farm, intersection of Routes 15 and 104, just west of Cambridge Village. The second story of this amazing shop/winery (see below) is filled with exquisite, locally made furniture and furnishings. Local crafts are also displayed downstairs.

FARMS AND A WINERY

Boyden Farm and Winery (644-8151), at the intersection of Routes 15 and 104, just west of Cambridge Village. Open Tuesday through Sunday 10–5 June through December, otherwise Friday through Sunday 10–5. At this fourth-generation working dairy, bordering the Lamoille River, David Boyden has turned an 1878 carriage barn into a microwinery producing both fruit and grape wines. Wine tours and tastings are offered and the apple wine we brought home ($6.95) was excellent. Maple syrup and Vermont products and crafts (see above) are also sold. Inquire about farm tours.

Pumpkin Harbor Farm (644-2019), 928 Pumpkin Harbor Road, Cambridge, 1 mile from Route 15. At this operating goat dairy, you can milk a goat, feed a kid.

Applecheek Farm (888-4482), 367 McFarlane Road, Hyde Park.. Call before coming. A dairy farm with Holsteins and Jerseys, maple-sugaring operation; other farm animals include llamas, emus, draft horses, miniature horses. Picnic with llama treks, barbecue with horse and wagon rides (see also *To Do—Llama Treks*).

SPECIAL STORES

Johnson Woolen Mills (635-7185; 1-877-635-WOOL), Main Street, Johnson. Open year-round 8–5 daily except Sunday; Saturday 9–4. Although wool is no longer manufactured in this picturesque mill, the fine line of clothing for which Johnson Woolen Mills has long been known is made on the premises. This mill's label can still be found in shops throughout the country, and its famous, heavy green wool work pants, a uniform of Vermont farmers, are especially popular in Alaska. Although there are few discounts at the factory store, the selection of wool jackets and pants—for men, women, and children—is exceptional. The mail-order catalog is filled with sweaters, wool ties, hunters jackets, blankets, and other staples available in the shop.

Butternut Mountain Country Store (635-2329), Main Street, Johnson, is open Monday through Saturday 9–5:30, Sunday 11–4. This is the retail outlet for the Marvin family's maple products, plus a variety of Vermont gifts.

The Studio Store (635-2203; 1-800-887-2203), Johnson, adjacent to the Vermont Studio Center (see *To See—Galleries*). Open Wednesday through Saturday 10–6, Sunday noon–6. A fully stocked artists supply store, independently owned.

Arthur's Department Store (888-3125), Morrisville. Arthur and Theresa Breault and their daughter, Adrienne, do their buying in New York and Boston; they have created an unexpectedly fine and friendly source of clothing and footwear for men, women, juniors, and children. **The Cellar Shop** offers genuine bargains.

Vermont Maple Outlet (644-5482), Route 15 between Jefferson and Cambrige. A nice selection of cheese, syrup, handmade jams, and gift boxes.

EVENTS

January: **Winterfest** (last weekend in January)—primitive biathlon, muzzle-loaders, and snowshoes.

March: **Marchfest.** Four weeks of special events at Smugglers' Notch Resort: Nordic, alpine races, broom-ball tournaments, crafts shows, folk dances, snow sculpture, fireworks, ball.

June: **Vermont Dairy Festival** (first weekend)—arts and crafts, horse pulling, stage shows, 2-hour Saturday parade, country-and-western jamboree Sunday. **Smug-a-Thon,** Jeffersonville—a mini-triathlon sponsored by the Smugglers Notch Area Chamber of Commerce: a 3-mile walk/jog on the Cambridge Greenway rec path (see *To Do—Bicycling*), a 4-mile downstream paddle on the Lamoille, and a 9.5-mile bicycle race.

July 4: **Celebration,** Jeffersonville. Outstanding small-town parade at 10 AM followed by a chicken barbecue, games, crafts, cow-flop bingo, and a frog-jumping contest on the green behind the elementary school. Evening music at Smugglers' Notch Resort (see *Lodging*), food, fireworks.

September: **Labor Day Festivities** in Cambridge—barbecue on the green, flea market; family road run (3.1 miles) from Jeffersonville to Cambridge along back roads.

VI. THE NORTHEAST KINGDOM

St. Johnsbury, Craftsbury, and Burke Mountain Area
Jay Peak Area
Newport and the North Country

Irasburg

KIM GRANT

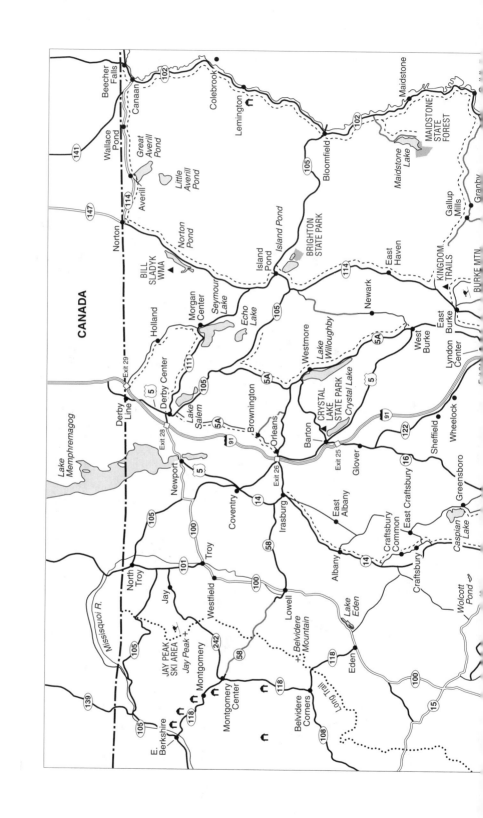

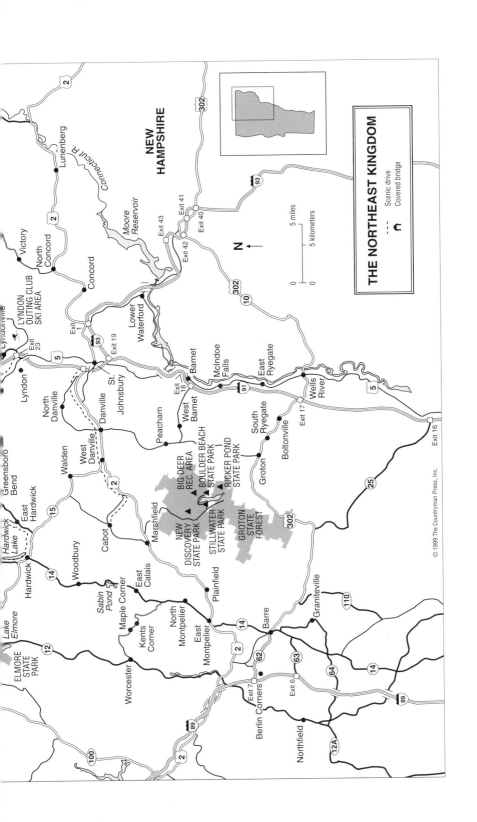

THE NORTHEAST KINGDOM

Scenic drive
Covered bridge

5 miles
5 kilometers

N

© 1999 The Countryman Press, Inc.

Introduction

You know, this is such beautiful country up here. It ought to be called the Northeast Kingdom of Vermont.

It was in 1949 that Sen. George Aiken made this remark to a group in Lyndonville. Since then, word has gotten around that that's what Vermont's three northeastern counties—Orleans, Caledonia, and Essex—should be calling themselves. This is, after all, a world unto itself: the state's most rural and lake-spotted corner, encompassing nearly 2,000 square miles. Aside from a few dramatic elevations, such as Jay Peak on its northwestern fringe and Burke Mountain at its heart, this is a predominantly high, open, glacially carved plateau of humped hills and rolling farmland, with some lonely lumbering country along the northern reaches of the Connecticut River. Neither of the ski areas draws patrons enough to change the look of the surrounding landscape. In the era of trains and steamboats, there were many more summer hotels than there are now; yet you can still stay in an unexpected range of places—from elegant country inns and full resorts to ski lodges and condominiums, from summer cottages to working farms. And all the amenities are here: golf, tennis, and horseback riding as well as plenty of hiking, fishing, canoeing, and winter sports that include ice fishing, tracking and snowshoeing, some of the state's best snowmobiling, and cross-country as well as downhill skiing. But they may take some searching out, and in the process you may stumble across some people and places of memorable beauty.

The Northeast Kingdom has a voice. Listen at a lunch counter, in a general store, at a church supper, at a county fair, or during the peerless Northeast Kingdom Foliage Festival. Admittedly it's fading, but you can sharpen your ear with Howard Frank Mosher's beautifully written books—*Northern Borders, Where the Rivers Run North, A Stranger in the Kingdom,* and *Disappearances.* Kingdom-based filmmaker and arts activist Jay Craven has turned the last three into films. Other local authors who evoke the look and feel of the Kingdom include Pulitzer Prize–winning poet Galway Kinnell (*Imperfect Thirst; Selected Poems*), Orleans native Leland Kinsey (*Family Drives*), and his sister, Natalie

Kinsey Warnock, whose children's books include *Canada Geese Quilt Book, The Fiddler and the Northern Lights,* and *The Wilderness Cats.*

Unfortunately, while this is the single most distinctive corner of the entire state, 2,000 square miles is too large an area to describe without dividing it into three smaller sections. If you have a particular passion such as canoeing, cross-country skiing, fishing, hiking, or mountain biking, check *To Do* under all three.

The **Northeast Kingdom Travel and Tourism Association,** (723-5300; 1-888-884-8001; fax: 723-5300; e-mail: info@travelthekingdom. com), a nonprofit umbrella organization representing 10 local chambers of commerce, publishes a useful *Four Season Guide* and a *Heritage Tour Map,* and also maintains an excellent web site, www.travelkingdom.com.

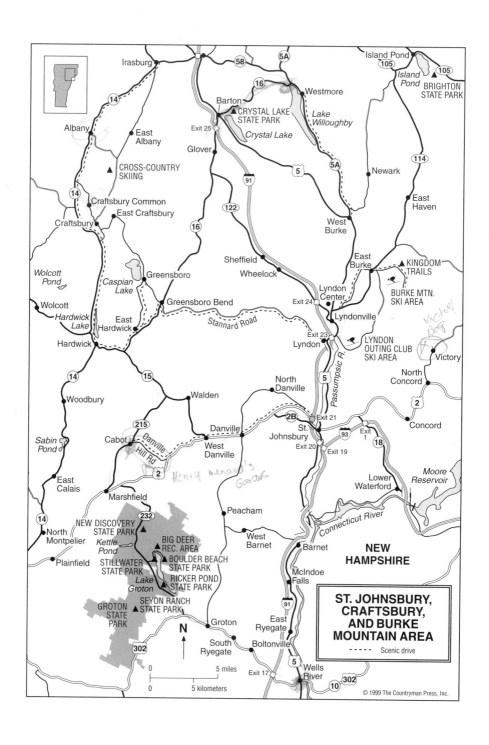

ST. JOHNSBURY,
CRAFTSBURY,
AND BURKE
MOUNTAIN AREA

- - - - Scenic drive

© 1999 The Countryman Press, Inc.

St. Johnsbury, Craftsbury, and Burke Mountain Area

With a population of 7,600, St. Johnsbury is the largest community in the Northeast Kingdom. Thanks to the Fairbanks family, who began manufacturing their world-famous scale here in the 1830s, it is graced with an outstanding museum of natural and local history, a handsome athenaeum, and an outstanding academy. The general late-19th-century affluence that St. Jay (as it is affectionately known) enjoyed as an active rail junction and industrial center has been commemorated in ornate brick along Railroad Street and sloping Eastern Avenue and in the fine mansions along Main Street, set high above the commercial downtown. In the 1960s, when Fairbanks became a division of a conglomerate—which threatened to move the scaleworks south—townspeople themselves raised the money to subsidize a new plant. The point is that this is a spirited community boasting one of the country's oldest town bands, a busy calendar of concerts, lectures, and plays, and all the shops and services needed by residents of the picturesque villages along the Connecticut River to the south, the rolling hills to the southwest and northwest, and the lonely woodlands to the east. Less than a dozen miles north, the wide, main street of Lyndonville is also lined with useful shops. Burke Mountain, a short way up Route 114, is accessible by car as well as by foot in summer and draws skiers from throughout the Northeast in winter.

As Route 2 climbs steeply west from St. J to Danville, a spectacular panorama of the White Mountains unfolds to the east. The village of Danville itself is a beauty and the back roads running south to Peacham and north to Walden follow ridges with long views. Continue northwest to Cabot and on to Craftsbury, where fields roll away like waves to the mountains in the distance.

Craftsbury is a composite of scattered villages, most of which you drive through in a trice. It's Craftsbury Common, with its common so vast that it dwarfs the surrounding white homes, academy, and church, that compels you to stop. It's so high that the countryside drops away on all sides.

Get lost in the surrounding web of well-maintained dirt roads.

491

Eventually you hit a paved, numbered road and in the meantime you find some of Vermont's most breathtaking farmscape, spotted with small lakes and large ponds. Don't miss Greensboro, an early-20th-century summer compound on Caspian Lake.

In Hardwick, a small trading center for the southwestern corner of the Kingdom, Main Street is unexpectedly Victorian, a reminder of the town's heyday as one of the world's largest granite processors. The granite was actually in Woodbury, 5 miles south, whence it arrived by rail. Thousands of skilled European craftsmen moved to town beginning in the 1870s and continuing into the 1920s; a number of French Canadians remain.

Barton, this area's northernmost commercial center, also obviously boomed in the late 19th century, when six passenger trains a day stopped in summer, bringing guests to fill the town's big (long gone) hotels or the gingerbread "camps" (still there) on Crystal Lake.

Lake Willoughby, between Barton and East Burke, is one of Vermont's most hauntingly beautiful lakes. Mounts Hor and Pisgah, which rise abruptly from opposite shores, create a fjordlike effect when viewed from the public beach in Westmore at the northern end or from the southern tip of the lake. Mostly undeveloped, Willoughby is surrounded for much of its length by state forest, and the water is stocked with salmon and rainbow trout. A well-known resort area in the days of grand hotels and steamboats, it now has a limited, loyal following of sailors, windsurfers (there is always a breeze here), and year-round fishermen.

GUIDANCE

Northeast Kingdom Chamber of Commerce (748-3678; 1-800-639-6379; web site: www.vermontnekchamber.org), 30 Western Avenue, St. Johnsbury 05819. The chamber maintains a year-round walk-in office, also a seasonal information booth at the corner of Main Street and Eastern Avenue; a source for lodging, dining, and general information for a 35-mile radius around St. Johnsbury.

The Lyndon Area Chamber of Commerce (626-9696), P.O. Box 886, Lyndonville 05851, publishes a leaflet guide and maintains a seasonal information booth on the common.

For cottage listings on Crystal Lake in Barton and Lake Parker in Glover, you can check with the **Barton Chamber of Commerce** (525-1137), P.O. Box 222, Barton 05822.

See also Northeast Kingdom Travel and Tourism Association under the Kingdom introduction.

GETTING THERE

By bus: Check with **Vermont Transit** (864-6811) about schedules to St. Johnsbury from Boston, New York, and Connecticut via White River Junction. At this writing, buses stop in Barnet, St. Johnsbury, Lyndonville, Barton, Orleans, and Newport.

By car: I-93, completed in the 1980s, makes the Northeast Kingdom far more accessible from the southeast than is still generally realized. Bostonians, for instance, can be in St. Johnsbury in 3 hours. It also enables you to bypass St. J entirely en route to the Craftsbury area.

Note that I-91 works like a fireman's pole, a quick way to move north–south through the Kingdom. In snow, beware the high, open, 16-mile stretch of highway between Lyndon Center and Barton.

MEDICAL EMERGENCY

Dial **911**.

Emergency services are available at **Northeastern Vermont Regional Hospital** (748-8141), St. Johnsbury; **Lyndon State College Rescue Squad** (626-5053), Lyndonville; Craftsbury (472-6666); Glover (525-3505); Barton (525-3505); Orleans (754-6366).

TOWNS AND VILLAGES

Peacham. High on a ridge overlooking the White Mountains, this is a tiny but aristocratic village settled just after the Revolution, with a library at the four corners, a fine historical house, and a general store specializing in fresh-baked croissants and gourmet fare. Peacham has an unusual number of retired professors, literati, artistic luminaries, and ambassadors per capita. All three Peachams (South, East, and Center) are worth exploring, as are the roads between.

Barnet. An old Scots settlement, the village of Barnet itself is on a curve of the Connecticut River, almost lost today in a curious intertwining of I-91 and Route 5. **Pearson's General Store** marks the middle of town, and **Goodwillie House** (633-2542), built in 1790 by a Scottish pastor, served as a stop on the Underground Railroad and now houses the collections of the Barnet Historical Society. Drive east to Barnet Center to find Harvey's Lake (good for both fishing and swimming) and the long-established **Karme-Choling Buddhist Meditation Center** (633-2384). From the road it appears to be a traditional white farmhouse, but inside the house has been dramatically altered to let in the sun and a sense of the surroundings, creating a Tibetan-style temple. It provides housing for guests, who are welcome to stay overnight, and for retreats. Drop-in visitors are also welcome. Child care is offered.

Danville. Until 1855, Danville was the shire town of Caledonia County. It is an exceptionally beautiful town set high on a plateau, around a large green complete with bandstand, Civil War monument, and general store. The imposing town hall was built as the county courthouse, and the small, square Passumpsic Savings Bank is one of the safest strongholds around, thanks to devices installed after it was last held up, in 1935. Danville is known primarily as the headquarters for the American Society of Dowsers. In **Dowsers' Hall** (684-3417), open weekdays 9–5 (occasionally on weekends), you learn that dowsing is the knack of finding water through the use of a forked stick, a pair of angle rods, or a pendulum. Staff are always willing to demonstrate the art or to turn on the introductory video. Dowsing equipment and books are sold. Occasional weekend workshops are also offered. The American Society of Dowsers boasts 5,600 members throughout the world. The owner of the **Danville Morgan Horse Farm** (see *To See—Farms*) provides tours and enjoys talking about the breed.

West Danville is a crossroads (Routes 15 and 2) village. **Hastings Store** is a great, old-fashioned general store–cum–post office, and one of the world's smallest libraries sits across the road at Joe's Pond. There is a public beach with picnic and sanitary facilities at the pond. The water from Joe's Pond (an old summer resort) is said to empty, eventually, into Long Island Sound, while that from Molly's Pond (a mile south, named for Joe's squaw) presumably winds up in the Gulf of St. Lawrence.

Cabot. Known during the War of 1812 for its distilleries (the whiskey was sold to Canadians), this distinctly upcountry village is now famed for its cheese. The **Cabot Farmers Co-op Creamery** is Vermont's major producer, and its visitors center is a popular attraction (see *Selective Shopping—Cheese*).

Lyndonville. An up-and-down roll of land encompassing the villages of Lyndonville, Lyndon Center, Lyndon Corner, Red Village, and East Lyndon, and the neighborhoods of Vail Hill, Pudding Hill, Darling Hill, and Squabble Hollow. Lyndon isn't a tourist town but it offers real, down-home hospitality and five covered bridges (see *To See*). The village of Lyndonville was developed by the Passumpsic River Railroad Co. in the 1860s. Besides a handsome (long gone) station and a number of brick rail shops, the company laid out broad streets, planted elm trees, and landscaped Bandstand Park. The former home of Dr. Vanila L. Shores is filled with Victoriana, town memorabilia, and special exhibits (see *To See—Museums*). **Lyndon State College** is on Vail Hill (T.N. Vail was the first president of AT&T; he came here to buy a horse and bought a farm, which eventually turned into 20 farms, much of which is now occupied by campus). Lyndonville's famous product is Bag Balm (see *Selective Shopping—Special Shops*).

East Burke. A small village with a beautiful library and historical society building (the **Old Museum,** 626-9823, open June through October, Wednesday and Saturday afternoons; also by appointment), some attractive lodging, shops, and restaurants geared to alpine skiers at Burke Mountain, known because of its excellent terrain and reasonable prices as the Vermonter's Mountain. Burke Mountain Cross-Country center also offers some 80 km of high, wooded trails (see *Winter Sports*).

Greensboro. Shaped like an hourglass, Caspian Lake has a century-old following. The unusual purity of its water is checked three times weekly in-season by its association of cottage owners—who include noted authors, educators, and socialites—all of whom mingle in **Willey's Store**

KIM GRANT

The Eaton House in Brownington

in the center of Greensboro (see *Selective Shopping—General Stores*). There is a public beach and resort facilities maintained by Highland Lodge, also open in winter for cross-country skiing. Greensboro also claims Vermont's oldest (nine-hole) golf course.

Craftsbury Common. Few places convey such a sense of tranquillity and order. In summer, petunias bloom in the post office window boxes, and the green of the grass contrasts crisply with the white fence. In winter, the general whitewash of this scene contrasts with the blue of the sky. Throughout the year there are nearby places to stay and books to check out at the desk beneath the imposing portraits of Ebenezer and Samuel Crafts in the village library.

Unlike most North Country pioneers, Ebenezer was university educated (Yale, class of 1740). Forced to sell his tavern in Sturbridge, Massachusetts (the still-popular Publick House), due to war debts, he made his way here over the Bayley-Hazen Military Road, eventually bringing his family and 150 of his Sturbridge neighbors this way on sleds. Ebenezer saw to it that a church and school were established soon after the saw- and gristmills. His son Samuel, a Harvard graduate who served two terms as Vermont's governor, founded the Academy, which still serves as the public high school for the town. The **Sterling College** campus adds to the variety.

Many farmers welcome visitors to their sugarhouses during "sugaring" season in late March and early April and sell syrup from their farmhouses year-round. Inns and B&Bs offer year-round lodging, and Craftsbury Outdoor Center offers basic accommodations and one of the most extensive and dependable cross-country-ski networks in New

England; its summer sculling program is also nationally recognized. Mountain biking, walking, Elderhostel, and a variety of other programs are offered. The extensive web of well-surfaced dirt roads meandering in all directions is beloved by bicyclists and horseback riders.

Barton. The hotels are now gone, but Crystal Lake remains beautiful, with a clifflike promontory on one side and public beaches at its northern rim. There is golf here, and the town of Barton itself packs an astounding number of services into its small downtown. The Crystal Lake Falls Historical Association maintains the **Pierce House Museum** (525-6251) on Water Street, next to the old-fashioned office of the *Barton Chronicle,* an excellent little weekly covering much of Orleans and Essex Counties.

Brownington Village is a crossroads full of outstanding, early-19th-century buildings, the core of a once proud hill town long since eclipsed by such valley centers as Barton, Orleans, and Newport. There are 19th-century gardens behind the **Eaton House** and a spectacular panorama from the wooden observatory set up in a meadow behind the church. A descriptive walking tour booklet is available at the Old Stone House Museum (see *To See—Museums*), the big attraction in the village.

Wolcott, a small village that fronts on Route 15 and backs on the Lamoille River, and has long been known for its big store. In the early decades of the century the store was Charles E. Haskell's, famed as the "most general store in the entire Northeast" (teakettles, church pews, whatever). Now O. C. Buck's, probably the largest furniture (and then some) store in Vermont, dominates the town in a startling way: Most village buildings are painted chocolate brown to show that they belong to Buck's. To the east of the village the Fisher Covered Bridge, built in 1908, is said to be the nation's only surviving covered railroad bridge. The Golden Maple Bed & Breakfast on the western edge of town specializes in fly-fishing.

TO SEE

MUSEUMS
The Fairbanks Museum and Planetarium (748-2372), Main and Prospect Streets, St. Johnsbury. Open daily, year-round, Monday through Saturday 10–4, Sunday 1–5; in July and August, 10–6 on weekdays; $5 adults, $3 seniors, $2.50 ages 17 and less; $12 families; nominal charge for planetarium shows which are Saturday and Sunday, 1:30 year-round, also weekdays at 11 and at 1:30 in July and August. This is still a wonderfully old-fashioned "Cabinet of Curiosities." Its main hall, which is capped by a 30-foot-high, barrel-vaulted ceiling, is filled with thousands of stuffed animals: from mice to moose, from bats to bears (including a superb polar bear), birds galore (from hummingbirds to passenger pigeons), reptiles and fish, insects' nests; also fossils, rocks, and minerals. Historical exhibits

are drawn from the collection of 95,000 objects and "ethnological" exhibits from a 5,000-piece collection representing most of the world's far corners. "I wish the museum to be the people's school . . . to teach the village the meaning of nature and religion," explained Franklin Fairbanks at the museum's 1890 dedication. In the upstairs planetarium, which seats just 50 people, you learn about the night sky as it appears in the Northeast Kingdom. The museum is a U.S. weather observation station, and daily forecasts are a popular feature on Vermont Public Radio. There is also a fine little gift shop. The Kitchel Center, a resource library for studies and information about the Northeast Kingdom, is open Tuesday and Thursday 2–4.

St. Johnsbury Athenaeum (748-8291), Main Street, St. Johnsbury. Open Monday and Wednesday 9–8, closed Sunday, otherwise 10–5:30. The big attraction is the art gallery in the rear of this fascinating public library. Said to be the oldest unaltered gallery in the country, it has a distinctly 19th-century feel. Smaller canvases and sculptures are grouped around the outsized painting *Domes of Yosemite,* by Albert Bierstadt. Natural light through an arched skylight enhances the effect of looking into the Yosemite Valley; this is the setting for frequent chamber music concerts and other special events.

Bread and Puppet Theater Museum (525-3031), Route 122, Glover. Open June through October, 10–5. The internationally known Bread and Puppet Theater tours in winter, but in summer its farmhouse on this back road displays the huge and haunting puppet dwarfs, giants, devils, and other fantastic figures of good and evil, the artistic expres-

ROBERT C. JENKS

Work in progress at the St. Johnsbury Atheneum

sions of Polish-born Peter Schumann. Inquire about Sunday-afternoon performances, staged in the meadow across the road.

The Old Stone House Museum (754-2022), off Route 58 east of Orleans in Brownington. Open May 15 through October 15 (call for hours); modest admission charge. This is the Orleans County Historical Society Museum, housed in a four-story granite building dating back to 1836, built as a dormitory for a rural academy. The structure resembles the earliest dorms at Middlebury College, from which Alexander Twilight, the school's principal and building's architect, graduated in 1823. There is some question about whether Twilight was—as Middlebury College claims—the first African American graduate of an American college. There is no question about the beauty of the building and the historical collections: Rooms represent 10 of the 18 towns in Orleans County and also hold 18th- and 19th-century weapons, tools, paintings, furniture, and decorative arts. Pick up a walking tour (see Brownington under *Villages*).

Shores Memorial Museum (626-8547), 202 Center Street, Lyndon Center. Open June through August, Saturday and Sunday 2–4 and by appointment. What you notice first is the portrait of Vanila Shores as a young woman. Both the girl's parents followed the poor scholar when she went to Bates College, again when she moved on to Smith College and then to Johns Hopkins. Shores's house is now filled with Victorian items—hair wreaths and horsehair couches, vintage clothing and old toys, and—most notably—tops once made in town and sold around the world. Changing exhibits.

OTHER

Cabot Creamery Visitors Center (563-2231), Cabot. Open year-round except January, daily June through October 9–5, Monday through Saturday the rest of the year, 9–4. Cabot was judged "Best cheddar in the world" at the 1998 world Championship Cheese Contest (the industry's Olympics). Now owned by Agri-Mark (a cooperative of 1,650 farms), the center showcases its 80-year history as a true Vermont cooperative. There's a video and half-hour tour of the plant ($1 includes samples). The store features every conceivable variety of cheese product, plus spreads and yogurt as well as other Vermont products.

Maple Grove Maple Museum (748-5141), Route 2 east, St. Johnsbury. Open May 30 through late October. Guided tours are offered daily 8–4:30 of "the world's largest maple candy factory." In business since 1904, this is an old-fashioned factory in which maple candy is made from molds. A film in the adjacent museum depicts maple production and displays tools of the trade.

John Woodruff Memorial Library (586-9692) in East Craftsbury, was a general store built in the 1840s by the grandfather of the late Miss Jean Simpson. She converted it into one of New England's most pleasant libraries; most titles are in the room once used for bolts of cloth and groceries (old shelves and counters remain), and there is a special back room for youngsters, with a Ping-Pong table amid the books. Open Wednesday and Saturday 9–noon, 2–5, and 7–9:30; Sunday noon–1:30.

COVERED BRIDGES

All five within northern Caledonia County are in Lyndonville—one 120-foot, 1865 bridge across the Passumpsic, 3 miles north of town off Route 114; one as you enter town, a genuine 1869 bridge moved from its original site; two in Lyndon Corner (one dating from 1879, the other from 1881, both west off Route 5); the fifth in Lyndon Center on Route 122.

FARMS

In Danville, the owner of the **Danville Morgan Horse Farm** (684-2251) provides tours and enjoys talking about the breed (call ahead), and just north of Danville Village at **Emergo Farm** (684-2215), the Websters "just love to show off" their fifth-generation, prizewinning dairy operation (see also *Lodging*). Susan Houston at **Maple Leaf Llamas** (586-2674) in Craftsbury Common welcomes visitors who call ahead, as does **Oooh Ahhh Baby Llamas** (563-2929; 1-800-674-8023) on Cobb Road in Hardwick. At **Cedar Grove Farm** (593-3650) in Peacham visitors are welcome to see how Jubilee beef cattle (a new breed) are raised and **Coburn Hill Blueberry Farm** (586-2202) in Craftsbury invites pick-your-own customers August through frost. We have not had a chance to check the **Perry Farm** (754-2396) in Brownington (a small dairy farm with Morgan horses and maple syrup) or **Garvin Hill Farm** (533-7436) in Greensboro, raising beefalo and free-range chicken, both offering B&B. Ditto for the **MacBain Homestead**, (563-2025), a working dairy farm offering a reasonably priced three-room apartment on Mack Mountain Road between East Cabot and Peacham (handy to Harvey's Lake). See also *Selective Shopping—Gardens* and *Sugarhouses*.

SCENIC DRIVES

Route 2 West from St. Johnsbury to Danville. As the road climbs steadily, the White Mountains rise like a white wall in the distance. This actually works better if you are driving east from Danville. Either way, be sure to pull off to appreciate the panorama.

Danville Hill Road. Continue west on Route 2 from West Danville, past Joe's Pond, and after the Craft Shop at Molly's Pond (see *Selective Shopping—Crafts Shops*) take the right-hand turn marked for Cabot. This is a high road with long mountain views; note the Birdman (see *Crafts Shops*) along the way and the Cabot Creamery Visitors' Center in Cabot.

Up Burke Mountain. A 2.5-mile auto road to the summit of Burke Mountain (3,267 feet) commands a sweeping view of the North Country; picnic areas are provided halfway and at the summit. This preserve was formerly the 10,000-acre Darling State Forest, donated to the state in 1933. The road was constructed by the Civilian Conservation Corps. The toll road and campsites in the Sugar House Campground are open May 25 through October 15.

Darling Hill Road from Route 114 in East Burke, 5 miles south to Route 114 in Lyndonville, follows a ridge past a magnificent former estate that once encompassed many old homesteads and still offers great views.

Greensboro Village to East Hardwick. The road passes through Hardwick Street (that's the name of the hamlet) and a fine collection of Federal and Greek Revival houses; from Greensboro Village to Hardwick it makes a beeline through high and open farm country; and from Craftsbury Common north to Route 14 through Albany and Irasburg, it follows the rich farmland of the Black River Valley.

West Burke to Westmore. The stretch of Route 5A along Lake Willoughby is one of the most breathtaking anywhere.

Greensboro Bend to Lyndon. An old ridge road with splendid views, 17-mile **Stannard Road** is unpaved but usually well graveled most of the way. Check locally, though, because there are occasional washouts.

TO DO

BIKING

Craftsbury Outdoor Center (586-7767; 1-800-729-7751), Craftsbury Common, rents 21-speed fat-tire bikes and offers instruction and guide service on 200 miles of dirt roads and more than 100 miles of cross-country-ski trails (see also *Lodging*).

East Burke Sports (626-3215), Route 114, East Burke Village. A full-service cycle shop whose owners have developed an extensive off-road trail system and offer maps, guided tours, and rentals. Owner John Worth has been instrumental in developing the extensive Kingdom Trails network (see *Biking and Walking Trails*); call the shop for details.

Northeast Kingdom Cycling (1-800-639-5234), Golden Maple Inn, Route 15, Wolcott, rents road and 21-speed hybrid mountain bikes for self-guided and inn-to-inn tours.

BIKING AND WALKING TRAILS

Bayley-Hazen Military Road. Begun at Wells River on the Connecticut River in 1776 by Gen. Jacob Bayley, continued in 1778–79 by Gen. Moses Hazen, this 48-mile road was a flop as the invasion route it was intended to be, but it served settlers well after the Revolution when it came time to establish towns in this area. A historical but not very practical map is available from the Northeastern Vermont Development Association (748-5181), 44 Main Street, St. Johnsbury. The beautiful dirt stretch from Hazen's Notch to Lowell is noted in the "Jay Peak Area" chapter; the next stretch to Albany is now a walking/riding trail. It continues unmarked through Craftsbury and is marked on its way through Greensboro, where a monument commemorates its story; the first couple of miles of the road is a pleasant walk, from the granite marker at the northern end of Main Street in Wells River to Ticklenaked Pond in Boltonville (a good place for a swim and a picnic).

Kingdom Trails (John Worth: 626-3215). The East Burke area is webbed with more than 75 miles of trails: alpine ski trails on Burke Mountain, cross-country-ski trails at the Burke touring center, several loops in East Burke Village, snowmobile trails maintained by VAST, cross-country trails up on Darling Hill, and several more miles of trails specifically maintained by this nonprofit organization. Hikers have the right-of-way but this is clearly mountain-biker heaven. For a map, send $4 ($3 for the map, $1 for handling) to Kingdom Trails, P.O. Box 204, East Burke 05832.

See also Craftsbury Outdoor Center trails under *Biking*, the Vermont Leadership Center Trails in "Newport and the North Country," and Hazen's Notch Association trails in "Jay Peak."

BOAT RENTALS

Indianjoe Motor Court (684-3430), Route 2, West Danville; **Harvey's Lake Campground** (633-2213), West Barnet; **Village Sport Shop** (626-8448), Lyndonville. (See also *Camping.*) Also **Anglin' Canoe & Boat Rental** on Crystal Lake in Barton (525-3750). See also *Canoeing* and *Sculling.* This area is pocked with lakes, and launches are shown on the state map.

CAMPING

Groton State Forest, Marshfield 05658. A 25,623-acre preserve with four separate campgrounds, a beach area, yet another area for fly-fishing, and one for group camping, all listed below (access is from the Marshfield-Groton Highway, Route 232). **New Discovery Campground** (584-3820) has a total of 47 campsites, 14 of them lean-tos; beach privileges and hiking trails; primitive camping. **Stillwater Campground** (584-3822), on the west side of Lake Groton, has a total of 63 tent sites, 16 lean-tos; campers' beach and boat launch; rental boats, dump station. **Ricker Pond Campground** (584-3821) has a total of 33 campsites, 22 lean-tos, on the south side of Ricker Pond; campers' beach, rental boats, nature trail, dump station. **Seyon Fly-Fishing Area** (584-3829), on Noyes Pond, features an old lodge, frequently booked by groups. (See *Fishing.*) **Kettle Pond** (584-3820). On the south side of Kettle Pond; walk-in fishing, group camping, hiking, and snowmobiling.

CANOEING

East of St. Johnsbury, the **Moore** and **Comerford Reservoirs,** created by dams, are good for canoeing (there are two boat launches in Lower Waterford) as we found out one evening, listening to birdcalls and watching a baby beaver swim steadily toward a beaver lodge beneath the pines. Below the Comerford Dam, the stretch of the Connecticut River south to McIndoe Falls (now the McIndoe Dam) is excellent, and the portage around the dam is not difficult. For a canoe/camping guide to the Connecticut from Wells River south, contact the **Upper Valley Land Trust** (603-643-6626). Other rivers that invite canoeing are the **Passumpsic** and **Moose,** which join the Sleeper at St. Johnsbury. A boat launch on the Moose River can be accessed from

Concord Avenue in St. J, and look for a boat launch on the Passumpsic in Passumpsic Village, 5 miles south of St. Johnsbury. For rentals, check with the outlets listed under *Boating*. (See also East Burke Sports and Craftsbury Outdoor Center under *Biking*.) For details about canoeing the uppermost stretch of the Connecticut River and the Clyde River, see "Newport and the North Country."

Golden Maple Inn (888-6614), Route 15, Wolcott Village (see *Lodging*), has Old Town canoe rentals that can be launched on the Lamoille River right behind the inn, with shuttle service back from the Route 15 bridge.

Highland Lodge (see *Lodging*) also has canoes for its guests, and **Craftsbury Outdoor Center** (see *Biking*) rents canoes for use on Great and Little Hosmer Ponds and on the Black River.

FISHING

Fishing is huge here. See the pamphlet *Vermont Guide to Fishing* available from the Vermont Fish and Wildlife Department in Waterbury (241-3711) or check the Northeast Kingdom Chamber of Commerce web site (see *Guidance*) for details about which fish are available where. Check the state highway map for local access points. Willoughby is known as the prime fishing lake, but Caspian and other lakes are also good for salmon, lake and rainbow trout, and perch. There are trout in the streams, too. (See also *To Do—Camping*.)

Willoughby Falls Wildlife Management Area. From Orleans drive east on Route 58 for 0.2 mile. At the BROWNINGTON sign bear left and drive 0.1 mile to the Vermont Fish and Wildlife parking area. Between the last week in April and the second week in May, wild rainbow trout climb the falls here, jumping high to clear the white water to reach their spawning ground.

    A handicapped-accessible fishing platform has been constructed in Passumpsic Village on the Passumpsic River.

Sugarmill Farm (525-3701), Route 16 south of Barton Village. Inquire about free fishing for rainbow trout (geared to kids) in its fish ponds. (See also *Selective Shopping—Sugarhouses*.)

Lodging geared to fishermen includes **Anglin B&B** (525-4548) on Crystal Lake in Barton, which offers fishing from its dock and also rental boats and canoes; **Golden Maple Inn** (888-6614; 1-800-639-5234), on the Lamoille River in Wolcott Village, which offers a fly-fishing school, canoe rentals, and guide services; **Seyon Ranch,** a lodge on Noyes Pond within the Seyon Recreation Area (May to October: 584-3829; otherwise: 479-3241), offers nominally priced group and individual reservations; trout fishing, with flies only, from boats rented at the site. See also Quimby Country and Seymour Lake Lodge in the "Newport and the North Country" section.

GOLF

Mountain View Country Club (533-9294), Greensboro, nine holes. Established 1898; open to nonmembers midweek only. Use of carts permitted only for health reasons.

St. Johnsbury Country Club (748-9894; 1-800-718-8899), off Route 5 north, open daily mid-May through October, PGA rated, 18 holes. (Original nine holes designed in 1923, added nine holes designed by Geoffrey Cornish.) Cart rentals, great little restaurant, lounge.

Orleans Country Club (754-9392), Route 58, near Lake Willoughby. April through November. 18 holes, rentals, instruction.

Barton Golf Course (525-1126), Telfer Hill. April through September. Nine holes, cart rentals, low fees.

HAY- AND SLEIGH RIDES

In the Craftsbury area, **Coachworks Farm** (586-2818), Page Pond Road, Albany, offers hayrides. On Darling Hill, both the **Wildflower Inn** in and the **Inn at Mountain View Creamery** offer sleigh rides (see Burke Mountain–area *Lodging*).

HEALTH SPAS

St. Johnsbury Academy Field House (748-8683), Main Street, St. Johnsbury, has a pool, track, weight room with Nautilus and free weights, and three racquetball courts. These are open to the public at certain hours; call ahead for times and rates.

Old Mill Racquet & Fitness Center (748-5313), Perkins Street, St. Johnsbury. Indoor tennis, racquetball, aerobics, Nautilus, free weights, sauna, Jacuzzi.

The Wellness Barn at CoachWorks Farm (755-6342), Page Pond Road, Albany near Craftsbury Common, is an amazingly sophisticated facility; there's an indoor lap pool, sauna, steam bath, massage, and weight machines.

HIKING AND WALKING

Mount Pisgah and **Mount Hor,** Lake Willoughby. Named respectively for the place where the Lord sent Moses to view the Promised Land and for the place Moses' brother Aaron died after the Lord commanded him to go there, these twin mountains, separated by a narrow stretch of lake, form Willoughby Gap. Both are within the 7,000-acre Willoughby State Forest and offer well-maintained hiking trails. Mount Pisgah (2,751 feet) on the east side of the lake (access marked from Route 5A) has fairly short climbs yielding spectacular views of the White Mountains; trails up Mount Hor (2,648 feet) begin on the Civilian Conservation Corps road, 1.8 miles west of its junction with Route 5A, and also offer panoramic views of the Green Mountains to the west. For details, consult *50 Hikes in Vermont* (Backcountry Publications) and *Day Hiker's Guide to Vermont* (Green Mountain Club).

Wheeler Mountain. The trail begins on Wheeler Mountain Road, which leaves the north side of Route 5, 8.3 miles north of West Burke and 5 miles south of Barton Village. From the highway, the unpaved road climbs to the trailhead, 1.9 miles.

Bald Mountain. There are excellent views from the abandoned fire tower at the summit of this, the tallest peak in the Willoughby Lake area. Trails ascend to the summit from both the north (Lookout's Trail, 2.8 miles) and the south (Long Pond Trail, 2.1 miles). From the north side of Bald Mountain, you can hike on trails and wilderness roads all the way to the summit of Mount Hor, and Haystack Mountain (a side trip) has excellent views and two trails. Details can be found in *Day Hiker's Guide to Vermont* (see *Hiking and Walking* in "What's Where").

Willoughby Gap Expeditions (626-5936, 626-8047). Naturalists Craig Erickson and Fife Hubbard lead expeditions Saturday and Sunday from East Burke Village to study the geology, flora, and fauna of Willoughby Gap. Private tours by appointment.

HORSEBACK RIDING

Rohan Farm (467-3701), East Burke. Brian Kelly offers trail rides and cross-country treks geared to intermediate and better riders over the web of bridle paths on Darling Ridge and the adjacent mountains.

Greenhope Horse Farm B&B (533-7772), Walden. A long established riding center with a summer camp and instruction, along with trail riding for experienced riders, on 140 acres connecting with local trails and dirt roads. Inquire about year-round B&B.

RUNNING

Craftsbury Outdoor Center (586-7767; 1-800-729-7751), Craftsbury Common, offers six 1-week camp sessions between June 30 and August 10; training for triathlons, marathons, the Stowe road race, and other excursions at around $500 per week.

SCULLING

Craftsbury Outdoor Center (586-7767; 1-800-729-7751), Craftsbury Common, offers a nationally acclaimed summer sculling program; novices welcome.

SWIMMING

Harvey's Lake in West Barnet; **Miles Pond** in Concord; public beaches in **Groton State Forest;** a small beach at **Ticklenaked Pond** in Boltonville; **Joe's Pond** in West Danville; **Molly's Pond** in Marshfield; public pools in St. Johnsbury and **Powers Park** in Lyndonville. In Glover, **Shadow Lake Beach,** marked from Route 16, is a delightful spot. There is also a public beach on **Caspian Lake,** near Greensboro Village. In Barton, **Crystal Lake State Beach** just east of the village on Route 15 is open daily in-season 10–8, with lifeguard, bathhouse, and picnic facilities; and **Pageant Park,** a mile farther east on Route 16, is a town-owned park open daily until 10 PM, also with a bathhouse and camping (primarily tenting).

Lake Willoughby has small public beaches at both its northern and southern tips. **Boulder Beach Day Use Area** (584-3820) in Groton State Forest has a public beach, picnic area, snack bar, bathhouse.

WINTER SPORTS

CROSS-COUNTRY SKIING

Inquire about the Ski the Kingdom Cross-country Trail Pass (1-800-729-7751), good on all 220 commercially maintained cross-country trails in

Cross-country skiing in Craftsbury Center

this area. *Note:* There are two exceptionally high, dependably snowy, and spectacularly beautiful trail systems in this area, one in Craftsbury and the second in and around East Burke.

Craftsbury Outdoor Center Nordic Ski Center (586-7767; 1-800-729-7751), Craftsbury Common, grooms 105 km of its 130 km marked and maintained trail system; it offers rentals, instruction, lodging packages (trail fee). The system connects with **Highland Lodge** (533-2647) in Greensboro, which offers a total of 60 km of trails, 15 of them well groomed. The only major New England cross-country system that's no-where near an alpine ski hill, the Craftsbury Outdoor Center/Highland Lodge trails web the kind of red barn–spotted farmscape that's equated with, but increasingly rare in, Vermont. They traverse rolling fields, woods, and maple and evergreen groves, with stunning views of the distant Green Mountains. Thanks to their elevation and Craftsbury's exceptional grooming, they also represent some of the most dependable cross-country skiing in the Northeast and usually remain skiable well into March and sugaring season.

Burke Mountain Cross-Country (626-8338; 1-800-786-8338), East Burke. Well-groomed trails begin at 1,300 feet and wind through woods that yield to panoramic views. Rentals, lessons, guided tours; 62 km of tracked trails, an 80-km system that connects with the evolving King-dom Trails (see *To Do—Biking and Walking Trails*). Trails climb to 2,400 feet.

The Wildflower Inn and the **Inn at Mountain View Creamery** (see *Lodging* for both) on Darling Hill between East Burke and Lyndonville offer adjoining trail systems with fabulous views; nominal donation.

Groton State Forest. Snowed-over roads, good for 20 km of cross-country skiing.

Sugarmill Farm (1-800-688-7978), Route 16, Barton. Eleven km of marked trails meander through the farm; 800- to 1,400-foot elevations. $5 trail fee.

See also Hazen's Notch in the "Jay Peak Area" chapter of this section.

DOWNHILL SKIING AND SNOWBOARDING

Burke Mountain (626-3305 and 1-800-541-5480; snow report: 1-877-754-2875; reservations: 1-877-287-5388; web site: burkemountain.com), East Burke. The first ski trails on this majestic mountain were cut in the 1930s when it became a state park. In 1955, a Poma lift was installed to the summit, and a shelter and parking lot were opened. Long known as the Vermonter's Mountain, it caters to local patrons, as well as to Canadians and Bostonians (Boston is less than 4 hours away via I-93). After a few years of uphill financial struggles, at the moment the mountain seems to be once again on a firm footing and has increased its snowmaking by 50 percent.

Lifts: One quad chairlift, one double chairlift, one Poma lift, one J-bar.

Trails and slopes: 43 trails; 32 cut and maintained, 11 glades/woods; 14 percent novice, 42 percent intermediate, 33 percent advanced, 11 percent expert only.

Vertical drop: 2,000 feet.

Snowmaking: 60 percent of skiable terrain.

Snowboarding: The Gap Park is a 5-acre technical playland; snowboarding is permitted on all trails.

Facilities: Sherburne Base Lodge includes a glass-walled restaurant, as well as a cafeteria, both serving Bavarian specialties and beer. Another base lodge serves the upper mountain; private and group lessons.

For children: A nursery for the 6-month- to 6-year-olds; a supervised program for children ages 7–14. Burke Mountain Academy, a prep school for aspiring racers, claims to have developed more competitors for the U.S. ski team than any other American program.

Rates: $25 midweek for everyone; weekends $42 adult, $37 teen and seniors, $28 per child 7–12.

Lyndon Outing Club (626-8465), Hill Street, Lyndonville. An old-fashioned, nonprofit town ski hill with a lodge, maintained by the Lyndon Outing Club since 1937. Open Tuesday, Wednesday, and Friday for night skiing 6:30–9:30, weekends 10–4; a T-bar is the workhorse lift and a rope tow serves the beginners trail; snowboarding is permitted and several cross-country trails are also maintained. Weekends $12 per adult, $8 weeknights.

SNOWMOBILING

The Northeast Kingdom Chamber of Commerce (see *Guidance*) publishes a local snowmobiling map and directs inquiries to the local club from which it's necessary to purchase a VAST membership in order to use local trails. Rentals are available from **All Around Power Equipment** (748-1413), Route 5 north, St. Johnsbury.

GREEN SPACE

Barr Hill Nature Preserve, Greensboro. Turn right at the town hall and go about a half mile to Bar Hill Road (another left). The trails at Barr Hill, managed by The Vermont Nature Conservancy, overlook Caspian Lake. Don't miss the view from the top of Barr Hill.

Victory Basin, alias Victory Bog. This 4,970-acre preserve administered by the Vermont Fish and Wildlife Department includes a 25-acre boreal bog with rare plant life, 1,800 acres of wetlands, 1,084 acres of hardwoods, and 71 acres of clearings and old fields. The dirt road access is via Victory; there are three parking areas: Mitchell's Landing, Lee Hill, and Damons Crossing.

Hurricane Brook Wildlife Management Area, off Route 114, south of Norton Pond: 9,500 forested acres, also accessible via a gravel road past Holland Pond from Holland Village. A detailed map is available from the Fish and WildlifeDepartment in Waterbury.

Waterford Dam at Moore Reservoir. New England Power offers guided tours of the huge complex of turbines. There are also picnic sites and a boat launch here. The approach is from the New Hampshire side of the Connecticut River, just below Lower Waterford, Vermont, off Route 135.

In St. Johnsbury

Fred Mold Park near the confluence of the Passumpsic and Moose Rivers is a great picnic spot by a waterfall and old mill. **The Arlington Preserve,** accessible from Waterman Circle, is a 33-acre nature preserve with woods, meadows, and rock outcroppings.

See also *Biking, Biking and Walking Trails,* and *Camping.*

LODGING

In the St. Johnsbury area

Rabbit Hill Inn (748-5168; 1-800-76-BUNNY), Route 18, Lower Waterford 05848. Brian and Leslie Mulcahy welcome you to this pillared landmark, an inn since 1795. All 15 rooms and five suites are romantic confections, with canopy beds, antiques, and "indulging" bathrooms. Twelve rooms have working fireplace; suites also have Jacuzzi for two and private porch. All have been painstakingly furnished, complete with a "room diary." Summer swimming and fishing in a freshwater pond, canoeing, and golf privileges; winter cross-country skiing and snowshoeing. Rooms $235–265, suites $300–370 per couple, breakfast, afternoon tea, and five-course, candlelit dinner included. Add 15 percent service charge.

Broadview Farm (748-9902), 2627 McDowell Road, North Danville 05828.

Open June through March. This shingle-style country mansion has been in Molly Newell's family since 1901. It's set on 300 acres with a panoramic view of mountains, on a farm road in North Danville that, Molly assures us, was once the Boston-Montreal Road. In the late 19th century, before its shingles and gables, this old farmhouse took in summer boarders, advertising its 2,000-foot elevation as a sure escape from malaria and hay fever. Today the elevation suggests dependable cross-country skiing. Molly has thoroughly renovated the old place, removing 4,000 pounds of radiators, replacing windows, and gutting and redesigning the kitchen, while preserving the fine woodwork, detailing, and maple floors throughout the house. The four guest rooms are furnished with family antiques (check out the great oak set in the Yellow Room). Baths are private or shared; $50–80 double includes a full breakfast.

The Albro Nichols House (751-8434), 7 Boynton Avenue, St. Johnsbury 05819. This 1840s Federal-style house sits up behind Arnold Park at the head of Main Street, a flowery, quiet setting that's still within strolling distance of St. Johnsbury's museums, galleries, theaters, shops, and restaurants. Margaret Ryan is a former prep school dean and a high school theater director who clues in guests to the Kingdom's cultural scene. The pleasant, square Rose Room with private bath ($60) is on the ground floor; the upstairs rooms (both $50), one with twin beds, the other with a double (this would be a delightful room for a single person, too), share a book-lined sitting room and a bath. Common rooms feature plenty of books and interesting art; a full breakfast is included.

Branch Brook Bed & Breakfast (626-8316; 1-800-572-7712), P.O. Box 143, South Whelk Road, Lyndon 05316. This is an exceptional house with long, graceful parlor windows, built in the 1830s, beautifully converted to a B&B by Ted and Ann Dolman. Both the room with a pencil-post bed locally crafted from cherrywood and the one with a canopy bed are worthy of brides; several rooms are tucked under exposed beams, furnished with antiques. All but two of the five have private bath. $60–80 per couple with a hearty breakfast; Ann Tolman has a food-service background and prides herself on breakfasts prepared on her English Aga cooker stove.

✎ **Emergo Farm B&B** (684-2215; 1-800-280-1898), 261 Webster Hill, Danville 05828. Just north of the village, this strikingly handsome farm is a prizewinning, fifth-generation working dairy farm. The upstairs apartment has two bedrooms, full kitchen, sitting room, and bath, ideal for a family or two couples (a pullout in the sitting room sleeps extra kids). Rooms are also available individually with shared bath. The farm's 200 acres include a hilltop with panoramic views of much of the Kingdom. Livestock includes a pet goat and turkeys as well as 130 head of cattle (80 milking cows). $65 per room includes breakfast, served downstairs in the dining room.

🐾✎ **Creamery Inn Bed & Breakfast** (563-2819), P.O. Box 187, Cabot 05647.

Dan and Judy Lloyd's Federal-style 1835 village home has three guest rooms, one with carefully restored stenciling, and a suite. All have private bath. Candlelight dining by reservation. Children welcome. Visiting dogs are housed in a kennel in back of the house. $55–85 per couple, including full breakfast.

🐾 **The Inn at Maplemont Farm** (633-4880; 1-800-230-1617), Route 5, Barnet 05821. Tom and Sherry Tolle's trim, well-kept, large yellow farmhouse sits in a bucolic setting on 43 acres across the road from the Connecticut River. The three guest rooms are pleasant, all with private bath; South Peacham, the ground-floor twin, is particularly attractive. Pet and livestock accommodations are available if you arrange in advance. $65–90 per night, with hearty breakfast and afternoon refreshments.

🏅 **Sherryland** (684-3354), Danville 05828. Caroline Sherry's large, 19th-century farmhouse is on a pleasant country road about a mile south of the village green. Five guest rooms are genuinely homelike. No meals; still only $32 double, $28 single, $5 per cot.

Echo Ledge Farm Inn (748-4750), Route 2, P.O. Box 46, East St. Johnsbury 05838. Open year-round. The Lamotte family runs this bed & breakfast on a farm established in 1793. Six comfortable bedrooms, five with private bath. Afternoon tea, plenty of books. $47–67; $5 less single, $10 extra for use of one or two daybeds.

Ha'Penny Gourmet (592-3317; 1-800-471-7655), Peacham 05862 (see also *Selective Shopping—General Stores*). Mark Moore and Karen Stawiecki, proprietors of the unusual Peacham Store, have three cozy bedrooms over the shop. $75–85 double, with a sumptuous breakfast of freshly made croissants and homemade jams. Dinner by reservation.

Long Meadow Inn (757-2538; 1-800-394-2538), Route 5, Wells River 05081. This stately brick Federal by the river, once a stagecoach stop, is now nicely restored (and extensively fireproofed) by Roy and Ellen Canlon. There are five pretty guest rooms, two with private bath. $25–30 per person, less for three or more days.

The Old Homestead (633-4016; 1-877-OLD-HOME), 1573 Route 5 south, Barnet 05821. Gail Arnaar is a musician who welcomes other musicians in particular, everyone in general, to this handsome old house. Guest rooms range from small ($48 single) to a $95 family room; inquire about $65 per weekend per couple.

MOTELS

🐾 **Fairbanks Motor Inn** (748-5666), 32 Western Avenue, St. Johnsbury 05819, near exit 21, I-91, Route 2 east. This three-story, 46-unit, quite luxurious motel has central air-conditioning, heated pool, and fitness center privileges. $59–110. Pets accepted.

🐾 **Aime's Motel** (748-3194; 1-800-504-6663), junction of Routes 2 and 18, Box 332, St. Johnsbury 05819. Jim Buck manages this small, family-geared motel next to a rushing stream. There are 16 rooms, which a reader tells us are sparkling clean. $37–70 double includes morning coffee. Pets accepted.

In the Burke Mountain area

✍ **The Wildflower Inn** (626-8310; 1-800-627-8310), Star Route, Lyndonville
05851. This is a fine old farmhouse set high on a ridge with a spectacular
view, surrounded by its own 500 acres including gardens and trails
maintained for hiking, mountain biking, and cross-country skiing. Jim
and Mary O'Reilly have eight children (five boys, three girls), and other
children are particularly welcome. There is a big playroom in the main
house; a daily (except Sunday) supervised morning arts, crafts, and
summer nature program for children ages 4 and up in the big barn; a
variety of animals to relate to in the petting barn; a sports complex with
basketball, a batting cage, and tennis court and playing field beyond.
Adult spaces include an attractive parlor and library—stocked with
games and the kind of books you really want to read—and a fine little art
gallery. The landscaped pool commands a spectacular view of rolling hills.
Dinner is a multicourse event (see *Dining Out*), but for families with
children, there's the option of eating early with food on plates the
moment they sit down. Breakfast is a three-course production, and tea is
also served. Upstairs in the main house, two family suites have great views.
There are nine more suites, including a romantic one off by itself in the
old schoolhouse, complete with whirlpool bath. There are also 10 rooms
in the former carriage house across the road. $85–250 per couple B&B
plus $15 per teen, $8 per child ages 6–12, and free for ages 5 and under.
Christmastime is especially festive here.

The Inn at Mountain View Creamery (626-9924), Darling Hill Road,
East Burke 05832. Like the Wildflower Inn, this is part of a onetime
9,000-acre hilltop estate owned by Elmer Darling, a Burke native, who
built this creamery in 1890 to supply dairy products to his Fifth Avenue
hotel (it used to churn out 600 pounds of butter a month and 70 pounds
of cheese per day). The inn is still set among restored barns and backed
by 440 acres that spread across a high ridge and are laced with trails,
maintained for walking, mountain biking, and cross-country skiing.
Marilyn Pastore has tastefully decorated the 12 guest rooms (private
baths) with antiques, wicker, and bright fabrics. The downstairs sitting
rooms are also nicely furnished, and a patio with tables, chairs, and
striped market umbrellas is set in perennial gardens. A weekend bistro
serves lunch and dinner (see *Dining Out*). This is a favorite for weddings and with bike groups. $115–180 per room includes a full break-
fast that might include a vegetable frittata as well as fruit, yogurt, muffins, and cereals. Inquire about the neighboring Victorian farmhouse,
sleeping six: two bedrooms, two baths, a Jacuzzi, full kitchen, and parlor, $1,800 per week.

🐾 **The Old Cutter Inn** (626-5152; 1-800-295-1943), Burke Hollow Road, East
Burke 05832. Closed April and November. This 1845 farmhouse just
minutes from Burke Mountain has been owned and operated by Swiss-

born chef Fritz Walther since 1977. It's a spotless, cozy inn with a suite plus nine rooms, five with private bath, and a two-bedroom apartment next to the barn. Its excellent dining room is open to the public every night except Wednesday (when it still serves guests); you can choose between the formal dining room (see *Dining Out*) and a friendly, less expensive pub. The grounds include a heated, landscaped swimming pool and views of Willoughby Gap. $54–66 double occupancy, $10 per extra person in room; MAP available; multi-day packages; cheaper in the off-season. Pets are welcome with advance notice.

The Village Inn of East Burke (626-3161, 793-4517), Box 186, East Burke 05832. This friendly bed & breakfast owned by Lorraine and George Willy offers five rooms, all large enough to accommodate families and all with private bath; in the common space are a woodstove, books, and games. Guests can use a separate kitchen with stove and refrigerator. $45 single, $60 per couple includes a light breakfast.

Burke Mountain Condominiums (626-8903; 1-800-541-5480), Burke Hollow Road, East Burke 05832. About 90 slope-side units in the rental pool are salted around the ski area's access roads. They range from studios to four-bedroom apartments accommodating 11. All have woodstove or fireplace, TV, and trail access; 2-night weekend packages from $199 per person; 5-night midweek, from $281 per person.

In the Craftsbury area

The Inn on the Common (586-9619; 1-800-521-2233), Craftsbury Common 05827. The most regal lodging in the Kingdom has been offered since 1978 by Michael and Penny Schmidt. Guest rooms and suites are impeccably tasteful, with matching paper and curtains, well-chosen antiques, brass and four-poster beds, and original art. The 16 rooms, 5 with woodstove or fireplace, some with canopy beds, are divided among three Federal-style buildings close to the common. Guests congregate in the library for cocktails and dine formally at candlelit tables (see *Dining Out*). In summer, you can take advantage of the solar-heated pool, the perennial gardens, lawn croquet, and the tennis court. Inquire about packages featuring mountain biking, running, sculling, and cross-country-skiing programs at nearby Craftsbury Outdoor Center (see *Winter Sports*), and the inn also offers access to superbly equipped Coachworks (see *Health Spas*). $150–265 single occupancy, $230–290 per couple, MAP, plus tax and 15 percent service. Children (special rates), smokers, and pets ($15 per stay) are all welcome.

Highland Lodge (533-2647), Greensboro 05841. Open May 30 through October 16 and December 20 through March 15. A fine, Victorian-era inn on the shore of Caspian Lake that manages to be both airy in warm weather and cozy in winter, now managed by the second generation of Smiths (David, Wilhelmina, and Alex)—hosts whose warmth is reflected in the atmosphere of their public rooms. Common rooms include a comfortable library with desks and armchairs, a game room and a living

room with fireplace, and a sitting room with baby grand piano. Upstairs
are 11 rooms, all with private bath. There are also 11 cottages (4 remain
open in winter). In summer, facilities include tennis and a pleasant beach
with bathhouse and boats, along with the nature trails on the property and
in the adjacent Barr Hill Nature Preserve (see *Green Space*); in winter the
draw is cross-country skiing on the extensive network radiating from the
inn's touring center, rising to unusual elevations with superb views.
Inside, there is plenty of space to read and get away from other guests,
along with nice corners in which to socialize. For children, there's an
organized summer program (ages 4–9). In the lodge, $95–120 per person,
$20–65 per child depending on age, MAP; in a cottage, $120–140 per
person; inquire about family rates; 15 percent gratuity, as well as breakfast
and dinner, is included. Less in May and weekdays in June, September,
October, January, and March.

Craftsbury Bed & Breakfast (586-2206), Craftsbury Common 05827.
Margaret Ramsdell welcomes guests to her farmhouse on Wylie Hill,
with views that (even by local standards) are hard to beat. Generally
known as Margie's Place, this friendly, informal B&B caters to skiers,
bicyclists, and hikers. The two upstairs rooms (sharing a bath) have the
longest views, but the four additional ground-floor guest rooms (sharing
two baths) are perfectly pleasant. There's an inviting living room with a
woodstove, and the door to the big country kitchen—with its glowing
soapstone stove, backed by gleaming copper—is always open. In winter
(December through early April), guests can ski out the door and onto
105 km of groomed trails maintained by the Craftsbury Outdoor Center
(see below). $60–75 ($55 single) includes a full breakfast (maybe cinna-
mon-apple pancakes or eggs with cheddar cheese). Dinner possible.

Craftsbury Outdoor Center (586-7767; 1-800-729-7751), Box 31,
Craftsbury Common 05827. Recreational facilities are the big attractions
here, with accommodations for 90 guests divided between two rustic
lodges: nine large doubles and 31 smaller rooms sharing lavatory-style
hall bathrooms, 3 larger rooms with private bath, two efficiency apartments, and three housekeeping cottages sleeping four. Three meals are
served, buffet-style, in the dining hall. Guests come for the programs
offered: running, sculling, walking, mountain biking, and cross-country
skiing; or they stay and enjoy the outdoors at their own pace (see *To Do*).
Facilities include swimming at Lake Hosmer, exercise rooms, sauna,
tennis courts, and 140 acres. From $65 per person and $115 per couple
including three plentiful meals with vegetarian options; family, and
multi-day rates available. (See also *Biking*, *Sculling*, *Running*, and *Cross-
Country Skiing*.)

Lakeview Inn (533-2291), Main Street, Greensboro 05841. Open year-
round. Built in 1872 as a summer boardinghouse, this handsome clapboard inn served that purpose right up until the 1980s (it housed the
musicians who performed in Summer Music from Greensboro), but it

had stood abandoned for eight years when Kathy Unser and John Hunt took it on, painstakingly restoring it. Much of the ground floor is now an informal restaurant (see *Eating Out*) and there is a small first-floor guest sitting room with a big-screen TV. Upstairs is another common room. All 12 guest rooms are furnished with antiques. One is handicapped-accessible and a top-floor three-bedroom suite sleeps six. $95–115 ($230 for the suite) includes breakfast.

✿ **Craftsbury Inn** (586-2848; 1-800-336-2848), Route 14, Craftsbury 05826, a village with a delightful general store just downhill from Craftsbury Common. The handsome 1850 Greek Revival–style inn run by Blake and Rebecca Gleason was built as a private residence in the 1850s with a second-story, wraparound porch. There are unusually attractive living and game rooms dressed with interesting artwork. Upstairs, the 10 guest rooms are also nicely decorated, some with canopy beds, all with quilts made to match the wallpaper. Dinner is taken seriously (see *Dining Out*). Rates $140–160 per couple, MAP; $90–110 B&B plus 15 percent for service. Midweek packages, single rates.

  Whetstone Brook Bed & Breakfast (586-6916), HCR 65, Box 4220, Craftsbury 05826-4220. An 1826 Vermont classic cape that, with additions, has been home to six generations of the Wilson family is now Audrey and Bryce Wilson's retirement project, a pleasant B&B. There's a piano in the living room, an Aga stove in the kitchen, and the small round tables in the dining room are positioned to view the meadow through the French doors. Two upstairs rooms share a bath (a third is rented if everyone belongs to the same group) and the ground-floor Apple Blossom Room has a queen bed and private bath. $60–80 includes a full breakfast.

🐾 **The Brick House** (472-5512), Box 128, Brick House Road, East Hardwick 05836. Judith and Rachel Kane preside over this early-19th-century, two-story brick house on the edge of East Hardwick Village. There are three elaborately furnished bedrooms, two sharing one and a half baths, one private (the beds have feather mattresses, feather pillows, and handmade quilts). There are books, a fireplace, and a dartboard in the sitting room. Amenities include woodland walks and trout fishing on the property. Innkeeper Judith Kane is British herself and serves English cream teas; see *Tea*. $60–75 per couple; "well-behaved pets" welcome, $5 extra.

  Somerset House (472-5484; 1-800-838-80744), 24 Highland Avenue, Hardwick 05843. A vernacular 1890s Victorian home with perennial flower gardens and four guest rooms, one with private bath, three sharing two baths. English hostess Ruth Gaillard serves a full breakfast with an egg entrée or crêpes, fresh fruit. Ask for a tower room. $69–80 double, $50–60 single.

  Golden Maple Inn (888-6614; 1-800-639-5234), Route 15, Wolcott Village 05680, offers three spacious guest rooms and a fireplace suite, all with private bath, in an 1865 riverside home. The inn offers canoe and

KIM GRANT

Lake Willoughby

bike rentals and inn-to-inn bike tours, but fly-fishing is the real specialty (a fly-fishing school and guide service can be arranged; see *To
Do—Fishing*). The ground-floor Geneve Suite with gas woodstove goes
for $74–84, and the second-floor Captain's Cabin and Alpen Glow, with
private baths, are $59–84. Breakfast includes a hot dish like baked
French toast, as well as homemade granola, served on china and linen.

Village House Inn (755-6722), P.O. Box 228, Route 14, Albany 05820. Jon
and Kate Fletcher have turned this fine Victorian village house with a
wraparound porch from a B&B into a full-service inn with eight bedrooms (private baths) just minutes from Craftsbury Common and adjacent to the Catamount cross-country-ski trail. From $65 per couple,
including breakfast. See also *Dining Out*.

Tranquility Farm (525-3646), Lake Parker, West Glover 05875. Olive and
Ray Griffin are avid birders, happy to guide guests when they are not
off on their own birding expeditions (usually limited to spring). There's
a two-bedroom apartment as well as rooms in the house. $45–55; RVs
$15 plus tax.

On Lake Willoughby

Fox Hall (525-6930), mailing address: RFD 1, Barton 05822. Ken and
Sherry Pyden have transformed the main house at a turn-of-the-
century mansion, which served for many decades as a girls camp, into a
comfortable bed & breakfast. Common space is ample and the eight
guest rooms, some round, four with private bath, are furnished with
antiques. All offer views of Lake Willoughby. The 76 acres include lake
frontage and a dock. Guests have access to canoes, paddleboats, and
windsurfers, and can swim off the dock. But they may never want to
leave the wide old porch, which commands one of the most dramatic

views in Vermont, right down Willoughby Gap. Sherry has a thing about moose—which she collects in many forms. Inquire about summer music and theater in the pavilion behind the inn. $79–109 in summer and fall, less mid-October through June, an exceptional breakfast included.

  ᕙ **Willoughvale Inn** (525-4123; 1-800-594-9102), RR 2, Box 403, Westmore 05860. This nifty place has an efficiency suite and seven unique upstairs rooms, one handicapped-accessible room downstairs, and 4 two-bedroom housekeeping cottages with fireplaces across the road, on the lake. The taproom and dining room are open to the public for dinner (see *Dining Out*); breakfast is also available for guests. The original farmhouse here dated back to the mid-1800s, and by the early 1900s it was a restaurant. After several years of vacancy, the old house was replaced by a new inn, tastefully built along traditional lines with windows that maximize the spectacular lake view. It is now owned and operated by the Gameroff family, who also own the Green Mountain Inn (see *Lodging* in "Stowe and Waterbury"). Elegant public areas give guests some private space beyond their quarters, some of which are quite spacious; all have private bath, furnishings specifically made for them, and water views. In the main inn, standard rooms with queen beds are $69–89 in low season and $109–139 in high; the Lupine Room, with four-poster and Jacuzzi, is $99–119 in low, $134–154 in high; and the Harter Suite, with living–dining room and kitchen, is $79–99 in low, $125–145 in high (plus $2 per room per night as housekeeping gratuity). The cottages are $109–119 in low season, $179–215 nightly, $1,170 weekly in high. Canoe and bicycle, snowshoe and snowmobile rentals are available on the premises. Inquire about packages that combine Willoughvale and Green Mountain Inn stays.

In the Barton/Orleans area

  ❀ **Heermansmith Farm Inn** (754-8866), Box 7, Heermanville Road, Coventry 05825. Up a hill and out a back road beyond a small village you will find this farm, which has been in the same family since 1807. Jack and Louise Smith offer six rooms upstairs in the snug, 1860s farmhouse that sits amid fields of hay and pastureland skirted by the Black River. It is well known as one of the region's leading restaurants (see *Dining Out*). Three of the rooms, with private bath, are in a new wing, and three others, also with private bath, are in the original part of the house, one about as Vermont as a guest room can be, complete with antique bed, handmade quilt, and a crazy window. Books line the walls throughout the inn, including in the dining rooms. Guests can enjoy the lounge by day. $50 single, $75 double, B&B.

  Brick House (754-2108), P.O. Box 33, Irasburg 05845. Roger and Jo Sweatt welcome you to their 1875 brick house just off the common in this small, very Vermont village. There are three guest rooms, one twin bedded with private bath and two (one with a lace-topped canopy bed and the other with a brass bed) sharing a bath. A breakfast, which might include Jo's crustless mushroom quiche, is included in $45 double, $30 single,

$50 for the family room with a pullout bed. Add $5 for 1-night stays on weekends.

Anglin B&B (525-4548), Route 5, Barton 05822. Fay Valley's trim white house sits right on Crystal Lake, and the view is across its width. The three rooms with private bath are bright, nicely furnished, with lake views. There are lots of books and reading alcoves. Guests can fish and swim from the dock, and boats and canoes can be rented. $65 per couple, $55 single includes breakfast. Children are welcome (Fay herself has 12).

CAMPGROUNDS
For a complete listing, see *To Do—Camping*.

WHERE TO EAT

DINING OUT

Inn on the Common (586-9619; 1-800-521-2233), Craftsbury Common. The menu at this elegant inn changes daily and is open to outside guests by reservation. Meals are in the formal dining room at either common or small tables (patrons tend to meet over cocktails in the library before dinner), or (weather permitting) on the adjoining patio. The menu changes nightly. On a late October evening you might begin with a shrimp, roasted pepper, and spinach appetizer, then a cream of celery soup followed by a salad. Then choose from pan-seared rib-eye buffalo, chicken breast sautéed with a sesame-honey-ginger glaze, or sautéed medallions of tuna with lemon caper buerre blanc. Dessert can be cheesecake with kiwi puree. $35 prix fixe includes after-dinner coffee and chocolates in the library. The wine list is a passion of innkeeper Michael Schmidt.

Heermansmith Farm Inn (754-8866), Heermanville Road, Coventry. Closed Monday and Tuesday in the off-season, otherwise open for dinner nightly, year-round. Reservations appreciated. The farm itself is locally known for the quality of its produce, especially strawberries. The restaurant is the candlelit interior of the old farmhouse, walls lined with books, white linen–covered tables well spaced. You might begin with mushrooms en cassoulet (sautéed in a sherried cream sauce and nestled in a warm pastry puff shell, $5.95) and dine on Duck Heermansmith, roasted crisp with a strawberry and Chambord fruit sauce ($16.95). A lighter menu is offered in the Library Lounge.

Willoughvale Inn and Restaurant (525-4123), Route 5A, Westmore. Open for lunch and dinner June through mid-October; in the off-season, Tuesday through Saturday for dinner and Sunday brunch. The dining room is spacious with large windows to maximize the view of Willoughby Lake and Gap, and in the evening it glows with candlelight reflected in the highly polished tables. The atmosphere is casual and the cuisine eclectic, featuring fresh seafood specialties, vegetarian fare, beef, and poultry. Chefs change but the specialty of the house remains (and we can vouch for it): Chicken Willoughvale, stuffed with apples and cheddar cheese. Lighter dishes are served in the adjoining Tap Room. Dinner entrées: $9.95–15.95.

Darling's (626-9924), the Inn at Mountain View Creamery, Darling Hill Road, East Burke. Open Friday, Saturday, and Sunday for lunch and dinner. Subtitled A Country Bistro, this brick-walled room, once the heart of a working creamery, is an attractive dining room with a varied menu that includes entrées ranging from a layered polenta terrine with roasted vegetables and French feta ($10.95) to roasted New Zealand lamb ($19.95). Specials vary each night, as do the featured wines.

The Wildflower Inn (626-8310), between Lyndonville and East Burke on Darling Hill Road. Open for dinner June through mid-October, Monday through Saturday; in winter Thursday, Friday, and Saturday. Positioned as it is at the rear of the inn, overlooking flower gardens and a spread of valley with mountains rolling into the distance, this is a delightful place to dine. Entrées might include salmon and sole lattice with pesto, Irish beef stew, and marinated rib-eye steak. $12–20.

Rabbit Hill Inn (748-5168; 1-800-76-BUNNY), Route 18 in Lower Waterford. Open to outside guests by reservation, space permitting. The elegant dining room holds just 15 tables, and both food and atmosphere are carefully orchestrated. There's candlelight and crystal, harp or flute music many nights, and a choice of five course dinners. Entrées might range from broccoli-cheddar crêpes filled with mushrooms, leeks, and sun-dried tomatoes; to poached red snapper in red peppercorn broth with olive pancetta; to smoked tenderloin of beef. Appetizer or soup, and bread, sorbet, salad, dessert, and beverage are included in the $37 prix fixe.

The Old Cutter Inn (626-5152), Burke Hollow Road, East Burke. Open for dinner daily except Wednesday, also for Sunday brunch; closed November and April. Owner Fritz Walther prepares a few of his native specialties, like Rahmschnitzel (pork medallions sautéed in butter with shallots, deglazed with white wine, and finished with fresh mushrooms in a light cream sauce). He is also known for his beef Wellington and veal dishes. Less formal fare, like smoked trout, Swiss bratwurst, and forster-schnitten, is served in the tavern, a favorite local gathering. Entrées $13.25–18.95, less in the tavern.

Creamery Restaurant (684-3616), Danville. Open Tuesday through Friday for lunch and dinner; Saturday for dinner only. A former creamery nicely converted into a gracious little restaurant that many feel is the best in the St. J area. A blackboard menu features homemade soups and salads, pies, and a choice of meat and seafood dishes. Moderate; less expensive pub menu downstairs.

The Village House Inn (755-6722), Route 14, Albany. Open for dinner year-round. Right in the middle of this small village, the inn—a Victorian home—rides a reputations for quality that chef-owner Jon Ryan established during the years he was chef at Heermansmith Farm, where wife Kate managed the dining room, as she does this one, a long, narrow, many-windowed space with tables on the porch, too, in warm weather. Entrées range from grilled Cajun chicken on a bed of spinach ($10.95), to fresh tomato fettuccine primavera pesto ($11.95), to veal Oscar ($17.95), to salmon en croute (which we can personally recommend, $16.95). Desserts are superior and wines are reasonably priced.

Craftsbury Inn (586-2848), Craftsbury. Dinner is open to the public by reservation May through October, Wednesday through Sunday 6:30–8:30. The small dining room has just eight tables and a choice of four entrées. Chef-owner Blake Gleason offers a limited menu that changes seasonally but might include sautéed mushrooms and goat cheese in puff pastry for starters ($4.75) and sautéed pork medallions served with apricot brandy sauce ($15.95).

Highland Lodge (533-2647), Greensboro. The inn is open late May through mid-October and Christmas week through mid-March. Breakfast, lunch (except Monday), and dinner (by reservation) are served in the inn's attractive dining room and, weather permitting, on the porch. Dinner entrées could include Vermont leg of lamb with roasted garlic sauce, farmed salmon fillet with mustard and tarragon, or triple orange chicken breast. Begin with wild mushroom soup and French walnut rolls and end with bittersweet chocolate cake. Lunch features interesting croissants, salads, and soups as well as the usual sandwiches. Specials, too, can be interesting. Dinner entrées $14.75–16.75, with a lighter menu available.

EATING OUT

River Garden Cafe (626-3514), Route 114, East Burke Village. Open daily for lunch and dinner. A hugely and justly popular place with an attractive decor and varied menu, from salads, burgers, pizza, eggplant Parmesan, and pastas to filet mignon ($19.50); homemade breads and desserts. A café atmosphere, casual and pleasant, with a year-round back porch and summer patio dining within earshot of the river.

Elliot's Restaurant (472-6770), Main Street, Hardwick. Dinner Tuesday through Saturday, lunch in summer. The dining room has a tin ceiling and stained-glass lighting fixtures, and there is a small, quiet bar area. The menu features vegetarian entrées as well as hand-cut steaks and homemade soups and desserts. Moderately priced.

Lakeview Inn (533-2291), Main Street, Greensboro. Open daily for breakfast, lunch, and light fare until 4, later in summer. This is a meeting spot for miles around, an expansive, comfortable dining room with a bakery and deli serving soups, chili, salads, and such. Definitely worth checking.

Big Bertha's (465-3032), West Burke Village. Open daily in summer, closed Wednesdays in the off-season, 10:30–8. Regulars call ahead to reserve orders because the BBQ ribs have been known to run out on weekends. Pizza, bread, and rolls are all made on the spot; burgers, salads, subs, and seafood plates are also on the menu.

Richie's (525-4673), Main Street, Barton. Open daily for breakfast, lunch, and dinner. Good pizza, but what's really excellent here are Polish specialties like pirogi stuffed with steamed ground beef and served with fried onions.

Village Restaurant (472-5701), junction of Routes 14 and 15, Hardwick, offers three squares in a basic, clean, comfortable, no-frills, dinerlike place in the center of town.

Miss Lyndonville Diner (626-9890), Route 5 south, Lyndonville. Open from 6 AM until supper, famed for strawberry pancakes with whipped cream for breakfast, pie, homemade French toast, and jumbo eggs.

Danville Restaurant (684-3484), Danville Village. Housed in a village house, open 6 AM–9 PM, this family restaurant is good for all three meals at reasonable prices in a friendly atmosphere. Both counter and table service, from hamburgers to full-course meals, daily specials.

In St. Johnsbury

Cucina de Gerardo (748-6772), 213 Railroad Street. Everyone's favorite place for gourmet pizzas, chicken pesto, and mussels marinara. Far closer to Italy than you might suspect you could come in St. J. Most entrées are in the $8.95–13.95 range.

Northern Lights Bookshop Cafe (748-4463), 79 Railroad Street. Open daily from 9:30 for bagels, croissants, currant scones, sour cream coffee cake, and assorted omelets; at lunch for soups, salads, and sandwiches; until 4 PM for pastries; and until 8:30 Thursday, Friday, and Saturday nights for dinner. Espresso, cappuccino, and teas all day. Begun as a bookstore café, this bright, imaginative space now fills a second storefront. The dinner menu features regional American dishes; beer and wine is served. Inquire about Thursday-evening jazz (see also *Selective Shopping—Bookstores*).

Anthony's Restaurant (748-3613), 50 Railroad Street. Open 6:30 AM–8 PM weekdays, from 7 Sunday. Anthony and Judy Proia have run this cheerful, family-geared diner since 1979, remodeling it several years ago to make it handicapped-accessible and give it a homier feel. Regulars still gather around the counter, and there are booths—but there are also curtains and a bookcase with reading material (including children's books). Breakfast is big: specialty omelets and just abut everything else you can think of, from sausage, gravy, and biscuits with homefries through French toast and pancakes. "Specials" are amazing bargains (our burger with all the fixings and cheese was $2.95), and Anthony takes special pride in the quality of the burgers, and of the homemade fries and soups. "Good food at a fair price" is his motto. Dinner specials, too.

St. Jay Diner (748-9751), Memorial Drive (Route 5 North). Open Sunday through Thursday 7:30 AM–8 PM, Friday and Saturday 7:30 AM–9 PM. Formerly the Miss Vermont Diner, now owned by the owners of Warners Gallery (see below). Known for reliable roadfood.

In Wells River

✎ **Warners Gallery Restaurant** (429-2120), Route 302. Open for dinner nightly and for Sunday brunch. Often crowded for dinner; reserve. Good range of moderately priced entrées like stuffed shrimp and prime ribs. Children's menu. Boasts "best Sunday brunch in the Northeast." All entrées come with the large salad bar (includes peel-and-eat shrimp and sticky buns); on Wednesday, the second dinner is half price. Children under 12 are free on Friday. Fully licensed.

Happy Hours Restaurant (757-3466), Route 5. Open daily 8 AM–9 PM. This solid, pine-paneled family restaurant in the middle of town serves all three meals, fully licensed.

P&H Truck Stop (429-2141), Route 302 just off I-91. Open 24 hours, a genuine trucker's haven with showers and hearty grub. Popular with families as well.

TEA

The Brick House (472-5512), East Hardwick, features 3 acres of perennial gardens, the backdrop for English cream teas, served by English-born and -bred Judith Kane. Aside from a variety of teas and lemonades, the teas include cucumber sandwiches, scones, ham, fresh cream, and pastries.

ENTERTAINMENT

Catamount Film and Arts Company (748-2600), 60 Eastern Avenue, St. Johnsbury. Established in 1975 as a nonprofit cultural organization serving northern Vermont and New Hampshire, Catamount stages a variety of "showcase events" at sites throughout the region, weekend film screenings at the Catamount Arts Center (the former St. Johnsbury post office), and changing shows in its gallery. Summer productions include performances of Circus Smirkus, a summerlong circus workshop for area youths ages 10–18.

Star Theater (748-4900, 748-9511), 18 Eastern Avenue, St. Johnsbury. Cinemas 1-2-3; first-run movies.

Lyndon Corner Grange (748-8829) sponsors dances every Saturday night at the Grange Hall. A three-piece band plays for the over-50 crowd. BYOB; dancing begins at 9 PM. $3 admission; call for reservations.

Summer Music from Greensboro, based at the Congregational church in Greensboro, is a series of chamber and choral music concerts in July and August.

Craftsbury Chamber Players have brought chamber music to northern Vermont for 25 years. The 6-week summer series runs mid-July through August, Thursday evenings, at the Hardwick Town House. There are also shorter, Thursday-afternoon free concerts at the Town House. Most performers are faculty members at the Juilliard School of Music in New York City.

The Vermont Symphony Orchestra plays regularly at Burke Mountain in summer; check local calendars for many other musical performances at Burke.

✐ **Vermont Children's Theater** (626-8838), Darling Hill Road, Lyndonville. Local youngsters perform amazingly well. Performances the last two weekends in July are by thespians ages 8–12 and, in August, ages 13–18.

✐ **Circus Smirkus** (533-7443; 1-800-532-7443) in Greensboro. A children's circus camp stages frequent performances in July and August.

Band concerts. St. Johnsbury Town Band concerts, weekly all summer at the bandstand in Town Hall Park. Monday 8 PM. **Lyndonville Town Band concerts,** every Wednesday in summer at 8 PM in the park. **Craftsbury band concerts** at the band shell on the common, Sundays at 7 in July and August.

In **Greensboro.** Concerts on the dock at Caspian Lake, sponsored by the Greensboro Association, summer Sundays at 7:30.

SELECTIVE SHOPPING

ANTIQUES SHOPS

Farr's Antiques (684-3333), Peacham Road, Danville. Oak tables, chairs, dressers, and other assorted furniture and furnishings fill three floors of a former granary.

Route 5 Collectibles (626-5430), Route 5, Lyndonville. A multi-dealer and consignment shop.

Norman Dion's (754-8770), Irasburg. Ask directions from the general store. It's just a short way out of the village, up a farm road; there's no sign, but you'll see the warehouselike complex on your right before you get to the Castle (you'll know when you do). This is a local institution, a vast collection of trash and treasure, well known to antiques dealers from near and far.

BOOKSTORES

The American Society of Dowsers Bookstore (748-8565; 1-800-711-9497), 99 Railroad Street, St. Johnsbury. This is an amazing store. Everything you ever wanted to know about dowsing and dowsing equipment is here, but also a host of New Age books and tapes on healing, chakras, earth mysteries, the esoteric and metaphysical, reiki, runes, and well-being, not to mention labyrinth T-shirts, crystals, and more.

✐ **Northern Lights Bookshop** (748-4463), 79 Railroad Street, St. Johnsbury. A bright, lively, full-service bookstore that's a real part of St. Johnsbury's cultural life. The stock is unusually extensive, with many Vermont-based writers, a large children's section, also cards, magazines, and children's toys. The popular café (see *Eating Out*) displays work by local artists (see *Galleries*). Inquire about author's readings and music.

The Galaxy Bookshop (472-5533), 7 Mill Street, Hardwick. Since Linda Ramsdell moved her shop into a vintage-1910 bank building, she offers not only ample space for her stock but also probably the only drive-through book and rental audiotape (call ahead) service in the country. Audiotapes? Local farmers listen while driving tractors and doing chores. This is a full-service bookstore specializing in Vermont writers and unusual titles; armchairs invite lingering.

Green Mountain Books & Prints (626-5051), 100 Broad Street, Lyndonville (Route 5 on the corner of the common). Open Monday through Thursday 10–4, Friday 10–6, Saturday 10–1. Ellen Doyle is the second generation of her family to preside over this book-lover's heaven: an unusual mix of new and used books; many new, discounted titles; new and old prints; and rare books. Doyle seems to know something about every book in this 4,000-plus square-foot space. Vermontiana, Native American, and children's books are specialties, but the range is wide and patrons are welcome to sit in a corner for as long as they wish. Bigger than it looks at first: There are separate children's and fiction rooms.

That Book Store (748-1722), 71 Eastern Avenue, St. Johnsbury. Monday through Saturday 10–8, Sunday 11–8 . . ."usually." A big old hardware space is filled with used and antiquarian books, postcards, and "paper ephemera."

Jolly's Books (626-3469), Main Street, Lyndonville. Open daily, Friday till 8 PM, Sunday to 4. Bibliophile John Knudsen has assembled an extraordinarily large and eclectic stock of new—and remaindered—books, most at discount prices.

CHEESE

Cabot Creamery Visitors Center (563-2231), Cabot. Open year-round except January, June through October 9–5 daily, in the off-season Monday through Saturday 9–4. For details, see *To See*.

Kingsey Cheese of Vermont (472-5763), Hardwick Industrial Park, Wolcott Street, Hardwick. Founded in Quebec, this is a rBGH-free milk cheese; check out the retail shop.

Northeast Kingdom Sheep Milk Cheese (533-2360), Akunk Hollow Farm, Greensboro. Visitors are discouraged at the farm itself, but this exceptional cheese is available at the Lake View Inn (see *Lodging*) and other locations in Greensboro.

CRAFTS SHOPS

Northeast Kingdom Artisans Guild (748-0158), 101 Railroad Street, St. Johnsbury. Open Monday through Saturday. This cooperative showcases some magnifcent work in many media.

The Peacham Corner Guild (592-3332), Route 2. Open June through October, daily 10–5, Sunday 11–5. Handcrafted gifts, small antiques.

Birdman (563-2877), Danville Hill Road between Route 2 and Cabot. Open July through October, Monday through Saturday 8–5; November through June by chance or appointment. Edmund Menard produces small, impressively fantailed birds: Christmas ornaments, a bird necklace, earrings, lapel pins, and more.

The Craft Shop at Molly's Pond, on Route 2, west of West Danville. Open June through November, closed Sunday. One of the state's first outstanding crafts shops, here for more than 30 years, specializing in original metal jewelry, fine pottery, weavings, blown glass, and Sabra Field prints. Shopkeeper Martha Price knows all the craftspeople personally.

The Miller's Thumb (533-2960), Greensboro Village. A former gristmill with a spectacular view of the stream churning down falls below, through a window in the floor. Open June through mid-September, a gallery with crafts. A trove of art, crafts, and gift items, many made locally; check out the furniture and clothing upstairs.

Steffi's Studio (754-6012), Irasburg green. Steffi Huess crafts gold and silver jewelry, and sells it along with other local arts and crafts right from the front room in her home.

GALLERIES

Note: St. Johnsbury's most famous art gallery is the St. Johnsbury Athenaeum (see *To See—Museums*), but an unusual quantity and quality of original art is displayed within a short walk along Eastern Avenue and Railroad Street:

Catamount Art Gallery (748-2600), 60 Eastern Avenue, mounts shows representing regional artists. Inquire about special August and December crafts sales.

Windhorse Visual Art Center (751-8303), 56 Eastern Avenue. This trio of octagonal buildings, set back above Eastern Avenue, has recently been developed as Windhorse Commons. The most striking of the buildings dates from 1854 and features a (recent) mural painted on the curved central stairwell, depicting Caledonia County history and landscapes. The gallery at the top of the stairs features changing exhibits.

Wool Away (748-5767), 13 Eastern Avenue. Open Tuesday through Saturday. This is an outstanding knitting-supply shop featuring fiber arts and the paintings, multimedia works, and sketches by Nicholas Piliero.

The St. Johnsbury Art League (748-6233), 71 Railroad Avenue. The restored Merchants National Bank block and its atrium constitute a gallery of architectural history and a fine showcase for changing exhibits, plus a room for the permanent display of paintings by Frank Mason.

The Art Cache (626-5711), East Burke. Marty Martin's long-established gallery in an 1856 schoolhouse exhibits a wide range of art from throughout the country.

Stephen Huneck Gallery (748-5593), RFD 1, St. Johnsbury. Huneck's stylish, carved wooden animals and bold, fanciful furniture, panels, jewelry, and even Christmas-tree ornaments are being widely exhibited and shown in the permanent collections of the Smithsonian and other museums.

See also Northern Lights Bookshop under *Bookstores* (shows change monthly and include crafts as well as traditional media) and Northeast

Kingdom Artisans Guild under *Crafts Shops* (paintings and prints are displayed).

GARDENS

Vermont Daylilies (533-7155), Barr Hill Road, Greensboro. David and Andrea Perham offer some 400 varieties of daylilies; also B&B.

Labour of Love Gardens (525-6695), Route 16, Glover. An acre of public gardens on the Barton River, mid-May until frost, plus antiques and crafts.

Stone's Throw Gardens (586-2805), East Craftsbury, features displays of perennials and roses around a restored 1795 farmhouse; nursery open May 1 through late August, Wednesday through Sunday.

Perennial Pleasures Nursery (472-5512), East Hardwick. Sited at the Brick House (see *Lodging*) and run by Rachel Kane, this unusual nursery specializes in authentic 17th-, 18th-, and 19th-century restoration gardens. There are 3 acres of flowering perennial and herb gardens, grassy walks, and arbors; more than 375 varieties of plants are available. See also *Tea*.

Stillmeadow Farm (755-671), South Albany. In their greenhouses at this handsome dairy farm that's been in the same family since the 1830s, Bruce and Elizabeth Urie now sell a variety of annuals; syrup too.

GENERAL STORES

Danville General Store (684-3691), on the green, includes a collection of local crafts and foods, such as Clover Hill Farm fudge, Julie Kempton's children's clothes, Partridge Lane Woodworks, and Marylyn Magnus's wool rugs. Mail-order catalog.

Hastings Store (684-3398), West Danville. See Danville under *Towns and Villages*.

Bailey's Country Store (626-3666), Route 114, East Burke. Open 6:30 AM–9 PM weekdays, 8–9 Sunday, closes at 8 in winter. This classic old general store has been nicely fancied up by longtime local residents Jeanne and Jerry Bailey. The second-floor gallery has been restored and displays work by local craftsmen. Downstairs are breads, pies, cookies, and coffee cakes baked daily right here; also a gourmet deli featuring cheeses, cold cuts, fresh fruits and vegetables, and basic staples. A selection of wines, coffees, and teas, and a back room full of wicker complete the scene.

Currier's Quality Market (525-8822), Glover. The number of stuffed (formerly live) animals festooned from the rafters and counters is impressive in this old-style emporium.

Craftsbury General Store (586-2811), Craftsbury Village. A genuine, old-style village store under the same ownership for many years; a source of information about the area and a full stock of everything.

Pierce's Store (525-3400), Barton: pharmacy, state liquor store, downstairs a separate fishing and hunting supply store. Vermont gifts and books, sports equipment and clothes, groceries, beer and wine, deli, hunting and fishing licenses.

Ha'Penny Gourmet, the Peacham Store (592-3310), Peacham Village.

Hastings General Store in West Danville

Crafts, collectibles, and specialty foods. Gourmet food to take out. It's the kind of place that grows as it comes into focus, especially if you check out the back rooms and the upstairs gallery.

Bayley-Hazen Country Store (592-3630), South Peacham. An upscale country store with a gallery featuring local artists.

Willey's Store (533-2621), Greensboro Village. One of the biggest and best general stores in the state; an extensive grocery, produce and meat section, hardware, toys, and just about everything else you should have brought for a vacation but forgot.

Lake Parker Country Market (525-6985; 1-800-893-6985), Main Street, West Glover. By Lake Parker. Good for basics plus sandwiches and baked goods.

Northern Exposure Country Store (525-3789), Route 5A at Lake Willoughby. Deli, grinders, fishing and hunting licenses, crafts, Green Mountain coffee.

SPECIAL SHOPS

Moose River Lake and Lodge Store (748-2423), 69 Railroad Street, St. Johnsbury, features an eye-popping collection of antiques, rustic furniture, and accessories for the home, camp, or cabin: taxidermy specialties, antlers and skulls, prints, pack baskets, fishing creels and snowshoes, folk art, and more.

The Old Forge (533-2241) at the Lake View Inn, Greensboro. Open daily, year-round, 10–5; 1–5 on Sunday. Karen Clobber Atwood's long-established outlet for Scottish designer sweaters and other woolens has moved from East Craftsbury to this old village inn (separate entrance; see *Lodging*).

Peter Glenn Ski & Sports (748-3433), 115 Railroad Street, St. Johnsbury. A full four-season sports shops, top quality at good prices.

Caplan's Army Store Work & Sportswear (748-3236), 112 Railroad Street, St. Johnsbury. Established in 1927 as a serious source of quilted jackets, skiwear, Woolrich sweaters, hunting boots, and such; good value and friendly service.

Bag Balm, Route 5, Lyndonville. Developed in 1899 as an antiseptic ointment for cattle, Bag Balm proved particularly effective for chapped udders and is still used by Vermont farmers. In recent years, its campy, old-fashioned green tins began to appear in Madison Avenue pharmacies and ski resort boutiques, at three or four times the price they fetch locally. The factory is an old, red, double-porched building at the southern end of town. Factory tours and sales are discouraged because the company, which turns out some 6,000 tins a day, has only four employees, so visit the Lyndonville Pharmacy, which stocks Bag Balm at realistic prices. The company is owned by John Norris, who inherited the business from his father in 1933.

Evansville Trading Post (754-6305), Route 58 between Orleans and Lake Willoughby. A crafts cooperative for local Abenaki Indian products and special events May through October. A big powwow is usually scheduled for the first weekend in August.

Trout River Brewing Company (626-3984; 1-888-BYO-BREW), Route 114, East Burke. Located in the middle of East Burke Village behind Bailey's Country Store. Open for tours daily 11–6, until 7 Friday and 4 on Sunday. The three signature beers here are a Rainbow Red (medium-bodied), a Caramel Porter (dark), and a Scottish Ale.

SUGARHOUSES

The Sugarmill Farm (525-3701), Route 16 south of Barton Village. The Auger family has turned its former dairy farm into a combination maple museum, working maple operation, dairy parlor, and gift shop selling its own syrup and locally crafted items. Attractions include a tractor-drawn wagon trip through the orchards, a covered bridge, a film on sugaring, a sugarhouse, a fish pond, vintage farm and sugaring tools, and picnic tables. Ben & Jerry's is served year-round; sugar-on-snow in-season.

Rowell Sugarhouse (563-2756), Route 15, Walden. Visitors are welcome year-round. Maple cream and candy as well as sugar; also Vermont honey and sheepskins.

LaPlant's Sugarhouse (467-3900), 3 miles north of West Burke on Route 5, offers horse-drawn sleigh- and hayrides as well as sugarhouse tours.

David and Myra Houston (223-7307), West Hill in Cabot. Here 250–500 taps and buckets are gathered with oxen; up to 10 visitors at a time are welcome during boiling off.

Tamarlane Farm (626-3265), Pudding Hill, Lyndonville. This family farm prides itself on the quality of its syrup.

Goodrich's Sugarhouse (563-9917), just off Route 2 by Molly's Pond in East Cabot. A family tradition for seven generations, open to visitors March through December with a full line of award-winning maple products.

Martin Calderwood (586-2297), South Albany Road, Craftsbury. Here 1,900 taps are gathered with a tractor and sled; arranges sugar parties on request.

Harry F. Sweat (586-2838), Craftsbury, on the road from the common to Craftsbury Center. There are 3,000 taps; arranges sugar parties.

Bruce and Elizabeth Urie (755-6713), at **Stillmeadow Farm,** South Albany, have a sugar shack right on this picturesque back road, across from the old red dairy barn. The farm has been in the Urie family since the 1820s, and the syrup is outstanding and reasonably priced.

Peter and Sandra Gebbie at **Maplehurst Farm** (533-2984), Greensboro, put out 7,000 taps and will arrange sugaring parties; syrup is sold year-round in their friendly kitchen.

Beverly and George Young (533-2964), Greensboro Bend, put out 1,100 taps and will arrange sugar parties.

See also *To See—Other.* Request the *Maple in Caledonia County* pamphlet, available from the Northeast Kindgom Chamber of Commerce (see *Guidance*).

SPECIAL EVENTS

February: **Snowflake Festival Winter Carnival,** Lyndonville-Burke. Events include a crafts show, snow sculpture, ski races for all ages and abilities, sleigh rides, music, and art.

March: **Open sugarhouses.**

May: In East Burke, the **Annual White-Water Canoe Race** on the Passumpsic River, May 1.

June: **Lumberman's Day** at Burke Mountain. In Lyndonville, the **Caledonia Classic Auto Show,** first Sunday in June.

July: **Antiques and Uniques Fair** in Craftsbury Common. **Strawberry Festival Dinner,** second Thursday, at North Congregational Church. **St. J Burklyn Summer Festival of Vermont Arts and Crafts,** Bandstand Park, Lyndonville. **Stars and Stripes Pageant,** Lyndonville, last weekend—big auction, parade featuring Bread and Puppet Uncle Sam, barbecue. **Hardwick Annual Fiddlers' Contest,** also the last weekend.

July and August: **Circus Smirkus** (533-7443), Greensboro. A children's circus camp stages frequent performances.

July through October: **Farmer's Market,** Saturday and Wednesday until noon at the Middle School on Western Avenue, St. Johnsbuy.

August: **Old Home Day,** Craftsbury Common (parade, games, crafts). **Danville Fair, Orleans County Fair** in Barton, old-fashioned event at the extensive fairground. **Old Stone House Day**—open house, picnic lunch, crafts demonstrations at the museum in Brownington Village. **Caledonia County Fair,** Lyndonville; fourth weekend, Thursday through Sunday. **Dowsers National Convention** (684-3410), held at Lyndon State College. Annual **Star Party** at Fairbanks Museum and Planetarium (see *To See—Museums*): a week of special events, St. Johnsbury.

September through October: **Northeast Kingdom Fall Foliage Festival,** the last week in September or first one in October. Eight towns take turns hosting visitors, feeding them breakfast, lunch, and dinner, and guiding them to beauty spots and points of interest within their borders. In Walden, the specialty is Christmas wreath making; in Cabot, there is a tour of the cheese factory; in Plainfield, farm tours; in Peacham, sugar-on-snow parties in the hillside sugarhouse; in Barnet, there's usually a ham dinner at the Barnet Center Church; and in St. Johnsbury, the windup. For details, contact Mrs. Lee Hatch (563-2472).

December: **Burklyn Christmas Crafts Fair,** the first weekend—a major gathering of North Country craftspeople and artists in St. J.

December 31: **First Night Celebrations** (748-4561).

Jay Peak Area

Jay Peak towers like a sentinel above a wide valley in which the state of Vermont and the province of Quebec meet at three border crossings and mingle not only in the waters of Lake Memphremagog but also in general ambience. The sentinel itself has fallen to the French. The face of Vermont's northernmost peak is owned by Mont-Saint-Saveur International, and more than half of the patrons at Jay Peak ski area hail from across the border. Montreal is, after all, less than 2 hours away.

From Jay's base lodge, a 60-passenger aerial tram runs in summer as well as winter to the 3,861-foot summit—which yields one of the most spectacular views in the state: from Lake Champlain on the west, off across Lake Memphremagog to the north, across the Northeast Kingdom to the east, and back down the Green Mountains as far as Camel's Hump to the south.

In winter, storms sweep down from Canada or roll in from Lake Champlain, showering the clutch of mountains around Jay with dependable quantities of snow—a fact more pertinent to cross-country than to downhill skiers in these days of snowmaking. A total of 100 km of trails link the five touring centers in the area. Aside from accommodations at Jay Peak itself, lodging is scattered along Route 242, which climbs steadily 9 miles from Montgomery Center to the ski area, then dips as steeply the 4 miles down to Jay Village (named for John Jay, who never saw it), which is just a crossroads inn, gas station, and general store. This land remains primarily farming and logging country with a special, haunting quality.

In contrast to most ski resort areas, this one does not attract transients. Its innkeepers, restaurateurs, and shopkeepers are a mix of self-sufficient natives and the interesting kind of people who tend to gather in the world's beautiful back-and-behind places.

GUIDANCE

Jay Peak Travel Service (988-2611; outside Vermont: 1-800-451-4449), Jay 05859; in winter arranges train and air tickets and serves as a source of lodging information for the entire area. Open 9–5 weekdays, until 7 on winter Saturdays, until 4 Sunday. In summer this number simply rings at the Hotel Jay front desk (see *Lodging*), but staff are generally helpful about suggesting local inns and B&Bs. Much of this area is also covered by the **Newport Area Chamber of Commerce** (334-7782), the Causeway, Newport 05855.

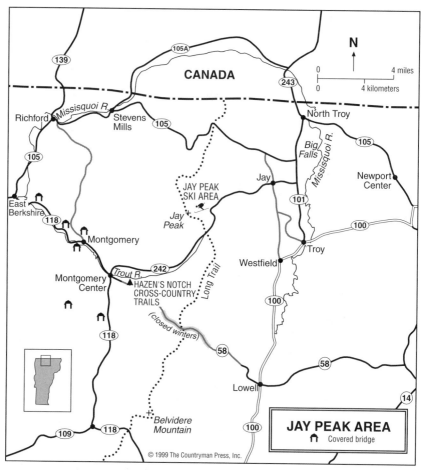

Jay Peak Area Association (988-2259; 1-800-882-7460), Welcome Center, Town Hall, Route 242, Jay 05859.

GETTING THERE

By air: Burlington International Airport, a 1½-hour drive.

By train: **Amtrak** service to St. Albans.

By bus: **Greyhound and Vermont Transit** service to Newport; host lodges will generally pick up.

MEDICAL EMERGENCY

Montgomery (933-4000); **North Country Hospital & Medical Center** (334-7331), Prouty Drive, Newport.

TO SEE

Jay Peak summit. The panorama from this peak is one of the finest in the East. (See the introduction to this section). It's accessible via the Jay Peak Tram (966-2611) at Jay Peak Resort, Route 242, Jay. The 60-passenger tram operates daily during ski season and from the last weekend in June through Labor Day, then in foliage season, 10–5. $8 adults, $5 children, $25 family pass.

Hazen's Notch. From Montgomery Center, an unpromising narrow road, Route 58, climbs steeply east, quickly changing to dirt. In winter, it is open only for the first 4 miles and is a popular ski-touring spot (see *Winter Sports—Cross-Country Skiing*). In summer, it's a beautiful road, dappled with sunlight through the thick foliage. A fine picnic spot has been provided near the height of land, close to a clear roadside spring. A historic site plaque says the road through the high pass was built by Gen. Moses Hazen in 1778–79, commissioned by George Washington himself. The road was begun in 1776, 48 miles to the southeast at Wells River on the Connecticut River, and was intended to reach St. John, Quebec. It was abandoned on this spot in April 1779 when the news that British patrols might use it as an invasion route (it was meant to work the other way) reached the camp at Hazen's Notch.

Montgomery covered bridges. Montgomery boasts a grand total of six Town lattice covered bridges: one right in Montgomery Village over Black Falls Creek; one south on Route 118; another nearby but 3 miles off Route 118 on West Hill on an abandoned side road over a waterfall; another northwest on Route 118 over the Trout River; and two in Montgomery Center, both a mile west of Route 118 over the Trout River (see area map).

Montgomery Village is the most picturesque village in the Jay area. It began as a lumbering center and was for a long time one of the world's major producers of timothy grass seed culture. The **Montgomery Historical Society**'s collection is housed in an 1835 wooden church, open June through September at stated hours; the society also sponsors Saturday-evening concerts on the common in July and August (see *Special Events*).

Big Falls of the Missisquoi, North Troy. The turn south off Route 105 east of North Troy may or may not be marked, but the gravel road is on the state map (and our map). It's a short way in to the pull-off, and the falls themselves can be magnificent; they're good for swimming, water permitting.

St. Benoit du Lac (819-843-4080), Austin, Quebec. Open daily. This noncloistered French Benedictine monastery, founded in 1912, is sited on the west shore of Lake Memphremagog in a fjordlike section. It's a handsome building, and the 50 resident monks welcome visitors for daily Mass at 11 AM and vespers (usually at 5 PM), at which Gregorian chant is sung. The monastery shop sells Gregorian music records, also hard cider, cheese, vestments, and religious articles. The easiest route from Newport is via the North Troy border crossing, then through Mansonville, South Bolton, and Austin.

TO DO

BICYCLE TOURING

In his classic 25 *Bicycle Tours in Vermont*, John Freidin describes a varying 22.6- or 33.7-mile ride that, according to Rita Kalsmith, is this cycling guru's favorite in all Vermont. It begins at the Black Lantern (see *Lodging—Inns*) in Montgomery Village, passes two covered bridges along Route 118 north, and takes you to East Berkshire; you can simply continue to Enosburg Falls, where Lake Carmi offers camping and swimming, turn onto the Richford Road, and loop back to Montgomery or loop up into Canada. The new Western Vermont Rail Trail to St. Albans is also a possibility. The terrain is right and the roads are little trafficked.

CANOEING

The 86-mile-long Missisquoi River makes a complete loop around Jay, passes briefly through Quebec, and continues across Vermont to empty into Lake Champlain. The upper half of the river near Jay offers spring fast water, and the lower reaches are gentle and broad, good spring and summer ground for beginners and those who enjoy traversing outstanding rural landscape. For canoes and boat rentals, contact the Missisquoi Riverbend B&B (744-9991), Route 100, Troy.

FISHING

The Trout River deserves its name. Brook trout can also be found in the Missisquoi, and Lake Memphremagog harbors smallmouth bass and salmon, among other species. See "Newport and the North Country" for boat rentals in Newport. See *To Do—Canoeing* for boat rentals.

HIKING

The Long Trail terminates its 262-mile route at the Canadian border, 10 miles north of Jay Peak, but the trek up Jay itself is what most hikers look for here. The most popular ascent is from Route 242, 1.2 miles east of the entrance to the ski area; the round-trip hike takes 3 hours. For details on this and the section of the trail between Hazen's Notch and Route 242, also for the final, fairly flat leg to the border, see the *Long Trail Guide*, published by the Green Mountain Club, which maintains the trail and four shelters in this area.

MOUNTAIN BIKING

The Jay Peak Ski and Summer Resort (988-2611; 1-800-451-4449) maintains a network of trails for experienced mountain bikers via its aerial tramway, which will transport them and their bikes to the 3,861-foot summit from which several routes descend: 20 miles of alpine and 15 miles of cross-country.

SWIMMING

A number of inns have their own pools. The most popular local swimming hole is at **Jay Four Corners,** downstream from the Route 101 bridge.

Jay Swim and Racquetball Club (988-2880). Day membership is available for the pool and courts.

TENNIS

🖉 **Jay Peak Resort** (988-2611) maintains tennis courts in warm-weather months.

WALKING

Hazen's Notch Association and Outdoor Education Center (326-4789), Route 58, Montgomery Center. Sharon and Rolf Anderson, who directed Vermont Voyageur Expeditions for 10 years, have reorganized their programs, offering nature and ecology day camps for children 6–9, Adventure Day and Overnight Camps for ages 10–12, and Voyageur Camp/Wilderness trips for ages 13–16. They also supervise the self-guided use of 10 miles of trails over 100 acres of privately owned lands for hiking and nature study in spring, summer, and fall; for showshoeing and cross-country skiing in winter. Park and walk 15 minutes to Bear Paw Pond. Inquire about frequent nature walks, fly-fishing workshops, and other special events.

Jay Peak Resort (988-2611) publishes a self-guiding nature walk from the top of the tram.

WINTER SPORTS

CROSS-COUNTRY SKIING

Hazen's Notch Cross-Country Ski Center (326-4708), Route 58, Montgomery Center. This outstanding touring center offers 30 km of meticulously tracked trails, some with fine views of Jay and the Cold Hollow Mountains. A total of 45 km of marked trails connect the network with the Catamount Trail. In business since 1978, when Val Schadinger and Rolf Anderson first laid out the trails, Hazen's Notch's rustic, non-commercial atmosphere has attracted a loyal following. Early and late in the season, this tends to be one of a half-dozen cross-country networks in New England that have snow (elevation: 1,000–1,670 feet). *Note:* B&B rooms are also offered.

Jay Peak Resort (988-2611) maintains 20 km of trails.

DOWNHILL SKIING

🖉 **Jay Peak** (information and reservations: 988-2611; 1-800-451-4449 including Canada; snow conditions: 988-9601; an unusually extensive web site with reservation capacity: www.jaypeakresort.com). The original trails are Stateside, on a shoulder of Jay Peak. Still considered some of the toughest runs in Vermont, they were carved 30 years ago by local residents. An enterprising Kiwanis group (it included the parish priest) convinced the Vermont legislature to reroute existing roads up over the high ridge from which Jay's access road arises, thus linking it to northwestern Vermont as well as to the Northeast Kingdom. They also imported an Austrian skimeister to create a true trail system and ski school. Some

Jay Peak

30,000 acres on and around Jay Peak were owned by Weyerhaeuser Corporation, and in the early '60s the mammoth lumber company—based in Tacoma, Washington—acquired the ski area. It installed a Swiss-built tramway to Jay's Peak, which it topped with a Sky Haus tram station, a building that emphasizes the crest of the summit and gives it a distinctly Matterhorn-like cap. Weyerhaeuser also built a large, sturdy, Tyrolean-style base complex that includes a 48-room hotel, and it laid out a winding access road to be lined with chalets.

And there it sat: a major mountain offering outstanding lifts, trails, one of New England's largest vertical drops (2,153 feet), and frequently the highest snowfall of any new England ski area. Since 1978 it has been owned by the Montreal-based owners of Saint-Saveur, a lucrative Laurentian ski area. The rebirth of Jay as a destination rather than a Montreal day-tripping place is relatively recent. But under a dynamic operations manager, lifts have been improved and condominiums have been proliferating. This is a great place for bargain-priced lodging and for spring skiing, but beware weekends, when it's mobbed by Montrealers.

Lifts: 60-passenger tram; one quad chair, one triple, two double, two T-bars. A new high-speed detachable quad is scheduled for winter 1999–2000, to augment service on trails served by the tram.

Trails and slopes: 64 trails, glades, and chutes totaling more than 50 miles of skiing, spread over two peaks, connected by a ridgeline.

Off-piste skiing: 150 acres.

Vertical drop: 2,153 feet.

Snowboarding: Permanent halfpipe course; Jay is now Burton Board demo center; rentals, instruction for beginners.

Snowmaking: 80 percent.

Snowshoeing: Weekly snowshoeing walks led by a naturalist.

Facilities: Austria Haus and Tram Haus base lodges with cafeteria, pub, and ski and rental shop. Sky Haus cafeteria at summit, nursery and daycare facilities. Full line of rentals, telemark rentals, and instruction available. A lighted skating rink and skate rentals. Van service is offered from Burlington Airport (80 miles away) and from the Amtrak station in St. Albans (a 45-minute drive).

Ski school: U.S. and Canadian certified instructors, adult and junior racing clinics.

For children: SKIwee program for both skiing and snowboarding 5- to 12-year-old group, kinderschool for ages 2–5. Daycare for children ages 2–7.

Rates: $44 per adult, $32 junior, $30 Vermonter. Two-day, half-day, and ski-week rates.

SLEIGH RIDES

Rose Apple Acres Farm (988-4300) *see Bed & Breakfasts.*

SNOWMOBILING

The area is webbed with Vermont Association of Snow Travelers (VAST) trails; check with the local inns.

TRACKING

Offered at **Hazen's Notch Association** (326-4789), Route 58, Montgomery Center (see *Walking*).

LODGING

On-mountain

Hotel Jay (1-800-451-4449), Route 242, Jay 05859. Located right at the lifts, an attractive lodge with 48 rooms, each with color TV and private bath; a pleasant public dining room, a game room, family room, sauna, Jacuzzi, outdoor pool (summer only). Rates are reasonable, especially in the off-season. In winter, a 2-day package including lift, lodging, two breakfasts, and one dinner can be had for $227 per person (except over the holidays).

Jay Peak Condominiums (from Vermont: 988-2611; from out of state: 1-800-451-4449). A total of 104 rental units, most of which you can ski directly to and from, constructed in clusters: studios and two- and three-bedroom units accommodate from 4 to 10 people; all have fireplace, living room, and fully equipped kitchen. The Village Townhouses accommodate up to six people and are unusually luxurious. From $50 per person in the off-season and from $199 including lifts for 2 nights during ski season.

INNS

Black Lantern Inn (326-4507; 1-800-255-8661), Montgomery 05470. A white-pillared, brick inn built in 1803 as the Montgomery Village stage stop. Ten guest rooms are small but nicely furnished with wicker and antiques, and all have private bath; there is a three-bedroom with a fireplace. Four more suites with fireplace and whirlpool bath in the neighboring Burdett House are not only luxurious but also truly comfortable (our fireplace drew beautifully and the rooms were thoughtfully furnished: hooked rugs, a few antiques, a TV—everything but a phone). The inn itself also offers a small reading-talking area, warmed by a soapstone stove; a cozy taproom; and a charming, seven-table dining room. Innkeepers Rita and Allan Kalsmith set an elegant table. This is not a place for children. Beyond the porch is this special village to explore, and from the back there is a view of Hazen's Notch (see *To See*). $60–85 per room, $85–145 per suite B&B; less in the off-season. EP and MAP rates also offered.

✍ **Inglenook Lodge** (988-2880; 1-800-331-4346), Route 242, Jay 05859. This classic ski lodge on the lower eastern slope of Jay Peak offers a great view. It has 10 large rooms and 8 smaller, a sunken lounge with circular fireplace, indoor swimming pool, Jacuzzi, and sauna. Dining by candlelight. From $69 per couple B&B, $138 MAP. Owner Janice Kruse also manages: Trillium Woods at Jay on Route 242 between the village and the mountain. These are town houses holding eight, with Jacuzzi, fireplace, sauna, $350 per night in ski season, available by the week and month in summer.

Jay Village Inn (988-2306; 1-800-565-5641), Jay Village 05859. There's a real warmth to this cozy lodge in the middle of Jay Village. The public rooms include a lounge, with fireplace and a player piano, and an outside hot tub. The dining room is attractive, and the menu reflects the owners' Italian accent (see Dining Out). The 15 rooms upstairs have all been attractively refurbished and furnished; each has a private bath. $55–69 per room B&B.

The Inn on Trout River (326-4391; 1-800-338-7049), Montgomery Center 05471. Built grandly by a lumber baron, this attractive village house offers 10 guest rooms with private bath, and one suite with a brass bed and woodstove. There are also hearths in the dining room, library, and foyer. The innkeepers are Michael and Lee Forman. The convivial Hobo Cafe and more formal Lemoine's Restaurant are open to the public (see *Dining Out*). $43–56 per person B&B.

BED & BREAKFASTS

Rose Apple Acres Farm (988-4300; fax: 988-2309), East Hill Road, North Troy 05859. There are three guest rooms, one with private bath, in the Meads' comfortable house with its own 52 acres, good for cross-country skiing. Located 10 miles from Jay Peak, near a covered bridge on the Missisquoi River; good for fishing. Sleigh rides by reservation. Camilla's porcelain doll studio (see *Selective Shopping*), blacksmith shop, Morgan horse breeding and sales. $25–35 per person includes breakfast.

✎ **Woodshed Lodge** (988-4444; 1-800-495-4445), Route 242, Jay 05459. Just 3 miles from Jay Peak, this landmark old lodge is maintained by John and Chris Engler, who cater to families. Three of the seven rooms have private bath, four share two baths. There's a sitting room upstairs and a library–TV lounge downstairs. $34–38 per person includes breakfast; there are 5-day and weekend specials; 20 percent discount for children 10 and under. Dinner by arrangement.

Hazen's Notch B&B and Cross-Country Ski and Hiking Center (326-4708), Route 58, Montgomery Center 05471. The B&B is an old farmhouse, restored and greatly improved, offering three newly decorated bedrooms and baths; a living room has wood-burning stove. Cross-country trails radiate from the doorstep; under the same ownership as the adjacent touring center. $50–60 per room, continental breakfast included.

Phineas Swann B&B (326-4306), Main Street, Montgomery Center 05471. Michael Bindler and Glen Bartolomeo are the hosts in this bright gingerbread Victorian with seven guest rooms, each decorated with period antiques and Laura Ashley patterns, equipped with TV and VCR. $69–89 per room, including full breakfast (like raspberry French toast) and afternoon tea. There are also three suites with sitting room, fireplace, and Jacuzzi in the Carriage House: $145 for two bedrooms, $125 for one bedroom. Add 13 percent gratuity in suites.

WHERE TO EAT

DINING OUT

Zack's on the Rocks (326-4500), Montgomery Center. Dinner by reservation for two nightly sittings (at 6 and 9), except Mondays, the month of November, and mud season. There is more than a touch of fantasy and dash of performance art to this place. Zack (he was born Zachadnykjon in Blackstone, Massachusetts) frequently greets guests in purple garb. "I'm a frustrated actor," says Zack, who built this aerie 38-some years ago ("I must be doing something right"), using "all the things I like—marble, rocks." The predominant color is purple in many shades, and it extends to the soapstone stove. Decorations mirror the season. Zack dislikes the word "gourmet," but the fact is that patrons come back often because the food is superb. The night's surprisingly large menu, hand-written on a paper bag, might include such entrées as chicken banana and roast duckling with fruit sauce. We can vouch for the veal Oscar served with lobster tail. Just beware the three kinds of bread and chocolate butter that are served the moment you sit down. Entrées $19–21.

Black Lantern Inn (326-4507), Montgomery Village. Dinner is served nightly in-season. The low-beamed dining room of this old inn is the setting for candlelight dinners that might feature filet mignon with mushrooms and onions, roast duck with berry and curry sauces, mustard-crusted rack of lamb, and walnut-crusted sole. Entrées $11–20. Full dinners for $15 Thursdays (in winter only).

Lemoine's at the Inn on Trout River (326-4391), Main Street, Montgomery Center. The lacy dining room in this handsome old house is the setting for heart-healthy meals featuring entrées like turkey tenderloin with celery sauce ($11.95) and grilled leg of lamb with pesto and sundried tomatoes ($15.95). Full dinners run $20.50–24.25.

Jay Village Inn and Restaurant (988-2643), Jay Village. A large, friendly dining room specializing in Italian dishes and prime rib. Entrées $8–15.95.

Hotel Jay (988-2611) at Jay Peak. Dinner is served 6–9, and reservations are a must in winter. In summer, dinner is served only Friday through Sunday. The room itself is cheery, and the menu features dishes like veal Gruyère and fillet of salmon Florentine; entrées include escargots dijonnaise and coquilles Saint-Jacques. Sunday brunch, a specialty (fall and summer only), is big here. Moderate.

✒ **North Troy Village Restaurant** (988-4063), Main Street, North Troy. Open at 5 PM daily except Tuesday. Irene McDermott has earned an admiring clientele for this nicely outfitted dining establishment in an exceptional old town house with two-story front porch. The menu is extensive, featuring seafood, a prime-rib special at $15.95, and rack of lamb for two at $28.95. There's a kids menu and "mini-meals," like a 5-ounce tournedo (why don't others do this?). Inexpensive to moderate.

EATING OUT

The Belfry (326-4400), Route 242, Montgomery Center. Open nightly 4 PM until late. A pleasant pub in an old schoolhouse with friendly wooden booths that patrons usually settle into for an hour or two. The soup is homemade, and there is a blackboard menu with daily specials like pan-blackened fish and grilled lamb chops, in addition to sliced London broil and BBQ chicken, salads, burgers, and fried mushrooms. Inquire about weekly music.

J. R.'s Café (326-4682), Main Street, Montgomery Center. Open 6:30 AM–10 PM, later on weekends. Bigger than it looks from its greenhouse-style front. A genuine gathering spot for the area, with cheerful wallpaper and wainscoting. Breakfast options include bagels, smoked salmon, and eggs any style. Soups are a luncheon specialty, and at dinner the menu ranges from sautéed scampi through pastas, to J. R.'s Texas rib platter. Beer and wine are served.

Hobo Cafe at the Inn at Trout River (326-4391). A pub atmosphere and menu, reasonably priced dinners like BBQ ribs and chicken.

Kilgore's General Store, Main Street, Montgomery Center. Open daily except Monday, 7 AM–6 PM. Steve and Karen Houghtaling operate this picturesque old store with an upstairs gallery and an old-style soda fountain, serving sandwiches and light fare.

Jay Country Store (988-4040). Open daily. The sandwiches at the counter are the best in the village, reflecting the quality of the store's deli.

Buon Amici (988-2299), North Troy. Open for dinner. Good Italian fare.

Junction 101 (744-2770), junction of Routes 100 and 101, Troy. Formerly Nutsy's Nest, this roadside eatery serves three perfectly fine meals.

SELECTIVE SHOPPING

Jay Country Store (988-4040), Jay Village. Open daily. Art and Peggy Moran's store forms the center of Jay Village, selling papers, gas, food and wine basics, also a deli (see *Eating Out*), plus an interesting assortment of gift items (we bought a stunning Vermont-designed Peruvian wool ski cap here), cards, books and an art gallery that has been growing over the years, featuring limited-edition prints by Will Moses (grandson of Grandma Moses), varied landscapes.

Kilgore's General Store (326-4681), Main Street, Montgomery Center. A fine old store with an interior balcony, nicely restored with a classic soda fountain and cases stocked with munchies (ideal for hikers and bikers). The store also sells crafts and natural-fiber clothing.

Vermont Voyageur Equipment (326-4789), Route 242, Montgomery Center. A quality line of shell parkas, pants, overmitts, and overboots is made in the VVE shop, sold primarily by commission and mail order but also available on the spot. This cross-country skier wouldn't be without the mitts and boots, which are waterproof and effective. A mosquito-proof, light net jacket is popular with summer hikers and bikers. VVE also makes flags.

Couture's Maple Shop (744-733; 1-800-845-2733), Route 100, Westfield. A long established maple producer: maple candy, cream, granulated sugar, pancake mix, and salad dressing, as well as syrup; will ship anywhere.

The Tickle Trunk (988-4731), Crossroads, Jay, is full of clocks, books, Victorian and country antiques, vintage clothing, and work by local artists and artisans.

Rose Apple Acres Dolls (988-4300), East Hill Road, North Troy. Modern porcelain figures (the idea is to make dolls resembling a particular child), plus sculpture and doll-making classes and supplies.

Montgomery Schoolhouse, Montgomery Village. A green box of a building that stands on the triangular green. The schoolhouse is open to the public; toys can be found in the ground-floor shop (Monday through Friday 8–4:30).

SPECIAL EVENTS

January: **Hazen's Notch Ski Race,** last Sunday.

Mid-February: **Winter Festival**—varied events including a race from the summit of Jay Peak to Jay Village.

July and August: **Concerts on the common,** presented by the Montgomery Historical Society on Saturday evening (326-4404), and during September in the Montgomery Village church.

Mid-August: **Jay Day.**

October: **Octoberfest,** Jay Peak—art show, special events.

Newport and the North Country

The Northeast Kingdom is blessed with some of the most beautiful lakes in Vermont. The largest of these is Memphremagog, stretching more than 30 miles from Newport, Vermont, to Magog, Quebec.

In the heyday of railroad passenger service, large wooden hotels sprang up near the shores of these lakes. In Newport, the 400-room Memphremagog House stood next to the railroad station, Newport House was across the street where the Chittenden Bank now stands, and the New City Hotel also stood nearby. Guests came by train from Boston and Philadelphia. Lindbergh came with his *Spirit of Saint Louis,* and there was a racetrack and a paddle wheeler. While the city only suggests the splendor captured in its Victorian-era photos, the brick library, courthouse, and state building remain and the new Waterfront Gateway is a downtown window on the water.

From Prospect Hill, where the spires of St. Mary, Star of the Sea, tower above everything, Newport slopes to the lake, which actually seems to surround it, as the downtown area separates the lake proper from South Bay. The shoreline offers access points for sailing, canoeing, fishing, and swimming.

Memphremagog (with the stress on the third syllable) has a split personality. The two-thirds of the lake north of the Canadian border is not only French-speaking (although there are English pockets like Georgeville) but also more of a resort area. Montreal is just an hour's drive from the French-speaking resort town of Magog, and Sherbrooke, a Canadian metropolis of 100,000, is much nearer; in stark contrast is the American end of the lake, which is the end of the road (I-91) from New York and Boston. It remains a delightful refuge for frugal flatlanders, especially those who like to fish, hike, observe wildlife, or generally steep themselves in the beauty of this high, rolling—still pastoral—countryside.

Less than a dozen miles northeast of Newport is the split-nationality community of Derby Line, Vermont–Rock Island, Province of Quebec. This is a major border crossing (I-91 continues north as highway #55), linking with the major east–west highway between Montreal and Quebec City. The international line runs right through the Haskell

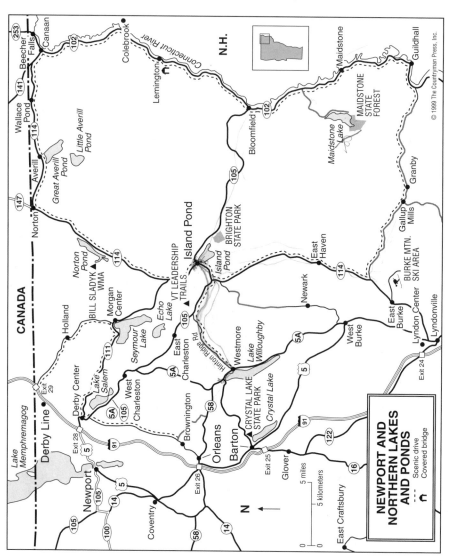

1 day

Opera House in Derby Line, with the audience in America attending concerts in Quebec.

West of Derby Center you are quickly in little-trafficked lake country: Lakes Derby and Salem, Seymour and Echo are all favored by fishermen, and there are dozens more, all with boat launches.

Island Pond is a town as well as a lake. A sign in front of the city-sized Island Pond depot reads, "Pioneer railroad planner John A. Poor's dream of an international railroad connecting Montreal, Canada, with the ice-free harbor of Portland, Maine, became a reality on July 18, 1854, when the first through trains met at this great halfway point on the Grand Trunk Railway." During the late 19th century and into the early 20th, Island Pond hummed with the business of servicing frequent passenger trains and freight trains transporting logs and wood pulp. It was also a booming manufacturing center. No longer, though. Today it is a sleepy village on a 2-mile-by-1-mile-long pond with a 20-acre island in its center.

For the traveler, Island Pond still looms large on the map, because you must pass through it to get to the empty (of people but teeming with moose, black bears, and other wildlife), lake-pocked land to the northeast. There's good fishing around Averill and the hauntingly lonely stretch of the Connecticut River between Guildhall and Canaan. Because this area is so sparsely populated, we have sketched our impressions of it by describing what lies along the area's back roads and byways (see *Scenic Drives*).

GUIDANCE

Vermont North Country Chamber of Commerce (334-7782; 1-800-635-4643; www.travelthekingdom.com), the Causeway, Newport 05855, serves most of this area.

Island Pond Chamber of Commerce (741-7301), Box 255, Island Pond 05846, maintains a seasonal information center in the Railroad Depot, which is also the seasonal office for the Northeast Kingdom Travel and Tourism Association (1-888-884-8001). Off-season and in winter, information services are based at the Lakefront Inn Motel and Marina (see *Lodging*).

North Country Chamber of Commerce (603-237-8939), Colebrook, New Hampshire 03476, also serves the upper reaches of the Connecticut Valley, including the Canaan, Vermont, area.

Magog Bureau du Tourisme (819-843-2744), 1032 Principale Ouest, Magog, Quebec J1X 2B6, Canada, serves the French-speaking shoreline. It's a good source of advice on area restaurants.

GETTING THERE

By bus: Newport is the northern terminus of **Vermont Transit**'s White River Junction route, with connections to Boston.

By car: Really the only way to get around. Note the link with I-93 that hooks up Newport and Derby Line directly with Boston, which you can reach within 4 hours.

MEDICAL EMERGENCY

911 service: for fire, police, and ambulance in Derby, Derby Line, East Charleston, Holland, Irasburg, Island Pond, Morgan, Newport, Newport Center, West Charleston. In Jay, Lowell, North Troy, Orleans: 988-4315. **Country Hospital & Health Center** (334-7331; emergency: 334-7900), Newport.

TO SEE

Jay Peak summit. Accessible by Vermont's only aerial Tramway, yields a spectacular overview of this region (see "Jay Peak Area").

Derby Line. As noted in the introduction to this section, the town straddles the Canadian border. The Haskell Free Library and Opera House on Caswell Avenue, a yellow-brick, neoclassical structure with a handsome library downstairs, has an upstairs opera house in which audiences sit in the United States, watching a stage in Canada. Walk in the front door in the United States and out the back in Canada (see *Entertainment*).

Newport. A city of 5,500 people, a former logging and rail center that is enjoying a renaissance. Main Street is a bustling shopping center, graced by some substantial gift and clothing stores as well as the 19th-century Goodrich Memorial Library (334-8902), with its historical collections, and a matching redbrick Orleans County Courthouse and State Building. See also the introduction to this chapter.

Cow Town Elk Ranch (766-5068), Derby Center, intersection of Routes 5 and 105. Visitors welcome anytime. Derby once had so many dairies that it was known as Cow Town, but Doug Nelson's is now the only big dairy operation left (1,000 head), and he also raises elk (the herd numbered 130 with 40 calves due when we last checked). There's parking and a sign answering the 10 most frequently asked questions. Nelson harvests the velvet for the Asian trade in June, so you might want to come before, when the antlers are at their most majestic. Spring is also calving time. Please don't feed the elk, and be cautious: They're friendly, but they're still wild animals.

LAKES

Lake Memphremagog, Vermont's second largest lake, 32 miles long, only 5 miles of which are within the United States. Memphremagog stretches north from Newport. See St. Benoit du Lac (see *To See* in "Jay Peak Area") and listings under *To Do* for *Boating, Fishing,* and *Swimming.*

Seymour Lake. There is a public beach in the tiny village of Morgan Center, also the spot to rent boats for fishing for landlocked salmon. In winter, this lake is peppered with fishing shanties, and there is an untracked system of cross-country trails.

Echo Lake. Much smaller than Seymour Lake and adjoining it on the south, this lake is circled by a dirt road and gently rolling hills. There is also public boat access good for trout and landlocked salmon.

Island Pond is actually a small lake with a 20-acre island off the sandy beach and a wooded campground in Brighton State Park (see *Green Space*). Boating and fishing are both easily accessible. See also *Boat Excursion* under *To Do*.

SCENIC DRIVES

Hinman Settler Road from Derby Center to Brownington (mostly unpaved but good gravel). It's better to start from Derby, as there are confusing forks from the other direction. The route terminates in Brownington Village's historic district, from which a paved road leads to Orleans and I-91. To find this route, head south on Main Street, Derby Center (Route 105). Where Route 105 curves sharply to the east at the lower end of the village, go straight to Brownington. You are rewarded by rolling hills, fields, and sweeping vistas.

Holland-Morgan Loop. Take the paved road east from I-91, Derby Line exit. After several miles, the road makes an S-curve through tiny Holland Village and continues to Seymour Lake in Morgan. Here, take Route 111 to Derby Center.

Island Pond shortcut to Lake Willoughby. Easy from Westmore on Lake Willoughby: Turn north in the middle of the village on Hinton Ridge Road and follow it through high, rolling farmland and forest (never mind name changes) until it reaches a T-intersection. Turn right and right again onto Route 105 into Island Pond. The reverse direction is even more beautiful but tricky at the beginning (left onto Hudson Road off Route 105 and then your second left onto Westmore Road).

Route 114 north from Island Pond. The Canadian National Railway's Grand Trunk line from Montreal to Portland, Maine, hugs the highway all the way to Norton. This railway was once Montreal's winter lifeline to Europe, as goods could not be shipped in or out of the frozen port of Montreal during the coldest months. The 16 miles between Island Pond and the border town of Norton is a lonely wilderness, much of the land owned by lumber and paper companies. About halfway to Norton, near the south end of long and slender Norton Pond (there's a boat launch on Route 114), a gravel road to the left leads into the Bill Sladyk Wildlife Management Area (see *Hiking*), a vast, undeveloped wilderness frequented by hunters, fishermen, and loggers. Just before reaching the tiny village of Norton (opposite slightly larger Stanhope, Quebec), the forest thins out and farmland reappears. Norton is the site of the notorious Earth People's Park, a 1960s-style, loosely governed hippie commune that has survived but has dwindled from hundreds to perhaps two dozen residents. The road passes several farms, a school, and two stores, then swings abruptly eastward to avoid the imposing Canadian port-of-entry. Perhaps the most French-Canadian town in Vermont, Norton is for practical purposes a satellite of nearby Coaticook, Quebec. Continuing eastward along the border, Route 114 reenters the forest, passing a series of lakes, most of which are dotted with hunting and fishing camps. The largest of the lakes is Big Averill, which you can see by pulling off the road at Averill Village (as directions to the boat launch).

Shortly after passing Big Averill, you leave the St. Lawrence watershed and begin a rapid descent into the Connecticut River Valley. Halfway from Averill to Canaan, the road skirts the south shore of sizable Wallace Pond, almost entirely within the province of Quebec.

Canaan, 14 miles east of Norton, is a pleasant pocket of civilization along the upper reaches of the Connecticut River. There are two villages. The first is Canaan itself, a village with a tiny green and a lovely little Greek Revival building that houses the Alice M. Ward Memorial Library (266-7135), a former station on the Underground Railroad, displaying a collection of antique lumbering tools.

A left at the junction of Routes 114 and 102 will take you a couple of miles north to Beecher Falls, another port-of-entry and a factory village, dominated by a huge Ethan Allen Furniture plant, the company's original factory site (to arrange a tour, call 266-3355). Occasionally in winter, you'll hear Canaan mentioned on your weather report as the coldest spot in the United States for the day. (There is an official U.S. weather observation station here.) Both villages hug the nascent Connecticut River, which originates not far to the northeast in extreme northern New Hampshire.

From Canaan, you can choose to drive southward on the more scenic Vermont side or via the faster New Hampshire side of the river. On the Vermont side (Route 102), you travel through river-bottom farmland, reaching the bridge to Colebrook, New Hampshire, in just under 10 miles.

Colebrook is the only big town on this northernmost end of the river. On the Vermont side, Route 102 continues south through Lemington, past the impressively long Columbia covered bridge, to the tiny village of Bloomfield. Along the way, the river valley alternately narrows and widens, and the road tunnels through forest, broken occasionally by farms, fields, and glimpses of impressive mountains. You pass the small town halls of Lemington, Brunswick, and Maidstone, but several of the townships, gores, and grants are unorganized and have to be governed from Montpelier. At Bloomfield (consisting of one store, with adjoining snack bar), the Grand Trunk railroad line to Portland crosses the road, bound for North Stratford, New Hampshire, on the other side of the river. Here in January 1933, the lowest recorded Vermont temperature (–50 degrees F) was measured.

Continuing south another 16 miles to Guildhall, Route 102 winds among the bluffs and oxbows of the ever-widening river. Glimpses of the White Mountains are more frequent. The town of Brunswick was once the site of a thriving mineral spring resort. The buildings are all gone, but the springs still run pure. Nearly halfway to Guildhall, a gravel road to the right leads to beautiful and isolated Maidstone State Park.

Entering Guildhall, you are informed by a billboard-sized sign that the town was "discovered" in 1754, chartered in 1761, and settled in 1764, making it the oldest town in northeastern Vermont (by contrast, Norton was not settled until 1860). You are further informed that the town has been the seat of Essex County since 1809. An attractive, square green is flanked by a host of historically interesting buildings: a tiny courthouse, church, town hall (the Guild Hall, 1798), and an ornate 1909 Classical Revival library with stained-glass windows. An unassuming white-clapboard house serves as a county lockup. There is also an attractive inn (see *Lodging*).

Two miles downriver from Guildhall, a town road marked GRANBY runs west off Route 102, beginning as a paved road but becoming gravel well before reaching the tiny hamlets of Granby and Gallup Mills, about 8 miles from Route 102. This is wild, wooded, and boggy country, good for spotting moose and bear. Lumber camps and sawmills once peppered this area, and there was even a steam railway.

The road finally descends about 8 miles west of Granby to reach Route 114, joining it a couple of miles north of East Burke (see "St. Johnsbury, Craftsbury, and Burke Mountain Area"). Take Route 114 some 12 miles north through rolling, mixed farm- and forestland to its junction with Route 105, 2 miles west of Island Pond.

Note: Pick up a copy of *A Day in the Kingdom* cultural heritage tour map published by the Northeast Kingdom Travel and Tourism Association (1-888-884-8001); inquire about the audio tour.

TO DO

BOATING

Aluminum boats (14 feet) with small motors, also pontoons and sailboats, may be rented at **Newport Marine** (334-5911) at Eastside Restaurant Docks, Farrants Point, on Lake Memphremagog in Newport. Rental boats are also available from **Trade Winds Country Store** (895-2975) on Seymour Lake. **Lakefront Inn Motel and Marina** (see *Lodging*) in Island Pond rents both canoes and motorboats and offers sculling lessons and expeditions. Boats are also available at both Brighton and Maidstone State Parks (see *Green Space*).

BOAT EXCURSION

Newport's Princess (334-6617), 225 Sias Avenue at Newport City Dock, Newport. This paddle-wheel riverboat offers daily cruises from mid-May to late October. There are three 1½-hour daily sight-seeing cruises ($9.25); 2-hour Saturday and Sunday brunch cruises at 10 AM ($15.95); Friday and Saturday buffet dinner trips ($22.95); and moonlight cruises at 10 PM Friday and Saturday ($10.25). In peak summer and foliage times, reservations are strongly recommended. Family, senior, and children's rates.

Newport lakefront

Lady of the Lake (723-6649), 1 mile east of town on Route 105, offers 1-hour narrated tours of Island Pond. $6 per adult, $3 per child.

CANOEING

Vermont Leadership Center (723-6011), Ten Mile Square Road, East Charleston (5 miles west of Island Pond), offers rental canoes on the Clyde River. On the Connecticut River, Canaan is a good place to put in, but there are several rapids at the start. Canoeing is also good below Colebrook, New Hampshire, for 3 miles but then rather fast for an equal distance. (See *Fishing*, below.)

FISHING

Quimby Country (see *Lodging*), a self-contained resort that includes 70-acre Forest Lake, is ¼ mile from 1,200-acre Big Averill, both lonely and remote but good for trout and salmon; rowboats can be rented here by the day.

Seymour Lake Lodge (see *Lodging*). David Benware, with more than 30 years of fly-fishing experience, offers day and half-day guidance, transportation, handcrafted flies, and instruction: $95–225.

See also the Vermont Leadership Center under *Canoeing;* for the Upper Connecticut, contact **Osprey Fishing Adventures** (603-922-3800). Ken Hastings of Columbia, New Hampshire, is the fishing guru for this stretch of the river. Check the state highway map for local access points to ponds. The Connecticut Lakes in adjacent northern New Hampshire offer world-class trout fishing. There are also landlocked salmon and brown, brook, lake, and rainbow trout in dozens of ponds with boat access, as well as in the lakes we describe here. There is a **state fish hatchery in Newark**; Newark Pond has an access and is good for yellow perch along with trout. Rental boats, bait, and tackle are available at the sites listed under *Boating*. Lake Memphremagog is good for smelts, smallmouth bass, and walleyes, in addition to salmon and trout. **Ice fishing** is particularly popular on Memphremagog. The pamphlet *Vermont Guide to Fishing*, prepared by the Vermont Fish and Wildlife Department, available locally, tells where to find what. For other guides, consult *Fishing* under "What's Where." See also *Lakes* under *To See*.

GOLF

Newport Country Club (334-7751), off Mount Vernon Street, overlooking the lake. Eighteen holes, rentals, instruction, restaurant; April through November.

Dufferin Heights Golf Club (819-876-5528), Stanstead, Quebec. May through November. Nine holes, cart rentals, restaurant. There are no golf courses in Essex County. The closest ones in New Hampshire are the **Colebrook Country Club** (9 holes), the **Balsams** in Dixville Notch (18 holes; magnificent site), and the **Waumbec Country Club** in Jefferson (18 holes).

Grandad's Invitational, Newark. This nine-hole course is a local legend. Ask around for directions and leave your fee in the mailbox.

HAYRIDES AND SLEIGH RIDES

Letourneau's Maple Hill Farm (766-2646), Nelson Hill Road, Holland (southeast of Derby Line), offers hayrides in summer and fall, and 1-day sugar-on-snow sleigh rides with live music and refreshments.

HIKING

Bluff Mountain (elevation: 2,380 feet) looms over Island Pond to the north. It is a popular climb, with spectacular views. The trail starts from Route 114, north of the village. Inquire locally for directions.

Monadnock Mountain (elevation: 3,140 feet), in Lemington, towers over the Connecticut River and Colebrook, New Hampshire. A trail runs west, beginning as a driveway off Route 102 near the bridge to Colebrook. An abandoned fire tower crowns the summit.

Bill Sladyk Wildlife Management Area, off Route 114, south of Norton Pond: 9,500 forested acres, also accessible via a gravel road past Holland Pond from Holland Village. A detailed map is available from the Fish and Wildlife Department in Waterbury (241-3700).

Vermont Leadership Center (723-6551), Ten Mile Square Road, East Charleston, offers 40 miles of hiking/mountain-biking/cross-country skiing trails. (See *Green Space*.)

HUNTING

Seymour Lake Lodge, Morgan (see *Lodging*). David Benware provides guided grouse and woodcock hunts on 600 acres of private land and on large tracts of public land; mid-September to late October is the best time. $140 per day.

MOUNTAIN BIKING

Rentals available from **Great Outdoors** (334-2831), 73 Main Street, Newport.

SWIMMING

In Newport, try **Pirouette Beach,** a public facility east of the city that also has tennis courts, picnic facilities, and campsites. On **Seymour Lake** there is a public beach in Morgan Center. There are state facilities at **Island Pond,** a large beach that is sandy and shallow for quite a way out, great for children; and at **Madison Lake** (small beach), nominal entrance fee charged.

WINTER SPORTS

CROSS-COUNTRY SKIING

There are no commercial cross-country centers in northern Essex County. With all the wild, open land, you might find paying to ski somewhat appalling. There is a vast network of wilderness snowmobile trails that are marked by snowmobile clubs and open to skiers. See also Vermont Leadership Center under *Green Space*.

DOWNHILL SKIING

On Lake Memphremagog, **Owl's Head** (514-292-5592), Masonville, Quebec, offers 25 trails, including a steep expert run down the face of the mountain. Snowmaking covers 80 percent of the terrain, and there are six double chairlifts, one quad. Facilities include condominiums and a new apartment hotel, moderately priced. Burke Mountain and Jay Peak are nearby (see "St. Johnsbury, Craftsbury, and Burke Mountain Area" and "Jay Peak Area").

SNOWMOBILING

Island Pond is the snowmobiling capital of the Northeast Kingdom, from which groomed VAST (Vermont Association of Snow Travelers) trails radiate in all directions. Check with **Kingdom Cat Corp.** (723-9602) for rentals and information about local sledding.

GREEN SPACE

Brighton State Park (723-4360), Island Pond, southeast of the village of Island Pond on the south shore of Island Pond and the west shore of Spectacle Pond. Facilities include 84 campsites, of which 21 have lean-tos; also a swimming beach, dump station, snack bar, picnic area, bathhouse, rental boats, nature trail, and naturalist in residence.

Maidstone State Forest (676-3930), near Bloomfield. Five miles south of Bloomfield on Route 102, then 5 miles on dirt road, this is a forest of maple, beech, and hemlock around a large lake, with a beach, picnic area, rental boats, picnic shelter, hiking trails, and 83 campsites, including 37 lean-tos.

Vermont Leadership Center (723-6551), Ten Mile Square Road, East Charleston (5 miles west of Island Pond), is a 60-acre nature preserve with 40 miles of walking/skiing and snowshoeing trails traversing neighboring private property. Aside from its formal nature hikes, guided canoeing, and other programs, the center also serves as an informal clearinghouse for local canoe, fishing, tracking, and nature guides.

LODGING

❀❀ Quimby Country (822-5533; off-season: 717-733-2234), Route 114, Forest Lake Road, Averill 05901, about as north (less than 3 miles from Canada) and as east (10 miles from New Hampshire) as you can get in the Kingdom. This unique 650-acre resort is a 19th-century lodge and grouping of 20 cabins overlooking 70-acre Forest Lake. It is also ¼ mile from 1,200-acre Big Averill, 4 miles from 400-acre Little Averill, and surrounded by its own woodland, which, in turn, is surrounded by forest owned by paper companies. Begun as a fishing lodge, Quimby Country evolved into a family-oriented resort under the proprietorship of Hortense Quimby, attracting a large following in the process. Fearful that the place might change when it came up for sale upon Miss Quimby's death, a number of regular guests formed a corporation and bought it. When the place is in full operation, late June through late August, the rates are $119–133 per adult, $58–69 per child depending on age, with all three meals and a supervised children's program geared to ages 6–15 that includes swimming, hiking, overnight camping, and rainy-day activities. Reasonable rates during spring fishing season (May 10 through June 27), and again August 30 through foliage season when cottages are available on a housekeeping basis. This is a great place for family reunions.

Seymour Lake Lodge (895-2752), Route 111, Morgan 05853. Newport natives Dave and Sue Benware maintain this landmark lodge. There are six bedrooms (one with private bath) and the living room has a decorative tin ceiling and knotty-pine walls and a woodstove. The lounge serves wines and beer, and the dining room is open for breakfast and dinner, with field lunches provided for anglers and hunters. Dave is an Orvis-endorsed fly-fishing guide who offers workshops and both hunting and fishing guide service. He also directs his guests to the best spots for landlocked salmon; brown, lake, and brook trout; and smallmouth bass. The inn is open for winter ice fishing and snowmobiling or cross-country skiing on the lake; local snowmobiling trails are at elevations of 1,300 feet and higher. Boat rentals, sports shop, fishing licenses. April through November, $95 double; December through March, $50 single; children 6–12, free. Rates include breakfast; dinner is $10 extra.

Lakefront Inn Motel & Marina (723-6507), Cross Street, Island Pond 05846. A tidy, upscale, two-story motel, also a building housing the lobby and suites with one, two or three bedrooms (some with fireplace), right in the center of the village. Enjoy sweeping views of Island Pond, which laps the edge of the property. There is no restaurant (but there are enough within walking distance). Four of the 20 units have built-in kitchenette. A small dock is reserved for motel guests, and a heated multi-bay garage is available for guests to work on servicing their snowmobiles in winter. Just across a vacant lot is an extensive public recreation complex, including tennis courts, beach, picnic area, boat launch, lighted ice hockey rink, and children's playground. Marcel and Anita Gervais charge $79 per room, $295 per efficiency for two people in winter (high season), $10 per extra person. Summer rates are lower.

Derby Village Inn (873-3604; fax: 873-3047), 46 Main Street, Derby Line 05830. Sheila Steplas and Catherine McCormick maintain their imposing mansion, built by retired Civil War general Butterfield in 1902. Detailing includes cherry wainscoting in the dining room, and intricate woodwork in the library, TV room, and double parlor. There are tables for puzzles and games and a sunporch for breakfast. The five double bedrooms upstairs all have private bath with original fixtures. The Passageway, a former sitting room, has a king bed and gas fireplace. $75–100 includes a full breakfast.

The Birchwood B&B (873-9104), 48 Main Street, Derby Line 05830. Betty and Dick Fletcher's handsome 1920s village house has three spacious, antiques-furnished (the couple own an antiques store), immaculate bedrooms with private bath. Rooms include the Double Bed Chamber (antique pineapple bed), the blue-and-white Queen Canopy Chamber, and the green-and-pink Twin Bed Room, $75 with a full breakfast in the stately dining room. The fireplace in the formally furnished living room is frequently lit, and guests gather around the long formal dining table for candlelit breakfasts.

Guildhall Inn (676-3720; 1-800-286-6557), Box 129, Guildhall 05905. Open weekends. Built in the early 1800s, this is a large, elegant old farmhouse with three rooms upstairs (shared bath), furnished with an assortment of country antiques. Families are welcome. It's on Route 102, just south of the Guildhall town green. Biking, canoeing, snowmobiling, cross-country skiing available. Steve and Eleanor Degnan include a full breakfast at $35–50.

CAMPGROUNDS
See Brighton State Park and Maidstone State Forest in *Green Space*.

WHERE TO EAT

DINING OUT
The East Side (334-2340), Lake Street, Newport. Open for lunch and dinner weekdays, for breakfast on weekends. Closed Monday. This is a great spot right on the lake, an old landmark (the Landing) now with new ownership (Dena and Pauline Gray are well-known local restaurateurs) and decor. It's unquestionably the best place to eat in town. An outside deck and dock are nice in summer. The reasonably priced lunch menu might include lamb stew and biscuits or grilled chicken salad; the

dinner menu is also moderately priced, and many locals come just for dessert (try the pecan ribbon). Live entertainment Friday and Saturday.

Abbie Lane (334-3900), Newport-Derby Road (Route 5), ½ mile west of I-91, exit 28. Open for dinner Tuesday through Sunday, 5–9 PM. The current new toast of the North Country: genuinely fine dining. You might begin with a bowl of mussels steamed in rice wine, tossed with fresh ginger, shallots, basil, mint, and cilantro ($5.95), and feast on porcini and morel mushroom–crusted seared pork loin stuffed with fresh mushrooms and herbs in a sauce of pan juices and red Dubonnet, potatoes au gratin, and sautéed vegetables ($11.95). Entrées $10.95–19.95; a three-course dinner is $15.95 between 5 and 6:30.

Quimby Country (822-5533), Route 114, Averill (see *Lodging*). Open to the public for dinner by reservation only, offering a rotating menu of two entrées, plus a children's entrée; Sunday-night buffet. Moderate.

Candlelight Restaurant (266-8119), Beecher Falls. A full-service restaurant in newly rebuilt, overdecorated but comfortable quarters on the edge of the Connecticut River. Moderate.

Sutton Place Restaurant (603-237-8842), 152 Main Street, Colebrook, New Hampshire. Lunch Tuesday through Saturday and dinner every night. Don and Carmela Kelsea have created an intimate dining place in the front parlors of a Queen Anne–style house in the center of town. Dinner entrées include steak, chicken, and seafood. Moderate.

EATING OUT

The Nickelodeon Cafe (334-8055), Main Street, Newport. Open 11 AM–late. Housed in a former bank and utilities building with a distinctive outdoor clock, really two separate spaces (one was formerly the Corner restaurant), one a restaurant, the other a lounge. Open for lunch and dinner.

The Brown Cow (334-7887), 900 East Main Street, Newport, open daily 6 AM–7 PM except Sunday, when it's 7–1. This is a nice spot to linger over breakfast (served all day); sandwich and salad lunches, reasonably priced dinners. Homemade ice cream on homemade pie.

Miss Newport Diner (334-7742), East Main Street, Newport. Open 5 AM–11 PM daily except Saturday, when it closes at 10:30 PM. Blueberry pancakes and fresh muffins are the specialty, along with homemade soup and friendly natives; choice of stools and booths.

The Border Motel Dining Room and Lounge (766-2213; 1-800-255-1559), Routes 5 and 105 in Derby. Seafood specials Friday night, veal and chicken dishes, liquor license; reservations a good idea on Friday and Saturday nights.

🏅 **Jennifer's** (723-6135), Island Pond, the town's gathering spot, a cheery restaurant known for good food. Hearty breakfasts sandwiches, and roast turkey, surf and turf for dinner. Seafood is a specialty. Beer and wine served.

Friendly Pizza (723-4616), Route 105 (Derby Street), Island Pond. John

Koxarakis offers a wine variety of pizzas, also steaks, spaghetti, sandwiches, grinders, and Greek salad in his small eatery on the southern fringe of the village. Eat in or take out.

Northland Restaurant and Lounge (266-9947), Canaan. A large, clean, comfortable place offering three squares. The spacious adjoining bar–lounge–dance floor hosts rock and country-rock bands Saturday evening.

ENTERTAINMENT

North Country Concert Association (723-6027), Box 601 in Newport, sponsors a dance, theater, and concert series in various locations throughout the area.

Haskell Opera House (373-3022), in Derby, is the scene of frequent and outstanding concerts.

Piggery Theater (819-842-2431), North Hatley, Quebec. June through August, summer theater.

Northsong Chorus (895-2747) presents concerts at various times and places throughout the year.

SELECTIVE SHOPPING

Sel-Bar Weaving (334-6565), in the old South School, Glen Road, Newport. Continue east on Main Street across Long Bridge (don't turn onto the Causeway) and take your first left. A small store at the factory selling 30 different styles of factory seconds and discontinued patterns, also fine place mats, napkins, and homespun linens. We use them day in and day out (they machine wash) and send them as wedding gifts to far places because they mail so well. Mats and tablecloths come in a variety of colors.

Bogner Factory Outlet (334-0135), 150 Main Street, Newport. Looking more like a boutique than the outlet it is—for the nationally known ski- and sportswear made in town.

Woodknot Books, (334-6720) Main Street, Newport. Open 9–5 except Sunday, Friday until 7. A good selection of books, magazines, and VCR tapes.

Country Thyme Vermont (1-800-639-1370), Derby Road, Newport, specializes in handcrafted gifts and fine food gift baskets.

Great Outdoors, (334-2851), Main Street, Newport. In summer, the store features an extensive array of fishing gear and sells fishing licenses; four-season sporting goods.

Simon the Tanner (723-4452), Cross and Main Streets, Island Pond. Open daily except Saturday, closing at 3 on Friday, otherwise 9–5, until 8 on Thursday. This is an unlikely spot for such a huge shoe store, but here it is selling a wide variety of name-brand shoes—Birkenstock and Clarks sandals, Dansko and Stegmann clogs, Doc Martens, work boots, winter boots, Tubbs snowshoes, and a big selection of athletic shoes, all at below-usual prices. There's also a bargain basement. Candles, specialty food, wrought iron, natural soaps, and body-care products made by the Twelve Tribes, an international sect that rooted in Island Pond several decades ago, restoring a number of houses and winning the respect of the community.

Lakeview Store (822-5570), Route 114, Averill. Open daily 8–7. A great general store with fabulous wools, handcrafted items: bowls, sweaters, baskets, also spinning wheels and weaving supplies. Pick a fleece at a nearby Swanson Oldfarm and the store's owner, Priscilla Roy, will spin and knit it.

SUGARHOUSES

Spates Maple Orchard (895-4012), Derby Line. 3,500 taps; use old and new methods.

Couture's Sugarhouse (744-2733), Route 100, Westfield. A modern sugarhouse with a wood-fired evaporator, open to the public whenever the evaporator is boiling. The maple shop at the farmhouse is open year-round.

SPECIAL EVENTS

February: **Newport Winter Carnival, Island Pond Snowmobile Races.**

March: **Sugaring** throughout the region.

July: **Memphremagog International Aquafest**—a swim race from Newport to Magog in Canada (32 miles), also a water-ski tournament, parade, public suppers, and more.

August: **North Country Moose Festival** (last week). Based in Colebrook, New Hampshire, a series of colorful events on both sides of the Connecticut River.

November: **Annual Hunters Supper**.

Index

574

Books from The Countryman Press

EXPLORER'S GUIDES

The alternative to mass-market guides with their homogenized listings, Explorer's Guides focus on independently owned inns, B&Bs, and restaurants, and on family and cultural activities reflecting the character and unique qualities of the area. Explorer's Guides are available for:

Cape Cod and the Islands, by Kim Grant
Massachusetts: Beyond Boston and Cape Cod, by Christina Tree
    & William Davis
Connecticut, by Barnett D. Laschever & Andi Marie Fusco
The Best of the Hudson Valley and Catskill Mountains, by Joanne
    Michaels & Mary-Margaret Barile
Maine, by Christina Tree & Elizabeth Roundy
New Hampshire, by Christina Tree & Christina Hamm
Rhode Island, by Phyllis Méras and Tom Gannon

A SELECTION OF OUR BOOKS ABOUT THE NORTHEAST

Canoe Camping Vermont & New Hampshire Rivers
Waterfalls of the White Mountains
Fishing Vermont's Streams and Lakes
In-Line Skate New England
Reading the Forested Landscape: A Natural History of New England
The New England Herb Gardener
Blue Ribbons and Burlesque: A Book of Country Fairs
Full Duty: Vermonters in the Civil War
Nine Months to Gettysburg: Stannard's Vermonters and the Repulse of
    Pickett's Charge
Lake Champlain: Key to Liberty
Covered Bridges of Vermont
30 Bicycle Tours in New Hampshire
25 Bicycle Tours in Vermont
25 Mountain Bike Tours in Vermont
50 Hikes in the White Mountains
50 More Hikes in New Hampshire
50 Hikes in Vermont

We offer many more books in hiking, fly fishing, travel, nature, and other subjects. Our books are available at bookstores and outdoor stores everywhere. For more information or a free catalog, please call 1-800-245-4151 or write to us at The Countryman Press, PO Box 748, Woodstock, VT 05091. You can find us on the Internet at www.countrymanpress.com.